BMW | 3-SERIES/Z4
1999-05 REPAIR MANUAL

CHILTON'S

Covers U.S. and Canadian models of BMW 3-series models (E46 chassis) and Z4

Does not include the 318ti, 323is, 328is, Z3 or information specific to M3 models or all-wheel drive models

by Robert Maddox and Joe L Hamilton

CHILTON *Automotive Books*

PUBLISHED BY **HAYNES NORTH AMERICA, Inc.**

Manufactured in USA
©2005 Haynes North America, Inc.
ISBN-13: 978-1-56392-609-9
ISBN-10: 1-56392-609-1
Library of Congress Control Number 2005

Haynes Publishing Group
Sparkford Nr Yeovil
Somerset BA22 7JJ England

Haynes North America, Inc
861 Lawrence Drive
Newbury Park
California 91320 USA

ABCDE
FGHIJ
KLMNO
PQRST

Contents

Mechanic and photographer with a 2004 BMW 330i

ACKNOWLEDGEMENTS

Wiring diagrams provided exclusively for the publisher by Valley Forge Technical Information Services.

While every attempt is made to ensure that the information in this manual is correct, no liability can be accepted by the authors or publishers for loss, damage or injury caused by any errors in, or omissions from, the information given.

About this manual

ITS PURPOSE

The purpose of this manual is to help you get the best value from your vehicle. It can do so in several ways. It can help you decide what work must be done, even if you choose to have it done by a dealer service department or a repair shop; it provides information and procedures for routine maintenance and servicing; and it offers diagnostic and repair procedures to follow when trouble occurs.

We hope you use the manual to tackle the work yourself. For many simpler jobs, doing it yourself may be quicker than arranging an appointment to get the vehicle into a shop and making the trips to leave it and pick it up. More importantly, a lot of money can be saved by avoiding the expense the shop must pass on to you to cover its labor and overhead costs. An added benefit is the sense of satisfaction and accomplishment that you feel after doing the job yourself.

USING THE MANUAL

The manual is divided into Chapters. Each Chapter is divided into numbered Sections. Each Section consists of consecutively numbered paragraphs.

At the beginning of each numbered Section you will be referred to any illustrations which apply to the procedures in that Section. The reference numbers used in illustration captions pinpoint the pertinent Section and the Step within that Section. That is, illustration 3.2 means the illustration refers to Section 3 and Step (or paragraph) 2 within that Section.

Procedures, once described in the text, are not normally repeated. When it's necessary to refer to another Chapter, the reference will be given as Chapter and Section number. Cross references given without use of the word "Chapter" apply to Sections and/or paragraphs in the same Chapter. For example, "see Section 8" means in the same Chapter.

References to the left or right side of the vehicle assume you are sitting in the driver's seat, facing forward.

Even though we have prepared this manual with extreme care, neither the publisher nor the author can accept responsibility for any errors in, or omissions from, the information given.

➡ NOTE

A *Note* provides information necessary to properly complete a procedure or information which will make the procedure easier to understand.

❋ CAUTION

A *Caution* provides a special procedure or special steps which must be taken while completing the procedure where the Caution is found. Not heeding a Caution can result in damage to the assembly being worked on.

❋ WARNING

A *Warning* provides a special procedure or special steps which must be taken while completing the procedure where the Warning is found. Not heeding a Warning can result in personal injury.

Introduction to the BMW 3-series and Z4

The models covered by this manual are equipped with either a 2.5, 2.8 or 3.0 liter six-cylinder engine. These engines are of the Dual Overhead Camshaft (DOHC) design. They also are equipped with a computer-controlled ignition and fuel delivery system with electronic fuel injection.

Transmissions are either five- or six-speed manual or four- or five-speed automatic with overdrive. Power is transmitted from the transmission to the rear axle through a two-piece driveshaft. The differential is bolted to a crossmember and drives the wheels through driveaxles equipped with inner and outer constant velocity joints.

The front suspension is of the MacPherson strut design, with the coil spring/shock absorber unit making up the upper suspension link. The rear suspension is a fully independent multi-link design. Power assisted rack-and-pinion steering is standard.

Power assisted front and rear disc brakes are standard on all models.

A wide range of standard and optional equipment is available for all models.

Recall information

Vehicle recalls are carried out by the manufacturer in the rare event of a possible safety-related defect. The vehicle's registered owner is contacted at the address on file at the Department of Motor Vehicles and given the details of the recall. Remedial work is carried out free of charge at a dealer service department.

If you are the new owner of a used vehicle which was subject to a recall and you want to be sure that the work has been carried out, it's best to contact a dealer service department and ask about your indi-

vidual vehicle - you'll need to furnish them your Vehicle Identification Number (VIN).

The table below is based on information provided by the National Highway Traffic Safety Administration (NHTSA), the body which oversees vehicle recalls in the United States. The recall database is updated constantly. For the latest information on vehicle recalls, check the NHTSA website at www.nhtsa.gov, or call the NHTSA hotline at 1-888-327-4236.

Recall date	Recall campaign number	Model(s) affected	Concern
3/26/1999	99V063000	1999 323i, 328i	Side-impact airbags and Head Protection System (HPS) might deploy during a non-crash impact, such as hitting a large pothole or speed bump
4/30/1999	99V100000	1999 323i, 328i	Brake booster pushrod might become detached from brake pedal, resulting in loss of braking
2/15/2000	00V048000	2000 323i, 328i	Brake light switch could fail, causing the lights to remain on, or not work at all
11/16/2000	00V383000	2001 325i, 330i	The wheels could have been damaged during tire mounting; tire failure could occur
6/15/2001, 5/10/2002	01V206000 02V138000	2001 325i, 325Ci, 325it, 330i	Engine auxiliary cooling fan control unit might fail, resulting in overheating. Control unit could also catch on fire
2/13/2002	02V057000	2002 325i, 330i	Strut upper mount thrust bearing may not have been properly positioned and secured; strut could separate from upper mount, resulting in loss of control
8/9/2002	02V223000	1999 323i, 328i 2000 323i, 328i	Side-impact airbags might deploy during a non-crash impact, such as hitting a large pothole or speed bump
1/27/2003	03V032000	2003 Z4	Seat belt-to-tensioner connection may fail in a crash
3/14/2003	03V124000	2003 325i, 325Ci	On some models with automatic transmission, idle speed could increase; with gear selected, vehicle could move
4/17/2003	03V160000	2003 325i, 325Ci, 330i	Window anti-pinching device might not function properly
5/15/2003	03V214000	2003 Z4	On some models with 18-inch wheels, the wheels could have been damaged during tire mounting; tire failure could occur
4/1/2004	04V182000	2004 Z4	Fuel pump prone to vapor lock; vehicle could stall
4/13/2004	04V247000	2003 Z4	Wrong airbag system processors may have been installed; airbags might not deploy in a crash

Vehicle Identification Numbers

VEHICLE IDENTIFICATION NUMBER

The Vehicle Identification Number (VIN) is located on the dashboard near the bottom of the windshield on the driver's side of the vehicle (see illustration), on the driver's side door and on the Manufacturer's Plate and on the right shock tower. It contains valuable information such as where and when the vehicle was manufactured, the model year and the body style. This number can be used to cross-check the registration and license.

ENGINE SERIAL NUMBER

The engine serial number is stamped on the left-hand face of the cylinder block near the base of the oil level dipstick, above the starter on the left rear side of the engine.

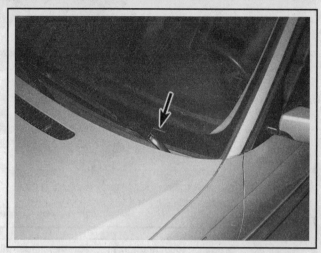

The Vehicle Identification Number is visible through the driver's side of the windshield

Buying parts

Replacement parts are available from many sources, which generally fall into one of two categories - authorized dealer parts departments and independent retail auto parts stores. Our advice concerning these parts is as follows:

Retail auto parts stores: Good auto parts stores will stock frequently needed components which wear out relatively fast, such as clutch components, exhaust systems, brake parts, tune-up parts, etc. These stores often supply new or reconditioned parts on an exchange basis, which can save a considerable amount of money. Discount auto parts stores are often very good places to buy materials and parts needed for general vehicle maintenance such as oil, grease, filters, spark plugs, belts, touch-up paint, bulbs, etc. They also usually sell tools and general accessories, have convenient hours, charge lower prices and can often be found not far from home.

Authorized dealer parts department: This is the best source for parts which are unique to the vehicle and not generally available elsewhere (such as major engine parts, transmission parts, trim pieces, etc.).

Warranty information: If the vehicle is still covered under warranty, be sure that any replacement parts purchased - regardless of the source - do not invalidate the warranty!

To be sure of obtaining the correct parts, have engine and chassis numbers available and, if possible, take the old parts along for positive identification.

Maintenance techniques, tools and working facilities

MAINTENANCE TECHNIQUES

There are a number of techniques involved in maintenance and repair that will be referred to throughout this manual. Application of these techniques will enable the home mechanic to be more efficient, better organized and capable of performing the various tasks properly, which will ensure that the repair job is thorough and complete.

Fasteners

Fasteners are nuts, bolts, studs and screws used to hold two or more parts together. There are a few things to keep in mind when work-ing with fasteners. Almost all of them use a locking device of some type, either a lockwasher, locknut, locking tab or thread adhesive. All threaded fasteners should be clean and straight, with undamaged threads and undamaged corners on the hex head where the wrench fits. Develop the habit of replacing all damaged nuts and bolts with new ones. Special locknuts with nylon or fiber inserts can only be used once. If they are removed, they lose their locking ability and must be replaced with new ones.

Rusted nuts and bolts should be treated with a penetrating fluid to ease removal and prevent breakage. Some mechanics use turpentine in a spout-type oil can, which works quite well. After applying the rust penetrant, let it work for a few minutes before trying to loosen the nut

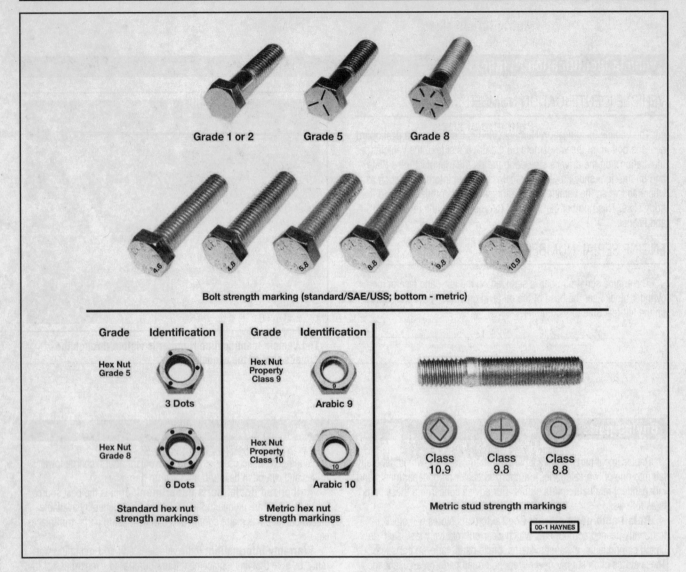

Grade 1 or 2   Grade 5   Grade 8

Bolt strength marking (standard/SAE/USS; bottom - metric)

Grade	Identification	Grade	Identification
Hex Nut Grade 5	3 Dots	Hex Nut Property Class 9	Arabic 9
Hex Nut Grade 8	6 Dots	Hex Nut Property Class 10	Arabic 10

Standard hex nut strength markings

Metric hex nut strength markings

Class 10.9   Class 9.8   Class 8.8

Metric stud strength markings

00-1 HAYNES

or bolt. Badly rusted fasteners may have to be chiseled or sawed off or removed with a special nut breaker, available at tool stores.

If a bolt or stud breaks off in an assembly, it can be drilled and removed with a special tool commonly available for this purpose. Most automotive machine shops can perform this task, as well as other repair procedures, such as the repair of threaded holes that have been stripped out.

Flat washers and lockwashers, when removed from an assembly, should always be replaced exactly as removed. Replace any damaged washers with new ones. Never use a lockwasher on any soft metal surface (such as aluminum), thin sheet metal or plastic.

Fastener sizes

For a number of reasons, automobile manufacturers are making wider and wider use of metric fasteners. Therefore, it is important to be able to tell the difference between standard (sometimes called U.S. or SAE) and metric hardware, since they cannot be interchanged.

All bolts, whether standard or metric, are sized according to diameter, thread pitch and length. For example, a standard 1/2 - 13 x 1 bolt is 1/2 inch in diameter, has 13 threads per inch and is 1 inch long. An M12 - 1.75 x 25 metric bolt is 12 mm in diameter, has a thread pitch of 1.75 mm (the distance between threads) and is 25 mm long. The two bolts are nearly identical, and easily confused, but they are not interchangeable.

In addition to the differences in diameter, thread pitch and length, metric and standard bolts can also be distinguished by examining the bolt heads. To begin with, the distance across the flats on a standard bolt head is measured in inches, while the same dimension on a metric bolt is sized in millimeters (the same is true for nuts). As a result, a standard wrench should not be used on a metric bolt and a metric wrench should not be used on a standard bolt. Also, most standard bolts have slashes radiating out from the center of the head to denote the grade or strength of the bolt, which is an indication of the amount of torque that can be applied to it. The greater the number of slashes, the greater the strength of the bolt. Grades 0 through 5 are commonly used on automobiles. Metric bolts have a property class (grade) number, rather than a slash, molded into their heads to indicate bolt strength. In this case, the higher the number, the stronger the bolt. Property class numbers 8.8, 9.8 and 10.9 are commonly used on automobiles.

Strength markings can also be used to distinguish standard hex nuts from metric hex nuts. Many standard nuts have dots stamped into one side, while metric nuts are marked with a number. The greater the number of dots, or the higher the number, the greater the strength of the nut.

Metric studs are also marked on their ends according to property class (grade). Larger studs are numbered (the same as metric bolts), while smaller studs carry a geometric code to denote grade.

Metric thread sizes

	Ft-lbs	Nm
M-6	6 to 9	9 to 12
M-8	14 to 21	19 to 28
M-10	28 to 40	38 to 54
M-12	50 to 71	68 to 96
M-14	80 to 140	109 to 154

Pipe thread sizes

	Ft-lbs	Nm
1/8	5 to 8	7 to 10
1/4	12 to 18	17 to 24
3/8	22 to 33	30 to 44
1/2	25 to 35	34 to 47

U.S. thread sizes

	Ft-lbs	Nm
1/4 - 20	6 to 9	9 to 12
5/16 - 18	12 to 18	17 to 24
5/16 - 24	14 to 20	19 to 27
3/8 - 16	22 to 32	30 to 43
3/8 - 24	27 to 38	37 to 51
7/16 - 14	40 to 55	55 to 74
7/16 - 20	40 to 60	55 to 81
1/2 - 13	55 to 80	75 to 108

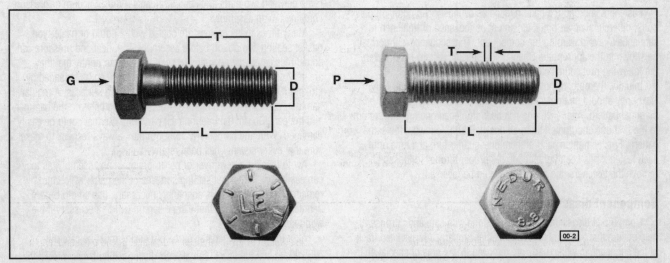

Standard (SAE and USS) bolt dimensions/grade marks

G   Grade marks (bolt strength)
L   Length (in inches)
T   Thread pitch (number of threads per inch)
D   Nominal diameter (in inches)

Metric bolt dimensions/grade marks

P   Property class (bolt strength)
L   Length (in millimeters)
T   Thread pitch (distance between threads in millimeters)
D   Diameter

It should be noted that many fasteners, especially Grades 0 through 2, have no distinguishing marks on them. When such is the case, the only way to determine whether it is standard or metric is to measure the thread pitch or compare it to a known fastener of the same size.

Standard fasteners are often referred to as SAE, as opposed to metric. However, it should be noted that SAE technically refers to a non-metric fine thread fastener only. Coarse thread non-metric fasteners are referred to as USS sizes.

Since fasteners of the same size (both standard and metric) may have different strength ratings, be sure to reinstall any bolts, studs or nuts removed from your vehicle in their original locations. Also, when replacing a fastener with a new one, make sure that the new one has a strength rating equal to or greater than the original.

Tightening sequences and procedures

Most threaded fasteners should be tightened to a specific torque value (torque is the twisting force applied to a threaded component such as a nut or bolt). Overtightening the fastener can weaken it and cause it to break, while undertightening can cause it to eventually come loose. Bolts, screws and studs, depending on the material they are made of and their thread diameters, have specific torque values, many of which are noted in the Specifications at the end of each Chapter. Be sure to follow the torque recommendations closely. For fasteners not assigned a specific torque, a general torque value chart is presented here as a guide. These torque values are for dry (unlubricated) fasteners threaded into steel or cast iron (not aluminum). As was previously mentioned, the size and grade of a fastener determine the amount of torque that can

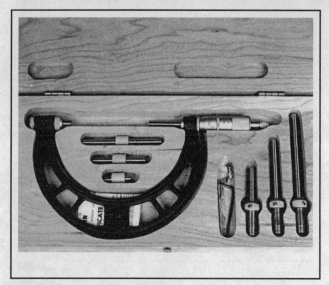

Micrometer set

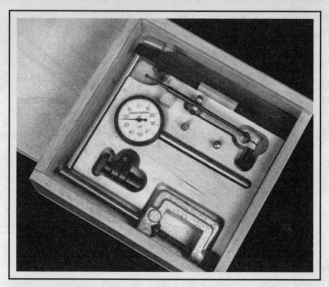

Dial indicator set

safely be applied to it. The figures listed here are approximate for Grade 2 and Grade 3 fasteners. Higher grades can tolerate higher torque values.

Fasteners laid out in a pattern, such as cylinder head bolts, oil pan bolts, differential cover bolts, etc., must be loosened or tightened in sequence to avoid warping the component. This sequence will normally be shown in the appropriate Chapter. If a specific pattern is not given, the following procedures can be used to prevent warping.

Initially, the bolts or nuts should be assembled finger-tight only. Next, they should be tightened one full turn each, in a criss-cross or diagonal pattern. After each one has been tightened one full turn, return to the first one and tighten them all one-half turn, following the same pattern. Finally, tighten each of them one-quarter turn at a time until each fastener has been tightened to the proper torque. To loosen and remove the fasteners, the procedure would be reversed.

Component disassembly

Component disassembly should be done with care and purpose to help ensure that the parts go back together properly. Always keep track of the sequence in which parts are removed. Make note of special characteristics or marks on parts that can be installed more than one way, such as a grooved thrust washer on a shaft. It is a good idea to lay the disassembled parts out on a clean surface in the order that they were removed. It may also be helpful to make sketches or take instant photos of components before removal.

When removing fasteners from a component, keep track of their locations. Sometimes threading a bolt back in a part, or putting the washers and nut back on a stud, can prevent mix-ups later. If nuts and bolts cannot be returned to their original locations, they should be kept in a compartmented box or a series of small boxes. A cupcake or muffin tin is ideal for this purpose, since each cavity can hold the bolts and nuts from a particular area (i.e. oil pan bolts, valve cover bolts, engine mount bolts, etc.). A pan of this type is especially helpful when working on assemblies with very small parts, such as the carburetor, alternator, valve train or interior dash and trim pieces. The cavities can be marked with paint or tape to identify the contents.

Whenever wiring looms, harnesses or connectors are separated, it is a good idea to identify the two halves with numbered pieces of masking tape so they can be easily reconnected.

Gasket sealing surfaces

Throughout any vehicle, gaskets are used to seal the mating surfaces between two parts and keep lubricants, fluids, vacuum or pressure contained in an assembly.

Many times these gaskets are coated with a liquid or paste-type gasket sealing compound before assembly. Age, heat and pressure can sometimes cause the two parts to stick together so tightly that they are very difficult to separate. Often, the assembly can be loosened by striking it with a soft-face hammer near the mating surfaces. A regular hammer can be used if a block of wood is placed between the hammer and the part. Do not hammer on cast parts or parts that could be easily damaged. With any particularly stubborn part, always recheck to make sure that every fastener has been removed.

Avoid using a screwdriver or bar to pry apart an assembly, as they can easily mar the gasket sealing surfaces of the parts, which must remain smooth. If prying is absolutely necessary, use an old broom handle, but keep in mind that extra clean up will be necessary if the wood splinters.

After the parts are separated, the old gasket must be carefully scraped off and the gasket surfaces cleaned. Stubborn gasket material can be soaked with rust penetrant or treated with a special chemical to soften it so it can be easily scraped off.

✸✸ CAUTION:

Never use gasket removal solutions or caustic chemicals on plastic or other composite components.

A scraper can be fashioned from a piece of copper tubing by flattening and sharpening one end. Copper is recommended because it is usually softer than the surfaces to be scraped, which reduces the chance of gouging the part. Some gaskets can be removed with a wire brush, but regardless of the method used, the mating surfaces must be left clean and smooth. If for some reason the gasket surface is gouged, then a gasket sealer thick enough to fill scratches will have to be used during reassembly of the components. For most applications, a non-drying (or semi-drying) gasket sealer should be used.

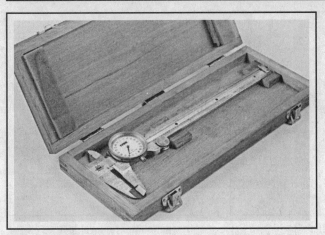

Dial caliper

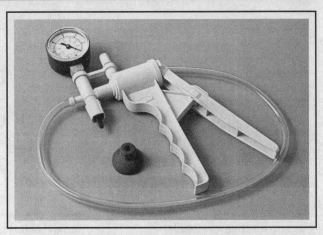

Hand-operated vacuum pump

Timing light

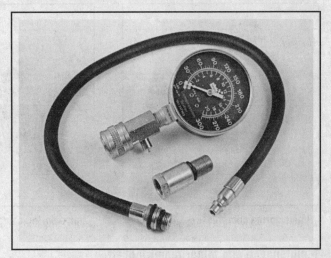

Compression gauge with spark plug hole adapter

Hose removal tips

✳✳ WARNING:

If the vehicle is equipped with air conditioning, do not disconnect any of the A/C hoses without first having the system depressurized by a dealer service department or a service station.

Hose removal precautions closely parallel gasket removal precautions. Avoid scratching or gouging the surface that the hose mates against or the connection may leak. This is especially true for radiator hoses. Because of various chemical reactions, the rubber in hoses can bond itself to the metal spigot that the hose fits over. To remove a hose, first loosen the hose clamps that secure it to the spigot. Then, with slip-joint pliers, grab the hose at the clamp and rotate it around the spigot. Work it back and forth until it is completely free, then pull it off. Silicone or other lubricants will ease removal if they can be applied between the hose and the outside of the spigot. Apply the same lubricant to the inside of the hose and the outside of the spigot to simplify installation.

As a last resort (and if the hose is to be replaced with a new one anyway), the rubber can be slit with a knife and the hose peeled from the spigot. If this must be done, be careful that the metal connection is not damaged.

If a hose clamp is broken or damaged, do not reuse it. Wire-type clamps usually weaken with age, so it is a good idea to replace them with screw-type clamps whenever a hose is removed.

TOOLS

A selection of good tools is a basic requirement for anyone who plans to maintain and repair his or her own vehicle. For the owner who has few tools, the initial investment might seem high, but when compared to the spiraling costs of professional auto maintenance and repair, it is a wise one.

To help the owner decide which tools are needed to perform the tasks detailed in this manual, the following tool lists are offered: *Maintenance and minor repair, Repair/overhaul and Special.*

The newcomer to practical mechanics should start off with the *maintenance and minor repair* tool kit, which is adequate for the simpler jobs performed on a vehicle. Then, as confidence and experience grow, the owner can tackle more difficult tasks, buying additional tools as they are needed. Eventually the basic kit will be expanded into the *repair and overhaul* tool set. Over a period of time, the experienced do-it-yourselfer will assemble a tool set complete enough for most repair and overhaul procedures and will add tools from the special category when it is felt that the expense is justified by the frequency of use.

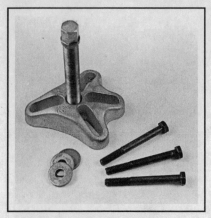

Damper/steering wheel puller

General purpose puller

Hydraulic lifter removal tool

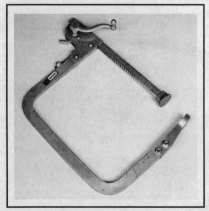

Valve spring compressor

Valve spring compressor

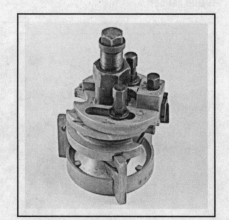

Ridge reamer

Maintenance and minor repair tool kit

The tools in this list should be considered the minimum required for performance of routine maintenance, servicing and minor repair work. We recommend the purchase of combination wrenches (box-end and open-end combined in one wrench). While more expensive than open end wrenches, they offer the advantages of both types of wrench.

Combination wrench set (1/4-inch to 1 inch or 6 mm to 19 mm)
Adjustable wrench, 8 inch
Spark plug wrench with rubber insert
Spark plug gap adjusting tool
Feeler gauge set
Brake bleeder wrench
Standard screwdriver (5/16-inch x 6 inch)
Phillips screwdriver (No. 2 x 6 inch)
Combination pliers - 6 inch
Hacksaw and assortment of blades
Tire pressure gauge
Grease gun
Oil can
Fine emery cloth
Wire brush
Battery post and cable cleaning tool
Oil filter wrench
Funnel (medium size)
Safety goggles
Jackstands (2)
Drain pan

➡**Note: If basic tune-ups are going to be part of routine maintenance, it will be necessary to purchase a good quality stroboscopic timing light and combination tachometer/ dwell meter. Although they are included in the list of special tools, it is mentioned here because they are absolutely necessary for tuning most vehicles properly.**

Repair and overhaul tool set

These tools are essential for anyone who plans to perform major repairs and are in addition to those in the maintenance and minor repair tool kit. Included is a comprehensive set of sockets which, though expensive, are invaluable because of their versatility, especially when various extensions and drives are available. We recommend the 1/2-inch drive over the 3/8-inch drive. Although the larger drive is bulky and more expensive, it has the capacity of accepting a very wide range of large sockets. Ideally, however, the mechanic should have a 3/8-inch drive set and a 1/2-inch drive set.

Socket set(s)
Reversible ratchet
Extension - 10 inch
Universal joint
Torque wrench (same size drive as sockets)
Ball peen hammer - 8 ounce
Soft-face hammer (plastic/rubber)
Standard screwdriver (1/4-inch x 6 inch)
Standard screwdriver (stubby - 5/16-inch)
Phillips screwdriver (No. 3 x 8 inch)
Phillips screwdriver (stubby - No. 2)
Pliers - vise grip

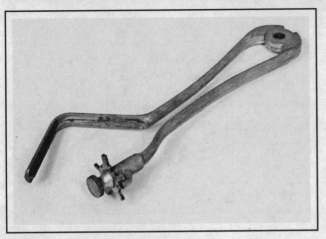

Piston ring groove cleaning tool

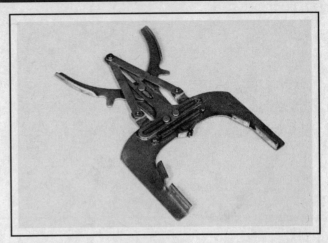

Ring removal/installation tool

Ring compressor

Cylinder hone

Brake hold-down spring tool

Pliers - lineman's
Pliers - needle nose
Pliers - snap-ring (internal and external)
Cold chisel - 1/2-inch
Scribe
Scraper (made from flattened copper tubing)
Centerpunch
Pin punches (1/16, 1/8, 3/16-inch)
Steel rule/straightedge - 12 inch
Allen wrench set (1/8 to 3/8-inch or 4 mm to 10 mm)
A selection of files
Wire brush (large)
Jackstands (second set)
Jack (scissor or hydraulic type)

➡**Note: Another tool which is often useful is an electric drill with a chuck capacity of 3/8-inch and a set of good quality drill bits.**

Special tools

The tools in this list include those which are not used regularly, are expensive to buy, or which need to be used in accordance with their manufacturer's instructions. Unless these tools will be used frequently, it is not very economical to purchase many of them. A consideration would be to split the cost and use between yourself and a friend or friends. In addition, most of these tools can be obtained from a tool rental shop on a temporary basis.

This list primarily contains only those tools and instruments widely available to the public, and not those special tools produced by the vehicle manufacturer for distribution to dealer service departments. Occasionally, references to the manufacturer's special tools are included in the text of this manual. Generally, an alternative method of doing the job without the special tool is offered. However, sometimes there is no alternative to their use. Where this is the case, and the tool cannot be purchased or borrowed, the work should be turned over to the dealer service department or an automotive repair shop.

Valve spring compressor
Piston ring groove cleaning tool
Piston ring compressor
Piston ring installation tool
Cylinder compression gauge
Cylinder ridge reamer
Cylinder surfacing hone
Cylinder bore gauge
Micrometers and/or dial calipers
Hydraulic lifter removal tool
Balljoint separator
Universal-type puller
Impact screwdriver
Dial indicator set
Stroboscopic timing light (inductive pick-up)
Hand operated vacuum/pressure pump
Tachometer/dwell meter
Universal electrical multimeter
Cable hoist
Brake spring removal and installation tools
Floor jack

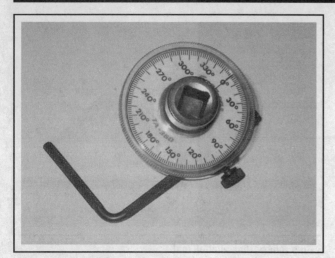

Torque angle gauge

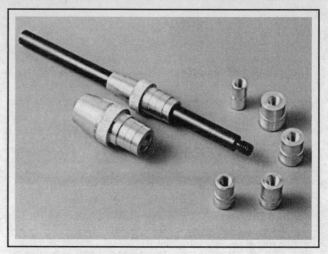

Clutch plate alignment tool

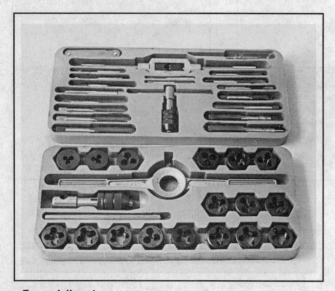

Tap and die set

Buying tools

For the do-it-yourselfer who is just starting to get involved in vehicle maintenance and repair, there are a number of options available when purchasing tools. If maintenance and minor repair is the extent of the work to be done, the purchase of individual tools is satisfactory. If, on the other hand, extensive work is planned, it would be a good idea to purchase a modest tool set from one of the large retail chain stores. A set can usually be bought at a substantial savings over the individual tool prices, and they often come with a tool box. As additional tools are needed, add-on sets, individual tools and a larger tool box can be purchased to expand the tool selection. Building a tool set gradually allows the cost of the tools to be spread over a longer period of time and gives the mechanic the freedom to choose only those tools that will actually be used.

Tool stores will often be the only source of some of the special tools that are needed, but regardless of where tools are bought, try to avoid cheap ones, especially when buying screwdrivers and sockets, because they won't last very long. The expense involved in replacing cheap tools will eventually be greater than the initial cost of quality tools.

Care and maintenance of tools

Good tools are expensive, so it makes sense to treat them with respect. Keep them clean and in usable condition and store them properly when not in use. Always wipe off any dirt, grease or metal chips before putting them away. Never leave tools lying around in the work area. Upon completion of a job, always check closely under the hood for tools that may have been left there so they won't get lost during a test drive.

Some tools, such as screwdrivers, pliers, wrenches and sockets, can be hung on a panel mounted on the garage or workshop wall, while others should be kept in a tool box or tray. Measuring instruments, gauges, meters, etc. must be carefully stored where they cannot be damaged by weather or impact from other tools.

When tools are used with care and stored properly, they will last a very long time. Even with the best of care, though, tools will wear out if used frequently. When a tool is damaged or worn out, replace it. Subsequent jobs will be safer and more enjoyable if you do.

HOW TO REPAIR DAMAGED THREADS

Sometimes, the internal threads of a nut or bolt hole can become stripped, usually from overtightening. Stripping threads is an all-too-common occurrence, especially when working with aluminum parts, because aluminum is so soft that it easily strips out.

Usually, external or internal threads are only partially stripped. After they've been cleaned up with a tap or die, they'll still work. Sometimes, however, threads are badly damaged. When this happens, you've got three choices:

1) *Drill and tap the hole to the next suitable oversize and install a larger diameter bolt, screw or stud.*
2) *Drill and tap the hole to accept a threaded plug, then drill and tap the plug to the original screw size. You can also buy a plug already threaded to the original size. Then you simply drill a hole to the specified size, then run the threaded plug into the hole with a bolt and jam nut. Once the plug is fully seated, remove the jam nut and bolt.*
3) *The third method uses a patented thread repair kit like Heli-Coil or Slimsert. These easy-to-use kits are designed to repair damaged threads in straight-through holes and blind holes. Both are available as kits which can handle a variety of sizes and thread*

patterns. Drill the hole, then tap it with the special included tap. Install the Heli-Coil and the hole is back to its original diameter and thread pitch.

Regardless of which method you use, be sure to proceed calmly and carefully. A little impatience or carelessness during one of these relatively simple procedures can ruin your whole day's work and cost you a bundle if you wreck an expensive part.

WORKING FACILITIES

Not to be overlooked when discussing tools is the workshop. If anything more than routine maintenance is to be carried out, some sort of suitable work area is essential.

It is understood, and appreciated, that many home mechanics do not have a good workshop or garage available, and end up removing an engine or doing major repairs outside. It is recommended, however, that the overhaul or repair be completed under the cover of a roof.

A clean, flat workbench or table of comfortable working height is an absolute necessity. The workbench should be equipped with a vise that has a jaw opening of at least four inches.

As mentioned previously, some clean, dry storage space is also required for tools, as well as the lubricants, fluids, cleaning solvents, etc. which soon become necessary.

Sometimes waste oil and fluids, drained from the engine or cooling system during normal maintenance or repairs, present a disposal problem. To avoid pouring them on the ground or into a sewage system, pour the used fluids into large containers, seal them with caps and take them to an authorized disposal site or recycling center. Plastic jugs, such as old antifreeze containers, are ideal for this purpose.

Always keep a supply of old newspapers and clean rags available. Old towels are excellent for mopping up spills. Many mechanics use rolls of paper towels for most work because they are readily available and disposable. To help keep the area under the vehicle clean, a large cardboard box can be cut open and flattened to protect the garage or shop floor.

Whenever working over a painted surface, such as when leaning over a fender to service something under the hood, always cover it with an old blanket or bedspread to protect the finish. Vinyl covered pads, made especially for this purpose, are available at auto parts stores.

Booster battery (jump) starting

➡**Note: The battery is located in the trunk with remote terminals provided in the engine compartment.**

Observe the following precautions when using a booster battery to start a vehicle:

a) Before connecting the booster battery, make sure the ignition switch is in the Off position.
b) Turn off the lights, heater and other electrical loads.
c) Your eyes should be shielded. Safety goggles are a good idea.
d) Make sure the booster battery is the same voltage as the dead one in the vehicle.
e) The two vehicles MUST NOT TOUCH each other.
f) Make sure the transmission is in Neutral (manual transmission) or Park (automatic transmission).

Connect the red jumper cable to the positive (+) terminals of each battery (or to the remote positive terminal in the engine compartment) (see illustration).

Connect one end of the black cable to the negative (-) terminal of the booster battery. The other end of this cable should be connected to a good ground on the engine block (or to the remote negative terminal in the engine compartment) (see illustration). Make sure the cable will not come into contact with the fan, drivebelts or other moving parts of the engine.

Start the engine using the booster battery, then, with the engine running at idle speed, disconnect the jumper cables in the reverse order of connection.

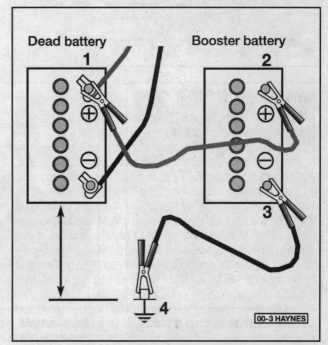

Make the booster battery cable connections in the numerical order shown (note that the negative cable of the booster battery is NOT attached to the negative terminal of the dead battery)

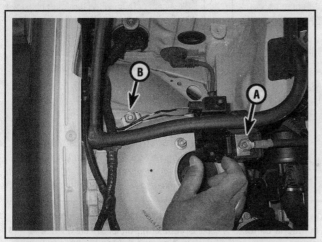

Remote locations for the positive (A) and negative (B) battery terminals are in the engine compartment behind the right shock tower

Jacking and towing

JACKING

The jack supplied with the vehicle should be used only for raising the vehicle when changing a tire or placing jackstands under the frame.

✳ WARNING:

Never crawl under the vehicle or start the engine when this jack is being used.

The vehicle should be on level ground with the wheels blocked and the transmission in Park (automatic) or Reverse (manual). Pry off the hub cap (if equipped) using the tapered end of the lug wrench. Loosen the wheel bolts one-half turn and leave them in place until the wheel is raised off the ground.

On all except Z4 and later 3-Series models, unscrew the access cover in the rocker panel nearest the wheel to be changed (see illustration). Engage the head of the jack with the hole in the rocker panel (see illustration). If you're working on a Z4 and later 3-Series model,

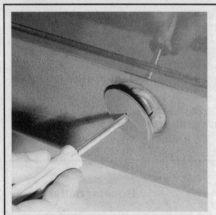

On early 3-Series models, unscrew the access cover from the rocker panel . . .

engage the head of the jack with the jacking point on the underside of the vehicle, directly behind the front wheel of right in front of the rear wheel (see illustration). Block the wheel opposite the one being changed. Make sure the jack is located on firm ground; if not, place a block of wood under it. Turn the jack handle clockwise until the wheel is raised off the ground, then unscrew the wheel bolts and remove the wheel.

Install the spare wheel and tighten the wheel bolts until they are snug. Lower the vehicle by turning the jack handle counterclockwise, then remove the jack and install the access cover (early 3-Series models). Tighten the bolts in a diagonal pattern to the torque listed in the Chapter 1 Specifications. If a torque wrench is not available, have the torque checked by a service station as soon as possible. Reinstall the hub cap, if equipped.

TOWING

Manual transmission-equipped vehicles can be towed with all four wheels on the ground. Automatic transmission-equipped vehicles can be towed with all four wheels on the ground if speeds do not exceed 35 mph and the distance is not over 50 miles, otherwise transmission damage can result. Towing equipment specifically designed for this purpose should be used and should be attached to the main structural members of the vehicle, not the bumper or brackets.

For pulling the vehicle with a strap or cable (to pull the vehicle onto a trailer with a winch), a towing eye is provided in the vehicle's tool kit. This tool can be screwed into the front or rear bumper after prying the small cover off to install it (see illustration). The tool should be stored during normal vehicle operation.

✳ WARNING:

As stated, this towing eye is only intended for use when pulling the vehicle onto a trailer or flatbed car carrier. Never use it for towing the vehicle on the road.

. . . and insert the jack into the hole

On Z4 and later 3-Series models, install the jack to the contact area on the underside of the vehicle

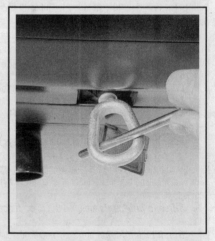

Pry off the access cover from the front or rear bumper, then screw the eye into position and tighten it securely

Automotive chemicals and lubricants

A number of automotive chemicals and lubricants are available for use during vehicle maintenance and repair. They include a wide variety of products ranging from cleaning solvents and degreasers to lubricants and protective sprays for rubber, plastic and vinyl.

CLEANERS

Carburetor cleaner and choke cleaner is a strong solvent for gum, varnish and carbon. Most carburetor cleaners leave a dry-type lubricant film which will not harden or gum up. Because of this film it is not recommended for use on electrical components.

Brake system cleaner is used to remove brake dust, grease and brake fluid from the brake system, where clean surfaces are absolutely necessary. It leaves no residue and often eliminates brake squeal caused by contaminants.

Electrical cleaner removes oxidation, corrosion and carbon deposits from electrical contacts, restoring full current flow. It can also be used to clean spark plugs, carburetor jets, voltage regulators and other parts where an oil-free surface is desired.

Demoisturants remove water and moisture from electrical components such as alternators, voltage regulators, electrical connectors and fuse blocks. They are non-conductive and non-corrosive.

Degreasers are heavy-duty solvents used to remove grease from the outside of the engine and from chassis components. They can be sprayed or brushed on and, depending on the type, are rinsed off either with water or solvent.

LUBRICANTS

Motor oil is the lubricant formulated for use in engines. It normally contains a wide variety of additives to prevent corrosion and reduce foaming and wear. Motor oil comes in various weights (viscosity ratings) from 0 to 50. The recommended weight of the oil depends on the season, temperature and the demands on the engine. Light oil is used in cold climates and under light load conditions. Heavy oil is used in hot climates and where high loads are encountered. Multi-viscosity oils are designed to have characteristics of both light and heavy oils and are available in a number of weights from 5W-20 to 20W-50.

Gear oil is designed to be used in differentials, manual transmissions and other areas where high-temperature lubrication is required.

Chassis and wheel bearing grease is a heavy grease used where increased loads and friction are encountered, such as for wheel bearings, balljoints, tie-rod ends and universal joints.

High-temperature wheel bearing grease is designed to withstand the extreme temperatures encountered by wheel bearings in disc brake equipped vehicles. It usually contains molybdenum disulfide (moly), which is a dry-type lubricant.

White grease is a heavy grease for metal-to-metal applications where water is a problem. White grease stays soft under both low and high temperatures (usually from -100 to +190-degrees F), and will not wash off or dilute in the presence of water.

Assembly lube is a special extreme pressure lubricant, usually containing moly, used to lubricate high-load parts (such as main and rod bearings and cam lobes) for initial start-up of a new engine. The assembly lube lubricates the parts without being squeezed out or washed away until the engine oiling system begins to function.

Silicone lubricants are used to protect rubber, plastic, vinyl and nylon parts.

Graphite lubricants are used where oils cannot be used due to contamination problems, such as in locks. The dry graphite will lubricate metal parts while remaining uncontaminated by dirt, water, oil or acids. It is electrically conductive and will not foul electrical contacts in locks such as the ignition switch.

Moly penetrants loosen and lubricate frozen, rusted and corroded fasteners and prevent future rusting or freezing.

Heat-sink grease is a special electrically non-conductive grease that is used for mounting electronic ignition modules where it is essential that heat is transferred away from the module.

SEALANTS

RTV sealant is one of the most widely used gasket compounds. Made from silicone, RTV is air curing, it seals, bonds, waterproofs, fills surface irregularities, remains flexible, doesn't shrink, is relatively easy to remove, and is used as a supplementary sealer with almost all low and medium temperature gaskets.

Anaerobic sealant is much like RTV in that it can be used either to seal gaskets or to form gaskets by itself. It remains flexible, is solvent resistant and fills surface imperfections. The difference between an anaerobic sealant and an RTV-type sealant is in the curing. RTV cures when exposed to air, while an anaerobic sealant cures only in the absence of air. This means that an anaerobic sealant cures only after the assembly of parts, sealing them together.

Thread and pipe sealant is used for sealing hydraulic and pneumatic fittings and vacuum lines. It is usually made from a Teflon compound, and comes in a spray, a paint-on liquid and as a wrap-around tape.

CHEMICALS

Anti-seize compound prevents seizing, galling, cold welding, rust and corrosion in fasteners. High-temperature anti-seize, usually made with copper and graphite lubricants, is used for exhaust system and exhaust manifold bolts.

Anaerobic locking compounds are used to keep fasteners from vibrating or working loose and cure only after installation, in the absence of air. Medium strength locking compound is used for small nuts, bolts and screws that may be removed later. High-strength locking compound is for large nuts, bolts and studs which aren't removed on a regular basis.

Oil additives range from viscosity index improvers to chemical treatments that claim to reduce internal engine friction. It should be noted that most oil manufacturers caution against using additives with their oils.

Gas additives perform several functions, depending on their chemical makeup. They usually contain solvents that help dissolve gum and varnish that build up on carburetor, fuel injection and intake parts. They also serve to break down carbon deposits that form on the inside surfaces of the combustion chambers. Some additives contain upper cylinder lubricants for valves and piston rings, and others contain chemicals to remove condensation from the gas tank.

MISCELLANEOUS

Brake fluid is specially formulated hydraulic fluid that can withstand the heat and pressure encountered in brake systems. Care must be taken so this fluid does not come in contact with painted surfaces or plastics. An opened container should always be resealed to prevent contamination by water or dirt.

Weatherstrip adhesive is used to bond weatherstripping around doors, windows and trunk lids. It is sometimes used to attach trim pieces.

Undercoating is a petroleum-based, tar-like substance that is designed to protect metal surfaces on the underside of the vehicle from corrosion. It also acts as a sound-deadening agent by insulating the bottom of the vehicle.

Waxes and polishes are used to help protect painted and plated surfaces from the weather. Different types of paint may require the use of different types of wax and polish. Some polishes utilize a chemical or abrasive cleaner to help remove the top layer of oxidized (dull) paint on older vehicles. In recent years many non-wax polishes that contain a wide variety of chemicals such as polymers and silicones have been introduced. These non-wax polishes are usually easier to apply and last longer than conventional waxes and polishes.

CONVERSION FACTORS

LENGTH (distance)

Inches (in)	X	25.4	= Millimeters (mm)	X 0.0394	= Inches (in)
Feet (ft)	X	0.305	= Meters (m)	X 3.281	= Feet (ft)
Miles	X	1.609	= Kilometers (km)	X 0.621	= Miles

VOLUME (capacity)

Cubic inches (cu in; in³)	X	16.387	= Cubic centimeters (cc; cm³)	X 0.061	= Cubic inches (cu in; in³)
Imperial pints (Imp pt)	X	0.568	= Liters (l)	X 1.76	= Imperial pints (Imp pt)
Imperial quarts (Imp qt)	X	1.137	= Liters (l)	X 0.88	= Imperial quarts (Imp qt)
Imperial quarts (Imp qt)	X	1.201	= US quarts (US qt)	X 0.833	= Imperial quarts (Imp qt)
US quarts (US qt)	X	0.946	= Liters (l)	X 1.057	= US quarts (US qt)
Imperial gallons (Imp gal)	X	4.546	= Liters (l)	X 0.22	= Imperial gallons (Imp gal)
Imperial gallons (Imp gal)	X	1.201	= US gallons (US gal)	X 0.833	= Imperial gallons (Imp gal)
US gallons (US gal)	X	3.785	= Liters (l)	X 0.264	= US gallons (US gal)

 Cubic inches (cu in; in^3), Cubic centimeters (cc; cm^3).

MASS (weight)

Ounces (oz)	X	28.35	= Grams (g)	X 0.035	= Ounces (oz)
Pounds (lb)	X	0.454	= Kilograms (kg)	X 2.205	= Pounds (lb)

FORCE

Ounces-force (ozf; oz)	X	0.278	= Newtons (N)	X 3.6	= Ounces-force (ozf; oz)
Pounds-force (lbf; lb)	X	4.448	= Newtons (N)	X 0.225	= Pounds-force (lbf; lb)
Newtons (N)	X	0.1	= Kilograms-force (kgf; kg)	X 9.81	= Newtons (N)

PRESSURE

Pounds-force per square inch (psi; lbf/in^2; lb/in^2)	X	0.070	= Kilograms-force per square centimeter (kgf/cm^2; kg/cm^2)	X 14.223	= Pounds-force per square inch (psi; lbf/in^2; lb/in^2)
Pounds-force per square inch (psi; lbf/in^2; lb/in^2)	X	0.068	= Atmospheres (atm)	X 14.696	= Pounds-force per square inch (psi; lbf/in^2; lb/in^2)
Pounds-force per square inch (psi; lbf/in^2; lb/in^2)	X	0.069	= Bars	X 14.5	= Pounds-force per square inch (psi; lbf/in^2; lb/in^2)
Pounds-force per square inch (psi; lbf/in^2; lb/in^2)	X	6.895	= Kilopascals (kPa)	X 0.145	= Pounds-force per square inch (psi; lbf/in^2; lb/in^2)
Kilopascals (kPa)	X	0.01	= Kilograms-force per square centimeter (kgf/cm^2; kg/cm^2)	X 98.1	= Kilopascals (kPa)

TORQUE (moment of force)

Pounds-force inches (lbf in; lb in)	X	1.152	= Kilograms-force centimeter (kgf cm; kg cm)	X 0.868	= Pounds-force inches (lbf in; lb in)
Pounds-force inches (lbf in; lb in)	X	0.113	= Newton meters (Nm)	X 8.85	= Pounds-force inches (lbf in; lb in)
Pounds-force inches (lbf in; lb in)	X	0.083	= Pounds-force feet (lbf ft; lb ft)	X 12	= Pounds-force inches (lbf in; lb in)
Pounds-force feet (lbf ft; lb ft)	X	0.138	= Kilograms-force meters (kgf m; kg m)	X 7.233	= Pounds-force feet (lbf ft; lb ft)
Pounds-force feet (lbf ft; lb ft)	X	1.356	= Newton meters (Nm)	X 0.738	= Pounds-force feet (lbf ft; lb ft)
Newton meters (Nm)	X	0.102	= Kilograms-force meters (kgf m; kg m)	X 9.804	= Newton meters (Nm)

VACUUM

Inches mercury (in. Hg)	X	3.377	= Kilopascals (kPa)	X 0.2961	= Inches mercury
Inches mercury (in. Hg)	X	25.4	= Millimeters mercury (mm Hg)	X 0.0394	= Inches mercury

POWER

Horsepower (hp)	X	745.7	= Watts (W)	X 0.0013	= Horsepower (hp)

VELOCITY (speed)

Miles per hour (miles/hr; mph)	X	1.609	= Kilometers per hour (km/hr; kph)	X 0.621	= Miles per hour (miles/hr; mph)

FUEL CONSUMPTION *

Miles per gallon, Imperial (mpg)	X	0.354	= Kilometers per liter (km/l)	X 2.825	= Miles per gallon, Imperial (mpg)
Miles per gallon, US (mpg)	X	0.425	= Kilometers per liter (km/l)	X 2.352	= Miles per gallon, US (mpg)

TEMPERATURE

Degrees Fahrenheit = (°C x 1.8) + 32   Degrees Celsius (Degrees Centigrade; °C) = (°F - 32) x 0.56

*It is common practice to convert from miles per gallon (mpg) to liters/100 kilometers (l/100km), where mpg (Imperial) x l/100 km = 282 and mpg (US) x l/100 km = 235

FRACTION/DECIMAL/MILLIMETER EQUIVALENTS

DECIMALS to MILLIMETERS

Decimal	mm	Decimal	mm
0.001	0.0254	0.500	12.7000
0.002	0.0508	0.510	12.9540
0.003	0.0762	0.520	13.2080
0.004	0.1016	0.530	13.4620
0.005	0.1270	0.540	13.7160
0.006	0.1524	0.550	13.9700
0.007	0.1778	0.560	14.2240
0.008	0.2032	0.570	14.4780
0.009	0.2286	0.580	14.7320
		0.590	14.9860
0.010	0.2540		
0.020	0.5080		
0.030	0.7620		
0.040	1.0160	0.600	15.2400
0.050	1.2700	0.610	15.4940
0.060	1.5240	0.620	15.7480
0.070	1.7780	0.630	16.0020
0.080	2.0320	0.640	16.2560
0.090	2.2860	0.650	16.5100
		0.660	16.7640
0.100	2.5400	0.670	17.0180
0.110	2.7940	0.680	17.2720
0.120	3.0480	0.690	17.5260
0.130	3.3020		
0.140	3.5560		
0.150	3.8100		
0.160	4.0640	0.700	17.7800
0.170	4.3180	0.710	18.0340
0.180	4.5720	0.720	18.2880
0.190	4.8260	0.730	18.5420
		0.740	18.7960
0.200	5.0800	0.750	19.0500
0.210	5.3340	0.760	19.3040
0.220	5.5880	0.770	19.5580
0.230	5.8420	0.780	19.8120
0.240	6.0960	0.790	20.0660
0.250	6.3500		
0.260	6.6040		
0.270	6.8580	0.800	20.3200
0.280	7.1120	0.810	20.5740
0.290	7.3660	0.820	21.8280
		0.830	21.0820
0.300	7.6200	0.840	21.3360
0.310	7.8740	0.850	21.5900
0.320	8.1280	0.860	21.8440
0.330	8.3820	0.870	22.0980
0.340	8.6360	0.880	22.3520
0.350	8.8900	0.890	22.6060
0.360	9.1440		
0.370	9.3980		
0.380	9.6520		
0.390	9.9060		
		0.900	22.8600
0.400	10.1600	0.910	23.1140
0.410	10.4140	0.920	23.3680
0.420	10.6680	0.930	23.6220
0.430	10.9220	0.940	23.8760
0.440	11.1760	0.950	24.1300
0.450	11.4300	0.960	24.3840
0.460	11.6840	0.970	24.6380
0.470	11.9380	0.980	24.8920
0.480	12.1920	0.990	25.1460
0.490	12.4460	1.000	25.4000

FRACTIONS to DECIMALS to MILLIMETERS

Fraction	Decimal	mm	Fraction	Decimal	mm
1/64	0.0156	0.3969	33/64	0.5156	13.0969
1/32	0.0312	0.7938	17/32	0.5312	13.4938
3/64	0.0469	1.1906	35/64	0.5469	13.8906
1/16	0.0625	1.5875	9/16	0.5625	14.2875
5/64	0.0781	1.9844	37/64	0.5781	14.6844
3/32	0.0938	2.3812	19/32	0.5938	15.0812
7/64	0.1094	2.7781	39/64	0.6094	15.4781
1/8	0.1250	3.1750	5/8	0.6250	15.8750
9/64	0.1406	3.5719	41/64	0.6406	16.2719
5/32	0.1562	3.9688	21/32	0.6562	16.6688
11/64	0.1719	4.3656	43/64	0.6719	17.0656
3/16	0.1875	4.7625	11/16	0.6875	17.4625
13/64	0.2031	5.1594	45/64	0.7031	17.8594
7/32	0.2188	5.5562	23/32	0.7188	18.2562
15/64	0.2344	5.9531	47/64	0.7344	18.6531
1/4	0.2500	6.3500	3/4	0.7500	19.0500
17/64	0.2656	6.7469	49/64	0.7656	19.4469
9/32	0.2812	7.1438	25/32	0.7812	19.8438
19/64	0.2969	7.5406	51/64	0.7969	20.2406
5/16	0.3125	7.9375	13/16	0.8125	20.6375
21/64	0.3281	8.3344	53/64	0.8281	21.0344
11/32	0.3438	8.7312	27/32	0.8438	21.4312
23/64	0.3594	9.1281	55/64	0.8594	21.8281
3/8	0.3750	9.5250	7/8	0.8750	22.2250
25/64	0.3906	9.9219	57/64	0.8906	22.6219
13/32	0.4062	10.3188	29/32	0.9062	23.0188
27/64	0.4219	10.7156	59/64	0.9219	23.4156
7/16	0.4375	11.1125	15/16	0.9375	23.8125
29/64	0.4531	11.5094	61/64	0.9531	24.2094
15/32	0.4688	11.9062	31/32	0.9688	24.6062
31/64	0.4844	12.3031	63/64	0.9844	25.0031
1/2	0.5000	12.7000	1	1.0000	25.4000

Safety first!

Regardless of how enthusiastic you may be about getting on with the job at hand, take the time to ensure that your safety is not jeopardized. A moment's lack of attention can result in an accident, as can failure to observe certain simple safety precautions. The possibility of an accident will always exist, and the following points should not be considered a comprehensive list of all dangers. Rather, they are intended to make you aware of the risks and to encourage a safety conscious approach to all work you carry out on your vehicle.

ESSENTIAL DOS AND DON'TS

DON'T rely on a jack when working under the vehicle. Always use approved jackstands to support the weight of the vehicle and place them under the recommended lift or support points.

DON'T attempt to loosen extremely tight fasteners (i.e. wheel lug nuts) while the vehicle is on a jack - it may fall.

DON'T start the engine without first making sure that the transmission is in Neutral (or Park where applicable) and the parking brake is set.

DON'T remove the radiator cap from a hot cooling system - let it cool or cover it with a cloth and release the pressure gradually.

DON'T attempt to drain the engine oil until you are sure it has cooled to the point that it will not burn you.

DON'T touch any part of the engine or exhaust system until it has cooled sufficiently to avoid burns.

DON'T siphon toxic liquids such as gasoline, antifreeze and brake fluid by mouth, or allow them to remain on your skin.

DON'T inhale brake lining dust - it is potentially hazardous (see *Asbestos* below).

DON'T allow spilled oil or grease to remain on the floor - wipe it up before someone slips on it.

DON'T use loose fitting wrenches or other tools which may slip and cause injury.

DON'T push on wrenches when loosening or tightening nuts or bolts. Always try to pull the wrench toward you. If the situation calls for pushing the wrench away, push with an open hand to avoid scraped knuckles if the wrench should slip.

DON'T attempt to lift a heavy component alone - get someone to help you.

DON'T rush or take unsafe shortcuts to finish a job.

DON'T allow children or animals in or around the vehicle while you are working on it.

DO wear eye protection when using power tools such as a drill, sander, bench grinder, etc. and when working under a vehicle.

DO keep loose clothing and long hair well out of the way of moving parts.

DO make sure that any hoist used has a safe working load rating adequate for the job.

DO get someone to check on you periodically when working alone on a vehicle.

DO carry out work in a logical sequence and make sure that everything is correctly assembled and tightened.

DO keep chemicals and fluids tightly capped and out of the reach of children and pets.

DO remember that your vehicle's safety affects that of yourself and others. If in doubt on any point, get professional advice.

ASBESTOS

Certain friction, insulating, sealing, and other products - such as brake linings, brake bands, clutch linings, torque converters, gaskets, etc. - may contain asbestos. Extreme care must be taken to avoid inhalation of dust from such products, since it is hazardous to health. If in doubt, assume that they do contain asbestos.

FIRE

Remember at all times that gasoline is highly flammable. Never smoke or have any kind of open flame around when working on a vehicle. But the risk does not end there. A spark caused by an electrical short circuit, by two metal surfaces contacting each other, or even by static electricity built up in your body under certain conditions, can ignite gasoline vapors, which in a confined space are highly explosive. Do not, under any circumstances, use gasoline for cleaning parts. Use an approved safety solvent.

Always disconnect the battery ground (-) cable at the battery before working on any part of the fuel system or electrical system. Never risk spilling fuel on a hot engine or exhaust component. It is strongly recommended that a fire extinguisher suitable for use on fuel and electrical fires be kept handy in the garage or workshop at all times. Never try to extinguish a fuel or electrical fire with water.

FUMES

Certain fumes are highly toxic and can quickly cause unconsciousness and even death if inhaled to any extent. Gasoline vapor falls into this category, as do the vapors from some cleaning solvents. Any draining or pouring of such volatile fluids should be done in a well ventilated area.

When using cleaning fluids and solvents, read the instructions on the container carefully. Never use materials from unmarked containers.

Never run the engine in an enclosed space, such as a garage. Exhaust fumes contain carbon monoxide, which is extremely poisonous. If you need to run the engine, always do so in the open air, or at least have the rear of the vehicle outside the work area.

If you are fortunate enough to have the use of an inspection pit, never drain or pour gasoline and never run the engine while the vehicle is over the pit. The fumes, being heavier than air, will concentrate in the pit with possibly lethal results.

THE BATTERY

Never create a spark or allow a bare light bulb near a battery. They normally give off a certain amount of hydrogen gas, which is highly explosive.

Always disconnect the battery ground (-) cable at the battery before working on the fuel or electrical systems.

If possible, loosen the filler caps or cover when charging the battery from an external source (this does not apply to sealed or maintenance-free batteries). Do not charge at an excessive rate or the battery may burst.

Take care when adding water to a non maintenance-free battery and when carrying a battery. The electrolyte, even when diluted, is very corrosive and should not be allowed to contact clothing or skin.

Always wear eye protection when cleaning the battery to prevent the caustic deposits from entering your eyes.

HOUSEHOLD CURRENT

When using an electric power tool, inspection light, etc., which operates on household current, always make sure that the tool is correctly connected to its plug and that, where necessary, it is properly grounded. Do not use such items in damp conditions and, again, do not create a spark or apply excessive heat in the vicinity of fuel or fuel vapor.

SECONDARY IGNITION SYSTEM VOLTAGE

A severe electric shock can result from touching certain parts of the ignition system (such as the spark plug wires) when the engine is running or being cranked, particularly if components are damp or the insulation is defective. In the case of an electronic ignition system, the secondary system voltage is much higher and could prove fatal.

Troubleshooting

CONTENTS

This section provides an easy reference guide to the more common problems which may occur during the operation of your vehicle. These problems and their possible causes are grouped under headings denoting various components or systems, such as Engine, Cooling system, etc. They also refer you to the chapter and/or section which deals with the problem.

Remember that successful troubleshooting is not a mysterious art practiced only by professional mechanics. It is simply the result of the right knowledge combined with an intelligent, systematic approach to the problem. Always work by a process of elimination, starting with the simplest solution and working through to the most complex - and never overlook the obvious. Anyone can run the gas tank dry or leave the lights on overnight, so don't assume that you are exempt from such oversights.

Finally, always establish a clear idea of why a problem has occurred and take steps to ensure that it doesn't happen again. If the electrical system fails because of a poor connection, check the other connections in the system to make sure that they don't fail as well. If a particular fuse continues to blow, find out why - don't just replace one fuse after another. Remember, failure of a small component can often be indicative of potential failure or incorrect functioning of a more important component or system.

ENGINE

1 Engine fails to rotate when attempting to start

1 Battery terminal connections loose or corroded (Chapter 1)
2 Battery discharged or faulty (Chapter 5)
3 Broken, loose or disconnected wiring in the starting circuit (Chapter 5)
4 Defective starter solenoid or switch (Chapter 5)
5 Defective starter motor (Chapter 5)
6 Starter pinion or flywheel ring gear teeth loose or broken (Chapters 2 or 5)
7 Engine ground strap broken or disconnected.

2 Engine rotates, but will not start

1 Fuel tank empty
2 Battery discharged (engine rotates slowly) (Chapter 5)
3 Battery terminal connections loose or corroded (Chapter 1)
4 Air filter element dirty or clogged (Chapter 1)
5 Low cylinder compressions (Chapter 2)
6 Major mechanical failure (broken timing chain, for example) (Chapter 2)
7 Ignition components damp or damaged (Chapter 5)
8 Fuel injection system fault (Chapter 4)
9 Worn, faulty or incorrectly gapped spark plugs (Chapter 1)
10 Broken, loose or disconnected wiring in ignition circuit (Chapter 5)

3 Engine difficult to start when cold

1 Battery discharged (Chapter 5)
2 Battery terminal connections loose or corroded (Chapter 1)
3 Air filter element dirty or clogged (Chapter 1)
4 Worn, faulty or incorrectly gapped spark plugs (Chapter 1)
5 Low cylinder compressions (Chapter 2)
6 Fuel injection system fault (Chapter 4)
7 Ignition system fault (Chapter 5)

4 Engine difficult to start when hot

1 Battery discharged (Chapter 5)
2 Battery terminal connections loose or corroded (Chapter 1)
3 Air filter element dirty or clogged (Chapter 1)
4 Fuel injection system fault (Chapter 4)

5 Starter motor noisy or excessively rough in engagement

1 Starter pinion or flywheel ring gear teeth loose or broken (Chapter 2 or 5)
2 Starter motor mounting bolts loose or missing (Chapter 5)
3 Starter motor internal components worn or damaged (Chapter 5)

6 Starter motor turns engine slowly

1 Battery discharged (Chapter 5)
2 Battery terminal connections loose or corroded (Chapter 1)
3 Ground strap broken or disconnected (Chapter 5)
4 Starter motor wiring loose (Chapter 5)
5 Starter motor internal fault (Chapter 5)

7 Engine starts, but stops immediately

1 Loose ignition system wiring (Chapter 5)
2 Dirt in fuel system (Chapter 4)
3 Fuel injector fault (Chapter 4)
4 Fuel pump or pressure regulator fault (Chapter 4)
5 Vacuum leak at throttle body, intake manifold or hoses (Chapters 2 and 4)

8 Engine idles erratically

1 Air filter element clogged (Chapter 1)
2 Idle air control system fault (Chapter 6)
3 Worn, faulty or incorrectly gapped spark plugs (Chapter 1)
4 Vacuum leak at throttle body, intake manifold or hoses (Chapters 2 and 4)
5 Uneven or low cylinder compressions (Chapter 2)
6 Timing chain incorrectly installed or tensioned (Chapter 2)
7 Camshaft lobes worn (Chapter 2)
8 Faulty fuel injector(s) (Chapter 4)

9 Engine misfires at idle speed

1 Faulty ignition coil(s) (Chapter 5)
2 Faulty fuel injector(s) (Chapter 4)
3 Fouled or cracked spark plug(s) (Chapter 1)
4 Uneven or low cylinder compressions (Chapter 2)
5 Disconnected, leaking, or deteriorated crankcase ventilation hoses (Chapter 4)
6 Vacuum leak at the throttle body, intake manifold or associated hoses (Chapter 4)

10 Engine misfires throughout the driving speed range

1 Fuel filter plugged (Chapter 1)
2 Fuel pump faulty, or delivery pressure low (Chapter 4)
3 Fuel tank vent blocked, or fuel pipes restricted (Chapter 4)
4 Uneven or low cylinder compressions (Chapter 2)
5 Worn, faulty or incorrectly gapped spark plugs (Chapter 1)
6 Faulty ignition coil(s) (Chapter 5)

11 Engine stalls

1 Fuel filter plugged (Chapter 1)
2 Blocked injector/fuel injection system fault (Chapter 4)
3 Fuel pump faulty, or delivery pressure low (Chapter 4)
4 Vacuum leak at the throttle body, intake manifold or associated hoses (Chapter 4)
5 Fuel tank vent blocked, or fuel pipes restricted (Chapter 4)

12 Engine lacks power

1 Fuel filter plugged (Chapter 1)

2 Timing chain incorrectly installed or tensioned (Chapter 2)
3 Fuel pump faulty, or delivery pressure low (Chapter 4)
4 Worn, faulty or incorrectly gapped spark plugs (Chapter 1)
5 Vacuum leak at the throttle body, intake manifold or associated hoses (Chapter 4)
6 Uneven or low cylinder compressions (Chapter 2)
7 Brakes binding (Chapters 1 and 9)
8 Clutch slipping (Chapter 8)
9 Blocked injector/fuel injection system fault (Chapter 4)

13 Engine backfires

1 Timing chain incorrectly installed (Chapter 2)
2 Faulty injector/fuel injection system fault (Chapter 4)

14 Oil pressure warning light illuminated with engine running

1 Low oil level, or incorrect oil grade (Chapter 1)
2 Faulty oil pressure sensor (Chapter 5)
3 Worn engine bearings and/or oil pump (Chapter 2)
4 Excessively high engine operating temperature (Chapter 3)
5 Oil pressure relief valve defective (Chapter 2)
6 Oil pick-up strainer clogged (Chapter 2)

➡**Note: Low oil pressure in a high-mileage engine at idle is not necessarily a cause for concern. Sudden pressure loss at speed is far more significant. In any event, check the gauge or warning light sender before condemning the engine.**

15 Engine runs-on after switching off

1 Excessive carbon build-up in engine (Chapter 2)
2 Excessively high engine operating temperature (Chapter 3)

16 Engine noises

1 Pre-ignition (pinging) or knocking during acceleration or under load
  a) *Excessive carbon build-up in engine (Chapter 2)*
  b) *Faulty fuel injector(s) (Chapter 4)*
  c) *Ignition system fault (Chapter 5)*
2 Whistling or wheezing noises
  a) *Leaking exhaust manifold gasket (Chapter 4)*
  b) *Leaking vacuum hose (Chapter 4 or 9)*
  c) *Blown cylinder head gasket (Chapter 2).*
3 Tapping or rattling noises
  a) *Worn valve gear or camshaft (Chapter 2)*
  b) *Auxiliary component fault (water pump, alternator, etc.) (Chapters 3, 5, etc.)*
4 Knocking or thumping noises
  a) *Worn connecting rod bearings (regular heavy knocking, perhaps less under load) (Chapter 2)*
  b) *Worn main bearings (rumbling and knocking, perhaps worsening under load) (Chapter 2)*
  c) *Piston slap (most noticeable when cold) (Chapter 2)*
  d) *Auxiliary component fault (water pump, alternator, etc.) (Chapters 3, 5, etc.)*

COOLING SYSTEM

17 Overheating

1 Insufficient coolant in system (Chapter 1)
2 Thermostat faulty (Chapter 3)
3 Radiator core blocked, or grille restricted (Chapter 3)
4 Cooling fan or viscous coupling faulty (Chapter 3)
5 Inaccurate temperature gauge sender unit (Chapter 3)
6 Airlock in cooling system (Chapter 3)
7 Expansion tank pressure cap faulty (Chapter 3)

18 Overcooling

1 Thermostat faulty (Chapter 3)
2 Inaccurate temperature gauge sender unit (Chapter 3)
3 Viscous coupling faulty (Chapter 3)

19 External coolant leakage

1 Deteriorated or damaged hoses or hose clips (Chapter 1)
2 Radiator or heater core leaking (Chapter 3)
3 Pressure cap faulty (Chapter 3)
4 Water pump internal seal leaking (Chapter 3)
5 Water pump-to-block seal leaking (Chapter 3)
6 Boiling due to overheating (Chapter 3)
7 Core plug leaking (Chapter 2)

20 Internal coolant leakage

1 Leaking cylinder head gasket (Chapter 2)
2 Cracked cylinder head or cylinder block (Chapter 2)

21 Corrosion

1 Infrequent draining and flushing (Chapter 1)
2 Incorrect coolant mixture or inappropriate coolant type (Chapter 1)

FUEL AND EXHAUST SYSTEMS

22 Excessive fuel consumption

1 Air filter element dirty or clogged (Chapter 1)
2 Fuel injection system fault (Chapter 4)
3 Ignition timing incorrect/ignition system fault (Chapters 1 and 5)
4 Tires under-inflated (Chapter 1)

23 Fuel leakage and/or fuel odor

  Damaged or corroded fuel tank, lines or connections (Chapter 4)

24 Excessive noise or fumes from exhaust system

1 Leaking exhaust system or manifold joints (Chapters 1 and 4)
2 Leaking, corroded or damaged mufflers or pipe (Chapters 1 and 4)
3 Broken mountings causing body or suspension contact (Chapter 1)

CLUTCH

25 Pedal travels to floor - no pressure or very little resistance

1 Brake fluid level low/air in the hydraulic system (Chapters 1 and 8)
2 Broken clutch release bearing or fork (Chapter 8)
3 Broken diaphragm spring in clutch pressure plate (Chapter 8)

26 Clutch fails to disengage (unable to select gears)

1 Brake fluid level low/air in the hydraulic system (Chapters 1 and 8)
2 Clutch disc sticking on transmission input shaft splines (Chapter 8)
3 Clutch disc sticking to flywheel or pressure plate (Chapter 8)
4 Faulty pressure plate assembly (Chapter 8)
5 Clutch release mechanism worn or incorrectly assembled (Chapter 8)

27 Clutch slips (engine speed increases, with no increase in vehicle speed)

1 Clutch disc linings excessively worn (Chapter 8)
2 Clutch disc linings contaminated with oil or grease (Chapter 8)
3 Faulty pressure plate or weak diaphragm spring (Chapter 8)

28 Shudder as clutch is engaged

1 Clutch disc linings contaminated with oil or grease (Chapter 8)
2 Clutch disc linings excessively worn (Chapter 8)
3 Faulty or distorted pressure plate or diaphragm spring (Chapter 8)
4 Worn or loose engine or transmission mountings (Chapter 2A or 2B)
5 Clutch disc hub or transmission input shaft splines worn (Chapter 8)

29 Noise when depressing or releasing clutch pedal

1 Worn clutch release bearing (Chapter 8)
2 Worn or dry clutch pedal bushings (Chapter 8)
3 Faulty pressure plate assembly (Chapter 8)
4 Pressure plate diaphragm spring broken (Chapter 8)
5 Broken clutch disc cushioning springs (Chapter 8)

MANUAL TRANSMISSION

30 Noisy in neutral with engine running

1 Input shaft bearings worn (noise apparent with clutch pedal released, but not when depressed) (Chapter 7)*
2 Clutch release bearing worn (noise apparent with clutch pedal depressed, possibly less when released) (Chapter 8)

31 Noisy in one particular gear

Worn, damaged or chipped gear teeth (Chapter 7)*

32 Difficulty engaging gears

1 Clutch fault (Chapter 8)
2 Worn or damaged shift linkage/cable (Chapter 7)
3 Incorrectly adjusted shift linkage/cable (Chapter 7)
4 Worn synchronizer units (Chapter 7)*

33 Jumps out of gear

1 Worn or damaged shift linkage/cable (Chapter 7)
2 Incorrectly adjusted shift linkage/cable (Chapter 7)
3 Worn synchronizer units (Chapter 7)*
4 Worn selector forks (Chapter 7)*

34 Vibration

1 Lack of oil (Chapter 1)
2 Worn bearings (Chapter 7)*

35 Lubricant leaks

1 Leaking differential output oil seal (Chapter 7)
2 Leaking housing joint (Chapter 7)*
3 Leaking input shaft oil seal (Chapter 7)*

*Although the corrective action necessary to remedy the symptoms described is beyond the scope of the home mechanic, the above information should be helpful in isolating the cause of the condition, so that the owner can communicate clearly with a professional mechanic.

AUTOMATIC TRANSMISSION

→Note: Due to the complexity of the automatic transmission, it is difficult for the home mechanic to properly diagnose and service this unit. For problems other than the following, the vehicle should be taken to a dealer service department or automatic transmission specialist. Do not be too hasty in removing the transmission if a fault is suspected, as most of the testing is carried out with the unit installed.

36 Fluid leakage

Automatic transmission fluid is usually dark in color. Fluid leaks should not be confused with engine oil, which can easily be blown onto the transmission by airflow.

To determine the source of a leak, first remove all built-up dirt and grime from the transmission housing and surrounding areas using a degreasing agent, or by steam-cleaning. Drive the vehicle at low speed, so airflow will not blow the leak far from its source. Raise and support the vehicle, and determine where the leak is coming from. The following are common areas of leakage:

a) Oil pan (Chapters 1 and 7)
b) Dipstick tube (Chapter 1 and 7)
c) Transmission-to-fluid cooler pipes/unions (Chapter 7)

37 Transmission fluid brown, or has burned smell

Transmission fluid level low, or fluid in need of replacement (Chapter 1)

38   General gear selection problems

Chapter 7B deals with checking and adjusting the selector cable on automatic transmissions. The following are common problems that may be caused by a poorly adjusted cable:

a) *Engine starting in gears other than Park or Neutral*
b) *Indicator panel indicating a gear other than the one actually being used*
c) *Vehicle moves when in Park or Neutral*
d) *Poor gear shift quality or erratic gear changes*

Refer to Chapter 7B for the selector cable adjustment procedure.

39   Transmission will not downshift (kickdown) with accelerator pedal fully depressed

1   Low transmission fluid level (Chapter 1)
2   Incorrect selector cable adjustment (Chapter 7)

40   Engine will not start in any gear, or starts in gears other than Park or Neutral

1   Incorrect starter/inhibitor switch adjustment (Chapter 7)
2   Incorrect selector cable adjustment (Chapter 7)

41   Transmission slips, shifts roughly, is noisy, or has no drive in forward or reverse gears

There are many probable causes for the above problems, but the home mechanic should be concerned with only one possibility - fluid level. Before taking the vehicle to a dealer or transmission specialist, check the fluid level and condition of the fluid as described in Chapter 1. Correct the fluid level as necessary, or change the fluid and filter if needed. If the problem persists, professional help will be necessary.

DIFFERENTIAL AND DRIVESHAFT

42   Vibration when accelerating or decelerating

1   Worn universal joint (Chapter 8)
2   Bent or distorted driveshaft (Chapter 8)

43   Low pitched whining; increasing with road speed

Worn differential (Chapter 8)

BRAKES

➡**Note: Before assuming that a brake problem exists, make sure that the tires are in good condition and correctly inflated, that the front wheel alignment is correct, and that the vehicle is not loaded with weight in an unequal manner. Apart from checking the condition of all pipe and hose connections, any faults occurring on the anti-lock braking system should be referred to a BMW dealer or other qualified repair shop for diagnosis.**

44   Vehicle pulls to one side under braking

1   Worn, defective, damaged or contaminated brake pads on one side (Chapters 1 and 9)
2   Seized or partially seized brake caliper piston (Chapters 1 and 9)
3   A mixture of brake pad lining materials (Chapters 1 and 9)
4   Worn or damaged steering or suspension components (Chapters 1 and 10)

45   Noise (grinding or high-pitched squeal) when brakes applied

1   Brake pad friction lining material worn down to metal backing (Chapters 1 and 9)
2   Excessive corrosion of brake disc. (May be apparent after the vehicle has been standing for some time (Chapters 1 and 9)
3   Foreign object (stone chipping, etc.) trapped between brake disc and shield (Chapters 1 and 9)

46   Excessive brake pedal travel

1   Faulty master cylinder (Chapter 9)
2   Air in hydraulic system (Chapters 1 and 9)

47   Brake pedal feels spongy when depressed

1   Air in hydraulic system (Chapters 1 and 9)
2   Deteriorated flexible rubber brake hoses (Chapters 1 and 9)
3   Master cylinder mounting nuts loose (Chapter 9)
4   Faulty master cylinder (Chapter 9)

48   Excessive brake pedal effort required to stop vehicle

1   Faulty brake booster (Chapter 9)
2   Disconnected, damaged or insecure brake booster vacuum hose (Chapter 9)
3   Primary or secondary hydraulic circuit failure (Chapter 9)
4   Seized brake caliper piston(s) (Chapter 9)
5   Brake pads incorrectly installed (Chapters 1 and 9)
6   Incorrect grade of brake pads installed (Chapters 1 and 9)
7   Brake pads or brake shoe linings contaminated (Chapters 1 and 9)

49   Shudder felt through brake pedal or steering wheel when braking

1   Excessive run-out or distortion of brake discs (Chapters 1 and 9)
2   Brake pad linings worn (Chapters 1 and 9)
3   Brake caliper mounting bolts loose (Chapter 9)
4   Wear in suspension or steering components (Chapters 1 and 10)

50   Brakes binding

1   Seized brake caliper piston(s) (Chapter 9)
2   Incorrectly adjusted parking brake mechanism (Chapter 9)
3   Faulty master cylinder (Chapter 9)

51 Brake pedal travels to the floor with little resistance

1 Little or no fluid in the master cylinder reservoir caused by leaking caliper piston(s), or loose, damaged or disconnected brake lines. Inspect the entire system and correct as necessary (Chapters 1 and 9).
2 Worn master cylinder seals (Chapter 9).

SUSPENSION AND STEERING

➡**Note: Before diagnosing suspension or steering faults, be sure that the trouble is not due to incorrect tire pressures, mixtures of tire types, or binding brakes.**

52 Vehicle pulls to one side

1 Defective tire (Chapter 1)
2 Excessive wear in suspension or steering components (Chapters 1 and 10)
3 Incorrect front wheel alignment (Chapter 10)
4 Accident damage to steering or suspension components (Chapter 1)

53 Wheel wobble and vibration

1 Front wheels out of balance (vibration felt mainly through the steering wheel) (Chapters 1 and 10)
2 Rear wheels out of balance (vibration felt throughout the vehicle) (Chapters 1 and 10)
3 Wheels damaged or distorted (Chapters 1 and 10)
4 Faulty or damaged tire (Chapter 1)
5 Worn steering or suspension joints, bushings or components (Chapters 1 and 10)
6 Wheel bolts loose (Chapters 1 and 10)

54 Excessive pitching and/or rolling around corners, or during braking

1 Defective shock absorbers (Chapters 1 and 10)
2 Broken or weak spring and/or suspension component (Chapters 1 and 10)
3 Worn or damaged stabilizer bar, bushings or links (Chapter 10)

55 Wandering or general instability

1 Incorrect front wheel alignment (Chapter 10)
2 Worn steering or suspension joints, bushings or components (Chapters 1 and 10)
3 Wheels out of balance (Chapters 1 and 10)
4 Faulty or damaged tire (Chapter 1)
5 Wheel bolts loose (Chapters 1 and 10)
6 Defective shock absorbers (Chapters 1 and 10)

56 Excessively stiff steering

1 Lack of power steering fluid (Chapter 10)
2 Seized tie-rod end balljoint or suspension balljoint (Chapters 1 and 10)
3 Broken or incorrectly adjusted drivebelt - power steering (Chapter 1)

4 Incorrect front wheel alignment (Chapter 10)
5 Steering rack or column bent or damaged (Chapter 10)

57 Excessive play in steering

1 Worn steering column intermediate shaft universal joint (Chapter 10)
2 Worn steering track rod end balljoints (Chapters 1 and 10)
3 Worn rack-and-pinion steering gear (Chapter 10)
4 Worn steering or suspension joints, bushings or components (Chapters 1 and 10)

58 Lack of power assistance

1 Broken or incorrectly adjusted drivebelt (Chapter 1)
2 Incorrect power steering fluid level (Chapter 1)
3 Restriction in power steering fluid hoses (Chapter 1)
4 Faulty power steering pump (Chapter 10)
5 Faulty rack-and-pinion steering gear (Chapter 10)

59 Tire wear excessive

1 Tires worn on inside or outside edges
   a) *Tires under-inflated (wear on both edges) (Chapter 1)*
   b) *Incorrect camber or caster angles (wear on one edge only) (Chapter 10)*
   c) *Worn steering or suspension joints, bushings or components (Chapters 1 and 10)*
   d) *Excessively hard cornering.*
   e) *Accident damage.*
2 Tire treads exhibit feathered edges
   Incorrect toe setting (Chapter 10)
3 Tires worn in center of tread
   Tires over-inflated (Chapter 1)
4 Tires worn on inside and outside edges
   Tires under-inflated (Chapter 1)
5 Tires worn unevenly
   a) *Tires/wheels out of balance (Chapter 1)*
   b) *Excessive wheel or tire run-out (Chapter 1)*
   c) *Worn shock absorbers (Chapters 1 and 10)*
   d) *Faulty tire (Chapter 1)*

ELECTRICAL SYSTEM

➡**Note: For problems associated with the starting system, refer to the faults listed under Engine earlier in this Section.**

60 Battery will not hold a charge for more than a few days

1 Battery defective internally (Chapter 5)
2 Battery terminal connections loose or corroded (Chapter 1)
3 Drivebelt worn or incorrectly adjusted (Chapter 1)
4 Alternator not charging at correct output (Chapter 5)
5 Alternator or voltage regulator faulty (Chapter 5)
6 Short-circuit causing continual battery drain (Chapters 5 and 12)

61 Ignition/no-charge warning light remains illuminated with engine running

1 Drivebelt broken, worn, or incorrectly adjusted (Chapter 1)
2 Alternator brushes worn, sticking, or dirty (Chapter 5)
3 Alternator brush springs weak or broken (Chapter 5)
4 Internal fault in alternator or voltage regulator (Chapter 5)
5 Broken, disconnected, or loose wiring in charging circuit (Chapter 5)

62 Ignition/no-charge warning light fails to come on

1 Warning light bulb blown (Chapter 12)
2 Broken, disconnected, or loose wiring in warning light circuit (Chapter 12)
3 Alternator faulty (Chapter 5)

63 Lights inoperative

1 Bulb blown (Chapter 12)
2 Corrosion of bulb or bulb holder contacts (Chapter 12)
3 Blown fuse (Chapter 12)
4 Faulty relay (Chapter 12)
5 Broken, loose, or disconnected wiring (Chapter 12)
6 Faulty switch (Chapter 12)

64 Instrument readings inaccurate or erratic

1 Instrument readings increase with engine speed
  Faulty voltage regulator (Chapter 12)
2 Fuel or temperature gauges give no reading
 a) *Faulty gauge sender unit (Chapters 3 and 4)*
 b) *Wiring open-circuit (Chapter 12)*
 c) *Faulty gauge (Chapter 12)*
3 Fuel or temperature gauges give continuous maximum reading
 a) *Faulty gauge sender unit (Chapters 3 and 4)*
 b) *Wiring short-circuit (Chapter 12)*
 c) *Faulty gauge (Chapter 12)*

65 Horn inoperative, or unsatisfactory in operation

1 Horn operates all the time
 a) *Horn push either grounded or stuck down (Chapter 12)*
 b) *Horn cable-to-horn switch grounded (Chapter 12)*
2 Horn fails to operate
 a) *Blown fuse (Chapter 12)*
 b) *Cable or cable connections loose, broken or disconnected (Chapter 12)*
 c) *Faulty horn (Chapter 12)*
3 Horn emits intermittent or unsatisfactory sound
 a) *Cable connections loose (Chapter 12)*
 b) *Horn mountings loose (Chapter 12)*
 c) *Faulty horn (Chapter 12)*

66 Windshield wipers inoperative, or unsatisfactory in operation

1 Wipers fail to operate, or operate very slowly

 a) *Wiper blades stuck to screen, or linkage seized or binding (Chapters 1 and 12)*
 b) *Blown fuse (Chapter 12)*
 c) *Cable or cable connections loose, broken or disconnected (Chapter 12)*
 d) *Faulty relay (Chapter 12)*
 e) *Faulty wiper motor (Chapter 12)*
2 Wiper blades sweep over too large or too small an area of the glass
 a) *Wiper arms incorrectly positioned on spindles (Chapter 1)*
 b) *Excessive wear of wiper linkage (Chapter 12)*
 c) *Wiper motor or linkage mountings loose or insecure (Chapter 12)*
3 Wiper blades fail to clean the glass effectively
 a) *Wiper blade inserts worn or deteriorated (Chapter 1)*
 b) *Wiper arm tension springs broken, or arm pivots seized (Chapter 12)*
 c) *Insufficient windshield washer additive to adequately remove road film (Chapter 1)*

67 Windshield washers inoperative, or unsatisfactory in operation

1 One or more washer jets inoperative
 a) *Blocked washer jet (Chapter 1)*
 b) *Disconnected, kinked or restricted fluid hose (Chapter 12)*
 c) *Insufficient fluid in washer reservoir (Chapter 1)*
2 Washer pump fails to operate
 a) *Broken or disconnected wiring or connections (Chapter 12)*
 b) *Blown fuse (Chapter 12)*
 c) *Faulty washer switch (Chapter 12)*
 d) *Faulty washer pump (Chapter 12)*
3 Washer pump runs for some time before fluid is emitted from jets
  Faulty one-way valve in fluid supply hose (Chapter 12)

68 Electric windows inoperative, or unsatisfactory in operation

1 Window glass will only move in one direction
  Faulty switch (Chapter 12)
2 Window glass slow to move
 a) *Regulator seized or damaged, or in need of lubrication (Chapter 11)*
 b) *Door internal components or trim fouling regulator (Chapter 11)*
 c) *Faulty motor (Chapter 11)*

69 Window glass fails to move

1 Blown fuse (Chapter 12)
2 Faulty relay (Chapter 12)
3 Broken or disconnected wiring or connections (Chapter 12)
4 Faulty motor (Chapter 11)

70 Power lock system inoperative, or unsatisfactory in operation

1 Complete system failure
 a) *Blown fuse (Chapter 12)*
 b) *Faulty relay (Chapter 12)*

c) *Broken or disconnected wiring or connections (Chapter 12)*
d) *Faulty motor (Chapter 11)*

2 Latch locks but will not unlock, or unlocks but will not lock

a) *Faulty master switch (Chapter 12)*
b) *Broken or disconnected latch operating rods or levers (Chapter 11)*
c) *Faulty relay (Chapter 12)*
d) *Faulty motor (Chapter 11)*

3 One solenoid/motor fails to operate

a) *Broken or disconnected wiring or connections (Chapter 12)*
b) *Faulty operating assembly (Chapter 11)*
c) *Broken, binding or disconnected latch operating rods or levers (Chapter 11)*
d) *Fault in door latch (Chapter 11)*

Section

1

TUNE-UP AND ROUTINE MAINTENANCE

Engine compartment layout (2.5 liter model shown - others similar)

1) Oil filter cover
2) Power steering fluid reservoir
3) Coolant expansion tank
4) Air filter housing

5) Engine oil dipstick
6) Brake and clutch fluid reservoir
7) Engine electrical box

8) Cabin air filter cover
9) Windshield washer fluid reservoir
10) Engine oil filler cap

Engine compartment underside components (2.5 liter model shown - others similar)

1) Oil drain plug	3) Lower control arm	5) Steering gear boot	7) Exhaust pipes
2) Steering rack	4) Coolant drain plug	6) Front brake caliper	

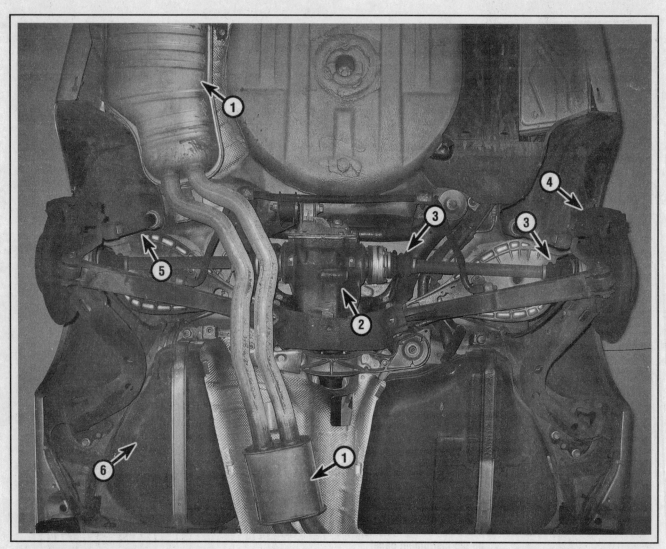

Rear underside components

1) Muffler
2) Differential
3) CV joint boot
4) Rear brake caliper
5) Shock absorber
6) Fuel tank

Maintenance schedule

→Note: Later models may come with a comprehensive maintenance plan where vehicle maintenance is included with vehicle
ownership for a certain amount of time. The BMW dealership
and owner's manual(s) have detailed information regarding any
type of maintenance plan your particular vehicle may have.

These models are equipped with a service display in the center of
the instrument panel, which shows the type of service next due, and the
distance remaining until the service is required. Once that distance is
reduced to zero, the display then shows the distance since the service
was due. Two types of service are specified, an Oil Service and an
Inspection Service. For more details, refer to the Owner's Handbook
supplied with the vehicle.

There are two different inspection services, Inspection I and Inspection II, these should be carried out alternately with some additional
items to be included every second Inspection II. If you are unclear as to
which inspection schedule was carried out last time start with Inspection II (including the additional items).

To reset the service interval display indicator on June 2000 and earlier models, a BMW service tool is required. Aftermarket alternatives to
the BMW tool are produced by several leading tool manufacturers and
should be available from larger car accessory shops.

EVERY 250 MILES (400 KM) OR WEEKLY

Check the engine oil level (Section 2)
Check the coolant level (Section 2)
Check the brake and clutch fluid level (Section 2)
Check the power steering fluid level (Section 2)
Tire condition and pressure (Section 2)
Windshield washer fluid level (Section 2)
Check the operation of all lights (Section 2)
Check the horn operation (Section 2)
Battery condition (Section 2)
Wiper blade condition (Section 2)
Electrical system condition (Section 2)

OIL SERVICE - 15,000 MILES (24,000 KM)

→Note: These vehicles are equipped with an oil life indicator
system that illuminates a message on the instrument panel
when the system deems it necessary to change the oil. A number of factors are taken into consideration to determine when
the oil should be considered worn out. Generally, this system
will allow the vehicle to accumulate more miles between oil
changes than the traditional 3000-mile interval, but we believe
that frequent oil changes are cheap insurance and will prolong
engine life. If you do decide not to change your oil every 3000
miles and rely on the oil life indicator instead, make sure you
don't exceed 15,000 miles before the oil is changed, regardless
of what the oil life indicator shows.

Replace the engine oil and filter (Section 3)
Reset the service interval display (Section 4)
Check the front brake pad thickness (Section 8)
Check the rear brake pad thickness (Section 9)
Check the operation of the parking brake (Section 10)
Replace the cabin filter (Section 14)

INSPECTION I - 30,000 MILES (48,000 KM) OR 24 MONTHS, WHICHEVER COMES FIRST

Check the manual transmission fluid level (if equipped) (Section 2)
Replace the engine oil and filter (Section 3)
Reset service interval display (Section 4)
Check all underhood components and hoses for fluid leaks
   (Section 5)
Check the condition of the drivebelts and replace if necessary
   (Section 6)
Check the condition of the steering and suspension components
   (Section 7)
Check the front brake pad thickness (Section 8)
Check the rear brake pad thickness (Section 9)
Check the operation of the parking brake (Section 10)
Check the exhaust system and mountings (Section 11)
Check the condition and operation of the seat belts (Section 12)
Lubricate all hinges and locks (Section 13)
Replace the cabin air filter (Section 14)
Check the headlight beam alignment (Section 15)
Check the operation of the windscreen/headlight washer system(s)
   (as applicable) (Section 16)
Check the engine management system (Section 17)
Carry out a road test (Section 18)

INSPECTION II - 60,000 MILES (96,000 KM) OR 48 MONTHS, WHICHEVER COMES FIRST

Carry out all the operations listed under Inspection I, along with the
following:

Reset the service interval display (Section 4)
Replace the spark plugs (Section 19)
Replace the air filter element (Section 20)
Check the condition of the driveshaft boots (Section 21)
Check the condition of the parking brake shoe linings (Section 22)

EVERY SECOND INSPECTION II

Replace the fuel filter (Section 23)

EVERY 2 YEARS

→Note: BMW states that the following should be carried out
regardless of mileage:

Replace the brake fluid (Section 24)

EVERY 4 YEARS

→Note: BMW states that the following should be carried out
regardless of mileage:

Replace the engine coolant (Section 25)

EVERY 100,000 MILES

Replace the automatic transmission fluid and filter (Section 26)

1   Introduction

1   This Chapter is designed to help the home mechanic maintain his/her vehicle for safety, economy, long life and peak performance.

2   The Chapter contains a master maintenance schedule, followed by Sections dealing specifically with each task in the schedule. Visual checks, adjustments, component replacement and other helpful items are included. Refer to the accompanying illustrations of the engine compartment and the underside of the vehicle for the locations of the various components.

3   Servicing your vehicle in accordance with the service indicator display and the following Sections will provide a planned maintenance program, which should result in a long and reliable service life. This is a comprehensive plan, so maintaining some items but not others at the specified service intervals, will not produce the same results.

4   As you service your vehicle, you will discover that many of the procedures can - and should - be grouped together, because of the particular procedure being performed, or because of the proximity of two otherwise-unrelated components to one another. For example, if the vehicle is raised for any reason, the exhaust can be inspected at the same time as the suspension and steering components.

5   The first step in this maintenance program is to prepare yourself before the actual work begins. Read through all the Sections relevant to the work to be carried out, then make a list and gather all the parts and tools required. If a problem is encountered, seek advice from a parts specialist, or a dealer service department.

2   Fluid level checks, general maintenance and tune-up information

FLUID LEVEL CHECKS

1   Fluids are an essential part of the lubrication, cooling, brake, clutch and other systems. Because these fluids gradually become depleted and/or contaminated during normal operation of the vehicle, they must be periodically replenished. See *Recommended lubricants and fluids* and *Capacities* at the end of this Chapter before adding fluid to any of the following components.

➡**Note: The vehicle must be on level ground before fluid levels can be checked.**

Engine oil

◗ **Refer to illustrations 2.2 and 2.4**

2   The engine oil level is checked with a dipstick located on the left side of the engine (see illustration). The dipstick extends through a metal tube from which it protrudes down into the engine oil pan.

3   The oil level should be checked before the vehicle has been driven, or about 5 minutes after the engine has been shut off. If the oil is checked immediately after driving the vehicle, some of the oil will remain in the upper engine components, producing an inaccurate reading on the dipstick.

4   Pull the dipstick from the tube and wipe all the oil from the end with a clean rag or paper towel. Insert the clean dipstick all the way back into its metal tube and pull it out again. Observe the oil at the end of the dipstick. At its highest point, the level should be between the upper and lower marks (see illustration).

5   It takes one quart of oil to raise the level from the lower mark to the upper mark on the dipstick. Do not allow the level to drop below the lower mark or oil starvation may cause engine damage. Conversely, overfilling the engine (adding oil above the upper mark) may cause oil-fouled spark plugs, oil leaks or oil seal failures.

6   Remove the filler cap to add oil (see illustration 2.2). Use a funnel to prevent spills if necessary. After adding the oil, install the filler cap hand tight. Start the engine for a minute and then turn it off. Check the oil level again after five minutes.

7   Checking the oil level is an important preventive maintenance step. A continually dropping oil level indicates oil leakage through damaged seals, from loose connections, or past worn rings or valve guides. If the oil looks milky in color or has water droplets in it, a cylinder head gasket may be blown or the oil cooler could be leaking. The engine should be checked immediately. The condition of the oil should also be checked. Each time you check the oil level, slide your thumb and index finger up the dipstick before wiping off the oil. If you see small dirt or metal particles clinging to the dipstick, the oil should be changed (see Section 3).

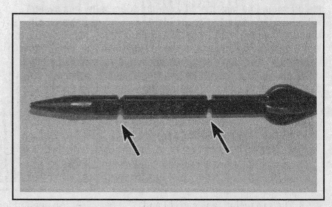

2.2 Check the oil level with the dipstick (A) and replenish oil through the filler cap (B)

2.4 The oil level should be between the two marks on the dipstick

Engine coolant

♦ Refer to illustrations 2.8 and 2.9

8 All vehicles covered by this manual are equipped with a pressurized coolant recovery system. A plastic expansion tank is located at the front of the engine compartment (see illustration). As the engine heats up during operation, the expanding coolant fills the tank.

9   The coolant level in the tank should be checked regularly.

The level in the tank varies with the temperature of the engine. When the engine is cold, the coolant level can be checked by removing the tank cap. The tank has a floating device which indicates the level of coolant (see illustration). If the level isn't correct, add a 50/50 mixture of ethylene glycol based antifreeze and water.

10 Drive the vehicle, let the engine cool completely then recheck the coolant level. If only a small amount of coolant is required to bring the system up to the proper level, water can be used. However, repeated additions of water will dilute the antifreeze and water solution. In order to maintain the proper ratio of antifreeze and water, always top up the coolant level with the correct mixture. An empty plastic milk jug or bleach bottle makes an excellent container for mixing coolant.

11 If the coolant level drops consistently, there may be a leak in the system. Inspect the radiator, hoses, filler cap, drain plugs and water pump (see Section 5). If no leaks are noted, have the expansion tank cap pressure tested by a service station.

12 If you have to remove the expansion tank cap, wait until the engine has cooled completely, then wrap a thick cloth around the cap and unscrew it slowly, stopping if you hear a hissing noise. If coolant or steam escapes, let the engine cool down longer, then remove the cap.

13 Check the condition of the coolant as well. It should be relatively clear. If it's brown or rust colored, the system should be drained, flushed and refilled. Even if the coolant appears to be normal, the corrosion inhibitors wear out, so it must be replaced at the specified intervals. Don't use rust inhibitors or additives.

Windshield washer fluid

➡Note: The windshield washer reservoir also provides fluid for the headlight washer system (if equipped).

14 Fluid for the windshield washer system is stored in a plastic reservoir that is located at the right front corner of the engine compartment - refer to the illustration at the beginning of this Chapter. In milder climates, plain water can be used to top up the reservoir, but the reservoir should be kept no more than 2/3 full to allow for expansion should the water freeze. In colder climates, the use of a specially designed windshield washer fluid, available at your dealer and any auto parts store, will help lower the freezing point of the fluid. Mix the solution with water in accordance with the manufacturer's directions on the container. Do not use regular antifreeze. It will damage the vehicle's paint.

Brake and clutch fluid

♦ Refer to illustration 2.16

15 The brake/clutch master cylinder is located on the driver's side of the engine compartment firewall.

16 The level should be maintained at the MAX mark on the reservoir (see illustration).

17 If additional fluid is necessary to bring the level up, use a rag to clean all dirt off the top of the reservoir. If any foreign matter enters the master cylinder when the cap is removed, blockage in the brake system lines can occur. Also, make sure all painted surfaces around the master cylinder are covered, since brake fluid will ruin paint. Carefully pour new, clean brake fluid into the master cylinder. Be careful not to spill the fluid on painted surfaces. Be sure the specified fluid is used; mixing different types of brake fluid can cause damage to the system. See *Recommended lubricants and fluids* at the end of this Chapter or your owner's manual.

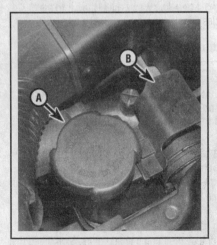

2.8 The expansion tank cap (A) and level information (B)

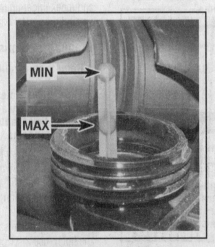

2.9 The coolant level indicator - when the upper (MIN) mark is level with the top of the filler neck, add coolant

2.16 The MAX and MIN marks are on the side of the master cylinder

18 At this time the fluid and the master cylinder can be inspected for contamination. If deposits, dirt particles or water droplets are seen in the fluid, the system should be drained, refilled and bled using new fluid (see Chapter 9).

19 Reinstall the master cylinder cap.

20 The brake fluid in the master cylinder will drop slightly as the brake shoes or pads at each wheel wear down during normal operation. If the master cylinder requires repeated replenishing to keep the level up, it's an indication of leaks in the brake system, which should be corrected immediately. Check all brake lines and connections, along with the wheel cylinders and booster (see Chapter 9 for more information).

21 If you discover that the reservoir is empty or nearly empty, the brake system should be filled, bled (see Chapter 9) and checked for leaks.

Power steering fluid

▶ Refer to illustration 2.26

22 Check the power steering fluid level periodically to avoid steering system problems, such as damage to the pump.

❋❋ CAUTION:

DO NOT hold the steering wheel against either stop (extreme left or right turn) for more than five seconds. If you do, the power steering pump could be damaged.

23 The power steering reservoir is located near the front of the engine compartment next to the oil filter cover - refer to the illustration at the beginning of this Chapter.

24 Park the vehicle on level ground and apply the parking brake.

25 Run the engine until it has reached normal operating temperature. With the engine at idle, turn the steering wheel back and forth about 10 times to get any air out of the steering system. Shut the engine off with the wheels in the straight-ahead position.

26 Remove the reservoir cap/dipstick and note the fluid level; it should be between the two marks (see illustration).

27 If necessary, add small amounts of fluid until the level is correct.

❋❋ CAUTION:

Do not overfill the reservoir. If too much fluid is added, remove the excess with a clean syringe or suction pump.

28 Check the power steering hoses and connections for leaks and wear.

Automatic transmission fluid

❋❋ CAUTION:

If you need to add fluid to your transmission to correct the level, it is extremely important that you use the appropriate fluid for your specific transmission. The correct type of fluid is found on a label on the bottom of the transmission. Failure to use the correct fluid could result in damage to the transmission. Consult a dealer parts department if there are any questions regarding which type of fluid to use for your specific transmission.

➡Note: On 5-speed automatic transmissions (2000 and later models), BMW recommends that the fluid level be checked by a

2.26 The fluid level should be between these two marks

BMW dealership or other qualified repair shop because the temperature of the fluid needs to be monitored to check the level properly.

29 The fluid level is checked by removing the filler/level plug from the transmission just above the fluid pan. If desired, raise the vehicle and support on jackstands to improve access, but make sure that the car is level.

30 The engine should be driven approximately 10 miles to warm the transmission fluid to the correct temperature range (between 85° to 120° degrees F). While the engine is idling, depress the brake pedal and move the selector lever through all the gear positions, beginning and ending in P.

31 Working under the car, place a container under the transmission fluid pan, then unscrew the filler/level plug.

32 The fluid level should be streaming slightly from the lower edge of the filler/level plug hole. Quickly replace the plug if the level is correct using a new gasket.

33 If necessary, top-up the fluid until it overflows from the plug hole.

34 The condition of the fluid should also be checked along with the level. If the fluid is black or a dark reddish-brown color, or if it smells burned, it should be replaced (see Section 26).

35 Install the filler/level plug (with a new gasket) and tighten it to the torque listed in this Chapter's Specifications.

36 Stop the engine and, where applicable, lower the car to the ground.

Manual transmission fluid

▶ Refer to illustration 2.37

➡Note: BMW states that the manual transmission is filled for life at the factory and no further service is necessary. We recommend that the fluid be checked every 30,000 miles (48,000 km) or 24 months.

37 The manual transmission does not have a dipstick. To check the fluid level, raise the vehicle and support it securely on jackstands. Remove the fluid fill-plug - located on the right side of the transmission case (see illustration). The fluid level is correct if it is up to the lower edge of the hole.

38 If the transmission needs more lubricant (if the level is not up to the hole), use a syringe or a gear oil pump to add more. Stop filling the transmission when the lubricant begins to run out the hole.

39 Install the plug and tighten it securely. Drive the vehicle a short distance and then check for leaks.

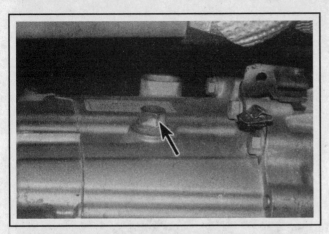

2.37 The transmission fill hole is on the side of the transmission

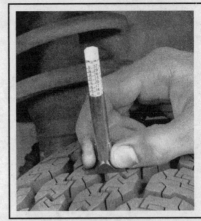

2.44 A tire tread depth indicator should be used to monitor tire wear - they are available at auto parts stores and service stations and cost very little

Rear differential fluid

➡Note: BMW states that the manual transmission is filled for life at the factory and no further service is necessary. We recommend that the fluid be checked every 30,000 miles (48,000 km) or 24 months.

40 To check the fluid level, raise the vehicle and support it securely on jackstands. On the axle housing, remove the check/fill plug. The fluid level is correct if it is up to the lower edge of the hole.

41 If the differential needs more lubricant (if the level is not up to the hole), use a syringe or a gear oil pump to add more. Stop filling the differential when the lubricant begins to run out the hole.

42 Install the plug and tighten it securely. Drive the vehicle a short distance and then check for leaks.

BASIC CHECKS AND MAINTENANCE

Tire condition and pressure

▶ Refer to illustrations 2.44, 2.45, 2.46a, 2.46b and 2.50

43 Periodic inspection of the tires may spare you from the inconvenience of being stranded with a flat tire. It can also provide you with vital information regarding possible problems in the steering and suspension systems before major damage occurs.

44 Normal tread wear can be monitored with a simple, inexpensive device known as a tread depth indicator (see illustration). When the tread depth reaches the specified minimum, replace the tire(s).

45 Note any abnormal tread wear (see illustration). Tread pattern irregularities such as cupping, flat spots and more wear on one side than the other are indications of front end alignment and/or balance

UNDERINFLATION

CUPPING

OVERINFLATION

Cupping may be caused by:
- Underinflation and/or mechanical irregularities such as out-of-balance condition of wheel and/or tire, and bent or damaged wheel.
- Loose or worn steering tie-rod or steering idler arm.
- Loose, damaged or worn front suspension parts.

INCORRECT TOE-IN OR EXTREME CAMBER

FEATHERING DUE TO MISALIGNMENT

2.45 This chart will help you determine the condition of your tires, the probable cause(s) of abnormal wear and the corrective action necessary

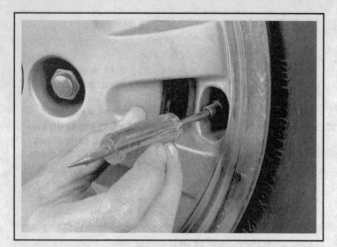

2.46a If a tire loses air on a steady basis, check the valve core first to make sure it's snug (special inexpensive wrenches are commonly available at auto parts stores)

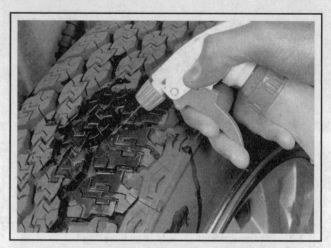

2.46b If the valve core is tight, raise the corner of the vehicle with the low tire and spray soapy water solution onto the tread as the tire is turned slowly - slow leaks will case small bubbles to appear

problems. If any of these conditions are noted, take the vehicle to a tire shop or service station to correct the problem.

46 Look closely for cuts, punctures and embedded nails or tacks. Sometimes a tire will hold its air pressure for a short time or leak down very slowly even after a nail has embedded itself into the tread. If a slow leak persists, check the valve core to make sure it is tight (see illustration). Examine the tread for an object that may have embedded itself into the tire or for a plug that may have begun to leak (radial tire punctures are repaired with a plug that is installed in a puncture). If a puncture is suspected, it can be easily verified by spraying a solution of soapy water onto the puncture area (see illustration). The soapy solution will bubble if there is a leak. Unless the puncture is inordinately large, a tire shop or gas station can usually repair the punctured tire.

47 Carefully inspect the inner side of each tire for evidence of brake fluid leakage. If you see any, inspect the brakes immediately.

48 Correct tire air pressure adds miles to the lifespan of the tires, improves mileage and enhances overall ride quality. Tire pressure cannot be accurately estimated by looking at a tire, particularly if it is a radial. A tire pressure gauge is therefore essential. Keep an accurate gauge in the glove box. The pressure gauges fitted to the nozzles of air hoses at gas stations are often inaccurate.

49 Always check tire pressure when the tires are cold. Cold, in this case, means the vehicle has not been driven over a mile in the three hours preceding a tire pressure check. A pressure rise of four to eight pounds is not uncommon once the tires are warm.

50 Unscrew the valve cap protruding from the wheel or hubcap and push the gauge firmly onto the valve (see illustration). Note the reading on the gauge and compare this figure to the recommended tire pressure shown on the tire placard on the left door jamb. Be sure to reinstall the valve cap to keep dirt and moisture out of the valve stem mechanism. Check all four tires and, if necessary, add enough air to bring them up to the recommended pressure levels.

51 Don't forget to keep the spare tire inflated to the specified pressure (consult your owner's manual). Note that the air pressure specified for the compact spare is significantly higher than the pressure of the regular tires.

Tire rotation (every 7500 miles [12,000 km] or 6 months)

▶ **Refer to illustrations 2.53a and 2.53b**

52 The tires should be rotated at the specified intervals and whenever uneven wear is noticed. Since the vehicle will be raised and the tires removed anyway, check the brakes (see Section 8) at this time.

53 Radial tires must be rotated in a specific pattern (see illustra-

2.50 To extend the life of your tires, check the air pressure at least once a week with an accurate gauge (don't forget the spare!)

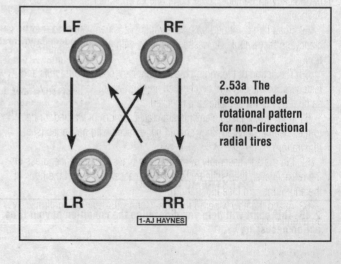

2.53a The recommended rotational pattern for non-directional radial tires

LF   RF

LR   RR

1-AJ HAYNES

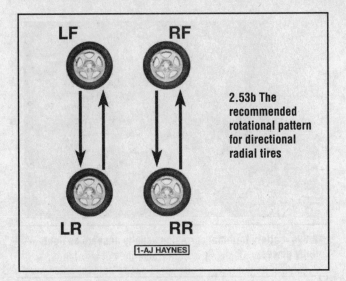

2.53b The recommended rotational pattern for directional radial tires

1-AJ HAYNES

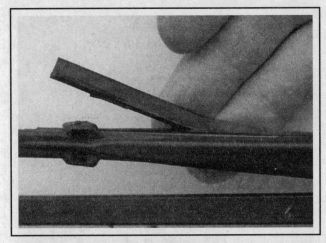

2.61 Replace worn or broken wiper blades

tions). Most models are equipped with non-directional tires, but some models may have directional tires, which have a different rotation pattern. When rotating tires, examine the sidewalls. Directional tires have arrows on the sidewall that indicate the direction they must turn, and a set of these tires includes two left-side tires and two right-side tires. The left and right side tires must not be rotated to the other side.

54 Refer to the information in *Jacking and towing* at the front of this manual for the proper procedures to follow when raising the vehicle and changing a tire. If the brakes are to be checked, do not apply the parking brake as stated. Make sure the tires are blocked to prevent the vehicle from rolling.

55 Preferably, the entire vehicle should be raised at the same time. This can be done on a hoist or by jacking up each corner and then lowering the vehicle onto jackstands placed under the frame rails. Always use four jackstands and make sure the vehicle is firmly supported.

56 After rotation, check and adjust the tire pressures as necessary and be sure to check the wheel bolt tightness. Ideally, wheel bolts should be tightened to the torque listed in this Chapter's Specifications with a torque wrench, and rechecked after 25 miles of driving.

57 For further information on the wheels and tires, refer to Chapter 10.

Wiper blades

▶ **Refer to illustrations 2.61 and 2.62**

58 The windshield wiper and blade assembly should be inspected periodically for damage, loose components and cracked or worn blade elements.

59 Road film can build up on the wiper blades and affect their efficiency, so they should be washed regularly with a mild detergent solution.

60 The action of the wiping mechanism can loosen bolts, nuts and fasteners, so they should be checked and tightened, as necessary, at the same time the wiper blades are checked.

61 If the wiper blade elements are cracked, worn or warped, or no longer clean adequately, they should be replaced with new ones (see illustration).

62 Lift the arm assembly away from the glass for clearance, press on the release lever, then slide the wiper blade assembly out of the hook at the end of the arm (see illustration).

63 Attach the new wiper to the arm. Connection can be confirmed by an audible click.

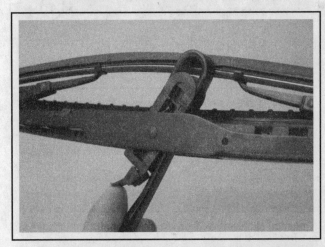

2.62 Swivel the blade at the arm and depress the locking tab and slide the blade from the hooked portion of the arm

Battery

▶ **Refer to illustrations 2.64, 2.69a, 2.69b, 2.70a and 2.70b**

✳✳ WARNING:

Certain precautions must be followed when checking and servicing the battery. Hydrogen gas, which is highly flammable, is always present in the battery cells, so keep lighted tobacco and all other open flames and sparks away from the battery. The electrolyte inside the battery is actually diluted sulfuric acid, which will cause injury if splashed on your skin or in your eyes. It will also ruin clothes and painted surfaces. When removing the battery cables, always detach the negative cable first and hook it up last!

64 A routine preventive maintenance program for the battery in your vehicle is the only way to ensure quick and reliable starts. But before performing any battery maintenance, make sure that you have the proper equipment necessary to work safely around the battery (see illustration on following page).

65 There are also several precautions that should be taken whenever battery maintenance is performed. Before servicing the battery, always turn the engine and all accessories off and disconnect the cable from

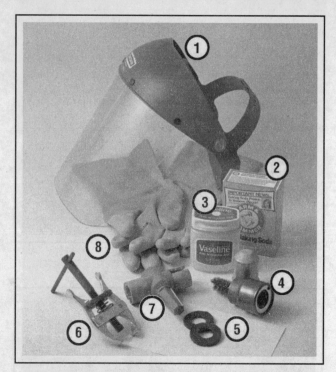

2.64 Tools and materials required for battery maintenance

1   **Face shield/safety goggles** - When removing corrosion with a brush, the acidic particles can easily fly up into your eyes
2   **Baking soda** - A solution of baking soda and water can be used to neutralize corrosion
3   **Petroleum jelly** - A layer of this on the battery posts will help prevent corrosion
4   **Battery post/cable cleaner** - This wire brush cleaning tool will remove all traces of corrosion from the battery posts and cable clamps
5   **Treated felt washers** - Placing one of these on each post, directly under the cable clamps, will help prevent corrosion
6   **Puller** - Sometimes the cable clamps are very difficult to pull off the posts, even after the nut/bolt has been completely loosened. This tool pulls the clamp straight up and off the post without damage
7   **Battery post/cable cleaner** - Here is another cleaning tool which is a slightly different version of number 4 above, but it does the same thing
8   **Rubber gloves** - Another safety item to consider when servicing the battery; remember that's acid inside the battery

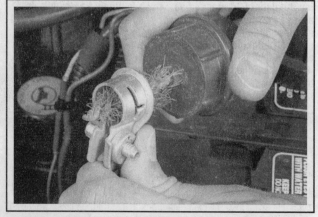

2.70a When cleaning the cable clamps, all corrosion must be removed

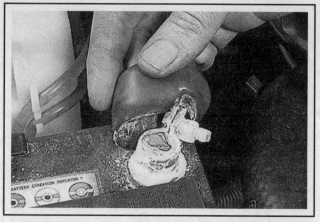

2.69a Battery terminal corrosion usually appears as light, fluffy powder

2.69b Removing a cable from the battery post with a wrench - sometimes a pair of special battery pliers are required for this procedure if corrosion has caused deterioration of the nut hex (always remove the ground (-) cable first and hook it up last!)

the negative terminal of the battery (see Chapter 5, Section 1).

66 The battery produces hydrogen gas, which is both flammable and explosive. Never create a spark, smoke or light a match around the battery. Always charge the battery in a ventilated area.

67 Electrolyte contains poisonous and corrosive sulfuric acid. Do not allow it to get in your eyes, on your skin on your clothes. Never ingest it. Wear protective safety glasses when working near the battery. Keep children away from the battery.

68 Note the external condition of the battery. If the positive terminal and cable clamp on your vehicle's battery is equipped with a rubber protector, make sure that it's not torn or damaged. It should completely cover the terminal. Look for any corroded or loose connections, cracks in the case or cover or loose hold-down clamps. Also check the entire length of each cable for cracks and frayed conductors.

69 If corrosion, which looks like white, fluffy deposits (see illustration) is evident, particularly around the terminals, the battery should be removed for cleaning. Loosen the cable clamp bolts with a wrench, being careful to remove the ground cable first, and slide them off the terminals (see illustration). Then disconnect the hold-down clamp bolt and nut, remove the clamp and lift the battery from the engine compartment.

70 Clean the cable clamps thoroughly with a battery brush or a

2.70b Regardless of the type of tool used to clean the battery posts, a clean, shiny surface should be the result

2.77 Failed bulbs are the most likely cause for a lamp that stops working

terminal cleaner and a solution of warm water and baking soda (see illustration). Wash the terminals and the top of the battery case with the same solution but make sure that the solution doesn't get into the battery. When cleaning the cables, terminals and battery top, wear safety goggles and rubber gloves to prevent any solution from coming in contact with your eyes or hands. Wear old clothes too - even diluted, sulfuric acid splashed onto clothes will burn holes in them. If the terminals have been extensively corroded, clean them up with a terminal cleaner (see illustration). Thoroughly wash all cleaned areas with plain water.

71 Make sure that the battery tray is in good condition and the hold-down clamp fasteners are tight. If the battery is removed from the tray, make sure no parts remain in the bottom of the tray when the battery is reinstalled. When reinstalling the hold-down clamp bolts, do not over-tighten them.

72 Information on removing and installing the battery can be found in Chapter 5. If you disconnected the cable(s) from the negative and/or positive battery terminals, see Chapter 5, Section 1. Information on jump starting can be found at the front of this manual.

73 Corrosion on the hold-down components, battery case and surrounding areas can be removed with a solution of water and baking soda. Thoroughly rinse all cleaned areas with plain water.

74 Any metal parts of the vehicle damaged by corrosion should be covered with a zinc-based primer, then painted.

Electrical systems

▶ **Refer to illustrations 2.77 through 2.79**

75 Check all external lights and the horn. Refer to the appropriate Sections of Chapter 12 for the details if any of the circuits are found to be inoperative

76 Visually check all accessible wiring connectors, harnesses and retaining clips for security, and for signs for chaffing or damage.

77 If a single indicator light, brake light or headlight has failed, it is likely that a bulb has blown and will need to be replaced. Refer to Chapter 12 for details. If both brake lights have failed, it is possible that the switch has failed (see illustration).

78 If more than one indicator light or taillight has failed, check that a fuse has not blown or that there is a fault in the circuit (see Chapter 12). The fuses are location in the fuse box in the passenger side glove box (see illustration). Details of the circuits protected by the fuses are shown on the card in the fuse box. Open the glove box, rotate the fasteners 90-degrees counterclockwise and lower the fuse box cover from the roof of the glove box.

2.78 The fuse box is located in the passengers side glove box

79 To replace a blown fuse, simply pull it out and install a new fuse of the correct amp rating (see illustration). If the fuse blows again, it is important that you find the cause (see Chapter 12).

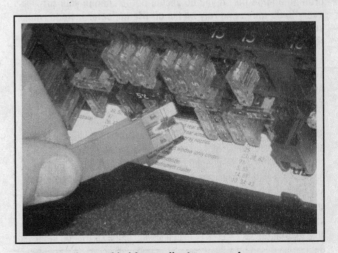

2.79 Use the provided fuse puller to remove fuses

※※ CAUTION:

Never replace a fuse using one with a different rating; This could result in major damage to the electrical system.

TUNE-UP

80 If the routine maintenance schedule is followed closely, especially from the time the vehicle is new, the engine will be kept in relatively good running condition and minimize the need for additional work in the future.

81 It is possible that there will be times when the engine is running poorly due to the lack of regular maintenance. This is even more likely if a used vehicle, which has not received regular and frequent maintenance checks, is purchased. In such cases, additional work may need to be carried out, outside of the regular maintenance intervals.

82 If engine wear is suspected, a compression test (see Chapter 2A) will provide valuable information regarding the overall performance of the main internal components. Such a test can be used as a basis to decide on the extent of the work to be carried out. If, for example, a compression test indicates serious internal engine wear, conventional maintenance as described in this Chapter will not greatly improve the

performance of the engine, and may prove a waste of time and money, unless extensive overhaul work is carried out first.

83 The following series of operations are those most often required to improve the performance of a generally poor-running engine:

Primary operations

a) Clean, inspect and test the battery (this section and Chapter 5).
b) Check all the engine-related fluids (this section).
c) Check the condition and tension of the drivebelts (Section 6).
d) Replace the spark plugs (Section 19).
e) Check the condition of the air filter, and replace if necessary (Section 20).
f) Check the fuel filter (Section 23).
g) Check the condition of all hoses, and check for fluid leaks (Section 5).

84 If the above operations do not prove fully effective, carry out the following secondary operations:

Secondary operations

All items listed under Primary operations, plus the following:

a) Check the charging system (see relevant Part of Chapter 5).
b) Check the ignition system (see relevant Part of Chapter 5).
c) Check the fuel system (see relevant Part of Chapter 4).

Inspection I

3 Engine oil and filter replacement

▶ Refer to illustrations 3.2, 3.5a, 3.5b, 3.8 and 3.14

➡Note: **These vehicles are equipped with an oil life indicator system that illuminates a light or message on the instrument panel when the system deems it necessary to change the oil. A number of factors are taken into consideration to determine when the oil should be considered worn out. Generally, this system will allow the vehicle to accumulate more miles between oil changes than the traditional 3000-mile interval, but we believe that frequent oil changes are cheap insurance and will prolong engine life. If you do decide not to change your oil every 3000 miles and rely on the oil life indicator instead, make sure you don't exceed 15,000 miles before the oil is changed, regardless of what the oil life indicator shows.**

1 Frequent oil and filter changes are the most important preventative maintenance work which can be undertaken by the home mechanic. As engine oil ages, it becomes diluted and contaminated, which leads to premature engine wear.

2 Before starting this procedure, gather together all the necessary tools and materials. Also make sure you have plenty of clean rags and newspapers handy, to mop up any spills. Ideally, the engine oil should be warm, as it will drain better, and more built-up sludge will be removed with it. Take care, however, not to touch the exhaust or any other hot parts of the engine when working under the car. To avoid any possibility of scalding, and to protect yourself from possible skin irritants and other harmful contaminants in used engine oils, it is advisable to wear gloves. Access to the underside of the car will be improved if it can be raised on a lift, driven onto ramps, or jacked up and supported on axle stands (see *Jacking and towing*). Whichever method is

3.2 Access to the drain plug is through a removable cover in the reinforcement plate

used, make sure the car remains level. On vehicles equipped with a front reinforcement plate between the front suspension lower control arms, access to the oil drain plug is through a removable cover in the plate (see illustration).

3 Working in the engine compartment, locate the oil filter housing at the front of the engine in front of the intake manifold.

4 Place a rag around the bottom of the housing to absorb any spilt oil.

3.5a Use an oil filter removal tool . . .

3.5b . . . or a strap wrench to remove the cover from the oil filter housing

5   Remove the oil filter housing cover using an oil filter wrench or equivalent (see illustrations). Remove the cover and lift the filter cartridge out.

6   Remove the O-rings from the cover.

7   Using a clean rag, wipe the mating faces of the housing and cover.

8   Install new O-rings to the cover (see illustration).

9   Place the new filter cartridge into the housing.

10 Apply a small amount of clean engine oil to the O-rings, install the cover and tighten it to the torque listed in this Chapter's Specifications.

11 Working under the car, loosen the oil drain plug about half a turn. Position the drain pan under the drain plug and then remove the plug completely.

➡**Note: It is very helpful to use gloves and keep pressure on the drain plug until it has cleared all of the threads of the oil pan and then remove it quickly.**

12 Recover the drain plug gasket (washer).

13 Allow some time for the old oil to drain. It may be necessary to reposition the drain pan as the oil flow slows to a trickle.

14 After all the oil has drained, wipe off the drain plug with a clean rag. Check the gasket condition, and replace it if necessary. Clean the area around the drain plug opening, then install and tighten the plug to the torque listed in this Chapter's Specifications (see illustration).

15 Remove the old oil and all tools from under the car and then lower the car to the ground (if applicable).

16 Remove the dipstick and then unscrew the oil filler cap. Fill the engine, using the correct grade and type of oil listed in this Chapter's Specifications. A funnel may help to reduce spillage. Pour in half the specified quantity of oil first, then wait a few minutes for the oil to fall to the oil pan. Continue adding oil a small quantity at a time until the level is up to the lower mark on the dipstick. Finally, bring the level up to the upper mark on the dipstick. Insert the dipstick, and install the filler cap.

17 Start the engine and run it for a few minutes. Check for leaks around the oil filter cover and the oil drain plug. The oil warning light should go off after a few seconds.

18 Turn off the engine, and wait a few minutes for the oil to settle in the oil pan once more. With the new oil circulated and the filter completely full, recheck the level on the dipstick and add more oil as necessary.

✳✳ CAUTION:

Be careful not to overfill the engine with oil. Having too much oil in the engine could cause considerable damage.

19 Dispose of the used filter and engine oil safely. Check on the Internet or with your local auto parts store, disposal facility or environmental agency to find where used oil is accepted for recycling. After the oil has cooled, it can be drained into containers (capped plastic jugs, topped bottles, milk cartons, etc.) for safe transport to an appropriate disposal site. DO NOT dispose of the oil any other way!

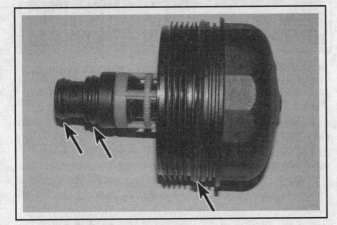

3.8 Install new O-rings to the cover

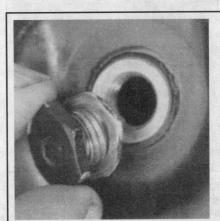

3.14 Check the condition of the oil drain plug gasket

4   Resetting the service interval display

JUNE 2000 AND EARLIER MODELS

➡**Note: The following requires use of a special BMW service tool and adapter. If an aftermarket tool is being used, refer to the instructions supplied by its manufacturer.**

1   Turn the ignition off, unscrew the cap, then plug BMW service interval resetting tool 62 1 110 into the engine compartment diagnostic socket. The socket is round with a protective cap and located near the jump start terminals in the right-rear part of the engine compartment.

2   Ensure that all electrical items are switched off then turn on the ignition switch.

➡**Note: Do not start the engine.**

3   To reset an Oil Service, press and hold the yellow button; the green light will illuminate. After about 3 seconds the yellow light will illuminate for about 12 seconds, and then go out.

4   To reset an Inspection Service, press and hold the red Inspection button; the green (function check) light will illuminate. After about 3 seconds the red lamp should also light, remain on for about 12 seconds, and then go out. Release the Inspection button and the green (function check) light will go out.

5   If the clock (annual service) symbol was illuminated at the same time as the oil service or inspection indicator, wait 20 seconds then repeat the operation in paragraph 4.

6   Turn off the ignition switch and disconnect the resetting tool and adapter from the diagnostic connector.

7   Turn the ignition switch on and check that the Service Interval Display has been reset.

JULY 2000 AND LATER MODELS

➡**Note: No special tool is necessary to reset the service interval display on these models.**

8   Press and hold the trip odometer reset button and then turn the ignition key to the accessory position.

9   After about 5 seconds the display will change, release the button once and then press and hold again for about 5 more seconds.

10 When the display begins to flash, release the button and press it once again briefly. After a few seconds, the display will change to END SIA.

11 The vehicle must be driven another 75 miles if any further resetting is needed.

12 You can interrupt the procedure by simply turning the ignition key off and start over if necessary.

5   Hose and fluid leak check

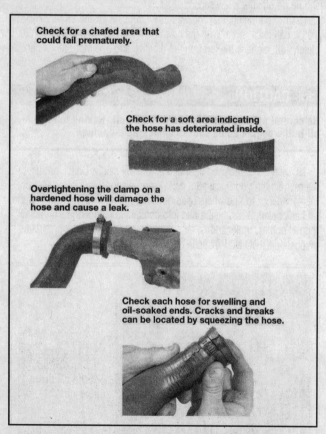

Check for a chafed area that could fail prematurely.

Check for a soft area indicating the hose has deteriorated inside.

Overtightening the clamp on a hardened hose will damage the hose and cause a leak.

Check each hose for swelling and oil-soaked ends. Cracks and breaks can be located by squeezing the hose.

5.3 Hoses, like drivebelts, have a habit of failing at the worst possible time - to prevent the inconvenience of a blown radiator or heater hose, inspect them carefully as shown here

▶ **Refer to illustration 5.3**

1   Visually inspect the engine joints, gaskets and seals for any signs of water or oil leaks. Pay particular attention to the areas around the camshaft cover, cylinder head, oil filter and oil pan. Keep in mind that, over a period of time, some very slight seepage from these areas is to be expected - what you are really looking for is any indication of a serious leak. Should a leak be found, replace the failing gasket or oil seal by referring to the appropriate Chapters in this manual.

2   Also check the security and condition of all the engine-related lines and hoses. Ensure that all cable-ties or securing clips are in place and in good condition. Clips that are broken or missing can lead to chafing of the hoses, lines or wiring, which could cause more serious problems in the future.

3   Carefully check the radiator hoses and heater hoses along their entire length. Replace any hose that is cracked, swollen or deteriorated. Cracks will show up better if the hose is squeezed. Pay close attention to the hose clips that secure the hoses to the cooling system components. Hose clips can pinch and puncture hoses, resulting in cooling system leaks (see illustration).

4   Inspect all the cooling system components (hoses, joints, etc) for leaks. Where any problems of this nature are found on system components, replace the component or gasket with reference to Chapter 3.

5   Where applicable, inspect the automatic transmission fluid cooler hoses for leaks or deterioration.

6   With the car raised, inspect the fuel tank and filler neck for punctures, cracks and other damage. The connection between the filler neck and tank is especially critical. Sometimes a rubber filler neck or connecting hose will leak due to loose retaining clamps or deteriorated rubber.

7   Carefully check all rubber hoses and metal fuel lines leading away from the fuel tank. Check for loose connections, deteriorated

hoses, crimped lines, and other damage. Pay particular attention to the vent lines and hoses, which often loop up around the filler neck and can become blocked or crimped. Follow the lines to the front of the car, carefully inspecting them all the way. Replace damaged sections as necessary.

8   Closely inspect the metal brake line which run along the car underbody. If they show signs of excessive corrosion or damage, they must be replaced.

9   From within the engine compartment, check the security of all fuel hose attachments and line fittings, and inspect the fuel hoses and vacuum hoses for kinks, chafing and deterioration.

10 Check the condition of the power steering fluid hoses and lines.

6   Drivebelt - check and replacement

CHECK

1   Due to their function and construction, the belts are prone to failure after a period of time, and should be inspected periodically to prevent problems.

2   The number of belts used on a particular car depends on the accessories installed. Drivebelts are used to drive the water pump, alternator, power steering pump and air conditioning compressor.

3   To improve access for belt inspection, if desired, remove the viscous cooling fan and cowl (if equipped) as described in Chapter 3.

4   With the engine stopped, using your fingers (and a light if necessary), move along the belts, checking for cracks and separation of the belt plies. Also check for fraying and glazing, which gives the belt a shiny appearance. Both sides of the belts should be inspected, which means the belt will have to be twisted to check the underside. If necessary turn the engine using a wrench or socket on the crankshaft pulley bolt so that the whole belt can be inspected.

REPLACEMENT

Air conditioning compressor

♦ **Refer to illustrations 6.6 and 6.7**

5   Access is most easily obtained from under the car. If desired, raise the front of the vehicle and support securely on jackstands. Remove the screws and remove the engine splash shield (see Section 25).

6   On models with a hydraulic tensioner, pry the cover from the center of the tensioner pulley. Engage a hexagon bit and extension bar with the tensioner bolt, and lever the tensioner clockwise (see illustration). Slide the belt from the pulleys.

7   On models with a mechanical tensioner, using a wrench on the hexagon section of the pulley arm, rotate the tensioner clockwise, and remove the belt from the pulleys (see illustration).

8   On all models, lever the tensioner until the drivebelt can be installed around the pulleys, then release the tensioner. Make sure that the belt is centered on the pulleys and engages the grooves correctly.

9   Install the splash shield and lower the car to the ground.

Water pump/alternator/power steering pump

♦ **Refer to illustrations 6.14 and 6.16**

10 Where applicable, remove the air conditioning compressor drivebelt as described previously in this Section.

11 If the drivebelt is to be re-used, mark the running direction of the belt before removal.

12 To improve access, remove the viscous cooling fan and shroud (if equipped) as described in Chapter 3.

13 Make a diagram of the routing of the drivebelt before removal.

14 Using a wrench on the hexagonal section of the pulley arm, rotate

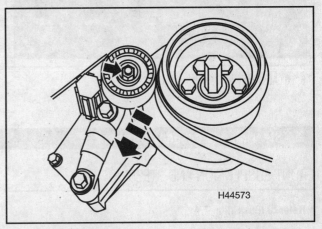

6.6 Insert the hexagon bit into the pulley center, and rotate the tensioner clockwise

6.7 Rotate the pulley arm clockwise

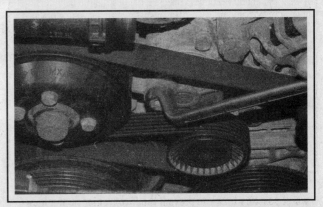

6.14 Rotate the tensioner clockwise and remove the belt

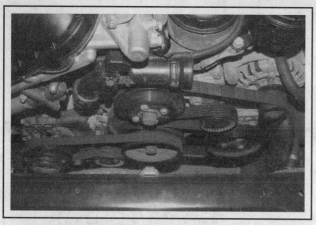

6.16 Auxiliary drivebelt routing

the tensioner clockwise, and remove the belt from the pulleys (see illustration).

15 If the original belt is being reinstalled, observe the running direction mark made before removal.

16 Compress the tensioner, and engage the belt with the pulleys, ensuring that it is routed as noted before removal. Make sure that the belt is centered on the pulleys and engages the grooves correctly (see illustration).

17 Where applicable, install the viscous cooling fan and shroud with reference to Chapter 3.

18 Where applicable, install the air conditioning compressor drivebelt as described previously in this Section.

7   Steering and suspension check

FRONT SUSPENSION AND STEERING

▶ **Refer to illustration 7.4**

1   Raise the front of the vehicle and support it securely on jackstands.

2   Visually inspect the balljoint dust covers and the steering rack-and-pinion boots for splits, chafing or deterioration. Any wear of these components will cause loss of lubricant, then dirt and water entry, resulting in rapid deterioration of the balljoints or steering gear.

3   Check the power steering fluid hoses for chafing or deterioration and the line and hose fittings for fluid leaks. Also check for signs of fluid leakage under pressure from the steering gear rubber boots, which would indicate failed fluid seals within the steering gear.

4   Grasp the wheel at the 12 o'clock and 6 o'clock positions, and try to rock it (see illustration). Very slight free play may be felt, but if the movement is appreciable, further investigation is necessary to determine the source. Continue rocking the wheel while an assistant depresses the brake. If the movement is now eliminated or significantly reduced, it is likely that the hub bearings are at fault. If the free play is still evident with the brake depressed, then there is wear in the suspension joints or mountings.

5   Now grasp the wheel at the 9 o'clock and 3 o'clock positions, and try to rock it as before. Any movement felt now may again be caused by wear in the hub bearings or the steering gear tie rod balljoints. If the inner or outer balljoint is worn, the visual movement will be obvious.

6   Using a large screwdriver or flat bar, check for wear in the suspension mounting bushings by levering between the relevant suspension component and its attachment point. Some movement is to be expected as the mountings are made of rubber, but excessive wear should be obvious. Also check the condition of any visible rubber bushings, looking for splits, cracks or contamination of the rubber.

7   With the car standing on its wheels, have an assistant turn the steering wheel back-and-forth about an eighth of a turn each way. There should be very little, if any, lost movement between the steering wheel and wheels. If this is not the case, closely observe the joints and mountings previously described, but in addition, check the steering column universal joints for wear, and the rack-and-pinion steering gear itself.

STRUT/SHOCK ABSORBER

8   Check for any signs of fluid leakage around the suspension strut/shock absorber body, or from the rubber boot around the piston rod. Should any fluid be noticed, the suspension strut/shock absorber is defective internally, and should be replaced.

➡**Note: Suspension struts/shock absorbers should always be replaced in pairs on the same axle.**

9   The efficiency of the suspension strut/shock absorber may be checked by bouncing the car at each corner. Generally speaking, the body will return to its normal position and stop after being depressed. If it rises and returns on a rebound, the suspension strut/shock absorber is probably suspect. Examine also the suspension strut/shock absorber upper and lower mountings for any signs of wear.

7.4 Check for wear in the hub bearings by grasping the wheel and trying to rock it

8   Front brake pad check

▶ **Refer to illustration 8.2**

1   Loosen the front wheel bolts. Firmly apply the parking brake, then raise the front of the vehicle and support it securely on jackstands. Remove the front wheels.

2   For a quick check, the thickness of friction material remaining on each brake pad can be measured through the top of the caliper body (see illustration). If any pad's friction material thickness is not within specification, all four pads must be replaced as a set.

3   For a comprehensive check, the brake pads should be removed and cleaned. The operation of the caliper can then also be checked, and the condition of the brake disc itself can be fully examined on both sides. Refer to Chapter 9 for further information.

8.2   Check the thickness of the brake pad friction material through the hole in the caliper body

9   Rear brake pad check

1   Loosen the front wheel bolts. Chock the front wheels, then raise the rear of the vehicle and support it securely on jackstands. Remove the rear wheels.

2   For a quick check, the thickness of friction material remaining on each brake pad can be measured through the top of the caliper body (see illustration 8.2). If any pad's friction material thickness is not within specification, all four pads must be replaced as a set.

3   For a comprehensive check, the brake pads should be removed and cleaned. This will permit the operation of the caliper to be checked, and the condition of the brake disc itself to be fully examined on both sides. Refer to Chapter 9 for further information.

10   Parking brake check

Check and, if necessary, adjust the parking brake as described in Chapter 9. Check that the parking brake cables are free to move easily and lubricate all exposed linkages/cable pivots.

11   Exhaust system check

▶ **Refer to illustration 11.2**

1   With the engine cold (at least an hour after the car has been driven), check the complete exhaust system from the engine to the end of the tailpipe. The exhaust system is most easily checked with the car raised on a hoist, or suitably supported on jackstands, so that the exhaust components are readily visible and accessible.

2   Check the exhaust pipes and connections for evidence of leaks, severe corrosion and damage. Make sure that all brackets and mountings are in good condition, and that all relevant nuts and bolts are tight (see illustration). Leakage at any of the joints or in other parts of the system will usually show up as a black sooty stain in the vicinity of the leak.

3   Rattles and other noises can often be traced to the exhaust system, especially the brackets and mountings. Try to move the pipes and mufflers. If the components are able to come into contact with the body or suspension parts, secure the system with new mountings. Otherwise separate the joints (if possible) and twist the pipes as necessary to provide additional clearance.

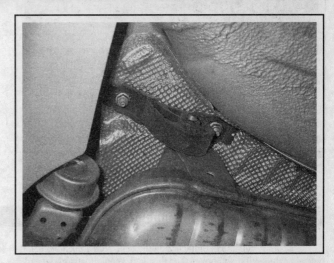

11.2   Check the condition of the exhaust rubber hangers/mounts

12 Seat belt check

1 Carefully examine the seat belt webbing for cuts or any signs of serious fraying or deterioration. If the seat belt is of the retractable type, pull the belt all the way out, and examine the full extent of the webbing.

2 Fasten and unfasten the belt, ensuring that the locking mechanism holds securely and releases properly when intended. If the belt is of the retractable type, check also that the retracting mechanism operates correctly when the belt is released.

3 Check the security of all seat belt mountings and attachments which are accessible, without removing any trim or other components, from inside the car.

13 Hinge and lock lubrication

1 Lubricate the hinges of the hood, doors and trunk with a light general-purpose oil. Similarly, lubricate all latches, locks and lock strikers. At the same time, check the security and operation of all the locks, adjusting them if necessary (see Chapter 11).

2 Lightly lubricate the hood release mechanism and cable with a suitable grease.

14 Cabin air filter replacement

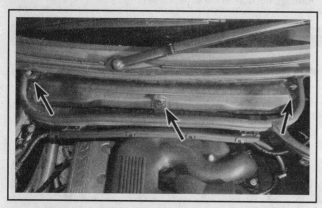

14.1a Rotate the three clips (arrowed) counterclockwise . . .

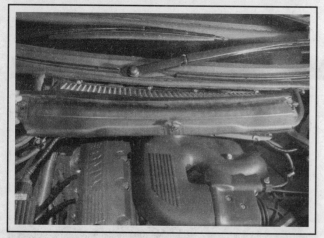

14.1b . . . and remove the filter cover

▶ **Refer to illustrations 14.1a, 14.1b and 14.2**

1 Working at the rear of the engine compartment, rotate the three retaining clips 90° counterclockwise and pull the filter cover out to the front (see illustrations).

2 Pull the filter up and to the front, and maneuver it from the housing (see illustration).

3 Install the new filter into the housing, ensuring that it's placed with the correct side up.

4 Install the filter cover, and secure it in place with the retaining clips.

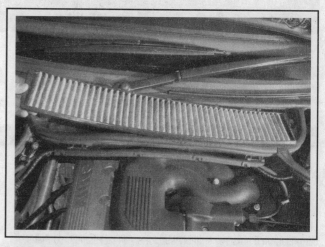

14.2 Remove the cabin air filter from the housing

15 Headlight beam alignment check

1 Accurate adjustment of the headlight beam is only possible using optical beam-setting equipment, and this work should therefore be carried out by a BMW dealer or service station with the necessary facilities.

2 Basic adjustments can be carried out in an emergency, and further details are given in Chapter 12.

16 Windshield/headlight washer system(s) check

▶ **Refer to illustration 16.1**

➡**Note: Not all models are equipped with a headlight washer system.**

1 Check that each of the washer jet nozzles are clear and that each nozzle provides a strong jet of washer fluid. The jets should be aimed to spray at a point slightly above the center of the windshield/headlight. On the windshield washer nozzles where there are two jets, aim one of the jets slightly above then center of the screen and aim the other just below to ensure complete coverage of the screen. If necessary, adjust the jets using a pin or length of fine, stiff wire (see illustration). Take great care not to damage the water channels in the jets.

2 Adjustment of the headlight washer jets requires the use of BMW special tool 00 9 100.

16.1 Use a fine pin to adjust the washer jet aim

17 Engine management system check

1 This check is part of the manufacturer's maintenance schedule, and involves testing the engine management system using a scan tool (see Chapter 6). Such testing will allow the test equipment to read any fault codes stored in the electronic control unit memory.

2 Unless a fault is suspected, this test is not essential, although it should be noted that it is recommended by the manufacturer.

3 If access to suitable test equipment is not possible, make a thorough check of all ignition, fuel and emission control system components, hoses, and wiring, for security and obvious signs of damage. Further details of the fuel system, emission control system and ignition system can be found in Chapters 4 and 5.

18 Road test

INSTRUMENTS AND ELECTRICAL EQUIPMENT

1 Check the operation of all instruments and electrical equipment.
2 Make sure that all instruments read correctly, and switch on all electrical equipment in turn, to check that it functions properly.

STEERING AND SUSPENSION

3 Check for any abnormalities in the steering, suspension, handling or road feel.
4 Drive the car, and check that there are no unusual vibrations or noises.
5 Check that the steering feels positive, with no excessive sloppiness, or roughness, and check for any suspension noises when cornering and driving over bumps.

DRIVETRAIN

6 Check the performance of the engine, clutch (where applicable), transmission and driveshafts.
7 Listen for any unusual noises from the engine, clutch and transmission.
8 Make sure that the engine runs smoothly when idling, and that there is no hesitation when accelerating.
9 Check that, where applicable, the clutch action is smooth and progressive, that the drive is taken up smoothly, and that the pedal travel is not excessive. Also listen for any noises when the clutch pedal is depressed.

10 On manual transmission models, check that all gears can be engaged smoothly without noise, and that the gear lever action is smooth and not abnormally vague or notchy.
11 On automatic transmission models, make sure that all gear-changes occur smoothly, without abrupt grabbing, and without an increase in engine speed between changes. Check that all the gear positions can be selected with the car at rest. If any problems are found, they should be referred to a BMW dealer or suitably-equipped specialist.

BRAKING SYSTEM

12 Make sure that the car does not pull to one side when braking, and that the wheels do not lock when braking hard.
13 Check that there is no vibration through the steering when braking.
14 Check that the parking brake operates correctly without excessive movement of the lever, and that it holds the car stationary on a slope.
15 Test the operation of the brake booster unit as follows. With the engine off, depress the brake pedal four or five times to remove the vacuum. With the brake pedal depressed, start the engine. As the engine starts, there should be a noticeable give in the brake pedal as vacuum increases in the booster. Allow the engine to run for at least two minutes, and then switch it off. If the brake pedal is depressed now, it should be possible to detect a hiss from the booster as the pedal is depressed. After about four or five applications, no further hissing should be heard, and the pedal should feel much harder.

Inspection II

19 Spark plug replacement

▶ **Refer to illustrations 19.5, 19.6 and 19.10**

1 Correct spark plug function is vital for proper engine operation. It is essential that the correct plugs are installed (the correct type is specified at the end of this Chapter or in your vehicle's owner's manual). If the correct plugs are used, and the engine is in good condition, the spark plugs should not need attention between scheduled replacement intervals. Spark plug cleaning is rarely necessary, and should not be attempted unless specialized equipment is available, as damage can easily be caused to the firing ends (electrodes).

2 The spark plugs are installed under the ignition coils in the center of the cylinder head.

3 Remove the valve cover (see Chapter 2A)

4 Remove the ignition coils (Chapter 5).

5 Unscrew the plugs using a spark plug wrench or a deep socket and extension bar (see illustration).

✳✳ CAUTION:

Keep the socket aligned with the spark plug - if the socket pushes against the top of the plug, it may break it.

6 Examination of the spark plugs will give a good indication of the condition of the engine. If the insulator nose of the spark plug is clean and white, with no deposits, this is indicative of a weak mixture or too hot a plug (a hot plug transfers heat away from the electrode slowly, a cold plug transfers heat away quickly). Compare your spark plugs with those shown in this chart (see illustration) to get an indication of the general running condition of the engine.

7 If the tip and insulator nose are covered with hard black-looking deposits, then this is indicative that the mixture is too rich. Should the plug be black and oily, then it is likely that the engine is fairly worn, as well as the mixture being too rich.

8 If the insulator nose is covered with light tan to grayish-brown deposits, then the mixture is correct, and it is likely that the engine is in good condition.

9 The spark plugs recommended by the manufacturer are either

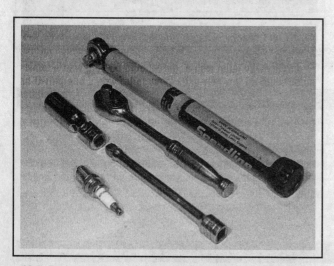

19.5 Tools required for spark plug removal and installation

 A **normally worn** spark plug should have light tan or gray deposits on the firing tip.

 A **carbon fouled** plug, identified by soft, sooty, black deposits, may indicate an improperly tuned vehicle. Check the air cleaner, ignition components and engine control system.

 An **oil fouled** spark plug indicates an engine with worn piston rings and/or bad valve seals allowing excessive oil to enter the chamber.

 This spark plug has been **left in the engine too long,** as evidenced by the extreme gap- Plugs with such an extreme gap can cause misfiring and stumbling accompanied by a noticeable lack of power.

 A **physically damaged** spark plug may be evidence of severe detonation in that cylinder. Watch that cylinder carefully between services, as a continued detonation will not only damage the plug, but could also damage the engine.

 A **bridged or almost bridged** spark plug, identified by a build up between the electrodes caused by excessive carbon or oil build-up on the plug.

19.6 Inspect the spark plug to determine engine running conditions

of the multi-ground electrode type or of the platinum or iridium type, all of which are pre-gapped to the proper setting and don't require adjustment. Additionally, attempting to adjust the gap on a platinum or iridium spark plug could scrape the platinum or iridium plating from the electrodes, which would severely shorten the spark plug's life.

10 Before installing the spark plugs, check that the threaded connector sleeves (on top of the plug) are tight, and that the plug exterior surfaces and threads are clean. It can be difficult to insert spark plugs into their holes without cross-threading them. One good method to use is to place a short piece of hose over the end of the spark plug to thread the plugs into the their holes (see Illustration).

11 Remove the hose (if used), and tighten the plug to the specified torque listed in this Chapter's Specifications using a spark plug socket and a torque wrench. Install the remaining plugs in the same way.

12 Install the ignition coils (see Chapter 5).

19.10 Using a piece of hose to thread the plug into its hole

20 Air filter replacement

▶ **Refer to illustrations 20.3 and 20.4**

➡ **Note: On 2003 and later models with an M56 engine, there is an additional carbon filter element fixed to the air filter housing that is not serviceable.**

1 The air cleaner assembly is located at the front left-hand corner of the engine compartment.

2 Release the retaining clips on the housing and the two clips that attach the air filter housing cover to the MAF sensor.

3 Separate the air inlet duct from the housing cover and then remove it from the housing (see illustration).

4 Lift out the air filter (see illustration).

5 Clean the inside of the air filter housing.

6 Place the new filter in position, carefully install the housing cover and secure all retaining clips.

20.3 Release the retaining clips (most clips are hidden in photo)

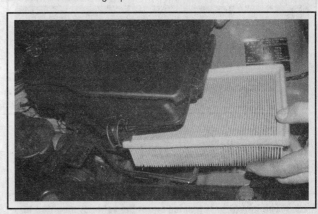

20.4 Lift out the filter element

21 Driveaxle boot check

▶ **Refer to illustration 21.1**

1 With the car raised and securely supported on stands, slowly rotate the rear wheel. Inspect the condition of the outer constant velocity (CV) joint rubber boots, squeezing the boots to open out the folds (see illustration). Check for signs of cracking, splits or deterioration of the rubber, which may allow the grease to escape and lead to water and grit entry into the joint. Also check the security and condition of the retaining clips. Repeat these checks on the inner CV joints. If any damage is found, the boots should be replaced (see Chapter 8).

2 At the same time, check the general condition of the CV joints themselves by first holding the driveaxle and attempting to rotate the wheel. Repeat this check by holding the inner joint and attempting to rotate the driveaxle. Any substantial movement indicates wear in the joints, wear in the driveaxle splines, or a loose driveaxle retaining nut.

21.1 Check the condition of the driveshaft boots

22 Parking brake shoe check

Referring to Chapter 9, remove the rear brake discs and inspect the parking brake shoes for signs of wear or contamination. Compare the shoe lining material thickness to the specification found at the end of this chapter. Replace the shoes if necessary.

Every second Inspection II

23 Fuel filter replacement

▶ **Refer to illustrations 23.3, 23.6a, 23.6b and 23.7**

➡**Note: On 2003 and later models with an M56 engine, the fuel filter is inside the fuel tank and is not serviceable.**

1   Depressurize the fuel system (see Chapter 4), then disconnect the cable(s) from the negative battery terminal(s) (see Chapter 5, Section 1).

2   Raise the vehicle and support it securely on jackstands. Remove the splash shield.

3   The fuel filter is located on a bracket bolted to the left-hand chassis member adjacent to the transmission (see illustration).

4   On models with the M54 engine, remove the screws and remove the cover from the fuel filter/regulator assembly.

5   On all models, note their fitted locations, and clamp the hoses to and from the fuel filter. Loosen the retaining clamps and disconnect the hoses from the filter. Be prepared for some fuel spillage.

6   On M54 engine models, disconnect the vacuum hose from the regulator (see illustrations).

➡**Note: The fuel pressure regulator is integral with the filter and the vacuum hose from the intake manifold is connected to the front of the regulator on the filter.**

7   Loosen the filter clamp fastener and slide the filter down from under the car (see illustration).

8   Installation is a reversal of removal, but make sure that the flow direction arrow on the filter points in the direction of fuel flow (i.e., towards the engine), and on completion, pressurize the fuel system with reference to Chapter 4 and check for leaks.

23.3   The fuel filter is located under the vehicle, mounted to the left side of the chassis

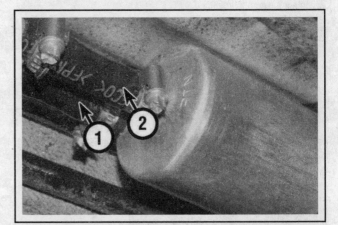

23.6a   Loosen the clamps and disconnect the fuel filter hoses at the rear . . .

    1)   From the fuel tank
    2)   Fuel return (M54 engines only)

23.6b   . . . and front of the filter

    3)   Fuel supply to injectors
    4)   Regulator vacuum hose (M54 engines only)

23.7   Unscrew the clamp nut and remove the filter

Every 2 years

24 Brake fluid replacement

✳✳ WARNING:

Brake hydraulic fluid can harm your eyes and damage painted surfaces, so use extreme caution when handling and pouring it. Do not use fluid that has been standing open for some time, as it absorbs moisture from the air. Excess moisture can cause a dangerous loss of braking effectiveness.

1 The procedure is similar to bleeding the hydraulic system as described in Chapter 9, except that the brake fluid in the reservoir should be replaced with new fluid before you begin. A clean poultry baster (or equivalent) works well for this.

✳✳ WARNING:

If a baster is used, never again use it for food preparation.

2 Working as described in Chapter 9, open the first bleed screw in the sequence and pump the brake pedal gently until nearly all the old fluid has been emptied from the master cylinder reservoir.

3 Top-up to the MAX level with new fluid, and continue pumping until only the new fluid remains in the reservoir, and new fluid can be seen emerging from the bleed screw. Tighten the screw, and top the reservoir level up to the MAX level again.

4 Work through all remaining bleed screws in sequence until new fluid can be seen at all of them. Be careful to keep the master cylinder reservoir topped-up to above the MIN level at all times, or air may enter the system and increase the length of the task.

5 When the operation is complete, check that all bleed screws are securely tightened (be careful not to over-tighten them) and re-install the dust caps. Wash off all traces of fluid with water and recheck the reservoir fluid level.

6 Check the operation of the brakes before taking the car on the road.

Every 4 years

25 Coolant replacement

COOLING SYSTEM DRAINING

▶ **Refer to illustrations 25.2, 25.3, 25.4a, 25.4b and 25.5**

✳✳ WARNING:

Wait until the engine is cold before starting this procedure. Do not allow antifreeze to come in contact with your skin, or with the painted surfaces of the car. Rinse off spills immediately with plenty of water. Never leave antifreeze lying around in an open container, or in a puddle in the driveway or on the garage floor. Children and pets are attracted by its sweet smell, but antifreeze can be fatal if ingested.

1 With the engine completely cold, cover the expansion tank cap with a rag, and slowly turn the cap counterclockwise to relieve the pressure in the cooling system (a hissing sound may be heard). Wait until all pressure in the system is released, then continue to turn the cap until it can be removed.

2 Unscrew the bleed screw from the top of the hose coupling above the expansion tank (see illustration).

3 Raise the front of the vehicle and support it securely on jackstands. Remove the retaining screws/clips and remove the splash shield from beneath the engine (see illustration).

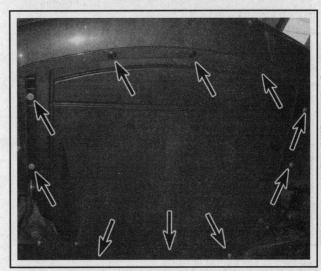

25.3 Engine splash shield fasteners

25.2 Unscrew the bleed screw

25.4a Open the expansion tank drain plug . . .

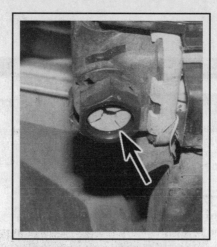

25.4b . . . and the radiator drain plug

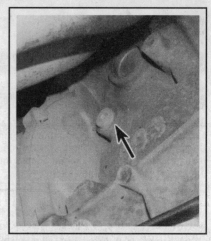

25.5 The cylinder block drain plug is located on the right-hand side

4   Position a suitable container beneath the drain plugs on the base of the radiator and the expansion tank. Unscrew the drain plugs and allow the coolant to drain into the container (see illustrations).

5   To fully drain the system, also unscrew the coolant drain plug from the right-hand side of the cylinder block and allow the remainder of the coolant to drain into the container (see illustration).

6   If the coolant has been drained for a reason other than replacement, then provided it is clean and less than two years old, it can be re-used, though this is not recommended.

7   Once all the coolant has drained, install the bleed screw to the hose coupling. Install a new gasket to the block drain plug and tighten it to the torque listed in this Chapter's Specifications.

COOLING SYSTEM FLUSHING

8   If coolant replacement has been neglected, or if the antifreeze mixture has become diluted, then in time, the cooling system may gradually lose efficiency, as the coolant passages become restricted due to rust, scale deposits, and other sediment. To restore cooling system efficiency, flush the cooling system.

9   The radiator should be flushed independently of the engine, to avoid unnecessary contamination.

Radiator flushing

10 To flush the radiator, disconnect the top and bottom hoses and any other relevant hoses from the radiator, with reference to Chapter 3.

11 Insert a garden hose into the radiator top inlet. Direct a flow of clean water through the radiator, and continue flushing until clean water emerges from the radiator bottom outlet.

12 If after a reasonable period, the water still does not run clear, the radiator can be flushed with a good proprietary cooling system cleaning agent. It is important that their manufacturer's instructions are followed carefully. If the contamination is particularly bad, insert the hose in the radiator bottom outlet, and reverse-flush the radiator.

Engine flushing

13 Fill the cooling system with clean water, following the Refilling procedure (see Step 17).

14 Start the engine and allow it to reach normal operating temperature, then rev up the engine a few times.

15 Turn the engine off and allow it to cool completely, then drain the system as described earlier.

16 Repeat Steps 13 through 15 until the water being drained is free of contaminants.

COOLING SYSTEM FILLING

17 Before attempting to fill the cooling system, make sure that all hoses and clamps are in good condition, and that the clamps are tight and the radiator and cylinder block drain plugs are securely tightened. Note that an antifreeze mixture must be used all year round, to prevent corrosion of the engine components (see following sub-Section).

18 Loosen the bleed screw on the upper radiator hose coupling (see illustration 25.2).

19 Turn on the ignition, and set the heater control to maximum temperature, with the fan speed set to low. This opens the heating valves.

20 Remove the expansion tank filler cap. Fill the system by slowly pouring the coolant into the expansion tank to prevent airlocks from forming.

21 If the coolant is being replaced, begin by pouring in a couple of liters of water, followed by the correct quantity of antifreeze, then top-up with more water.

➡**Note: Use of a large clean bucket to pre-mix the coolant with the correct amount of water is best.**

22 As soon as coolant free from air bubbles emerges from the bleed screw, tighten the screw securely.

23 Once the level in the expansion tank starts to rise, squeeze the radiator top and bottom hoses to help expel any trapped air in the system. Once all the air is expelled, top-up the coolant level to the MAX mark and install the expansion tank cap.

24 Start the engine and run it until it reaches normal operating temperature, then stop the engine and allow it to cool.

25 Check for leaks, particularly around disturbed components. Check the coolant level in the expansion tank, and top-up if necessary. Note that the system must be cold before an accurate level is indicated in the expansion tank. If the expansion tank cap is removed while the engine is still warm, cover the cap with a thick cloth, and unscrew the cap slowly to gradually relieve the system pressure (a hissing sound will normally be heard). Wait until all pressure remaining in the system is released, then continue to turn the cap until it can be removed.

ANTIFREEZE MIXTURE

26 The antifreeze should always be replaced at the specified intervals. This is necessary not only to maintain the antifreeze properties, but also to prevent corrosion which would otherwise occur as the corrosion inhibitors become progressively less effective.

27 Always use a long-life ethylene-glycol based antifreeze which is suitable for use in mixed-metal cooling systems. The correct quantity of antifreeze is indicated in the Specifications at the end of the Chapter.

28 Before adding antifreeze, the cooling system should be completely drained, preferably flushed, and all hoses checked for condition and security.

29 After filling with antifreeze, a label should be attached to the expansion tank, stating the type and concentration of antifreeze used, and the date installed. Any subsequent topping-up should be made with the same type and concentration of antifreeze.

30 Do not use engine antifreeze in the windshield washer system because it will damage the paint; use a product labeled specifically for the windshield washer systems.

Every 100,000 miles

26 Automatic transmission fluid and filter replacement

▶ **Refer to illustrations 26.3**

➥**Note: A new drain plug gasket will be required on installation.**

1 The transmission fluid should be drained with the transmission at operating temperature. If the car has just been driven at least 10 miles, the transmission can be considered warm.

2 Immediately after driving the car, park it on a level surface, apply the parking. If desired, jack up the car and support on axle stands to improve access, but make sure that the car is level.

3 Working under the car, loosen the transmission fluid pan drain plug about half a turn (see illustration). Position a draining container under the drain plug, then remove the plug completely. If possible, try to keep the plug pressed into the fluid pan while unscrewing it by hand the last couple of turns. Measure the amount of fluid drained.

4 Recover the gasket from the drain plug.

5 Install the drain plug, using a new gasket and tighten it to the torque listed in this Chapter's Specifications.

6 Remove all the mounting fasteners for the transmission oil pan.

7 Remove the pan gasket and clean the mating surfaces on the oil pan and transmission.

8 Remove the mounting fasteners (if equipped) for the transmission oil filter and remove it.

➥**Note: Use a seal puller to remove the seal from the transmission if it does not come out with the filter.**

9 Install a new filter along with new seals.

10 Clean the inside of the pan and the magnet(s) (if equipped).

❊❊ **CAUTION:**

Only use lint-free rags or solvent with compressed air when cleaning the oil pan and magnet(s).

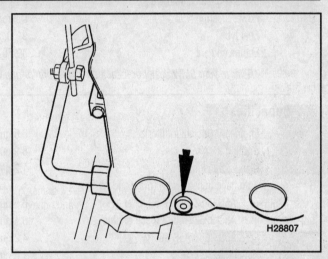

26.3 Automatic transmission fluid drain plug (5-speed transmission shown, others similar)

11 Using a new pan gasket, install the oil pan and tighten the fasteners to the torque listed in this Chapter's Specifications.

12 Fill the transmission with the specified type of fluid - fill the transmission through the filler/level plug hole (see Section 2). Start with the amount recorded in Step 3, so as not to overfill the transmission.

13 Check the fluid level, keeping in mind that the new fluid will not yet be at operating temperature (see Section 2).

14 With the parking brake applied and the transmission selector lever in position P, start the engine and run it at idle for a few minutes to warm up the new fluid; recheck the fluid level. Note that it may be necessary to drain off a little fluid once the new fluid has reached operating temperature.

Specifications

Recommended lubricants and fluids

➡ **Note: The fluids and lubricants listed here are those recommended by the manufacturer at the time this manual was written. Vehicle manufacturers occasionally upgrade their fluid and lubricant specifications, so check with your local auto parts store for the most current recommendations.**

Engine oil	
Type	BMW long-life oil or fully synthetic, API SJ/CD, EC II "Certified for gasoline engines"
Viscosity	SAE 5W-30 or 5W-40
Automatic Transmission fluid	BMW Lifetime Transmission oil*
Manual Transmission fluid	BMW Lifetime Transmission oil MTF-LT-1
Rear differential fluid	SAE 75W/90*
Brake and clutch fluid type	DOT 4 brake fluid
Power steering fluid	Dexron III*
Fuel type	91 Octane (or higher) is recommended
Engine coolant	50/50 mixture of long-life ethylene glycol based antifreeze and water*

Refer to your BMW dealer or local auto parts store for brand name and type recommendations

Capacities*

Engine oil (including filter)	6.9 quarts (6.5 liters)
Cooling system	8.9 quarts (8.4 liters)
Manual transmission	1.2 quarts (1.1 liters)
Automatic transmission (drain and refill)	
A5S 325Z (with 2.5 liter engine)	6.5 quarts (6.2 liters)**
A5S 325Z (with 3.0 liter engine)	6.4 quarts (6.1 liters)**
A5S 360R/A5S 390R	4.2 quarts (4.0 liters)**
Differential	1.8 quarts (1.7 liters)
Power-assisted steering	1.6 quarts (1.5 liters)
Fuel tank	17.2 gallons (65 liters)

All capacities approximate. Add as necessary to bring to appropriate level.

**If you want to flush the converter during a fluid change, purchase twice the amount of fluid listed here.*

Ignition system

Spark plugs	
Type	NGK BKR6 EQUP or equivalent
Gap	Do not adjust (see Section 19)

Brakes

Brake pad friction material minimum thickness	0.079 inch (2.0 mm)
Parking brake shoe friction material minimum thickness	0.059 inch (1.5 mm)

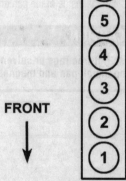

FRONT

18022-specs-HAYNES

Cylinder locations

Torque specifications	Ft-lbs (unless otherwise indicated)	Nm
Automatic transmission fluid pan bolts		
A5S 325Z	48 in-lbs	6
A5S 360R/A5S 390R	84 in-lbs	10
Automatic transmission drain plug		
A5S 325Z	26	35
A5S 360R/A5S 390R	14	18
Cylinder block coolant drain plug	18	25
Engine oil drain plug	18	25
Oil filter housing cover	18	25
Spark plugs	18	25
Wheel bolts	74	100

Notes

Section

2A

ENGINES

1 General information

HOW TO USE THIS CHAPTER

This Part of Chapter 2 describes the repair procedures that can reasonably be carried out on the engine while it remains in the vehicle. If the engine has been removed from the vehicle and is being disassembled or replaced as described in Part B, any preliminary disassembly procedures can be ignored.

Note that, while it may be possible physically to overhaul items such as the piston/connecting rod assemblies while the engine is in the car, such tasks are not usually carried out as separate operations. Usually, several additional procedures are required (not to mention the cleaning of components and oilways); for this reason, all such tasks are classed as major overhaul procedures, and are described in Part B of this Chapter.

Part B describes the removal of the engine/transmission from the car, and the overhaul or replacement procedures that can then be carried out.

ENGINE DESCRIPTION

General

The M52, M54 and M56 engines are of 6-cylinder double overhead camshaft design, mounted in-line, with the transmission bolted to the rear end. The main differences between the engines are that the M54 and M56 units are equipped with fully electronic throttle control, and tuned for lower emissions.

A timing chain drives the exhaust camshaft, and the intake camshaft is driven by a second chain from the end of the exhaust camshaft. Hydraulic lifters are installed between the camshafts and the valves. Each camshaft is supported by seven bearings incorporated in bearing castings in the cylinder head.

The crankshaft runs in seven main bearings of the usual bearing-type. Endplay is controlled by thrust bearings on the Number 6 main bearing.

The pistons are selected to be of matching weight, and incorporate fully-floating wrist pins retained by circlips.

The oil pump is chain-driven from the front of the crankshaft.

Variable camshaft timing control

On all models, a variable camshaft timing control system, known as VANOS, is installed. The VANOS system uses data supplied by the DME engine management system (see Chapter 6), to adjust the timing of both the intake and exhaust camshafts independently via a hydraulic control system using engine oil as the hydraulic fluid. The camshaft timing is varied according to engine speed. Retarding the timing (opening the valves later) at low and high engine speeds improves low-speed driveability and maximum power respectively. At medium engine speeds, the camshaft timing is advanced (opening the valves earlier) to increase mid-range torque and to improve exhaust emissions.

REPAIRS WITH ENGINE IN PLACE

The following operations can be carried out without having to remove the engine from the vehicle:

a) Removal and installation of the cylinder head.
b) Removal and installation of the timing chain and sprockets.
c) Removal and installation of the camshafts
d) Removal and installation of the oil pan.
e) Removal and installation of the connecting rod bearings, connecting rods, and pistons.*
f) Removal and installation of the oil pump.
g) Replacement of the engine/transmission mounts.
h) Removal and installation of the flywheel/driveplate.

* Although it is possible to remove these components with the engine in place, for reasons of access and cleanliness it is recommended that the engine is removed.

2 Compression test - description and interpretation

1   When engine performance is down, or if misfiring occurs which cannot be attributed to the ignition or fuel systems, a compression test can provide diagnostic clues as to the engine's condition. If the test is performed regularly, it can give warning of trouble before any other symptoms become apparent.

2   The engine must be fully warmed-up to normal operating temperature and the battery must be fully charged.

3   Remove the fuel pump fuse (located in the passenger compartment fuse box), and if possible, start the engine and allow it to run until the residual fuel in the system is exhausted. Failure to do so could result in damage to the catalytic converter.

4   Remove the spark plugs (see Chapter 1). Install a compression tester in the No 1 cylinder spark plug hole - the type of tester which screws into the plug hole is preferred.

❈❈ WARNING:

Make sure all of the electrical connectors are disconnected from the ignition coils.

5   Block the throttle wide open, then crank the engine with the starter motor for at least six compression strokes. The compression pressure should build-up to a maximum figure, and then stabilize. Record the highest reading obtained.

6   Repeat the test on the remaining cylinders, recording the pressure in each.

7   All cylinders should produce very similar pressures; a difference of more than approximately 29 psi (2 bar) between any two cylinders indicates a fault. Note that the compression should build-up quickly in a healthy engine; low compression on the first stroke, followed by gradually increasing pressure on successive strokes, indicates worn piston rings. A low compression reading on the first stroke, which does not build-up during successive strokes, indicates leaking valves or a blown head gasket (a cracked head could also be the cause). Deposits on the undersides of the valve heads can also cause low compression.

8   BMW minimum values for compression pressures are given in the Specifications.

9   If the pressure in any cylinder is low, carry out the following test to isolate the cause. Introduce a teaspoonful of clean oil into that cylinder through its spark plug hole, and repeat the test.

10 If the addition of oil temporarily improves the compression pressure, this indicates that bore or piston wear is responsible for the pressure loss. No improvement suggests that leaking or burnt valves, or a blown head gasket, may be to blame.

11 A low reading from two adjacent cylinders is almost certainly due to the head gasket having blown between them. The presence of coolant in the engine oil will confirm this.

12 If one cylinder is about 20 percent lower than the others and the

engine has a slightly rough idle, a worn camshaft lobe could be the cause.

13 If the compression reading is unusually high, the combustion chambers are probably coated with carbon deposits. If this is the case, the cylinder head should be removed and decarbonized.

14 On completion of the test, reinstall the spark plugs (see Chapter 1) and reinstall the fuel pump fuse.

3 Top Dead Center (TDC) for Number 1 piston - locating

▶ **Refer to illustrations 3.4, 3.5, 3.8a, 3.8b, 3.10, 3.11a and 3.11b**

➡ **Note: Special tools are required to check the position of the camshafts by locking the engine in the TDC position and resetting the VANOS units. Obtain the special tools from a dealer parts department or specialty tool distributor. Some of the tools may be fabricated using shop tools. Read through the text prior to attempting the procedure.**

1 Top Dead Center (TDC) is the highest point in the cylinder that each piston reaches as it travels up and down when the crankshaft turns. Each piston reaches TDC at the end of the compression stroke and again at the end of the exhaust stroke, but TDC generally refers to piston position on the compression stroke. Number 1 piston is at the front (timing chain end) of the engine.

2 Positioning Number 1 piston at TDC is an essential part of many procedures, such as timing chain removal and camshaft removal.

3 Remove the valve cover as described in Section 4.

4 Unclip the plastic cover from the intake camshaft (see illustration).

5 In order to accurately set the positions of the camshafts, the VANOS units must be set as follows. Unscrew the VANOS unit oil pressure pipe from the intake camshaft VANOS unit, and install special BMW tool 11 3 450 to the port on the VANOS unit (see illustration).

6 Using a clean cloth, cover the top of the VANOS unit as, when compressed air is applied, some oil will be sprayed out.

7 Connect a compressed air line to the union of the special tool, and apply a pressure of 28 to 86 psi (2.0 to 8.0 bar). This pressure will reset the VANOS units as the engine is rotated.

8 Using a socket and wrench on the crankshaft pulley bolt, turn

3.4 Release the retaining clips and remove the cover from the intake camshaft

the engine clockwise at least two complete revolutions until the tips of the front camshaft lobes on the exhaust and intake camshafts face one another. Note that the square flanges on the rear of the camshafts should be positioned with the sides of the flanges exactly at right-angles to the top surface of the cylinder head. BMW special tools 11 3 240 are available to lock the camshafts in this position. The tools slide over the square flanges of the camshafts and hold them at 90-degrees to the cylinder head upper surface, once the two outer valve cover studs have been removed. If the tools are not available, an alternative can be

3.5 Install the BMW special tool to the VANOS oil port

3.8a With the No 1 piston at TDC, the tips of the front camshaft lobes face each other

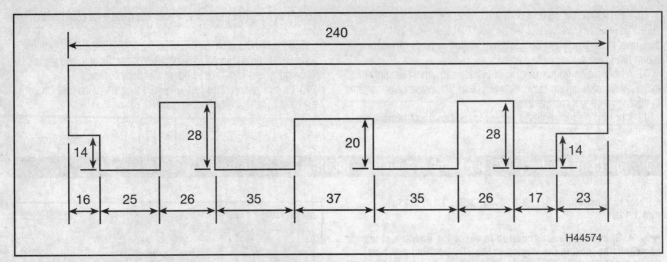

240

14 28 20 28 14

16 25 26 35 37 35 26 17 23

H44574

3.8b A camshaft holding fixture can be made from a piece of metal plate (steel or aluminum), cut to these dimensions. The plate must be thick enough not to distort when valve spring pressure tries to turn the camshafts (All dimensions in mm)

fabricated from steel or aluminum plate (see illustrations).

9   Pull the blanking plug from the timing hole in the left-hand, rear corner flange of the engine block. Access is improved if the starter motor is removed (see Chapter 5).

10 To lock the crankshaft in position, a special tool will now be required. BMW tool 11 2 300 can be used, but one can be made up by machining a length of steel rod (see illustration).

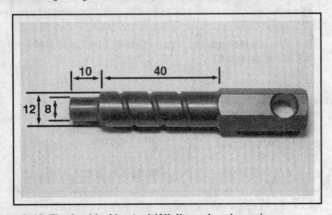

10 40

12 8

3.10 Flywheel locking tool (All dimensions in mm)

11 Insert the rod through the timing hole. If necessary, turn the crankshaft slightly until the rod enters the TDC hole in the flywheel (see illustrations).

12 The crankshaft is now locked in position with Number 1 piston at TDC. Disconnect the compressed air from the VANOS oil port.

✳ WARNING:

If, for any reason, it is necessary to turn either or both of the camshafts with Number 1 piston positioned at TDC, and either of the timing chain tensioners slackened or removed (or the timing chains removed), the following precaution must be observed. Before turning the camshaft(s), the crankshaft must be turned approximately 30-degrees counterclockwise away from the TDC position (remove the locking rod from the TDC hole in the flywheel to do this) to prevent the possibility of piston-to-valve contact.

13 Do not attempt to turn the engine with the flywheel or camshaft(s) locked in position, as engine damage may result. If the engine is to be left in the locked state for a long period of time, it is a good idea to disconnect the battery and to place suitable warning notices inside the vehicle, and in the engine compartment. This will reduce the possibility of the engine being cranked on the starter motor.

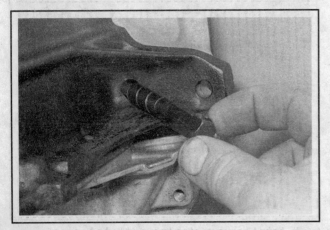

3.11a Insert the rod through the timing hole . . .

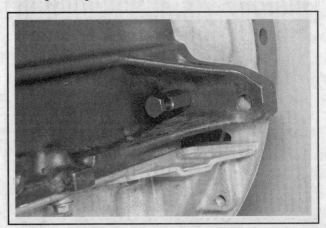

3.11b . . . until it enters the TDC hole in the flywheel - engine removed for clarity

4 Valve cover - removal and installation

➡**Note: New gaskets and/or seals may be required on installation - see text.**

REMOVAL

▶ **Refer to illustrations 4.2a, 4.2b, 4.4a, 4.4b, 4.5a, 4.5b, 4.6,
4.8 and 4.9**

1 Disconnect the cable from the negative terminal of the battery
(see Chapter 5, Section 1).
2 To allow sufficient clearance for the valve cover to be removed,
remove the heater/ventilation intake air duct from the rear of the engine
compartment (see illustrations).

a) *Remove the in-cabin filter cover from the rear of the engine compartment (see Chapter 1). Pull the filter forward and remove it.*
b) *Remove the four retaining clips and thread the cable out of the
harness.*
c) *Remove the screws and pull the filter housing forward to remove
it.*
d) *Pull up the rubber strip, rotate the two fasteners counterclockwise,
and move the dividing panel in the left-hand corner of the engine
compartment forward a little.*

**4.2a Unclip the
cable ducts**

e) *Remove the screws and remove the intake ducting upwards and
out of the engine compartment.*

3 Remove the engine oil filler cap.
4 Remove the plastic covers from the fuel rail and the top of the
valve cover. To remove the plastic covers, pry out the cover caps and
unscrew the two retaining nuts. To remove the cover from the cylinder
head, lift and pull the cover forwards, then manipulate the cover over
the oil filler neck (see illustration).
5 Unbolt the ground strap from the valve cover adjacent to the

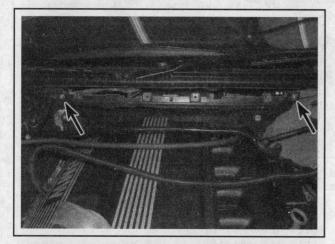

4.2b Remove the two Torx screws and remove the intake ducts

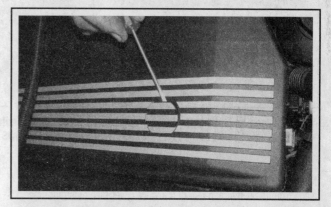

**4.4a Some models are equipped with caps that can be
removed to access the cover bolts**

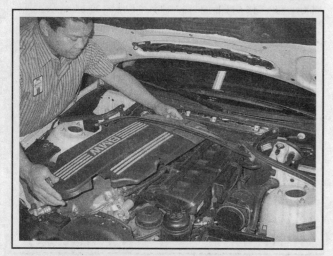

**4.4b Other models are equipped with clips that snap fit onto
the engine components**

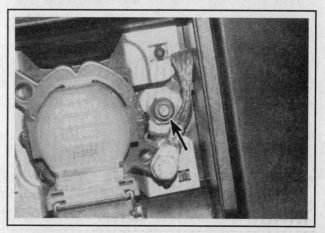

**4.5a Unbolt the ground strap from next to the No 1 spark
plug hole . . .**

4.5b . . . and the center of the cylinder head

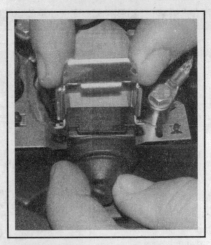

4.6 Slide up the locking elements and disconnect the coil plugs

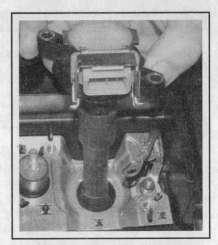

4.8 Remove the ignition coil bolts and pull the coils up from the spark plugs

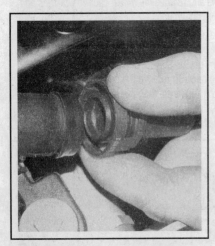

4.9 Disconnect the breather hose from the valve cover

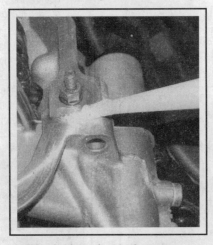

4.13a Apply sealant to the areas where the VANOS unit contacts the cylinder head . . .

4.13b . . . and the semi-circular cut-out sections

Number 1 spark plug hole and, where applicable, unbolt the ground leads from the center and rear of the valve cover (see illustrations).

6 Disconnect the electrical connectors from the ignition coils (see illustration).

7 Release the wiring from the clips on the valve cover, then move the complete ducting/wiring assembly to one side, clear of the valve cover.

8 Unscrew the ignition coil bolts, then carefully pull the coils from the spark plugs (see illustration). Note the locations of the ground leads and the coil wiring brackets.

9 Release the retaining clip and disconnect the PCV breather hose from the side of the valve cover (see illustration).

10 Unclip the oxygen sensor harness connectors from the right-side of the valve cover and lay them to one side.

11 Unscrew the retaining bolts/nuts (including the ones in the center of the cover) and lift off the valve cover. Note the locations of all washers, seals and gaskets, and recover any which are loose.

INSTALLATION

▶ **Refer to illustrations 4.13a, 4.13b and 4.13c**

12 Before installation, check the condition of all seals and gaskets.

Replace any which are deteriorated or damaged.

13 Clean the gasket/sealing faces of the cylinder head and the valve cover, then apply a bead of RTV sealant to the area where the VANOS unit meets the cylinder head, and the corners of the semi-circular cut-out sections at the rear of the cylinder head and VANOS unit. Lay the

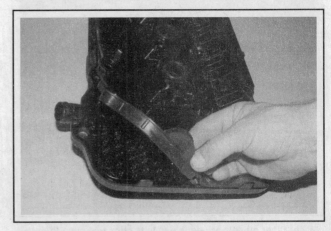

4.13c Ensure the gaskets are in position

main (outer) gasket and the spark plug hole (center) gaskets in position on the valve cover (see illustrations).

14 Set the valve cover in position, taking care not to disturb the gaskets. Check that the tabs on the rear of the main gasket are correctly positioned in the cut-outs in the rear of the cylinder head.

15 Reinstall the valve cover screws/nuts, ensuring that the seals are positioned as noted during removal, then tighten the bolts progressively to the torque listed in this Chapter's Specifications.

16 Further installation is the reverse of the removal procedure, bearing in mind the following points.

a) *Check that the ignition coil ground leads are correctly positioned as noted before removal.*

b) *Tighten the ignition coil retaining nuts/screws to the torque listed in this Chapter's Specifications.*

c) *Check that the rubber seals are in place when reconnecting the ignition wires to the coils.*

5 Crankshaft vibration damper/pulley and pulley hub - removal and installation

➡**Note 1: Models built before January 2000 are equipped with a two piece vibration damper and pulley assembly. Models built after January 2000 are equipped with a one piece damper/pulley assembly.**

➡**Note 2: If the pulley hub is removed, a new retaining bolt will be required on installation, and a torque wrench capable of providing 302 ft-lbs (410 Nm) of torque will be required.**

REMOVAL

1 Remove the engine splash shields (see Chapter 11).
2 Remove the viscous cooling fan/electric cooling fan and fan cowl

assembly as described in Chapter 3.

3 Remove the drivebelts (see Chapter 1).

4 Two different designs of damper/pulley and hub may be installed. On some models the pulley/damper is bolted to the hub (two piece), and on others the hub is integral with the damper/pulley (one piece).

Two-piece damper/pulley and hub

▶ **Refer to illustrations 5.5, 5.7, 5.9 and 5.10**

5 Unscrew the retaining bolts, and remove the vibration damper/pulley from the hub (see illustration). If necessary, lock the hub using a socket or wrench on the hub retaining bolt.

6 To remove the hub, the retaining bolt must be unscrewed.

❊❊ WARNING:

The crankshaft pulley hub bolt is very tight. A tool will be required to lock the hub as the bolt is unscrewed. Do not attempt the job using inferior or poorly-improvised tools, as injury or damage may result.

7 Make up a tool to hold the pulley hub. A suitable tool can be fabricated using two lengths of steel bar, joined by a large pivot bolt. Bolt the holding tool to the pulley hub using the pulley-to-hub bolts. If you can obtain them, use special tools 11 2 150 and 11 2 410 available from BMW dealers or automotive tool specialists (see illustration).

8 Using a socket and a long breaker bar, loosen the pulley hub bolt.

9 Unscrew the pulley hub bolt, and remove the washer (see illustration). Discard the bolt - a new one must be used on installation.

10 Withdraw the hub from the end of the crankshaft (see illustra-

5.5 Remove the bolts and remove the damper/pulley from the hub

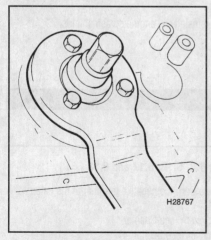

5.7 BMW special tool used to hold the crankshaft pulley hub

5.9 Unscrew the hub bolt and remove the washer . . .

5.10 . . . then withdraw the hub

5.12a Use BMW special tools to prevent the pulley/hub from turning . . .

5.12b . . . or use a strap wrench to hold it

tion). If the hub is tight, use a puller to draw it off.

11 Recover the Woodruff key from the end of the crankshaft if it is loose.

One piece damper/pulley and hub

▶ Refer to illustrations 5.12a and 5.12b

12 In order to prevent the hub from rotating while removing the central bolt, BMW specifies the use of tools 11 8 190 and 11 8 200, which engage in the holes between the webs of the pulley hub. In the absence of these tools, it may be possible to prevent the hub from rotating by using a strap wrench around the pulley (see illustrations). The bolt is very tight, and assistance may be required.

13 Remove the hub bolt and the washer. Discard the bolt - a new one must be installed.

14 Withdraw the hub from the end of the crankshaft. If the hub is tight, use a puller to draw it off.

15 Recover the Woodruff key from the end of the crankshaft if it is loose.

INSTALLATION

16 If the pulley hub has been removed, it is advisable to take the opportunity to replace the oil seal in the lower timing chain cover (see Section 6).

17 If the pulley hub has been removed, proceed as follows, other-

wise proceed to Step 20 (two piece damper/pulley and hub).

18 Where applicable, reinstall the Woodruff key to the end of the crankshaft, then align the groove in the pulley hub with the key, and slide the hub onto the end of the crankshaft.

19 Reinstall the washer, noting that the shoulder on the washer must face the hub, and install a new hub bolt.

Two piece damper/pulley and hub

20 Bolt the holding tool to the pulley hub, as during removal, then tighten the hub bolt to the torque listed in this Chapter's Specifications. Take care to avoid injury and/or damage.

21 Where applicable, unbolt the holding tool, and reinstall the vibration damper/pulley, ensuring that the locating dowel on the hub engages with the corresponding hole in the damper/pulley.

22 Reinstall the damper/pulley retaining bolts, and tighten to the torque listed in this Chapter's Specifications. Again, immobilize the pulley, if necessary, when tightening the bolts.

One piece damper/pulley and hub

23 Immobilize the hub using the method employed during removal, and tighten the bolt to the torque listed in this Chapter's Specifications.

All models

24 Reinstall the drivebelts as described in Chapter 1.

25 Reinstall the viscous cooling fan and cowl as described in Chapter 3.

26 Where applicable, reinstall the engine splash shields.

6 Timing chain cover - removal and installation

❋❋ WARNING:

The engine must be completely cool before beginning this procedure.

➠Note: New timing cover gaskets and a new crankshaft front oil seal will be required on installation. RTV sealant will be required at the joint where the cover meets the cylinder head/engine block - see text.

REMOVAL

▶ Refer to illustrations 6.8, 6.10, 6.12 and 6.13

1 Disconnect the cable from the negative terminal of the battery (see Chapter 5, Section 1).

2 Drain the cooling system (see Chapter 1).

3 Remove the valve cover (see Section 4).

4 Remove the drivebelts (see Chapter 1).

5 Remove the thermostat (see Chapter 3).

6.8 Unscrew the tensioner bolts (lower bolt not visible in this photo)

6.10 Drive the locating dowels out of the timing chain cover

6   Remove the crankshaft pulley/damper and hub (see Section 5).

7   Remove the oil pan (see Section 12).

8   Remove the two bolts and remove the drivebelt tensioner (see illustration).

9   The water pump pulley must now be removed. Prevent the pulley from turning by holding it with a strap wrench, then unscrew the retaining bolts and withdraw the pulley.

10 Working at the top of the timing chain cover, drive out the two cover dowels. Drive out the dowels towards the rear of the engine, using a pin-punch (less than 5.0 mm diameter) (see illustration).

11 It is now necessary to remove the VANOS adjustment unit (see Section 9), for access to the timing chain cover-to-cylinder head bolts.

12 Unscrew the three timing chain cover-to-cylinder head bolts, and lift the bolts from the cylinder head. Note that one of the bolts also secures the secondary timing chain guide (see illustration).

13 Unscrew the timing chain cover-to-engine block bolts, then withdraw the cover from the front of the engine (see illustration). Remove the gaskets.

INSTALLATION

▶ **Refer to illustrations 6.16 and 6.19**

14 Remove the oil seal from the timing chain cover.

6.12 Remove the timing chain cover-to-cylinder head bolts

15 Thoroughly clean the mating faces of the cover, engine block and cylinder head.

16 Install a new oil seal to the timing chain cover, using a large socket or a block of wood to drive the seal into position (see illustration).

6.13 Timing chain cover-to-engine block bolt locations

6.16 Drive the new oil seal squarely into the timing chain cover

17 Drive the cover dowels into position in the top of the cover so that they protrude from the rear (engine block mating) face of the cover by approximately 2.0 to 3.0 mm.

18 Position new gaskets on the cover, and hold them in position using a little grease.

19 Apply a little RTV sealant to the cylinder head/engine block joint at the two points where the timing chain cover contacts the cylinder head gasket (see illustration).

20 Lift the cover into position, ensuring that the gaskets stay in place. Make sure that the dowels engage with the engine block, and install the cover retaining bolts. Tighten the bolts finger-tight only at this stage.

21 Drive in the cover dowels until they are flush with the outer face of the cover.

22 Progressively tighten the cover retaining bolts to the torque listed in this Chapter's Specifications (do not forget the three cylinder head-to-cover bolts).

23 Reinstall the VANOS adjustment unit as described in Section 9.

24 Reinstall the crankshaft damper/pulley hub and damper/pulley as described in Section 5.

25 The remainder of installation is a reversal of removal, bearing in mind the following points.

a) *Ensure the drivebelt hydraulic tensioner strut is installed correctly (see Chapter 1). The TOP/OBEN arrow must point upwards.*

b) *Install the drivebelts (see Chapter 1).*

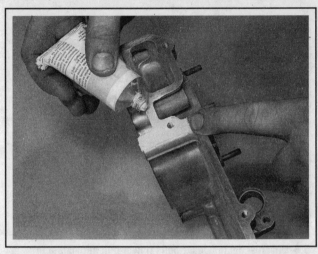

6.19 Apply sealant to the area where the timing chain cover contacts the cylinder head gasket

c) *Install the thermostat and housing (see Chapter 3).*

d) *Install the valve cover (see Section 4).*

e) *Install the oil pan (see Section 12).*

f) *On completion, refill the cooling system as described in Chapter 1.*

---

7 Timing chains - removal, inspection and installation

SECONDARY CHAIN

Removal

▶ **Refer to illustrations 7.2, 7.4, 7.5, 7.6 and 7.7**

1 Position the engine at TDC for cylinder no. 1 (see Section 3). Remove the VANOS adjustment unit (see Section 9).

2 Unscrew the timing chain tensioner plunger from the right-hand side of the engine (see illustration). Discard the sealing ring, a new one must be installed.

✳ WARNING:

The chain tensioner plunger has a strong spring. Take care when unscrewing the cover plug.

3 If the tensioner is to be re-used, compress and release the tensioner plunger a few times, to drain any oil inside.

4 Press down the secondary chain tensioner plunger and lock it in place by inserting a suitable drill bit (see illustration).

5 Remove the nuts and remove the camshaft position sensor wheel

7.2 Unscrew the timing chain tensioner from the right-hand side of the engine

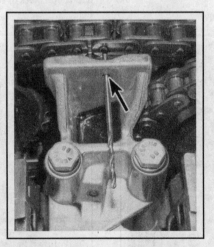

7.4 Use a drill bit to lock down the secondary chain tensioner

7.5 Remove the camshaft position sensor wheel from the exhaust camshaft sprocket

7.6 Remove the three nuts and remove the corrugated washer from the sprocket

7.7 Remove the exhaust sprocket with the chain, friction washer, intake sprocket and the intake camshaft splined shaft

from the exhaust camshaft sprocket, then remove the plate spring (see illustration).

6   Remove the three intake camshaft sprocket nuts and remove the corrugated washer (see illustration).

7   Remove the three screws from the exhaust camshaft sprocket and lift away the secondary chain together with the sprockets, friction washer and intake camshaft splined shaft (see illustration). If these items are to be re-used, store them together in order that they are reinstalled to their original locations.

Inspection

8   The chain should be replaced if the sprockets are worn or if the chain is worn (indicated by excessive lateral play between the links, and excessive noise in operation). It is wise to replace the chain in any case if the engine is disassembled for overhaul. Note that the rollers on a very badly worn chain may be slightly grooved. To avoid future problems, if there is any doubt at all about the condition of the chain, replace it.

9   Examine the teeth on the sprockets for wear. Each tooth forms an inverted V. If worn, the side of each tooth under tension will be slightly concave in shape when compared with the other side of the tooth (the teeth will have a hooked appearance). If the teeth appear worn, the sprockets must be replaced. Also check the chain guide and tensioner

contact surfaces for wear, and replace any worn components as necessary.

Installation

▶ **Refer to illustrations 7.11, 7.12, 7.13, 7.14, 7.17, 7.18 and 7.22**

10   Ensure that Number 1 piston is still positioned at TDC, with the crankshaft locked in position. Check the position of the camshafts using the holding fixture described in Section 3.

11   Check that the primary chain and sprocket on the exhaust camshaft is still in place. Install special tool 11 4 220 into the primary tensioner aperture, then turn the adjuster screw on the tool until the end of the screw just touches the tensioning rail (see illustration).

12   In order to establish the correct relationship between the two sprockets and the chain, use BMW special tool 11 6 180. Insert the two sprockets into the chain and lay the assembly in the special tool. In the absence of the special tool, arrange the sprockets so that there are 15 chain pins between the ends of the cutouts on the sprockets, as shown (see illustration).

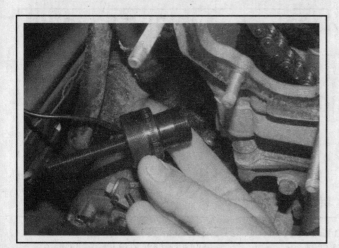

7.11 Install the BMW tool into the tensioner aperture

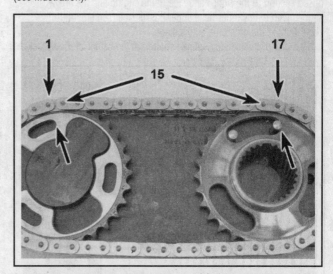

7.12 Insert the chain and sprockets into the special tool. If the tool is not available, arrange the sprockets so there are 15 pins between the positions indicated (and the ends of the cutouts in the sprockets aligned with pin 1 and pin 17)

7.13 The gaps in the intake sprocket and camshaft must align

7.14 Insert the splined shaft locking pin or master spline into the tooth gaps

7.17 Install the spring plate with the F at the front

13 Install the chain and sprockets over the end of the camshafts so that the alignment gap on the inner diameter of the intake sprocket splines aligns exactly with the alignment gap on the splined shaft protruding from the end of the camshaft (see illustration).

14 Reinstall the splined shaft into the end of the intake camshaft, and make sure the large spline installs into the alignment gap in both the camshaft and sprocket (see illustration). Push the splined shaft into the intake sprocket until approximately 1 mm of the splines can still be seen.

15 Reinstall the corrugated washer onto the intake sprocket with the FRONT marking forward. Reinstall the retaining nuts, but only hand-tighten them at this stage.

16 Reinstall the screws to the exhaust sprocket, tighten them to 44 in-lbs (5 Nm), then unscrew them 180-degrees.

17 Install the friction washer and plate spring to the exhaust sprocket. Note that the spring must be installed with the F mark facing forward. If the mark is no longer visible, install the spring with the convex side to the front (see illustration).

18 Reinstall the exhaust camshaft position sensor wheel with the raised section to the right-hand side of the engine and the arrow aligned with the cylinder head upper gasket face (see illustration). Hand-tighten the nuts only at this stage.

19 Pull out the exhaust splined shaft from the center of the sprocket as far as it will go.

20 Compress the secondary chain tensioner plunger and remove the locking pin/drill bit.

21 Using a torque wrench, apply a torque of 6 in-lbs (0.7 Nm) to the adjusting screw on the special tool 11 4 220 installed to the primary chain tensioner aperture. In the absence of a suitable torque wrench, turn the adjusting screw by hand just enough to remove any play in the chain. Check that all play has been removed by attempting to turn the primary chain sprocket on the exhaust camshaft by hand.

22 To ensure that the splined shafts in the sprockets, and the sprockets themselves are correctly centered, BMW tool 11 6 150 must be installed in place of the VANOS unit. Position the tool over the VANOS unit mounting studs (without the gasket), and evenly tighten the nuts until the tool is in full contact with the cylinder head. This tool positions the splined shafts, and holds them in place while the sprocket bolts/nuts are tightened (see illustration). This tool is critical to the timing of the camshafts, and its use is essential.

23 Evenly and progressively tighten the screw-in pins and sprockets nuts to the Step 1 torque listed in this Chapter's Specifications, beginning with the Torx screw-in pins of the exhaust sprocket, followed by the exhaust camshaft sprocket nuts, and then the intake sprocket nuts. Repeat the sequence tightening the screw-in pins and nuts to the Step 2 torque. With the sprockets tightened and the BMW tool 11 6 150 still in

7.18 Install the sensor wheel so that the arrow aligns with the upper gasket surface

7.22 Use the special BMW tool to center the splined shafts and sprockets

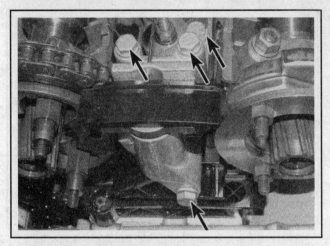

7.28 Remove the secondary chain tensioner bolts

7.29 Remove the three screw-in pins from the exhaust sprocket

place, remove the crankshaft/flywheel locking pin and the locking tool from the rear ends of the camshafts. Using a wrench or socket on the crankshaft pulley bolt, rotate the crankshaft two complete revolutions clockwise until the crankshaft locking pin can be re-inserted.

24 Check the position of the camshafts with the locking tools/template, and ensure the camshaft timing is correct.

➡**Note: Due to the rubber-insulated sprocket(s), tolerance in the VANOS unit and the splined shafts running clearance, the tool locking the intake camshaft may misalign by up to 1.0 mm with the square flange, but the timing would still be considered correct.**

25 Remove the splined shaft/sprocket centering/positioning tool, and reinstall the VANOS adjustment unit as described in Section 9.

PRIMARY CHAIN

Removal

▶ **Refer to illustrations 7.28, 7.29 and 7.32**

26 Remove the secondary timing chain as described previously in this Section.

27 Remove the splined shaft and sleeve from the center of the exhaust camshaft sprocket.

28 Remove the four bolts and remove the secondary chain tensioner (see illustration).

29 Remove the three screw-in pins from the exhaust sprocket, lift the chain and remove the sprocket from the end of the camshaft (see illustration). Note which way round the sprocket is installed.

30 Remove the timing chain cover (see Section 6).

31 Note the routing of the chain in relation to the tensioner rail and the chain guide.

32 Manipulate the tensioner rail as necessary to enable the chain to be unhooked from the crankshaft sprocket and lifted from the engine (see illustration).

✳✳ WARNING:

Once the primary timing chain has been removed, do not turn the crankshaft or the camshafts, as there is a danger of the valves hitting the pistons.

33 The tensioner rail can now be removed after removing the clip from the lower pivot (see illustration).

34 Similarly, the chain guide can be removed after releasing the upper and lower retaining clips. Take care when releasing the retaining clips, as the clips are easily broken (see illustration).

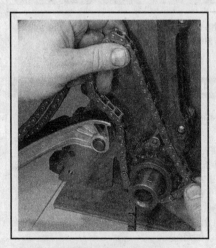

7.32 Unhook the chain from the crankshaft sprocket

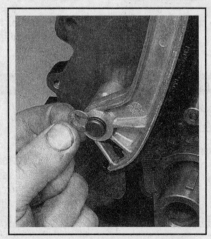

7.33 Remove the clip from the lower pivot to remove the tensioner rail

7.34 Release the retaining clips to remove the chain guide

Installation

▶ **Refer to illustrations 7.38, 7.43 and 7.44**

35 Ensure Number 1 piston is still at TDC, with the crankshaft locked in position. Check the position of the camshafts using the template.

36 Start installation by engaging the chain with the crankshaft sprocket.

37 Where applicable, reinstall the chain guide and the tensioner rail, ensuring that the chain is correctly routed in relation to the guide and tensioner rail, as noted before removal. Take care when installing the chain guide, as the clips are easily broken.

38 Manipulate the exhaust camshaft primary chain sprocket until the timing arrow on the sprocket is aligned with the upper edge of the cylinder head, then engage the chain with the sprocket (see illustration). Install the sprocket to the exhaust camshaft. Ensure that the sprocket is installed the correct way as noted before removal, and that the timing arrow is still in alignment with the upper edge of the cylinder head.

39 Reinstall the timing chain cover as described in Section 6.

40 Install special tool 11 4 220 into the tensioner aperture (see Section 9), then turn the adjuster screw on the tool until the end of the screw just touches the tensioning rail. Note that the exhaust camshaft sprocket may now have moved counterclockwise - if necessary reposition the sprocket in the chain so that the timing arrow re-aligns with the upper surface of the cylinder head (see illustration 7.38).

41 Insert the three screw-in pins through the exhaust sprocket, and tighten them to the torque listed in this Chapter's Specifications.

7.38 Align the arrow on the sprocket with the upper edge of the cylinder head

42 Reinstall the secondary timing chain tensioner and tighten the bolts securely.

43 Reinstall the splined shaft and sleeve to the exhaust camshaft sprocket so that the alignment gap in the sleeve aligns exactly with the corresponding alignment gap in the end of the camshaft. Note that the splined shaft incorporates a pin or large spline which must engage in both alignment gaps (see illustration).

44 Push the exhaust camshaft splined shaft in until the threaded holes in the camshaft sprocket are centered with respect to the oval holes in the tooth sleeve (see illustration).

45 Reinstall the secondary timing chain as described in Steps 10 to 25 of this Section.

7.43 The large spline must engage with the corresponding alignment gaps in the camshaft and sleeve

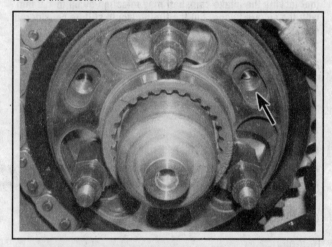

7.44 The holes in the sprocket must be centered in the oval holes in the splined sleeve

---

8 Timing chain sprockets and tensioners - removal, inspection and installation

CAMSHAFT SPROCKETS

1 Removal, inspection and installation of the sprockets is described as part of the secondary timing chain removal and installation procedure in Section 7.

CRANKSHAFT SPROCKET

Removal

2 The sprocket is combined with the oil pump drive sprocket. On some engines, the sprocket may be a press-install on the end of the crankshaft.

3 Remove the primary timing chain as described in Section 7.

4 Slide the sprocket from the front of the crankshaft. If the sprocket is a press-install, use a three-jawed puller to remove the sprocket from the crankshaft. Protect the threaded bore in the front of the crankshaft by installing the pulley hub bolt, or by using a metal spacer between the puller and the end of the crankshaft. Note which way the sprocket is installed to ensure correct installation.

5 Once the sprocket has been removed, recover the Woodruff key from the slot in the crankshaft if it is loose.

Inspection

6   Inspection is described with the timing chain inspection procedure in Section 7.

Installation

7   Where applicable, reinstall the Woodruff key to the slot in the crankshaft.

8   Slide the sprocket into position on the crankshaft. Ensure that the sprocket is installed the correct way as noted before removal. If a press-install sprocket is to be reinstalled, before installation, the sprocket must be heated to a temperature of 302-degrees F (150-degrees C). Do not exceed this temperature, as damage to the sprocket may result.

9   Once the sprocket has been heated to the given temperature, align the slot in the sprocket with the Woodruff key, then tap the sprocket into place with a socket or metal tube.

✳✳ WARNING:

When the sprocket is heated, take precautions against burns - the metal will stay hot for some time.

10 Reinstall the primary timing chain as described in Section 7.

SECONDARY CHAIN TENSIONER

Removal

▶ **Refer to illustration 8.13**

11 Remove the secondary timing chain as described in Section 7.

12 Unscrew the retaining bolts and withdraw the chain tensioner housing from the cylinder head (see illustration 7.28).

13 Remove the tool locking the secondary timing chain tensioner in position, then withdraw the plunger, spring and plunger housing (see illustration).

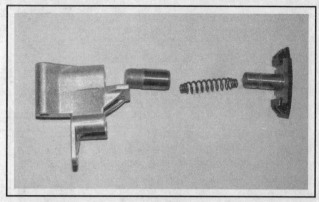

8.13 Details of the secondary timing chain tensioner plunger, spring, and plunger housing

Inspection

14 Inspect the tensioner, and replace if necessary. Check the plunger and the plunger housing for wear and damage. Inspect the chain contact face of the plunger slipper for wear, and check the condition of the spring. Replace any components which are worn or damaged.

15 When installing the plunger to the tensioner, note that the cut-out in the plunger should be positioned on the right-hand side of the engine when the assembly is reinstalled.

Installation

16 Reinstall the chain tensioner and tighten the bolts securely.

17 Reinstall the tool to lock the tensioner in position.

18 Reinstall the secondary timing chain (see Section 7).

PRIMARY CHAIN TENSIONER

19 Removal and installation is described as part of the primary timing chain removal procedure in Section 7.

9   Variable valve timing (VANOS) components - removal, inspection and installation

VANOS ADJUSTMENT UNIT

Removal

▶ **Refer to illustrations 9.3, 9.4, 9.8, 9.9 and 9.10**

1   Remove the viscous cooling fan/electric cooling fan and fan cowl assembly (see Chapter 3).

2   Remove the valve cover (see Section 4).

3   Unscrew the union bolt, and disconnect the oil feed pipe from the front of the VANOS adjustment unit (see illustration). Recover the sealing rings.

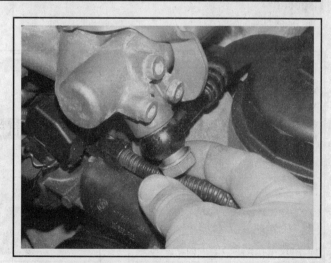

9.3 Disconnect the oil feed pipe from the VANOS unit

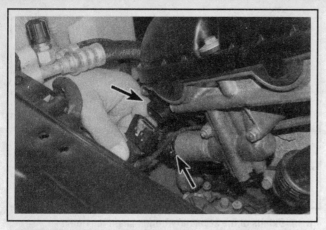

9.4 Disconnect the camshaft position sensor and the solenoid valve

9.8 Unscrew the cover plugs from the VANOS unit

4   Disconnect the exhaust camshaft position sensor and solenoid valve electrical connectors (see illustration).

5   Unscrew the retaining nut and bolt, and remove the engine lifting bracket from the front of the engine.

6   Unclip the plastic cover from the intake camshaft.

7   Position the crankshaft and camshafts at TDC on Number 1 piston (see Section 3).

8   Unscrew the two cover plugs from the front of the VANOS adjustment unit (see illustration). Be prepared for oil spillage and discard the sealing rings (new ones must be installed).

9   Using a pair of needle-nose pliers, pull the sealing caps from the end of the camshafts (see illustration).

10 Using a Torx bit, unscrew the setscrews from the end of the camshafts (see illustration).

➡**Note: The setscrews have left-hand threads (turn clockwise to loosen).**

11 Remove the retaining nuts and remove the VANOS adjustment unit from the front of the engine. Remove the gasket.

12 Do not rotate the crankshaft, camshafts or move the splined shaft in the end of the camshafts with the VANOS unit removed, otherwise the pistons may come in contact with the valves.

Inspection

13 To test the operation of the VANOS adjustment unit, special equipment is required. Testing must therefore be entrusted to a BMW dealer service department or other repair facility with the proper equipment.

Installation

▶ **Refer to illustration 9.16**

14 Ensure that the crankshaft and camshafts are still at TDC on Number 1 cylinder (see Section 3).

15 Make sure that the dowel sleeves are in position on the top VANOS adjustment unit retaining studs in the cylinder head.

16 Apply a thin film of sealant to the corners of the joint surfaces between the cylinder head and the VANOS adjustment unit, then install a new gasket over the studs on the cylinder head (see illustration).

17 Reinstall the VANOS adjustment unit and tighten the nuts to the torque listed in this Chapter's Specifications.

18 Reinstall the setscrews into the ends of the camshafts and tighten them to the torque listed in this Chapter's Specifications. Note that the setscrews are *left-hand thread* (turn counterclockwise to tighten). Check the condition of the O-ring seals and reinstall the sealing caps into the ends of the camshafts.

19 The remainder of the installation procedure is a reversal of removal, bearing in mind the following points.

   a) *Use new sealing rings when reconnecting the oil feed pipe to the VANOS adjustment unit.*

9.9 Use a pair of needle-nose pliers to remove the sealing caps

9.10 The setscrews in the end of the camshafts have a left-hand thread

9.16 Apply a little sealant to the top of the gasket surface on each side of the cylinder head

9.22 Unscrew the VANOS solenoid valve

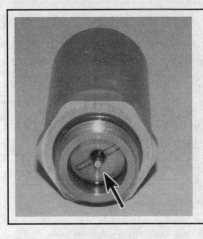

9.23 Check that the solenoid plunger moves freely

b) Reinstall the valve cover (see Section 4).
c) Reinstall the viscous cooling fan and cowl assembly (see Chapter 3).
d) Ensure the crankshaft locking tool is removed prior to starting the engine.

VANOS SOLENOID VALVE

➡**Note: A new sealing ring will be required on installation.**

Removal

▶ **Refer to illustration 9.22**

20 Ensure that the ignition is switched off.

21 Disconnect the solenoid valve electrical connector, which is clipped to the engine wiring harness behind the oil filter assembly.
22 Using an open-ended wrench, unscrew the solenoid valve and recover the seal (see illustration).

Inspection

▶ **Refer to illustration 9.23**

23 Check that the solenoid plunger can be pulled freely back and forth by hand (see illustration). If not, the solenoid must be replaced.

Installation

24 Installation is a reversal of removal, but use a new sealing ring. Tighten the solenoid valve to the torque listed in this Chapter's Specifications.

10 Camshafts and hydraulic lifters - removal, inspection and installation

✳✳ CAUTION:

BMW tool 11 3 260 will be required for this operation. Do not attempt to remove and reinstall the camshafts without the aid of this special tool, as expensive damage to the camshafts and/or bearings may result.

REMOVAL

▶ **Refer to illustrations 10.7, 10.11, 10.12, 10.13 and 10.14**

1 Remove the VANOS adjustment unit (see Section 9).
2 Remove the secondary timing chain (see Section 7).
3 Remove the splined shaft and sleeve from the center of the exhaust camshaft sprocket.
4 Unscrew the four bolts and remove the secondary chain tensioner (see illustration 7.28).
5 Remove the three screw-in pins from the exhaust sprocket, lift the chain and remove the sprocket from the end of the camshaft. Note which direction the sprocket is installed.
6 Remove the crankshaft locking pin then, holding the primary timing chain under tension with your hand, carefully rotate the crankshaft 30-degrees counterclockwise to prevent accidental piston-to-valve contact. Use a length of wire or a cable tie through the primary timing chain and secure it to the cylinder head to prevent the chain falling

down into the timing cover and/or disengaging from the crankshaft sprocket.
7 If required, remove the three screw-in pins on the end of the intake camshaft and remove the thrust washer and camshaft sensor wheel (see illustration).
8 Remove the template from the camshafts.
9 Unscrew the spark plugs from the cylinder head.
10 Check the camshaft bearing caps for identification marks. The caps are numbered from the timing chain end of the engine, and the

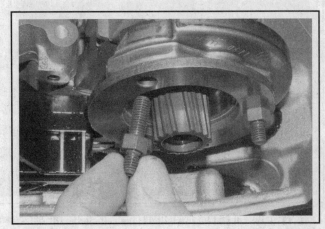

10.7 Remove the screw-in pins from the end of the camshaft

10.11 Unscrew the four camshaft cover retaining studs

10.12 No 1 camshaft bearing cap is centered by adapter sleeves (this cap must be removed before the other caps are loosened)

marks can normally be read from the exhaust side of the engine. The exhaust camshaft bearing caps are marked A1 to A7, and the intake camshaft caps are marked E1 to E7.

11 Unscrew the four camshaft cover retaining studs from the center of the cylinder head (see illustration).

12 As the intake camshaft No 1 bearing cap is located by adapter sleeves, unscrew the nuts and remove the cap to prevent the cap from binding while the camshaft is removed (see illustration).

13 Assemble BMW special tool 11 3 260, and mount the tool on the cylinder head by screwing the mounting bolts into the spark plug holes. Position the tool so that the plungers are located over the relevant camshaft bearing caps (intake or exhaust camshaft) (see illustration).

14 Apply force to the camshaft bearing caps by turning the eccentric shaft on the tools using a wrench (see illustration).

15 Unscrew the remaining camshaft bearing cap nuts.

✳✳ CAUTION:

Do not attempt to unscrew the camshaft bearing cap nuts without the special tools in place, as damage to the camshaft and/or bearings may result.

16 Slowly turn the special tool shaft to release the force from the bearing caps, then unbolt the tool from the cylinder head.

17 Lift off the bearing caps, keeping them in order, then lift out the camshaft.

18 The camshaft bearing casting can now be lifted from the cylinder head. This should be done very slowly, as the camshaft hydraulic lifters will be released as the casting is lifted off - if the casting is lifted off awkwardly, the camshaft hydraulic lifters may fall out. Do not allow the camshaft hydraulic lifters to fall out and get mixed up, as they must be installed to their original locations.

19 With the bearing casting removed, lift the camshaft hydraulic lifters from the cylinder head. Identify the hydraulic lifters for location, and store them upright in a container of clean engine oil to prevent the oil from draining from inside the hydraulic lifters.

20 Repeat the procedure on the remaining camshaft. Do not forget to mark the camshaft hydraulic lifters Intake and Exhaust.

INSPECTION

21 Clean all the components, including the bearing surfaces in the bearing castings and bearing caps. Examine the components carefully for wear and damage. In particular, check the bearing and camshaft lobe surfaces of the camshaft(s) for scoring and pitting. Examine the surfaces of the camshaft hydraulic lifters for signs wear or damage. Replace components as necessary.

10.13 BMW special tool installed to the cylinder head

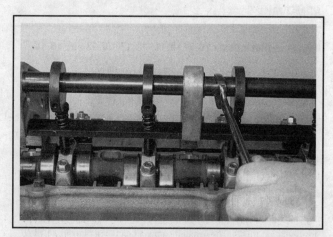

10.14 Use a wrench to turn the eccentric shaft, and apply force to the bearing caps

INSTALLATION

▶ **Refer to illustration 10.22**

22 If the camshaft lower bearing castings have been removed, check that the mating faces of the bearing castings and the cylinder head are clean, and check that the bearing casting locating dowels are in position on the studs at Nos. 2 and 7 bearing locations (see illustration).

23 The bearing casting(s) and camshaft hydraulic lifters must now be reinstalled.

24 The simplest method of installing these components is to retain the camshaft hydraulic lifters in the bearing casting, and reinstall the components as an assembly.

25 Oil the bearing casting contact surfaces of the camshaft hydraulic lifters (avoid allowing oil onto the top faces of the hydraulic lifters at this stage), then install each follower to its original location in the bearing casting.

26 Once all the hydraulic lifters have been installed, they must be retained in the bearing casting, so that they do not fall out as the assembly is reinstalled to the cylinder head.

27 With the camshaft hydraulic lifters retained in the bearing casting, reinstall the casting to the cylinder head. Note that the exhaust side casting is marked A and the intake side casting is marked E. When the castings are reinstalled, the marks should face each other at the timing chain end of the cylinder head.

✳✳ CAUTION:

The camshaft hydraulic lifters expand when not subjected to load by the camshafts, and therefore require some time before they can be compressed. If the camshaft installation operation is carried out rapidly, there is a possibility that the closed valves will be forced open by the expanded camshaft hydraulic lifters, resulting in piston-to-valve contact.

28 To minimize the possibility of piston-to-valve contact after installing the camshaft(s) observe the delays listed in the following table before turning the crankshaft back to the TDC position:

Temperature	Delay
Room temperature (68-degrees F)	4 minutes
50 to 68-degrees F	11 minutes
32 to 50-degrees F	30 minutes

29 First identify the camshafts to ensure that they are installed in the correct locations. The intake camshaft has a triangular front flange and the exhaust camshaft has a circular front flange. Ensure that the crankshaft is still positioned at 30-degrees counterclockwise from the TDC position.

30 Position the camshaft on the cylinder head, so that the tips of the front camshaft lobes on the exhaust and intake camshafts face one another. Note also that the square flanges on the rear of the camshaft should be positioned with the sides of the flanges exactly at right-angles to the top surface of the cylinder head (this can be checked using a set-square), and the side of the flange with holes drilled into it uppermost. Feed the primary timing chain over the end of the exhaust camshaft as it is installed.

31 Place the bearing caps in position, noting that the caps carry identification marks. The exhaust camshaft caps are marked A1 to A7, and the intake camshaft caps are marked E1 to E7. Place the bearing caps in their original locations as noted before removal.

10.22 Bearing casting location dowel on the cylinder head stud at No 2 bearing location (there's one at No 7 location, too)

32 Reassemble BMW special tool 11 3 260, and reinstall it to the cylinder head as during removal.

✳✳ CAUTION:

Again, do not attempt to reinstall the camshafts without the aid of the special tools.

33 Apply pressure to the relevant bearing caps by turning the eccentric shaft on the tools using a wrench.

34 With pressure applied to the bearing caps, reinstall the bearing cap retaining nuts, and tighten them as far as possible by hand.

35 Tighten the bearing cap nuts to the torque listed in this Chapter's Specifications, working progressively in a diagonal sequence.

36 Once the bearing cap nuts have been tightened, unbolt the tool used to apply pressure to the bearing caps.

37 Repeat the procedure on the remaining camshaft.

38 Reinstall the spark plugs, and reinstall the camshaft cover studs to the cylinder head.

39 Reinstall the special tool/camshaft holding fixture used to check the position of the camshafts. If necessary, turn the camshaft(s) slightly using a wrench on the flats provided until the fixture can be installed.

✳✳ CAUTION:

Note the caution in Step 27 before proceeding.

40 Turn the crankshaft back 30-degrees clockwise to the TDC position, then re-engage the locking tool with the flywheel to lock the crankshaft in position.

41 Reinstall the camshaft sprockets and timing chains as described in Section 7.

42 Reinstall the VANOS adjustment unit as described in Section 9.

43 To minimize the possibility of piston-to-valve contact, after installing the camshaft(s), observe the following delays before cranking the engine:

Temperature	Delay
Room temperature (68 degrees F)	10 minutes
50 to 68 degrees F	30 minutes
32 to 50 degrees F	75 minutes

11 Cylinder head - removal and installation

➡**Note: New cylinder head bolts and a new cylinder head gasket will be required on installation.**

REMOVAL

▶ **Refer to illustrations 11.5 and 11.8**

1   Drain the cooling system (see Chapter 1).
2   Remove the intake and exhaust manifolds (see Chapter 4).
3   Remove the camshafts and hydraulic lifters (see Section 10).
4   Trace the wiring back from the camshaft position sensors, then disconnect the sensor connectors. Unscrew the retaining bolts and remove the sensors from the cylinder head.
5   Remove the two Torx screws and remove the secondary timing chain guide from the cylinder head (see illustration).
6   Unscrew the bolts retaining the lower timing chain cover to the cylinder head.
7   Remove the thermostat (see Chapter 3).
8   Remove the two bolts and separate the coolant pipe from the intake side of the cylinder head. To improve access, if necessary, remove the union bolt and disconnect the VANOS adjustment unit oil feed pipe from the rear of the oil filter housing (see illustration). Recover the oil pipe sealing washers.
9   Disconnect the electrical connectors from the temperature sensor located in the left-hand side of the cylinder head.
10 Progressively loosen the cylinder head bolts, working in the reverse of the tightening sequence (see illustration 11.27).
11 Remove the cylinder head bolts and washers. Note that some of the washers may be captive in the cylinder head, in which case they cannot be withdrawn.
12 Release the cylinder head from the engine block and locating dowels by rocking it. Do not pry between the mating faces of the cylinder head and block, as this may damage the gasket faces.
13 Ideally, two assistants will now be required to help remove the cylinder head. Have one assistant hold the timing chain up, clear of the cylinder head, making sure that tension is kept on the chain. With the aid of another assistant, lift the cylinder head from the block - be careful, as the cylinder head is heavy. As the cylinder head is removed, feed the timing chain through the aperture in the front of the cylinder head, and support it from the engine block using the wire.
14 Remove the cylinder head gasket.

INSPECTION

15 Cylinder head dismantling and reassembly should be performed by a qualified automotive machinist.
16 The mating surfaces of the cylinder head and block must be perfectly clean before installing the head. Use a scraper to remove all traces of gasket and carbon, and also clean the tops of the pistons. Take particular care with the aluminum cylinder head, as the soft metal is easily damaged. Make sure that debris is not allowed to enter the oil and water passages. Using adhesive tape and paper, seal the water, oil and bolt holes in the engine block. To prevent carbon entering the gap between the pistons and bores, smear a little grease in the gap. After cleaning each piston, rotate the crankshaft so that the piston moves down the bore, then wipe out the grease and carbon with a cloth rag.
17 Check the block and head for nicks, deep scratches and other damage. If slight, they may be removed from the engine block carefully with a file. More serious damage may be repaired by machining, but this is a specialist job.
18 If warpage of the cylinder head is suspected, use a straightedge to check it for distortion. Compare your measurements with the warpage limit listed in this Chapter's Specifications. Have the cylinder head resurfaced by a machine shop if necessary.
19 Clean out the bolt holes in the block using a pipe cleaner or thin rag and a screwdriver. Make sure that all oil and water is removed, otherwise there is a possibility of the block being cracked by hydraulic pressure when the bolts are tightened.
20 Examine the threads in the engine block for damage. If necessary, use the correct size tap to chase out the threads in the block.

11.5 Remove the Torx bolts securing the secondary timing chain guide

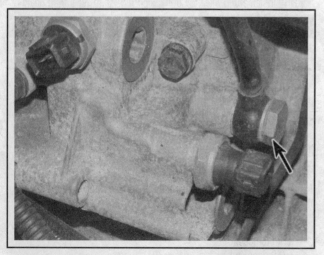

11.8 If necessary, remove the VANOS oil feed pipe from behind the oil filter housing

11.24 Install a new cylinder head gasket

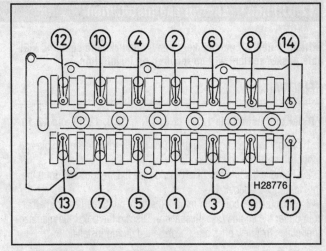

11.27 Cylinder head bolt tightening sequence

INSTALLATION

♦ **Refer to illustrations 11.24 and 11.27**

✳✳ CAUTION:

Since the camshafts have been removed from the cylinder head, note the cautions given in Section 10, regarding expanded camshaft hydraulic lifters.

21 To minimize the possibility of piston-to-valve contact after installing the camshaft(s), observe the following delays before installation the cylinder head.

Temperature	Delay
Room temperature	
(68 degrees F)	4 minutes
50 to 68 degrees F	11 minutes
32 to 50 degrees F	30 minutes

22 Ensure that the mating faces of the engine block and head are spotlessly clean, that the cylinder head bolt threads are clean and dry, and that they screw in and out of their locations. Check that the cylinder head locating dowels are correctly positioned in the engine block.

✳✳ CAUTION:

To avoid any possibility of piston-to-valve contact when installing the cylinder head, it is necessary to ensure that none of the pistons are at TDC. Before proceeding further, if not already done, turn the crankshaft to position No 1 piston at TDC (check that the locking rod can be engaged with the flywheel, then remove the locking rod and turn the crankshaft approximately 30-degrees counterclockwise using a wrench or socket on the crankshaft pulley hub bolt.

23 Apply a thin bead of RTV sealant to the area where the engine block meets the timing cover.

24 Install a new cylinder head gasket to the block, locating it over the dowels. Make sure that it is positioned with the correct side up (see illustration). The word OBEN should face up. Note that thicker-than-standard gaskets are available for use if the cylinder head has been machined (see Chapter 2B). Consult with a machine shop for the correct thickness cylinder head gasket.

25 Lower the cylinder head onto the block, engaging it over the dowels.

26 Apply a light coat of clean engine oil to the threads and washer contact areas then install the new cylinder head bolts, complete with new washers, where necessary, and tighten the bolts as far as possible by hand. Ensure that the washers are correctly seated in their locations in the cylinder head.

➡**Note: Do not install washers to any bolts which are installed to locations where there are already captive washers in the cylinder head. If a new cylinder head is installed (without captive washers), ensure that new washers are installed to all the bolts.**

27 Tighten the bolts in the correct sequence (see illustration) and the correct torque as listed in this Chapter's Specifications.

28 Reinstall and tighten the bolts securing the lower timing chain cover to the cylinder head.

29 Reinstall the secondary timing chain guide to the cylinder head and tighten the Torx screws securely.

30 Reinstall the camshafts and hydraulic lifters as described in Section 10.

31 Turn the crankshaft 30-degrees clockwise back to the TDC position, then re-engage the locking rod with the flywheel to lock the crankshaft in position.

32 The remainder of installation is a reverse of removal. On completion, refill the cooling system as described in Chapter 1.

12 Oil pan - removal and installation

➡**Note: A new oil pan gasket, a new dipstick tube seal and suitable gasket sealant will be required on installation.**

REMOVAL

◆ **Refer to illustrations 12.2, 12.3, 12.8, 12.9, 12.14 and 12.19**

1 Apply the parking brake, then jack up the front of the vehicle and support it securely on jackstands.

2 Remove the engine splash shield (see illustration) and drain the engine oil (see Chapter 1).

3 Unscrew the bolts and remove the front reinforcement frame/bar from under the engine (see illustration). Discard the bolts; the manufacturer states that new ones must be installed during installation.

➡**Note: Sedan models are equipped with a triangulated reinforcement bar while coupes and convertibles are equipped with a conventional square reinforcement frame.**

4 Unscrew the retaining bolts and/or nuts, and remove the alternator air ducting from the front of the vehicle.

5 Remove the air filter housing (see Chapter 4).

6 In order to remove the oil pan, the engine must be suspended and the front crossmember must be lowered. This can be accomplished with an engine lifting hoist and lifting chain or sling attached to the eye at the front of the cylinder head, or with an engine support fixture attached to the lifting eye. Take up the weight of the engine.

7 On automatic transmission models, disconnect the transmission fluid lines from the transmission oil pan. Be prepared for fluid spillage.

8 Remove the retaining bolt and detach the oil return hose from the oil separator, and pull the dipstick guide tube and return hose from the oil pan (see illustration). Discard the O-ring seal; a new one must be installed.

9 Check that the steering wheel is facing straight-ahead, and engage the steering lock. Make alignment marks between the steering column joint flange and the steering rack pinion, then loosen the pinch-bolt, and pull the joint from the pinion. While the column is separated from the rack, it is essential that neither the steering wheel nor front

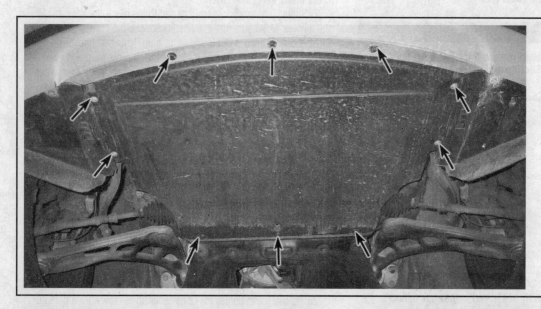

12.2 Location of the engine splash shield retaining screws and plastic expansion rivets

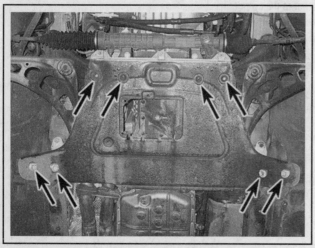

12.3 Location of the reinforcement plate/frame bolts

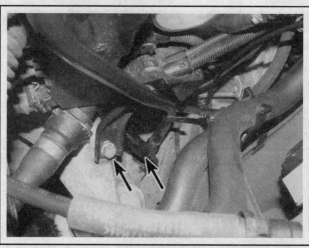

12.8 Dipstick guide tube, oil return hose and mounting bracket bolt

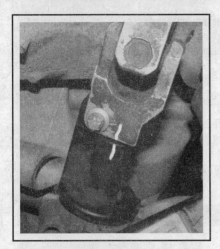

12.9 Remove the pinch-bolt and pull the joint from the pinion

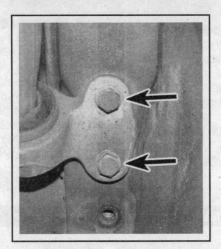

12.14 Remove the control arm-to-chassis bolts on each side

12.16 Remove the crossmember-to-chassis bolts on each side

wheels are moved from their positions (see illustration). To prevent the steering wheel from turning, make sure the steering column lock is engaged, or run the seat belt through the steering wheel and clip it into place.

10 Remove the drivebelt as described in Chapter 1.

11 Unbolt the power steering support bracket from the rear of the pump, then unbolt the pump mounting bracket from the alternator mounting bracket, and move the pump to one side, clear of the engine, leaving the fluid lines connected. Make sure that the pump is adequately supported, and do not strain the fluid lines.

12 Unscrew the nuts securing the left and right-hand engine mounts to the chassis. Using the engine hoist or support fixture, raise the engine approximately 10 to 15 mm, ensuring that the rear of the cylinder head does not crush or trap the brake lines along the engine compartment firewall.

✳✳ CAUTION:

Do not lift the engine excessively or the radiator cooling fan and/or radiator may be damaged.

13 Where applicable, unclip any lines, hoses and/or wiring from the engine mounting brackets, and oil pan.

14 Remove the bolts and detach the left and right-hand control arm brackets from the chassis (see illustration). Also separate the left inner balljoint from the chassis (see Chapter 10).

15 Unscrew the stabilizer bar clamp bolts (see Chapter 10).

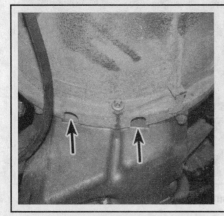

12.19 The rear oil pan bolts are accessible through the cutouts in the transmission housing

16 Support the crossmember with a floor jack, then remove the crossmember-to-chassis bolts (see illustration). Slowly lower the crossmember, taking care not to strain the power steering hoses. Where installed, remove the rubber bushings from between the crossmember and the oil pan.

17 Disconnect the front suspension ride-level sensor, if equipped.

18 Disconnect the oil level sensor harness connector located at the bottom of the oil pan.

19 Working under the vehicle, progressively remove all the oil pan retaining bolts. Note that the rear oil pan retaining bolts are accessible through the holes in the transmission bellhousing (see illustration). Also note that the three lower transmission-to-engine bolts must be removed, as they screw into the oil pan.

20 Lower the oil pan to the ground.

21 Remove the oil pan gasket.

INSTALLATION

▶ **Refer to illustration 12.23**

22 Start installation by thoroughly cleaning the mating surfaces of the oil pan and engine block.

23 Lightly coat the areas where the crankshaft rear oil seal housing and front timing chain cover join the engine block with RTV sealant (see illustration).

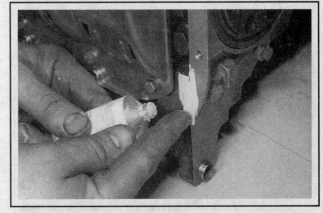

12.23 Apply sealant to the area where the rear oil seal housing and front timing chain cover join the engine block

24 Place the gasket in position on the oil pan flange.

25 Install the oil pan to the engine block, ensuring that the gasket stays in place, and reinstall the oil pan retaining bolts, tightening them finger-tight only at this stage.

26 Tighten the oil pan-to-engine block bolts a little at a time, working from the center bolts outward, to the torque listed in this Chapter's Specifications.

27 Tighten the transmission-to-engine bolts to the torque listed in this Chapter's Specifications.

28 Further installation is a reversal of removal, noting the following points.

a) When raising the crossmember into position, make sure that no pipes, hoses and/or wiring are trapped.

b) Install new crossmember and reinforcement frame/bar bolts, and tighten them to the torque listed in this Chapter's Specifications.

c) Tighten the suspension fasteners to the torque listed in the Chapter 10 Specifications.

d) Tighten the engine mount nuts securely.

e) Install the drivebelt (see Chapter 1).

f) When installing the dipstick tube, replace the O-ring seal.

g) On completion, refill the engine with oil as described in Chapter 1.

h) On automatic transmission models, check the transmission fluid level as described in Chapter 7B.

13 Oil pump and drive chain - removal, inspection and installation

OIL PUMP

➡ Note: A new pick-up pipe O-ring, a new relief valve spring cap O-ring and a new relief valve snap-ring will be required on installation.

Removal and installation

♦ Refer to illustrations 13.2, 13.5 and 13.6

➡ Note: Models built before January 2000 are equipped with an integral (one-piece) oil pump and baffle plate assembly. Models built after January 2000 are equipped with a separate oil pump and baffle plate.

1 Remove the oil pan (see Section 12).

2 Unscrew the nut securing the sprocket to the oil pump shaft (see illustration).

➡ Note: The nut has left-hand threads. Turn it clockwise to loosen it.

3 Pull the sprocket and chain from the oil pump shaft.

4 On models where the pump is integral with the oil pan baffle plate, remove the bolts and remove the plate complete with the pump and pick-up tube.

5 On models where the pump is separate from the baffle plate, remove the two bolts securing the pick-up pipe to the baffle plate, and the bolt securing the pipe to the pump (see illustration). Remove the pipe.

6 Remove the four bolts and remove the oil pump (see illustration).

Inspection

♦ Refer to illustrations 13.7, 13.10a, 13.10b, 13.11, 13.12a, 13.12b and 13.12c

7 Unbolt the cover from the front of the pump (see illustration).

8 Withdraw the driveshaft/rotor and the outer rotor from the pump body.

9 Check the pump body, rotors and cover for any signs of scoring,

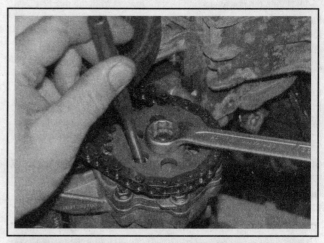

13.2 Unscrew the oil pump sprocket retaining nut - it has a left-hand thread

13.5 Unscrew the oil pick-up pipe bolts

13.6 Oil pump mounting bolts

13.7 Oil pump cover bolts

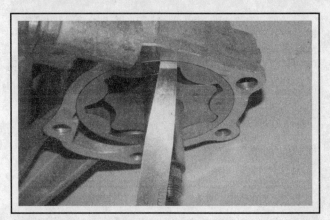

13.10a Measure the clearance between the outer oil pump rotor and the pump body . . .

13.10b . . . and the rotor endplay

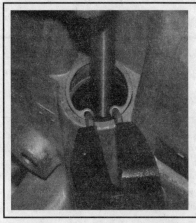

13.11 Extract the snap-ring using special pliers

wear or cracks. If any wear or damage is evident, install new rotors or replace the complete pump, depending on the extent of the damage. Note that it is wise to replace the complete pump as a unit.

10 Reinstall the rotors to the pump body, then using feeler gauges, measure the clearance between the outer rotor and the pump body. Using the feeler gauges and a straight-edge, measure the clearance (endplay) between each of the rotors and the oil pump cover mating face (see illustrations). Compare the measurements with the values given in the Specifications, and if necessary, replace any worn compo-

nents, or replace the complete pump as a unit.

11 To remove the pressure relief valve components, press the valve into its housing slightly, using a metal tool, then extract the snap-ring from the top of the housing using snap-ring pliers (see illustration).

❋❋ WARNING:

The relief valve has a strong spring. Take care when removing the snap-ring.

12 Withdraw the spring cap, spring and piston from the relief valve housing (see illustrations).

13.12a Withdraw the oil pressure relief valve spring cap . . .

13.12b . . . spring . . .

13.12c . . . and piston

13 Install a new O-ring seal to the top of the relief valve spring cap, then reinstall the components to the housing using a reversal of the removal procedure. Take care not to damage the surface of the spring cap during installation, and secure the components using a new O-ring.

14 Reinstall the rotors to the pump body, then reinstall the cover to the pump. Ensure that the locating dowels are in position in the pump cover. Reinstall and tighten the cover bolts to the torque listed in this Chapter's Specifications.

15 The remainder of installation is a reversal of removal, noting the following points:

a) *Where applicable, replace the oil pick-up tube O-ring seal.*
b) *Tighten the oil pump sprocket retaining nut (left-hand thread) to the torque listed in this Chapter's Specifications.*

OIL PUMP DRIVE CHAIN

Removal

16 Remove the primary timing chain (see Section 7).
17 Remove the oil pump drive chain from the crankshaft sprocket.

Inspection

18 Proceed as described for the secondary timing chain in Section 7.

Installation

19 Reinstall the chain to the crankshaft sprocket, then reinstall the primary timing chain as described in Section 7.

14 Oil seals - replacement

CRANKSHAFT FRONT OIL SEAL

1 The procedure is described as part of the timing chain cover removal and installation procedure in Section 6.

CRANKSHAFT REAR OIL SEAL

▶ **Refer to illustration 14.11**

2 Remove the flywheel/driveplate (see Section 15).
3 Working at the bottom of the oil seal housing, unscrew the bolts securing the rear of the oil pan to the housing.
4 Unscrew the bolts securing the oil seal housing to the engine block.
5 If the housing is stuck to the oil pan gasket, run a sharp, thin blade between the housing and the oil pan gasket. Take care not to damage the oil pan gasket.
6 Withdraw the housing from the engine block. If the housing is stuck, tap it gently using a soft-faced mallet. Do not pry between the housing and the engine block, as this may damage the gasket surfaces.
7 Remove the gasket.
8 Thoroughly clean all traces of old gasket and sealant from the mating faces of the oil seal housing and the engine block. Again, take care not to damage the oil pan gasket. If the oil pan gasket has been damaged during removal, it is advisable to install a new one with reference to Section 12.
9 Support the oil seal housing on blocks of wood, then drive out the seal from the rear of the housing using a hammer and drift.
10 Clean the seal mating surfaces in the housing.
11 The seal must only be installed with the aid of the seal protector (supplied with the seal). Leave the seal protector installed into the center of the seal at this stage. Do not touch the sealing lip with your fingers, the lip is very sensitive and must not be kinked. Carefully drive it into position in the housing, using a seal driver to avoid damage to the seal (see illustration).
12 Ensure that the locating dowels are in position in the rear of the engine block, then locate a new oil seal housing gasket over the dowels.

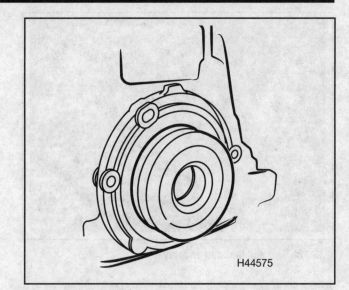

14.11 Leave the seal protector in the center of the seal and drive it into place

➡**Note: A new oil seal housing gasket will be required on installation.**

13 Carefully install the housing to the engine block, sliding the oil seal protector over the crankshaft flange, and push the seal and housing into place. Take care not to damage the oil seal lips.
14 Reinstall the housing-to-engine block and the oil pan-to-housing bolts, and tighten them lightly by hand.
15 Tighten the housing-to-engine block bolts to the torque listed in this Chapter's Specifications, then tighten the oil pan-to-housing bolts to the torque listed in this Chapter's Specifications.
16 Reinstall the flywheel/driveplate as described in Section 15.

CAMSHAFT OIL SEALS

17 As this is a timing chain engine, no camshaft oil seals are installed. Sealing is provided by the valve cover gasket and the timing chain cover gaskets.

15 Flywheel/driveplate - removal and installation

➡Note: New flywheel/driveplate retaining bolts will be required on installation, and thread-locking compound may be required.

REMOVAL

▶ **Refer to illustration 15.3**

1   Remove the manual transmission as described in Chapter 7A, or the automatic transmission as described in Chapter 7B.

2   On models with a manual transmission, remove the clutch as described in Chapter 8.

3   In order to remove the bolts, the flywheel/driveplate must be locked in position. This can be done by bolting a flywheel locking tool (engage the tooth with the starter ring gear) to the engine block using one of the transmission-to-engine bolts (see illustration).

4   Progressively loosen and remove the retaining bolts, then withdraw the flywheel/driveplate from the crankshaft. Note that the flywheel/driveplate locates on dowels.

✳ WARNING:

Take care as the flywheel/driveplate is heavy.

5   Remove the engine/transmission intermediate plate (where installed), noting its orientation.

INSTALLATION

▶ **Refer to illustrations 15.6, 15.7 and 15.8**

6   Reinstall the engine/transmission intermediate plate (where installed), ensuring that it is correctly located on the dowel(s) (see illustration).

7   Reinstall the flywheel/driveplate to the end of the crankshaft, ensuring that the locating dowel engages. Note that on dual-mass flywheels, the position of the dowel is indicated by one or two notches in the flywheel adjacent to the relevant locating hole (see illustration).

8   Examine the threads of the new retaining bolts. If the threads are not already coated with thread-locking compound, apply a non-hardening thread-locking compound to them, then reinstall the bolts (see illustration).

15.3 Tool used to lock the flywheel in position when unscrewing flywheel bolts

15.6 Ensure the engine/transmission intermediate plate is correctly located

9   Tighten the bolts progressively in a diagonal sequence to the torque listed in this Chapter's Specifications. Lock the flywheel/driveplate by reversing the tool used during removal.

10 Where applicable, reinstall the clutch as described in Chapter 8.

11 Reinstall the transmission as described in Chapter 7A or 7B.

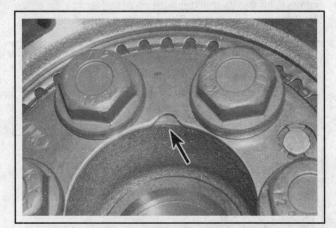

15.7 The notch indicates the position of the locating hole for the dowel

15.8 If the bolt threads are not already coated with thread locking compound, apply some

16 Crankshaft pilot bearing - replacement

▶ **Refer to illustrations 16.1 and 16.6**

1   On manual transmission models, a bearing is installed in the end of the crankshaft to support the end of the transmission input shaft (see illustration).

2   Special pilot bearing pullers are available at most auto parts stores. If one is not available, this alternative method works:

3   Remove the flywheel (see Section 15).

4   Pack the space behind, and the center bore, of the bearing with general purpose grease.

5   Position a metal rod or bolt in the entrance of the bearing bore. The rod/bolt diameter should be just less than the diameter of the bearing bore. Cover the rod near the flywheel with a rag to catch any grease that might squirt out.

❄❄ WARNING:

Wear eye protection before performing this Step.

6   Strike the end of the rod/bolt with a hammer several times (see illustration). As the rod/bolt is struck, the compressed grease forces the bearing from position. Continue until the bearing is removed.

7   Thoroughly clean the bearing housing in the end of the crankshaft.

8   Tap the new bearing into position, up to the stop, using a bearing driver or socket on the bearing outer race.

9   Reinstall the flywheel (see Section 15).

16.1 Crankshaft pilot bearing

16.6 Use grease and a close-installing rod to extract the pilot bearing

17 Engine/transmission mounts - inspection and replacement

INSPECTION

1   Two engine mounts are used, one on either side of the engine.

2   If improved access is required, raise the front of the vehicle and support it securely on jackstands.

3   Check the mount rubber to see if it is cracked, hardened or separated from the metal at any point. Replace the engine mounts if any such damage or deterioration is evident.

4   Check that all the mount bolts and nuts are securely tightened.

5   Using a large screwdriver or a crowbar, check for wear in the mounts by carefully prying against it to check for free play. Where this is not possible, enlist the aid of an assistant to move the engine/transmission back-and-forth, or from side-to-side, while you observe the mounts. While some freeplay is to be expected, even from new components, excessive wear should be obvious. If excessive freeplay is found, check first that the fasteners are correctly secured, then replace any worn components as required.

REPLACEMENT

▶ **Refer to illustrations 17.7a and 17.7b**

6   Support the engine, either using a hoist and lifting chain con-

nected to the engine lifting brackets (refer to *Engine - removal and installation* in Part B of this Chapter), or by positioning a jack and block of wood under the oil pan. Ensure that the engine is adequately supported before proceeding.

7   Remove the nuts securing the left and right-hand engine mount brackets to the mounts, then unbolt the mount brackets from the engine block, and remove the mounts. Disconnect the engine ground straps

17.7a Unbolt the engine mounting bracket from the engine block

from the mount (see illustrations).

8 Remove the nuts securing the mounts to the body, then remove the mounts.

9 Installation is the reverse of removal, but ensure that the metal protector plates are in position on the mounts, and securely tighten all fasteners.

17.7b A ground strap is installed to the right-hand engine mounting bracket

18 Oil pressure, level and temperature switches - removal and installation

OIL PRESSURE SWITCH

▶ **Refer to illustration 18.3**

➡**Note: On some models it may be necessary to remove the intake manifold to access the oil pressure switch (see Chapter 4).**

1 Unscrew the oil filter cap. This allows the oil within the filter to flow back into the oil pan, reducing the amount lost during switch replacement.

2 Remove the air filter housing (see Chapter 4).

3 Disconnect the electrical connector and unscrew the switch from the base of the oil filter housing (see illustration).

4. Install the new switch, and tighten it to the torque listed in this Chapter's Specifications.

5 Reinstall the air filter housing and oil filter cap. Check the oil level as described in Chapter 1.

OIL LEVEL SWITCH

▶ **Refer to illustration 18.8**

6 Drain the engine oil (see Chapter 1).

7 Remove the engine splash shield (see Chapter 11).

8 Disconnect the electrical connector, remove the three retaining nuts and remove the level switch (see illustration).

9 Ensure that the oil pan mating surface is clean.

10 Complete with a new seal, install the oil level switch and tighten the retaining nuts securely.

11 Reinstall the engine splash shield and refill the crankcase with the proper type and quantity of engine oil as described in Chapter 1.

OIL TEMPERATURE SWITCH

▶ **Refer to illustration 18.14**

12 Unscrew the oil filter cap. This precaution allows the oil within the filter to flow back into the oil pan, reducing the amount lost during switch replacement.

13 Remove the air filter housing (see Chapter 4).

14 Disconnect the electrical connector and unscrew the switch from the base of the oil filter housing (see illustration).

15 Install the new switch, and tighten it to the torque listed in this Chapter's Specifications.

16 Reinstall the air filter housing and oil filter cap. Check the oil level as described in Chapter 1.

18.3 Disconnect the electrical connector from the oil pressure switch

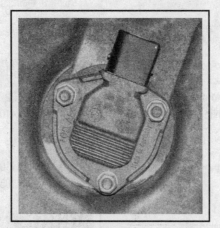

18.8 The oil level switch is retained by three nuts

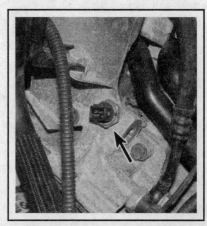

18.14 Disconnect the electrical connector from the oil temperature switch

Specifications

General

Engine code

M52 TU B25	152 cu. In. (2494 cc)
M52 TU B28	170 cu. In. (2793 cc)
M54 B25	152 cu. In. (2494 cc)
M54 B30	182 cu. In. (2979 cc)
M56 B25	152 cu. In. (2494 cc)
Direction of engine rotation	Clockwise (viewed from front of vehicle)
No 1 cylinder location	Timing chain end
Firing order	1-5-3-6-2-4
Minimum compression pressure	142 to 156 psi (10.0 to 11.0 bar)
Cylinder head warpage limit	0.002 inch (0.050 mm)

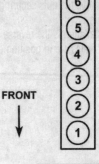

18022-specs-HAYNES

Cylinder locations

Camshafts

Endplay	0.006 to 0.013 inch (0.150 to 0.330 mm)

Lubrication system

Oil pump rotor clearances

Outer rotor to pump body	0.004 to 0.007 inch (0.100 to 0.176 mm)
Inner rotor endplay	0.001 to 0.003 inch (0.030 to 0.080 mm)
Outer rotor endplay	0.002 to 0.004 inch (0.040 to 0.090 mm)

Torque specifications

	Ft-lbs (unless otherwise indicated)	Nm
Camshaft bearing cap nuts	11	14
Camshaft screw-in pins		
Step 1	44 in-lbs	5
Step 2	15	20
Camshaft sprocket nuts		
Step 1	44 in-lbs	5
Step 2	89 in-lbs	10
Camshaft set-screw (left-hand thread)	89 in-lbs	10
Chain tensioner cover plug	30	40
Chain tensioner plunger cylinder	52	70
Chain guide (secondary, lower) Torx bolts	89 in-lbs	10
Crankshaft rear oil seal housing bolts		
M6 bolts	89 in-lbs	10
M8 bolts	16	22
Crankshaft vibration damper/pulley-to-hub bolts	16	22
Crankshaft vibration damper/pulley hub bolt*	303	410
Crossmember-to-chassis bolts*		
Grade 8.8	57	77
Grade 10.9	81	110
Grade 12.9	77	105
Cylinder head bolts*		
Step 1	30	40
Step 2	Tighten an additional 90-degrees	
Step 3	Tighten an additional 90-degrees	

Torque specifications	Ft-lbs (unless otherwise indicated)	Nm
Driveplate bolts*	89	120
Flywheel bolts*	77	105
Oil feed pipe banjo bolt-to-VANOS unit	24	32
Oil pressure switch	20	27
Oil temperature switch	20	27
Oil pump bolts	16	22
Oil pump cover	79 in-lbs	9
Oil pump sprocket nut (left-hand thread)	18	25
Oil pump pick-up tube bolts	89 in-lbs	10
Reinforcement plate/bar bolts*		
Bar type	31	42
Plate style		
Step 1	43	59
Step 2	Tighten an additional 90-degrees	
Oil pan oil drain plug	18	25
Oil pan to block		
M6 Grade 8.8	89 in-lbs	10
M6 Grade 10.9	106 in-lbs	12
Oil pan lower section to upper section	89 in-lbs	10
Timing chain cover-to-engine block bolts		
M6	89 in-lbs	10
M7	132 in-lbs	15
M8	16	22
M10	34	47
Valve cover bolts	18	25
VANOS solenoid valve	22	30
VANOS oil feed pipe to oil filter housing	24	32
VANOS unit-to-cylinder head nuts		
M6	89 in-lbs	10
M7	120 in-lbs	14
VANOS sealing plugs	37	50

*Do not re-use

Notes

Section

Reference to other Chapters

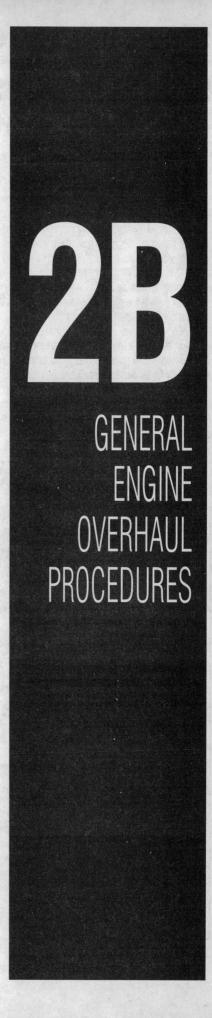

2B

GENERAL ENGINE OVERHAUL PROCEDURES

1 General information - engine overhaul

▶ **Refer to illustrations 1.1, 1.2, 1.3, 1.4, 1.5 and 1.6**

Included in this portion of Chapter 2 are general information and diagnostic testing procedures for determining the overall mechanical condition of your engine.

The information ranges from advice concerning preparation for an overhaul and the purchase of replacement parts and/or components to detailed, step-by-step procedures covering removal and installation.

The following Sections have been written to help you determine whether your engine needs to be overhauled and how to remove and install it once you've determined it needs to be rebuilt. For information concerning in-vehicle engine repair, see Chapter 2A.

It's not always easy to determine when, or if, an engine should be completely overhauled, because a number of factors must be considered.

High mileage is not necessarily an indication that an overhaul is needed, while low mileage doesn't preclude the need for an overhaul. Frequency of servicing is probably the most important consideration. An engine that's had regular and frequent oil and filter changes, as well as other required maintenance, will most likely give many thousands of miles of reliable service. Conversely, a neglected engine may require an overhaul very early in its service life.

Excessive oil consumption is an indication that piston rings, valve seals and/or valve guides are in need of attention. Make sure that oil leaks aren't responsible before deciding that the rings and/or guides are bad. Perform a cylinder compression check to determine the extent of the work required (see Chapter 2A). Also check the vacuum readings under various conditions (see Section 3).

Check the oil pressure with a gauge installed in place of the oil pressure sending unit and compare it to this Chapter's Specifications (see Section 2). If it's extremely low, the bearings and/or oil pump are probably worn out.

Loss of power, rough running, knocking or metallic engine noises, excessive valve train noise and high fuel consumption rates may also point to the need for an overhaul, especially if they're all present at the same time. If a complete tune-up doesn't remedy the situation, major mechanical work is the only solution.

An engine overhaul involves restoring the internal parts to the specifications of a new engine. During an overhaul, the piston rings are replaced and the cylinder walls are reconditioned (rebored and/or honed) (see illustrations 1.1 and 1.2). If a rebore is done by an automotive machine shop, new oversize pistons will also be installed. The main bearings, connecting rod bearings and camshaft bearings are generally replaced with new ones and, if necessary, the crankshaft may

1.1 An engine block being bored. An engine rebuilder will use special machinery to recondition the cylinder bores

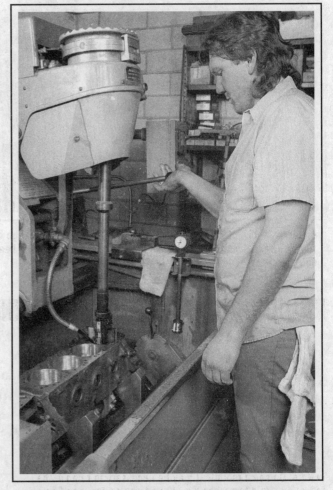

1.2 If the cylinders are bored, the machine shop will normally hone the engine on a machine like this

be reground to restore the journals (see illustration 1.3). Generally, the valves are serviced as well, since they're usually in less-than-perfect condition at this point. While the engine is being overhauled, other components, such as the distributor, starter and alternator, can be rebuilt as well. The end result should be similar to a new engine that will give many trouble free miles.

→**Note: Critical cooling system components such as the hoses, drivebelts, thermostat and water pump should be replaced with new parts when an engine is overhauled. The radiator should be checked carefully to ensure that it isn't clogged or leaking (see Chapter 3). If you purchase a rebuilt engine or short block, some rebuilders will not warranty their engines unless the radiator has been professionally flushed. Also, we don't recommend overhauling the oil pump - always install a new one when an engine is rebuilt.**

Overhauling the internal components on today's engines is a difficult and time-consuming task which requires a significant amount of specialty tools and is best left to a professional engine rebuilder (see illustrations 1.4, 1.5 and 1.6). A competent engine rebuilder will handle the inspection of your old parts and offer advice concerning the reconditioning or replacement of the original engine, never purchase parts or have machine work done on other components until the block has been thoroughly inspected by a professional machine shop. As a general rule, time is the primary cost of an overhaul, especially since the vehicle may be tied up for a minimum of two weeks or more. Be

1.3 A crankshaft having a main bearing journal ground

aware that some engine builders only have the capability to rebuild the engine you bring them while other rebuilders have a large inventory of rebuilt exchange engines in stock. Also be aware that many machine shops could take as much as two weeks time to completely rebuild your engine depending on shop workload. Sometimes it makes more sense to simply exchange your engine for another engine that's already rebuilt to save time.

1.4 A machinist checks for a bent connecting rod, using specialized equipment

1.5 A bore gauge being used to check the main bearing bore

1.6 Uneven piston wear like this indicates a bent connecting rod

2   Oil pressure check

1   Low engine oil pressure can be a sign of an engine in need of rebuilding. A "low oil pressure" indicator (often called an "idiot light") is not a test of the oiling system. Such indicators only come on when the oil pressure is dangerously low. Even a factory oil pressure gauge in the instrument panel is only a relative indication, although much better for driver information than a warning light. A better test is with a mechanical (not electrical) oil pressure gauge.

2   Locate the oil pressure switch. The oil pressure switch is mounted at the base of the oil filter housing (see Chapter 2A).

→**Note: On some models it may be necessary to remove the intake manifold to access the oil pressure switch (see Chapter 4).**

3   Unscrew and remove the oil pressure sending unit and then screw in the hose for your oil pressure gauge. If necessary, install an adapter fitting. Use Teflon tape or thread sealant on the threads of the adapter and/or the fitting on the end of your gauge's hose.

4   Connect an accurate tachometer to the engine, according to the tachometer manufacturer's instructions.

5   Check the oil pressure with the engine running (normal operating temperature) at the specified engine speed, and compare it to this Chapter's Specifications. If it's extremely low, the bearings and/or oil pump are probably worn out.

3 Vacuum gauge diagnostic checks

▶ **Refer to illustrations 3.4 and 3.6**

A vacuum gauge provides inexpensive but valuable information about what is going on in the engine. You can check for worn rings or cylinder walls, leaking head or intake manifold gaskets, restricted exhaust, stuck or burned valves, weak valve springs, improper ignition or valve timing and ignition problems.

Unfortunately, vacuum gauge readings are easy to misinterpret, so they should be used in conjunction with other tests to confirm the diagnosis.

Both the absolute readings and the rate of needle movement are important for accurate interpretation. Most gauges measure vacuum in inches of mercury (in-Hg). The following references to vacuum assume the diagnosis is being performed at sea level. As elevation increases (or atmospheric pressure decreases), the reading will decrease. For every 1,000 foot increase in elevation above approximately 2,000 feet, the gauge readings will decrease about one inch of mercury.

Connect the vacuum gauge directly to an intake manifold vacuum source, not to ported (throttle body) vacuum (see illustration). Use a

3.4 A simple vacuum gauge can be handy in diagnosing engine condition and performance

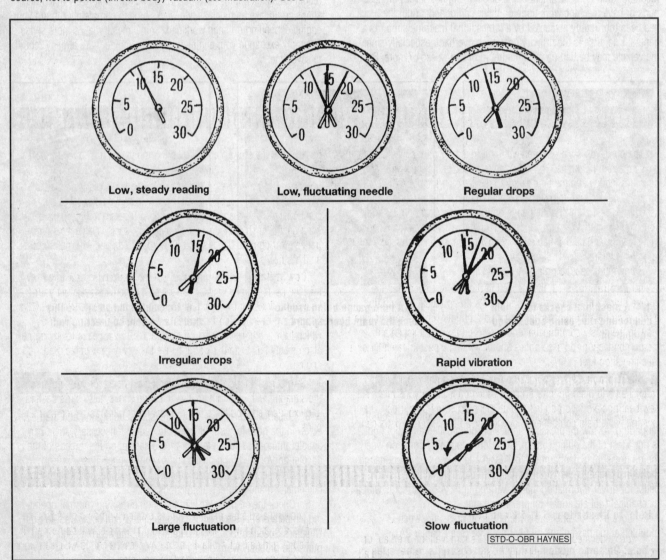

Low, steady reading

Low, fluctuating needle

Regular drops

Irregular drops

Rapid vibration

Large fluctuation

Slow fluctuation

STD-O-OBR HAYNES

3.6 Typical vacuum gauge readings

T-fitting to access the vacuum signal. Be sure no hoses are left disconnected during the test or false readings will result.

Before you begin the test, allow the engine to warm up completely. Block the wheels and set the parking brake. With the transmission in Park, start the engine and allow it to run at normal idle speed.

✳✳ WARNING:

Keep your hands and the vacuum gauge clear of the fans.

Read the vacuum gauge; an average, healthy engine should normally produce about 17 to 22 in-Hg with a fairly steady needle (see illustration). Refer to the following vacuum gauge readings and what they indicate about the engine's condition:

1   A low, steady reading usually indicates a leaking gasket between the intake manifold and cylinder head(s) or throttle body, a leaky vacuum hose, late ignition timing or incorrect camshaft timing. Check ignition timing with a timing light and eliminate all other possible causes, utilizing the tests provided in this Chapter before you remove the timing chain cover to check the timing marks.

2   If the reading is three to eight inches below normal and it fluctuates at that low reading, suspect an intake manifold gasket leak at an intake port or a faulty fuel injector.

3   If the needle has regular drops of about two-to-four inches at a steady rate, the valves are probably leaking. Perform a compression check or leak-down test to confirm this.

4   An irregular drop or down-flick of the needle can be caused by a sticking valve or an ignition misfire. Perform a compression check or leak-down test and read the spark plugs.

5   A rapid vibration of about four in-Hg vibration at idle combined with exhaust smoke indicates worn valve guides. Perform a leak-down test to confirm this. If the rapid vibration occurs with an increase in engine speed, check for a leaking intake manifold gasket or head gasket, weak valve springs, burned valves or ignition misfire.

6   A slight fluctuation, say one inch up and down, may mean ignition problems. Check all the usual tune-up items and, if necessary, run the engine on an ignition analyzer.

7   If there is a large fluctuation, perform a compression or leak-down test to look for a weak or dead cylinder or a blown head gasket.

8   If the needle moves slowly through a wide range, check for a clogged PCV system, incorrect idle fuel mixture, throttle body or intake manifold gasket leaks.

9   Check for a slow return after revving the engine by quickly snapping the throttle open until the engine reaches about 2,500 rpm and let it shut. Normally the reading should drop to near zero, rise above normal idle reading (about 5 in-Hg over) and then return to the previous idle reading. If the vacuum returns slowly and doesn't peak when the throttle is snapped shut, the rings may be worn. If there is a long delay, look for a restricted exhaust system (often the muffler or catalytic converter). An easy way to check this is to temporarily disconnect the exhaust ahead of the suspected part and redo the test.

4   Engine rebuilding alternatives

The do-it-yourselfer is faced with a number of options when purchasing a rebuilt engine. The major considerations are cost, warranty, parts availability and the time required for the rebuilder to complete the project. The decision to replace the engine block, piston/connecting rod assemblies and crankshaft depends on the final inspection results of your engine. Only then can you make a cost effective decision whether to have your engine overhauled or simply purchase an exchange engine for your vehicle.

Some of the rebuilding alternatives include:

Individual parts - If the inspection procedures reveal that the engine block and most engine components are in reusable condition, purchasing individual parts and having a rebuilder rebuild your engine may be the most economical alternative. The block, crankshaft and piston/connecting rod assemblies should all be inspected carefully by a machine shop first.

Short block - A short block consists of an engine block with a crankshaft and piston/connecting rod assemblies already installed. All new bearings are incorporated and all clearances will be correct. The existing valve train components, cylinder head and external parts can be bolted to the short block with little or no machine shop work necessary.

Long block - A long block consists of a short block plus an oil pump, oil pan, cylinder head, valve cover, camshaft and valve train components, timing sprockets and chain or gears and timing cover. All components are installed with new bearings, seals and gaskets incorporated throughout. The installation of manifolds and external parts is all that's necessary.

Low mileage used engines - Some companies now offer low mileage used engines which is a very cost effective way to get your vehicle up and running again. These engines often come from vehicles which have been totaled in accidents or come from other countries which have a higher vehicle turn over rate. A low mileage used engine also usually has a similar warranty like the newly remanufactured engines.

Give careful thought to which alternative is best for you and discuss the situation with local automotive machine shops, auto parts dealers and experienced rebuilders before ordering or purchasing replacement parts.

5   Engine removal - methods and precautions

▶ **Refer to illustrations 5.1, 5.2 and 5.3**

If you've decided that an engine must be removed for overhaul or major repair work, several preliminary steps should be taken. Read all removal and installation procedures carefully prior to committing to this job.

Locating a suitable place to work is extremely important. Adequate work space, along with storage space for the vehicle, will be needed. If a shop or garage isn't available, at the very least a flat, level, clean work surface made of concrete or asphalt is required.

Cleaning the engine compartment and engine before beginning the

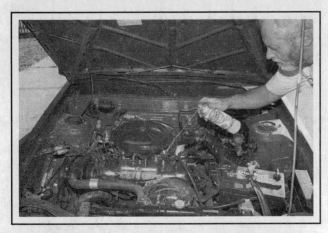

5.1 After tightly wrapping water-vulnerable components, use a spray cleaner on everything, with particular concentration on the greasiest areas, usually around the valve cover and lower edges of the block. If one section dries out, apply more cleaner

5.2 Depending on how dirty the engine is, let the cleaner soak in according to the directions and then hose off the grime and cleaner. Get the rinse water down into every area you can get at; then dry important components with a hair dryer or paper towels

5.3 Get an engine stand sturdy enough to firmly support the engine while you're working on it. Stay away from three-wheeled models; they have a tendency to tip over more easily, so get a four-wheeled unit.

removal procedure will help keep tools clean and organized (see illustrations 5.1 and 5.2).

An engine hoist will also be necessary. Make sure the hoist is rated in excess of the combined weight of the engine and transmission. Safety is of primary importance, considering the potential hazards involved in removing the engine from the vehicle.

If you're a novice at engine removal, get at least one helper. One person cannot easily do all the things you need to do to remove a big heavy engine from the engine compartment. Also helpful is to seek advice and assistance from someone who's experienced in engine removal.

Plan the operation ahead of time. Arrange for or obtain all of the tools and equipment you'll need prior to beginning the job (see illustration 5.3). Some of the equipment necessary to perform engine removal and installation safely and with relative ease are (in addition to an engine hoist) a heavy duty floor jack (preferably fitted with a transmission jack head adapter), complete sets of wrenches and sockets as described in the front of this manual, wooden blocks, plenty of rags and cleaning solvent for mopping up spilled oil, coolant and gasoline.

Plan for the vehicle to be out of use for quite a while. A machine shop can do the work that is beyond the scope of the home mechanic. Machine shops often have a busy schedule, so before removing the engine, consult the shop for an estimate of how long it will take to rebuild or repair the components that may need work.

6 Engine - removal and installation

❄❄ WARNING 1:

Gasoline is extremely flammable, so take extra precautions when you work on any part of the fuel system. Don't smoke or allow open flames or bare light bulbs near the work area, and don't work in a garage where a gas-type appliance (such as a water heater or clothes dryer) is present. Since gasoline is carcinogenic, wear fuel-resistant gloves when there's a possibility of being exposed to fuel, and, if you spill any fuel on your skin, rinse it off immediately with soap and water. Mop up any spills immediately and do not store fuel-soaked rags where they could ignite. The fuel system is under constant pressure, so, if any fuel lines are to be disconnected, the fuel pressure in the system must be relieved first (see Chapter 4 for more information). When you perform any kind of work on the fuel system, wear safety glasses and have a Class B type fire extinguisher on hand.

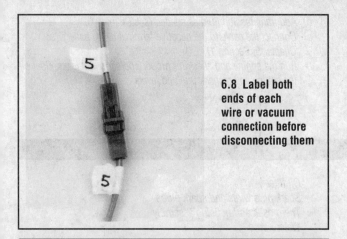

6.8 Label both ends of each wire or vacuum connection before disconnecting them

➡Note: Take instant photos or sketch the locations of components and brackets to help with reassembly

REMOVAL

▶ **Refer to illustrations 6.8 and 6.24**

1 Relieve the fuel system pressure (see Chapter 4).

2 Disconnect the cable from the negative terminal of the battery (see Chapter 5, Section 1).

3 Remove the air filter housing and air intake duct (see Chapter 4).

4 Remove the engine cover (see Chapter 2A).

5 Remove the hood (see Chapter 11) or open it up all the way into the service position.

6 Remove the intake manifold (see Chapter 4).

7 Working at the engine compartment fuse/relay center, disconnect the engine harness connectors and position the harness over the engine. If necessary, tape the harness looms together to prevent them from interfering with other components during engine removal.

8 Label and disconnect all vacuum hoses and any other wires from the engine (that aren't connected to the main harnesses that were disconnected in the previous Step) (see illustration). Masking tape and/or a touch-up paint applicator work well for marking items.

9 Disconnect the accelerator cable, if equipped, from the throttle body (see Chapter 4).

10 Remove the secondary air injection (AIR) pump (see Chapter 6).

11 Disconnect the fuel lines at the engine (see Chapter 4) and plug the lines to prevent fuel loss.

12 Raise the vehicle and support it securely on jackstands.

13 Drain the cooling system and remove the drivebelt(s) (see Chapter 1).

14 Remove the power steering reservoir and power steering pump, without disconnecting the hoses, and tie it out of the way (see Chapter 10).

15 Remove the air conditioning compressor, without disconnecting the refrigerant lines, and tie it out of the way (see Chapter 3).

16 Remove the engine reinforcement plate/bar (see Chapter 2A, Section 12).

17 Remove the starter (see Chapter 5).

18 Support the rear of the engine from above with an engine support

6.24 Attach the engine hoist cable or chain to the lifting brackets at the front and rear of the engine

fixture, then remove the transmission (see Chapter 7).

19 Drain the engine oil (see Chapter 1).

20 Remove the transmission cooler lines and brackets from the engine (see Chapter 7).

21 Lower the vehicle.

22 Remove the radiator hoses and the recirculation hoses in the engine compartment (see Chapter 3).

23 Remove the fan shrouds and the engine cooling fan, the coolant reservoir and the radiator (see Chapter 3).

24 Support the engine from below with a floor jack and block of wood placed under the oil pan. Remove the engine support fixture, then support the engine from above with a hoist (see illustration). Attach the hoist chain to the engine lifting bracket at the front of the engine and to the bracket or hole in the casting at the rear of the engine block. If no brackets are present, you will have to obtain some, or fasten the chains to some substantial part of the engine - one that is strong enough to take the weight, but in a location that will provide good balance. If you're attaching a chain to a stud on the engine, or are using a bolt passing through the chain and into a threaded hole, place a washer between the nut or bolt head and the chain and tighten the nut or bolt securely.

25 Use the hoist to take the weight off the engine mounts, and remove the engine mount through-bolts or mount-to-mount bracket bolts (see Chapter 2A).

26 Check to make sure everything is disconnected, then slowly lift the engine out of the vehicle. The engine will probably need to be tilted and/or maneuvered as it's lifted out, so have an assistant handy.

27 Remove the flywheel/driveplate and mount the engine on an engine stand or set the engine on the floor and support it so it doesn't tip over. Then disconnect the engine hoist.

INSTALLATION

28 Installation is the reverse of the removal procedure, noting the

following points:

a) Check the engine mounts. If they're worn or damaged, replace them.
b) Change the engine oil filter and fill the crankcase with engine oil (see Chapter 1).
c) Refill the cooling system (see Chapter 1).

d) Add transmission fluid as needed (see Chapter 1).
e) Connect the cable to the negative terminal of the battery (see Chapter 5, Section 1)
f) Run the engine and check for proper operation and leaks. Shut off the engine and recheck the fluid levels.

7 Engine overhaul - disassembly sequence

1 It's much easier to remove the external components if it's mounted on a portable engine stand. A stand can often be rented quite cheaply from an equipment rental yard. Before the engine is mounted on a stand, the driveplate should be removed from the engine.

2 If a stand isn't available, it's possible to remove the external engine components with it blocked up on the floor. Be extra careful not to tip or drop the engine when working without a stand.

3 If you're going to obtain a rebuilt engine, all external components must come off first, to be transferred to the replacement engine. These components include:

Driveplate/flywheel
Ignition system components
Emissions-related components
Engine mounts and mount brackets
Intake/exhaust manifolds
Fuel injection components
Oil filter
Spark plug wires and spark plugs
Thermostat and housing assembly
Water pump

➡Note: When removing the external components from the engine, pay close attention to details that may be helpful or important during installation. Note the installed position of gaskets, seals, spacers, pins, brackets, washers, bolts and other small items.

4 If you're going to obtain a short block (assembled engine block, crankshaft, pistons and connecting rods), then remove the timing chain, cylinder heads, oil pan, oil pump pick-up tube, oil pump and water pump from your engine so that you can turn in your old short block to the rebuilder as a core. See *Engine rebuilding alternatives* for additional information regarding the different possibilities to be considered.

8 Pistons and connecting rods - removal and installation

REMOVAL

▶ Refer to illustrations 8.1, 8.3, 8.4a and 8.4b

➡Note: Prior to removing the piston/connecting rod assemblies, remove the cylinder head, oil pan, oil pan baffle plate and oil pump (see Chapter 2A).

1 Use your fingernail to feel if a ridge has formed at the upper limit of ring travel (about 1/4-inch down from the top of each cylinder). If carbon deposits or cylinder wear have produced ridges, they must be completely removed with a special tool (see illustration). Follow the manufacturer's instructions provided with the tool. Failure to remove the ridges before attempting to remove the piston/connecting rod assemblies may result in piston breakage.

2 After the cylinder ridges have been removed, turn the engine so the crankshaft is facing up.

3 Before the main bearing cap assembly and connecting rods are removed, check the connecting rod endplay with feeler gauges. Slide them between the first connecting rod and the crankshaft throw until the play is removed (see illustration). Repeat this procedure for each connecting rod. The endplay is equal to the thickness of the feeler gauge(s). Check with an automotive machine shop for the endplay service limit (a typical endplay limit should measure between 0.005 to 0.015 inch [0.127 to 0.369 mm]). If the play exceeds the service limit, new connecting rods will be required. If new rods (or a new crankshaft) are installed, the endplay may fall under the minimum allowable. If it does, the rods will have to be machined to restore it. If necessary, consult an automotive machine shop for advice.

4 Check the connecting rods and caps for identification marks. If they aren't plainly marked, use paint or marker (see illustrations) to clearly identify each rod and cap (1, 2, 3, etc., depending on the cylinder they're associated with). Do not interchange the rod caps. Install the exact same rod cap onto the same connecting rod.

✳✳ CAUTION:

Do not use a punch and hammer to mark the connecting rods or they may be damaged.

8.1 Before you try to remove the pistons, use a ridge reamer to remove the raised material (ridge) from the top of the cylinders

8.3 Checking the connecting rod endplay (side clearance)

5   Loosen each of the connecting rod cap bolts 1/2-turn at a time until they can be removed by hand.

✳✳ CAUTION:

New connecting rod cap bolts must be used when reassembling the engine, but save the old bolts for use when checking the connecting rod bearing oil clearance.

6   Remove the number one connecting rod cap and bearing insert. Don't drop the bearing insert out of the cap.

7   Remove the bearing insert and push the connecting rod/piston assembly out through the top of the engine. Use a wooden or plastic hammer handle to push on the upper bearing surface in the connecting rod. If resistance is felt, double-check to make sure that all of the ridge was removed from the cylinder.

8   Repeat the procedure for the remaining cylinders.

9   After removal, reassemble the connecting rod caps and bearing

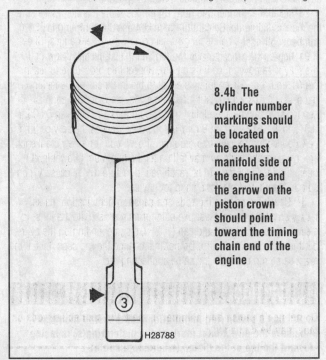

8.4b The cylinder number markings should be located on the exhaust manifold side of the engine and the arrow on the piston crown should point toward the timing chain end of the engine

H28788

8.4a If the connecting rods or caps are not marked, use permanent ink or paint to mark the caps to the rods by cylinder number (for example, this would be number 4 cylinder connecting rod)

inserts in their respective connecting rods and install the cap bolts finger tight. Leaving the old bearing inserts in place until reassembly will help prevent the connecting rod bearing surfaces from being accidentally nicked or gouged.

10 The pistons and connecting rods are now ready for inspection and overhaul at an automotive machine shop.

PISTON RING INSTALLATION

▶ **Refer to illustrations 8.13, 8.14, 8.15, 8.21 and 8.22**

11 Before installing the new piston rings, the ring end gaps must be checked. It's assumed that the piston ring side clearance has been checked and verified correct.

12 Lay out the piston/connecting rod assemblies and the new ring sets so the ring sets will be matched with the same piston and cylinder during the end gap measurement and engine assembly.

13 Insert the top (number one) ring into the first cylinder and square it up with the cylinder walls by pushing it in with the top of the piston (see illustration). The ring should be near the bottom of the cylinder, at the lower limit of ring travel.

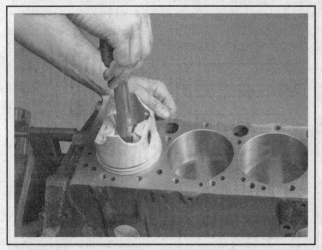

8.13 Install the piston ring into the cylinder then push it down into position using a piston so the ring will be square in the cylinder

8.14 With the ring square in the cylinder, measure the ring end gap with a feeler gauge

14 To measure the end gap, slip feeler gauges between the ends of the ring until a gauge equal to the gap width is found (see illustration). The feeler gauge should slide between the ring ends with a slight amount of drag. A typical ring gap should fall between 0.010 and 0.020 inch [0.25 to 0.50 mm] for compression rings and up to 0.020 inch [0.50 mm] for the oil rings. If the gap is larger or smaller than specified, double-check to make sure you have the correct rings before proceeding.

15 If the gap is too small, it must be enlarged or the ring ends may come in contact with each other during engine operation, which can cause serious damage to the engine. If necessary, increase the end gaps by filing the ring ends very carefully with a fine file. Mount the file in a vise equipped with soft jaws, slip the ring over the file with the ends contacting the file face and slowly move the ring to remove material from the ends. When performing this operation, file only by pushing the ring from the outside end of the file towards the vise (see illustration).

16 Excess end gap isn't critical unless it's greater than 0.040 inch (1.01 mm). Again, double-check to make sure you have the correct ring type.

17 Repeat the procedure for each ring that will be installed in the first cylinder and for each ring in the remaining cylinders. Remember to keep rings, pistons and cylinders matched up.

8.15 If the ring end gap is too small, clamp a file in a vise as shown and file the piston ring ends - be sure to remove all raised material

18 Once the ring end gaps have been checked/corrected, the rings can be installed on the pistons.

19 The oil control ring (lowest one on the piston) is usually installed first. First insert the expander into the ring groove, then install the oil control ring using a ring installation tool (see illustration 8.22), with the gap in the ring positioned 180-degrees from the gap in the expander.

20 After the oil ring components have been installed, check to make sure that the ring can be rotated smoothly inside the ring groove.

21 The number two (middle) ring is installed next. It's usually stamped with a mark which must face up, toward the top of the piston. Do not mix up the top and middle rings, as they have different cross-sections (see illustration).

➡ **Note: Always follow the instructions printed on the ring package or box - different manufacturers may require different approaches.**

22 Use a piston ring installation tool and make sure the identification mark is facing the top of the piston, then slip the ring into the middle groove on the piston (see illustration). Don't expand the ring any more than necessary to slide it over the piston.

23 Install the number one (top) ring in the same manner. Make sure the mark is facing up. Be careful not to confuse the number one and number two rings.

24 Repeat the procedure for the remaining pistons and rings.

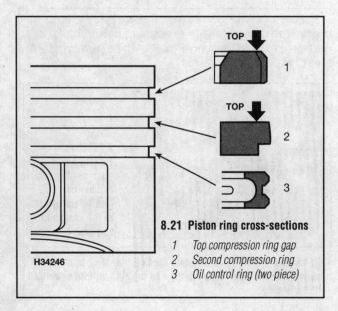

8.21 Piston ring cross-sections

1   *Top compression ring gap*
2   *Second compression ring*
3   *Oil control ring (two piece)*

H34246

8.22 Use a piston ring installation tool to install the rings - be sure the directional mark on the piston ring(s) is facing toward the top of the piston (where applicable)

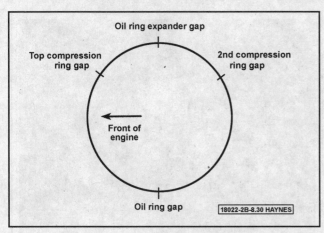

8.30 Position the piston ring end gaps as shown here before installing the piston/connecting rod assemblies into the engine

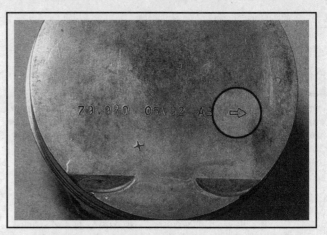

8.33 The arrow must face the front of the engine

INSTALLATION

25 Before installing the piston/connecting rod assemblies, the cylinder walls must be perfectly clean, the top edge of each cylinder bore must be chamfered, and the crankshaft must be in place.

26 Remove the cap from the end of the number one connecting rod (refer to the marks made during removal). Remove the original bearing inserts and wipe the bearing surfaces of the connecting rod and cap with a clean, lint-free cloth. They must be kept spotlessly clean.

Connecting rod bearing oil clearance check

▶ **Refer to illustrations 8.30, 8.33, 8.35, 8.37 and 8.41**

27 Clean the back side of the new upper bearing insert, then lay it in place in the connecting rod.

28 Make sure the tab on the bearing fits into the recess in the rod. Don't hammer the bearing insert into place and be very careful not to nick or gouge the bearing face. Don't lubricate the bearing at this time.

29 Clean the back side of the other bearing insert and install it in the rod cap. Again, make sure the tab on the bearing fits into the recess in the cap, and don't apply any lubricant. It's critically important that the mating surfaces of the bearing and connecting rod are perfectly clean and oil free when they're assembled.

30 Position the piston ring gaps at 120-degree intervals around the piston, as shown (see illustration).

31 Lubricate the piston and rings with clean engine oil and attach a piston ring compressor to the piston. Leave the skirt protruding about

1/4-inch to guide the piston into the cylinder. The rings must be compressed until they're flush with the piston.

32 Rotate the crankshaft until the number one connecting rod journal is at BDC (bottom dead center) and apply a liberal coat of engine oil to the cylinder walls. Refer to the TDC locating procedure in Chapter 2A for additional information.

33 With the arrow, notch or mark on the top of the piston facing the front of the engine, gently insert the piston/connecting rod assembly into the number one cylinder bore and rest the bottom edge of the ring compressor on the engine block (see illustration).

34 Tap the top edge of the ring compressor to make sure it's contacting the block around its entire circumference.

35 Gently tap on the top of the piston with the end of a wooden or plastic hammer handle (see illustration) while guiding the end of the connecting rod into place on the crankshaft journal. The piston rings may try to pop out of the ring compressor just before entering the cylinder bore, so keep some downward pressure on the ring compressor. Work slowly, and if any resistance is felt as the piston enters the cylinder, stop immediately. Find out what's hanging up and fix it before proceeding. Do not, for any reason, force the piston into the cylinder - you might break a ring and/or the piston.

36 Once the piston/connecting rod assembly is installed, the connecting rod bearing oil clearance must be checked before the rod cap is permanently installed.

37 Cut a piece of the appropriate size Plastigage slightly shorter than the width of the connecting rod bearing and lay it in place on the number one connecting rod journal, parallel with the journal axis (see illustration).

8.35 Use a plastic or wooden hammer handle to push the piston into the cylinder

8.37 Place Plastigage on each connecting rod bearing journal parallel to the crankshaft centerline

38 Clean the connecting rod cap bearing face and install the rod cap. Make sure the mating mark on the cap is on the same side as the mark on the connecting rod (see illustration 8.4).

39 Install the old rod bolts, at this time, and tighten them to the torque listed in this Chapter's Specifications.

➡Note: Use a thin-wall socket to avoid erroneous torque readings that can result if the socket is wedged between the rod cap and the bolt. If the socket tends to wedge itself between the fastener and the cap, lift up on it slightly until it no longer contacts the cap.

DO NOT rotate the crankshaft at any time during this operation.

40 Remove the fasteners and detach the rod cap, being very careful not to disturb the Plastigage. Discard the cap bolts at this time as they cannot be reused.

41 Compare the width of the crushed Plastigage to the scale printed on the Plastigage envelope to obtain the oil clearance (see illustration). The connecting rod oil clearance is usually about 0.001 to 0.002 inch (0.025 to 0.050 mm). Consult an automotive machine shop for the clearance specified for the rod bearings on your engine.

42 If the clearance is not as specified, the bearing inserts may be the wrong size (which means different ones will be required). Before deciding that different inserts are needed, make sure that no dirt or oil was between the bearing inserts and the connecting rod or cap when the clearance was measured. Also, recheck the journal diameter. If the Plastigage was wider at one end than the other, the journal may be tapered. If the clearance still exceeds the limit specified, the bearing will have to be replaced with an undersize bearing.

✳✳ CAUTION:

When installing a new crankshaft always use a standard size bearing.

Final installation

43 Carefully scrape all traces of the Plastigage material off the rod journal and/or bearing face. Be very careful not to scratch the bearing - use your fingernail or the edge of a plastic card.

44 Make sure the bearing faces are perfectly clean, then apply a uniform layer of clean moly-base grease or engine assembly lube to both of them. You'll have to push the piston into the cylinder to expose the face of the bearing insert in the connecting rod.

45 Slide the connecting rod back into place on the journal, install

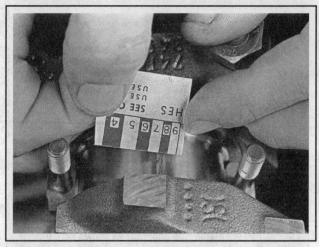

8.41 Use the scale on the Plastigage package to determine the bearing oil clearance - be sure to measure the widest part of the Plastigage and use the correct scale; it comes with both standard and metric scales

the rod cap, install the new bolts and tighten them to the torque listed in this Chapter's Specifications.

46 Repeat the entire procedure for the remaining pistons/connecting rods.

47 The important points to remember are:

a) Keep the back sides of the bearing inserts and the insides of the connecting rods and caps perfectly clean when assembling them.
b) Make sure you have the correct piston/rod assembly for each cylinder.
c) The mark on the piston must face the front of the engine.
d) Lubricate the cylinder walls liberally with clean oil.
e) Lubricate the bearing faces when installing the rod caps after the oil clearance has been checked.

48 After all the piston/connecting rod assemblies have been correctly installed, rotate the crankshaft a number of times by hand to check for any obvious binding.

49 As a final step, check the connecting rod endplay again. If it was correct before disassembly and the original crankshaft and rods were reinstalled, it should still be correct. If new rods or a new crankshaft were installed, the endplay may be inadequate. If so, the rods will have to be removed and taken to an automotive machine shop for resizing.

9   Crankshaft - removal and installation

REMOVAL

▶ **Refer to illustrations 9.1 and 9.3**

➡Note: The crankshaft can be removed only after the engine has been removed from the vehicle. It's assumed that the flywheel or driveplate, crankshaft pulley, timing chain, oil pan, oil pan baffle plate, oil pump, oil filter and piston/connecting rod assemblies have already been removed. The rear main oil seal retainer must be unbolted and separated from the block before proceeding with crankshaft removal.

1   Before the crankshaft is removed, measure the endplay. Mount a dial indicator with the indicator in line with the crankshaft and touching the end of the crankshaft (see illustration).

2   Pry the crankshaft all the way to the rear and zero the dial indicator. Next, pry the crankshaft to the front as far as possible and check the reading on the dial indicator. The distance traveled is the endplay. A typical crankshaft endplay will fall between 0.003 to 0.010 inch (0.07 to 0.25 mm). If it is greater than that, check the crankshaft thrust washer/bearing assembly surfaces for wear after it's removed. If no wear is evident, new main bearings should correct the endplay. Refer to Step 11 for the location of the thrust washer/bearing assembly on each engine.

9.1 Checking crankshaft endplay with a dial indicator

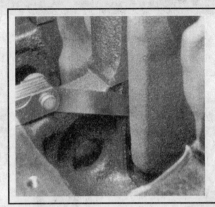

9.3 Checking crankshaft endplay with feeler gauges at the thrust bearing journal

3   If a dial indicator isn't available, feeler gauges can be used. Gently pry the crankshaft all the way to the front of the engine. Slip feeler gauges between the crankshaft and the front face of the thrust bearing or washer to determine the clearance (see illustration).

4   Loosen the main bearing cap bolts 1/4-turn at a time each, until they can be removed by hand.

❊❊ CAUTION:

New main bearing cap bolts must be used when reassembling the engine, but save the old bolts for use when checking the oil clearance

5   Gently tap the main bearing caps with a soft-face hammer around the perimeter of the assembly. Pull the main bearing cap straight up and off the cylinder block. Try not to drop the bearing inserts if they come out with the assembly.

6   Carefully lift the crankshaft out of the engine. It may be a good idea to have an assistant available, since the crankshaft is quite heavy and awkward to handle. With the bearing inserts in place inside the engine block and main bearing caps, reinstall the main bearing caps onto the engine block and tighten the bolts finger tight. Make sure you install the main bearing cap with the arrow facing the front of the engine.

INSTALLATION

▶ **Refer to illustration 9.10**

7   Crankshaft installation is the first step in engine reassembly. It's assumed at this point that the engine block and crankshaft have been cleaned, inspected and repaired or reconditioned.

8   Position the engine block with the bottom facing up. Remove the mounting bolts and lift off the main bearing cap assembly.

9   If they're still in place, remove the original bearing inserts from the block and from the main bearing cap assembly. Wipe the bearing surfaces of the block and main bearing cap assembly with a clean, lint-free cloth. They must be kept spotlessly clean. This is critical for determining the correct bearing oil clearance.

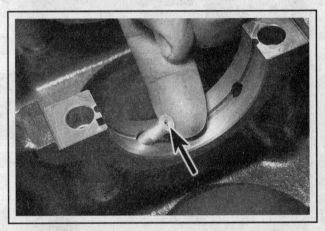

9.10 Some models are equipped with piston oil spray jets that fit in bores under the main bearing inserts

10 If equipped, remove the oil jet tubes and clean them, then reinstall them in the main bearing saddles (see illustration).

MAIN BEARING OIL CLEARANCE CHECK

▶ **Refer to illustrations 9.11, 9.17, 9.18 and 9.21**

11 Without mixing them up, clean the back sides of the new upper main bearing inserts (with grooves and oil holes) and lay one in each main bearing saddle in the block. Each upper bearing has an oil groove and oil hole in it.

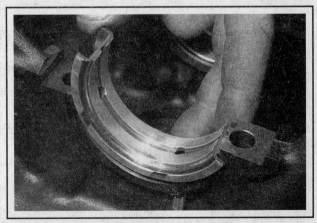

9.11 The thrust bearing insert is located on the number 6 main bearing saddle

ENGINE BEARING ANALYSIS

Debris

Babbitt bearing embedded with debris from machinings

Microscopic detail of debris

Microscopic detail of gouges

Overplated copper alloy bearing gouged by cast iron debris

Aluminum bearing embedded with glass beads

Microscopic detail of glass beads

Damaged lining caused by dirt left on the bearing back

Misassembly

Result of a lower half assembled as an upper - blocking the oil flow

Excessive oil clearance is indicated by a short contact arc

Polished and oil-stained backs are a result of a poor fit in the housing bore

Result of a wrong, reversed, or shifted cap

Overloading

Damage from excessive idling which resulted in an oil film unable to support the load imposed

Damaged upper connecting rod bearings caused by engine lugging; the lower main bearings (not shown) were similarly affected

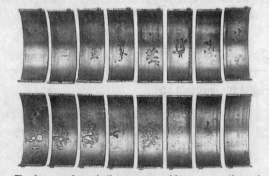

The damage shown in these upper and lower connecting rod bearings was caused by engine operation at a higher-than-rated speed under load

Misalignment

A warped crankshaft caused this pattern of severe wear in the center, diminishing toward the ends

A poorly finished crankshaft caused the equally spaced scoring shown

A tapered housing bore caused the damage along one edge of this pair

A bent connecting rod led to the damage in the "V" pattern

Lubrication

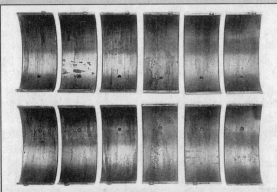

Result of dry start: The bearings on the left, farthest from the oil pump, show more damage

Result of a low oil supply or oil starvation

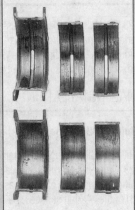

Severe wear as a result of inadequate oil clearance

Corrosion

Microscopic detail of corrosion

Corrosion is an acid attack on the bearing lining generally caused by inadequate maintenance, extremely hot or cold operation, or interior oils or fuels

Microscopic detail of cavitation

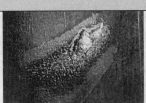

Example of cavitation - a surface erosion caused by pressure changes in the oil film

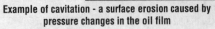

Damage from excessive thrust or insufficient axial clearance

Bearing affected by oil dilution caused by excessive blow-by or a rich mixture

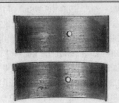

9.17 Place the Plastigage onto the crankshaft bearing journal as shown

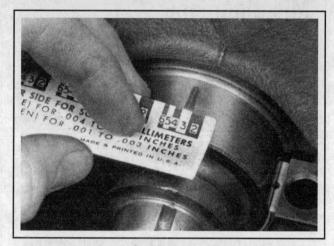

9.21 Use the scale on the Plastigage package to determine the bearing oil clearance - be sure to measure the widest part of the Plastigage and use the correct scale; it comes with both standard and metric scales

✳✳ CAUTION:

The oil holes in the block must line up with the oil holes in the upper bearing inserts.

The thrust washer/bearing insert is installed on the number 6 main bearing saddle (see illustration). Clean the back sides of the lower main bearing inserts and lay them in the corresponding location in the main bearing cap. Make sure the tab on the bearing insert fits into the recess in the block or main bearing cap. The upper bearings with the oil holes are installed into the engine block while the lower bearings without the oil holes are installed in the main bearing caps.

✳✳ CAUTION:

Do not hammer the bearing insert into place and don't nick or gouge the bearing faces. DO NOT apply any lubrication at this time.

12 Clean the faces of the bearing inserts in the block and the crankshaft main bearing journals with a clean, lint-free cloth.

13 Check or clean the oil holes in the crankshaft, as any dirt here can go only one way - straight through the new bearings.

14 Once you're certain the crankshaft is clean, carefully lay it in position in the cylinder block.

15 Before the crankshaft can be permanently installed, the main bearing oil clearance must be checked.

16 Cut several strips of the appropriate size of Plastigage. They must be slightly shorter than the width of the main bearing journal.

17 Place one piece on each crankshaft main bearing journal, parallel with the journal axis as shown (see illustration).

18 Clean the faces of the bearing inserts in the main bearing caps. Hold the bearing inserts in place and install the caps. DO NOT disturb the Plastigage. Make sure you install the main bearing caps with the arrow facing the front (timing chain end) of the engine.

19 Apply clean engine oil to the old bolt threads prior to installation (don't use the new bolts at this stage). Install the main bearing cap bolts and tighten them to the torque listed in this Chapter's Specifications. Don't rotate the crankshaft at any time during this operation!

20 Remove the bolts and carefully lift the main bearing cap assembly straight up and off the block. Do not disturb the Plastigage or rotate the crankshaft. If the main bearing caps are difficult to remove, tap it gently from side-to-side with a soft-face hammer to loosen it. Discard the cap bolts at this time as they cannot be reused.

21 Compare the width of the crushed Plastigage on each journal to the scale printed on the Plastigage envelope to determine the main bearing oil clearance (see illustration). Check with an automotive machine shop for the oil clearance for your engine.

22 If the clearance is not as specified, the bearing inserts may be the wrong size (which means different ones will be required). Before deciding if different inserts are needed, make sure that no dirt or oil was between the bearing inserts and the cap assembly or block when the clearance was measured. If the Plastigage was wider at one end than the other, the crankshaft journal may be tapered. If the clearance still exceeds the limit specified, the bearing insert(s) will have to be replaced with an undersize bearing insert(s).

✳✳ CAUTION:

When installing a new crankshaft always install a standard bearing insert set.

23 Carefully scrape all traces of the Plastigage material off the main bearing journals and/or the bearing insert faces. Be sure to remove all residue from the oil holes. Use your fingernail or the edge of a credit card - don't nick or scratch the bearing faces.

FINAL INSTALLATION

▶ **Refer to illustration 9.28**

24 Carefully lift the crankshaft out of the cylinder block.

25 Clean the bearing insert faces in the cylinder block, then apply a thin, uniform layer of moly-base grease or engine assembly lube to each of the bearing surfaces. Be sure to coat the thrust faces of the thrust bearing, too.

26 Make sure the crankshaft journals are clean, then lay the crankshaft back in place in the cylinder block.

27 Clean the bearing insert faces in the bearing caps and apply the same lubricant to them.

28 Install the main bearing caps, making sure the arrow faces the front of the engine (see illustration).

29 Prior to installation, apply clean engine oil to all bolt threads, wiping off any excess, then install all bolts finger-tight.

✳✳ CAUTION:

Remember - new bolts must be used.

30 Pry the crankshaft slightly back and forth in the block to seat the thrust bearings. Tighten all main bearing cap bolts to the torque listed in this Chapter's Specifications.

31 Recheck crankshaft endplay with a feeler gauge or a dial indicator. The endplay should be correct if the crankshaft thrust faces aren't worn or damaged and if new bearings have been installed.

32 Rotate the crankshaft a number of times by hand to check for any obvious binding. It should rotate with a running torque of 50 in-lbs or less. If the running torque is too high, correct the problem at this time.

33 Install a new rear main oil seal (see Chapter 2A).

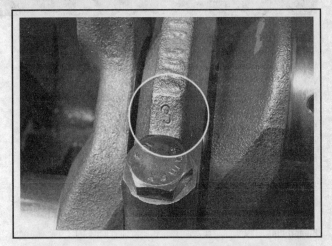

9.28 The main bearing caps should be numbered from 1 to 7 on the exhaust side of the engine starting from the timing chain end of the engine

10 Engine overhaul - reassembly sequence

1   Before beginning engine reassembly, make sure you have all the necessary new parts, gaskets and seals as well as the following items on hand:

Common hand tools
A 1/2-inch drive torque wrench
New engine oil
Gasket sealant
Thread locking compound

2   If you obtained a short block it will be necessary to install the cylinder head, the oil pump and pick-up tube, the oil pan, the water pump, the timing chain and timing chain cover, and the valve cover (see Chapter 2A). In order to save time and avoid problems, the exter-

nal components must be installed in the following general order:

Thermostat and housing cover
Water pump
Intake and exhaust manifolds
Fuel injection components
Emission control components
Spark plugs
Ignition coils
Oil filter
Engine mounts and mount brackets
Flywheel/driveplate

11 Initial start-up and break-in after overhaul

✳✳ WARNING:

Have a fire extinguisher handy when starting the engine for the first time.

1   Once the engine has been installed in the vehicle, double-check the engine oil and coolant levels.

2   With the spark plugs out of the engine, the electrical connectors disconnected from all of the ignition coils and the fuel pump fuse removed, crank the engine until oil pressure registers on the gauge or the light goes out.

3   Install the spark plugs and ignition coils, and the fuel pump fuse.

4   Start the engine. It may take a few moments for the fuel system to build up pressure, but the engine should start without a great deal of effort.

5   After the engine starts, it should be allowed to warm up to normal operating temperature. While the engine is warming up, make a thorough check for fuel, oil and coolant leaks.

6   Shut the engine off and recheck the engine oil and coolant levels.

7   Drive the vehicle to an area with minimum traffic, accelerate from 30 to 50 mph, then allow the vehicle to slow to 30 mph with the throttle closed. Repeat the procedure 10 or 12 times. This will load the piston rings and cause them to seat properly against the cylinder walls. Check again for oil and coolant leaks.

8   Drive the vehicle gently for the first 500 miles (no sustained high speeds) and keep a constant check on the oil level. It is not unusual for an engine to use oil during the break-in period.

9   At approximately 500 to 600 miles, change the oil and filter.

10 For the next few hundred miles, drive the vehicle normally. Do not pamper it or abuse it.

11 After 2000 miles, change the oil and filter again and consider the engine broken in.

GLOSSARY

B

Backlash - The amount of play between two parts. Usually refers to how much one gear can be moved back and forth without moving gear with which it's meshed.

Bearing Caps - The caps held in place by nuts or bolts which, in turn, hold the bearing surface. This space is for lubricating oil to enter.

Bearing clearance - The amount of space left between shaft and bearing surface. This space is for lubricating oil to enter.

Bearing crush - The additional height which is purposely manufactured into each bearing half to ensure complete contact of the bearing back with the housing bore when the engine is assembled.

Bearing knock - The noise created by movement of a part in a loose or worn bearing.

Blueprinting - Dismantling an engine and reassembling it to EXACT specifications.

Bore - An engine cylinder, or any cylindrical hole; also used to describe the process of enlarging or accurately refinishing a hole with a cutting tool, as to bore an engine cylinder. The bore size is the diameter of the hole.

Boring - Renewing the cylinders by cutting them out to a specified size. A boring bar is used to make the cut.

Bottom end - A term which refers collectively to the engine block, crankshaft, main bearings and the big ends of the connecting rods.

Break-in - The period of operation between installation of new or rebuilt parts and time in which parts are worn to the correct fit. Driving at reduced and varying speed for a specified mileage to permit parts to wear to the correct fit.

Bushing - A one-piece sleeve placed in a bore to serve as a bearing surface for shaft, piston pin, etc. Usually replaceable.

C

Camshaft - The shaft in the engine, on which a series of lobes are located for operating the valve mechanisms. The camshaft is driven by gears or sprockets and a timing chain. Usually referred to simply as the cam.

Carbon - Hard, or soft, black deposits found in combustion chamber, on plugs, under rings, on and under valve heads.

Cast iron - An alloy of iron and more than two percent carbon, used for engine blocks and heads because it's relatively inexpensive and easy to mold into complex shapes.

Chamfer - To bevel across (or a bevel on) the sharp edge of an object.

Chase - To repair damaged threads with a tap or die.

Combustion chamber - The space between the piston and the cylinder head, with the piston at top dead center, in which air-fuel mixture is burned.

Compression ratio - The relationship between cylinder volume (clearance volume) when the piston is at top dead center and cylinder volume when the piston is at bottom dead center.

Connecting rod - The rod that connects the crank on the crankshaft with the piston. Sometimes called a con rod.

Connecting rod cap - The part of the connecting rod assembly that attaches the rod to the crankpin.

Core plug - Soft metal plug used to plug the casting holes for the coolant passages in the block.

Crankcase - The lower part of the engine in which the crankshaft rotates; includes the lower section of the cylinder block and the oil pan.

Crank kit - A reground or reconditioned crankshaft and new main and connecting rod bearings.

Crankpin - The part of a crankshaft to which a connecting rod is attached.

Crankshaft - The main rotating member, or shaft, running the length of the crankcase, with offset throws to which the connecting rods are attached; changes the reciprocating motion of the pistons into rotating motion.

Cylinder sleeve - A replaceable sleeve, or liner, pressed into the cylinder block to form the cylinder bore.

D

Deburring - Removing the burrs (rough edges or areas) from a bearing.

Deglazer - A tool, rotated by an electric motor, used to remove glaze from cylinder walls so a new set of rings will seat.

E

Endplay - The amount of lengthwise movement between two parts. As applied to a crankshaft, the distance that the crankshaft can move forward and back in the cylinder block.

F

Face - A machinist's term that refers to removing metal from the end of a shaft or the face of a larger part, such as a flywheel.

Fatigue - A breakdown of material through a large number of loading and unloading cycles. The first signs are cracks followed shortly by breaks.

Feeler gauge - A thin strip of hardened steel, ground to an exact thickness, used to check clearances between parts.

Free height - The unloaded length or height of a spring.

Freeplay - The looseness in a linkage, or an assembly of parts, between the initial application of force and actual movement. Usually perceived as slop or slight delay.

Freeze plug - See Core plug.

G

Gallery - A large passage in the block that forms a reservoir for engine oil pressure.

Glaze - The very smooth, glassy finish that develops on cylinder walls while an engine is in service.

H

Heli-Coil - A rethreading device used when threads are worn or damaged. The device is installed in a retapped hole to reduce the thread size to the original size.

I

Installed height - The spring's measured length or height, as installed on the cylinder head. Installed height is measured from the spring seat to the underside of the spring retainer.

J

Journal - The surface of a rotating shaft which turns in a bearing.

K

Keeper - The split lock that holds the valve spring retainer in position on the valve stem.

Key - A small piece of metal inserted into matching grooves machined into two parts fitted together - such as a gear pressed onto a shaft - which prevents slippage between the two parts.

Knock - The heavy metallic engine sound, produced in the combustion chamber as a result of abnormal combustion - usually detonation. Knock is usually caused by a loose or worn bearing. Also referred to as detonation, pinging and spark knock. Connecting rod or main bearing knocks are created by too much oil clearance or insufficient lubrication.

L

Lands - The portions of metal between the piston ring grooves.

Lapping the valves - Grinding a valve face and its seat together with lapping compound.

Lash - The amount of free motion in a gear train, between gears, or in a mechanical assembly, that occurs before movement can begin. Usually refers to the lash in a valve train.

Lifter - The part that rides against the cam to transfer motion to the rest of the valve train.

M

Machining - The process of using a machine to remove metal from a metal part.

Main bearings - The plain, or babbitt, bearings that support the crankshaft.

Main bearing caps - The cast iron caps, bolted to the bottom of the block, that support the main bearings.

O

O.D. - Outside diameter.

Oil gallery - A pipe or drilled passageway in the engine used to carry engine oil from one area to another.

Oil ring - The lower ring, or rings, of a piston; designed to prevent excessive amounts of oil from working up the cylinder walls and into the combustion chamber. Also called an oil-control ring.

Oil seal - A seal which keeps oil from leaking out of a compartment. Usually refers to a dynamic seal around a rotating shaft or other moving part.

O-ring - A type of sealing ring made of a special rubberlike material; in use, the O-ring is compressed into a groove to provide the sealing action.

Overhaul - To completely disassemble a unit, clean and inspect all parts, reassemble it with the original or new parts and make all adjustments necessary for proper operation.

P

Pilot bearing - A small bearing installed in the center of the flywheel (or the rear end of the crankshaft) to support the front end of the input shaft of the transmission.

Pip mark - A little dot or indentation which indicates the top side of a compression ring.

Piston - The cylindrical part, attached to the connecting rod, that moves up and down in the cylinder as the crankshaft rotates. When the fuel charge is fired, the piston transfers the force of the explosion to the connecting rod, then to the crankshaft.

Piston pin (or wrist pin) - The cylindrical and usually hollow steel pin that passes through the piston. The piston pin fastens the piston to the upper end of the connecting rod.

Piston ring - The split ring fitted to the groove in a piston. The ring contacts the sides of the ring groove and also rubs against the cylinder wall, thus sealing space between piston and wall. There are two types of rings: Compression rings seal the compression pressure in the combustion chamber; oil rings scrape excessive oil off the cylinder wall.

Piston ring groove - The slots or grooves cut in piston heads to hold piston rings in position.

Piston skirt - The portion of the piston below the rings and the piston pin hole.

Plastigage - A thin strip of plastic thread, available in different sizes, used for measuring clearances. For example, a strip of plastigage is laid across a bearing journal and mashed as parts are assembled. Then parts are disassembled and the width of the strip is measured to determine clearance between journal and bearing. Commonly used to measure crankshaft main-bearing and connecting rod bearing clearances.

Press-fit - A tight fit between two parts that requires pressure to force the parts together. Also referred to as drive, or force, fit.

Prussian blue - A blue pigment; in solution, useful in determining the area of contact between two surfaces. Prussian blue is commonly used to determine the width and location of the contact area between the valve face and the valve seat.

R

Race (bearing) - The inner or outer ring that provides a contact surface for balls or rollers in bearing.

Ream - To size, enlarge or smooth a hole by using a round cutting tool with fluted edges.

Ring job - The process of reconditioning the cylinders and installing new rings.

Runout - Wobble. The amount a shaft rotates out-of-true.

S

Saddle - The upper main bearing seat.

Scored - Scratched or grooved, as a cylinder wall may be scored by abrasive particles moved up and down by the piston rings.

Scuffing - A type of wear in which there's a transfer of material between parts moving against each other; shows up as pits or grooves in the mating surfaces.

Seat - The surface upon which another part rests or seats. For example, the valve seat is the matched surface upon which the valve face rests. Also used to refer to wearing into a good fit; for example, piston rings seat after a few miles of driving.

Short block - An engine block complete with crankshaft and piston and, usually, camshaft assemblies.

Static balance - The balance of an object while it's stationary.

Step - The wear on the lower portion of a ring land caused by excessive side and back-clearance. The height of the step indicates the ring's extra side clearance and the length of the step projecting from the back wall of the groove represents the ring's back clearance.

Stroke - The distance the piston moves when traveling from top dead center to bottom dead center, or from bottom dead center to top dead center.

Stud - A metal rod with threads on both ends.

T

Tang - A lip on the end of a plain bearing used to align the bearing during assembly.

Tap - To cut threads in a hole. Also refers to the fluted tool used to cut threads.

Taper - A gradual reduction in the width of a shaft or hole; in an engine cylinder, taper usually takes the form of uneven wear, more pronounced at the top than at the bottom.

Throws - The offset portions of the crankshaft to which the connecting rods are affixed.

Thrust bearing - The main bearing that has thrust faces to prevent excessive end-play, or forward and backward movement of the crankshaft.

Thrust washer - A bronze or hardened steel washer placed between two moving parts. The washer prevents longitudinal movement and provides a bearing surface for thrust surfaces of parts.

Tolerance - The amount of variation permitted from an exact size of measurement. Actual amount from smallest acceptable dimension to largest acceptable dimension.

U

Umbrella - An oil deflector placed near the valve tip to throw oil from the valve stem area.

Undercut - A machined groove below the normal surface.

Undersize bearings - Smaller diameter bearings used with re-ground crankshaft journals.

V

Valve grinding - Refacing a valve in a valve-refacing machine.

Valve train - The valve-operating mechanism of an engine; includes all components from the camshaft to the valve.

Vibration damper - A cylindrical weight attached to the front of the crankshaft to minimize torsional vibration (the twist-untwist actions of the crankshaft caused by the cylinder firing impulses). Also called a harmonic balancer.

W

Water jacket - The spaces around the cylinders, between the inner and outer shells of the cylinder block or head, through which coolant circulates.

Web - A supporting structure across a cavity.

Woodruff key - A key with a radiused backside (viewed from the side).

Specifications

General

Engine code	
M52 TU B25	152 cubic inches (2494 cc)
M52 TU B28	170 cubic inches (2793 cc)
M54 B25	152 cubic inches (2494 cc)
M54 B30	182 cubic inches (2979 cc)
M56 B25	152 cubic inches (2494 cc)
Bore	
M52 TU B25	3.307 inches (84.0 mm)
M52 TU B28	3.307 inches (84.0 mm)
M54 B25	3.307 inches (84.0 mm)
M54 B30	3.307 inches (84.0 mm)
M56 B25	3.307 inches (84.0 mm)
Stroke	
M52 TU B25	2.953 inches (75.0 mm)
M52 TU B28	3.307 inches (84.0 mm)
M54 B25	2.953 inches (75.0 mm)
M54 B30	3.528 inches (89.6 mm)
M56 B25	2.953 inches (75.0 mm)
Direction of engine rotation	Clockwise (viewed from front of vehicle)
No 1 cylinder location	Timing chain end
Firing order	1-5-3-6-2-4
Minimum compression pressure	See Chapter 2A
Minimum oil pressure at idle speed	7 psi (0.5 bar)
Regulated oil pressure (maximum)	59 psi (4.0 bar)

Torque specifications

	Ft-lbs (unless otherwise indicated)	Nm
Connecting rod bearing cap bolts*		
1999 and 2000		
Step 1	17	23
Step 2	Tighten an additional 70-degrees	
2001 and later		
Step 1	44 in-lbs	5
Step 2	15	20
Step 3	Tighten an additional 70-degrees	
Main bearing cap bolts*		
1999 and 2000		
Step 1	18	24
Step 2	Tighten an additional 70-degrees	
2001 and later		
Step 1	20	27
Step 2	Tighten an additional 70-degrees	
Transmission-to-engine bolts	See Chapter 7A or 7B	

* Use new bolts

Section

Reference to other Chapters

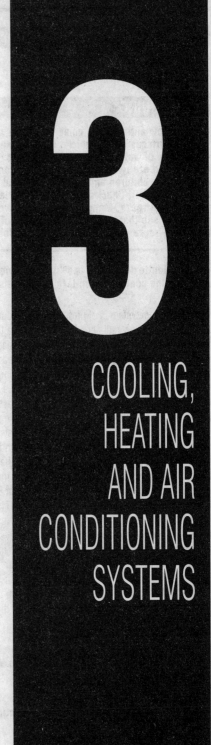

3

COOLING, HEATING AND AIR CONDITIONING SYSTEMS

1   General information and precautions

GENERAL INFORMATION

✳✳ WARNING:

Do not allow antifreeze to come in contact with your skin or painted surfaces of the vehicle. Rinse off spills immediately with plenty of water. Antifreeze is highly toxic if ingested. Never leave antifreeze lying around in an open container or in puddles on the floor; children and pets are attracted by it's sweet smell and may drink it. Check with local authorities about disposing of used anti-freeze. Many communities have collection centers which will see that antifreeze is disposed of safely. Never dump used anti-freeze on the ground or into drains.

➡**Note: Non-toxic coolant is available at most auto parts stores. Although the coolant is non-toxic, proper disposal is still required.**

The cooling system is of pressurized type, consisting of a pump, an aluminum crossflow radiator, cooling fan, and a thermostat. The system functions as follows. Cold coolant from the radiator passes through the hose to the water pump where it is pumped around the cylinder block and head passages. After cooling the cylinder bores, combustion surfaces and valve seats, the coolant reaches the underside of the ther-mostat, which is initially closed. The coolant passes through the heater and is returned through the cylinder block to the water pump.

When the engine is cold, the coolant circulates only through the cylinder block, cylinder head, expansion tank and heater. When the coolant reaches a predetermined temperature, the thermostat opens and the coolant passes through to the radiator. The thermostat opening and closing is controlled by the engine management ECM by a heating ele-ment within the wax capsule of the thermostat. This allows fine control of the engine running temperature, resulting in less emissions, and better fuel consumption. As the coolant circulates through the radiator it is cooled by the inrush of air when the car is in forward motion. Airflow is supplemented by the action of the cooling fan. Upon reaching the radiator, the coolant is now cooled and the cycle is repeated.

Two different engine cooling fan systems are used, depending on the model. On automatic transmission models, the main engine cooling fan is electric and is mounted in front of the radiator (bumper side). A mechanical fan with a viscous coupling driven by a drivebelt also cools the radiator. The fan clutch (viscous coupling) controls the speed of the fan depending upon the engine compartment temperature. On manual transmission models, one multi-speed cooling fan mounted on the engine side of the radiator cools the radiator coolant. On both manual and automatic models, the electric cooling fan is operated using a pulse width modulated signal from the ECM and is protected by a 50 amp fuse. The electric cooling fan and coolant temperatures are controlled using 15 different speed selections depending upon the radiator outlet temperature, the catalytic converter temperature, the vehicle speed, the battery voltage and the air conditioning pressure.

Refer to Section 11 for information on the air conditioning system.

PRECAUTIONS

✳✳ WARNING:

Do not attempt to remove the expansion tank filler cap or dis-turb any part of the cooling system while the engine is hot, as there is a high risk of scalding. If the expansion tank filler cap must be removed before the engine and radiator have fully cooled (even though this is not recommended) the pressure in the cooling system must first be relieved. Cover the cap with a thick layer of cloth, to avoid scalding, and slowly unscrew the filler cap until a hissing sound can be heard. When the hissing has stopped, indicating that the pressure has reduced, slowly unscrew the filler cap until it can be removed; if more hissing sounds are heard, wait until they have stopped before unscrew-ing the cap completely. At all times keep well away from the filler cap opening.

Do not allow antifreeze to come into contact with skin or painted surfaces of the vehicle. Rinse off spills immediately with plenty of water. Never leave antifreeze lying around in an open container or in a puddle in the driveway or on the garage floor. Children and pets are attracted by its sweet smell. Antifreeze can be fatal if ingested.

Refer to Section 11 for precautions to be observed when working on models equipped with air conditioning.

2   Cooling system hoses - disconnection and replacement

◆ **Refer to illustrations 2.3a and 2.3b**

➡**Note: Refer to the warnings given in Section 1 of this Chapter before proceeding.**

1   If the checks described in Chapter 1 reveal a faulty hose, it must be replaced as follows.

2   First drain the cooling system (see Chapter 1). If the coolant is not due for replacement, it may be re-used if it is collected in a clean container.

3   To disconnect a hose union from a fitting (such as at the radia-tor), pry up the wire retaining clip and pull the hose union from its fitting (see illustrations). Some hoses are secured to their unions using traditional hose clamps. To disconnect these type hoses, loosen the clamps, then move them along the hose, clear of the relevant inlet/out-

2.3a Pry up the wire locking clip . . .

let union. Carefully work the hose free. While the hoses can be removed with relative ease when new, or when hot, do not attempt to disconnect any part of the system while it is still hot.

4 Note that the radiator inlet and outlet are fragile; do not use excessive force when attempting to remove the hoses. If a hose proves to be difficult to remove, try to release it by rotating the hose ends before attempting to free it.

5 To reinstall a hose, simply push the end over the fitting until the retaining clip engages and lock the hose in place. Pull the hose to make sure it's locked in place. When installing a hose with traditional hose clamps, first slide the clamps onto the hose, then work the hose into position. If the hose is stiff, use a little soapy water as a lubricant, or soften the hose by soaking it in hot water. Work the hose into position, checking that it is correctly routed, then slide each clamp along the hose until it passes over the flared end of the relevant inlet/outlet union, before securing it in position.

6 Refill the cooling system (see Chapter 1).

7 Check thoroughly for leaks as soon as possible after disturbing any part of the cooling system.

2.3b . . . and pull the hose union from the fitting (the union shown here has two clips, one for each fitting)

3 Radiator - removal, inspection and installation

※※ WARNING:

The engine must be completely cool before beginning this procedure.

➡Note: Some models are equipped with a specialized radiator designed to consume ground level ozone. Do not replace the radiator with a radiator not equipped with this special coating.

REMOVAL

▶ **Refer to illustrations 3.6, 3.7, 3.8, 3.11a, 3.11b and 3.11c**

1 Disconnect the cable from the negative terminal of the battery (see Chapter 5, Section 1).

2 Drain the cooling system (see Chapter 1).

3 Remove the air filter housing (see Chapter 4).

4 On automatic transmission models, remove the cooling fan and viscous coupling (see Section 5). On manual transmission models remove the electric cooling fan (see Section 6)

➡Note: On automatic transmission models; there is no need to remove the electric cooling fan on the front (bumper) side of the radiator.

5 Pry out the locking wire clips and disconnect the upper coolant hose union from the radiator and expansion tank (see illustration 2.3b).

6 Pry out the locking wire clip and disconnect the hose from the expansion tank (see illustration).

7 Pry out the locking wire clip and disconnect the lower hose from the expansion tank (see illustration).

3.6 Disconnect the hose from the expansion tank

3.7 Pry out the locking wire clip and disconnect the lower hose from the expansion tank

3.8 Disconnect the level sensor wiring connector, and pull out the expansion tank retaining clip

3.11a The radiator on some models is secured by a Torx screw located in the upper right-hand corner of the radiator . . .

3.11b . . . and a plastic expansion rivet in the left-hand corner

8 Reach underneath the expansion tank and disconnect the wiring from the coolant level sensor. Pull out the retaining clip from the base of the expansion tank (see illustration).

9 Pull the expansion tank away from the radiator and lift it up off the brackets located at the bottom of the radiator and remove it.

10 Disconnect the transmission fluid cooler lines from the external transmission cooler, if equipped (see Chapter 7B).

11 Depending no model, remove the Torx screw at the upper right corner of the radiator, the plastic rivet at the upper left corner, and/or the plastic bolts at the top of the radiator, then lift the radiator upwards and out of the engine compartment (see illustrations).

INSPECTION

12 If the radiator has been removed due to suspected blockage, reverse flush it as described in Chapter 1.

13 Clean dirt and debris from the radiator fins, using an air line (in which case, wear eye protection) or a soft brush. Be careful, as the fins are easily damaged, and are sharp.

14 If necessary, a radiator specialist can perform a flow test on the radiator, to establish whether an internal blockage exists.

15 A leaking radiator must be referred to a specialist for permanent repair. Do not attempt to weld or solder a leaking radiator, as damage may result.

16 Inspect the radiator lower rubber mounts for signs of damage or deterioration and replace if necessary.

INSTALLATION

▶ **Refer to illustration 3.17**

17 Installation is the reverse of removal, noting the following points.

a) *Ensure that the lower mount bushings are correctly located in the body, then lower the radiator into position, engage it with the mounts and secure it in position with the retaining bolts/clip (see illustration).*

b) *Ensure that the fan cowl is correctly located with the lugs on the radiator and secure it in position with the clips.*

c) *Reconnect the hoses and ensure the retaining clips engage securely.*

d) *Check the condition of the O-ring seals in the end of the radiator fittings. Replace any that are defective.*

e) *On completion, reconnect the battery (see Chapter 5, Section 1) and refill the cooling system (see Chapter 1).*

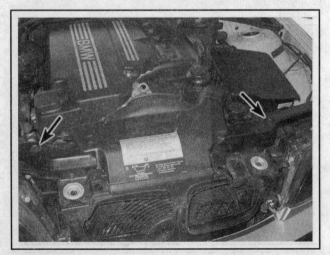

3.11c The radiator on other models is secured by two plastic bolts at the top of the radiator support

3.17 The radiator must sit in the V in the mounting

4 Thermostat - removal and installation

❄❄ WARNING 1:

Do not allow antifreeze to come in contact with your skin or painted surfaces of the vehicle. Rinse off spills immediately with plenty of water. Antifreeze is highly toxic if ingested. Never leave antifreeze lying around in an open container or in puddles on the floor; children and pets are attracted by it's sweet smell and may drink it. Check with local authorities about disposing of used anti-freeze. Many communities have collection centers which will see that antifreeze is disposed of safely. Never dump used anti-freeze on the ground or into drains.

❄❄ WARNING 2:

The engine must be completely cool before beginning this procedure.

➡ Note 1: Non-toxic coolant is available at most auto parts stores. Although the coolant is non-toxic, proper disposal is still required.

➡ Note 2: A new thermostat sealing ring and (where fitted) housing gasket/seal will be required on installation.

REMOVAL

1 Disconnect the cable from the negative terminal of the battery

(see Chapter 5, Section 1).

2 Drain the cooling system (see Chapter 1).

3 Where applicable, to improve access to the thermostat housing, remove the cooling fan and viscous coupling (see Section 5).

4 Pry out the locking wire clips and disconnect the coolant hose(s) from the thermostat housing on the front of the cylinder head/timing chain cover (as applicable). Disconnect the electrical connector from the thermostat housing.

5 Unscrew the retaining bolts and remove the thermostat housing. Recover the housing gasket/seal. It will be necessary to unbolt the engine lifting bracket to allow the housing to be removed.

6 Note that the thermostat is integral with the housing. Recover the sealing ring.

INSTALLATION

7 Installation is the reverse of removal, bearing in mind the following points.

  a) Replace the thermostat housing O-ring seal.
  b) Tighten the thermostat housing bolts to the torque listed in this Chapter's Specifications.
  c) Reinstall the cooling fan as described in Section 5.
  d) On completion, refill the cooling system (see Chapter 1).

5 Cooling fan and viscous coupling (automatic transmission models) - removal and installation

➡ Note: A special 32 mm narrow open-ended wrench (tool number 11 5 040) will be required to remove the fan and viscous coupling assembly.

REMOVAL

▶ Refer to illustrations 5.5a and 5.5b

1 Remove the expansion rivets mounting the fan shroud to the radiator. Where plastic expansion rivets are installed, lift up the center

pin, then pry the entire rivet from place.

2 Disconnect the cooling ducts from the shroud and remove them from the engine compartment.

3 Disconnect the electrical connectors from the right side of the shroud assembly.

4 Release the fan shroud upper retaining clips by pulling out their center pins then lift the shroud upwards and out of position.

5 Using the special open-ended wrench (tool number 11 5 040), unscrew the viscous coupling from the water pump and remove the cooling fan (see illustrations).

5.5a Loosen the cooling fan hub nut using the special open-ended wrench (it has a left-hand thread; turn it clockwise to loosen it) . . .

5.5b . . . and remove the cooling fan

➡**Note: The viscous coupling has a left-hand thread.**

If necessary, use a strip of metal bolted to the drive pulley to counterhold the nut.

6　Remove the retaining bolts and separate the cooling fan from the coupling noting which way direction the fan is installed.

INSTALLATION

7　Reinstall the fan to the viscous coupling and tighten the bolts to the torque listed in this Chapter's Specifications. Make sure the fan is installed facing the correct direction. Screw the fan onto the water pump and tighten the hub nut to the torque listed in this Chapter's Specifications.

➡**Note: If the fan is installed the wrong way the efficiency of the cooling system will be significantly reduced.**

8　Engage the fan shroud with the lugs on the radiator and secure it in position with the retaining clips.
9　Reconnect the cooling ducts (where equipped) to the shroud then securely tighten its retaining screws.

6　Electric cooling fan and shroud - removal and installation

REMOVAL

Cooling fan (manual transmission models)

▶ **Refer to illustrations 6.1, 6.3, 6.5a, 6.5b, 6.7 and 6.8**

1　Remove the expansion rivets mounting the fan shroud to the radiator (see illustration). Where plastic expansion rivets are installed, lift up the center pin, then pry the entire rivet from place.
2　Disconnect the cooling ducts from the shroud and remove them from the engine compartment.

3　Disconnect the electrical connectors from the right side of the shroud assembly (see illustration).
4　Where applicable, remove the hoses from the clips on the lower part of the shroud.
5　Remove the screw and the expansion rivet from the radiator and the fan shroud (see illustrations).
6　Lift the fan upwards and out of the engine compartment. Take care not to damage the radiator while lifting the fan shroud assembly.
7　Remove the three screws and remove the fan motor from the shroud (see illustration).

6.1　Pry up the center pin, then remove the expansion rivet

6.3　Remove the connectors from the shroud

6.5a　Remove the screw in the right-hand corner . . .

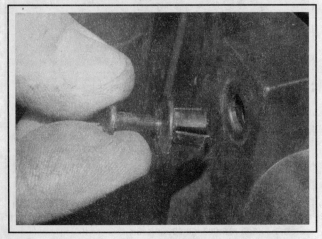

6.5b　. . . and the plastic expanding rivet in the left-hand corner

6.7　The fan motor is secured by three screws

6.8 Remove the four screws and remove the timer unit

6.9 Pry out the expansion rivets and remove the intake hood

➡**Note: Do not lift the assembly by the fan blades or the balance of the fan may be disturbed, resulting in excessive noise while the fan is in use.**

8   If required, remove the four screws and remove the timer unit from the shroud (see illustration).

Primary cooling fan (automatic transmission models)

▶ **Refer to illustration 6.9**

9   Remove the expansion rivets mounting the fan shroud to the radiator (see illustration). Where plastic expansion rivets are installed,

lift up the center pin, then pry the entire rivet out.
10   Remove the front bumper (see Chapter 11).
11   Unclip and disconnect the fan motor electrical connector.
12   Pry out the four expansion rivets, and remove the fan shroud.
13   Remove the four nuts and withdraw the fan and motor.

INSTALLATION

14   Installation is a reversal of removal, ensuring the lugs on the lower edge of the shroud engage in the corresponding slots in the radiator edge.

---

7   Cooling system electrical switches - testing, removal and installation

---

RADIATOR OUTLET SWITCH

Testing

1   Testing of the switch should be entrusted to a BMW dealer or other qualified repair shop.

Removal

▶ **Refer to illustration 7.5**

❊❊ **WARNING:**

The engine must be completely cool before beginning this procedure.

2   The switch is located in the radiator lower hose. The engine and radiator must be cold before removing the switch.
3   Disconnect the cable from the negative terminal of the battery (see Chapter 5, Section 1).
4   Either drain the cooling system to below the level of the switch (as described in Chapter 1), or have ready a suitable plug which can be used to plug the switch aperture in the radiator while the switch is removed. If a plug is used, take great care not to damage the radiator, and do not use anything which will allow foreign matter to enter the radiator.
5   Disconnect the wiring connector from the switch (see illustration).

7.5 The radiator outlet switch is located in the lower hose

6   Release the retaining clip, and remove the switch. Recover the sealing ring.

Installation

7   Installation is a reverse of removal using a new sealing washer. On completion, refill the cooling system as described in Chapter 1.
8   Start the engine and run it until it reaches normal operating temperature, then continue to run the engine and check that the cooling fan cuts in and functions correctly.

COOLANT TEMPERATURE SENSOR

Testing

9 Testing of the sensor should be entrusted to a BMW dealer or other qualified repair shop.

Removal

▶ **Refer to illustration 7.12**

10 Either partially drain the cooling system to just below the level of the sensor (as described in Chapter 1), or have ready a suitable plug which can be used to plug the sensor aperture while it is removed. If a plug is used, take great care not to damage the sensor unit aperture, and do not use anything which will allow foreign matter to enter the cooling system.

11 The sensor is screwed into the left-hand side of the cylinder head, under the intake manifold.

12 Disconnect the wiring from the sensor. Unscrew the sensor unit from the cylinder head and recover its sealing washer (see illustration).

Installation

13 Install a new sealing washer to the sensor unit and reinstall the

7.12 Coolant temperature sensor (shown with the intake manifold removed)

sensor, tightening it securely.

14 Reconnect the wiring connector then refill the cooling system (see Chapter 1).

.8   Water pump - removal and installation

❊❊ WARNING 1:

Do not allow antifreeze to come in contact with your skin or painted surfaces of the vehicle. Rinse off spills immediately with plenty of water. Antifreeze is highly toxic if ingested. Never leave antifreeze lying around in an open container or in puddles on the floor; children and pets are attracted by it's sweet smell and may drink it. Check with local authorities about disposing of used anti-freeze. Many communities have collection centers which will see that antifreeze is disposed of safely. Never dump used anti-freeze on the ground or into drains.

❊❊ WARNING 2:

The engine must be completely cool before beginning this procedure.

➡Note 1: Non-toxic coolant is available at most auto parts stores. Although the coolant is non-toxic, proper disposal is still required.

➡Note 2: A new sealing ring will be required on installation.

REMOVAL

▶ **Refer to illustrations 8.3, 8.5 and 8.6**

1 Drain the cooling system (see Chapter 1).

2 Remove the cooling fan (see Section 5 or 6).

3 Loosen the water pump pulley bolts (see illustration) then remove the auxiliary drivebelt (see Chapter 1).

4 Unscrew the retaining bolts/nuts and remove the pulley from the pump, noting which way around it is installed.

5 Loosen and remove the pump retaining bolts/nuts (as applicable) and withdraw the pump. If the pump is a tight fit, screw two M6 bolts into the jacking holes on either side of the pump and use the bolts to

8.3 Remove the water pump pulley bolts (if necessary, wedge a screwdriver between one of the bolts and the hub to prevent it from turning)

8.5 If the water pump is a tight fit, separate the pump using two jacking bolts

draw the pump out of position (see illustration).

6   Recover the sealing ring from the rear of the pump (see illustration).

INSTALLATION

7   Install the new sealing ring to the rear of the pump and lubricate it with a smear of grease to ease installation.

8   Place the pump in position and reinstall the retaining bolts/nuts. Tighten the bolts/nuts evenly and progressively to the torque listed in this Chapter's Specifications, making sure the pump is drawn squarely into position.

9   Reinstall the pulley to the pump, making sure it is the correct way around, and screw in its retaining bolts. Tighten the bolts to the torque listed in this Chapter's Specifications.

10 Reinstall the drivebelt as described in Chapter 1 then securely tighten the pulley bolts.

11 Reinstall the cooling fan assembly (where applicable) as described in Section 5 or 6.

12 Refill the cooling system (see Chapter 1).

8.6 Recover the sealing ring from the rear of the water pump

9   Heating and ventilation system - general information

1   The Integrated Heating Cooling Climate Control (IHKA) system offers efficient cooling and heating operation in manual and automatic modes.

2   Heating and air conditioning functions are selected using the center console mounted control panel. The control unit controls the electrically operated door flap valves to deflect and mix the air flowing through the various parts of the heating/ventilation system. The flap valves are contained in the air distribution housing, which acts as a central distribution unit, passing air to the various ducts and vents.

3   Cold air enters the system through the grille at the rear of the engine compartment. An in-cabin filter is installed in the air inlet to filter out dust, spores and soot from the incoming air.

4   The airflow, which can be boosted by the blower, then flows through the various ducts, according to the settings of the controls. Stale air is expelled through ducts at the rear of the vehicle. If warm air is required, the cold air is passed through the heater core, which is heated by the engine coolant.

5   If necessary, the outside air supply can be closed off, allowing the air inside the vehicle to be recirculated. This can be useful to prevent unpleasant odors entering from outside the vehicle, but should only be used briefly, as the recirculated air inside the vehicle will soon deteriorate.

6   Certain models are equipped with rear window defogger systems that are integrated into the programming functions of the IHKA system. The temperature is regulated automatically by a sensor and can be set at different levels, controlled by switches on the instrument panel.

10   Heater/ventilation components - removal and installation

✳✳ WARNING:

The models covered by this manual are equipped with Supplemental Restraint systems (SRS), more commonly known as airbags. Always disarm the airbag system before working in the vicinity of any airbag system component to avoid the possibility of accidental deployment of the airbag, which could cause personal injury (see Chapter 12). Do not use a memory saving device to preserve the PCM's memory when working on or near airbag system components.

1   Disconnect the cable from the negative terminal of the battery (see Chapter 5, Section 1).

INTEGRATED HEATING COOLING ASSEMBLY (IHKA) CONTROL PANEL

3 series models

▶ **Refer to illustration 10.9**

2   Working below the IHKA control panel, open the utility compartment door.

3   Push up in the center of the utility compartment door to release the locking tabs.

4   Remove the utility compartment from the dash.

5   Pry the shift lever bezel from the center console (see Chapter 7).

10.9 Reach in with your hand and push the control panel out of the dash

6 Remove the shift knob or lever (see Chapter 7). Unclip the boot from around the shift panel and move the rubber boot up and around the shift lever. Do not remove the boot from the console.

7 Remove the mounting screws from the rear of the shift panel and lift the trim to unhook the assembly from the front of the console.

8 Remove the mounting screws from the front and rear of the ash-tray assembly and remove it from the console.

9 Reach in from the opening and push the control panel out of the dash (see illustration).

10 Disconnect the electrical connectors from the back of the IHKA control panel.

11 Use an anti-static pad and disconnect the IHKA control module from the control panel.

12 Installation is the reverse of removal. Be sure to use a BMW scan tool to program the IHKA module after it has been installed back into the dash. Consult with a dealer service department or other qualified automotive repair facility.

Z4 models

13 Remove the radio (see Chapter 12).

14 Using a panel removal tool, carefully pry the trim panel below the control panel assembly out of the dash.

15 Disconnect the electrical connectors from behind the control panel.

16 Position a protective cover below the control panel covering the center console.

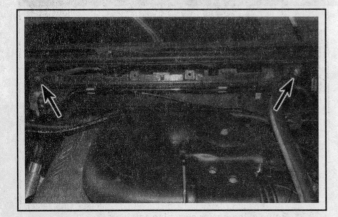

10.23 Remove the two Torx screws and remove the inlet ducting

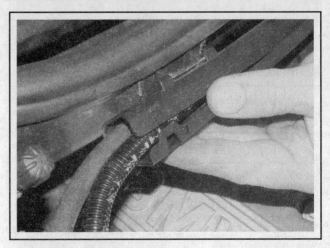

10.22 Unclip the cable ducting

17 Press the controls on the panel into the dash, move the control panel assembly away from the dash and lower the assembly out the bottom through the opening.

18 Installation is the reverse of removal. Be sure to use a BMW scan tool to program the IHKA module after it has been installed back into the dash. Consult with a dealer service department or other qualified automotive repair facility.

HEATER CORE

19 Have the air conditioning system refrigerant discharged by a BMW dealer or suitably-equipped specialist.

20 Drain the engine coolant (see Chapter 1).

3 series models

▶ **Refer to illustrations 10.22, 10.23, 10.25, 10.28, 10.29, 10.31 and 10.32**

21 Remove the in-cabin air filter (see Chapter 1).

22 Release the wire harness holder locking tabs and remove the harness and hoses from the holder (see illustration).

23 Remove the screws and separate the ducting from the cowl (see illustration).

24 Working in the passenger compartment, remove the center console and the instrument panel (see Chapter 11).

25 Working in the engine compartment, disconnect the heater hoses at the firewall (see illustration). Use shop towels or suitable plugs to prevent coolant spillage.

10.25 Loosen the clamps and disconnect the heater hoses from the firewall

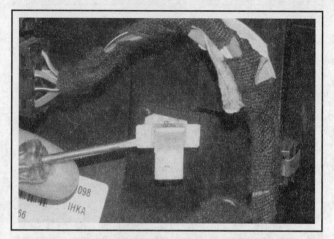

10.28 Pry the temperature sensor from the heater box

10.29 Release the clip and remove the core cover

26 Working in the passenger compartment, remove the right side air duct from the IHKA housing.

27 Disconnect the electrical connectors from the housing. Label each connector carefully.

28 Remove the heater core temperature sensor (see illustration).

29 Remove the retaining clips from the heater core housing cover (see illustration).

30 Remove the heater core cover and unhook the tabs located in the rear of the housing.

31 Remove the screw securing the coolant pipes (see illustration).

32 Disconnect the coolant pipes at the heater core (see illustration). Tilt the heater core to remove it from the IHKA housing.

33 Unbolt any brackets securing the heater box, and disconnect any wiring connectors, having noted their locations and harness routing. Remove the heater core from the vehicle.

34 Be prepared for coolant spillage and position a suitable container beneath the union on the end of the core.

35 Installation is the reverse of removal. Use new sealing rings. On completion, refill the cooling system as described in Chapter 1.

Z4 models

36 Remove the control panel (see Steps 13 through 18).

37 Remove the lower section of the steering column (see Chapter 10).

38 Remove the instrument panel (see Chapter 11).

39 Working in the engine compartment, disconnect the heater hoses at the firewall. Use shop towels or suitable plugs installed into the hose ends to prevent coolant overflow.

40 Working directly next to the heater hoses, remove the bolts for the air conditioning lines.

41 Working under the dash, remove the heater assembly mounting bolts from below the steering column.

42 Remove the nuts from the brace at the left and right corners of the passenger compartment.

43 Remove the screws from the center console area of the heater assembly.

44 Remove the brace from the passenger compartment.

45 Lower the heater assembly from the dash area.

46 Unbolt the adapter plate securing the heater box, and disconnect any wiring connectors, having noted their locations and harness routing. Remove the heater core from the heater assembly.

47 Be prepared for coolant spillage and position a suitable container beneath the union on the end of the core.

48 Installation is the reverse of removal. Use new sealing rings. On completion, refill the cooling system as described in Chapter 1.

HEATER BLOWER MOTOR

49 Have the air conditioning system refrigerant discharged by a BMW dealer or suitably-equipped specialist.

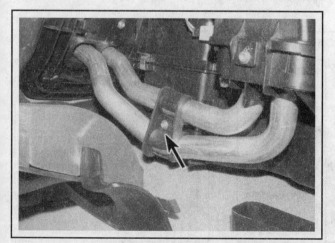

10.31 Heater pipe bracket retaining screw

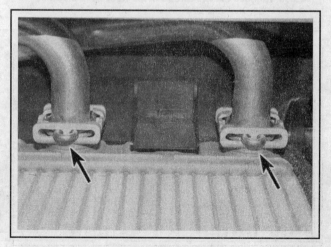

10.32 Remove the heater core pipe retainers

10.57 Lift the spindle lever to remove the flap

10.58 Remove the screw, release the clips and remove the blower motor cover

3 series models

▶ **Refer to illustration 10.57, 10.58, 10.59a, 10.59b, 10.60 and 10.61**

50 Remove the in-cabin air filter (see Chapter 1).
51 Release the wire harness holder locking tabs and remove the harness and hoses from the holder.

10.59a Remove the two screws at the right-hand side . . .

52 Remove the lower housing screws and separate the housing from the cowl (see illustration 10.16).
53 Remove the engine compartment side trim panel.
54 Remove the heater firewall cover mounting screws and lift the cover from the engine compartment.
55 Remove the engine cover (see Chapter 2A).
56 Peel away the rubber sealing strip from the housing opening.
57 Pull up the right-hand flap spindle lever, and remove the flap (see illustration).
58 Remove the single screw, release the two retaining clips and remove the heater motor front cover (see illustration).
59 Remove the three screws and remove the right-hand cover from the motor (see illustrations).
60 Disconnect the motor wiring connector and, using a spiked-tool, push the retaining clip down and release the motor (see illustration). Maneuver the motor out through the passenger side of the opening.
61 Installation is a reversal of removal. Ensure that the locating lug in the motor housing engages correctly with the rectangular hole in the motor casing (see illustration).

Z4 models

62 Remove the right side glovebox housing.
63 Remove the footwell and trim panel from the passenger's side foot area.

10.59b . . . and one screw in the center

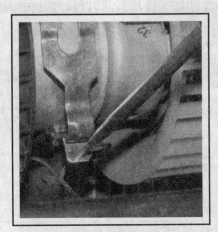

10.60 Push down the retaining clip to release the motor

10.61 Ensure the lug engages with the corresponding hole in the motor casing

64 Remove the screws from the current distributor located directly in front of the blower motor and push the assembly forward to remove it.

65 Working below the glovebox area, unlock the plug connectors and disconnect them.

66 Remove the wiring harness and position it off to the side.

67 Remove the heater blower motor fan mounting screws and remove the fan with the motor.

68 Installation is a reversal of removal.

Heater blower motor resistor

69 Refer to the information given in Section 12 regarding *Blower limit switch.*

Heater core valve

70 The heater core valve is mounted in the left-hand side of the engine compartment. Unscrew the expansion tank cap (referring to the *Warning* note in Section 1) to release any pressure present in the cooling system then securely reinstall the cap.

71 Clamp both heater hoses as close to the coolant valve as possible to minimize coolant loss.

72 Disconnect the valve wiring connector(s).

73 Loosen the retaining clips and disconnect the hoses from the valve then unclip the valve and remove it from the engine compartment.

74 Installation is the reverse of removal.

11 Air conditioning system - general information and precautions

GENERAL INFORMATION

1 The Integrated Heating Cooling Climate Control (IHKA) system offers efficient cooling and heating operation in automatic and programmed modes. The IHKA air conditioning system enables the temperature of incoming air to be lowered, and dehumidifies the air, which makes for rapid defogging and increased comfort.

2 The cooling side of the system works in the same way as a domestic refrigerator. Refrigerant gas is drawn into a belt-driven compressor and passes into a condenser mounted in front of the radiator, where it loses heat and becomes liquid. The liquid passes through an expansion valve to an evaporator, where it changes from liquid under high pressure to gas under low pressure. This change is accompanied by a drop in temperature, which cools the evaporator. The refrigerant returns to the compressor and the cycle begins again.

3 Air blown through the evaporator passes to the air distribution unit, where it is mixed with hot air blown through the heater core to achieve the desired temperature in the passenger compartment.

4 The operation of the system is controlled by an electronic control unit, with a self-diagnosis system. Any problems with the system should be referred to a BMW dealer or suitably-equipped specialist.

PRECAUTIONS

5 It is necessary to observe special precautions whenever dealing with any part of the system, its associated components and any items which require disconnection of the system. If for any reason the system must be disconnected, entrust this task to your BMW dealer or a suitably-equipped specialist.

❊❊ WARNING 1:

The refrigerant is potentially dangerous and should only be handled by qualified persons. If it is splashed onto the skin it can cause frostbite. It is not itself poisonous, but in the presence of a flame (including a cigarette) it forms a poisonous gas. Uncontrolled discharging of the refrigerant is dangerous and potentially damaging to the environment.

❊❊ WARNING 2:

Do not operate the air conditioning system if it is known to be short of refrigerant, as this may damage the compressor.

12 Air conditioning system components - removal and installation

❊❊ WARNING:

The models covered by this manual are equipped with Supplemental Restraint systems (SRS), more commonly known as airbags. Always disarm the airbag system before working in the vicinity of any airbag system component to avoid the possibility of accidental deployment of the airbag, which could cause personal injury (see Chapter 12). Do not use a memory saving device to preserve the PCM's memory when working on or near airbag system components.

EVAPORATOR

1 Have the air conditioning refrigerant discharged by a BMW dealer or suitably-equipped specialist.

3 series models

▶ Refer to illustrations 12.7a, 12.7b and 12.9

2 Working in the engine compartment, remove the in-cabin air filter and heater/ventilation inlet air ducting from the rear of the engine compartment (see Section 10).

3 Remove the heater core (see Section 10).

4 Remove the instrument panel (see Chapter 11).

5 Working in the engine compartment on the right side of the cowl, pull up on the spindle lever and release the right air intake flap from the blower housing (see illustration 10.57).

6 Remove the fasteners, and disconnect the air conditioning lines from the engine compartment firewall. Use special tool 64 5 102 to disconnect the A/C lines. Discard the O-ring seals, new ones must be installed.

12.7a The heater housing is secured by two bolts at the top (one on each side) . . .

12.7b . . . and two at the bottom (one on each side) of the heater motor aperture

12.9 Disconnect the temperature sensor wiring connector

7   Remove the screws securing the heater housing to the engine compartment firewall (see illustrations).

8   Remove the air conditioning blower limit switch as described in this Section.

9   Disconnect the wiring connector and remove the temperature sensor from the evaporator housing (see illustration).

10 Unclip the linkage from the servo motor, disconnect any wiring connectors and release any wiring harnesses from the retaining clips, having noted their installed locations.

11 Release the retaining clips, remove the lower part of the evaporator housing, and remove the evaporator.

➡Note: Take care not to damage any of the evaporator cooling fins. If necessary straighten any that are bent.

12 Installation is the reverse of removal. Have the refrigerant recharged by a BMW dealer or specialist, and top up the coolant level as described in Chapter 1.

Z4 models

13 Working inside the vehicle, remove the heater assembly (see Steps 36 through 45 in Section 10).

14 Remove the adapter plate from the heater assembly.

15 Remove the cable and unclip the retainers from the evaporator cover.

16 Remove the screw and retaining clips from the upper cover and lift the upper cover from the heater assembly.

17 Remove the expansion valve (see Step 19) and the evaporator mounting screws. Lift evaporator from the heater assembly.

18 Installation is the reverse of removal. Have the refrigerant recharged by a BMW dealer or specialist, and top up the coolant level as described in Chapter 1.

EXPANSION VALVE

19 Have the air conditioning refrigerant discharged by a BMW dealer or suitably-equipped specialist.

3 series models

20 Working in the engine compartment, remove the in-cabin air filter and heater/ventilation inlet air ducting from the rear of the engine compartment (see Section 10).

21 Working in the engine compartment on the right side of the cowl, pull up on the spindle lever and release the right air intake flap from the

blower housing (see illustration 10.57).

22 Remove the fasteners, and disconnect the air conditioning lines from the engine compartment firewall. Use special tool 64 5 102 to disconnect the A/C lines. Discard the O-ring seals, new ones must be installed.

23 Remove the nut and disconnect the dual pipe coupling from the expansion valve.

24 Remove the two screws and remove the expansion valve. Discard the O-ring seals, new ones must be installed.

25 Installation is the reverse of removal. Have the refrigerant recharged by a BMW dealer or specialist, and top up the coolant level as described in Chapter 1.

Z4 models

26 Working in the engine compartment, remove the mounting bolts from the refrigerant line clamps and the receptacle at the firewall.

27 Remove the air conditioning lines from the firewall.

28 Remove the adapter plate mounting bolt and separate the adapter plate from the firewall grommet.

29 Remove the grommet from the firewall.

30 Remove the two expansion valve mounting bolts and push the valve down slightly to separate it from the evaporator line. Install new seals and firewall grommet.

31 Installation is the reverse of removal. Have the refrigerant recharged by a BMW dealer or specialist, and top up the coolant level as described in Chapter 1.

RECEIVER/DRIER

▶ Refer to illustrations 12.34 and 12.36

32 The receiver/drier should be replaced when:

a) There is dirt in the air conditioning system.
b) The compressor has been replaced.
c) The condenser or evaporator has been replaced.
d) A leak has emptied the air conditioning system.
e) The air conditioning system has been opened for more than 24 hours.

33 Have the air conditioning refrigerant discharged by a BMW dealer or suitably-equipped specialist.

34 The receiver/drier is located in the right-hand corner of the engine compartment. Remove the retaining screws and lift the pipes

12.34 Remove the screws and disconnect the couplings

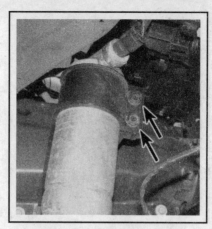

12.36 Remove the clamp screws securing the receiver/drier

12.41 Disconnect the compressor wiring connector

and coupling from the top of the unit (see illustration). Discard the O-ring seals, new ones must be installed.

➡**Note: If the drier is to be left unconnected for more than one hour, plug the openings.**

35 Remove the right-hand front fender liner as described in Chapter 11, Section 23.

➡**Note: On Z4 models, the receiver drier is accessible without removing the fender liner.**

36 Remove the clamp screws and lower the receiver/drier from the clamp (see illustration).

37 Installation is the reverse of removal. Have the refrigerant recharged by a BMW dealer or specialist, and top up the coolant level as described in Chapter 1.

COMPRESSOR

▶ **Refer to illustrations 12.41 and 12.42**

38 Have the air conditioning refrigerant discharged by a BMW dealer or suitably-equipped specialist.

39 Firmly apply the handbrake, then raise the vehicle and secure it on jack stands. Remove the engine splash shield (see Chapter 2A). Remove the drivebelt (see Chapter 1).

40 Remove the front windshield wiper fluid reservoir.

41 Disconnect the compressor wiring connector (see illustration).

42 Remove the two bolts and disconnect the air conditioning lines from the compressor (see illustration). Discard the O-ring seals, new ones must be installed.

43 Remove the three mounting bolts, and remove the compressor.

44 Installation is a reversal of removal, noting the following points:

a) *Prior to installing the compressor, it is essential that the correct amount of refrigerant oil is added - refer to your dealer for the correct amount and specification.*

b) *Always use new seals when reconnecting the refrigerant lines.*

c) *Upon completion, have the refrigerant recharged by a BMW dealer or specialist.*

PRESSURE SENSOR

45 The pressure sensor is installed to the top of the receiver/drier. Have the air conditioning refrigerant discharged by a BMW dealer or suitably-equipped specialist.

46 Disconnect the sensor wiring connector, and unscrew the sensor.

47 Installation is a reversal of removal, tighten the sensor securely, and have the refrigerant recharged by a BMW dealer or specialist.

CONDENSER

▶ **Refer to illustrations 12.50, 12.51a and 12.51b**

48 Have the air conditioning refrigerant discharged by a BMW dealer or suitably-equipped specialist.

49 Remove the air filter housing (see Chapter 4). The condenser is located in front of the radiator. Remove the radiator (see Section 3).

50 Remove the two bolts and disconnect the refrigerant lines from the condenser (see illustration). Discard the O-ring seals, new ones

12.42 Remove the bolts and disconnect the refrigerant lines

12.50 Remove the two bolts and disconnect the refrigerant lines from the condenser

12.51a Remove the two plastic screws . . .

12.51b . . . release the clips and lift out the condenser

12.54 Disconnect the linkage arm from the servo motor

must be installed.

51 Remove the two plastic screws securing the condenser through the cross panel. Lift the condenser up and disengage it from the mounting bracket (see illustrations).

52 Installation is a reversal of removal, noting the following points:

a) *Prior to installation, the condenser it is essential that the correct amount of refrigerant oil is added - refer to your dealer for the correct amount and specification.*

b) *Always use new seals when reconnecting the refrigerant pipes.*

c) *Upon completion, have the refrigerant recharged by a BMW dealer or specialist.*

BLOWER LIMIT SWITCH

♦ **Refer to illustrations 12.54 and 12.55**

53 Unclip the right-hand footwell air duct from the heater housing.

54 Carefully pry the linkage arm from the servo motor. Remove the two screws (one above, one below) and remove the bracket and servo motor (see illustration).

12.55 Remove the blower limit switch screws

55 Disconnect the wiring connector, remove the two retaining screws, push back the retaining clip and remove the blower limit switch (see illustration).

56 Installation is the reverse of removal.

Specifications

General

Antifreeze type	See Chapter 1
Expansion tank cap opening pressure	29 psi (2.0 bar)

Torque specifications	Ft-lbs (unless otherwise indicated)	Nm
Water pump bolts/nuts		
M6	89 in-lbs	10
M7	132 in-lbs	15
M8	16	22
Water pump pulley bolts	89 in-lbs	10
Cooling fan hub nut-to-water pump (left-hand thread)		
With tool 11 5 040	22	30
Without tool 11 5 040	29	40
Cooling fan viscous coupling-to-fan assembly	89 in-lbs	10
Thermal switch to radiator	132 in-lbs	15
Thermostat housing bolts	89 in-lbs	10

Section

Reference to other Chapters

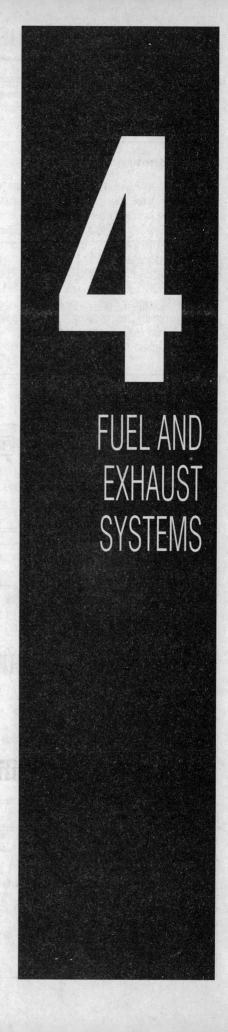

4

FUEL AND EXHAUST SYSTEMS

1 General information and precautions

GENERAL INFORMATION

▸ **Refer to illustration 1.1**

The fuel supply system consists of a fuel tank (which is mounted under the rear of the vehicle, with an electric fuel pump immersed in it), a fuel filter, fuel feed and return lines. The fuel pump supplies fuel to the fuel rail, which acts as a reservoir for the four fuel injectors that inject fuel into the inlet tracts. The fuel filter incorporated in the feed line from the pump to the fuel rail ensures that the fuel supplied to the injectors is clean. On M52TU engines, a fuel pressure regulator is installed on the fuel injection rail, where the fuel then returns to the tank. On M54 engines, the pressure regulator is incorporated into the fuel filter assembly (see illustration). On M56 engines, the pressure regulator is mounted inside the fuel tank.

Refer to Section 7 for further information on the operation of the

fuel injection system, and to Section 14 for information on the exhaust system.

325I MODELS WITH AN M56 ENGINE

Specific 2003 and later 325i models, with automatic transmissions, are equipped with the M56 engine. These models are sold in California, Massachusetts, New York and Vermont (2004 and later) during the time this book was written. These models are designed to meet higher standards for lower emissions. The fuel delivery and emissions equipment, although similar, varies in these vehicles. As a result, the home mechanic will be limited to certain repairs due to the special tools and equipment necessary to service these systems. Moreover, these models have a sealed stainless steel fuel tank with certain fuel system components inside. If any of the components fail, the fuel tank will have to be replaced as an assembly (at least this was the case at the time this

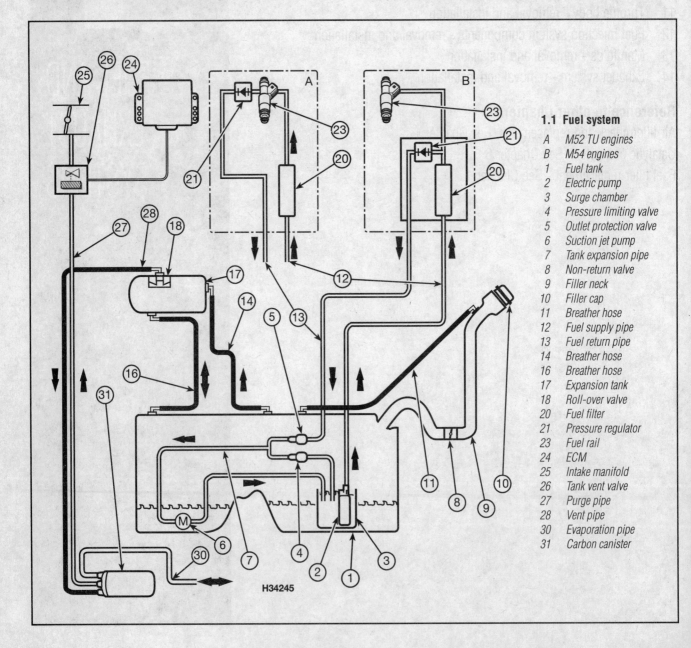

1.1 Fuel system

A M52 TU engines
B M54 engines
1 Fuel tank
2 Electric pump
3 Surge chamber
4 Pressure limiting valve
5 Outlet protection valve
6 Suction jet pump
7 Tank expansion pipe
8 Non-return valve
9 Filler neck
10 Filler cap
11 Breather hose
12 Fuel supply pipe
13 Fuel return pipe
14 Breather hose
16 Breather hose
17 Expansion tank
18 Roll-over valve
20 Fuel filter
21 Pressure regulator
23 Fuel rail
24 ECM
25 Intake manifold
26 Tank vent valve
27 Purge pipe
28 Vent pipe
30 Evaporation pipe
31 Carbon canister

H34245

manual was written).

On the M56 engine, BMW warrants emission components (along with specified fuel delivery components) for a period of 15 years or 150,000 miles; whichever occurs first from the date the vehicle was first put into service. If the vehicle falls within this time period, take the vehicle to a BMW dealer for warranty service.

PRECAUTIONS

> ❄❄ **WARNING:**
>
> **Gasoline is extremely flammable, so take extra precautions**

when you work on any part of the fuel system. Don't smoke or allow open flames or bare light bulbs near the work area, and don't work in a garage where a gas-type appliance (such as a water heater or a clothes dryer) is present. Since gasoline is carcinogenic, wear fuel-resistant gloves when there's a possibility of being exposed to fuel, and, if you spill any fuel on your skin, rinse it off immediately with soap and water. Mop up any spills immediately and do not store fuel-soaked rags where they could ignite. The fuel system is under constant pressure, so, if any fuel lines are to be disconnected, the fuel pressure in the system must be relieved first (see Section 8). When you perform any kind of work on the fuel system, wear safety glasses and have a Class B type fire extinguisher on hand.

2   Air cleaner assembly - removal and installation

REMOVAL

▶ **Refer to illustration 2.3**

1   Release the engine wiring harness from the retaining bracket on the air cleaner housing.
2   Release the clips and disconnect the intake hose from the top section of the housing.
3   Unscrew the two retaining bolts and remove the air cleaner hous-

ing from the engine compartment, disengaging it from the inlet ducting as it is withdrawn (see illustration).

INSTALLATION

▶ **Refer to illustration 2.4**

4   Installation is a reverse of removal, but ensure that the lower mounting engages with the plastic lug on the body (see illustration), and where a rubber seal is installed between the intake hose and the housing, apply a little acid-free grease to the seal to ease installation.

2.3 Air cleaner housing mounting bolts (2004 shown, others similar)

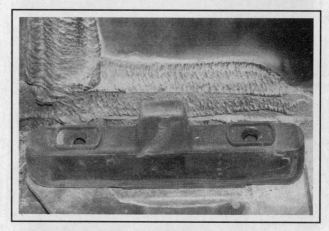

2.4 The plastic bracket on the inner fender used for mounting the air cleaner housing

3   Fuel tank - removal and installation

> ❄❄ **WARNING:**
>
> **Refer to the *Warning* in Section 1 before proceeding.**

M52TU AND M54 ENGINES

Removal

▶ **Refer to illustrations 3.6a, 3.6b, 3.7, 3.8, 3.9, 3.11 and 3.13**

1   Relieve the fuel system pressure (see Section 8), then disconnect

the cable from the negative battery terminal (see Chapter 5, Section 1).
2   Before removing the fuel tank, it is best that the level of fuel be near empty. There is no drain plug for the gas tank. If necessary, siphon the fuel into an approved fuel container.

> ❄❄ **WARNING:**
>
> **Do not start the siphoning action by mouth. Use a siphoning kit (available at most auto parts stores).**

3   Raise the rear of the vehicle and support it securely on jackstands.

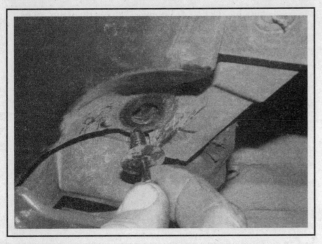

3.6a Pry up the center pins, pull out the rivets . . .

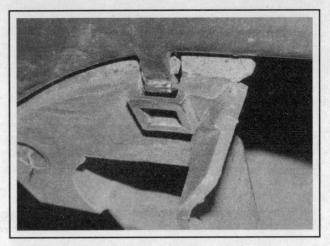

3.6b . . . and remove the trim panels from either side of the fuel tank

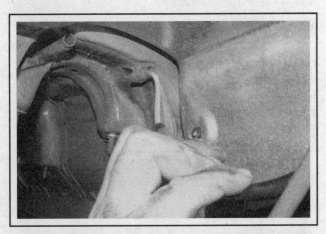

3.7 Pull the parking brake cables from the guide tubes

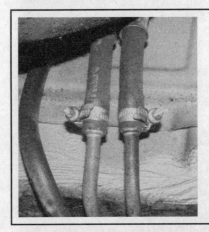

3.8 Disconnect the fuel supply and return hoses

4 Detach the parking brake cables from the parking brake lever as described in Chapter 9.

5 Remove the driveshaft as described in Chapter 8.

6 Working under the vehicle, pry up the center pins and remove the plastic expansion rivets, then remove the trim panel from under the left-hand side of the tank, and the sill trim (see illustrations). Repeat this procedure on the right-hand side of the tank.

7 Pull the parking brake cables from the guide tubes (see illustration).

8 Mark the fuel supply and return hoses to aid reinstallation, then loosen the clamps and disconnect them (see illustration). Be prepared for fuel spillage, and clamp or plug the open ends of the hoses and lines to prevent dirt entry and further fuel spillage.

9 Loosen the hose clamp, then disconnect the fuel filler hose from the tank neck (see illustration).

10 Support the fuel tank using a jack and a block of wood.

11 Remove the retaining bolt in the center-rear of the tank, and the bolts securing the tank retaining straps (see illustration).

12 Lower the tank slightly and disconnect the wiring connector(s)

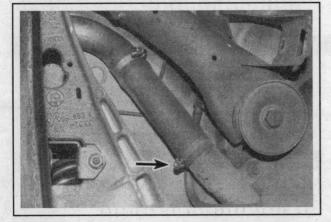

3.9 Loosen the clamp and disconnect the fuel filler hose

3.11 Remove the fuel tank center bolt

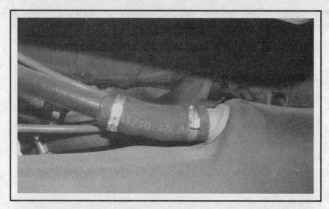

3.13 Cut the clamp and disconnect the tank breather pipe (replace the clamp with a screw-type clamp upon installation)

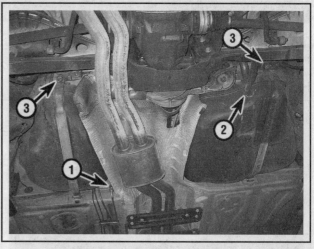

3.22 Fuel tank details for M56 engine models:

1)	Fuel feed line fitting	3)	Fuel tank retaining strap
2)	Fuel tank vent line		bolts

after noting their installed positions.

13 Release the clamp and disconnect the breather hose from the tank (see illustration). Lower the tank, and maneuver it from under the vehicle.

Installation

14 Installation is a reversal of removal. Note that once the tank is installed, at least 1-1/3 gallons of fuel must be added to allow the fuel system to function correctly.

M56 ENGINES

Removal

▶ **Refer to illustrations 3.22**

15 Proceed as described in Steps 1 to 3.

16 Remove the bottom portion of the rear seat (see Chapter 11).

17 Move the floor trim and insulation away from the seal cover and fasteners.

18 Remove the seal cover fasteners and cover.

19 Disconnect the electrical connector from the fuel tank by turning it counterclockwise.

20 Remove the rear differential (see Chapter 8).

21 Remove the wheel well cover from the right-rear wheel.

22 Detach the feed line using a flare nut wrench on the line fitting (see illustration).

23 Detach the vent line from the fuel tank (see illustration 3.22).

24 Detach the fuel filler pipe and the fueling vent line.

25 Support the fuel tank using a jack and a block of wood.

26 Remove the bolts securing the tank retaining straps (see illustration 3.22) and carefully lower the tank.

Installation

27 Installation is a reversal of removal. Note that once the tank is installed, at least 1-1/3 gallons of fuel must be added to allow the fuel system to function correctly.

---

4 Fuel expansion tank - removal and installation

▶ **Refer to illustration 4.3**

✳✳ WARNING:

Refer to the _Warning_ in Section 1 before proceeding.

1 Loosen the right-rear wheel lug nuts, raise the right-hand rear side of the vehicle and support it securely on jackstands. Remove the right-rear wheel.

2 Remove the plastic nuts/screws/expansion rivets and remove the liner in the right-rear wheel well (see Chapter 12).

3 Remove the retaining nut, disconnect the lower hose, and pull the bottom of the tank forward (see illustration).

4 Note their installed positions, then loosen the clamps and disconnect the remaining two breather hoses from the tank. Remove the tank.

5 Installation is a reversal of removal.

4.3 Remove the expansion tank retaining nut

5 Throttle cable - removal, installation and adjustment

➡**Note: On 2001 and later models, no throttle cable is used (the throttle is electronically motor-driven).**

REMOVAL

▸ **Refer to illustrations 5.1, 5.2, 5.3, 5.5 and 5.6**

1   Unscrew the two screws, and remove the plastic cover from the

5.1 Remove the screws and detach the cover

5.2 Squeeze together the sides of the grommet and push it out from the throttle lever

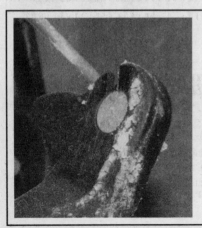

5.5 Disengage the throttle cable end from the lever

top of the throttle body (see illustration).

2   Use a pair a pliers to squeeze together the sides of the end fitting grommet, slide the grommet from the throttle lever and feed the cable through the slot in the lever (see illustration).

3   Pull the outer cable, then the rubber grommet, from the supporting bracket (see illustration).

4   Working inside the vehicle, release the retaining clips/screws, and withdraw the driver's side lower dash panel (see Chapter 11).

5   Disengage the inner throttle cable from the top of the throttle operating lever (see illustration).

6   Working under the dash, squeeze together the two retaining clips, and push the cable outer end fitting from the firewall (see illustration).

7   Note the correct routing, then free the cable from any retaining clips/grommets and maneuver it from the engine compartment.

INSTALLATION

8   Installation is a reversal of removal, ensuring that the cable is routed as before. Carry out the adjustment procedure as follows.

ADJUSTMENT

➡**Note: Vehicles equipped with automatic transmissions must have the throttle cable adjusted by a BMW dealer or suitably equipped specialist.**

5.3 Pull the outer cable, then the grommet, from the supporting bracket

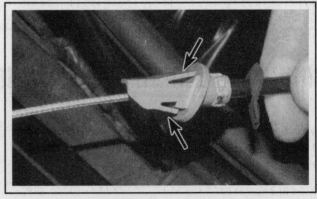

5.6 Throttle outer cable retaining clips

9 In order to accurately adjust the throttle cable, a specialized BMW diagnostic scan tool is required to establish the throttle potentiometer position expressed as a percentage. However, the basic position for manual transmission models can be established as follows, providing that a BMW dealer or suitably equipped specialist checks the setting afterwards.

10 Check that the accelerator pedal and throttle are in the idle position.

11 Rotate the knurled cable adjustment sleeve on the outer cable to eliminate freeplay in the cable.

12 Screw the sleeve a quarter of a turn to allow a little freeplay in the cable.

13 Have an assistant fully depress and hold the accelerator pedal, check that there is still 0.020-inch (0.5 mm) of freeplay at the throttle valve in the throttle body.

14 If necessary, turn the pedal full-throttle stop (screwed into the floor) to give the correct amount of freeplay. On some models, it will be necessary to loosen a locknut before the stop can be adjusted.

6 Throttle pedal - removal and installation

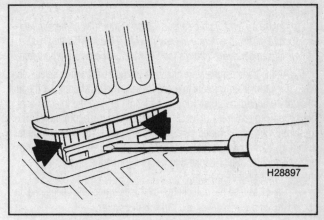

6.1 **Release the throttle pedal from the floor**

⁑ WARNING:

Once the throttle pedal has been removed, it MUST be replaced. Removal will damage the pedal retaining clips, and if the original pedal is installed, it could work loose, causing an accident.

MODELS WITH A THROTTLE CABLE (2000 AND EARLIER)

▶ **Refer to illustration 6.1**

1 Press down on the carpet under the pedal, then bend back the lower pedal retaining clips, and lever the pedal upwards to release it from the floor (see illustration). Maneuver the pedal and free it from the throttle cable operating lever. Discard the pedal, a new one must used on installation.

2 Engage the new pedal with the throttle cable operating lever.

3 Push the pedal down to engage the lower retaining clips with the floor plate. Ensure that the clips snap securely into place.

4 Check the throttle cable adjustment as described in Section 5.

MODELS WITHOUT A THROTTLE CABLE (ELECTRONIC, 2001 AND LATER)

➥**Note: The accelerator pedal has a pedal position sensor integrated into the assembly. If the sensor fails, the entire assembly must be replaced.**

5 Using a flat-bladed screwdriver, depress the retaining clip and slide the pedal assembly towards the center of the cabin (see illustration). Disconnect the wiring connector as the assembly is withdrawn.

6 To install, reconnect the wiring connector and slide the assembly into the mounting, ensuring that it is correctly located. Two clicks should be heard as the clips engage, and the right-hand side of the assembly should be flush with the side of the mounting.

6.5 **Depress the clip, and slide the pedal assembly towards the center of the cabin**

7 Fuel injection system - general information

1 An integrated engine management system known as DME (Digital Motor Electronics) is used for all models. The system controls all fuel injection and ignition system functions using a central ECM (Electronic Control Module).

2 On all models, the system incorporates a closed-loop catalytic converter and an evaporative emission control system, and complies with the very latest emission control standards. Refer to Chapter 5 for information on the ignition side of the system; the fuel side of the system operates as follows.

3 The fuel pump (which is immersed in the fuel tank) supplies fuel from the tank to the fuel rail, via a filter. A pressure regulator controls fuel pressure. When the optimum operating pressure of the fuel system is exceeded, the regulator allows excess fuel to return to the tank.

4   The electrical control system consists of the ECM, along with the following sensors:

a) *Hot film air mass meter - informs the ECM of the quantity and temperature of air entering the engine.*

b) *Coolant temperature sensor(s) - informs the ECM of engine temperature.*

c) *Crankshaft position sensor - informs the ECM of the crankshaft position and speed of rotation.*

d) *Camshaft position sensor(s) - informs the ECM of the camshaft(s) position.*

e) *Oxygen sensor(s) - informs the ECM of the oxygen content of the exhaust gases (explained in greater detail in Chapter 6).*

f) *Vehicle speed sensor - informs the ECM of the vehicle's road speed.*

g) *Intake air temperature sensor - informs the ECM of the temperature of the air entering the engine (M52TU and M54 engines).*

h) *Oil temperature - informs the ECM of the engine oil temperatue.*

5   All the above signals are analyzed by the ECM, which selects the fueling response appropriate to those values. The ECM controls the fuel injectors (varying the pulse width - the length of time the injectors are held open - to provide a richer or weaker mixture, as appropriate). The mixture is constantly varied by the ECM, to provide the best setting for cranking, starting (with a hot or cold engine), warm-up, idle, cruising and acceleration. See Chapter 6 for more information on the engine management system sensors.

6   The ECM also has full control over the engine idle speed, via an auxiliary air valve that bypasses the throttle valve. When the throttle valve is closed, the ECM controls the opening of the valve, which in turn regulates the amount of air entering the manifold, and so controls the idle speed.

7   The ECM controls the exhaust and evaporative emission control systems, which are described in Chapter 6.

8   On all engines, a Differential Air Inlet System (DISA) is installed. Variable length inlet tracts incorporated in the inlet manifold are operated by a butterfly valve according to engine speed and load. This improves engine torque at low and medium engine speeds. The butterfly valve is installed under the manifold and operated by a vacuum actuator.

9   If there is an abnormality in any of the readings obtained from the sensors, the ECM enters its back-up mode. In this event, it ignores the abnormal sensor signal and assumes a preprogrammed value that will allow the engine to continue running (at reduced efficiency). If the ECM enters this back-up mode, the relevant fault code will be stored in the ECM memory.

10   If a fault is suspected, the vehicle should be taken to a BMW dealer at the earliest opportunity. A complete test of the engine management system can then be carried out, using a special electronic diagnostic test unit connected to the system's diagnostic connector. The OBD-II 16-pin socket is located under the dash on the driver's side, while the BMW diagnostic socket is located in the right-hand corner of the engine compartment or under the dash on the driver's side; Refer to Section 10 of this Chapter for further details regarding testing.

8   Fuel injection system - depressurization and priming

✳✳ WARNING:

Refer to the *Warning* in Section 1 before proceeding.

DEPRESSURIZATION

1   Remove the fuel pump fuse from the fuse box. The fuse is located in the main fuse box in the passenger glove box, and the exact location is given on the fuse box cover (see Chapter 12).

2   Start the engine and allow it to stall. Switch off the ignition.

3   Remove the fuel filler cap.

4   The fuel system is now depressurized.

➡Note: Place a rag around any fuel lines before disconnecting them, to prevent any residual fuel from spilling onto the engine.

5   Disconnect the cable from the negative battery terminal before working on any part of the fuel system (see Chapter 5, Section 1).

PRIMING

6   Reconnect the negative battery cable (see Chapter 5, Section 1).

7   Install the fuel pump fuse, then switch on the ignition and wait for a few seconds for the fuel pump to run, building-up fuel pressure. Switch off the ignition unless the engine is to be started.

9   Fuel pump/fuel level sensors - removal and installation

✳✳ WARNING:

Refer to the *Warning* in Section 1 before proceeding.

➡Note: On 2003 and later 325i models with an M56 engine, the fuel pump and other components are permanently sealed within the fuel tank and cannot be serviced. The fuel tank must be replaced if the pump is faulty; refer to Section 1 of this chapter for more information.

REMOVAL

1   There are two level sensors installed in the fuel tank - one in the left-hand side of the tank, and one in the right-hand side. The pump is integral with the right-side sensor, and at the time of writing can only be replaced as a complete unit.

Right-hand sensor/fuel pump

▶ Refer to illustrations 9.5, 9.6, 9.7, 9.8a and 9.8b

2   Relieve the fuel system pressure (see Section 8). Before remov-

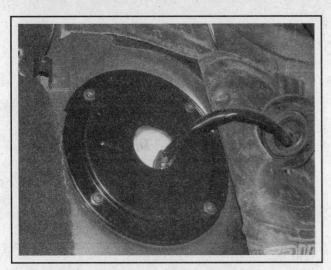

9.5 Unscrew the four nuts and remove the access cover

9.6 Slide out the locking element (arrow) to disconnect the connector, then snip the hose clamp

ing the fuel pump/level sensor, all fuel should be drained from the tank. Since a fuel tank drain plug is not provided, it is preferable to carry out the removal operation when the tank is nearly empty. If necessary, siphon the fuel into an approved fuel container.

⁜ WARNING:

Do not start the siphoning action by mouth. Use a siphoning kit (available at most auto parts stores).

3   Remove the rear bench seat as described in Chapter 11.

4   Unclip the rubber wiring grommet, and fold back the rubber matting to expose the access cover.

5   Remove the four nuts and detach the access cover from the floor (see illustration).

6   Slide out the locking element to disconnect the wiring connector, then cut the original metal hose clamp from place using side-cutters (or equivalent) and disconnect the fuel hose (see illustration). Be prepared

for fuel spillage.

7   Unscrew the fuel pump/level sensor unit locking ring and remove it from the tank. Although a BMW tool 16 1 020 is available for this task, it can be accomplished using a large pair of pliers to push on two opposite raised ribs on the locking ring. Alternatively, a home-made tool can be fabricated to engage with the raised ribs of the locking ring. Turn the ring counterclockwise until it can be unscrewed by hand (see illustration).

8   Carefully lift the fuel pump/level sensor unit from the tank, taking care not to bend the sensor float arm (gently push the float arm towards the unit if necessary). Recover the sealing ring. If necessary the strainer on the base of the pump can be unclipped for cleaning (see illustrations), but no further dismantling is recommended.

Left-hand sensor

▶ **Refer to illustration 9.9**

9   Removal of the left-hand sensor is almost identical to the right-hand sensor described previously, except that the wiring connector is

9.7 Using a home-made tool to unscrew the locking ring

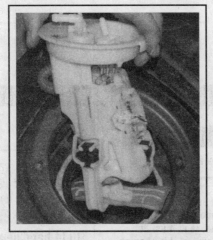

9.8a Carefully lift the assembly from the fuel tank

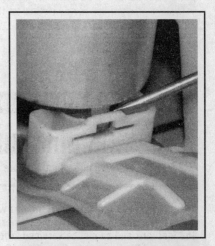

9.8b Depress the clip, and remove the strainer from the base of the pump

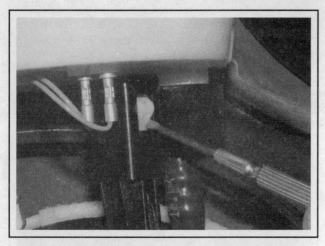

9.9 Press in the detent and disconnect the wiring connector

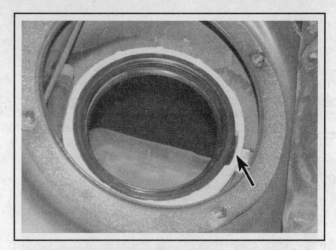

9.10 Note the slot in the fuel tank collar

clipped into place. When lifting out the sensor unit, depress the detent and disconnect the expansion tank line from the unit (see illustration).

INSTALLATION

▶ **Refer to illustration 9.10**

10 Installation is a reversal of removal, noting the following points:

a) Use a new sealing ring.
b) To allow the unit to pass through the aperture in the fuel tank, press the float arm against the fuel pick-up strainer.
c) When the unit is installed, the locating lug on the unit must engage with the corresponding slot in the fuel tank collar (see illustration).
d) Use a new hose clamp to secure the fuel hose.

10 Fuel injection system - testing and adjustment

TESTING

▶ **Refer to illustrations 10.2a and 10.2b**

1 If a fault appears in the fuel injection system, first ensure that all the system wiring connectors are securely connected and free of corrosion. Ensure that the fault is not due to poor maintenance. A dirty air filter element, poor spark plug connections, fouled or incorrectly gapped spark plugs, poor or uneven cylinder compression pressures, or clogged engine breather hoses can adversely affect the fuel injection system; refer to the relevant Parts of Chapters 1, 2 and 5 for further information.

2 If the above concerns fail to reveal the cause of the problem, the vehicle should be taken to a BMW dealer or suitably equipped specialist for testing. A wiring block connector is incorporated in the engine management circuit, into which a special electronic diagnostic tester (scan tool) can be connected. On June 2000 and earlier models, the BMW diagnostic connector is clipped to the right-hand shock tower (see illustration). On later models, it is located under the dash in the driver's footwell incorporated with the OBD (On-Board Diagnostic) 16-pin socket (see illustration). The tester (scan tool) is used to help locate the fault.

10.2a Unscrew the cap to expose the BMW diagnostic connector (used for June 2000 and earlier models)

10.2b The OBD 16-pin diagnostic socket is near the left kick panel under the dash

ADJUSTMENT

3   Experienced home mechanics with a considerable amount of skill and equipment (including a tachometer and an accurately calibrated exhaust gas analyzer) may be able to check the exhaust CO level and the idle speed. However, if these are found to be in need of adjustment, the car must be taken to a BMW dealer or specialist for further testing.

11 Throttle body - removal and installation

M52TU ENGINES

Removal

▶ **Refer to illustrations 11.9 and 11.11**

1   Disconnect the cable from the negative battery terminal (see Chapter 5, Section 1).

2   Remove the air cleaner housing as described in Section 2.

3   Remove the mass airflow sensor and ducting as described in Chapter 6.

4   Disconnect the throttle cable(s) from the throttle quadrant and support bracket.

5   Release the retaining clips, and disconnect the air intake ducting from the throttle body and the idle speed control valve.

6   Note their installed locations, and disconnect any wiring connectors attached to the throttle body.

7   Disconnect the electrical connectors from the oil pressure and oil temperature switches, adjacent to the oil filter housing.

8   Unclip the fuel lines and fuel regulator vacuum hose (where installed) from the retaining bracket on the oil dipstick guide tube.

9   Disconnect the oil return line from the dipstick guide tube, undo the retaining bolt and remove the guide tube. Discard the O-ring seal - a new one must be installed (see illustration).

10   Remove the three screws/nuts securing the cable duct mounting.

11   Rotate the connector collar counterclockwise, and disconnect the wiring connector from the throttle body (M52TU engines) or release the retaining clip and disconnect the wiring connector (M54 engines) (see illustration), unscrew the four bolts and remove the throttle body from the intake manifold.

Installation

▶ **Refer to illustration 11.13**

12   Examine the throttle body-to-intake manifold O-ring seal. If it is

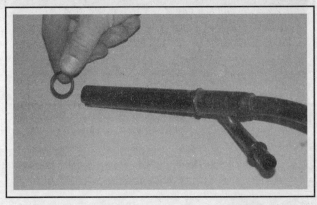

11.9 Be sure to install a new O-ring on the dipstick tube

good condition, it can be re-used. Install the throttle body to the manifold, and tighten the four bolts securely.

13   Prior to reconnecting the throttle body wiring connector on M52TU engines, rotate the connector collar until the red locking pin is visible though the opening in the collar. Align the arrow on the collar with the arrow on the throttle body terminal. Push the wiring connector on, rotating the collar clockwise until the second arrow on the collar aligns (see illustration). On M54 engines, simply install the wiring connector.

14   The remainder of installation is a reversal of removal. Note that if a new throttle body has been installed, the (learned) stored values in the engine management ECM, must be reset using dedicated test equipment. Have this carried out be a BMW dealer or suitably equipped specialist.

➡**Note: On M54 engines, it may be possible to perform ECM adaptation by performing the following steps:**

a)   *Turn the ignition ON for 10 seconds. Don't start the engine at this time.*

b)   *Turn the ignition OFF for 10 seconds.*

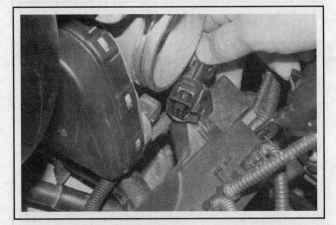

11.11 Disconnect the throttle body wiring connector (M54 engine shown)

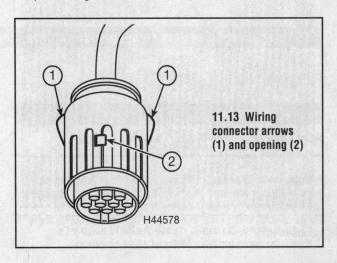

11.13 Wiring connector arrows (1) and opening (2)

H44578

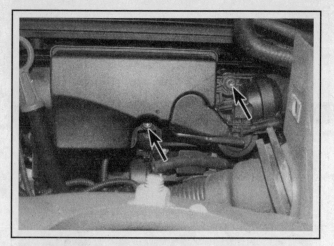

11.18 Remove the screws and detach the DISA adjustment unit

11.19 Remove the bolt securing the suction jet tube

c) Start the engine. It may take a few trips before full adaptation occurs. If the vehicle does not run correctly after driving in various conditions, have the vehicle inspected by a BMW dealership or other qualified repair facility.

M54 AND M56 ENGINES

Removal

▶ **Refer to illustrations 11.18, 11.19 and 11.23**

15 Disconnect the cable from the negative battery terminal (see Chapter 5, Section 1).

16 Remove the air cleaner housing as described in Section 2.

17 Release the retaining clips, disconnect the wiring connector and vacuum hose, and remove air cleaner housing-to-connecting piece intake ducting.

18 Disconnect the wiring connector, unscrew the two Torx screws, and remove the DISA adjustment unit from the intake manifold (see illustration).

19 Unscrew the bolt securing the suction jet tube to the intake manifold (see illustration).

20 Release the clamps and disconnect the intake ducting from the throttle body and idle speed control valve.

21 Disconnect the idle speed control valve wiring connector.

11.23 Disconnect the tank vent valve wiring connector

22 Disconnect the wiring connectors for the oil temperature and oil pressure switches adjacent to the oil filter housing.

23 Press in the retaining clip to unlock the wiring connector, and detach it from the tank venting valve (see illustration).

24 Proceed as described in Steps 8 through 11.

Installation

25 Installation is as described in Steps 12 through 14.

12 Fuel injection system components - removal and installation

FUEL RAIL AND INJECTORS

➡Note: On 2003 and later 325i models with an M56 engine, special fittings are used on the fuel rail and injectors. Removal must performed by a BMW dealer or specialist using the appropriate special tools; refer to Section 1 of this chapter for more information.

1 Depressurize the fuel system as described in Section 8, then disconnect the cable from the negative battery terminal (see Chapter 5, Section 1).

M52TU engines

▶ **Refer to illustrations 12.3, 12.4, 12.5, 12.6, 12.7 and 12.12**

2 Working at the rear of the engine compartment, turn the fasteners 90° counterclockwise and remove the cabin filter cover. Slide the filter from the housing. If necessary, refer to Chapter 1.

3 Release the retaining clips and remove the cable from the ducting on the air intake housing (see illustration).

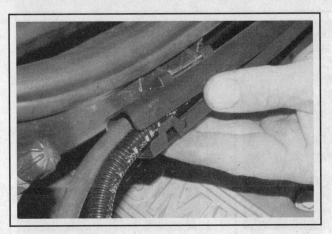

12.3 Unclip the cable ducting

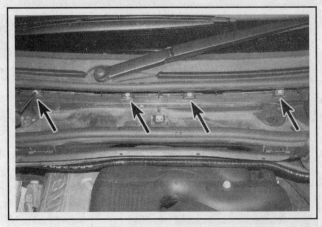

12.4 The cabin filter housing is secured by four screws

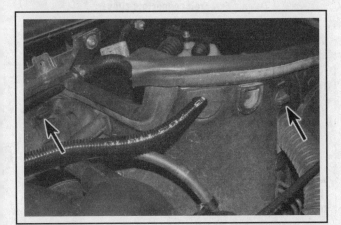

12.5 Pull up the sealing strip, loosen the two fasteners and pull the panel forwards

12.6 Unscrew the Torx screws and remove the heater inlet housing

4   Remove the four screws and pull the cabin filter housing to the front (see illustration).

5   In the left-rear corner of the engine compartment, pull up the sealing strip, remove the two fasteners and pull the trim panel forwards a little (see illustration).

6   Remove the two Torx screws, and lift out the heater intake housing (see illustration).

7   Pry out the plastic caps, remove the two screws, and remove the plastic cover from the injectors (see illustration).

8   Disconnect the fuel regulator vacuum hose.

9   Disconnect the air intake temperature sensor wiring connector, then pull the wiring rail from the fuel injectors.

10 Mark the two oxygen sensor wiring connectors to aid installation, disconnect and release them from the retaining clips.

11 Label the fuel supply and return pipes, then disconnect the pipes at the quick-release connectors.

12 Remove the four bolts and remove the fuel rail complete with the injectors (see illustration).

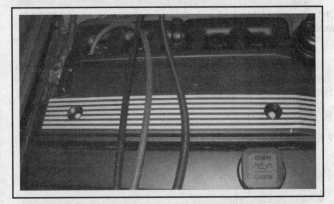

12.7 Remove the screws and detach the plastic cover from the injectors

12.12 Fuel rail mounting bolts

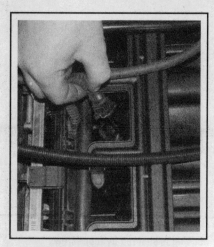

12.20a Disconnect the air intake temperature sensor . . .

12.20b . . . and the VANOS solenoid . . .

12.20c . . . then release the wiring rail connectors clips

13 To remove a fuel injector from the fuel rail, proceed as follows.

a) *Pry off the metal securing clip, using a screwdriver.*

b) *Pull the fuel injector from the fuel rail.*

➡**Note: Whether you're replacing an injector or a leaking O-ring, it's a good idea to remove all the injectors from the fuel rail and replace all the O-rings.**

14 Lightly lubricate the fuel injector O-rings with a little petroleum jelly, or acid-free grease.

✳✳ CAUTION:

Do not use silicone grease; it will clog the injectors.

15 Reinstall the injectors to the fuel rail, and retain them in place with the clips pushed into the grooves.

16 Further installation is a reversal of removal.

M54 engines

◆ **Refer to illustrations 12.20a, 12.20b, 12.20c and 12.21**

17 Proceed as described in Paragraphs 2 to 6.

18 Pry out the plastic caps, undo the two screws, and remove the plastic cover from over the injectors (see illustration 12.7).

19 Mark the two oxygen sensor wiring connectors to aid installation, disconnect and release them from the retaining clips.

20 Disconnect the air intake temperature sensor wiring connector,

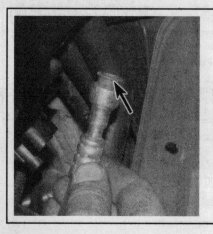

12.21 Depress the collar and disconnect the fuel supply hose

the VANOS solenoid wiring connector, and release the retaining clips and pull the wiring rail from the fuel injectors (see illustrations).

21 Disconnect the fuel supply pipe at the quick-release connector (see illustration).

22 Unscrew the four screws and remove the fuel rail complete with the injectors (see illustration 12.12).

23 To remove a fuel injector from the fuel rail, proceed as follows.

a) *Pry off the metal securing clip, using a screwdriver.*

b) *Pull the fuel injector from the fuel rail.*

➡**Note: Whether you're replacing an injector or a leaking O-ring, it's a good idea to remove all the injectors from the fuel rail and replace all the O-rings.**

24 Lightly lubricate the fuel injector O-rings with a little petroleum jelly or acid-free grease.

✳✳ CAUTION:

Do not use silicone grease; it will clog the injectors.

25 Reinstall the injectors to the fuel rail, and retain them in place with the clips pushed into the grooves.

26 Further installation is a reversal of removal.

FUEL PRESSURE REGULATOR

✳✳ WARNING:

Refer to the *Warning* in Section 1 before proceeding.

➡**Note: On 2003 and later 325i models with an M56 engine, the fuel pressure regulator is sealed within the fuel tank and cannot be serviced. Fuel tank replacement is necessary if the regulator is found to be defective; refer to Section 1 of this chapter for more information.**

27 Depressurize the fuel system as described in Section 8, then disconnect the cable from the negative battery terminal (see Chapter 5, Section 1).

M52TU engines

◆ **Refer to illustration 12.30**

28 To allow sufficient clearance, remove the heater/ventilation inlet

air ducting from the rear of the engine compartment as follows.

a) *Rotate the three fasteners 90° counterclockwise and remove the cabin filter cover from the rear of the engine compartment. Pull the filter forward and remove it.*

b) *Undo the four retaining clips and thread the cable out of the ducting (see illustration 12.3).*

c) *Unscrew the four screws and pull the filter housing forwards and remove it (see illustration 12.4).*

d) *Unscrew the two screws and remove the inlet ducting upwards ad out of the engine compartment (see illustration 12.6).*

29 Pry up the two caps, undo the screws and remove the plastic cover from above the fuel rail.

30 Pull the vacuum hose from the fuel regulator (see illustration).

31 Remove the circlip, then twist and pull the regulator from the fuel rail.

32 Before installation, check the O-rings, and replace if necessary.

33 Installation is a reversal of removal, bearing in mind the following points.

a) *Ensure that the regulator is pushed firmly into position in the end of the fuel rail.*

b) *Make sure that the circlip correctly engages with the recess in the fuel rail.*

c) *On completion, pressurize the fuel system (reinstall the fuel pump fuse and switch on the ignition) and check for leaks before starting the engine.*

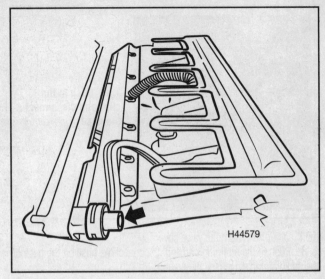

12.30 Pull the vacuum hose from the regulator

M54 engines

34 On these engines, the regulator is integral with the fuel filter assembly. If defective, replace the complete filter housing (see Chapter 1).

---

13 Manifolds - removal and installation

INTAKE MANIFOLD

▸ **Refer to illustrations 13.3, 13.6, 13.9a and 13.9b**

➡**Note: On vehicles with the M56 engine, fuel rail removal requires special tools and expertise that may only be available at a BMW dealership. Removal of the intake manifold requires fuel rail removal; see Section 1 for more details.**

1 To allow sufficient clearance, remove the heater/ventilation inlet air ducting from the rear of the engine compartment as follows.

a) *Rotate the three fasteners 90° counterclockwise and remove the cabin filter cover from the rear of the engine compartment. Pull the filter forward and remove it.*

b) *Undo the four retaining clips and thread the cable out of the ducting (see illustration 12.3).*

c) *Unscrew the four screws and pull the filter housing forwards and remove it (see illustration 12.5).*

d) *Pull up the rubber strip, rotate the two fasteners counterclockwise, and move the dividing panel in the left-hand corner of the engine compartment forward a little (see illustration 12.5).*

e) *Undo the two screws and remove the inlet ducting upwards and out of the engine compartment (see illustration 12.6).*

2 Depressurize the fuel system (see Section 8), then disconnect the cable from the negative terminal of the battery (see Chapter 5, Section 1). Remove the fuel rail and injectors (see Section 12).

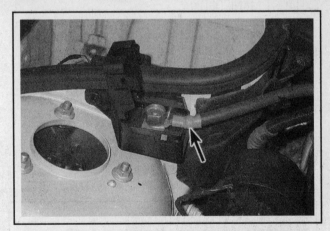

13.3 Disconnect the starter motor supply lead from the engine compartment terminal

➡**Note: For M56 engine models, refer to the note at the beginning of this section.**

3 Open the jump-starting connection point on the right-hand side of the engine compartment, then disconnect the starter motor supply lead (see illustration).

4 Disconnect the VANOS solenoid wiring connector at the left-front side of the cylinder head (if not already done so).

5 Squeeze together the sides of the locking collar and disconnect

13.6 Push in the clip, and disconnect the hose

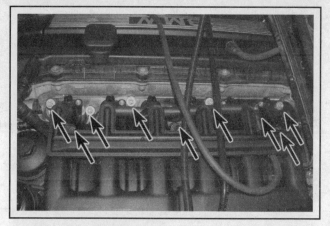

13.9a Intake manifold nuts

the breather hose from the valve cover.

6 Push in the retaining clip and disconnect the hose on the base of the tank venting valve (see illustration).

7 Note their installed positions, then release any wiring harness(s) from the retaining clips on the manifold and support bracket (under the manifold).

8 To disconnect the power brake booster vacuum hose above the manifold, cut off the hose clamp with a pair of side-cutters, and pull the plastic tube from the rubber hose.

9 Remove the nuts securing the manifold to the cylinder head, and the nut securing the manifold support bracket to the cylinder block (under the manifold), and remove the manifold from the cylinder head. As the manifold is withdrawn, feed the starter motor cable through the manifold, and on M54 engines disconnect the fuel pressure regulator vacuum hose (see illustrations). Recover the seals.

10 Check the condition of the seals and replace if necessary.

11 Installation is a reversal of removal.

EXHAUST MANIFOLD

12 To allow sufficient clearance, remove the heater/ventilation inlet air ducting from the rear of the engine compartment as follows.

   a) *Rotate the three fasteners 90° counterclockwise and remove the cabin filter cover from the rear of the engine compartment. Pull the filter forward and remove it.*

   b) *Undo the four retaining clips and thread the cable out of the ducting (see illustration 12.3).*

   c) *Unscrew the four screws and pull the filter housing forwards and remove it (see illustration 12.4).*

   d) *Undo the two screws and remove the inlet ducting upwards and out of the engine compartment (see illustration 12.6).*

13 Raise the front of the vehicle and support it securely on jackstands. Remove the screws and remove the engine splash shield.

14 Remove the front axle reinforcement plate/bar bolts (see Chapter 2, Section 12). Discard the bolts, new ones must be installed.

15 Attach an engine hoist or engine support fixture to the lifting eye at the front of the cylinder head and take the weight off the engine.

16 Working underneath the vehicle, remove the right-hand engine mounting complete with support arm.

17 Pry out the plastic caps, remove the two screws, and remove the plastic cover from the over the injectors.

18 Trace back the wiring from the oxygen sensor(s), and disconnect the wiring connectors. Label the connectors to ensure correct installation. Unclip the cable harness from any retainers on the manifolds.

19 Remove the nuts/bolts and separate the exhaust pipe from the manifold.

13.9b Remove the manifold support bracket nut

20 Using the engine hoist, raise the engine approximately 1/4-inch (6 mm).

21 Starting with the front exhaust manifold, remove the nuts and maneuver the manifold from the engine compartment (see illustration). Take great care not to damage the oxygen sensor installed to the manifold. Discard the gasket.

13.21 Withdraw the front exhaust manifold from the cylinder head

22 Remove the nuts and remove the rear exhaust manifold. Again take great care not to damage the oxygen sensor. Discard the gasket.

23 Installation is a reversal of removal, noting the following points:

 a) *Apply some anti-seize high-temperature grease to the manifold studs.*

 b) *Always replace the manifold gaskets.*
 c) *Tighten the manifold nuts to the torque listed in this Chapter's Specifications.*
 d) *Tighten the front axle reinforcement plate bolts to the torque listed in the Chapter 2A Specifications.*

14 Exhaust system - removal and installation

➡**Note: New exhaust front section-to-manifold gaskets and securing nuts will be required on installation.**

REMOVAL

1 Raise the vehicle and support securely on jackstands. Remove the screws and remove the engine splash shield.

2 Unscrew the fasteners and disconnect the front section of the exhaust from the manifold. Recover the gasket (see illustration).

3 Unscrew the clamp bolt securing the two halves of the transmission exhaust mounting bracket together, then unscrew the clamp pivot bolt, and pivot the clamp halves away from the exhaust system (see illustration).

4 Unscrew the bolts and remove the reinforcement plates from across the transmission tunnel. Note that the rear reinforcement plate is attached to the exhaust system by rubber mounts (see illustration).

5 Slide the rear exhaust mounting rubber from the brackets on the exhaust system.

6 Withdraw the complete exhaust system from under the vehicle.

7 To remove the heat shield, remove the nuts and bolts, then lower it to the ground.

INSTALLATION

8 Installation is a reversal of removal, bearing in mind the following points.

 a) *Use new gaskets when reconnecting the exhaust front section to the manifold. Also use new nuts, and coat the threads of the new*

14.2 Remove the exhaust front section-to-manifold nuts

 nuts with copper grease.
 b) *Check the position of the tailpipes in relation to the cut-out in the rear valence, and if necessary adjust the exhaust mountings to give sufficient clearance between the system and the valence.*
 c) *Once the mountings have been reconnected and tightened, loosen the two nuts and bolts securing the exhaust mounting bracket to the transmission bracket, and if necessary slide the bracket within the elongated holes to release any sideways tension on the system. Once the system is correctly positioned, tighten the nuts and bolts.*

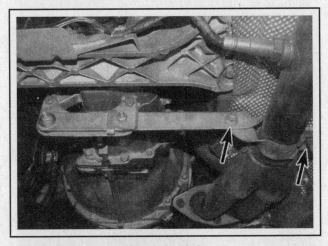

14.3 Exhaust clamp bolt and pivot bolt

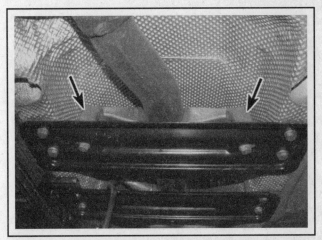

14.4 The rear reinforcement plate is secured to the exhaust by rubber mounts

Specifications

System type

M52TU 6-cylinder engines	DME (Digital Motor Electronics) MS42 engine management
M54 6-cylinder engines	DME (Digital Motor Electronics) MS43 engine management
M56 6-cylinder engines	DME (Digital Motor Electronics) MS45.1 engine management

Fuel system data

Fuel pump type	Electric, immersed in tank
Fuel pressure regulator rating	50.7 ± 2.9 psi (3.5 ± 0.2 bar)
Specified idle speed	Not adjustable - controlled by ECM

Torque specifications

	Ft-lbs (unless otherwise indicated)	Nm
Exhaust manifold nuts*		
M6 nuts	84 in-lbs	10
M7 nuts	15	20
M8 nuts	16	22
Front axle reinforcement plate bolts	See Chapter 2A	
Fuel rail-to-inlet manifold bolts	84 in-lbs	10
Fuel tank mounting bolts	17	23
Fuel tank retaining strap bolts	72 in-lbs	8
Inlet manifold nuts:		
M6 nuts	84 in-lbs	10
M7 nuts	132 in-lbs	15
M8 nuts	16	22

*Do not re-use

Section

Reference to other Chapters

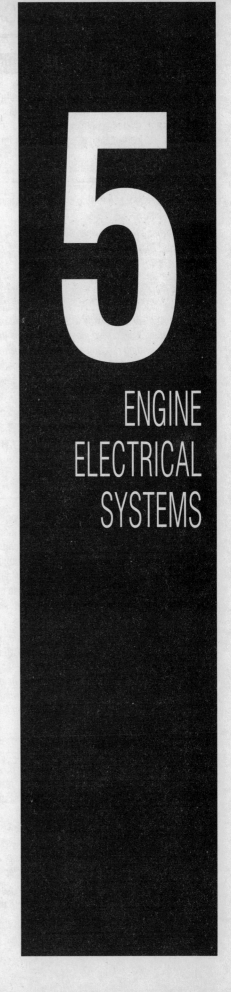

5

ENGINE ELECTRICAL SYSTEMS

1 General information, precautions and battery disconnection

The engine electrical systems include all ignition, charging and starting components. Because of their engine-related functions, these components are covered separately from body electrical devices such as the lights, the instruments, etc. (which you'll find in Chapter 12).

PRECAUTIONS

Always observe the following precautions when working on the electrical system:

a) *Be extremely careful when servicing engine electrical components. They are easily damaged if checked, connected or handled improperly.*

b) *Never leave the ignition switched on for long periods of time when the engine is not running.*

c) *Never disconnect the battery cables while the engine is running.*

d) *Maintain correct polarity when connecting battery cables from another vehicle during jump starting - see the "Booster battery (jump) starting" section at the front of this manual.*

e) *Always disconnect the cable from the negative battery terminal before working on the electrical system, but read the following battery disconnection procedure first.*

It's also a good idea to review the safety-related information regarding the engine electrical systems located in the "Safety first!" section at the front of this manual, before beginning any operation included in this Chapter.

BATTERY DISCONNECTION

Some systems on the vehicle require battery power to be available at all times, either to maintain continuous operation (alarm system, power door locks, etc.), or to maintain control unit memory (radio station presets, Powertrain Control Module and other control units). When the battery is disconnected, the power that maintains these systems is cut. So, before you disconnect the battery, please note the following points to ensure that there are no unforeseen consequences of this action:

a) *The radio is equipped with pre-set selections that will be erased once the battery is disconnected. Record all the programs and stations before disconnecting the battery.*

b) *When the battery is disconnected, the engine management system's Electronic Control Module (ECM) will lose some diagnostic trouble codes. Check for trouble codes after the proper drive cycle (see Chapter 6).*

c) *When the battery is disconnected, the on-board instrument panel module (computer) will lose programmed information and clock time. It will be necessary to re-set all the driver's information (refer to owner's manual). On Z4 models, reactivate the sliding sunroof and the AFS system (electric assisted steering), if equipped (see owner's manual).*

d) *On a vehicle with power door locks, it's a wise precaution to remove the key from the ignition and to keep it with you, so that it does not get locked inside if the power door locks should engage accidentally when the battery is reconnected!*

Devices known as "memory-savers" can be used to avoid some of these problems. Precise details vary according to the device used. The typical memory saver is plugged into the cigarette lighter and is connected to a spare battery. Then the vehicle battery can be disconnected from the electrical system. The memory saver will provide sufficient current to maintain audio unit security codes, ECM memory, etc. and will provide power to "always hot" circuits such as the clock and radio memory circuits.

✳✳ WARNING 1:

Some memory savers deliver a considerable amount of current in order to keep vehicle systems operational after the main battery is disconnected. If you're using a memory saver, make sure that the circuit concerned is actually open before servicing it.

✳✳ WARNING 2:

If you're going to work near any of the airbag system components, the battery MUST be disconnected and a memory saver must NOT be used. If a memory saver is used, power will be supplied to the airbag, which means that it could accidentally deploy and cause serious personal injury.

✳✳ WARNING 3:

Some Z4 models are equipped with a dual battery system. The negative battery terminal on both batteries must be disconnected to properly deactivate the vehicle's battery power.

To disconnect the battery for service procedures requiring power to be cut from the vehicle, remove the battery cover (see Section 3), loosen the cable clamp nut and disconnect the cable from the negative battery post. Isolate the cable end to prevent it from coming into accidental contact with the battery post.

REPROGRAMMING AFTER COMPONENT REPLACEMENT

These vehicles are equipped with systems that require reprogramming after the battery has been disconnected and components in that system have been replaced or reinstalled. For example, independent systems such as the Integrated Heating Cooling Climate Control (IHKA) system require that the control module be programmed after installation. A BMW scan tool can access the software for the IHKA system to activate the module.

These models are equipped with the Central Body Electronic (ZKE-V) system. Each individual system is linked to a centralized control module that allows efficient and accurate troubleshooting. This control module governs the windshield wipers and washers, the central locking and anti-theft system, the power windows, the interior lights, the alarm system and the electronic consumer sleep mode. If any of the components in this system are replaced or re-installed, it will be necessary to reprogram the Controller Area Network (CAN) module.

All these systems will require a BMW scan tool to reactivate or reprogram. In the event the vehicle's electronic systems are repaired, have the vehicle checked and reprogrammed by a dealer service department or other qualified automotive repair facility.

2   Battery - emergency jump starting

Refer to the *Booster battery (jump) starting* procedure at the front of this manual.

3   Battery - check and replacement

✳✳ WARNING 1:

Always disconnect the cable from the negative battery terminal FIRST and hook it up LAST or the battery may be shorted by the tool being used to loosen the cable clamps.

✳✳ WARNING 2:

Some Z4 models are equipped with a dual battery system. The negative battery terminal on both batteries must be disconnected to properly deactivate the vehicle's battery power.

CHECK

◆ **Refer to illustrations 3.2 and 3.3**

➡**Note: The battery's surface charge must be removed before accurate voltage measurements can be made. Turn on the high beams for ten seconds, then turn them off and let the vehicle stand for two minutes.**

1   Remove the battery cover (see Section 3). Disconnect the negative battery cable, then the positive cable from the battery(ies) (see Section 1).

2   Check the battery state of charge. Visually inspect the indicator eye on the top of the battery; if the indicator eye is black in color, charge the battery as described in Chapter 1. If the indicator eye is yellow in color, the battery is defective. Replace the battery. Next perform an open voltage circuit test using a digital voltmeter (see illustration). Touch the negative probe of the voltmeter to the negative terminal of the battery and the positive probe to the positive terminal of the battery. The battery voltage should be 11.5 to 12.5 volts or slightly above. If the voltage is less than specified, charge the battery before proceeding to the next test. Do not proceed with the battery load test unless the battery charge is correct.

3   Perform a battery load test. An accurate check of the battery condition can only be performed with a load tester (available at most auto parts stores). This test evaluates the ability of the battery to operate the starter and other accessories during periods of high current draw. Hook up a special load tester to the battery terminals (see illustration). Maintain the load on the battery for 15 seconds or less and observe that the battery voltage does not drop below 9.6 volts. If the battery condition is weak or defective, the tool will indicate this condition immediately.

➡**Note: Cold temperatures will cause the voltage readings to drop slightly. Follow the chart given in the tool manufacturer's instructions to compensate for cold climates. Minimum load voltage for freezing temperatures (32-degrees F) should be approximately 9.1 volts.**

REPLACEMENT

◆ **Refer to illustrations 3.5 and 3.6**

➡**Note: The 3 series convertible models are equipped with a battery designed to withstand extreme vehicle vibration. Replace the battery in convertibles only with this specific vibration-resistant battery. Consult with a dealer parts department or other qualified auto parts store.**

4   Remove the floor and right-side trim panels in the trunk.

✳✳ WARNING:

Some Z4 models are equipped with a dual battery system. The negative battery terminal on both batteries must be disconnected to properly deactivate the vehicle's battery power.

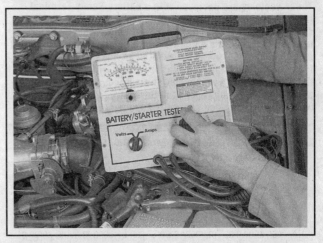

3.2 To test the open circuit voltage of the battery, touch the black probe of the voltmeter to the negative terminal and the red probe to the positive terminal of the battery; a fully charged battery should be about 12.6 volts

3.3 Some battery load testers (like this one) are equipped with an ammeter that allows you to vary the amount of the load on the battery (a less expensive tester only has a load switch that puts the battery under a fixed load)

3.5 Unscrew the fasteners and remove the tray for access to the battery

5   Remove the battery cover (see illustration).

6   Disconnect the cable(s) from the negative battery terminal(s) first, then *(and only then!)* disconnect the cable(s) from the positive battery terminal(s) (see illustration).

7   Remove the battery hold-down clamp nuts (see illustration 3.6) and remove the hold-down clamp.

8   Lift out the battery. Be careful - it's heavy.

➡Note: Battery straps and handlers are available at most auto parts stores for a reasonable price. They make it easier to remove and carry the battery.

9   While the battery is out, inspect the area under the battery for corrosion. If corrosion is present, clean the deposits from the metal with a solution of warm water and baking soda to prevent further corrosion.

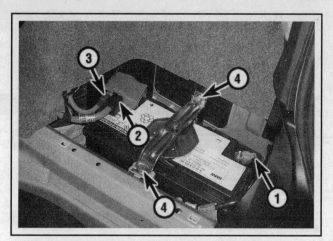

3.6 Battery mounting details (3 series BMW shown - others similar)

1   *Negative cable clamp (always disconnect this one first and hook it up last)*
2   *Battery Safety Terminal (BST) (cable clamp under cover)*
3   *Positive battery cable to main harness fuse box*
4   *Hold-down cable clamp bolt/nut*

➡Note: 3 series convertible models are equipped with shock-proof mounts to prevent excessive vibration to the battery.

10   If you are replacing the battery, make sure you get one that's identical, with the same dimensions, amperage rating, cold cranking rating, etc.

11   Installation is the reverse of removal. Be sure to connect the positive cable(s) first and the negative cable(s) last.

4   Battery cables - check and replacement

▶ **Refer to illustration 4.4**

❊❊ **WARNING:**

These vehicles are equipped with a Battery Safety Terminal (BST) device incorporated into to the battery positive cable's clamp. The BST incorporates a pyrotechnic device that automatically disconnects battery power to the engine compartment electrical components in the event of an impact of sufficient force to deploy the airbags. Battery power will be available to the exterior lights and the interior electrical components. If the positive cable clamp requires replacement, be sure to replace it with a genuine replacement part, not a generic cable clamp.

➡Note: To gain access to the battery, refer to Section 3.

1   Periodically inspect the entire length of each battery cable for damage, cracked or burned insulation and corrosion. Poor battery cable connections can cause starting problems and decreased engine performance.

2   Inspect the cable-to-terminal connections at the ends of the cables for cracks, loose wire strands and corrosion. The presence of white, fluffy deposits under the insulation at the cable terminal connection means that the cable is corroded and should be replaced. Also inspect the battery posts for distortion and corrosion. If they're corroded, clean them up as described in Chapter 1.

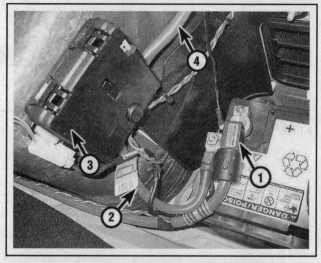

4.4 Positive battery cable details

1   *Positive battery cable with the Battery Safety Terminal (BST)*
2   *Positive battery cable to the main harness fuse box*
3   *Main harness fuse box*
4   *Positive battery cable leading to the engine compartment*

3   When removing the cables, always disconnect the cable from the negative battery terminal first and hook it up last, or you might accidentally short out the battery with the tool you're using to loosen the cable clamps. Even if you're only replacing the cable for the positive terminal, be sure to disconnect the negative cable from the battery first (see Section 1).

4   Disconnect the old cables from the battery, then trace each cable to its opposite end and disconnect it (see illustration). Be sure to note the routing of each cable before disconnecting it to ensure correct installation. Separate the starter cable from the other wiring. Then, after you've installed the new starter cable, carefully bunch the wiring - including the starter cable - back together again. Tape it to hold it together tightly, re-cover it with the conduit, then finish taping all exposed wiring.

5   When purchasing battery cables, *take the old one(s) with you when buying new cables*. It is vitally important that you replace the cables with identical parts.

6   Clean the threads of the solenoid or ground connection with a wire brush to remove rust and corrosion. Apply a light coat of battery terminal corrosion inhibitor or petroleum jelly to the threads to prevent future corrosion.

7   Attach the cable to the solenoid or ground connection and tighten the mounting nut/bolt securely.

8   Before connecting a new cable to the battery make sure that it reaches the battery post without having to be stretched.

9   Connect the cable to the positive battery terminal first, then connect the ground cable to the negative battery terminal (see Section 1).

5   Ignition system - general information

✳✳ WARNING:

Because of the high voltage generated by the ignition system, be extremely careful when performing any procedure involving ignition components.

GENERAL INFORMATION

The ignition system is controlled by the engine management system (see Chapter 6), known as DME (Digital Motor Electronics). The DME system controls all ignition and fuel injection functions using a central ECM (Electronic Control Module).

The ignition timing is based on inputs provided to the ECM by various sensors supplying information on engine load, engine speed, coolant temperature and inlet air temperature (see Chapter 6).

Some engines are equipped with knock sensors to detect knocking (also known as pinging or detonation). The knock sensors are sensi-
tive to vibration and detect the knocking which occurs when a cylinder starts to detonate. The knock sensor provides a signal to the ECM which in turn retards the ignition advance setting until the knocking ceases.

A distributorless ignition system is used, with a separate ignition coil for each cylinder. No distributor is used, and the coils provide the high voltage signal directly to each spark plug.

The ECM uses the inputs from the various sensors to calculate the required ignition advance and the coil charging time.

PRECAUTIONS

Refer to the precautions in Section 1.

Testing of ignition system components should be entrusted to a BMW dealer or other qualified repair shop. Improvised testing techniques are time-consuming and run the risk of damaging the engine management ECM.

6   Ignition coil(s) - removal and installation

REMOVAL

▶ **Refer to illustrations 6.5, 6.6, 6.7, 6.8 and 6.9**

1   Each spark plug is fed by its own coil, and the coils are mounted directly on top of the spark plugs, in the valve cover.

2   Ensure the ignition is switched off.

3   Remove the engine oil filler cap.

4   Remove the in-cabin air filter (see Chapter 1) and the heater/ventilation inlet air ducting from the rear of the engine compartment (see Chapter 2A, Section 4).

5   Pry up the plastic caps, remove the retaining screws, and remove the plastic cover from above the injectors (see illustration).

6.5 Unscrew the bolts and remove the plastic cover from above the injectors

6.6 Pry up the caps, remove the nuts, and remove the cover

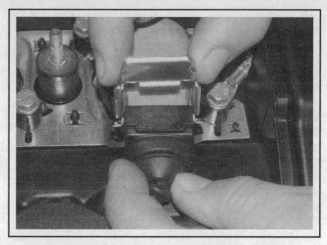

6.7 Lift the clip and disconnect the electrical connector

6   Remove the plastic cover from the top of the cylinder head cover. To remove the cover, pry out the cover plates (see illustration) and unscrew the two securing nuts, then lift and pull the cover forwards. Manipulate the cover over the oil filler neck.

7   Lift the securing clip, and disconnect the electrical connector from the relevant coil (see illustration). If all the coils are to be removed, disconnect all the connectors, then unscrew the nut securing the coil wiring ground lead to the stud on the front of the timing chain cover - the wiring harness can then be unclipped from the camshaft cover and moved to one side.

8   Unscrew the two coil securing bolts, noting the locations of any ground leads and/or brackets secured by the bolts (see illustration). Note that the coil connectors are spring-loaded, so the top of the coil will lift as the bolts are unscrewed.

9   Pull the coil from the valve cover and spark plug, and withdraw it from the engine (see illustration).

Installation

10   Installation is a reversal of removal, but ensure that any ground leads and brackets are in position as noted before removal.

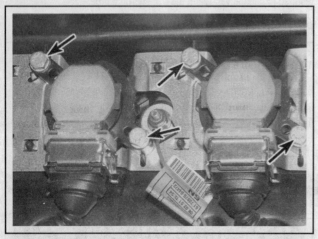

6.8 Remove the coil bolts

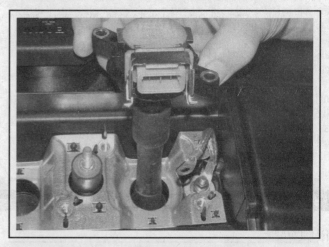

6.9 Lift the ignition coil from the cylinder head

7   Knock sensor - removal and installation

REMOVAL

▶ **Refer to illustration 7.6**

1   Two knock sensors are used, bolted to the left-hand side of the cylinder block. One sensor detects knocking in Numbers 1 to 3 cylinders, and the other sensor detects knocking in Numbers 4 to 6 cylinders.

2   Disconnect the cable from the negative terminal of the battery (see Section 1).

3   Remove the intake manifold (see Chapter 4).

4   Locate the sensor connector bracket which is located beneath the idle speed control valve.

✳✳ **WARNING:**

If both knock sensors are to be removed, mark the wiring connectors to ensure correct installation. Incorrect reconnection may result in engine damage.

5   Unclip the connector from the retaining clip, and disconnect the sensor wiring connector(s).

7.6 The knock sensors are located just below the cylinder head on the engine block

6   Unscrew the retaining bolt and remove the knock sensor, noting the routing of the wiring. The sensor for cylinders 1 to 3 is located beneath the temperature sensors in the cylinder head (see illustration).

The sensor for cylinders 4 to 6 is located to the rear of the sensor wiring connector bracket.

INSTALLATION

7   Commence installation by thoroughly cleaning the mating faces of the sensor and the cylinder block.
8   Install the sensor to the cylinder block, tightening the securing bolt to the torque listed in this Chapter's Specifications.
9   Route the wiring as noted before removal, then reconnect the connector(s), and clip the connector to the bracket, ensuring that the connectors are positioned as noted before removal.

❋❋ WARNING:

Ensure that the wiring connectors are correctly connected as noted before removal. If the connectors are incorrectly connected mixed up), engine damage may result.

10 Install the intake manifold (see Chapter 4).

8   Charging system - testing

1   If the ignition warning light fails to illuminate when the ignition is switched on, first check the alternator wiring connections for security. If satisfactory, check that the warning light bulb has not blown, and that the bulb holder is secure in its location in the instrument panel. If the light still fails to illuminate, check the continuity of the warning light feed wire from the alternator to the bulb holder. If all is satisfactory, the alternator is at fault and should be replaced or taken to an auto-electrician for testing and repair.
2   If the ignition warning light illuminates when the engine is running, stop the engine and check that the drivebelt is correctly tensioned (see Chapter 1) and that the alternator connections are secure. If all is so far satisfactory, have the alternator checked by an automotive electrician for testing and repair.
3   If the alternator output is suspect even though the warning light

functions correctly, the regulated voltage may be checked as follows.
4   Connect a voltmeter across the battery terminals and start the engine.
5   Increase the engine speed until the voltmeter reading remains steady; the reading should be at least 12.66 volts, and no more than 14.2 volts.
6   Switch on as many electrical accessories as possible (headlights, heated rear window and heater blower, etc.), and check that the alternator maintains the regulated voltage at around 13 to 14 volts.
7   If the regulated voltage is not as stated, the fault may be due to worn alternator brushes, weak brush springs, a faulty voltage regulator, a faulty diode, a severed phase winding or worn or damaged slip-rings. The alternator should be replaced or taken to an automotive electrician for testing and repair.

9   Alternator - removal and installation

REMOVAL

▶ **Refer to illustrations 9.7 and 9.8**

1   Disconnect the cable(s) from the negative battery terminal(s) (see Section 1).
2   Remove the air filter housing (see Chapter 4) and the mass airflow (MAF) sensor (see Chapter 6).
3   Remove the engine cooling fan (see Chapter 3). On automatic transmission models, remove the cooling fan and viscous coupling.
4   Remove the drivebelt (see Chapter 1).
5   Reach beneath the alternator and pull the air cooling hose down and off of the alternator rear cover.
6   Remove the alternator cover rear mounting nuts and the rear cover.
7   Remove the fasteners and disconnect the wiring from the rear of the alternator (see illustration).

9.7 To disconnect the alternator wiring, remove the rubber cover, unscrew the nut then unplug the connector

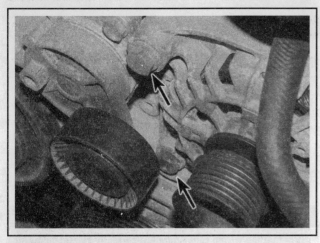

9.8 Alternator mounting bolts

8 Remove the upper and lower alternator securing bolts (see illustration).

9 Withdraw the alternator from the engine.

INSTALLATION

10 Installation is a reversal of removal, bearing in mind the following points.

a) *When installing the tensioner idler pulley, ensure that the lug on the rear of the pulley assembly engages with the corresponding cut-out in the mounting bracket.*

b) *Install the all parts in the reverse order of removal.*

10 Alternator - testing and overhaul

If the alternator is thought to be suspect, it should be removed from the vehicle and taken to an automotive electrician for testing. Most automotive electricians will be able to supply and replace brushes at a reasonable cost. However, check on the cost of repairs before proceeding as it may prove more economical to obtain a new or exchange alternator.

11 Starting system - testing

1 If the starter motor fails to operate when the ignition key is turned to the appropriate position, the following possible causes may be to blame.

a) *The battery is faulty.*

b) *The electrical connections between the switch, solenoid, battery and starter motor are somewhere failing to pass the necessary current from the battery through the starter to ground.*

c) *The solenoid is faulty.*

d) *The starter motor is mechanically or electrically defective.*

2 To check the battery, switch on the headlights. If they dim after a few seconds, this indicates that the battery is discharged - recharge or replace the battery. If the headlights glow brightly, operate the ignition switch and observe the lights. If they dim, then this indicates that current is reaching the starter motor, therefore the fault must lie in the starter motor. If the lights continue to glow brightly (and no clicking sound can be heard from the starter motor solenoid), this indicates that there is a fault in the circuit or solenoid - see following paragraphs. If the starter motor turns slowly when operated, but the battery is in good condition, then this indicates that either the starter motor is faulty, or there is considerable resistance somewhere in the circuit.

3 If a fault in the circuit is suspected, disconnect the battery leads (including the ground connection to the body), the starter/solenoid wiring and the engine/transmission ground strap. Thoroughly clean the connections, and reconnect the leads and wiring, then use a voltmeter or test lamp to check that full battery voltage is available at the battery positive lead connection to the solenoid, and that the ground is sound. Apply petroleum jelly around the battery terminals to prevent corrosion - corroded connections are amongst the most frequent causes of electrical system faults.

4 If the battery and all connections are in good condition, check the circuit by disconnecting the wire from the solenoid blade terminal. Connect a voltmeter or test lamp between the wire end and a good ground, and check that the wire is live when the ignition switch is turned to the 'start' position. If it is, then the circuit is sound - if not the circuit wiring can be checked as described in Chapter 12.

5 The solenoid contacts can be checked by connecting a voltmeter or test lamp between the battery positive feed connection on the starter side of the solenoid, and ground. When the ignition switch is turned to the 'start' position, there should be a reading or lighted bulb, as applicable. If there is no reading or lighted bulb, the solenoid is faulty and should be replaced.

6 If the circuit and solenoid are proved sound, the fault must lie in the starter motor. In this event, it may be possible to have the starter motor overhauled by a specialist, but check on the cost of spares before proceeding, as it may prove more economical to obtain a new or exchange motor.

12 Starter motor - removal and installation

REMOVAL

1 Disconnect the cable(s) from the negative battery terminal(s) (see Section 1).v

3 series models

▶ **Refer to illustration 12.5**

➡**Note: The following procedure describes removing the starter from underneath the vehicle. On some models it may be easier to remove the starter from above, after removing the intake manifold. Check your vehicle carefully to asses which method will be more appropriate.**

2 Apply the parking brake, then raise the vehicle and support it securely on jackstands. Remove the engine splash shield (see Chapter 2A).

3 Remove the reinforcement plate/bar from below the engine compartment (see Chapter 2A, Section 12).

➡**Note: The vehicle must not be driven with the reinforcement removed, or damage may result.**

4 Remove the fuel filter and position the fuel lines off to the side to make clearance (see Chapter 4).

5 Note their installed positions, then remove the nuts and disconnect the wiring from the starter motor (see illustration).

6 Using a socket, ratchet and long extension, remove the starter motor mounting bolts from the transmission bellhousing.

7 Pull the starter motor forward and maneuver it downwards.

Z4 models

8 Remove the air filter housing (see Chapter 4).

9 Note their installed positions, then remove the nuts and discon-

12.5 Note their locations, then disconnect the starter motor connectors

nect the wiring from the starter motor.

10 Remove the starter motor mounting bolts from the transmission bellhousing.

11 Lift the starter from the engine compartment.

INSTALLATION

12 Installation is a reversal of removal, noting the following points:

a) *Tighten all nuts/bolts to the specified torque where given.*

b) *On 3 series models, new bolts must be used when installing the underbody reinforcement plate/bar. Tighten the bolts to the torque listed in the Chapter 2A Specifications.*

13 Starter motor - testing and overhaul

If the starter motor is thought to be suspect, it should be removed from the vehicle and taken to an automotive electrician for testing. Most automotive electricians will be able to supply and install brushes at a reasonable cost. However, check on the cost of repairs before proceeding as it may prove more economical to obtain a new or exchange motor.

14 Ignition switch - removal and installation

The ignition switch is integral with the steering column lock, and can be removed as described in Chapter 10.

Specifications

General

Firing order	1-5-3-6-2-4
Battery voltage	
Engine off	12.0 to 12.6 volts
Engine running	Approximately 13.5

Torque specifications	Ft-lbs (unless otherwise indicated)	Nm
Knock sensor retaining bolt	15	20
Starter motor support bracket-to-engine bolts	35	47
Starter motor support bracket-to-starter motor nuts	44 in-lbs	5
Starter motor-to-transmission bolts	35	47

Section

1 General information
2 On Board Diagnostic (OBD) system and trouble codes
3 Emission control systems - component replacement
4 Catalytic converter - general information and precautions
5 Engine management system components - removal and installation

Reference to other Chapters

6

EMISSIONS
AND ENGINE
CONTROL
SYSTEMS

1 General information

▶ **Refer to illustration 1.5**

All models have various built-in fuel system features that help to minimize emissions, including a crankcase emission control system, catalytic converter, and an evaporative emission control system. M52TU and M56 engine models are also equipped with secondary air injection to shorten the catalytic converter warm-up phase.

To prevent pollution of the atmosphere from incompletely burned and evaporating gases, and to maintain good driveability and fuel economy, a number of emission control systems are incorporated. They include the:

Catalytic converter
Evaporative Emissions Control (EVAP) system
Intake Manifold Runner Control
On-Board Diagnostic-II (OBD-II) system
Positive Crankcase Ventilation (PCV) system
Electronic Fuel Injection system (part of the computerized engine control system)
Secondary air injection
Variable Valve Timing (VANOS)

This Chapter includes general descriptions of these and other emissions-related devices and component replacement procedures (where possible) for most of the systems listed above. Before assuming that an emissions control system is malfunctioning, check the fuel and ignition systems carefully. The diagnosis of most emission control devices requires specialized tools, equipment and training. If a procedure is beyond your ability, consult a dealer service department or other repair shop. Remember, the most frequent cause of emissions problems is simply a loose or broken wire or vacuum hose, so always check all hose and wiring connections first.

Pay close attention to any special precautions outlined in this Chapter. It should be noted that the illustrations of the various systems might not exactly match the system installed on your vehicle because of annual changes made by the manufacturer during production and because of running changes made during a model year.

A Vehicle Emissions Control Information (VECI) label (see illustration) is located in the engine compartment, either on the underside of the hood or attached to the radiator support or one of the strut towers. This label specifies the important emissions systems on the vehicle and it provides the important specifications for tune-ups. Part of the VECI label, the Vacuum Hose Routing Diagram, provides a vacuum hose schematic with emissions components identified. When servicing the engine or emissions systems, the VECI label and the vacuum hose routing diagram should always be checked for up-to-date information.

CRANKCASE EMISSION CONTROL

To reduce the emission of unburned hydrocarbons from the crankcase into the atmosphere, the engine is sealed, and the blow-by gases and oil vapor are drawn from the crankcase and the cylinder head cover, through an oil separator, into the intake tract, to be burned by the engine during normal combustion.

Under conditions of high manifold vacuum (idling, deceleration) the gases will be sucked positively out of the crankcase. Under conditions of low manifold vacuum (acceleration, full-throttle running) the gases are forced out of the crankcase by the (relatively) higher crankcase pressure; if the engine is worn, the raised crankcase pressure (due to increased blow-by) will cause some of the flow to return under all manifold conditions.

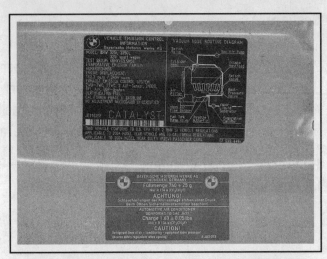

1.5 The Vehicle Emission Control Information (VECI) label specifies the emission-control systems on your vehicle; including important information and a vacuum hose routing diagram

EXHAUST EMISSION CONTROL

To minimize the amount of pollutants which escape into the atmosphere, all models are installed with a catalytic converter in the exhaust system. The system is of the "closed-loop" type; one or two oxygen (lambda) sensors in the exhaust system provides the fuel injection/ignition system ECM with constant feedback, enabling the ECM to adjust the mixture to provide the best possible conditions for the converter to operate.

The oxygen sensor(s) has a built-in heating element, controlled by the ECM, to quickly bring the sensor's tip to an efficient operating temperature. The sensor's tip is sensitive to oxygen, and sends the ECM a varying voltage depending on the amount of oxygen in the exhaust gases. If the intake air/fuel mixture is too rich, the exhaust gases are low in oxygen, so the sensor sends a low-voltage signal. The voltage rises as the mixture weakens and the amount of oxygen in the exhaust gases rises. Peak conversion efficiency of all major pollutants occurs if the intake air/fuel mixture is maintained at the chemically-balanced ratio for the complete combustion of gasoline - 14.7 parts (by weight) of air to 1 part of fuel (the "stoichiometric" ratio). The sensor output voltage alters in a large step at this point, the ECM using the signal change as a reference point, and correcting the intake air/fuel mixture accordingly by altering the fuel injector pulse width (the length of time that the injector is open).

EVAPORATIVE EMISSION CONTROL

To minimize the escape into the atmosphere of unburned hydrocarbons, an evaporative emissions control system is fitted to all models. The fuel tank filler cap is sealed, and a charcoal canister, mounted under the rear of the vehicle, collects the gasoline vapors generated in the tank when the car is parked. The canister stores them until they can be cleared from the canister (under the control of the fuel injection/ignition system ECM) via the purge solenoid valve. When the valve is opened, the fuel vapors pass into the intake tract, to be burned by the engine during normal combustion.

To ensure that the engine runs correctly when it is cold and/or idling, the ECM does not open the purge control valve until the engine has warmed-up and is under load; the valve solenoid is then modulated on and off, to allow the stored vapor to pass into the intake tract.

SECONDARY AIR INJECTION

M52TU and M56 engine models are equipped with a system that is designed to shorten the amount of time the catalytic converter takes to warm-up. In order to function correctly, the catalytic converter needs to be at a temperature of at least 300°C. This temperature level is achieved by the action of the exhaust gases passing through. In order to reduce the catalyst warm-up phase, a secondary air injection pump injects fresh air just behind the exhaust valves in the exhaust manifold. This oxygen rich mixture causes an "afterburning" effect in the exhaust, greatly increasing the gas temperature, and therefore the catalyst temperature. The system is only active during cold starts (up to 91-degees F [33°C] coolant temperature), and only operates for approximately 2 minutes.

2   On Board Diagnostic (OBD) system and trouble codes

SCAN TOOL INFORMATION

♦ **Refer to illustration 2.1**

1   Hand-held scanners are the most powerful and versatile tools for analyzing engine management systems used on later model vehicles (see illustration). Early model scanners handle codes and some diagnostics for many systems. Each brand scan tool must be examined carefully to match the year, make and model of the vehicle you are working on. Often, interchangeable cartridges are available to access the particular manufacturer (Chrysler, Ford, GM, Honda, Toyota etc.). Some manufacturers will specify by continent (Asia, Europe, USA, etc.).

➡**Note: An aftermarket generic scanner should work with any model covered by this manual. Before purchasing a generic scan tool, make sure that it will work properly with the OBD-II system you want to scan. If necessary, of course, you can always have the codes extracted by a dealer service department or an independent repair shop.**

OBD SYSTEM GENERAL DESCRIPTION

2   All models are equipped with the second generation OBD-II system. This system consists of an on-board computer known as an Electronic Control Module (ECM) or a Powertrain Control Module (PCM), and information sensors, which monitor various functions of the engine and send data to the ECM. This system incorporates a series of diagnostic monitors that detect and identify fuel injection and emissions control system faults and store the information in the computer memory. This updated system also tests sensors and output actuators, diagnoses drive cycles, freezes data and clears codes.

3   This powerful diagnostic computer must be accessed using an OBD-II scan tool and the 16-pin Data Link Connector (DLC) located under the driver's dash area. The ECM is located in a protected area of the engine compartment mounted to the firewall. The ECM is the brain of the electronically controlled fuel and emissions systems. It receives data from a number of sensors and other electronic components (switches, relays, etc.). Based on the information it receives, the ECM generates output signals to control various relays, solenoids (i.e. fuel injectors) and other actuators. The ECM is specifically calibrated to optimize the emissions, fuel economy and driveability of the vehicle.

4   It isn't a good idea to attempt diagnosis or replacement of the ECM or emission control components at home while the vehicle is under warranty. Because of a Federally mandated warranty which covers the emissions system components and because any owner-induced damage to the ECM, the sensors and/or the control devices may void this warranty, take the vehicle to a dealer service department if the ECM or a system component malfunctions.

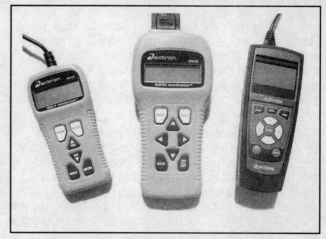

2.1 Scan-tools like these from Actron and AutoXray can provide advanced diagnostic assistance and information regarding your vehicle's engine management system

INFORMATION SENSORS

5   **Brake Pedal Position (BPP) switch** - The BPP switch is located at the top of the brake pedal. It's a normally open switch that closes when the brake pedal is applied and sends a signal to the ECM, which interprets this signal as its cue to disengage the torque converter clutch. The BPP switch is also used to disengage the brake/shift interlock. For information regarding the replacement and adjustment of the BPP switch, refer to Chapter 9.

6   **Camshaft Position (CMP) sensor** - The CMP sensor produces a signal that the ECM uses to identify the number 1 cylinder and to time the firing sequence of the fuel injectors.

7   **Crankshaft Position (CKP) sensor** - The CKP sensor produces a signal that the ECM uses to determine the position of the crankshaft.

8   **Engine Coolant Temperature (ECT) sensor** - The ECT sensor is a thermistor (temperature-sensitive variable resistor) that sends a voltage signal to the ECM, which uses this data to determine the temperature of the engine coolant. The ECT sensor helps the ECM control the air/fuel mixture ratio and ignition timing.

9   **Fuel tank pressure sensor** - The fuel tank pressure sensor measures the fuel tank pressure when the ECM tests the EVAP system, and it's also used to control fuel tank pressure by signaling the EVAP system to purge the tank when the pressure becomes excessive.

10 **Input shaft (mainshaft) speed sensor** - The input shaft speed sensor is located inside the transmission. The ECM uses the signal produced by this sensor for many functions involving the powertrain.

11 **Intake Air Temperature (IAT) sensor** - The IAT sensor monitors the temperature of the air entering the engine and sends a signal to the ECM. The IAT sensor is located at the top of the intake manifold near the center.

12 **Knock sensor(s)** - The knock sensor is a piezoelectric crystal that oscillates in proportion to engine vibration. (The term piezoelectric refers to the property of certain crystals that produce a voltage when subjected to shock.) The oscillation of the piezoelectric crystal produces a voltage output that is monitored by the ECM, which retards the ignition timing when the oscillation exceeds a certain threshold. When the engine is operating normally, the knock sensor oscillates consistently and its voltage signal is steady. When detonation occurs, engine vibration increases, and the oscillation of the knock sensor exceeds a design threshold. (Detonation is an uncontrolled explosion, after the spark occurs at the spark plug, which spontaneously combusts the remaining air/fuel mixture, resulting in a pinging or slapping sound.) If allowed to continue, detonation can damage the engine. The knock sensor is bolted to the engine block.

13 **Manifold Absolute Pressure (MAP) sensor** - The MAP sensor, monitors the pressure or vacuum downstream from the throttle plate, inside the intake manifold. The MAP sensor measures intake manifold pressure and vacuum on the absolute scale, i.e. from zero instead of from sea-level atmospheric pressure (14.7 psi). The MAP sensor converts the absolute pressure into a variable voltage signal that changes with the pressure. The ECM uses this data to determine engine load so that it can alter the ignition advance and fuel enrichment.

14 **Output shaft (countershaft) speed sensor** - The output shaft speed sensor is located inside the transmission. The ECM uses the signal produced by this sensor for many functions involving the powertrain.

15 **Oxygen sensors** - An oxygen sensor generates a small variable voltage signal in proportion to the difference between the oxygen content in the exhaust stream and the oxygen content in the ambient air. The ECM uses this voltage signal to maintain a stoichiometric air/fuel ratio of 14.7:1 by constantly adjusting the on-time of the fuel injectors. There are four oxygen sensors: two upstream sensors (ahead of the catalytic converter) and two downstream oxygen sensors (after the catalyst).

16 **Throttle Position (TP) sensor** - The TP sensor is a potentiometer that receives a constant voltage input from the ECM and sends back a voltage signal that varies in relation to the opening angle of the throttle plate inside the throttle body. This voltage signal tells the ECM when the throttle is closed, half-open, wide open or anywhere in between. The ECM uses this data, along with information from other sensors, to calculate injector pulse width (the interval of time during which an injector solenoid is energized by the ECM). The TP sensor is located on the throttle body, on the end of the throttle plate shaft. The TP sensor is not removable on any model. If it's defective, replace the throttle body.

17 **Transmission range switch** - The transmission range switch is located inside the transmission. It is used only on automatics and functions like a conventional Park/Neutral Position (PNP) switch: it prevents the engine from starting in any gear other than Park or Neutral, and it closes the circuit for the back-up lights when the shift lever is moved to Reverse. The ECM monitors the voltage output signal from the switch, which corresponds to the position of the shift lever. Thus the ECM is able to determine the gear selected and is able to control the operation of the transmission.

18 **Vehicle Speed Input** - The speed signal is obtained by the ABS system and used by the Electronic Control Module (ECM) for various functions in the engine management system.

OUTPUT ACTUATORS

19 **EVAP canister purge valve** - The purge valve is normally closed. But when ordered to do so by the ECM, it allows the fuel vapors that are stored in the EVAP canister to be drawn into the intake manifold, where they're mixed with intake air, then burned along with the normal air/fuel mixture, under certain operating conditions.

20 **Three/two-way valve** - The three/two-way valve is located just ahead of the fuel filter underneath the vehicle and covered by a shield. It is controlled by the ECM and regulates fuel volume going to the fuel rail and injectors.

21 **Fuel injectors** - The fuel injectors spray a very fine mist of fuel into the intake ports where it is mixed with incoming air. The injectors operate like solenoids and are controlled by the ECM. For more information about the injectors, see Chapter 4.

22 **Idle Air Control (IAC) valve** - The IAC valve controls the amount of air allowed to bypass the throttle plate when the throttle plate is at its (nearly closed) idle position. The IAC valve is controlled by the ECM. When the engine is placed under an additional load at idle (running the air conditioning compressor during low-speed maneuvers, for example), the engine can run roughly, stumble and even stall. To prevent this from happening, the ECM opens the IAC valve to increase the idle speed enough to overcome the extra load imposed on the engine. The IAC valve is mounted on the throttle body.

23 **Ignition coils** - There is one ignition coil per spark plug. The coils are located on top of the valve cover, directly over the spark plugs. The ignition coils are under the control of the Electronic Control Module (ECM). There is no separate ignition control module. Instead, coil drivers inside the ECM turn the primary side of the coils on and off. For more information about the ignition coils, see Chapter 5.

24 **Variable Valve Timing (VANOS)** - Variable valve timing is achieved by the use of solenoids and actuators allowing oil pressure to act upon both camshafts (intake and exhaust) to provide a dynamic range of valve timing adjustment. The system is controlled by the ECM and offers many benefits including an increase in performance and fuel economy, lowered emissions (NOx), and smoother idle.

OBTAINING AND CLEARING DIAGNOSTIC TROUBLE CODES (DTCS)

25 All models covered by this manual are equipped with on-board diagnostics. When the ECM recognizes a malfunction in a monitored emission control system, component or circuit, it turns on the Malfunction Indicator Light (MIL) on the dash. This light may read, Check Engine or Service Engine Soon or may just be a symbol depending on when the vehicle was made. The ECM will continue to display the MIL until the problem is fixed and the Diagnostic Trouble Code (DTC) is cleared from the ECM's memory. You'll need a scan tool to access any DTCs stored in the ECM.

26 Before accessing any DTCs stored in the ECM, thoroughly inspect ALL electrical connectors and hoses. Make sure that all electrical connections are tight, clean and free of corrosion. And make

sure that all hoses are correctly connected, fit tightly and are in good condition (no cracks or tears). Also, make sure that the engine is tuned up. A poorly running engine is probably one of the biggest causes of emission-related malfunctions. Often, simply giving the engine a good tune-up will correct the problem.

Accessing the DTCs

▶ **Refer to illustration 2.27**

27 On these models, all of which are equipped with On-Board Diagnostic II (OBD-II) systems, the Diagnostic Trouble Codes (DTCs) can only be accessed with a scan tool. Professional scan tools are expensive, but relatively inexpensive generic scan tools (see illustration 2.1) are available at most auto parts stores. Simply plug the connector of the scan tool into the vehicle's diagnostic connector (see illustration). Follow the instructions included with the scan tool to extract the DTCs.

28 Once you have obtained (and written down) all of the stored DTCs, look them up on the accompanying DTC chart.

29 After troubleshooting the source of each DTC make any necessary repairs or replace the defective component(s).

Clearing the DTCs

30 Clear the DTCs with the scan tool in accordance with the instructions provided by the scan tool's manufacturer.

2.27 The Data Link Connector (DLC) is located under the dash near the left kick panel

DIAGNOSTIC TROUBLE CODES

31 The accompanying tables list several Diagnostic Trouble Codes (DTCs) that can be accessed by the home mechanic. More codes exist for the vehicle by the manufacturer but only a professional scan tool and software (which is quite expensive) can get them.

OBD-II TROUBLE CODES

➡ **Note: Not all trouble codes apply to all models.**

Code	Probable cause
P0011	Camshaft (A) position timing over-advanced or performance problem (Bank 1)
P0012	Camshaft (A) position timing over-retarded or performance problem (Bank 1)
P0014	Camshaft (B) position timing over-advanced or performance problem (Bank 1)
P0015	Camshaft (B) position timing over-retarded or performance problem (Bank 1)
P0030	Upstream oxygen sensor, heater circuit malfunction (Bank 1 Sensor 1)
P0031	Upstream oxygen sensor heater circuit, low voltage input (Bank 1 Sensor 1)
P0032	Upstream oxygen sensor heater circuit, high voltage input (Bank 1 Sensor 2)
P0036	Downstream oxygen sensor, heater circuit malfunction (Bank 1 Sensor 2)
P0037	Downstream oxygen sensor heater circuit, low voltage input (Bank 1 Sensor 2)
P0038	Downstream oxygen sensor heater circuit, high voltage input (Bank 1 Sensor 1)
P0040	Oxygen sensor signal Bank 1 Sensor 1 is crossed with Bank 2 Sensor 1
P0041	Oxygen sensor signal Bank 1 Sensor 2 is crossed with Bank 2 Sensor 2
P0050	Upstream oxygen sensor, heater circuit malfunction (Bank 2 Sensor 1)
P0051	Upstream oxygen sensor heater circuit, low voltage input (Bank 2 Sensor 1)
P0052	Upstream oxygen sensor heater circuit, high voltage input (Bank 2 Sensor 2)
P0056	Downstream oxygen sensor, heater circuit malfunction (Bank 2 Sensor 2)
P0057	Downstream oxygen sensor heater circuit, low voltage input (Bank 2 Sensor 2)

OBD-II TROUBLE CODES (CONTINUED)

➡Note: Not all trouble codes apply to all models.

Code	Probable cause
P0058	Downstream oxygen sensor heater circuit, high voltage input (Bank 2 Sensor 1)
P0101	Mass Air Flow (MAF) sensor circuit range or performance problem
P0102	Mass or Volume Air Flow (MAF) sensor circuit, low input voltage
P0103	Mass or Volume Air Flow (MAF) sensor circuit, high input voltage
P0107	MAP or Barometric pressure sensor circuit, low input voltage
P0108	MAP or Barometric pressure sensor circuit, high input voltage
P0111	Intake Air Temperature (IAT) sensor, range or performance problem
P0112	Intake Air Temperature (IAT) sensor, low input voltage
P0113	Intake Air Temperature (IAT) sensor, high input voltage
P0116	Engine Coolant Temperature (ECT) sensor circuit, range or performance problem
P0117	Engine Coolant Temperature (ECT) sensor circuit, low input voltage
P0118	Engine Coolant Temperature (ECT) sensor circuit, high input voltage
P0120	Throttle Position (TP) sensor, circuit "A" malfunction
P0121	Throttle/pedal position sensor, "A" circuit range or performance problem
P0122	Throttle/pedal position sensor, "A" circuit low voltage input
P0123	Throttle/pedal position sensor, "A" circuit high voltage input
P0125	Insufficient coolant temperature for closed loop fuel control
P0128	Engine Coolant Temperature, insufficient coolant temperature for closed loop
P0130	Upstream oxygen sensor, circuit malfunction (Bank 1 Sensor 1)
P0131	Upstream oxygen sensor circuit, low voltage input (Bank 1 Sensor 1)
P0132	Upstream oxygen sensor circuit, high voltage input (Bank 1 Sensor 1)
P0133	Upstream oxygen sensor circuit, slow response (Bank 1 Sensor 1)
P0134	Upstream oxygen sensor circuit, no activity detected (Bank 1 Sensor 1)
P0135	Upstream oxygen sensor heater, circuit malfunction (Bank 1 Sensor 1)
P0136	Downstream oxygen sensor, circuit malfunction (Bank 1 Sensor 2)
P0137	Downstream oxygen sensor circuit, low voltage input (Bank 1 Sensor 2)
P0138	Downstream oxygen sensor circuit, high voltage input (Bank 1 Sensor 2)
P0139	Downstream oxygen sensor circuit, slow response (Bank 1 Sensor 2)
P0140	Downstream oxygen sensor circuit, no activity detected (Bank 1 Sensor 2)
P0141	Downstream oxygen sensor heater, circuit malfunction (Bank 1 Sensor 2)
P0150	Upstream oxygen sensor, circuit malfunction (Bank 2 Sensor 1)
P0151	Upstream oxygen sensor circuit, low voltage input (Bank 2 Sensor 1)

Code	Probable cause
P0152	Upstream oxygen sensor circuit, high voltage input (Bank 2 Sensor 1)
P0153	Upstream oxygen sensor circuit, slow response (Bank 2 Sensor 1)
P0154	Upstream oxygen sensor circuit, no activity detected (Bank 2 Sensor 1)
P0155	Upstream oxygen sensor heater, circuit malfunction (Bank 2 Sensor 1)
P0156	Downstream oxygen sensor, circuit malfunction (Bank 2 Sensor 2)
P0157	Downstream oxygen sensor circuit, low voltage input (Bank 2 Sensor 2)
P0158	Downstream oxygen sensor circuit, high voltage input (Bank 2 Sensor 2)
P0159	Downstream oxygen sensor circuit, slow response (Bank 2 Sensor 2)
P0160	Downstream oxygen sensor circuit, no activity detected (Bank 2 Sensor 2)
P0161	Downstream oxygen sensor heater, circuit malfunction (Bank 2 Sensor 2)
P0170	Fuel trim malfunction (Bank 1)
P0171	Fuel system too lean (Bank1)
P0172	Fuel system too rich (Bank 1)
P0173	Fuel trim malfunction (Bank 2)
P0174	Fuel system too lean (Bank 2)
P0175	Fuel system too rich (Bank 1)
P0197	Engine oil temperature sensor, low input voltage
P0198	Engine oil temperature sensor, high input voltage
P0201	Cylinder No. 1 fuel injector, circuit malfunction
P0202	Cylinder No. 2 fuel injector, circuit malfunction
P0203	Cylinder No. 3 fuel injector, circuit malfunction
P0204	Cylinder No. 4 fuel injector, circuit malfunction
P0205	Cylinder No. 5 fuel injector, circuit malfunction
P0206	Cylinder No. 6 fuel injector, circuit malfunction
P0221	Throttle/pedal position sensor, "B" circuit range or performance problem
P0222	Throttle/pedal position sensor, "B" circuit low voltage input
P0223	Throttle/pedal position sensor, "B" circuit high voltage input
P0261	Cylinder No. 1 fuel injector circuit, low voltage input
P0262	Cylinder No. 1 fuel injector circuit, high voltage input
P0264	Cylinder No. 2 fuel injector circuit, low voltage input
P0265	Cylinder No. 2 fuel injector circuit, high voltage input
P0267	Cylinder No. 3 fuel injector circuit, low voltage input
P0268	Cylinder No. 3 fuel injector circuit, high voltage input
P0270	Cylinder No. 4 fuel injector circuit, low voltage input

OBD-II TROUBLE CODES (CONTINUED)

➡**Note: Not all trouble codes apply to all models.**

Code	Probable cause
P0271	Cylinder No. 4 fuel injector circuit, high voltage input
P0273	Cylinder No. 5 fuel injector circuit, low voltage input
P0274	Cylinder No. 5 fuel injector circuit, high voltage input
P0276	Cylinder No. 6 fuel injector circuit, low voltage input
P0277	Cylinder No. 6 fuel injector circuit, high voltage input
P0300	Random or multiple cylinder misfires detected
P0301	Cylinder no. 1 misfire detected
P0302	Cylinder no. 2 misfire detected
P0303	Cylinder no. 3 misfire detected
P0304	Cylinder no. 4 misfire detected
P0305	Cylinder no. 5 misfire detected
P0306	Cylinder no. 6 misfire detected
P0313	Misfire detected with low fuel
P0316	Misfire detected at start up (within first 1000 revolutions)
P0325	Knock sensor 1, circuit malfunction (Bank 1)
P0327	Knock sensor 1, low voltage input (Bank 1)
P0328	Knock sensor 1, high voltage input (Bank 1)
P0330	Knock sensor 2, circuit malfunction (Bank 2)
P0332	Knock sensor 2, low voltage input (Bank 2)
P0335	Crankshaft Position (CKP) sensor, circuit "A" malfunction
P0339	Crankshaft Position (CKP) sensor, intermittent "A" circuit
P0340	Camshaft Position (CMP) sensor, circuit "A" malfunction (Bank 1)
P0344	Camshaft Position (CMP) sensor, intermittent "A" circuit (Bank 1)
P0363	Misfire detected ñ fueling disabled
P0365	Camshaft Position (CMP) sensor, "B" circuit malfunction (Bank 1)
P0369	Camshaft Position (CMP) sensor, intermittent "B" circuit (Bank 1)
P0370	Timing Reference High Resolution Signal A
P0385	Crankshaft Position (CKP) sensor, circuit "B" malfunction
P0411	Secondary Air Injection System incorrect flow detected
P0412	Secondary Air Injection switching valve circuit "A" malfunction
P0413	Secondary Air Injection System switching valve open circuit "A"
P0414	Secondary Air Injection System switching valve shorted circuit "A"

Code	Probable cause
P0420	Catalyst system efficiency below threshold (Bank 1)
P0430	Catalyst system efficiency below threshold (Bank 2)
P0440	Evaporative Emission Control (EVAP) system malfunction
P0441 (pre-2002)	Evaporative Emission Control (EVAP) system, incorrect purge flow
P0441 (2002 and later)	Evaporative Emission Control (EVAP) system purge control valve stuck open
P0442	Evaporative Emission Control (EVAP) system, small leak detected
P0443	Evaporative Emission Control (EVAP) system purge control valve, circuit malfunction
P0444	Evaporative Emission Control (EVAP) system, purge control valve circuit open
P0445	Evaporative Emission Control (EVAP) system, purge control valve circuit shorted
P0455	Evaporative Emission Control (EVAP) system, large leak detected
P0456	Evaporative Emission Control (EVAP) system, very small leak detected
P0491	Secondary Air Injection System insufficient flow
P0492	Secondary Air Injection System insufficient flow (Bank 2)
P0500	Vehicle Speed Sensor (VSS), circuit "A" malfunction
P0505	Idle control system malfunction
P0600	Serial Communication Link malfunction
P0601	Powertrain Control Module (PCM), memory checksum error
P0604	PCM Random Access Memory (RAM) error
P0700	Transmission Control Request (MIL Request)

3 Emission control systems - component replacement

➡Note: Emission components are usually covered by a warranty that lasts longer than the bumper-to-bumper warranty (depending also on the state in which the vehicle was first sold). Be sure to consult with a BMW dealership before pursuing any repairs on the emission or fuel controls.

CRANKCASE EMISSION CONTROL

1   The components of this system require no routine attention, other than to check that the hoses are clear and undamaged at regular intervals.

CHARCOAL CANISTER REPLACEMENT

▶ Refer to illustrations 3.3, 3.4a and 3.4b

➡Note: The canister on M56 engine models is stainless steel and uses line fittings. The canister is covered under the emissions warranty for 15 years/150,000 miles - see Chapter 4 for more details.

2   The canister is located under the rear of the vehicle. Jack up the rear and support it securely on jackstands.

3   Remove the screws/expansion rivet, and remove the cover and long plastic panel (if equipped) at the right-hand side of the spare wheel well (see illustration).

3.3 Pry out the expansion rivet and remove the panel

3.4a Squeeze together the sides of the locking collars to disconnect the hoses

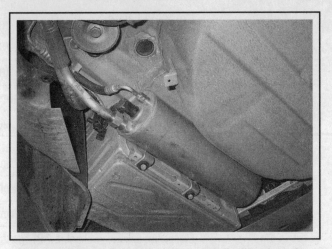

3.4b Use a flare-nut wrench to disconnect the lines from the canister on M56 engine models

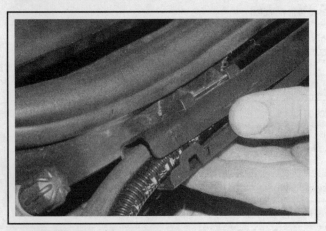

3.7a Unclip the cable ducting

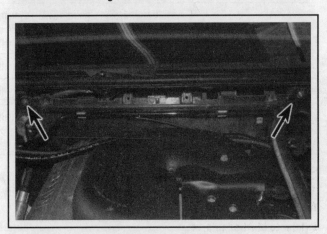

3.7b Unscrew the two Torx screws and remove the inlet housing

4   Disconnect the hoses (or lines) from the canister. If the hoses are secured by plastic locking clips, squeeze the sides of the clips to release them from the connection on the canister. On M56 engine models, use a flare nut wrench to remove the lines from the canister. Note the hose locations to ensure correct installation (see illustrations).

5   Unscrew the securing screws, and withdraw the canister/bracket assembly.

3.8 Disconnect the purge solenoid valve wiring connector

6   Installation is a reversal of removal, but ensure that the hoses are correctly reconnected as noted before removal, and make sure that the hose securing clips are correctly engaged.

PURGE SOLENOID VALVE REPLACEMENT

♦ **Refer to illustrations 3.7a, 3.7b and 3.8**

7   The valve is located under the intake manifold. To allow sufficient clearance, remove the heater/ventilation inlet air ducting from the rear of the engine compartment as follows.

   a) *Rotate the three fasteners 90° counterclockwise and remove the cabin filter cover from the rear of the engine compartment. Pull the filter forward and remove it.*

   b) *Undo the four retaining clips and thread the cable out of the ducting (see illustration).*

   c) *Unscrew the four screws and pull the filter housing forwards and remove it.*

   d) *Undo the two screws and remove the inlet ducting upwards and out of the engine compartment (see illustration).*

8   Reach under the manifold, and disconnect the valve wiring connector (see illustration).

9   Depress the locking catch and disconnect the hose from the underside of the valve.

3.14 Unscrew the two nuts and remove the secondary air injection valve (M52TU engine shown, others similar)

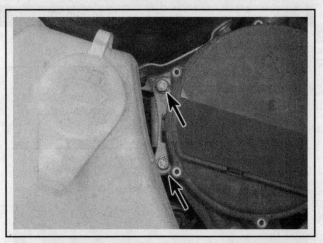

3.17 Secondary air injection pump and fasteners (M52TU engine shown, others are similar)

10 Disconnect the remaining hose and pull the valve from the rubber holder.

11 Installation is a reversal of removal.

CATALYTIC CONVERTER REPLACEMENT

12 The catalytic converters are integral with the exhaust manifolds. In order to replace them, it is necessary to replace the manifolds (see Chapter 4).

SECONDARY AIR INJECTION SYSTEM

Air injection valve

▶ **Refer to illustration 3.14**

13 The air injection valve is located above the exhaust manifold on the right-side of the cylinder head. Squeeze together the sides of the locking collar, and disconnect the pump-to-valve hose fitting.

14 Unscrew the two retaining nuts and remove the valve from the cylinder head (see illustration). Recover the gaskets.

15 Installation is the reversal of removal, tightening the retaining nuts securely.

Air pump

▶ **Refer to illustration 3.17**

16 The air pump is located on the right-hand inner fender. Loosen the clamp and disconnect the hose from the pump.

17 Unscrew the fasteners and remove the pump (see illustration). Disconnect the wiring connector as the pump is removed.

➡ **Note: The M56 engine models are equipped with a MAF sensor in the duct leading to the pump from its air filter.**

4 Catalytic converter - general information and precautions

The catalytic converter is a reliable and simple device, which needs no maintenance in itself, but there are some facts of which an owner should be aware, if the converter is to function properly for its full service life.

a) *DO NOT use leaded gasoline in a car equipped with a catalytic converter - the lead will coat the precious metals, reducing their converting efficiency, and will eventually destroy the converter.*

b) *Always keep the ignition and fuel systems well-maintained in accordance with the manufacturer's schedule.*

c) *If the engine develops a misfire, do not drive the car at all (or at least as little as possible) until the fault is cured.*

d) *DO NOT push- or tow-start the car - this will soak the catalytic converter in unburned fuel, causing it to overheat when the engine does start.*

e) *DO NOT switch off the ignition at high engine speeds.*

f) *DO NOT use fuel or engine oil additives - these may contain substances harmful to the catalytic converter.*

g) *DO NOT continue to use the car if the engine burns oil to the extent of leaving a visible trail of blue smoke.*

h) *Remember that the catalytic converter operates at very high temperatures. DO NOT, therefore, park the car in dry undergrowth, or over long grass or piles of dead leaves after a long run.*

i) *Remember that the catalytic converter is FRAGILE - do not strike it with tools during servicing work.*

j) *In some cases, a sulphurous smell (like that of rotten eggs) may be noticed from the exhaust. This is common to many catalytic converter-equipped cars, and once the car has covered a few thousand miles the problem should disappear.*

k) *The catalytic converter, used on a well-maintained and well-driven car, should last for between 50,000 and 100,000 miles - if the converter is no longer effective, it must be replaced.*

5 Engine management system components - removal and installation

ELECTRONIC CONTROL MODULE (ECM)

▶ **Refer to illustrations 5.2 and 5.3**

1 Disconnect the cable from the negative battery terminal (see Chapter 5, Section 1).

5.2 Loosen the screws and remove the electrical box cover

➡**Note: Disconnecting the battery will erase any fault codes stored in the ECM. Any stored codes should be retrieved before the battery is disconnected. Entrust this task to a BMW dealer or suitably equipped specialist.**

2 Working in the left-hand corner of the engine compartment, loosen the fasteners and remove the cover from the electrical box (see illustration).

3 Disconnect the module wiring connectors and remove it from the box (see illustration).

4 Installation is a reversal of removal.

➡**Note: If a new module has been installed, it will need to be coded using special test equipment. Entrust this task to a BMW dealer or suitably equipped specialist.**

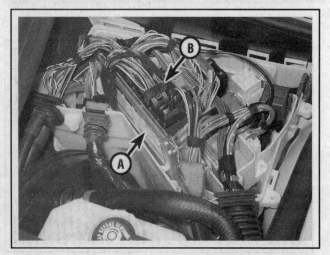

5.3 The ECM module (A) and one of the electrical connectors (B)

After reconnecting the battery, the vehicle must be driven for several miles under various conditions so that the ECM can learn its basic settings. If the engine runs erratically after being driven, service by a BMW dealer or specialist (using specialized equipment) will be required to reinstate the settings.

MASS AIRFLOW SENSOR (MAF)

M52TU engines

➡**Note: A new airflow sensor seal may be required on installation.**

5 Ensure the ignition is turned off, and disconnect the wiring connector from the sensor (see illustration 5.8).

6 Pull the vacuum hose from the intake ducting, release the retaining clips, and remove the sensor complete with the intake ducting. Recover the seal.

7 Installation is a reversal of removal, but check the condition of the seal and replace if necessary.

M54 and M56 engines

▶ **Refer to illustration 5.8**

➡**Note 1: A new airflow sensor seal may be required on installation.**

➡**Note 2: The M56 engine also utilizes a mass airflow sensor on the air duct to the secondary air injection pump.**

8 Ensure the ignition is turned off, and disconnect the wiring connector from the sensor (see illustration).

9 Release the retaining clips and detach the intake ducting from the sensor, and the sensor from the air cleaner housing. Recover the seal.

10 Installation is a reversal of removal, but check the condition of the seal and replace if necessary.

THROTTLE POSITION SENSOR (TPS)

11 The throttle position sensor is integral with the throttle body and cannot be replaced individually. Remove the throttle body as described in Chapter 4.

12 Note that if a new throttle body/position sensor has been installed, it is likely that values in the engine management ECM may

5.8 Mass airflow sensor

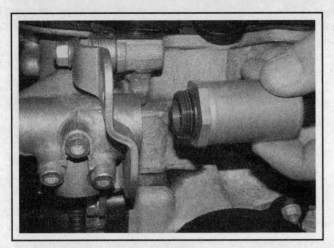

5.24 Unscrew the VANOS solenoid

5.26 Remove the screw and pull out the camshaft position sensor

need to be cleared and reset. If you don't have a specialized scan tool to clear values, seek assistance from a BMW dealer or suitably equipped specialist. Once cleared, new values will be "learned" as the engine is started and used.

COOLANT TEMPERATURE SENSOR (ECT)

✳✳ WARNING:

The engine must be completely cool before performing this procedure.

13 The sensor is located in the left side of the cylinder head under the intake manifold. Partially drain the cooling system as described in Chapter 1, and remove the intake manifold, as described in Chapter 4.

14 Disconnect the sensor wiring connector, and unscrew it from the cylinder head.

15 Installation is a reversal of removal. Tighten the sensor to the torque listed in this Chapter's Specifications, and top up the coolant as described in Chapter 1.

CRANKSHAFT POSITION SENSOR (CKP)

M52TU engines

16 Raise the front of the vehicle and support it securely on jackstands. Remove the screws and remove the engine splash shield.

17 The sensor is located below the starter motor. Disconnect the sensor wiring connector, unscrew the retaining screw and remove the sensor. Recover the seal.

18 Installation is a reversal of removal. Check the condition of the seal and replace if necessary.

M54 and M56 engines

19 Raise the front of the vehicle and support it securely on jackstands. Remove the screws and remove the engine splash shield.

20 Unscrew the bolts and remove the reinforcement plate from between the lower control arms (see Chapter 2A, Section 12). Note that new bolts will be needed upon installation.

21 The sensor is located under the starter motor. Disconnect the sensor wiring connector, remove the fastener and remove the sensor. Recover the seal.

22 Installation is a reversal of removal. Tighten the fastener to the

torque listed in this Chapter's Specifications, use new bolts when installing the front axle reinforcement plate, and tighten the reinforcement plate bolts to the torque listed in the Chapter 2A Specifications.

CAMSHAFT POSITION SENSORS (CMP)

Intake camshaft

▶ **Refer to illustrations 5.24 and 5.26**

23 Ensure the ignition is turned off, and remove the air cleaner housing as described in Section 2.

24 Disconnect the wiring connector, then unscrew the VANOS (variable valve timing system) solenoid valve to access the sensor (see illustration).

25 Trace the wiring back from the sensor, and disconnect the wiring connector where it clips to the cable ducting behind the alternator.

26 Remove the retaining fastener and pull the sensor from the cylinder head (see illustration). Recover the seal.

Exhaust camshaft

▶ **Refer to illustration 5.28**

27 Ensure the ignition is switched off.

28 Disconnect the sensor wiring connector (see illustration), remove the retaining fastener and remove the sensor. Recover the seal.

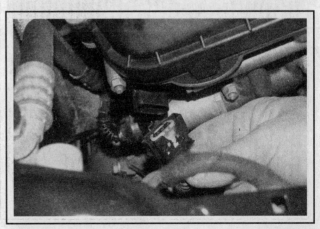

5.28 Disconnect the exhaust camshaft sensor wiring connector

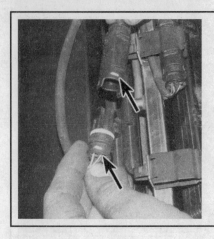

5.35 Mark or label the oxygen sensor wiring connector

29 Installation is a reversal of removal. Check the condition of the seal and replace it if necessary.

OXYGEN SENSOR (HO2S)

▶ **Refer to illustration 5.35**

➡**Note: Ensure that the exhaust system is cool before attempting to remove the oxygen sensor.**

30 The oxygen sensors are located at the front exhaust down pipes before and after the catalytic converters.

31 Ensure the ignition is switched off.

32 Apply the parking brake, then raise the front of the vehicle and support it securely on jackstands. Remove the screws and remove the engine splash shield.

➡**Note: Due to limited access, if the sensor for cylinders 4 to 6 is to be removed, the complete exhaust system must be removed.**

33 To allow sufficient clearance, remove the heater/ventilation inlet air ducting from the rear of the engine compartment as follows.

   a) *Rotate the three fasteners 90° counterclockwise and remove the cabin filter cover from the rear of the engine compartment. Pull the filter forward and remove it.*
   b) *Detach the four retaining clips and thread the cable out of the ducting (see illustration 3.7a).*
   c) *Unscrew the four screws and pull the filter housing forwards and remove it.*
   d) *Pull up the rubber strip, rotate the two fasteners counterclockwise, and move the dividing panel in the left-hand corner of the engine compartment forward a little.*
   e) *Unscrew the two screws and remove the inlet ducting upwards and out of the engine compartment (see illustration 3.7b).*

34 Pry out the plastic caps, remove the two screws, and remove the plastic cover from over the injectors.

35 Unclip the oxygen sensor cables from the retainer, and disconnect the wiring connectors. Label the connectors to ensure they are installed to their original locations (see illustration).

36 Remove the exhaust manifolds as described in Chapter 4.

37 Using a oxygen sensor removal socket, unscrew the sensor and remove it from the exhaust pipe.

38 Installation is a reverse of the removal procedure, noting the following points:

   a) *Tighten the sensor to the torque listed in this Chapter's Specifications.*

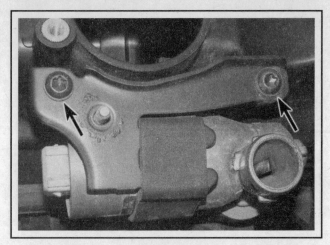

5.45 Idle speed control valve mounting screws

   b) *Check that the wiring is correctly routed, and in no danger of contacting the exhaust system.*
   c) *Ensure that no lubricant or dirt comes into contact with the sensor probe.*
   d) *Apply a small amount of copper based, high temperature anti-seize grease to the sensor threads prior to installation.*

IDLE SPEED CONTROL VALVE

▶ **Refer to illustration 5.45**

39 Disconnect the cable from the negative battery terminal (see Chapter 5, Section 1).

40 The idle speed control valve is located below the intake manifold, and above the throttle body.

41 Remove the air cleaner housing as described in Section 2.

42 Pull the throttle cable outer (if equipped) from the support bracket on the throttle body.

43 Loosen the two clamps and disconnect the intake ducting from the throttle body and idle speed control valve.

44 Disconnect the wiring connectors from the idle speed control valve and the manifold resonance flap actuator solenoid valve.

45 Remove the nut securing the cable support bracket, and the two screws securing the idle speed control valve bracket. Maneuver the valve from the manifold (see illustration). Discard the seal between the valve and the manifold - a new one must be installed.

46 Apply a small amount of grease to the new seal and install it to the intake manifold. Push the idle speed control valve into place and securely tighten the bracket retaining screws/nuts.

47 The remainder of installation is a reversal of removal.

FUEL PUMP RELAY

▶ **Refer to illustrations 5.52 and 5.53**

48 Disconnect the cable from the negative battery terminal (see Chapter 5, Section 1).

49 Remove the passenger side glove box, as described in Chapter 11.

50 Insert a flat-bladed screwdriver into the slot in the end of the glove box light and carefully pry it from place. Disconnect the wiring connector as the light is withdrawn.

51 Remove the five screws, release the expanding rivet and remove

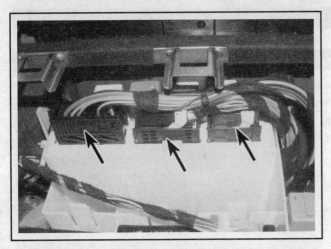

5.52 Disconnect the general control module wiring connectors

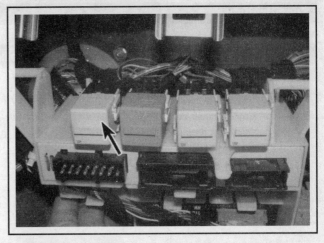

5.53 Fuel pump relay

the glove box frame from the dash (see Chapter 11 if necessary).

52 Undo the locking levers, and disconnect the wiring connectors from the general control module (see illustration).

53 Pull the fuel pump relay from the relay plate (see illustration).

54 Installation is a reversal of removal.

MAIN ENGINE MANAGEMENT RELAY

▶ **Refer to illustration 5.57**

55 Ensure the ignition is switched off.

56 Working in the left-hand corner of the engine compartment, loosen the four screws, and remove the cover from the electrical box

(see illustration 5.2).

57 Pull the relay from the relay socket (see illustration).

58 Installation is a reversal of removal.

INTAKE MANIFOLD DIFFERENTIAL PRESSURE SENSOR

▶ **Refer to illustration 5.60**

59 Ensure the ignition is switched off, undo the two nuts, lift the front edge, and pull the plastic engine cover to the front and remove it.

60 Disconnect the wiring connector, undo the screws and remove the sensor from the manifold (see illustration).

61 Installation is a reversal of removal.

5.57 Engine management relay

5.60 Unscrew the two screws and remove the differential pressure sensor

Specifications

Torque specifications	Ft-lbs (unless otherwise indicated)	Nm
Oxygen sensor to exhaust system	37	50
Camshaft position sensor bolt	60 in-lbs	7
Coolant temperature sensor	120 in-lbs	13
Crankshaft position sensor bolt	84 in-lbs	10

Section

Reference to other Chapters

Manual transmission lubricant level check/change - See Chapter 1

7A

MANUAL TRANSMISSION

1 General information

The transmission is a 5 or 6-speed unit, and is contained in a cast-alloy casing bolted to the rear of the engine.

Drive is transmitted from the crankshaft via the clutch to the input shaft, which has a splined extension to accept the clutch friction disc. The output shaft transmits the drive via the driveshaft to the rear differential.

The input shaft runs in line with the output shaft. The input shaft and output shaft gears are in constant mesh with the countershaft gear cluster. Selection of gears is achieved by sliding synchromesh hubs that lock the appropriate output shaft gears to the output shaft.

Gear selection is via a floor-mounted shift lever.

The selector mechanism causes the appropriate selector fork to move its respective synchro-sleeve along the shaft, to lock the gear pinion to the synchro-hub. Since the synchro-hubs are splined to the output shaft, this locks the pinion to the shaft, so that drive can be transmitted. To ensure that shifting can be made quickly and quietly, a synchromesh system is installed on all forward gears, consisting of balk rings and spring-loaded fingers, as well as the gear pinions and synchro-hubs. The synchromesh cones are formed on the mating faces of the balk rings and gear pinions.

The transmission is filled with oil during production, and is then considered filled for life. Refer to Chapter 1 for the alternate recommended service interval.

2 Gear selector components - removal and installation

SHIFT LEVER

▶ **Refer to illustrations 2.4, 2.5 and 2.9**

➡ **Note: A new shift lever bearing will be required on installation.**

1   Raise the vehicle and support it securely on jackstands.
2   Remove the knob from the shift lever by pulling it sharply upwards.

➡ **Note: Do not twist the knob or damage will result to the turning lock.**

3   Carefully pry the shift lever boot from the center console, and withdraw the boot over the shift lever. Where applicable, also remove the foam insulation.

4   Working under the vehicle, pry the securing clip from the end of the gear selector rod pin. Withdraw the selector rod pin from eye on the end of the shift lever, and recover the washers (see illustration).

5   It is now necessary to release the shift lever lower bearing retaining ring from the gear selector arm. A special tool is available for this purpose, but two screwdrivers, with the tips engaged in opposite slots in the bearing ring can be used instead. To unlock the bearing ring, turn it a quarter-turn counterclockwise (see illustration).

6   The bearing can now be pushed up through the housing, and the shift lever can be withdrawn from inside the vehicle.

7   If desired, the bearing can be removed from the shift lever ball by pressing it downwards. To withdraw the bearing over the lever eye, rotate the bearing until the eye passes through the slots provided in the bearing.

8   Install a new bearing using a reversal of the removal process. Ensure that the bearing is pressed securely into position on the shift lever ball.

9   Reinstall the lever using a reversal of the removal process, bearing in mind the following points.

   a) *Grease the contact faces of the bearing before installing.*
   b) *Lower the shift lever into position, ensuring that the arrow on the shift lever grommet points towards the front of the vehicle.*
   c) *Make sure that the shift lever grommet is correctly engaged with the gear selector arm and with the opening in the vehicle floor (see illustration).*

2.4 Slide the retaining clip from the selector rod pin

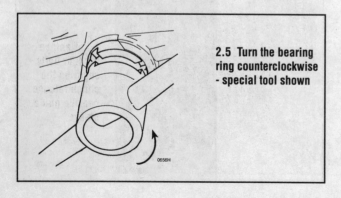

2.5 Turn the bearing ring counterclockwise - special tool shown

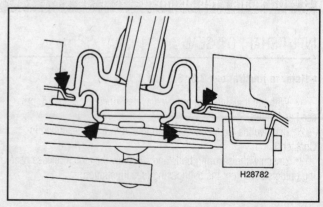

2.9 The gear lever grommet correctly positioned with the selector arm and vehicle chassis

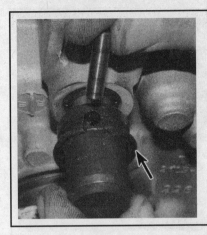

2.13 Slide back the circlip and drive out the pin

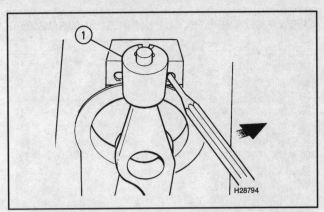

2.19 Lever the gear selector arm rear mounting sleeve (1) from the body bracket

d) When engaging the bearing with the selector arm, make sure that the arrows or tabs (as applicable) on the top of the bearing point towards the rear of the vehicle.

e) To lock the bearing in position in the selector arm, press down on the top of the bearing retaining tab locations until the tabs are heard to click into position.

f) Grease the selector rod pin before engaging it with the shift lever eye.

a) Before installation, check the condition of the rubber washer in the end of the selector shaft eye and replace if necessary.

b) Use a new roll-pin to secure the eye to the selector shaft.

c) Grease the selector rod pin.

d) Reconnect the driveshaft to the transmission flange as described in Chapter 8.

GEAR SELECTOR SHAFT EYE

▶ **Refer to illustration 2.13**

➡**Note: A new selector shaft eye securing roll-pin will be required on installation.**

10 Raise the vehicle and support it securely on jackstands.

11 Disconnect the driveshaft from the transmission flange, and support it clear of the transmission using wire or string. Refer to Chapter 8 for details.

12 Pry the retaining clip from the end of the gear selector rod pin. Withdraw the selector rod pin from the selector shaft eye, and recover the washers.

13 Slide back the locking sleeve, then drive out the roll-pin securing the gear selector shaft eye to the end of the gear selector shaft (see illustration).

14 Pull the gear selector shaft eye off the end of the selector shaft.

15 Installation is a reversal of removal, bearing in mind the following points.

GEAR SELECTOR ARM REAR MOUNTING

▶ **Refer to illustration 2.19**

16 Raise the vehicle and support it securely on jackstands.

17 Disconnect the driveshaft from the transmission flange, and support it clear of the transmission using wire or string. See Chapter 8 for details.

18 Remove the shift lever as described previously in this Section.

19 Using a screwdriver or a small pin-punch, lever the mounting sleeve from the bracket on the body (see illustration).

20 Pull the mounting from the selector arm.

21 Grease the mounting, then push the mounting onto the selector arm, with the cut-out facing the rear of the vehicle, and the arrow pointing vertically upwards.

22 Clip the mounting into position in the bracket, making sure that the mounting is securely located.

23 Reconnect the driveshaft to the transmission flange as described in Chapter 8, then lower the vehicle to the ground.

3 Oil seals - replacement

INPUT SHAFT OIL SEAL

▶ **Refer to illustrations 3.3, 3.5 and 3.7**

1 With the transmission removed as described in Section 5, proceed as follows.

2 Remove the clutch release bearing and lever as described in Chapter 8.

3 Unscrew the securing bolts and withdraw the clutch release bearing guide sleeve from the bellhousing (see illustration).

3.3 Remove the four bolts securing the clutch release bearing guide sleeve

3.5 Drill a small hole in the oil seal

3.7 Insert a self-tapping screw into the hole, and pull the seal out with a pair of pliers

4 Note the fitted depth of the now-exposed input shaft oil seal.

5 Drill one small hole in the oil seal (two small pilot holes should be provided at opposite points on the seal. Coat the end of the drill bit with grease to prevent any metal shavings from entering the transmission from the holes (see illustration).

6 Using a small drift, tap one side of the seal (opposite to the hole) into the bellhousing as far as the stop.

7 Screw a small self-tapping screw into the opposite side of the seal, and use pliers to pull out the seal (see illustration).

8 Clean the oil seal seating surface. Also make sure there are no metal chips present from the drilling operation.

9 Lubricate the lips of the new oil seal with a little clean transmission oil, then carefully slide the seal over the input shaft into position in the bellhousing.

10 Tap the oil seal into the bellhousing to the previously noted depth.

11 Reinstall the guide sleeve to the transmission housing, tighten the retaining bolts securely, using a drop of locking compound on the threads of the bolts.

12 Reinstall the clutch release lever and bearing as described in Chapter 8.

13 Reinstall the transmission as described in Section 5, then check the transmission oil level as described in Chapter 1.

OUTPUT FLANGE OIL SEAL

▶ **Refer to illustrations 3.17, 3.18, 3.19 and 3.21**

➡**Note: Thread-locking compound will be required for the transmission flange nut on installation.**

14 Raise the vehicle and support it securely on jackstands.

15 Disconnect the driveshaft from the transmission flange, and support it clear of the transmission using wire or string. See Chapter 8 for details.

16 Where applicable, pry the transmission flange nut cover plate from the flange using a screwdriver. Discard the cover plate - it is not required on installation. If necessary, support the transmission, and remove the transmission crossmember to improve access.

17 Hold the transmission flange by bolting a forked or two-legged tool to two of the flange bolt holes, then unscrew the flange securing nut using a deep socket and extension bar (see illustration).

18 Using a puller, draw the flange from the end of the transmission output shaft (see illustration). Be prepared for oil spillage.

19 Note the fitted depth of the oil seal then, then using a puller (take care to avoid damage to the transmission output shaft), pull the oil seal from the transmission casing (see illustration).

3.17 Hold the output flange and remove the nut using a deep socket

3.18 Use a three-jaw puller to remove the output flange

3.19 Carefully pull the seal from place

3.21 Tap the seal into place using a seal driver or a socket which only contacts the hard outer edge of the seal

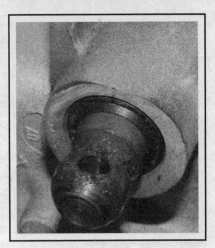

3.31 Tap the new selector shaft oil seal into position

20 Clean the oil seal seating surface.

21 Lubricate the lips of the new oil seal with a little clean transmission oil, then carefully tap the seal into the transmission casing to the to the previously noted depth (see illustration).

22 Reinstall the flange to the output shaft.

➡ **Note: To ease reinstallation of the flange, immerse it in hot water for a few minutes, then install it on the shaft.**

23 Tighten the flange nut to the Stage one torque setting, then loosen and remove the nut (Stage two). Coat the threads of the flange nut with a non-hardening thread-locking compound, then tighten the nut to the Stage three torque as specified. Hold the flange the same way as removal in step 17.

24 If a flange nut cover plate was originally fitted, discard it. There is no need to fit a cover plate on installation.

25 Reconnect the driveshaft to the transmission flange as described in Chapter 8, then check the transmission oil level as described in Chapter 1, and lower the vehicle to the ground.

GEAR SELECTOR SHAFT OIL SEAL

▸ **Refer to illustration 3.31**

➡ **Note: A new selector shaft eye securing roll-pin will be required on installation.**

26 Raise the vehicle and support it securely on jackstands.

27 Disconnect the driveshaft from the transmission flange, and support it clear of the transmission using wire or string. See Chapter 8 for details. For improved access, support the transmission, and remove the transmission crossmember.

28 Slide back the locking collar, then slide out the pin securing the gear selector shaft eye to the end of the gear selector shaft.

29 Pull the gear selector shaft eye (complete with gear linkage) off the end of the selector shaft, and move the linkage clear of the selector shaft.

30 Using a small flat-bladed screwdriver, pry the selector shaft oil seal from the transmission casing.

31 Clean the oil seal seating surface, then tap the new seal into position using a seal driver or a small socket of the correct diameter (see illustration).

32 Check the condition of the rubber washer in the end of the selector shaft eye and replace if necessary.

33 Push the selector shaft eye back onto the end of the selector shaft, then align the holes in the eye and shaft and secure the eye to the shaft using the pin.

34 Slide the locking collar into position over the roll-pin.

35 Reconnect the driveshaft to the transmission flange as described in Chapter 8.

36 Check the transmission oil level as described in Chapter 1, then lower the vehicle to the ground.

---

4 Back-up light switch - testing, removal and installation

TESTING

1 The back-up light circuit is controlled by a plunger-type switch screwed into the left-hand side of the Getrag transmission casing, and the right-hand side of the ZF transmission casing. If a fault develops in the circuit, first ensure that the circuit fuse has not blown.

2 To test the switch, disconnect the wiring connector, and use a multimeter (set to the resistance function) or a battery-and-bulb test circuit to check that there is continuity between the switch terminals only when reverse gear is selected. If this is not the case, and there are no obvious breaks or other damage to the wires, the switch is faulty, and must be replaced.

REMOVAL

▸ **Refer to illustration 4.4**

3 Raise the vehicle and support it securely on jackstands.

4.4 Back-up light switch

5   Manual transmission - removal and installation

➡Note: This is an involved operation. Read through the procedure thoroughly before starting work, and ensure that adequate lifting and/or jacking/support equipment is available.

REMOVAL

▶ Refer to illustrations 5.6, 5.11a, 5.11b, 5.16 and 5.17

1   Disconnect the cable from the negative battery terminal (see Chapter 5, Section 1).

2   Raise the vehicle and support it securely on jackstands. Note that the car must be raised sufficiently to allow clearance for the transmission to be removed from under the car. Remove the screws and remove the engine/transmission shields.

3   Remove the engine intake air duct located over the radiator and leading to the air cleaner (See Chapter 4).

4   Remove the starter motor as described in Chapter 5.

5   Remove the driveshaft as described in Chapter 8.

6   Working under the car, pry the retaining clip from the end of the gear selector rod pin. Withdraw the selector rod pin from the eye on the end of the transmission selector shaft, and recover the washers. Similarly, disconnect the selector rod pin from the end of the gear lever, and withdraw the selector rod (see illustration).

4   Disconnect the wiring connector, then unscrew the switch from the transmission casing (see illustration).

INSTALLATION

5   Screw the switch back into position in the transmission housing and tighten it securely. Reconnect the wiring connector, and test the operation of the circuit.

6   Lower the vehicle to the ground.

7   Working at the bellhousing, unscrew the nuts, and withdraw the clutch slave cylinder from the studs on the bellhousing. Support the slave cylinder away from the working area, but do not strain the hose.

✴ CAUTION:

Do not depress the clutch pedal with the slave cylinder removed.

8   Note their installed locations, then disconnect all wiring connectors, and release any wiring harnesses from the transmission casing.

9   Remove the exhaust mounting bracket from the rear of the transmission casing.

10 Unscrew the securing bolts, and remove the front suspension reinforcement plate/brace (see Chapter 2A, Section 12).

11 Remove the heater/ventilation inlet air ducting from the rear of the engine compartment as follows (see illustrations).

a) Rotate the three fasteners 90° counterclockwise and remove the cabin filter cover from the rear of the engine compartment. Pull the filter forward and remove it.

b) Loosen the four retaining clips and thread the cable out of the ducting.

5.6 Remove the retaining clips and remove the selector rod

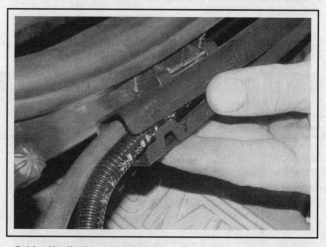

5.11a Unclip the cable ducting

5.11b Remove the two Torx screws and remove the inlet housing

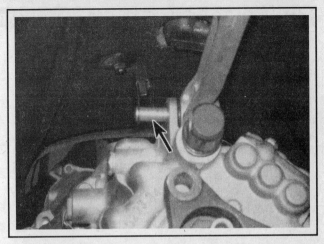

5.16 Pry up the retaining clip and slide the pivot pin out

c) *Unscrew the four screws and pull the filter housing forwards and remove it.*

d) *Pull up the rubber strip, rotate the two fasteners counterclockwise, and move the dividing panel in the left-hand corner of the engine compartment forward a little.*

e) *Remove the two screws and remove the inlet ducting upwards and out of the engine compartment.*

12 Support the engine from above using an engine hoist or an engine support fixture. Connect it to the engine lifting eye at the rear left-hand corner of the cylinder block (incorporated in the rear flange of the cylinder block casting).

13 Place a jack under the transmission casing, just behind the bellhousing. If available, use a transmission jack and secure the transmission to the jack with safety chains. Raise the jack just enough to take the weight of the transmission.

14 Remove the crossmember and mounts from the rear of the transmission.

15 Using the jack and engine hoist, lower the engine and transmission until the rear of the engine cylinder head/manifold assembly is almost touching the engine compartment firewall. Check that the assembly is not resting against any hoses/lines on the firewall.

16 Working at the top of the transmission, pry up the clip securing the gear selector arm pivot pin to the transmission casing, then pull out the pivot pin to release the selector arm from the transmission (see illustration).

17 Where applicable, unscrew the bolt securing the engine/transmission adapter plate to the right-hand side of the bellhousing and/or remove the flywheel lower cover plate (see illustration).

18 Unscrew the engine-to-transmission bolts, and recover the washers, then slide the transmission rearwards to disengage the input shaft from the clutch. Take care during this operation to ensure that the weight of the transmission is not allowed to hang on the input shaft. As the transmission is released from the engine, check to make sure that the engine is not forced against the heater hose connections or the firewall.

19 Lower the transmission and carefully withdraw it from under the car. If the transmission is to be removed for some time, ensure that the engine is adequately supported in the engine compartment.

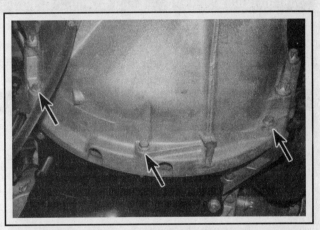

5.17 Unscrew the three bolts and remove the flywheel lower cover plate

INSTALLATION

20 Refer to Chapter 8 and inspect the clutch components (now would be a good time to replace them).

21 Ensure that the clutch friction disc is centered as described in Chapter 8.

22 Inspect and grease the clutch release bearing and lever as described in Chapter 8.

23 The remainder of the installation procedure is a reversal of removal, bearing in mind the following points.

a) *Check that the transmission positioning dowels are securely in place at the rear of the engine.*

b) *Make sure that the washers are in place on the engine-to-transmission bolts.*

c) *Tighten all fasteners to the specified torque.*

d) *Lightly grease the gear selector arm pivot pin and the gear selector rod pin before installation.*

e) *Reconnect the driveshaft to the transmission flange as described in Chapter 8.*

f) *Reinstall the starter motor as described in Chapter 5.*

g) *Check the transmission lubricant level as described in Chapter 1.*

6   Manual transmission overhaul - general information

Overhauling a manual transmission is a difficult and involved job for the home mechanic. In addition to dismantling and reassembling many small parts, clearances must be precisely measured and, if necessary, changed by selecting shims and spacers. Internal transmission components are also often difficult to obtain, and in many instances, extremely expensive. Because of this, if the transmission develops a fault or becomes noisy, the best course of action is to have the unit overhauled by a qualified specialist, or to obtain an exchange reconditioned unit. Be aware that some transmission repairs can be carried out with the transmission in the car.

Nevertheless, it is not impossible for the more experienced mechanic to overhaul the transmission, provided the special tools are available, and the job is done in a deliberate step-by-step manner, so that nothing is overlooked.

The tools necessary for an overhaul include internal and external circlip pliers, bearing pullers, a slide hammer, a set of pin punches, a dial test indicator, and possibly a hydraulic press. In addition, a large, sturdy workbench and a vice will be required.

During dismantling of the transmission, make careful notes of how each component is installed, to make reassembly easier and more accurate.

Before dismantling the transmission, it will help if you have some idea what area is malfunctioning. Certain problems can be closely related to specific areas in the transmission, which can make component examination and replacement easier. Refer to the *Troubleshooting* Section at the beginning of this manual for more information.

Specifications

Lubrication

Oil capacity	See Chapter 1

Torque specifications

	Ft-lbs (unless otherwise indicated)	Nm
Transmission crossmember-to-body bolts:		
M8 bolts	15	21
M10 bolts	31	42
Transmission mounting-to-transmission nuts:		
M8 nuts	15	21
M10 nuts	31	42
Transmission-to-engine bolts:		
Hexagon head bolts:		
M8 bolts	18	25
M10 bolts	36	49
M12 bolts	55	74
Torx head bolts:		
M8 bolts	16	22
M10 bolts	32	43
M12 bolts	53	72
Oil drain plug	37	50
Oil filler/level plug	37	50
Output flange-to-output shaft nut*:		
Stage 1	140	190
Stage 2	Remove nut and apply locking compound	
Stage 3	89	120
Back-up light switch	15	21

Coat the threads of the nut with thread-locking compound.

Section

Reference to other Chapters

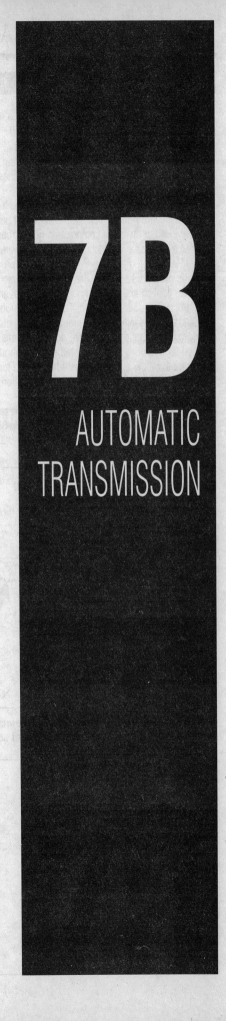

7B

AUTOMATIC TRANSMISSION

1 General information

Depending on model, a four- or five-speed automatic transmission may be installed, consisting of a torque converter, an epicyclic geartrain and hydraulically-operated clutches and brakes.

The torque converter provides a fluid coupling between engine and transmission, acting as a clutch, and also provides a degree of torque multiplication when accelerating.

The epicyclic geartrain provides either of the forward or reverse gear ratio, according to which of its component parts are held stationary or allowed to turn. The components of the transmission are held or released by brakes and clutches which are activated by a hydraulic control unit. A fluid pump within the transmission provides the necessary hydraulic pressure to operate the brakes and clutches.

Driver control of the transmission is by a seven-position selector lever, and a four-position switch. The transmission has a 'drive' position, and a 'hold' facility on the first three gear ratios (four-speed transmission) or gear ratios 2 to 4 (five-speed transmissions). The 'drive' position (D) provides automatic shifting throughout the range of all forward gear ratios, and is the position selected for normal driving. An automatic kickdown facility shifts the transmission down a gear if the accelerator pedal is fully depressed. The 'hold' facility is very similar, but limits the number of gear ratios available - i.e., when the selector lever is in the 3 position, only the first three ratios can be selected; in the 2 position, only the first two can be selected, and so on. The lower ratio 'hold' is useful when travelling down steep gradients, or for preventing unwanted selection of top gear on twisty roads. Three driving programs are provided for selection by the switch; 'Economy', 'Sport', and 'Manual' (four-speed transmission) or 'Winter' (five-speed transmission).

Certain models are available with Steptronic shifting where the driver is able to control shift points; moving the shift lever forward to up-shift and backward to down-shift. This is an additional feature to typical automatic transmission operation.

Due to the complexity of the automatic transmission, any repair or overhaul work must be left to a BMW dealer or specialist with the necessary special equipment for fault diagnosis and repair. The contents of the following Sections are therefore confined to supplying general information, and any service information and instructions that can be used by the owner.

2 Gear selector lever - removal and installation

REMOVAL

▶ Refer to illustration 2.2, 2.6, 2.8 and 2.9

1   Raise the vehicle and support it securely on jackstands. Ensure the selector lever is in position P.

2   Working underneath the vehicle, loosen the selector cable clamping nut on the transmission lever (see illustration).

3   Unscrew the locknut securing the selector outer cable and remove the cable from the support bracket on the transmission.

4   Working in the passenger cabin, pull the knob from the selector lever with a strong tug.

➡Note: Do not twist the knob or damage will result to the turning lock in the lever.

5   Carefully pry up the lever trim (complete with lever boot) from the center console. Disconnect the wiring connectors from the underside of the trim noting their installed locations before disconnecting them.

6   Remove the two trim retaining screws at the rear of the selector lever opening. Starting at the rear, lift the trim and disconnect the wiring connectors from the underside of the trim (having noted their installed locations) (see illustration). Remove the trim.

7   Pull out the storage tray from above the ashtray.

8   Remove the four retaining screws, and pull the ashtray/switch

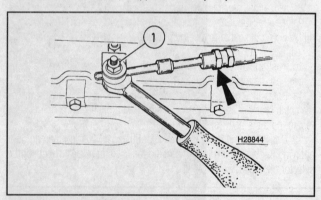

2.2 Hold the clamp bolt, and loosen the selector cable securing nut (1). Arrow points to the cable-to-bracket securing nut

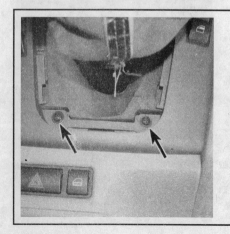

2.6 Remove the two screws at the rear of the selector lever opening

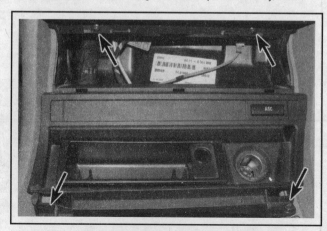

2.8 Remove the four screws and remove the frame

frame back from the center console. Press the switches out of the frame, and disconnect their wiring connectors (having noted their installed positions) (see illustration). Remove the frame.

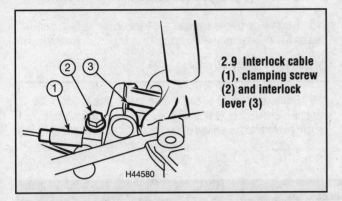

2.9 Interlock cable (1), clamping screw (2) and interlock lever (3)

9 Loosen the interlock cable clamping screw (see illustration).

10 Note their installed positions, then disconnect any wiring connectors attached to the selector lever assembly.

11 Remove the three screws securing the lever assembly to the floor, maneuver the assembly up from its location, unhooking the interlock cable as it is withdrawn.

INSTALLATION

12 Installation is a reversal of removal, noting the following points:

   a) *Adjust the interlock cable as described in this Chapter.*

   b) *Prior to installing the gear knob, push the boot down the lever until the locking groove in the lever is exposed.*

   c) *On completion, adjust the selector cable as described in Section 3.*

---

3   Gear selector cable - removal, installation and adjustment

REMOVAL

1 Disconnect the cable from the selector lever assembly as described in Section 2.

2 To improve access, apply the parking brake, then raise the front of the vehicle and support securely on jackstands.

3 Working at the end of the cable, hold the clamp bolt, and loosen the securing nut. Take care not to bend the end of the cable (see illustration 2.2).

4 Loosen the securing nut, and release the cable from the bracket on the transmission.

5 Slide the end of the cable from the end fitting.

6 Withdraw the cable down from under the car, noting its routing to ensure correct installation.

INSTALLATION

7 Installation is a reversal of removal, bearing in mind the following points.

   a) *Do not tighten the cable end securing nut and bolts until the cable has been adjusted.*

   b) *Reconnect the cable to the selector lever assembly with reference to Section 2.*

   c) *On completion, adjust the cable as described in the following paragraphs.*

ADJUSTMENT

▶ **Refer to illustration 3.11**

8 Move the selector lever to position P.

9 If not already done, hold the clamp bolt and loosen the clamp nut securing the cable to the end fitting (the car should be raised for access).

10 Push the operating lever on the transmission away from the cable bracket on the transmission (towards the Park position).

11 Press the end of the cable in the opposite direction (i.e., towards the cable bracket), then release the cable and tighten the clamp nut (again, hold the bolt) (see illustration).

12 Check that the cable is correctly adjusted by starting the engine, applying the brakes firmly, and moving the selector lever through all the selector positions.

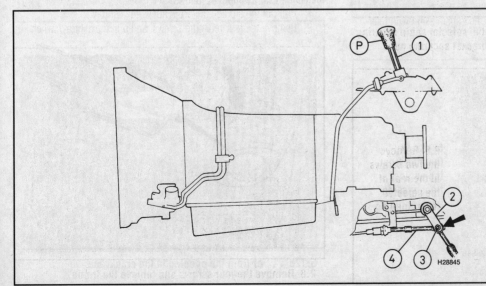

3.11 Adjusting the selector cable

P   Park position
1   Selector lever
2   Operating lever
3   Clamp nut
4   Selector cable

4 Fluid seals - replacement

TORQUE CONVERTER SEAL

1 Remove the transmission and the torque converter as described in Section 5.

2 Using a hooked tool, pry the old oil seal from the bellhousing. Alternatively, drill a small hole, then screw a self-tapping screw into the seal and use pliers to pull out the seal.

3 Lubricate the lip of the new seal with clean fluid, then carefully drive it into place using a large socket or tube.

4 Remove the old O-ring seal from the input shaft, and slide a new one into place. Apply a small amount of petroleum jelly to the new O-ring.

5 Reinstall the torque converter and transmission as described in Section 5.

OUTPUT FLANGE OIL SEAL

6 Replacement of the oil seal involves partial dismantling of the transmission, which is a complex operation. Oil seal replacement should be entrusted to a BMW dealer or other qualified repair shop.

5 Automatic transmission - removal and installation

➡Note: This is an involved operation. Read through the procedure thoroughly before starting work, and ensure that adequate lifting and/or jacking/support equipment is available. A suitable tool will be required to align the torque converter when installing the transmission, and new fluid line O-rings may be required.

REMOVAL

▶ Refer to illustrations 5.12a, 5.12b, 5.15a, 5.15b, 5.17 and 5.25

1 Disconnect the cable(s) from the negative battery terminal(s) (see Chapter 5, Section 1).

2 Raise the vehicle and support it securely on jackstands. Note that the car must be raised sufficiently to allow clearance for the transmission to be removed from under the car. Remove the screws and remove the engine/transmission under-shield from the vehicle.

3 Unscrew the bolts and remove the front reinforcement brace/plate from under the transmission.

4 Remove the starter motor as described in Chapter 5.

5 Remove the exhaust system and heat shield, then unbolt the exhaust mounting crossmember from under the car.

6 Remove the drive shaft as described in Chapter 8.

7 Drain the automatic transmission fluid as described in Chapter 1.

8 Disconnect the selector cable from the transmission with reference to Section 3.

9 Disconnect the transmission wiring harness connectors after carefully noting their installed locations. Release the wiring harness from the brackets and clips on the transmission.

10 Release the oxygen sensor from the bracket on the transmission.

11 Unbolt the fluid cooler line brackets and clamps. Unscrew the fittings and disconnect the fluid lines - be prepared for fluid spillage.

12 Pry the plug from the opening in the engine/transmission adapter plate, above the pan, or from the opening in the crankcase, depending on model, for access to the torque converter securing bolts (see illustrations).

13 Unscrew the three torque converter bolts, turning the crankshaft using a wrench or socket on the pulley hub bolt for access to each bolt in turn.

14 Support the transmission using a jack and a wood plank to distribute the weight evenly. If available, use a transmission jack and secure the transmission to the jack with safety chains.

✳✳ CAUTION:

The transmission is heavy, so make sure that it is adequately supported.

15 Remove the heater/ventilation inlet air ducting from the rear of the engine compartment as follows.

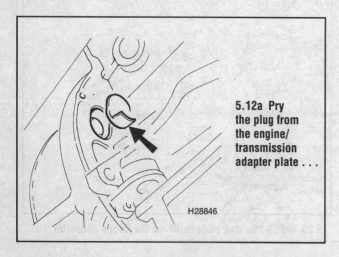

5.12a Pry the plug from the engine/transmission adapter plate . . .

H28846

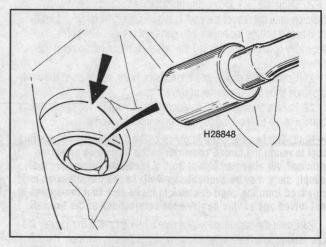

H28848

5.12b . . . or from the opening in the crankcase

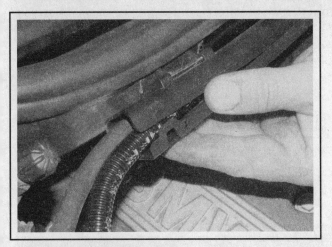

5.15a Unclip the cable ducting

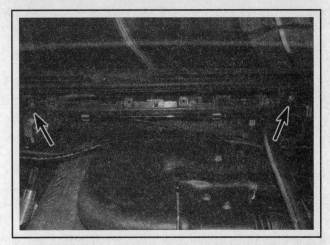

5.15b Remove the two Torx screws and remove the inlet housing

a) Rotate the three fasteners 90° counterclockwise and remove the cabin filter cover from the rear of the engine compartment. Pull the filter forward and remove it.

b) Detach the four retaining clips and thread the cable out of the ducting (see illustration).

c) Unscrew the four screws and pull the filter housing forwards and remove it.

d) Pull up the rubber strip, rotate the two fasteners counterclockwise, and move the dividing panel in the left-hand corner of the engine compartment forward a little.

e) Remove the two screws and remove the inlet ducting upwards and out of the engine compartment (see illustration).

16 Support the engine with a hoist or engine support fixture using the engine lifting eye at the rear left-hand corner of the cylinder block (incorporated in the rear flange of the cylinder block casting).

17 Where applicable, unbolt the transmission front mounting assembly (see illustration).

18 Check to ensure that the engine and transmission are adequately supported then, working under the car, unscrew the nuts securing the transmission rubber mountings to the lugs on the transmission casing.

19 Remove the bolts securing the transmission crossmember to the body, then withdraw the crossmember from under the car. If necessary, bend back or unbolt the exhaust heat shield for access to the crossmember bolts.

20 Using the jack and engine hoist, lower the engine and transmission until the rear of the engine cylinder head/manifold assembly is almost touching the engine compartment firewall. Check that the assembly is not resting against the heater hose connections on the firewall.

21 Unscrew the engine-to-transmission bolts, and recover the washers, then slide the transmission rearwards.

22 Insert a suitable metal or wooden lever through the slot in the bottom of the bellhousing to retain the torque converter.

➡Note: The lever is used in place of the special (manufacturer) tool to retain the torque converter to the transmission during removal. An aftermarket tool from a specialty automotive tool supply store may be available as well. As the transmission is released from the engine, check to make sure that the engine is not forced against the heater hose connections or the firewall.

23 Lower the transmission and carefully withdraw it from under the car, making sure that the torque converter is held in position. If the transmission is to be removed for some time, ensure that the engine is adequately supported in the engine compartment.

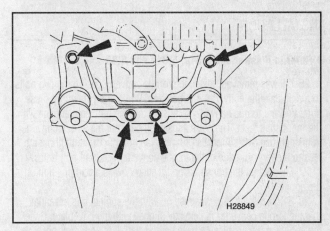

5.17 Where applicable, unscrew the bolts and remove the transmission front mounting assembly

24 To remove the torque converter, first remove any retaining levers or tools installed in step 22.

25 Fit two long bolts to two of the torque converter securing bolt holes, and use the bolts to pull the torque converter from the transmission (see illustration). Pull evenly on both bolts. Be prepared for fluid spillage.

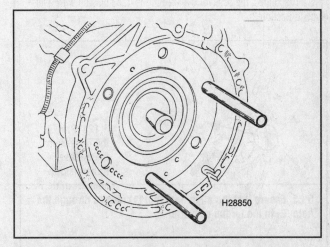

5.25 Install two long bolts to lift out the torque converter

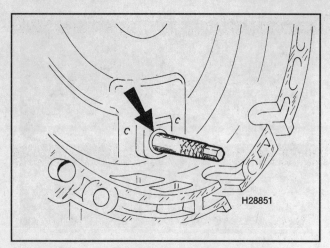

5.31a Alignment tool screws into the driveplate, aligned with the opening in the bottom of the pan/bellhousing

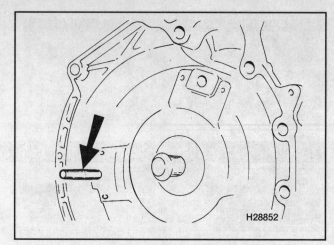

5.31b Alignment tool screws into the driveplate aligned with the opening in the engine/transmission adapter plate (5-speed transmission)

INSTALLATION

▶ **Refer to illustrations 5.31a, 5.31b and 5.35**

26 If it was removed, install the torque converter, using the two bolts to manipulate the converter into position. While applying slight pressure, turn the torque converter to ensure that the hub teeth engage with the input shaft teeth. The correct installed depth of the torque converter is greater than 1-3/16 inches (30 mm) (approx.) from the bellhousing face to the forward edge of the torque converter securing bolt holes.

27 Ensure that the transmission locating dowels are in position on the engine.

28 Before mating the transmission with the engine, it is essential that the torque converter is perfectly aligned with the driveplate. Once the engine and transmission have been mated, it is no longer possible to turn the torque converter to allow re-alignment.

29 To align the driveplate with the torque converter, BMW uses a special tapered tool which screws into the driveplate. It may be possible to improvise a suitable tool using an old torque converter-to-driveplate bolt with the head cut off, or a length of threaded bar - note that the

end of the bolt or bar must either have a slot cut in the end, or flats machined on it to allow it to be unscrewed once the engine and transmission have been mated.

30 Turn the flywheel to align one of the torque converter-to-driveplate bolt holes with the opening in the bottom of the pan/bellhousing (for access to the pan securing bolt), or with the opening in the engine/transmission adapter plate (as applicable). This is essential to enable the alignment stud to be removed after the engine and transmission have been mated.

31 Screw the alignment tool into the relevant hole in the driveplate (see illustrations).

32 Where applicable, remove the retaining lever from the torque converter.

33 Ensure that the transmission is adequately supported, and maneuver it into position under the car.

34 Turn the torque converter to align one of the torque converter-to-driveplate bolt holes with the alignment tool installed to the driveplate, then place the transmission into position.

35 Ensure that the alignment tool passes through the hole in the torque converter, then install and tighten the engine-to-transmission bolts, ensuring that the washers are in place (see illustration).

36 Unscrew the alignment tool from the driveplate, then install the torque converter-to-driveplate bolt. Tighten the bolt to the specified torque.

37 Turn the crankshaft as during removal for access to the remaining two torque converter-to-driveplate bolt locations. Install and tighten the bolts.

38 Further installation is a reversal of removal, bearing in mind the following points.

a) *Tighten all fasteners to their specified torque, where applicable.*
b) *Check the condition of the transmission fluid line O-rings and replace if necessary.*
c) *Install the drive shaft (see Chapter 8).*
d) *Install the starter motor (see Chapter 5).*
e) *Reconnect and adjust the selector cable as described in Section 3.*
f) *On completion, refill the transmission with the correct fluid as described in Chapter 1.*

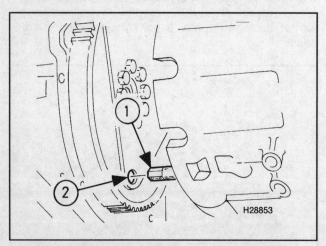

5.35 Ensure that the alignment tool (1) passes through the hole (2) in the torque converter

6   Automatic transmission overhaul - general information

In the event of a fault occurring with the transmission, it is first necessary to determine whether it is of an electrical, mechanical or hydraulic nature, and to do this special test equipment is required. It is therefore essential to have the work carried out by a BMW dealer or suitably-equipped specialist if a transmission fault is suspected.

Do not remove the transmission from the car for possible repair before professional fault diagnosis has been carried out, since most tests require the transmission to be in the car.

7   Electronic components/sensors - removal and installation

1   The turbine speed sensor, output speed sensor and transmission range switch are all contained within the transmission casing. Replacement of the components involves removal of the oil pan and partial dismantling of the transmission, therefore this should be entrusted to a BMW dealer or suitably-equipped specialist.

2   The transmission electronic control module (ECM) is located in the 'E-box' in the left-hand corner of the engine compartment. Loosen the screws, remove the E-box lid, disconnect the wiring connector and remove the ECM.

Specifications

Torque specifications	Ft-lbs (unless otherwise indicated)	Nm
Engine-to-transmission bolts		
Hexagon bolts:		
M8 bolts	18	24
M10 bolts	33	45
M12 bolts	61	82
Torx bolts:		
M8 bolts	15	21
M10 bolts	31	42
M12 bolts	53	72
Engine/transmission adapter plate bolt	17	23
Output flange nut*		
Stage 1	140	190
Stage 2	Loosen 360°	
Stage 3	89	120
Torque-converter-to-driveplate bolts		
M8 bolts	19	26
M10 bolts	36	49
Transmission crossmember-to-body bolts		
M8 bolts	15	21
M10 bolts	31	42
Transmission mounting-to-transmission nuts		
M8 nuts	15	21
M10 nuts	31	42

*Use thread-locking compound

Section

8

CLUTCH AND DRIVELINE

1 General information

CLUTCH

All models with a manual transmission are equipped with a single dry plate clutch which consists of five main components; a friction disc, pressure plate, diaphragm spring, cover and release bearing.

The friction disc is free to slide along the splines of the transmission input shaft, and is held in position between the flywheel and the pressure plate by the pressure exerted on the pressure plate by the diaphragm spring. Friction lining material is riveted to both sides of the friction disc. These models utilize a Self-Adjusting Clutch (SAC), which compensates for friction disc wear by altering the attitude of the diaphragm spring fingers by means of a sprung mechanism within the pressure plate cover. This ensures a consistent clutch pedal feel over the life of the clutch.

The diaphragm spring is mounted on pins, and is held in place in the cover by circular fulcrum rings.

The release bearing is located on a guide sleeve at the front of the transmission, and the bearing is free to slide on the sleeve under the action of the release arm, which pivots inside the bellhousing.

The release mechanism operates by the clutch pedal and hydraulic pressure. The pedal acts on the master cylinder pushrod and then hydraulically on a slave cylinder that's mounted on the bellhousing. This operates a clutch release lever by a pushrod from the slave cylinder.

When the clutch pedal is depressed, the release arm pushes the release bearing against the center of the diaphragm spring, thus pushing the center of the diaphragm spring inward. The diaphragm spring acts against the fulcrum rings in the cover, and so as the center of the spring is pushed in, the outside of the spring is pushed out, so allowing the pressure plate to move backwards away from the friction disc.

When the clutch pedal is released, the diaphragm spring forces the pressure plate into contact with the friction linings on the friction disc, and simultaneously pushes the friction disc forward on its splines, forcing it against the flywheel. The friction disc is now firmly sandwiched between the pressure plate and the flywheel, and drive is taken up.

DRIVELINE

Power is transmitted from the transmission to the rear axle by a two-piece driveshaft, joined behind the center bearing by a slip joint - a sliding, splined coupling. The slip joint allows slight fore-and-aft movement of the driveshaft. The forward end of the driveshaft is attached to the output flange of the transmission either by a flexible rubber coupling or a universal flange joint. On some models, a vibration damper is mounted between the front of the driveshaft and coupling. The middle of the driveshaft is supported by a center bearing that is bolted to the vehicle body. Universal joints are located at the center bearing and at the rear end of the driveshaft, to compensate for movement of the transmission and differential on their mountings and for any flexing of the chassis.

The differential assembly includes the drive pinion, the ring gear, the differential and the output flanges. The drive pinion, which drives the ring gear, is also known as the differential input shaft and is connected to the driveshaft via an input flange. The differential is bolted to the ring gear and drives the rear wheels through a pair of output flanges bolted to driveaxles with constant velocity (CV) joints at either end. The differential allows the wheels to turn at different speeds when cornering.

The driveaxles deliver power from the differential output flanges to the rear wheels. The driveaxles are equipped with constant velocity (CV) joints at each end. The inner CV joints are bolted to the differential flanges and the outer CV joints engage the splines of the wheel hubs, and are secured by a large nut.

Major repair work on the differential assembly components (drive pinion, ring-and-pinion, and differential) requires many special tools and a high degree of expertise, and therefore should not be attempted by the home mechanic. If major repairs become necessary, we recommend that they be performed by a BMW service department or other qualified repair shop.

2 Clutch assembly - removal, inspection and installation

✳✳ WARNING:

Dust created by clutch wear and deposited on the clutch components, is a health hazard. DO NOT blow it out with compressed air, or inhale any of it. DO NOT use gasoline (or petroleum-based solvents) to clean off the dust. Brake system cleaner should be used to flush the dust into a suitable receptacle. After the clutch components are wiped clean with rags, dispose of the contaminated rags and cleaner in a sealed, marked container.

➡**Note: If the clutch pressure plate is to be re-used, BMW tool 21 2 170 will be required to compress the diaphragm spring prior to removal of the clutch cover. Tool 21 2 142 may be required to center the friction plate.**

REMOVAL

◗ **Refer to illustration 2.3**

1 Remove the transmission as described in Chapter 7A.

2 If the original clutch is to be reinstalled, make alignment marks between the clutch cover and the flywheel, so that the clutch can be installed in its original position.

3 If the original pressure plate is to be re-used, engage the three legs of the BMW clutch compressing tool (No 21 2 170) with the clutch cover in the area of the adjusting springs (see illustration). Screw down the knurled collar to lock the legs in place, then tighten down the spindle to compress the diaphragm spring.

2.3 Use BMW tool 21 2 170 to compress the diaphragm spring

4   Regardless of whether the pressure plate is to be replaced, progressively unscrew the bolts securing the clutch cover to the flywheel and, where applicable, recover the washers.

5   Withdraw the clutch cover from the flywheel. Be prepared to catch the clutch friction disc, which may drop out of the cover as it is withdrawn, and note which way the friction disc is installed - the two sides of the disc are normally marked Engine side and Transmission side. The greater projecting side of the hub faces away from the flywheel.

INSPECTION

6   With the clutch assembly removed, clean off all traces of dust using a dry cloth. Although most friction discs now have asbestos-free linings, some do not, and it is wise to take suitable precautions; asbestos dust is harmful, and must not be inhaled.

7   Examine the linings of the friction disc for wear and loose rivets, and the disc for distortion, cracks, and worn splines. The surface of the friction linings may be highly glazed, but, as long as the friction material pattern can be clearly seen, this is satisfactory. If there is any sign of oil contamination, indicated by a continuous, or patchy, shiny black discoloration, the disc must be replaced. The source of the contamination must be traced and rectified before installing new clutch compo-

nents; typically, a leaking crankshaft rear oil seal or transmission input shaft oil seal - or both - will be to blame (replacement procedures are given in the relevant Part of Chapter 2, and Chapter 7A respectively). The disc must also be replaced if the lining thickness has worn down to, or just above, the level of the rivet heads. Note that BMW specifies a minimum friction material thickness above the heads of the rivets (see Specifications).

8   Check the machined faces of the flywheel and pressure plate. If either is grooved, or heavily scored, replacement is necessary. The pressure plate must also be replaced if any cracks are apparent, or if the diaphragm spring is damaged or its pressure suspect.

9   With the clutch removed, it is advisable to check the condition of the release bearing, as described in Section 3.

10 Check the pilot bearing in the end of the crankshaft. Make sure that it turns smoothly and quietly. If the transmission input shaft contact face on the bearing is worn or damaged, install a new bearing, as described in the relevant Part of Chapter 2.

INSTALLATION

▶ **Refer to illustrations 2.13a, 2.13b, 2.14, 2.15 and 2.18**

11 If new clutch components are to be installed, ensure that all anti-corrosion preservative is cleaned from the friction material on the disc, and the contact surfaces of the pressure plate. Use brake system cleaner to clean the surfaces.

12 It is important to ensure that no oil or grease gets onto the friction disc linings, or the pressure plate and flywheel faces. It is advisable to install the clutch assembly with clean hands, and to wipe down the pressure plate and flywheel faces with a clean rag before assembly begins.

13 Apply a small amount of molybdenum disulfide grease to the splines of the friction disc hub. Match the disc to the flywheel, with the greater projecting side of the hub facing away from the flywheel (most friction discs will have an Engine side or Transmission side marking which should face the flywheel or transmission as applicable) (see illustration). Using tool BMW tool 21 2 142, center the friction disc in the flywheel (see illustration).

14 If the original pressure plate and cover is to be installed, engage the legs of BMW tool 21 2 170 with the cover (if removed), and compress the diaphragm spring fingers as described in Paragraph 3.

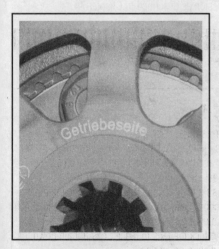

2.13a The friction disc may be marked Getriebeseite meaning Transmission side

2.13b Use a clutch alignment tool to center the friction disc

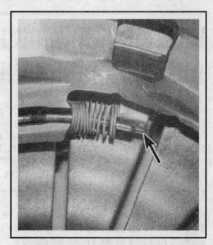

2.14a Push the adjustment ring thrust pieces fully counterclockwise . . .

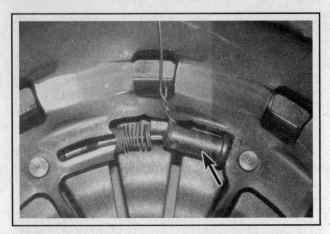

2.14b . . . and insert metal spacers between the thrust pieces and the cover

2.14c A special BMW tool is available to reset the adjustment ring thrust pieces

Using a screwdriver, reset the self-adjusting mechanism by pushing the adjustment ring thrust pieces fully anti-clockwise, while undoing the special tool spindle only enough to allow the adjustment ring to move. With the adjustment ring reset, tighten down the special tool spindle to compress the spring fingers, while preventing the adjustment ring thrust pieces from moving by inserting metal spacers in the gap between the thrust pieces and the cover. Note that a special tool is available from BMW to reset the adjustment ring (see illustrations)

15 Install the clutch cover assembly, aligning the marks on the flywheel and clutch cover (where applicable). Ensure that the clutch cover locates over the dowels on the flywheel (see illustration). Insert the securing bolts and washers, and tighten them to the specified torque.

16 If a new pressure plate cover was installed, insert a 14 mm Allen key into the center of the diaphragm spring locking piece, and turn it clockwise and remove it to release the spring.

17 Where the original pressure plate cover was installed, undo the spindle and knurled collar, then remove the compression tool from the cover. Pry out the metal spacers holding the adjustment ring thrust pieces in place (see illustration).

2.15 Ensure the cover locates over the flywheel dowels

✳✳ CAUTION:

As the last spacer is withdrawn, the adjustment ring may spring into place. Ensure your fingers are clear of the area.

---

18 Remove the clutch friction disc centering tool by screwing a 10 mm bolt into its end and pulling using a pair of pliers or similar (see illustration).

19 Install the transmission as described in Chapter 7A.

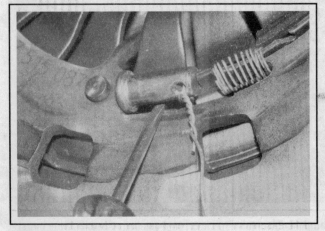

2.17 Keep your fingers away when removing the metal spacers

2.18 Thread the bolt into the end of the centering tool, then pull it out

3   Clutch release bearing and lever - removal, inspection and installation

❊❊ WARNING:

Dust created by clutch wear and deposited on the clutch components, is a health hazard. DO NOT blow it out with compressed air, or inhale any of it. DO NOT use gasoline (or petroleum-based solvents) to clean off the dust. Brake system cleaner should be used to flush the dust into a suitable receptacle. After the clutch components are wiped clean with rags, dispose of the contaminated rags and cleaner in a sealed, marked container.

RELEASE BEARING

Removal

◗ **Refer to illustration 3.2**

1   Remove the transmission as described in Chapter 7A.
2   Pull the bearing forwards, and slide it from the guide sleeve in the bellhousing (see illustration).

Inspection

3   Spin the release bearing, and check it for excessive roughness. Hold the outer race, and attempt to move it laterally against the inner race. If any excessive movement or roughness is evident, replace the bearing. If a new clutch has been installed, it is wise to replace the release bearing as a matter of course.

Installation

4   Clean and then lightly apply high-temperature grease to the release bearing contact surfaces on the release lever and guide sleeve.
5   Slide the bearing into position on the guide sleeve, ensuring that the bearing engages correctly with the release lever.
6   Install the transmission, referring to Chapter 7A.

RELEASE LEVER

Removal

◗ **Refer to illustration 3.8**

7   Remove the release bearing, as described previously in this Section.

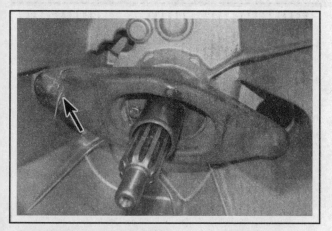

3.8 Slide the release lever sideways to disengage the retaining clip

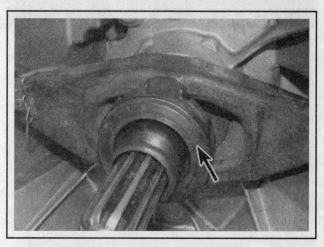

3.2 Pull the release bearing from the guide sleeve

8   Slide the release lever sideways to release it from the retaining spring clip and pivot, then pull the lever forwards from the guide sleeve (see illustration).

Inspection

9   Inspect the release bearing, pivot and slave cylinder pushrod contact faces on the release lever for wear. Replace the lever if excessive wear is evident.
10 Check the release lever retaining spring clip, and replace if necessary. It is advisable to replace the clip as a matter of course.

Installation

◗ **Refer to illustration 3.11**

11 Slide the release lever into position over the guide sleeve, then push the end of the lever over the pivot, ensuring that the retaining spring clip engages correctly over the end of the release lever (see illustration).
12 Install the release bearing as described previously in this Section.

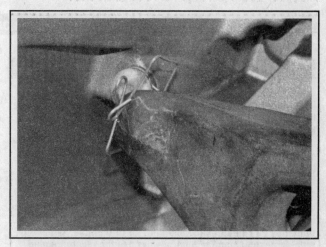

3.11 Ensure that the lever engages correctly with the retaining clip

4 Clutch slave cylinder - removal, inspection and installation

REMOVAL

▸ **Refer to illustration 4.4**

1 Remove the brake fluid reservoir cap, and siphon out sufficient brake fluid so that the fluid level is below the level of the reservoir fluid hose connection to the clutch master cylinder (the brake fluid reservoir feeds both the brake and clutch hydraulic systems). Do not empty the reservoir, as this will draw air into the brake hydraulic circuits.

2 To improve access, raise the vehicle and support it securely on jackstands.

3 Where applicable, remove the underbody shield for access to the bellhousing.

4 Place a container beneath the hydraulic line connection on the clutch slave cylinder to catch escaping brake fluid. Unscrew the fitting nuts and disconnect the fluid line. Remove the nut securing the line bracket to the slave cylinder (see illustration)

5 Remove the remaining securing nut, and withdraw the slave cylinder from the mounting studs on the bellhousing.

INSPECTION

6 Inspect the slave cylinder for fluid leaks and damage, and replace if necessary. No spare parts are available for the slave cylinder, and if faulty, the complete unit must be replaced.

INSTALLATION

7 Installation is the reverse of removal, noting the following points.
   a) *Before installation, clean and lightly grease the end of the slave cylinder pushrod.*
   b) *Tighten the mounting nuts to the specified torque.*
   c) *On completion, top-up the brake fluid level and bleed the clutch hydraulic circuit as described in Section 6.*

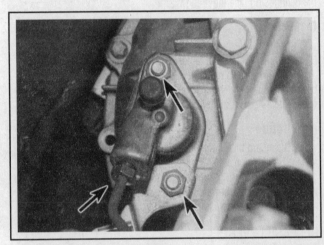

4.4 Disconnect the line fitting, then remove the retaining nuts

5 Clutch master cylinder - removal, inspection and installation

REMOVAL

▸ **Refer to illustrations 5.5, 5.6, and 5.7**

1 Remove the brake fluid reservoir cap, and siphon out sufficient brake fluid so that the fluid level is below the level of the reservoir fluid hose connection to the clutch master cylinder (the brake fluid reservoir feeds both the brake and clutch hydraulic systems). Do not empty the reservoir, as this will draw air into the brake hydraulic circuits.

2 Disconnect the clutch master cylinder hose from the brake fluid reservoir. Be prepared for fluid spillage, and plug the open end of the hose to prevent dirt entry.

3 Working inside the vehicle, remove the securing screws, and remove the driver's side lower dash trim panel (see Chapter 11).

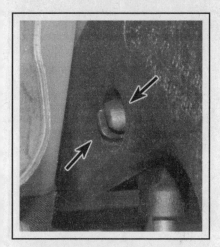

5.5 Squeeze together the ends and remove the pivot pin

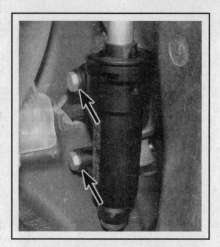

5.6 Remove the master cylinder bolts

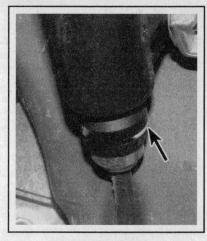

5.7 Pry out the retaining clip

4   Disconnect the electrical connector, and remove the clutch pedal switch by depressing the pedal, pulling out the switch red sleeve to its full extent, then squeeze together the two retaining clips and pull the switch from the bracket.

5   Squeeze together the two ends then press out the master cylinder pushrod pivot pin from the clutch pedal (see illustration).

6   Remove the fasteners securing the master cylinder to the pedal bracket in the footwell (see illustration).

7   Using a small screwdriver, pry out the retaining clip and then pull the master cylinder from the hydraulic pressure hose (which goes to the slave cylinder) (see illustration). Withdraw the master cylinder, and carefully ease the fluid supply hose through the firewall.

INSPECTION

8   Inspect the master cylinder for fluid leaks and damage, and replace if necessary. No spare parts are available for the master cylinder, and if faulty, the complete unit must be replaced.

INSTALLATION

9   Installation is the reverse of removal, noting the following points.

a) *Take care not to strain the master cylinder fluid supply hose during installation.*

b) *On completion, top up the fluid level in the reservoir, then bleed the clutch hydraulic system (see Section 6).*

6 Clutch hydraulic system - bleeding

✵ WARNING:

Brake fluid is poisonous; wash off immediately and thoroughly in the case of skin contact, and seek immediate medical advise if any fluid is swallowed or gets into the eyes. Certain types of brake fluid are flammable and may ignite when allowed into contact with hot components; when servicing any hydraulic system, it is safest to assume that the fluid is flammable, and to take precautions against the risk of fire as though it is gasoline that is being handled. Brake fluid is also an effective paint stripper, and will attack plastics; if any is spilled, it should be washed off immediately, using copious quantities of fresh water. Finally, it is hygroscopic (it absorbs moisture from the air) - old fluid may be contaminated and unfit for further use. When topping-up or replacing the fluid, always use the recommended type, and ensure that it comes from a freshly-opened sealed container.

➡**Note: BMW recommends the use of pressure-bleeding equipment to bleed the clutch hydraulic system.**

GENERAL

♦ **Refer to illustration 6.7**

1   The correct operation of any hydraulic system is only possible after removing all air from the components and circuit; this is achieved by bleeding the system.

2   During the bleeding procedure, add only clean, unused brake fluid of the recommended type; never re-use fluid that has already been bled from the system. Ensure that sufficient fluid is available before starting work.

3   If there is any possibility of incorrect fluid being already in the system, the brake and clutch components and circuit must be flushed completely with uncontaminated, correct fluid, and new seals should be installed to the various components.

4   If brake fluid has been lost from the system, or air has entered because of a leak, ensure that the fault is cured before proceeding further.

5   To improve access, apply the parking brake, then jack up the

front of the vehicle, and support it securely on jackstands.

6   Remove the screws and remove the underbody shield for access to the bellhousing.

7   Check that the clutch hydraulic line(s) and hose(s) are secure, that the fittings are tight, and that the bleed screw on the rear of the clutch slave cylinder (mounted under the vehicle on the lower left-hand side of the bellhousing) is closed. Clean any dirt from around the bleed screw (see illustration).

8   Unscrew the brake fluid reservoir cap, and top the fluid up to the MAX level line; install the cap loosely, and remember to maintain the fluid level at least above the MIN level line throughout the procedure, or there is a risk of further air entering the system. Note that the brake fluid reservoir feeds both the brake and clutch hydraulic systems.

9   It is recommended that pressure-bleeding equipment is used to bleed the system. Alternatively, there are a number of one-man, do-it-yourself brake bleeding kits currently available from motor accessory shops. These kits greatly simplify the bleeding operation, and also reduce the risk of expelled air and fluid being drawn back into the system. If such a kit is not available, the basic (two-man) method must be used, which is described in detail below.

10   If pressure-bleeding equipment or a one-man kit is to be used, prepare the vehicle as described previously, and follow the equipment/kit manufacturer's instructions, as the procedure may vary slightly according to the type being used; generally, they are as outlined below in the relevant sub-section.

11   Whichever method is used, the same basic process must be followed to ensure that all air is removed from the system.

BLEEDING

Basic (two-man) method

12   Using a clean glass jar, a suitable length of plastic or rubber tubing which is a tight fit over the bleed screw, and a flare nut wrench for the screw. The help of an assistant will also be required.

13   Where applicable, remove the dust cap from the bleed screw. Apply the wrench and tube to the screw, place the other end of the tube in the jar, and pour in sufficient fluid to cover the end of the tube.

14   Ensure that the reservoir fluid level is maintained at least above the MIN level line throughout the procedure.

15   Have the assistant fully depress the clutch pedal several times to build-up pressure, then maintain it on the final downstroke.

16   While pedal pressure is maintained, unscrew the bleed screw (approximately one turn) and allow the fluid (along with any air) to flow into the jar. The assistant should maintain pedal pressure, following it down to the floor if necessary, and should not release it until instructed to do so. When the flow slows, tighten the bleed screw again, have the assistant release the pedal slowly, and recheck the reservoir fluid level.

17   Repeat the steps given in Steps 15 and 16 until the fluid emerging from the bleed screw is free from air bubbles.

18   When no more air bubbles appear, tighten the bleed screw securely. Do not overtighten the bleed screw.

19   Temporarily disconnect the bleed tube from the bleed screw, and move the container of fluid to one side.

20   Unscrew the two securing nuts, and withdraw the slave cylinder from the bellhousing, taking care not to strain the fluid hose.

21   Reconnect the bleed tube to the bleed screw, and submerge the end of the tube in the container of fluid.

22   With the bleed screw pointing vertically upwards, unscrew the bleed screw (approximately one turn), and slowly push the slave cylinder pushrod into the cylinder until no more air bubbles appear in the fluid.

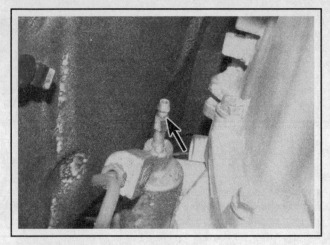

6.7 Clutch slave cylinder bleed screw

23   Hold the pushrod in position, then tighten the bleed screw.

24   Slowly allow the pushrod to return to its rest position. Do not allow the pushrod to return quickly, as this will cause air to enter the slave cylinder.

25   Remove the tube and wrench, and install the dust cap to the bleed screw.

26   Install the slave cylinder to the bellhousing, and tighten the securing nuts to the specified torque.

Using a one-way valve kit

27   As their name implies, these kits consist of a length of tubing with a one-way valve installed to prevent expelled air and fluid being drawn back into the system; some kits include a translucent container, which can be positioned so that the air bubbles can be more easily seen flowing from the end of the tube.

28   The kit is connected to the bleed screw, which is then opened. The user returns to the driver's seat, depresses the clutch pedal with a smooth, steady stroke, and slowly releases it; this is repeated until the expelled fluid is clear of air bubbles.

29   Note that these kits simplify work so much that it is easy to forget the reservoir fluid level; ensure that this is maintained at least above the MIN level line at all times.

Using a pressure-bleeding kit

30   These kits are usually operated by the reservoir of pressurized air contained in the spare tire. However, note that it will probably be necessary to reduce the pressure to a lower level than normal; refer to the instructions supplied with the kit.

31   By connecting a pressurized, fluid-filled container to the fluid reservoir, bleeding can be carried out simply by opening the bleed screw, and allowing the fluid to flow out until no more air bubbles can be seen in the expelled fluid.

32   This method has the advantage that the large reservoir of fluid provides an additional safeguard against air being drawn into the system during bleeding.

All methods

33   If after following the instructions given, it is suspected that air is still present in hydraulic system, remove the slave cylinder (Section 4) without disconnecting the hydraulic lines, push the cylinder piston all the way in, and holding the cylinder with the bleed screw pointing up, bleed the system again.

➡Note: Steps must be taken to ensure that the slave cylinder piston is prevented from extending during the bleeding procedure. If necessary, use a metal strip and two threaded bars to fabricate a tool to hold the piston in.

34 When bleeding is complete, and firm pedal feel is restored, wash off any spilt fluid, check that the bleed screw is tightened securely, and install the dust cap.

➡Note: Be careful not to overtighten the bleed screw.

35 Check the brake fluid level in the reservoir, and top-up if necessary (see Chapter 1).

36 Discard any brake fluid that has been bled from the system; it is not fit for re-use.

37 Check the feel of the clutch pedal. If it feels at all spongy, air must still be present in the system, and further bleeding is required. Failure to bleed satisfactorily after a reasonable repetition of the bleeding procedure may be due to worn master or slave cylinder seals.

38 On completion, where applicable install the underbody shield and lower the vehicle to the ground.

7 Clutch pedal - removal and installation

➡Note: A new self-locking nut should be used to secure the clutch master cylinder on installation.

REMOVAL

▶ **Refer to illustration 7.6**

1 Working inside the vehicle, release the retaining clips/screws, and withdraw the driver's side lower dash panel (see Chapter 11).

2 Where applicable, remove the clutch pedal switch, by depressing the pedal, pulling out the switch red sleeve to its full extent, then squeeze together the two retaining clips and pull the switch from the bracket.

3 Squeeze together the two halves of the end, then press out the master cylinder pushrod pivot pin from the clutch pedal (see illustration 5.5).

4 Carefully disconnect the return spring from the pedal using a pair of pliers.

5 Remove the two plastic nuts, and place the anti-theft ECM to one side.

6 Pry off the clip securing the pedal to the pivot shaft, then slide to the right, and remove the clutch pedal. Recover the pivot bushings if they are loose (see illustration).

INSTALLATION

7 Before installation of the pedal to the pivot shaft, check the condition of the pivot bushings, and replace if necessary. Apply a little grease to the bushings.

8 Installation is a reversal of removal. Ensure that the clutch switch plunger is fully extended prior to installation.

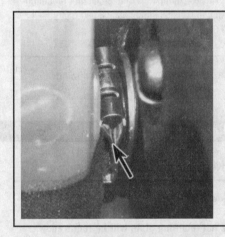

7.6 Pry off the pedal shaft clip

8 Differential - removal and installation

➡Note: New driveshaft rear coupling nuts and driveshaft retaining bolts will be required on installation.

REMOVAL

▶ **Refer to illustrations 8.9a and 8.9b**

1 Chock the front wheels. Loosen the rear wheel bolts, raise the rear of the vehicle and support it securely on jackstands. Remove both rear wheels. If necessary, drain the differential unit as described in Chapter 1.

2 Using paint or a suitable marker pen, make alignment marks between the driveshaft and differential unit flange. Unscrew the nuts securing the driveshaft to the differential unit and discard them; new ones must be used on installation.

3 Loosen and remove the retaining bolts and plates securing the right-hand driveshaft to the differential unit flange and support the driveshaft by tying it to the vehicle underbody using a piece of wire.

➡Note: Do not allow the driveshaft to hang under its own weight as the CV joint may be damaged. Discard the bolts, new ones should be used on installation.

4 Disconnect the left-hand driveshaft from the differential as described in Paragraph 3.

5 Unscrew the nuts/bolts and remove the heat shield panel from the left-hand end of the tension strut beneath the differential input shaft flange.

6 Disconnect the electrical connector from the speedometer drive on the rear of the differential unit (if equipped).

7 Loosen and remove the left- and right-hand stabilizer bar mounts (see Chapter 10).

8 Move a jack into position and raise it so that it is supporting the weight of the differential unit.

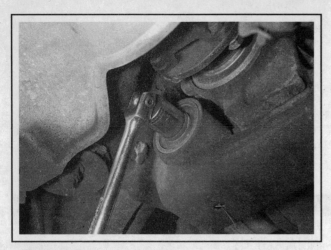

8.9a Unscrew the front . . .

8.9b . . . and rear differential mounting bolts

9   Making sure the differential unit is safely supported, remove the two bolts securing the front of the unit in position and the single bolt securing the rear of the unit in position (see illustrations).

10   Carefully lower the differential unit out of position and remove it from underneath the vehicle. Examine the differential unit mounting bushings for signs of wear or damage and replace if necessary.

INSTALLATION

11   Installation is a reversal of removal noting the following.

a) Raise the differential unit into position and engage it with the driveshaft rear joint, making sure the marks made prior to removal are correctly aligned.
b) Tighten the differential unit mounting bolts to the specified torque setting.
c) Install the new driveshaft joint nuts and tighten them to the specified torque.
d) Install the stabilizer bar mountings (see Chapter 10).
e) Install the new driveshaft joint retaining bolts and plates and tighten them to the specified torque.
f) On completion, refill/top-up the differential unit with oil as described in Chapter 1.

9   Differential oil seals - replacement

DRIVESHAFT FLANGE OIL SEAL

◆ Refer to illustration 9.3

➡Note: A new flange nut retaining plate will be required.

1   Drain the differential as described in Chapter 1.

2   Remove the differential unit as described in Section 8 and carefully secure the unit in a vise (or equivalent).

3   Remove the retaining plate and make alignment marks between the drive flange nut, the drive flange and pinion (see illustration). Discard the retaining plate a new one must be used on installation.

4   Hold the drive flange stationary by bolting a length of metal bar to it, then unscrew the nut noting the exact number of turns necessary to remove it.

5   Using a suitable puller, draw the drive flange from the pinion and remove the dust cover. If the dust cover shows signs of wear, replace it.

6   Pry the oil seal from the differential casing with a screwdriver or seal removal tool and clean the oil seal seat.

7   Apply a little oil on the sealing lip of the new oil seal, then press it squarely into the casing until it is flush with the outer face. If necessary, the seal can be tapped into position using a metal tube that only contacts its hard outer edge.

8   Install the dust cover and locate the drive flange on the pinion aligning the marks made on removal. Install the flange nut, screwing it on by the exact number of turns counted on removal, so that the alignment marks match.

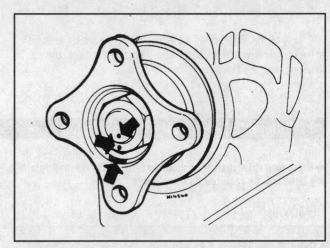

9.3 Make alignment marks on the flange, the pinion shaft and nut to ensure proper reassembly

✳✳ WARNING:

Do not overtighten the flange nut. If the nut is overtightened, the collapsible spacer behind the flange will be deformed necessitating its replacement. This is a complex operation requiring the differential unit to be disassembled (see Section 1).

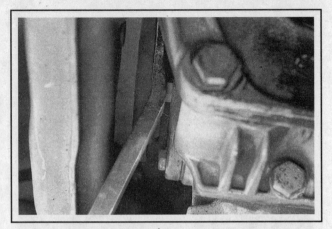

9.13 Use a suitable lever to remove the driveshaft flange from the differential unit

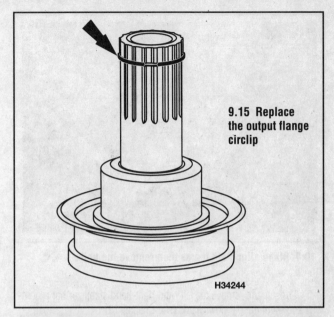

9.15 Replace the output flange circlip

9   Secure the nut in position with the new retaining plate, tapping it squarely into position.

10 Install the differential as described in Section 8 and refill it with oil as described in Chapter 1.

DRIVEAXLE FLANGE OIL SEAL

▶ **Refer to illustrations 9.13, 9.15 and 9.17**

➡**Note: New driveaxle joint retaining bolts and a driveshaft flange circlip will be required.**

11 Drain the differential oil as described in Chapter 1.

12 Loosen and remove the bolts securing the driveshaft constant velocity joint to the differential unit and recover the retaining plates. Position the driveshaft clear of the flange and tie it to the vehicle underbody using a piece of wire.

➡**Note: Do not allow the driveshaft to hang under its own weight as the CV joint may be damaged.**

13 Using a suitable lever, carefully pry the driveshaft flange out from the differential unit taking care not to damage the dust seal or casing (see illustration). Remove the flange and recover dust seal. If the dust seal shows signs of damage, replace it.

14 Carefully pry the oil seal out from the differential unit and clean the oil seal seat.

15 With the flange removed, pry out the circlip from the end of the splined shaft (see illustration).

16 Install a new circlip, making sure its is correctly located in the splined shaft groove.

17 Apply a little differential oil on the sealing lip of the new oil seal, then press it squarely into the casing until it reaches its stop. If neces-

9.17 Tap the new seal into position using a socket which only contacts the hard outer edge of the seal

sary, the seal can be tapped into position using a large socket that only contacts its hard outer edge (see illustration).

18 Install the dust cover and insert the drive flange. Push the drive flange fully into position and check that it is securely retained by the circlip.

19 Align the driveshaft with the flange and install the new retaining bolts and plates, tightening them to the specified torque.

20 Refill the differential unit with oil as described in Chapter 1.

10 Driveaxle - removal and installation

➡**Note: New driveshaft retaining fasteners will be required on installation.**

REMOVAL

▶ **Refer to illustration 10.7**

1   Remove the wheel trim/hub cap (as applicable) and loosen the driveaxle retaining nut with the vehicle resting on its wheels. Also loosen the wheel bolts.

2   Chock the front wheels, then raise the rear of the vehicle and support it on jackstands.

3   Remove the relevant rear wheel.

4   If the left-hand driveaxle is to be removed, remove the exhaust system tailpipe to improve access.

10.7 Make alignment marks then remove the bolts

10.10 When the driveshaft nut has been fully tightened, stake the nut using a punch

5   Loosen and remove the left- and right-hand stabilizer bar mountings and pivot the bar downwards (see Chapter 10).

6   Remove the driveaxle nut.

7   Make alignment marks, then loosen and remove the bolts securing the driveaxle constant velocity joint to the differential unit and recover the retaining plates (if equipped) (see illustration). Position the driveaxle clear of the flange and tie it to the vehicle underbody using a piece of wire.

➡**Note: Do not allow the driveaxle to hang under its own weight, as the CV joint may be damaged.**

8   Withdraw the driveaxle outer constant velocity joint from the hub assembly. The outer joint will be very tight; carefully tap the joint out of the hub using a soft-faced hammer. If this fails to free it from the hub, the joint will have to be pressed out using a suitable tool.

9   Remove the driveaxle from underneath the vehicle.

INSTALLATION

▶ **Refer to illustration 10.10**

10 Installation is the reverse of removal noting the following points.

a) *Apply a drop of clean oil to the new driveaxle nut (where it contacts the flange) prior to installing it and tighten it to the specified torque. If necessary, wait until the vehicle is lower to the ground and then tighten the nut to the specified torque. Once tightened, use a hammer and punch to stake the nut (see illustration).*

b) *Install new inner joint retaining bolts and plates (if equipped) and tighten to the specified torque.*

11 Driveaxle boots - replacement

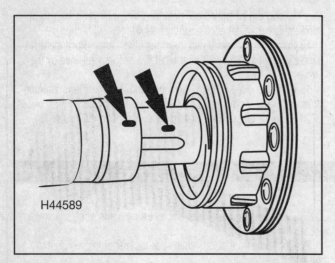

H44589

11.4 Make alignment marks, then slide the joint from the tube

1   Remove the driveaxle (see Section 10).

2   Clean the driveaxle and carefully mount it in a vise.

TELESCOPIC DRIVEAXLES

▶ **Refer to illustration 11.4**

3   Some models are equipped with a driveaxle where the inner CV joint is mounted on a short shaft which slides into the main driveaxle body. Release the two inner joint boot retaining clips and slide the boot away from the joint.

4   Make alignment marks between the CV joint shaft and the driveaxle tube, then slide the CV joint and shaft from the driveaxle (see illustration).

5   Release the two outer joint boot retaining clips and slide both boots from the inner end of the shaft.

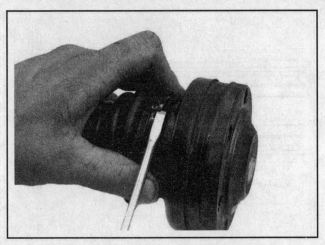

11.6 Release the boot retaining clips and slide the boot down the shaft

11.7 Carefully remove the sealing cover from the inner end of the joint

OTHER DRIVEAXLES

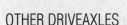 **Refer to illustrations 11.6, 11.7, 11.8, 11.9 and 11.10**

6   Release the two inner joint boot retaining clips and free the boot and dust cover from the joint (see illustration).

7   Lever off the sealing cover from the end of the inner constant velocity (CV) joint (see illustration).

8   Scoop out excess grease and remove the inner joint circlip from the end of the driveaxle (see illustration).

9   Securely support the joint inner member and tap the driveaxle out of position using a hammer and suitable drift (see illustration). If the joint is a tight fit, a suitable puller will be required to draw off the joint. Do not dismantle the inner joint.

10   With the joint removed, slide the inner boot and dust cover off from the end of the driveaxle (see illustration).

11   Release the outer joint boot retaining clips then slide the boot along the shaft and remove it.

ALL DRIVEAXLES

12   Thoroughly clean the constant velocity joints using a suitable solvent and dry it thoroughly. Carry out a visual inspection as follows.

11.8 Remove the inner joint circlip from the driveshaft

13 Move the inner splined driving member from side-to-side to expose each ball in turn at the top of its track. Examine the balls for cracks, flat spots or signs of surface pitting.

14 Inspect the ball tracks on the inner and outer members. If the tracks have widened, the balls will no longer be a tight fit. At the same

11.9 Support the inner joint inner member then tap the driveshaft out of position . . .

11.10 . . . and slide off the boot

time check the ball cage windows for wear or cracking between the windows.

15 If on inspection any of the constant velocity joint components are found to be worn or damaged, it must be replaced. The inner joint is available separately but if the outer joint is worn it will be necessary to replace the complete joint and driveaxle assembly. If the joints are in satisfactory condition, obtain new boot repair kits which contain boots, retaining clips, an inner constant velocity joint circlip and the correct type and quantity of grease required.

TELESCOPIC DRIVEAXLES

▶ **Refer to illustration 11.18**

16 Slide the new boots over the inner end of the driveaxle. Note that the outer boot has a length of 55 mm, and the inner boot is 65 mm long.

17 Repack both CV joints using the grease supplied in the boot kits.

18 Apply grease to the splines of the inner CV joint shaft. Align the previously made marks, and insert the CV joint shaft into the end of the driveshaft as far as it will go, then pull it back out so that the edge of the joint is the correct distance from the end of the driveaxle (see illustration).

19 Ease the boots over the joints and ensure the boot lips are correctly located on the driveshaft and CV joints. Lift the outer sealing lips of the boots to equalize air pressure within the boots.

20 Position the inner joint boot clips so that the fasteners are in line with the rivet on the flange. Secure the retaining clips in position.

21 Position the outer joint boot clips so that the fasteners are on the other side of the shaft from the inner clips fasteners, i.e. 180° offset.

OTHER DRIVEAXLES

▶ **Refer to illustrations 11.29a and 11.29b**

22 Tape over the splines on the end of the driveaxle.

23 Slide the new outer boot onto the end of the driveaxle.

24 Pack the outer joint with the grease supplied in the boot kit. Work the grease well into the bearing tracks while twisting the joint, and fill the rubber boot with any excess.

11.29a Fill the inner joint with the grease supplied . . .

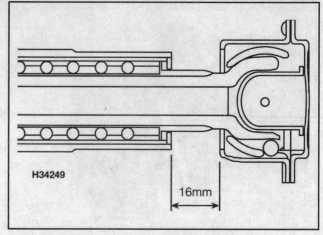

11.18 After greasing the shaft, push it in as far as it will go, then pull it out so that the gap is 16 mm (approx.)

25 Ease the boot over the joint and ensure that the boot lips are correctly located on both the driveaxle and constant velocity joint. Lift the outer sealing lip of the boot to equalize air pressure within the boot.

26 Install the large metal retaining clip to the boot. Pull the retaining clip tight then bend it back to secure it in position and cut off any excess clip. Secure the small retaining clip using the same procedure.

27 Engage the new inner boot with its dust cover and slide the assembly onto the driveaxle.

28 Remove the tape from the driveaxle splines and install the inner constant velocity joint. Press the joint fully onto the shaft and secure it in position with a new circlip.

29 Work the grease supplied fully into the inner joint and fill the boot with any excess (see illustrations).

30 Slide the inner boot into position and press the dust cover onto the joint, making sure the retaining bolt holes are correctly aligned. Lift the outer sealing lip of the boot, to equalize air pressure within the boot, and secure it in position with the retaining clips (see paragraph 26).

31 Apply a small amount of suitable sealant (BMW recommends BMW sealing gel) and press the new sealing cover fully onto the end of the inner joint.

ALL DRIVEAXLES

32 Check that both constant velocity joints are free to move easily then install the driveaxle as described in Section 10.

11.29b . . . and work it into the bearing tracks

12 Driveshaft - removal and installation

➡Note: New driveshaft front and rear coupling nuts will be required on installation.

REMOVAL

▸ Refer to illustrations 12.4, 12.5 and 12.7

1 Chock the front wheels. Jack up the rear of the vehicle and support it on jackstands.
2 Remove the exhaust system and heat shield as described in Chapter 4. Where necessary, unbolt the exhaust system mounting bracket(s) in order to gain the necessary clearance required to remove the driveshaft.
3 On models where the front of the driveshaft is bolted straight onto the transmission output flange, make alignment marks between the shaft and transmission flange then loosen and remove the retaining nuts. Discard the nuts - new ones should be used on installation.
4 On models where a rubber coupling is installed between the front end of the driveshaft and transmission output flange, make alignment marks between the shaft, transmission flange and rubber coupling. Loosen and remove the nuts and bolts securing the coupling to the transmission (see illustration). Discard the nuts - new ones should be used on installation.
5 Using a large open-ended wrench, or suitable adjustable pliers, loosen the threaded sleeve nut, which is situated near the support bearing, a couple of turns (see illustration).
6 Using paint or a suitable marker pen, make alignment marks between the driveshaft and differential unit flange. Unscrew the nuts securing the driveshaft to the differential unit and discard them; new ones must be used on installation.
7 With the aid of an assistant, support the driveshaft then unscrew the center support bearing bracket retaining nuts (see illustration). Slide the two halves of the shaft towards each other then lower the center of the shaft and disengage it from the transmission and differential unit. Remove the shaft from underneath the vehicle.

➡Note: Do not separate the two halves of the shaft without first making alignment marks. If the shafts are incorrectly joined, the driveshaft assembly may become unbalanced, leading to noise and vibration during operation.

8 Inspect the rubber coupling (if equipped), the support bearing and shaft universal joints as described in Sections 13, 14 and 15. Inspect the transmission flange locating pin and driveshaft bushing for signs of wear or damage and replace as necessary.

12.4 Loosen and remove the bolts securing the coupling to the transmission flange

12.5 Unscrew the large threaded sleeve a couple of turns

INSTALLATION

▸ Refer to illustration 12.9

9 Apply a small amount of molybdenum disulfide grease to the transmission pin and shaft bushing and maneuver the shaft into position (see illustration).

12.7 Remove the center bearing bracket retaining nuts

12.9 Apply moly-based grease to the transmission pin

10 Align the marks made prior to removal and engage the shaft with the transmission and differential unit flanges. With the marks correctly aligned, install the support bracket retaining nuts, tightening them lightly only at this stage.

11 Install new retaining bolts to the rear coupling of the driveshaft and tighten them to the specified torque.

12 On models where the driveshaft is bolted straight onto the transmission flange, install the new retaining nuts and tighten them to the specified torque.

13 On models with a rubber coupling, insert the bolts and install the new retaining nuts. Tighten them to the specified torque, noting that the nut/bolt should only be rotated on the flange side to avoid stressing the rubber coupling.

14 Tighten the driveshaft threaded sleeve nut securely.

15 Loosen the center bearing bracket nuts. Slide the bracket forwards to remove all free play, then preload the bearing by moving the bracket forwards another 4 to 6 mm. Hold the bracket in this position and tighten its retaining nuts to the specified torque.

16 Install the exhaust system and associated components as described in Chapter 4.

13 Driveshaft rubber coupling - check and replacement

➡ **Note: A rubber coupling is not installed on all models. On some models, a universal joint is installed to the front of the driveshaft instead.**

13.5 Coupling-to-driveshaft retaining bolts

CHECK

1 Firmly apply the parking brake, then raise the front of the vehicle and support it securely on jackstands.

2 Closely examine the rubber coupling, linking the driveshaft to the transmission, looking for signs of damage such as cracking or splitting or for signs of general deterioration. If necessary, replace the coupling as follows.

REPLACEMENT

▶ **Refer to illustrations 13.5 and 13.7**

➡ **Note: New driveshaft coupling nuts will be required.**

3 Carry out the operations described in Steps 1, 2, 4 and 5 of Section 12.

4 Slide the front half of the driveshaft to the rear then disengage it from the transmission locating pin and pivot it downwards.

5 Loosen and remove the nuts securing the coupling to the shaft and remove it (see illustration). If necessary, also remove the vibration damper; the damper should also be replaced if it shows signs of wear or damage.

6 Aligning the marks made on removal, install the vibration damper (if equipped) to the driveshaft.

7 Install the new rubber coupling noting that the arrows on the side of the coupling must point towards the driveshaft/transmission flanges (see illustration). Install the new retaining nuts and tighten them to the specified torque.

8 Apply a smear of molybdenum disulfide grease to the transmission pin and shaft bushing and maneuver the shaft into position.

9 Align the marks made prior to removal and engage the shaft with the transmission flange. With the marks correctly aligned, insert the bolts and install the new retaining nuts. Tighten them to the specified torque, noting that the nut/bolt should only be rotated on the flange side to avoid stressing the rubber coupling.

10 Tighten the driveshaft threaded sleeve securely.

11 Install the exhaust system and associated components as described in Chapter 4.

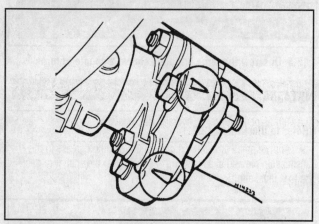

13.7 If the coupling has directional arrows, make sure the arrows are pointing towards the driveshaft/transmission flanges and not the bolt heads

14 Driveshaft support bearing - check and replacement

CHECK

1 Wear in the support bearing will lead to noise and vibration when the vehicle is driven. The bearing is best checked with the driveshaft removed (see Section 12). To gain access to the bearing with the shaft in position, remove the exhaust system and heat shields as described in Chapter 4.

2 Rotate the bearing and check that it turns smoothly with no sign of freeplay; if it's difficult to turn, or if it has a gritty feeling, replace it. Also inspect the rubber portion. If it's cracked or deteriorated, replace it.

REPLACEMENT

3   Remove the driveshaft as described in Section 12.

4   Make alignment marks between the front and rear sections of the driveshaft then unscrew the threaded sleeve nut and separate the two halves. Recover the sleeve nut, washer and bushing noting their correct locations.

5   Remove the circlip and slide off the support bearing rear dust cover.

6   Draw the support bearing off from the driveshaft using a suitable puller then remove the front dust cover in the same way.

7   Firmly support the support bearing bracket and press out the bearing with a suitable tubular spacer.

8   Install the new bearing to the bracket and press it into position using a tubular spacer that bears only on the bearing's outer race.

9   Thoroughly clean the shaft splines and carefully press the new front dust seal onto the driveshaft, making sure it is installed correctly.

10 Press the support bearing fully onto the driveshaft using a tubular spacer that only contacts the bearing's inner race.

11 Check that the bearing is free to rotate smoothly, then install the new rear dust seal.

12 Apply a small amount of molybdenum disulfide grease to the splines and install the threaded sleeve, washer and bushing to the front section of the driveshaft.

13 Align the marks made prior to separation and joint the front and rear sections of the driveshaft.

14 Install the driveshaft as described in Section 12.

15 Driveshaft universal joints - check and replacement

➡**Note: On some models a rubber coupling is installed between the driveshaft and transmission instead of a universal joint.**

CHECK

1   Wear in the universal joints is characterized by vibration in the transmission, noise during acceleration, and metallic squeaking and grating sounds as the bearings disintegrate. The joints can be checked with the driveshaft still installed noting that it will be necessary to remove the exhaust system and heat shields (see Chapter 4) to gain access.

2   If the driveshaft is in position on the vehicle, try to turn the driveshaft while holding the transmission/differential flange. Freeplay between the driveshaft and the front or rear flanges indicates excessive wear.

3   If the driveshaft is already removed, you can check the universal joints by holding the shaft in one hand and turning the yoke or flange with the other. If the axial movement is excessive, replace the driveshaft.

REPLACEMENT

4   At the time of writing, no spare parts were available to enable replacement of the universal joints to be carried out. Therefore, if any joint shows signs of damage or wear the complete driveshaft assembly must be replaced. Consult your BMW dealer for latest information on parts availability.

5   If replacement of the driveshaft is necessary, it may be worthwhile seeking the advise of an driveline specialist. They may be able to repair the original shaft assembly or supply a reconditioned shaft on an exchange basis.

Specifications

Type	Single clutch disc with diaphragm spring, hydraulically-operated

Clutch disc

Minimum lining thickness above rivet head	3/64-inch (1.0 mm)

Differential

Type	Unsprung, attached to rear suspension crossmember

Driveaxles

Type	Steel shafts with ball-and-cage type constant velocity joints at each end
Constant velocity joint grease capacity	80g in each joint

Driveshaft

Type	Two-piece tubular shaft with center bearing, center and rear universal joint. Front joint is either rubber coupling or universal joint (depending on model)

Torque specifications	Ft-lbs	Nm
Clutch cover-to-flywheel bolts	18	24
Clutch master cylinder bolts	16	22
Clutch release cylinder nuts	16	22
Hydraulic line fitting bolts	15	20
Differential mounting bolt		
Front bolt	70	95
Rear bolts	128	174
Oil filler and drain plug	52	70
Driveshaft flange retaining nut (approximate - see text)		
M20 nut	129	175
M22 nut	137	185
Vibration damper on bracket (if equipped)	57	77
Driveaxle		
Driveaxle retaining nut*		
M22 nut	148	200
M24 nut	185	250
M27 nut	221	300
Driveaxle-to-differential flange bolts		
Allen bolts:		
M10 bolts		
Bolts with serrations under bolt head	71	96
Bolts without serrations	61	83
M12 bolts	81	110
Torx bolts		
M10 bolts		
Plain bolts	61	83
Black bolts with serrations under bolt head	74	100
Silver bolts with serrations under bolt head	59	80
M8 bolts	47	64
M12 bolts	100	135
Driveshaft		
M10 bolts		
Strength grade 8.8 (see head of bolt)	35	48
Strength grade 10.9 (see head of bolt)	47	64
M12 bolts		
Strength grade 8.8 (see head of bolt)	60	81
Strength grade 10.9 (see head of bolt)	74	100
M14 bolts	103	140
Support bearing bracket nuts	15	21
Wheel bolts	See Chapter 1	

*Do not re-use

Section

Reference to other Chapters

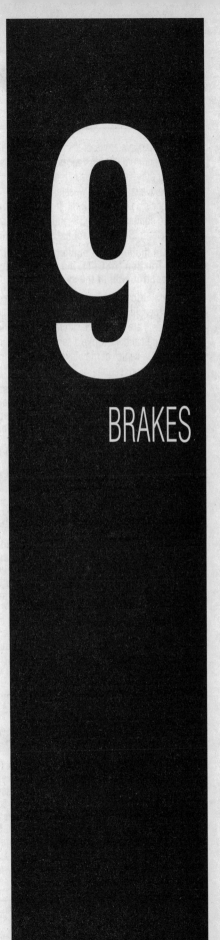

1 General information

GENERAL INFORMATION

The braking system is of the power-assisted, dual-circuit hydraulic type. Under normal circumstances, both circuits operate in unison. However, if there is hydraulic failure in one circuit, full braking force will still be available at two wheels.

All models are equipped with front and rear disc brakes. Most models are equipped with ABS, and was offered as an option on other models (refer to Section 19 for further information on ABS operation).

➡**Note: On models also equipped with Automatic Stability Control plus Traction (ASC+T), the ABS system also operates the traction control side of the system.**

The front disc brakes are actuated by single-piston sliding type calipers, which ensure that equal pressure is applied to each disc pad.

All models are equipped with rear disc brakes, actuated by single-piston sliding calipers, while a separate drum brake arrangement is installed in the center of the brake disc to provide a separate means of parking brake application.

➡**Note: When servicing any part of the system, work carefully and methodically; also observe scrupulous cleanliness when overhauling any part of the hydraulic system. Always replace components if in doubt about their condition (in axle sets,** where applicable), and use genuine BMW replacement parts, or parts of known good quality.

PRECAUTIONS

There are some general cautions and warnings involving the brake system on this vehicle:

a) *Only use the specified brake fluid conforming to DOT specifications.*

b) *The brake pads and linings contain fibers that are hazardous to your health if inhaled. Whenever you work on brake system components, clean all parts with brake system cleaner. Do not allow the fine dust to become airborne. Also, wear an approved filtering mask.*

c) *Safety should be paramount whenever any servicing of the brake components is performed. Do not use parts or fasteners that are not in perfect condition, and be sure that all clearances and torque specifications are adhered to. If you are at all unsure about a certain procedure, seek professional advice. Upon completion of any brake system work, test the brakes carefully in a controlled area before putting the vehicle into normal service. If a problem is suspected in the brake system, don't drive the vehicle until it's fixed.*

2 Hydraulic system - bleeding

✳✳ WARNING 1:

Brake fluid is poisonous; wash it off immediately and thoroughly in the case of skin contact, and seek immediate medical advice if any fluid is swallowed or gets into the eyes. Certain types of brake fluid are flammable, and may ignite when allowed into contact with hot components; when servicing any hydraulic system, it is safest to assume that the fluid is flammable, and to take precautions against the risk of fire as though it were gasoline. Brake fluid is also an effective paint stripper, and will attack plastics; if any is spilled, it should be washed off immediately, using copious quantities of fresh water. Finally, it is hygroscopic (it absorbs moisture from the air) - old fluid may be contaminated and unfit for further use. When topping-off or replacing the fluid, always use the recommended type, and ensure that it comes from a freshly-opened sealed container.

✳✳ WARNING 2:

On models with ABS (with or without ASC+T), if the high-pressure hydraulic system linking the master cylinder, hydraulic unit and accumulator (if equipped) has been disturbed, then bleeding of the brakes should be entrusted to a BMW dealer or other qualified repair shop. They will have access to the special service tester that is needed to operate the ABS modulator pump and bleed the high-pressure hydraulic system safely.

GENERAL

1   The correct operation of any hydraulic system is only possible after removing all air from the components and circuit; this is achieved by bleeding the system.

2   During the bleeding procedure, add only clean, unused brake fluid of the recommended type; never re-use fluid that has already been bled from the system. Ensure that sufficient fluid is available before starting work.

3   If there is any possibility of incorrect fluid being already in the system, the brake components and circuit must be flushed completely with uncontaminated, correct fluid, and new seals should be fitted to the various components.

4   If brake fluid has been lost from the system, or air has entered because of a leak, ensure that the fault is cured before continuing further.

5   Park the vehicle on level ground, switch off the engine and select first or reverse gear, then chock the wheels and release the parking brake.

6   Check that all lines and hoses are secure, fittings tight and bleed screws closed. Clean any dirt from around the bleed screws.

7   Unscrew the master cylinder reservoir cap, and fill the master cylinder reservoir to the MAX level line; install the cap loosely, and remember to maintain the fluid level at least above the MIN level line throughout the procedure, or there is a risk of further air entering the system.

8   There are a number of one-man, do-it-yourself brake bleeding kits currently available from motor accessory shops. It is recommended that one of these kits is used whenever possible, as they greatly simplify the bleeding operation, and reduce the risk of expelled air and fluid being drawn back into the system. If such a kit is not available, the basic (two-man) method must be used, which is described in detail below.

9   If a kit is to be used, prepare the vehicle as described previously, and follow the kit manufacturer's instructions, as the procedure may vary slightly according to the type being used; generally, they are as outlined below in the relevant sub-section.

10 Whichever method is used, the same sequence must be followed (paragraphs 11 and 12) to ensure the removal of all air from the system.

BLEEDING SEQUENCE

11 If the system has been only partially disconnected, and suitable precautions were taken to minimize fluid loss, it should be necessary only to bleed that part of the system.

12 If the complete system is to be bled, then it should be done working in the following sequence:

a) *Right-rear brake*
b) *Left-rear brake*
c) *Right-front brake*
d) *Left-front brake*

✳✳ WARNING:

On models with ABS (with or without ASC+T), after bleeding, the operation of the braking system should be checked at the earliest possible opportunity by a BMW dealer or suitably-equipped specialist.

Basic (two-man) method

13 Collect a clean glass jar, a suitable length of plastic or rubber tubing which is a tight fit over the bleed screw, and a flare-nut wrench to fit the screw. The help of an assistant will also be required.

14 Remove the dust cap from the first screw in the sequence. Fit the wrench and tube to the screw, place the other end of the tube in the jar, and pour in sufficient fluid to cover the end of the tube.

15 Ensure that the master cylinder reservoir fluid level is maintained at least above the MIN level line throughout the procedure.

16 Have the assistant fully depress the brake pedal several times to relieve the power brake booster's vacuum and create hydraulic pressure, then hold it down on the final downstroke.

17 While pedal pressure is maintained, unscrew the bleed screw (approximately one turn) and allow the fluid (along with any air) to flow into the jar. The assistant must maintain pedal pressure until instructed to release it. When the flow slows, tighten the bleed screw again, have the assistant release the pedal slowly, and recheck the reservoir fluid level.

18 Repeat the steps in paragraphs 16 and 17 until the fluid emerging from the bleed screw is free from air bubbles. If the master cylinder has been drained and refilled, and air is being bled from the first screw in the sequence, allow about 5 seconds between cycles for the master cylinder passages to refill.

19 When no more air bubbles appear, tighten the bleed screw securely, remove the tube and wrench, and install the dust cap. Be careful not to over-tighten the bleed screw.

20 Repeat the procedure on the remaining screws in the sequence, until all air is removed from the system and the brake pedal feels firm.

Using a one-way valve kit

▶ **Refer to illustration 2.21**

21 As their name implies, these kits consist of a length of tubing with a one-way valve installed, to prevent expelled air and fluid being drawn back into the system; some kits include a translucent container, which can be positioned so that the air bubbles can be more easily seen flowing from the end of the tube (see illustration).

22 The kit is connected to the bleed screw, which is then opened. The user returns to the driver's seat, depresses the brake pedal with a smooth, steady stroke, and slowly releases it; this is repeated until the expelled fluid is clear of air bubbles.

23 Note that these kits simplify work so much that it is easy to forget the master cylinder reservoir fluid level; ensure that this is maintained at least above the MIN level line at all times.

Using a pressure-bleeding kit

24 These kits are usually operated by the reservoir of pressurized air contained in the spare tire. However, note that it will probably be necessary to reduce the pressure to a lower level than normal; refer to the instructions supplied with the kit.

➡**Note: BMW specifies that a pressure of 2 bar (29 psi) should not be exceeded.**

25 By connecting a pressurized, fluid-filled container to the master cylinder reservoir, bleeding can be carried out simply by opening each screw in turn (in the specified sequence), and allowing the fluid to flow out until no more air bubbles can be seen in the expelled fluid.

26 This method has the advantage that the large reservoir of fluid provides an additional safeguard against air being drawn into the system during bleeding.

27 Pressure-bleeding is particularly effective when bleeding difficult systems, or when bleeding the complete system at the time of routine fluid replacement.

All methods

28 When bleeding is complete, and firm pedal feel is restored, wash off any spilled fluid, tighten the bleed screws securely, and install their dust caps.

29 Check the brake fluid level in the master cylinder reservoir, and top-off if necessary (see Chapter 1).

30 Properly discard any brake fluid that has been bled from the system; it will not be fit for re-use.

31 Check the feel of the brake pedal. If it feels at all spongy, air must still be present in the system, and further bleeding is required. Failure to bleed the system satisfactorily after a reasonable repetition of the bleeding procedure may be due to worn master cylinder seals.

2.21 Bleeding a rear brake caliper using a one-way valve kit

3 Hydraulic lines and hoses - replacement

✳✳ WARNING:

On models with ABS (with or without ASC+T), under no circum-stances should the hydraulic lines/hoses linking the master cylinder, hydraulic unit and the accumulator (if equipped) be disturbed. If these fittings are disturbed and air enters the high-pressure hydraulic system, bleeding of the system can only be safely carried out by a BMW dealer or suitably-equipped spe-cialist using the special service tester.

→Note: Before starting work, refer to the precautions in Sec-tion 1 and the warnings at the beginning of Section 2.

1   If any line or hose is to be replaced, minimize fluid loss by first removing the master cylinder reservoir cap, then tightening it down onto a piece of cellophane to obtain an airtight seal. Alternatively, flex-ible hoses can be sealed, if required, using a proprietary brake hose clamp; metal brake line fittings can be plugged (if care is taken not to allow dirt into the system) or capped immediately they are discon-nected. Place a wad of rag under any fitting that is to be disconnected, to catch any spilled fluid.

2   If a flexible hose is to be disconnected, unscrew the brake line fitting nut before removing the spring clip which secures the hose to its mounting bracket.

3   Use a flare-nut wrench to loosen the brake line fittings (these are available at most automotive retail stores). Always clean the fitting and surrounding area before disconnecting it. If disconnecting a component with more than one fitting, make a careful note of the connections before disturbing any of them.

4   If a brake line is to be replaced, it can be obtained, cut to length and with the fitting nuts and end flares in place, from BMW dealers. All that is then necessary is to bend it to shape, following the line of the original, before installing it to the car. Alternatively, most motor acces-sory shops can make up brake lines from kits, but this requires very careful measurement of the original, to ensure that the replacement is of the correct length. The safest answer is usually to take the original to the shop as a pattern.

5   On installation, do not over-tighten the line fittings.

6   Ensure that the lines and hoses are correctly routed, with no kinks, and that they are secured in the clips or brackets provided. After installation, remove the cellophane from the reservoir, and bleed the hydraulic system as described in Section 2. Wash off any spilled fluid, and check carefully for fluid leaks.

4 Front brake pads - replacement

4.2a Lever the spring away from the hub . . .

▶ Refer to illustrations: 4.2a, 4.2b, 4.3a, 4.3b, 4.4, 4.5a, 4.5b, 4.5c, 4.6a, 4.6b, 4.7, 4.10, 4.12, 4.13 and 4.16

✳✳ WARNING:

Replace both sets of front brake pads at the same time - never replace the pads on only one wheel, as uneven braking may result. Note that the dust created by wear of the pads is a health hazard. Never blow it out with compressed air, and do not inhale any of it. An approved filtering mask should be worn when working on the brakes. DO NOT use petrol or petroleum-based solvents to clean brake parts; use brake cleaner only.

→Note: Before starting work, refer to the precautions in Sec-tion 1 and the warnings at the beginning of Section 2.

1   Apply the parking brake, then jack up the front of the vehicle and support it on jackstands. Remove the front wheels.

2   Using a screwdriver, carefully unclip the anti-rattle spring from

4.2b . . . then lever it out from the caliper

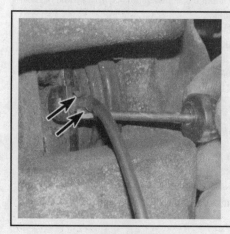

4.3a Release the clips . . .

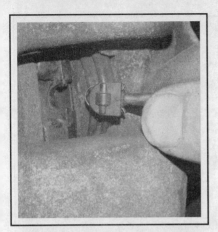

4.3b . . . and slide the wear sensor from the brake pad

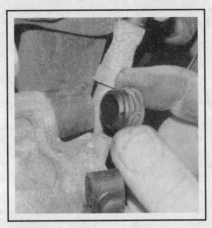

4.4 Remove the plastic caps to access the caliper guide pin bolts

4.5a Loosen . . .

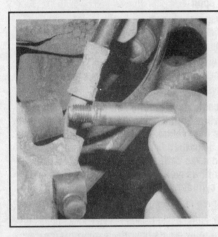

4.5b . . . and remove the caliper guide pin bolts

4.5c Tie the caliper mounting bracket to the suspension

the side of the brake caliper, noting its installed position (see illustrations).

3   Slide the brake pad wear sensor from the brake pad (if equipped) and remove it from the caliper aperture (see illustrations).

4   Remove the plastic caps from the caliper guide bushings to gain access to the guide pin bolts (see illustration).

5   Loosen and remove the guide pin bolts. Lift the caliper away from the caliper mounting bracket, and tie it to the suspension strut using

a suitable piece of wire (see illustrations). Do not allow the caliper to hang unsupported on the flexible brake hose.

6   Unclip the inner brake pad from the caliper piston, and withdraw the outer pad from the caliper mounting bracket (see illustrations).

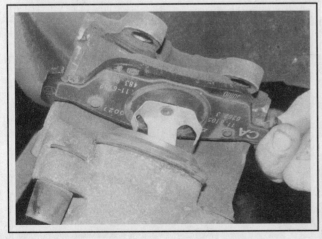

4.6a Unclip the inner pad from the caliper piston . . .

4.6b . . . and remove the outer pad from the caliper mounting bracket

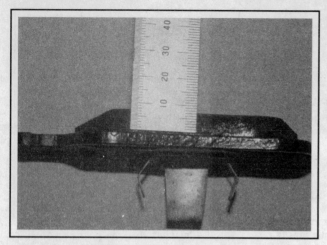

4.7 Measure the thickness of the friction material

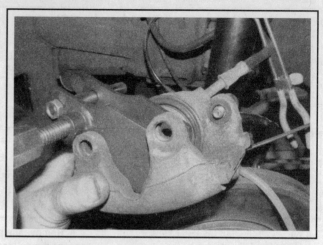

4.10 Using a piston retraction tool, with the hose clamped, and the bleed screw open

7   First measure the thickness of each brake pad's friction material (see illustration). If either pad is worn at any point to the specified minimum thickness or less, all four pads must be replaced. Also, the pads should be replaced if any are fouled with oil or grease; there is no satisfactory way of degreasing friction material, once contaminated. If any of the brake pads are worn unevenly, or are fouled with oil or grease, trace and rectify the cause before reassembly.

8   If the brake pads are still serviceable, carefully clean them using a clean, fine wire brush or similar, paying particular attention to the sides and back of the metal backing. Clean out the grooves in the friction material (where applicable), and pick out any large embedded particles of dirt or debris. Carefully clean the pad locations in the caliper body/mounting bracket.

9   Prior to installing the pads, check that the guide pins are a light, sliding fit in the caliper bushings, with little sign of free play. Brush the dust and dirt from the caliper and piston, but do not inhale it, as it is a health hazard. Inspect the dust seal around the piston for damage, and the piston for evidence of fluid leaks, corrosion or damage. If attention to any of these components is necessary, refer to Section 8.

10 If new brake pads are to be installed, the caliper piston must be pushed back into the cylinder to make room for them. Either use a piston retraction tool, a C-clamp or use suitable pieces of wood as levers. Clamp off the flexible brake hose leading to the caliper then connect a

brake bleeding kit to the caliper bleed screw. Open the bleed screw as the piston is retracted; the surplus brake fluid will then be collected in the bleed kit vessel (see illustration). Close the bleed screw just before the caliper piston is pushed fully into the caliper. This should ensure no air enters the hydraulic system.

➡Note: The ABS unit contains hydraulic components that are very sensitive to impurities in the brake fluid. Even the smallest particles can cause the system to fail through blockage. The pad retraction method described here prevents any debris in the brake fluid expelled from the caliper from being passed back to the ABS hydraulic unit, as well as preventing any chance of damage to the master cylinder seals.

11 Apply a small amount of brake anti-squeal compound to the backing plate of each pad, and the pad backing plate contact points on the caliper bracket; do not apply excess grease, nor allow the grease to contact the friction material.

12 Install the outer pad to the caliper mounting bracket, ensuring that its friction material is against the brake disc (see illustration).

13 Clip the inner pad into the caliper piston, and maneuver the caliper assembly into position (see illustration).

14 Install the caliper guide pin bolts, and tighten them to the specified torque setting. Install the covers to the ends of the caliper guide pins.

4.12 Install the outer pad to the caliper bracket

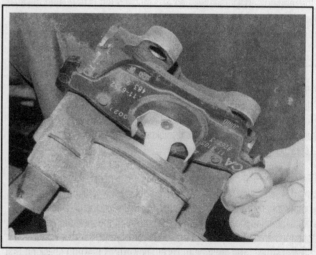

4.13 Clip the inner pad into the caliper piston

15 Clip the pad wear sensor back into position in the outer pad (if equipped), making sure its wiring is correctly routed (see illustrations 4.3a and 4.3b).

16 Clip the anti-rattle spring into position in the caliper (see illustration). Depress the brake pedal repeatedly, until the pads are pressed into firm contact with the brake disc, and normal (non-assisted) pedal pressure is restored.

17 Repeat the above procedure on the remaining front brake caliper.

18 Install the wheels, then lower the vehicle to the ground and tighten the wheel bolts to the torque listed in the Chapter 1 Specifications.

4.16 Install the anti-rattle spring

5 Rear brake pads - replacement

The rear brake calipers are virtually identical to those installed at the front. Refer to Section 4 for pad inspection and replacement details.

6 Front brake disc - inspection, removal and installation

→**Note 1: Before starting work, refer to the precautions in Section 1 and the warnings at the beginning of Section 2.**

→**Note 2: If either disc requires replacement, BOTH should be replaced at the same time, to ensure even and consistent braking. New brake pads should also be installed.**

INSPECTION

▶ **Refer to illustration 6.3**

1 Apply the parking brake, then jack up the front of the car and support it on jackstands. Remove the appropriate front wheel.

2 Slowly rotate the brake disc so that the full area of both sides can be checked; remove the brake pads if better access is required to the inboard surface (see Section 4). Light scoring is normal in the area swept by the brake pads, but if heavy scoring or cracks are found, the disc must be replaced.

3 It is normal to find a lip of rust and brake dust around the disc's perimeter; this can be scraped off if required. If, however, a lip has formed due to excessive wear of the brake pad swept area, then the disc's thickness must be measured using a micrometer (see illustration). Take measurements at several places around the disc, at the inside and outside of the pad swept area; if the disc has worn at any point to the specified minimum thickness or less, the disc must be replaced.

4 If the disc is thought to be warped, it can be checked for run-out. Either use a dial gauge mounted on any convenient fixed point, while the disc is slowly rotated, or use feeler blades to measure (at several points all around the disc) the clearance between the disc and a fixed point, such as the caliper mounting bracket. If the measurements obtained are at the specified maximum or beyond, the disc is excessively warped, and must be replaced; however, it is worth checking first

that the hub bearing is in good condition (see Chapter 10). If the run-out is excessive, the disc must be replaced.

5 Check the disc for cracks, especially around the wheel bolt holes, and any other wear or damage, and replace if necessary.

REMOVAL

▶ **Refer to illustrations 6.7a and 6.7b**

6 Unscrew the two bolts securing the brake caliper mounting bracket to the steering knuckle, then slide the caliper assembly off the disc. Using a piece of wire or string, tie the caliper to the front suspension coil spring, to avoid placing any strain on the hydraulic brake hose.

6.3 Measure the disc thickness using a micrometer

6.7a Remove the retaining screw . . .

6.7b . . . and remove the brake disc from the hub

7   Loosen and remove the screw securing the brake disc to the hub, and then remove the disc (see illustrations). If it is tight, lightly tap its rear face with a hide or plastic mallet.

INSTALLATION

8   Installation is the reverse of the removal procedure, noting the following points:

  a) Ensure that the mating surfaces of the disc and hub are clean and flat.

  b) Position the disc on the hub, install the disc retaining screw and tighten it to the specified torque.
  c) If a new disc has been installed, use a suitable solvent to wipe any preservative coating from the disc, before installing the caliper.
  d) Slide the caliper into position over the disc, making sure the pads pass either side of the disc. Tighten the caliper mounting bolts to the specified torque setting.
  e) Install the wheel, then lower the vehicle to the ground and tighten the wheel bolts to the specified torque. On completion, repeatedly depress the brake pedal until normal (non-power assisted) pedal pressure returns.

7   Rear brake disc - inspection, removal and installation

➡**Note 1: Before starting work, refer to the precautions in Section 1 and the warnings at the beginning of Section 2.**

➡**Note 2: If either disc requires replacement, BOTH should be replaced at the same time, to ensure even and consistent braking. New brake pads should also be installed.**

INSPECTION

1   Firmly chock the front wheels, then raise the rear of the vehicle and support it securely on jackstands. Remove the appropriate rear wheel. Release the parking brake.
2   Inspect the disc as described in Section 6.

REMOVAL

▶ **Refer to illustrations 7.3 and 7.4**

3   Unscrew the two bolts securing the brake caliper mounting bracket in position, then slide the caliper assembly off the disc. Using a piece of wire or string, tie the caliper to the rear suspension coil spring, to avoid placing any strain on the hydraulic brake hose (see illustration). If necessary unclip the brake hose from the lower mounting bracket to provide enough slack to maneuver the caliper and bracket.

7.3 Slide the rear caliper assembly off the disc

4   Remove the brake disc retaining screw (see illustration).

5   It should now be possible to withdraw the brake disc from the hub by hand. If it is tight, lightly tap its rear face with a hide or plastic mallet. If the parking brake shoes are binding, first check that the parking brake is fully released, then continue as follows.

6   Referring to Section 14 for further details, fully loosen the parking brake adjustment to obtain maximum free play in the cable.

7   Insert a screwdriver through one of the wheel bolt holes in the brake disc, and rotate the adjuster knurled wheel on the upper pivot to retract the shoes (see illustrations 14.5a and 14.5b). The brake disc can then be withdrawn.

INSTALLATION

8   If a new disc is been installed, use a suitable solvent to wipe any preservative coating from the disc.

9   Position the disc on the hub, install the disc retaining screw and tighten it to the specified torque.

10 Slide the caliper into position over the disc, making sure the pads pass either side of the disc. Tighten the caliper bracket mounting bolts to the specified torque setting.

11 Adjust the parking brake shoes and cable as described in Section 14.

12 Install the wheel, then lower the car to the ground, and tighten

7.4 Remove the retaining screw and slide the rear disc off the hub

the wheel bolts to the torque listed in the Chapter 1 Specifications. On completion, repeatedly depress the brake pedal until normal (non-power assisted) pedal pressure returns. Recheck the parking brake adjustment.

8   Front brake caliper - removal and installation

➡️Note: Before starting work, refer to the precautions in Section 1 and the warnings at the beginning of Section 2.

REMOVAL

1   Apply the parking brake, then jack up the front of the vehicle and support it on jackstands. Remove the appropriate wheel.

2   Minimize fluid loss by using a brake hose clamp, a C-clamp or a similar tool to clamp the flexible hose.

3   Clean the area around the fitting, then loosen the brake hose fitting nut.

4   Remove the brake pads (see Section 4).

5   Unscrew the caliper from the end of the brake hose and remove it from the vehicle.

INSTALLATION

6   Screw the caliper fully onto the flexible hose fitting.

7   Install the brake pads (see Section 4).

8   Securely tighten the brake line fitting nut.

9   Remove the brake hose clamp or cellophane, as applicable, and bleed the hydraulic system as described in Section 2. Note that, if the precautions described were taken to minimize brake fluid loss, it should only be necessary to bleed the relevant front brake.

10 Install the wheel, then lower the vehicle to the ground and tighten the wheel bolts to the torque listed in the Chapter 1 Specifications. On completion, check the brake fluid level as described in Chapter 1.

9   Rear brake caliper - removal and installation

➡️Note: Before starting work, refer to the precautions in Section 1 and the warnings at the beginning of Section 2.

REMOVAL

1   Chock the front wheels, then jack up the rear of the vehicle and support on jackstands. Remove the relevant rear wheel.

2   Minimize fluid loss by first removing the master cylinder reservoir cap, and then tightening it down onto a piece of cellophane, to obtain an airtight seal. Alternatively, use a brake hose clamp, a C-clamp or a similar tool to clamp the flexible hose.

3   Clean the area around the fitting, then loosen the brake hose fitting nut.

4   Remove the brake pads as described in Section 4.

5   Unscrew the caliper from the end of the flexible hose, and remove it from the vehicle.

INSTALLATION

6   Screw the caliper fully onto the flexible hose fitting.

7   Install the brake pads (refer to Section 4).

8   Securely tighten the brake line fitting nut.

9   Remove the brake hose clamp or cellophane, as applicable, and bleed the hydraulic system as described in Section 2. Note that, providing the precautions described were taken to minimize brake fluid loss, it should only be necessary to bleed the relevant rear brake.

10 Install the wheel, then lower the vehicle to the ground and tighten the wheel bolts to the torque listed in the Chapter 1 Specifications. On completion, check the brake fluid level as described in Chapter 1.

10 Master cylinder - removal and installation

➡ **Note 1: Before starting work, refer to the precautions in Section 1 and the warnings at the beginning of Section 2.**

➡ **Note 2: New master cylinder retaining nuts will be required on installation.**

➡ **Note 3: If the master cylinder is faulty, it must be replaced. Repair kits are not available from BMW dealers so the cylinder must be treated as a sealed unit. Replace the master cylinder O-ring seal and reservoir seals regardless of their apparent condition.**

MODELS WITH ABS

1   On models fitted with ABS, although it is possible for the home mechanic to remove the master cylinder, if the hydraulic fittings are disconnected from the master cylinder, air will enter the high-pressure hydraulic system linking the master cylinder and hydraulic unit. Bleeding of the high-pressure system can only be safely carried out by a BMW dealer or specialist who has access to the service tester (see Section 2). Consequently, once the master cylinder has been installed, the vehicle must be taken on a trailer or transporter to a suitably-equipped BMW dealer or specialist.

ALL MODELS

Removal

▶ **Refer to illustrations 10.3 and 10.5**

2   Remove the heater/ventilation inlet air ducting from the rear of the engine compartment as follows:

a) *Rotate the three fasteners 90° counterclockwise and remove the cabin filter cover from the rear of the engine compartment. Pull the filter forward and remove it.*

b) *Detach the four retaining clips and thread the cable out of the ducting.*

c) *Unscrew the four screws and pull the filter housing forwards and remove it.*

d) *Remove the two screws and remove the inlet ducting upwards and out of the engine compartment.*

3   Remove the master cylinder reservoir cap, and siphon the brake fluid from the reservoir.

➡ **Note: Do not siphon the fluid by mouth, as it is poisonous; use a syringe or a hand-held vacuum pump. Alternatively, open any convenient bleed screw in the system, and gently pump the brake pedal to expel the fluid through a plastic tube connected to the screw until the level of fluid drops below that of the reservoir (see Section 2). Disconnect the wiring connector(s) from the brake fluid reservoir (see illustration).**

4   Disconnect the fluid hose(s) from the side of the reservoir, and plug the hose end(s) to minimize fluid loss.

5   Remove the master cylinder reservoir retaining screw (see illustration).

6   Carefully ease the fluid reservoir out from the top of the master cylinder. Recover the reservoir seals, and plug the cylinder ports to prevent dirt entry.

7   Wipe clean the area around the brake line fittings on the side of the master cylinder, and place absorbent rags beneath the line fittings to catch any surplus fluid. Make a note of the correct installed positions of the fittings, then unscrew the fitting nuts and carefully withdraw the lines. Plug or tape over the line ends and master cylinder orifices, to minimize the loss of brake fluid, and to prevent the entry of dirt into the system. Wash off any spilled fluid immediately with cold water.

8   Loosen and remove the two nuts and washers securing the master cylinder to the power brake booster, then withdraw the unit from the engine compartment. Remove the O-ring from the rear of the master cylinder. Discard the retaining nuts, new ones should be used on installation.

Installation

9   Remove all traces of dirt from the master cylinder and power brake booster mating surfaces, and fit a new O-ring to the groove on the master cylinder body.

10   Install the master cylinder ensuring that the booster pushrod enters the master cylinder bore correctly. Use new master cylinder retaining nuts and washers, and tighten them to the specified torque.

11   Wipe clean the brake line fittings, then install them to the master cylinder ports and tighten them securely.

12   Press the new reservoir seals firmly into the master cylinder ports, then ease the reservoir into position. Tighten the reservoir retaining bolt securely. Reconnect the fluid hose(s) to the reservoir, and reconnect the electrical connector(s).

13   Refill the master cylinder reservoir with new fluid, and bleed the complete hydraulic system as described in Section 2.

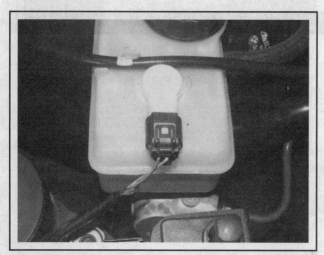

10.3 Disconnect the fluid level sensor electrical connector

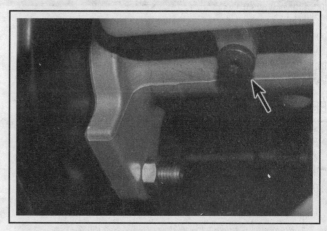

10.5 Remove the brake fluid reservoir retaining screw

11 Brake pedal - removal and installation

REMOVAL

▶ **Refer to illustrations 11.4**

1   Disconnect the cable from the negative battery terminal (see Chapter 5, Section 1).

2   Remove the brake light switch as described in Section 18.

3   Using a pair of pliers, carefully unhook the return spring from the brake pedal.

4   Slide off the retaining clip and remove the clevis pin securing the brake pedal to the power brake booster pushrod (see illustration).

5   Slide off the pedal pivot pin retaining clip and remove the pedal from the pivot.

6   Carefully clean and inspect all components, replacing any that are worn or damaged.

INSTALLATION

7   Installation is the reverse of removal. Apply a small amount of multi-purpose grease to the pedal pivot and clevis pin.

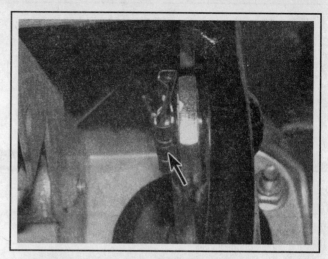

11.4 Remove the clip and slide out the clevis pin

12 Power brake booster - testing, removal and installation

➡**Note: On models with ABS and Traction control (ASC+T) or Dynamic stability control (DSC), removal of the power brake booster involves removal of the ABS/ASC+T and/or DSC control unit. Due to the need for special diagnostic equipment, this task should only be carried out be a BMW dealer or suitably-equipped specialist.**

TESTING

1   To test the operation of the power brake booster, depress the brake several times to remove the vacuum, then start the engine while keeping the pedal firmly depressed. As the engine starts, there should be a noticeable give in the brake pedal as vacuum increases. Allow the engine to run for at least two minutes, then switch it off. If the brake pedal is now depressed it should feel normal, but further applications should result in the pedal feeling firmer, with the pedal stroke decreasing with each application.

2   If the booster does not operate as described, first inspect the booster's check valve as described in Section 13.

3   If the power brake booster still fails to operate satisfactorily, the fault lies within the unit itself. Repairs to the unit are not possible - if faulty, the power brake booster must be replaced.

REMOVAL

▶ **Refer to illustration 12.8**

➡**Note: New retaining nuts will be required on installation.**

4   Remove the master cylinder as described in Section 10.

12.8 Remove the power brake booster retaining nuts

5   Disconnect the vacuum hose from the power brake booster check valve.

6   Loosen and remove the retaining screws securing the driver's side lower dash panel. Unclip the panel and remove it from the vehicle.

7   Referring to Section 11, unhook the brake pedal return spring, then slide off the retaining clip and remove the clevis pin securing the pedal to the power brake booster pushrod (see illustration 11.4).

8   Loosen and remove the power brake booster retaining nuts, then return to the engine compartment and remove the power brake booster from the vehicle (see illustration).

INSTALLATION

9   Installation is the reverse of removal, noting the following points.

a) *Check the power brake booster check valve sealing grommet for signs of damage or deterioration, and replace if necessary.*

b) *If a new power brake booster is being installed, remove the sound insulation material from the original, and transfer it to the new one.*

c) *Ensure that the power brake booster pushrod is correctly engaged with the brake pedal, then fit the new retaining nuts and tighten them to the specified torque.*

d) *Apply a small amount of grease to the booster pushrod clevis pin, and secure it in position with the retaining clip.*

e) *Install the master cylinder as described in Section 10 of this Chapter.*

f) *Install the brake-light switch as described in Section 18.*

g) *On completion, start the engine and check for air leaks at the vacuum hose-to-power brake booster connection; check the operation of the braking system.*

13 Power brake booster check valve - removal, testing and installation

REMOVAL

1   Disconnect the vacuum hose from the power brake booster check valve, mounted on the booster.

2   Carefully ease the check valve out of the power brake booster, taking care not to displace the grommet.

TESTING

3   Examine the check valve for signs of damage, and replace if necessary.

4   The valve may be tested by blowing through it in both directions; air should flow through the valve in one direction only - when blown through from the power brake booster end of the valve. Replace the valve if this is not the case.

5   Examine the power brake booster rubber sealing grommet for signs of damage or deterioration, and replace as necessary.

INSTALLATION

6   Ensure that the sealing grommet is correctly installed to the power brake booster.

7   Ease the valve into position in the booster, taking great care not to displace or damage the grommet.

8   Reconnect the vacuum hose securely to the valve.

9   On completion, start the engine and ensure there are no air leaks at the check valve-to-power brake booster connection.

14 Parking brake - adjustment

▶ **Refer to illustration 14.3, 14.4, 14.5a and 14.5b**

1   Applying normal moderate pressure, pull the parking brake lever to the fully applied position, counting the number of clicks emitted from the parking brake ratchet mechanism. If adjustment is correct, there should be approximately 7 or 8 clicks before the parking brake is fully applied. If there are more than 10 clicks, adjust as follows.

2   Loosen and remove one wheel bolt from each rear wheel then chock the front wheels, jack up the rear of the vehicle and support it on jackstands.

3   Access to the parking brake cable adjusting nuts can be gained by removing the parking brake lever boot from the center console (see illustration). If greater access is required, the rear section of the center console will have to be removed (see Chapter 11).

4   With the parking brake fully released, unscrew the cable locknuts and release the adjusting nuts until all tension in the cables is released (see illustration).

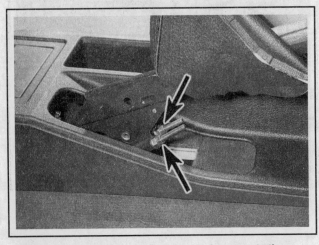

14.3 Unclip the parking brake boot to gain access to the parking brake cable adjustment nuts

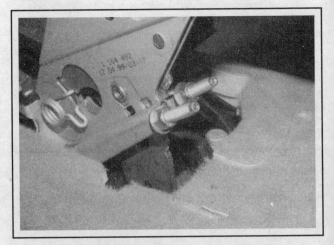

14.4 Loosen the parking brake cable adjusting nuts

14.5a Position one of the wheel bolt holes as shown, then insert a screwdriver through the hole . . .

14.5b . . . and rotate the adjuster knurled ring (shown with disc removed)

5   Starting on the left-hand rear wheel, fully release the parking brake and position the wheel/disc so the exposed bolt hole is positioned towards the rear at 65° from the vertical position. Make sure the parking brake lever is fully released, then insert a screwdriver in through the bolt hole and fully expand the parking brake shoes by rotating the adjuster knurled ring. When the wheel/disc can no longer be turned, back the knurled ring off by 10 teeth (catches) so that the wheel is free to rotate easily (see illustrations).

6   Repeat Step 5 on the right-hand wheel.

7   With the parking brake set on the sixth notch of the ratchet mechanism, rotate the cables adjusting nuts equally until it is difficult to turn both rear wheels. Once this is so, fully release the parking brake

lever, and check that the wheels rotate freely. Slowly apply the parking brake, and check that the brake shoes start to contact the drums when the parking brake is set to the second notch of the ratchet mechanism. Check the adjustment by applying the parking brake fully, counting the clicks emitted from the parking brake ratchet and, if necessary, re-adjust.

8   Once adjustment is correct, hold the adjusting nuts and securely tighten the locknuts. Check the operation of the parking brake warning light switch, then install the center console section/parking brake lever boot (as applicable). Install the wheels, then lower the vehicle to the ground and tighten the wheel bolts to the specified torque.

15 Parking brake lever - removal and installation

REMOVAL

▶ **Refer to illustration 15.3**

1   Remove the rear section of the center console and armrest (if equipped) as described in Chapter 11 to gain access to the parking brake lever.

2   Loosen and remove both the parking brake cable locknuts/adjusting nuts, and detach the cables from the lever.

3   Unscrew the retaining bolt, and remove the lever from the vehicle (see illustration).

INSTALLATION

4   Installation is a reversal of the removal. Prior to installing the center console, adjust the parking brake as described in Section 14.

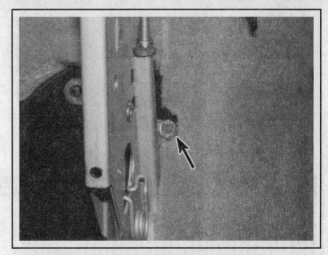

15.3 Remove the parking brake lever bracket bolt

16 Parking brake cables - removal and installation

REMOVAL

▶ **Refer to illustrations 16.5, 16.8a and 16.8b**

1   Remove the rear section of the center console as described in Chapter 11 to gain access to the parking brake lever. The parking brake cable consists of two sections, a right- and a left-hand section, which are connected to the lever. Each section can be removed individually.

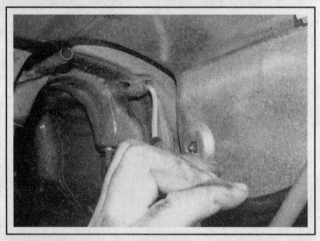

16.5 Withdraw the cable from the support guide

2   Loosen and remove the relevant parking brake cable locknut and adjusting nut, and disengage the inner cable from the parking brake lever.

3   Firmly chock the front wheels, then raise the rear of the vehicle and support it on jackstands.

4   Referring to the relevant Part of Chapter 4, remove the exhaust system heat shield to gain access to the parking brake cables. Note that on some models (M52TU engine codes), it may also be necessary to remove part of the exhaust system.

5   Free the front end of the outer cable from the body, and withdraw the cable from its support guide (see illustration).

6   Working back along the length of the cable, noting its correct routing, and free it from all the relevant retaining clips.

7   Remove the relevant rear disc as described in Section 7.

8   Slide the cable core in the direction of the expander lock up to the stop, depress the nipple and pull out the cable core from the expander (see illustrations)

INSTALLATION

9   Insert the cable into the brake backing plate, and push it in up to the stop on the cable outer sleeve.

10 Grip the sleeve of the cable end, and push it in to the expander until it snaps into place.

11 Installation is a reversal of the removal procedure. Prior to installing the center console, adjust the parking brake as described in Section 14.

16.8a Unfold the expander, then withdraw the pin . . .

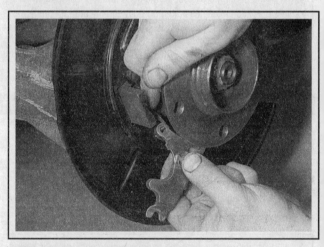

16.8b . . . and detach the expander from the end of the parking brake cable

17 Parking brake shoes - removal and installation

➡**Note: Before starting work, refer to the precautions in Section 1.**

REMOVAL

▶ **Refer to illustrations 17.2a, 17.2b, 17.3a, 17.3b, 17.4 and 17.6**

1   Remove the rear brake disc as described in Section 7, and make

a note of the correct installed position of all components.

2   Using a pair of pliers, carefully unhook and remove the parking brake shoe return springs (see illustrations).

3   Release the shoe retaining pins using pliers by depressing them and rotating them through 90°, then remove the pins and springs (see illustrations).

4   Remove both parking brake shoes, and recover the shoe adjuster mechanism, noting which way around it is installed (see illustration).

17.2a Using pliers, unhook and remove the parking brake shoe front . . .

17.2b . . . and rear return springs

17.3a Rotate the retainer pins through 90° . . .

17.3b . . . then remove the pins and springs . . .

17.4 . . . and parking brake shoes

5   Inspect the parking brake shoes for wear or contamination, and replace if necessary. It is recommended that the return springs are replaced as a matter of course.

6   While the shoes are removed, clean and inspect the condition of the shoe adjuster and expander mechanisms, replace them if they show signs of wear or damage. If all is well, apply a fresh coat of brake grease (BMW recommend Molykote Paste G) to the threads of the adjuster and sliding surfaces of the expander mechanism (see illustration). Do not allow the grease to contact the shoe friction material.

INSTALLATION

▶ **Refer to illustration 17.9**

7   Prior to installation, clean the backing plate, and apply a small amount of high-temperature brake grease or anti-seize compound to all those surfaces of the backing plate which bear on the shoes. Do not allow the lubricant to foul the friction material.

8   Offer up the parking brake shoes, and secure them in position with the retaining pins and springs.

9   Make sure the lower ends of the shoes are correctly engaged with

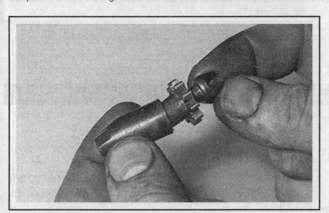

17.6 Clean the adjuster assembly and coat it with fresh brake grease

17.9 Install the adjuster assembly, making sure it is correctly engaged with both parking brake shoes

the expander, then slide the adjuster mechanism into position between the upper ends of the shoes (see illustration).

10 Check that all components are correctly installed, and fit the upper and lower return springs using a pair of pliers.

11 Center the parking brake shoes, and install the brake disc as described in Section 7.

12 Prior to installing the wheel, adjust the parking brake as described in Section 14.

18 Brake light switch - removal and installation

REMOVAL

▶ **Refer to illustrations 18.4a and 18.4b**

1 The brake light switch is located on the pedal bracket behind the dash.

2 Loosen and remove the retaining screws securing the driver's side lower dash panel. Unclip the panel and remove it from the vehicle.

3 Reach up behind the dash and disconnect the electrical connector from the switch.

4 Pull the switch from the mounting. If required, depress the clips and withdraw the switch mounting from the pedal bracket (see illustrations).

INSTALLATION

5 Fully depress the brake pedal and hold it down, then maneuver the switch into position. Hold the switch fully in position, then slowly release the brake pedal and allow it to return to its stop. This will automatically adjust the brake light switch.

➡**Note: If the pedal is released too quickly, the switch will be incorrectly adjusted.**

6 Reconnect the wiring connector, and check the operation of the brake lights. The brake lights should illuminate after the brake pedal has traveled approximately 3/16-inch (5 mm). If the switch is not functioning correctly, it is faulty and must be replaced; no other adjustment is possible.

7 On completion, install the driver's side lower dash panel.

18.4a Pull the switch from the switch mounting

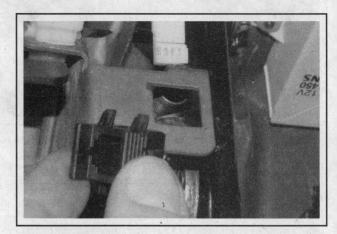

18.4b Press the retaining clips and remove the switch mounting

19 Anti-lock braking system (ABS) - general information

➡**Note: On models equipped with traction control, the ABS unit is a dual function unit, and works both the anti-lock braking system (ABS) and traction control function of the Automatic Stability Control plus Traction (ASC+T) system.**

1 Most models are equipped with ABS as standard, and was available as an option on all others. The system consists of a hydraulic block that contains the hydraulic solenoid valves and the electrically-driven return pump, the four wheel sensors (one installed to each wheel), and the electronic control unit (ECU). The purpose of the system is to prevent the wheel(s) locking during heavy braking. This is achieved by automatic release of the brake on the relevant wheel, followed by re-application of the brake.

2 The solenoids are controlled by the ECU, which itself receives signals from the four wheel sensors (one installed on each hub), which monitor the speed of rotation of each wheel. By comparing

these signals, the ECU can determine the speed at which the vehicle is travelling. It can then use this speed to determine when a wheel is decelerating at an abnormal rate, compared to the speed of the vehicle, and therefore predicts when a wheel is about to lock. During normal operation, the system functions in the same way as a non-ABS braking system. In addition to this, the brake pedal position sensor (which is installed to the vacuum power brake booster) also informs the ECU of how hard the brake pedal is being depressed.

3 If the ECU senses that a wheel is about to lock, it operates the relevant solenoid valve in the hydraulic unit, which then isolates the brake caliper on the wheel which is about to lock from the master cylinder, effectively sealing-in the hydraulic pressure.

4 If the speed of rotation of the wheel continues to decrease at an abnormal rate, the ECU switches on the electrically-driven return pump operates, and pumps the brake fluid back into the master cylinder,

releasing pressure on the brake caliper so that the brake is released. Once the speed of rotation of the wheel returns to an acceptable rate, the pump stops; the solenoid valve opens, allowing the hydraulic master cylinder pressure to return to the caliper, which then re-applies the brake. This cycle can be carried out at up to 10 times a second.

5   The action of the solenoid valves and return pump creates pulses in the hydraulic circuit. When the ABS system is functioning, these pulses can be felt through the brake pedal.

6   The operation of the ABS system is entirely dependent on electrical signals. To prevent the system responding to any inaccurate signals, a built-in safety circuit monitors all signals received by the ECU. If an inaccurate signal or low battery voltage is detected, the ABS system is automatically shut down, and the warning light on the instrument panel is illuminated, to inform the driver that the ABS system is not opera-

tional. Normal braking should still be available, however.

7   If a fault does develop in the ABS system, the vehicle must be taken to a BMW dealer or suitably-equipped specialist for fault diagnosis and repair.

8   On models equipped with ASC+T, an accumulator is also incorporated into the hydraulic system. As well as performing the ABS function as described above, the hydraulic unit also works the traction control side of the ASC+T system. If the ECU senses that the wheels are about to lose traction under acceleration, the hydraulic unit momentarily applies the rear brakes to prevent the wheel(s) spinning. In the same way as the ABS, the vehicle must be taken to a BMW dealer or suitably-equipped specialist for testing if a fault develops in the ASC+T system.

20 Anti-lock braking system (ABS) components - removal and installation

HYDRAULIC UNIT

1   Although it is possible for the home mechanic to remove the hydraulic unit, the unit's self-diagnosis system must be interrogated by dedicated test equipment before and after removal, and the unit must be bled by BMW service test equipment. Consequently, we recommend that removal and installation of the hydraulic unit should be entrusted to a BMW dealer or suitably-equipped specialist.

ACCUMULATOR (MODELS WITH ASC+T)

2   For the same reasons given in Step 1, we recommend that removal and installation of the accumulator should be entrusted to a BMW dealer or other qualified repair shop.

ELECTRONIC CONTROL UNIT (ECU)

3   In order to remove the ABS/ASC+T ECU, the hydraulic unit must first be removed, as the ECU is screwed to the side of the hydraulic unit. Consequently, we recommend that removal and installation of the ECU is entrusted to a BMW dealer or other qualified repair shop.

FRONT WHEEL SENSOR

Removal

▶ **Refer to illustrations 20.4 and 20.5**

4   Chock the rear wheels, then firmly apply the parking brake, jack up the front of the vehicle and support on jackstands. Remove the appropriate front wheel. Trace the wiring back from the sensor to the connector that is located in a protective plastic box. Unclip the lid, then free the wiring connector and disconnect it from the main harness (see illustration).

5   Loosen and remove the bolt securing the sensor to the steering knuckle, and remove the sensor and lead assembly from the vehicle (see illustration).

➡**Note: On some models, the front wheel sensors are handed, and are marked L and R accordingly. Additionally, the right-hand sensor has two green markings between the sensor and the grommet.**

Installation

6   Prior to installation, apply a thin coat of multi-purpose grease to the sensor tip (BMW recommend the use of Staborax NBU 12/k).

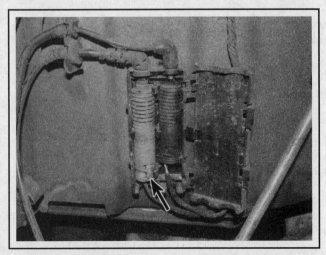

20.4 Unclip the lid, release and disconnect the ABS sensor electrical connector

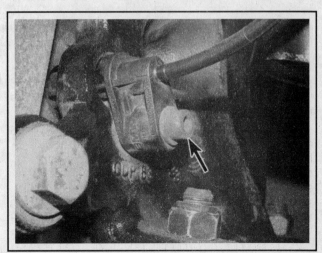

20.5 Remove sensor retaining bolt

7 Ensure that the sensor and steering knuckle sealing faces are clean and then fit the sensor to the knuckle. Ensure that, where applicable, the sensor is installed to the correct side of the vehicle (see Paragraph 5). Install the retaining bolt and tighten it to the specified torque.

8 Ensure that the sensor wiring is correctly routed and retained by all the necessary clips, and reconnect it to its wiring connector. Install the sensor connector into the box and securely clip the lid in position.

9 Install the wheel, then lower the vehicle to the ground and tighten the wheel bolts to the torque listed in the Chapter 1 Specifications.

REAR WHEEL SENSOR

Removal

10 Chock the front wheels, then jack up the rear of the vehicle and support it on jackstands. Remove the appropriate wheel.

11 Remove the sensor as described in paragraphs 4 and 5.

Installation

12 Install the sensor as described above in paragraphs 6 to 9.

FRONT RELUCTOR RINGS

13 The front reluctor rings are fixed onto the rear of wheel hubs. Examine the rings for damage such as chipped or missing teeth. If replacement is necessary, the complete hub assembly must be dismantled and the bearings replaced, with reference to Chapter 10.

REAR RELUCTOR RINGS

14 The rear reluctor rings are pressed onto the driveaxle outer joints. Examine the rings for signs of damage such as chipped or missing teeth, and replace as necessary. If replacement is necessary, the driveaxle assembly must be replaced (see Chapter 8).

Specifications

Brake fluid type	See Chapter 1

Front brakes

Disc minimum thickness	Refer to the dimension marked on the disc
Maximum disc run-out	0.007 inch (0.18 mm)
Brake pad friction material minimum thickness	See Chapter 1

Rear disc brakes

Disc minimum diameter	Refer to the dimension marked on the disc
Maximum disc run-out	0.007 inch (0.18 mm)
Brake pad friction material minimum thickness	See Chapter 1
Parking brake drum diameter (maximum)	6.304 inches (160 mm)

Torque specifications

	Ft-lbs (unless otherwise indicated)	Nm
ABS pressure sensors to master cylinder	168 in-lbs	19
ABS wheel sensor retaining bolts	60 in-lbs	8
Brake disc retaining screw	144 in-lbs	16
Brake hose fittings		
M10 thread	156 in-lbs	17
M12 thread	168 in-lbs	19
Front brake caliper		
Guide pin bolts	26	35
Mounting bracket bolts	81	110
Master cylinder mounting nuts*	19	26
Rear brake caliper		
Guide pin bolts	26	35
Mounting bracket bolts	49	67
Power brake booster mounting nuts*	16	22
Wheel bolts	See Chapter 1	

*Do not re-use

Section

Reference to other Chapters

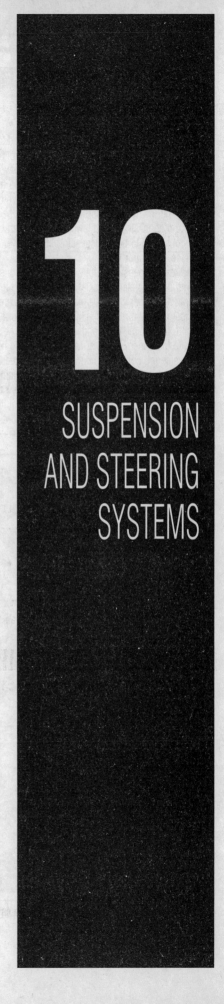

10

SUSPENSION AND STEERING SYSTEMS

1 General information

▶ **Refer to illustrations 1.1 and 1.2**

The independent front suspension is of the MacPherson strut type, incorporating coil springs and integral telescopic shock absorbers. The MacPherson struts are located by transverse lower suspension arms, which use rubber inner mounting bushings and incorporate a balljoint at the outer ends. The front steering knuckle, which carry the brake calipers and the hub/disc assemblies, are attached to the MacPherson struts, and connected to the lower arms through balljoints. A stabilizer bar is connected to both suspension struts/lower arms by connecting links (see illustration).

The rear suspension is fully independent consisting of a trailing arm with an integrated knuckle, which is linked to the rear axle carrier by upper and lower control arms. Coil springs are installed between the upper control arms and vehicle body, and shock absorbers are connected to the vehicle body and trailing arms. The stabilizer bar is connected to the upper control arms by connecting links (see illustration).

The steering column is connected to the steering gear by an intermediate shaft, which incorporates a universal joint.

The steering gear is mounted onto the front subframe, connects to the steering knuckles using tie-rods with balljoints on the ends. The tie-rod ends are threaded, to facilitate adjustment.

Power-assisted steering is standard. The hydraulic steering system is powered by a belt-driven pump, which is driven off the crankshaft pulley.

➡**Note: The information contained in this Chapter is applicable to the standard suspension set-up. On models with M-sport suspension, slight differences will be found. Refer to your BMW dealer for details.**

Frequently, when working on the suspension or steering system components, you may come across fasteners which seem impossible to loosen. These fasteners on the underside of the vehicle are continually subjected to water, road grime, mud, etc., and can become rusted or "frozen," making them extremely difficult to remove. In order to unscrew these stubborn fasteners without damaging them (or other components), be sure to use lots of penetrating oil and allow it to soak in for a while. Using a wire brush to clean exposed threads will also ease removal of the nut or bolt and prevent damage to the threads. Sometimes a sharp blow with a hammer and punch is effective in breaking the bond between a nut and bolt threads, but care must be taken to prevent the punch from slipping off the fastener and ruining the threads. Heating the stuck fastener and surrounding area with a torch sometimes helps too, but isn't recommended because of the obvious dangers associated with fire. Long breaker bars and extension, or

1.1 Front suspension components (2004 325i model shown)

1)	Lower control arm	3)	Strut	5)	Front reinforcement plate
2)	Tie-rod end	4)	Stabilizer bar		

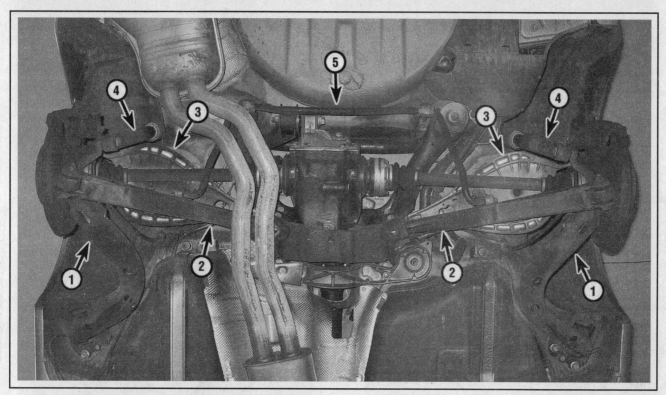

1.2 Rear suspension components (2004 325i model shown)

1)	Trailing arm with integrated knuckle	3)	Upper control arm	5)	Stabilizer bar
2)	Lower control arm	4)	Shock absorber		

"cheater," pipes will increase leverage, but never use an extension pipe on a ratchet - the ratcheting mechanism could be damaged. Sometimes, turning the nut or bolt in the tightening (clockwise) direction first will help to break it loose. Fasteners that require drastic measures to unscrew should always be replaced with new ones.

Since most of the procedures that are dealt with in this Chapter involve jacking up the vehicle and working underneath it, a good pair of jackstands will be needed. A hydraulic floor jack is the preferred type of jack to lift the vehicle, and it can also be used to support certain components during various operations.

✳✳ WARNING:

Never, under any circumstances, rely on a jack to support the vehicle while working on it. Whenever any of the suspension or steering fasteners are loosened or removed they must be inspected and, if necessary, be replaced with new ones of the same part number or of original equipment quality and design. Torque specifications must be followed for proper reassembly and component retention. Never attempt to heat or straighten any suspension or steering component. Instead, replace any bent or damaged part with a new one.

---

2 Front hub assembly - removal and installation

➡Note: Don't remove the hub assembly unless you intend to replace it. The manufacturer states that the hub assembly must be replaced whenever it is removed because of damage to the wheel bearing during removal. A new hub nut and grease cap will be required for installation.

REMOVAL

▶ Refer to illustrations 2.3, 2.4 and 2.5

1 Remove the front brake disc (see Chapter 9).
2 Remove the retaining screw and remove the front ABS wheel sensor (see Chapter 9).
3 Tap the grease cap out from the center of the hub (see illustration).

2.3 Tap out the grease cap from the center of the hub

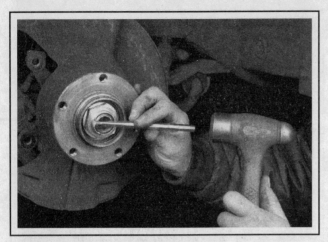

2.4 Using a hammer and pointed-nose chisel, tap out the hub nut staking

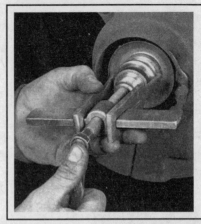

2.5 If the hub bearing inner race remains on the spindle, use a puller to remove it

4   Using a hammer and chisel, unstake the hub retaining nut, and then remove it (see illustration).

5   Attach a suitable puller to the hub assembly and draw it off the steering knuckle. If the bearing's inner race remains on the knuckle's spindle, a knife-edge type puller will be required to remove it (see illustration).

➡**Note: The wheel bearings are not available separately. The hub and wheel bearing must be replaced as an assembly.**

6   If required, remove the fasteners and detach the disc guard from the steering knuckle.

INSTALLATION

▶ **Refer to illustration 2.8**

7   If removed, reinstall the disc guard to the steering knuckle and tighten the fasteners securely.

8   Position the hub on the steering knuckle. Tap or press the hub assembly onto the steering knuckle using a tubular spacer (or equivalent) which only contacts the bearing's inner race (see illustration).

9   Install the hub nut and tighten it to the torque listed in this Chapter's Specifications. Lock the hub nut in position by staking it firmly into the stub axle groove using a hammer and punch.

2.8 Tap the hub assembly into position using a socket which only contacts the inner race of the new bearing

10 Check that the hub rotates freely, and press the new grease cap into the hub center.

11 Reinstall the brake disc and ABS wheel sensor as described in Chapter 9.

12 Tighten the wheel bolts to the torque listed in the Chapter 1 Specifications.

3   Steering knuckle - removal and installation

⁜ **WARNING:**

Dust created by the brake system is harmful to your health. Never blow it out with compressed air and don't inhale any of it. Do not, under any circumstances, use petroleum-based solvents to clean brake parts. Use brake system cleaner only.

➡**Note: New suspension strut-to-knuckle bolt, and tie-rod balljoint and lower arm balljoint nuts, will be required on installation.**

REMOVAL

▶ **Refer to illustration 3.6**

1   Firmly apply the parking brake, then raise the front of the vehicle

and support it securely on jackstands. Remove the relevant front wheel.

2   If steering knuckle is to be replaced, do not attempt to reuse the hub assembly (see Section 2).

3   If the steering knuckle is to be reinstalled, loosen and remove the two bolts securing the brake caliper mounting bracket and then slide the caliper assembly off the disc. Using a piece of wire or string, tie the caliper to the front suspension coil spring, to avoid placing any strain on the hydraulic brake hose. On models with ABS, also remove the wheel sensor (see Chapter 9).

4   Loosen and remove the nut securing the tie-rod balljoint to the steering knuckle and release the balljoint tapered shank using a universal balljoint separator.

5   Unscrew the lower arm balljoint nut, and release the balljoint tapered shank from the knuckle using a universal balljoint separator.

6   Loosen and remove the bolt securing the suspension strut to the

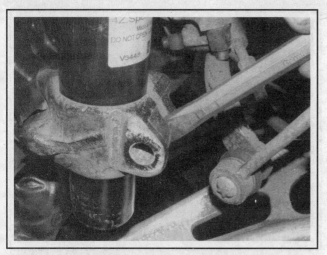

3.6 Use a large screwdriver to gently spread the clamp

3.10 Ensure that the locating pin slides into the slot in the clamp

knuckle. Slide the knuckle down and off from the end of the strut. To ease removal, insert a large screwdriver into the slot on the back of the steering knuckle and slightly spread it's clamp (see illustration). Take care to spread the clamp only as much as absolutely necessary, as excessive force will cause damage.

7 Examine the steering knuckle for signs of wear or damage, and replace if necessary.

INSTALLATION

▶ **Refer to illustration 3.10**

8 Prior to installation, clean the threads of the strut-to-steering knuckle bolt hole by running a tap of the correct thread size and pitch down it.

9 Engage the knuckle with the lower arm balljoint stud, and install the new retaining nut.

10 Position the knuckle on the suspension strut, ensuring that the locating pin on the strut slides into the slot in the knuckle's clamp (see illustration). Slide the knuckle up until it contacts the stop on the strut. Install the new strut-to-knuckle bolt and tighten it to the specified torque.

11 Tighten the lower arm balljoint nut to the specified torque.

12 Engage the tie-rod balljoint in the steering knuckle, then install a new retaining nut and tighten it to the specified torque.

13 If a replacement steering knuckle is being installed, install a new hub assembly (see Section 2).

14 On models where the hub was not disturbed, slide the caliper into position over the disc, making sure the pads pass either side of the disc. Clean the threads of the caliper bracket mounting bolts prior to installation and tighten them to the specified torque setting (see Chapter 9).

15 Reinstall the wheel, then lower the car to the ground and tighten the wheel bolts to the torque listed in the Chapter 1 Specifications.

4 Front suspension strut - removal, overhaul and installation

➡**Note: New strut upper mounting nuts and a strut-to-steering knuckle bolt will be required for installation.**

REMOVAL

▶ **Refer to illustrations 4.3 and 4.7**

1 Loosen the wheel bolts, chock the rear wheels, apply the parking brake, then raise the front of the vehicle and support it securely on jackstands. Remove the appropriate wheel.

2 To prevent the lower arm assembly hanging down while the strut is removed, screw a wheel bolt into the hub, then wrap a piece of wire around the bolt and tie it to the car body. This will support the weight of the steering knuckle. Alternatively, support the steering knuckle with a jack.

3 Unclip the brake hose and wiring harness from the clips on the base of the strut (see illustration).

4 Loosen and remove the retaining nut and washer, then disconnect the stabilizer bar link from the strut. Use a wrench to hold the sta-

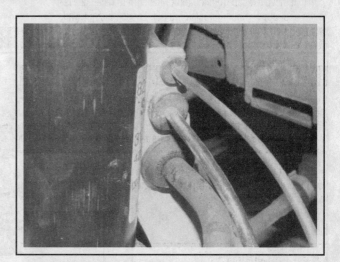

4.3 Pull the brake hose and wiring harness grommets from the bracket

bilizer bar link balljoint while loosening the nut.

5   On models equipped with a ride height sensor for headlamp range adjustment, unscrew the nut and remove the link bracket from the lower control arm.

6   Loosen and remove the bolt securing the suspension strut to the steering knuckle. Slide the steering knuckle down and off from the end of the strut. To ease removal, insert a large screwdriver into the slot on the back of the steering knuckle and slightly spread the steering knuckle clamp (see illustration 3.6). Take care to spread the steering knuckle clamp only as much as absolutely necessary, as excessive force will cause damage.

7   From within the engine compartment, unscrew the strut upper mounting nuts, then carefully lower the strut assembly out from underneath the wing. On some models, a centering pin fixed to the strut upper mounting plate aligns with a corresponding hole in the strut tower. On models where no centering pin is installed, make alignment marks between the mounting plate studs and strut tower before removing the strut (see illustration). It is essential that the mounting plate is installed to its original location to preserve the strut camber angle.

OVERHAUL

▶ Refer to illustrations 4.9, 4.10a, 4.10b, 4.17a, 4.17b, 4.17b, 4.18, 4.19 and 4.20a through 4.20d

❋❋ WARNING:

Disassembling a strut spring is potentially dangerous and utmost attention must be directed to the job, or serious injury may result. Use only a high-quality spring compressor and carefully follow the manufacturer's instructions furnished with the tool. After removing the coil spring from the shock assembly, set it aside in a safe, isolated area.

➡Note: A new mounting plate nut will be required.

8   With the strut removed from the car, clean away all external dirt, then mount it upright in a vice.

9   Install the spring compressor, and compress the coil spring until all tension is relieved from the upper spring seat (see illustration).

10 Remove the cap from the top of the strut to gain access to the strut upper mounting retaining nut. Loosen the nut while retaining the strut piston with a suitable tool (see illustrations).

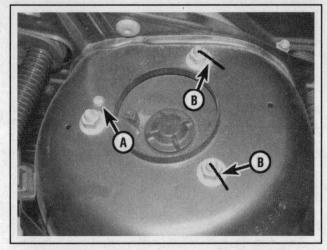

4.7 The location of the centering pin (A) and two strut mounting studs and nuts with index marks (B)

4.9 Install the spring compressor

11 Remove the mounting nut, and lift off the mounting plate complete with thrust bearing. Remove the conical washer and flat washer, followed by the upper spring plate and upper spring seat.

12 Lift off the coil spring, followed by the bump stop, boot and lower spring seat.

4.10a Remove the plastic cap . . .

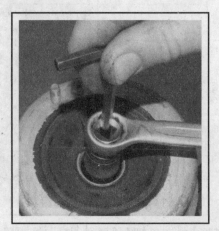

4.10b . . . and remove the nut

4.17a Reinstall the lower seat . . .

4.17b . . . followed by the boot and bump stop

13 With the strut assembly now completely dismantled, examine all the components for wear, damage or deformation, and check the upper mounting bearing for smoothness of operation. Replace any of the components as necessary.

14 Examine the strut for signs of fluid leakage. Check the strut piston for signs of pitting along its entire length, and check the strut body for signs of damage. While holding it in an upright position, test the operation of the strut by moving the piston through a full stroke, and then through short strokes of 2 to 4-inches (50 to 100 mm). In both cases, the resistance felt should be smooth and continuous. If the resistance is jerky, or uneven, or if there is any visible sign of wear or damage to the strut, replacement is necessary.

15 If any doubt exists about the condition of the coil spring, carefully remove the spring compressors, and check the spring for distortion and signs of cracking. Replace the spring if it is damaged or distorted, or if there is any doubt as to its condition.

16 Inspect all other components for damage or deterioration, and replace any that are suspect.

17 Reinstall the lower spring seat, and slide the bump stop and boot onto the strut piston (see illustrations).

18 Install the coil spring onto the strut, making sure the rubber seat and spring are correctly located (see illustration).

19 Install the upper spring seat so that the spring end is against the seat stop (see illustration).

20 Reinstall the flat washer followed by the conical washer (concave side up) and the upper mounting plate. Install the new mounting plate nut and tighten it to the specified torque (see illustrations). If the damper rod rotates while attempting to tighten the nut, a special cutaway socket is available from BMW dealers and good tool retailers that allows an Allen key to be inserted into the top of the damper rod while the torque wrench is used.

4.18 Note the spring will only fit into the lower seat in one position

4.19 Ensure the spring end is against the seat stop

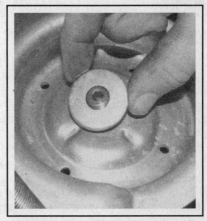

4.20a Install the flat washer . . .

4.20b . . . followed by the conical washer, concave side up . . .

4.20c . . . then reinstall the upper mounting . . .

4.20d . . . and install the new nut

21 Ensure the spring ends and seats are correctly placed, then carefully release the compressor and remove it from the strut. Reinstall the cap to the top of the strut.

INSTALLATION

22 Prior to installation, ensure that the threads on the steering knuckle clamp for the strut are clean. If necessary, clean the threads of the of the old strut-to-steering knuckle bolt with a wire wheel (or equivalent) and use it to clean the threads of the clamp on the steering knuckle.

23 Maneuver the strut assembly into position, aligning the centering pin with its corresponding hole, or previously made marks, and install the new upper mounting nuts.

24 Locate the steering knuckle correctly with the suspension strut (see Section 3), and insert the retaining bolt. Tighten the bolt to the specified torque. Note that the wiring/hose support bracket is also retained by the bolt.

25 Tighten the strut upper mounting nuts to the specified torque.

26 Where applicable, reinstall the suspension height sensor link bracket to the lower control arm, and tighten the retaining nut securely.

27 Engage the stabilizer bar connecting link with the strut. Make sure the flat on the balljoint shank is correctly located against the lug on the strut, then install the washer and new retaining nut and tighten to the specified torque.

28 Clip the hose/wiring back onto the strut, then reinstall the wheel. Lower the car to the ground and tighten the wheel bolts to the specified torque.

5 Front lower control arm - removal, overhaul and installation

➡**Note: New lower control arm front balljoint nuts be required on installation.**

REMOVAL

▶ **Refer to illustrations 5.5a, 5.5b and 5.6**

1 Chock the rear wheels, firmly apply the parking brake, then raise the front of the vehicle and support on jackstands. Remove the appropriate front wheel.

2 Remove the screws and remove the engine splash shield.

3 Unscrew the bolts and remove the reinforcement cross brace, or plate from under the vehicle (see Chapter 2A).

4 On models installed with suspension ride height sensors, unscrew the retaining nut and remove the sensor link bracket from the lower arm.

5 Unscrew the lower arm balljoint nut, and release the arm from the steering knuckle using a universal balljoint separator (see illustrations).

6 Loosen and remove the two bolts securing the lower arm rear mounting bracket from the chassis (see illustration).

7 Unscrew the nut from the arm's inner balljoint, and remove the lower arm assembly from underneath the car. Note that the balljoint may be a tight install in the crossmember, and may need to be tapped out of position.

OVERHAUL

8 Thoroughly clean the lower arm and the area around the arm mountings, removing all traces of dirt and underseal if necessary, then check carefully for cracks, distortion or any other signs of wear or damage, paying particular attention to the mounting bushings and balljoint. If either the bushing or the balljoint requires replacement, the lower arm should be taken to a BMW dealer or suitably-equipped garage. A hydraulic press and suitable spacers are required to press the bushings out of position and install the new ones.

INSTALLATION

9 Ensure the balljoint studs and mounting holes are clean and dry, then place the lower arm in position.

5.5a Hold the balljoint with an Allen key while removing the nut

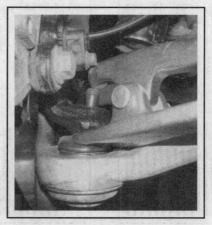

5.5b Use a balljoint separator to release the lower arm

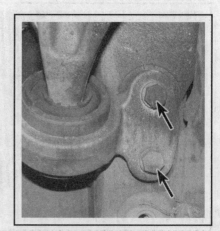

5.6 Unscrew the two lower arm-to-chassis bolts

10 Locate the inner mounting stud in the crossmember, and engage the balljoint stud with the steering knuckle. If necessary, press the inner balljoint stud into position by using a jack beneath the arm.

11 Install a new nut to the inner balljoint stud and tighten it to the specified torque.

12 Install a new nut to the outer balljoint stud, and tighten it to the specified torque setting.

13 Reinstall the lower arm rear mounting bracket bolts and tighten them to the specified torque setting.

14 On models equipped with suspension ride height sensors, reinstall the sensor link bracket to the lower arm and tighten the retaining nut securely.

15 Reinstall the reinforcement cross brace or plate to the underside of the vehicle and tighten the bolts to the specified torque.

16 Reinstall the engine splash shield.

17 Reinstall the wheel, then lower the car to the ground and tighten the wheel bolts to the specified torque.

6 Front suspension lower arm balljoint - replacement

Front suspension lower arm balljoint replacement requires the use of a hydraulic press and several suitable spacers if it is to be carried out safely and successfully. If replacement is necessary, then the arm should be removed (see Section 5) and taken to a BMW dealer or suitably-equipped workshop.

7 Front suspension stabilizer bar - removal and installation

➡**Note: New mounting clamp nuts and connecting link nuts will be required on installation.**

REMOVAL

▶ **Refer to illustrations 7.2 and 7.3**

1 Loosen the front wheel lug bolts. Chock the rear wheels, firmly apply the parking brake, then raise the front of the vehicle and support on jackstands. Remove the screws and remove the engine splash shield, then remove both front wheels.

2 Unscrew the retaining nuts, and free the connecting link from each end of the stabilizer bar using a second wrench to hold the balljoint stud (see illustration).

3 Make alignment marks between the bushings and stabilizer bar, then loosen the stabilizer bar mounting clamp retaining nuts (see illustration).

4 Remove both clamps from the subframe, and maneuver the stabilizer bar out from underneath the car. Remove the mounting bushings from the bar.

5 Carefully examine the stabilizer bar components for signs of wear, damage or deterioration, paying particular attention to the mounting bushings. Replace worn components as necessary.

INSTALLATION

6 Install the rubber bushings to the stabilizer bar, aligning them with the marks made prior to removal. Rotate each bushing so that the split side faces downward.

7 Maneuver stabilizer bar into position. Reinstall the mounting clamps, ensuring that their ends are correctly located in the hooks on the subframe, and install the new retaining nuts. Ensure that the bushing markings are still aligned with the marks on the bars, then tighten the mounting clamp retaining nuts to the specified torque.

8 Engage the stabilizer bar connecting links with the bar. Make sure the flats on the balljoint shank are correctly located against the lugs on the bar then install the new retaining nuts and tighten to the specified torque.

9 Reinstall the wheels then lower the car to the ground and tighten the wheel bolts to the specified torque.

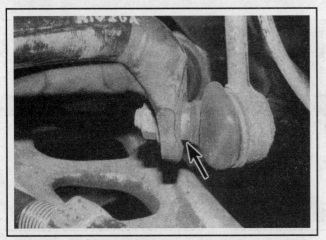

7.2 Use an open-end wrench to hold the balljoint stud on the stabilizer bar link

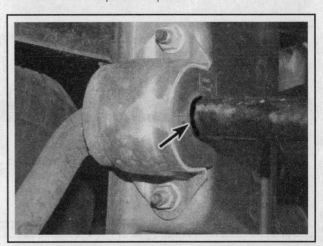

7.3 Remove the front stabilizer bar clamp nuts after marking the relationship of the bushing to the bar

8   Front suspension stabilizer bar connecting link - removal and installation

▶ **Refer to illustration 8.3**

➡**Note: New connecting link nuts will be required on installation.**

1   Firmly apply the parking brake, then raise the front of the vehicle and support it securely on jackstands.

2   Unscrew the retaining nut, and free the connecting link from the stabilizer bar using a second wrench to hold the link balljoint stud.

3   Loosen and remove the nut securing the link to the suspension strut, using a second wrench to hold the link balljoint stud (see illustration).

4   Check the connecting link balljoints for signs of wear. Check that each balljoint is free to move easily, and that the rubber boots are undamaged. If necessary replace the connecting link.

5   Installation is a reverse of the removal sequence, using new nuts and tightening them to the specified torque setting.

8.3 Use an open-ended wrench to hold the stabilizer bar link balljoint stud (removed for clarity)

9   Rear hub assembly - removal and installation

➡**Note 1: The hub assembly should not be removed unless it, or the hub bearing, is to be replaced. The hub is a press fit in the bearing's inner race removing the hub will damage the bearing. If the hub is to be removed, be prepared to replace the hub bearing at the same time.**

➡**Note 2: A long bolt or length of threaded bar and suitable washers will be required for installation.**

REMOVAL

1   Remove the relevant driveaxle as described in Chapter 8.

2   Remove the brake disc as described in Chapter 9.

3   Bolt a slide hammer to the hub surface, and use the hammer to draw the hub out from the bearing. If the bearing's inner race stays attached to the hub, a puller will be required to draw it off.

4   With the hub removed, replace the bearing as described in Section 10.

INSTALLATION

5   Lightly apply oil to the hub surface and then place it in the bearing's inner race.

6   Draw the hub into position by using a long bolt or threaded length of bar and two nuts. Install a large washer to both ends of the bolt or bar, so that the inner washer contacts the bearing's inner race, and the outer washer contacts the hub. Slowly tighten the nut(s) until the hub is pulled fully into position.

➡**Note: Do not force the hub into position using a hammer and drift as this will damage the bearing.**

7   Remove the bolt or threaded bar and washers (as applicable), and check that the hub bearing rotates smoothly and easily.

8   Reinstall the brake disc referring to Chapter 9.

9   Reinstall the driveshaft referring to Chapter 8.

10   Rear hub bearings - replacement

1   Remove the rear hub as described in Section 9.

2   Remove the hub bearing retaining snap-ring from the trailing arm.

3   Tap the hub bearing out from the trailing arm using a hammer and suitable punch.

4   Thoroughly clean the trailing arm bore, removing all traces of dirt and grease, and polish away any burrs or raised edges which might hinder reassembly. Replace the snap-ring if there is any doubt about its condition.

5   On reassembly, apply a light film of clean engine oil to the bearing outer race to aid installation.

6   Align the bearing in the trailing arm and tap it fully into position, ensuring that it enters the arm squarely, using a suitable tubular spacer that only contacts the bearing's outer race.

7   Secure the bearing in position with the snap-ring, making sure it is fully seated in the trailing arm groove.

8   Install the rear hub as described in Section 9.

11 Rear suspension shock absorber - removal, overhaul and installation

➡Note: New shock absorber upper mounting nuts and a new mounting gasket will be required on installation.

REMOVAL

▶ Refer to illustrations 11.2a, 11.2b, 11.5 and 11.6

1   Check the front wheels, then raise the rear of the vehicle and support it securely on jackstands. To improve access, remove the rear wheel.

2   On Sedan and Coupe models, lift up the floor panel in the trunk and remove the liner that covers the shock. On the left-hand side, remove the warning triangle, pry out the plastic rivet, and remove the warning triangle bracket. Pry out the retaining clips securing the side trim cover in position, and remove the trim and insulation panel to gain access to the shock absorber upper mounting fasteners (see illustrations).

3   On wagon models, remove the interior trim panel as described in Chapter 11, Section 27.

4   Position a jack underneath the trailing arm, and raise the jack so that it is supporting the weight of the arm. This will prevent the arm dropping when the shock absorber is unbolted.

5   Loosen and remove the bolt securing the shock absorber to the trailing arm (see illustration).

6   From inside the trunk, remove the upper mounting nuts (see illustration). Lower the shock absorber out from underneath the car and recover the gasket which is installed between the upper mounting and body.

OVERHAUL

➡Note: A new piston nut will be required.

7   Remove the trim cap from the top of the shock absorber, then remove all traces of dirt. Loosen and remove the piston nut and dished washer, noting which way around it is installed.

8   Lift off the upper mounting plate and remove the dust cover.

9   Slide the spacer and rubber stop off from the shock absorber piston.

10   Examine the shock absorber for signs of fluid leakage. Check the piston for signs of pitting along its entire length, and check the body for signs of damage. While holding it in an upright position, test the operation of the shock absorber by moving the piston through a full

11.2a Pry out the warning triangle bracket plastic rivet

stroke, and then through short strokes of 2 to 4-inches (50 to 100 mm). In both cases, the resistance felt should be smooth and continuous. If the resistance is jerky, or uneven, or if there is any visible sign of wear or damage, replacement is necessary.

11   Inspect all other components for signs of damage or deterioration, and replace any that are suspect.

12   Slide the rubber stop and spacer onto the shock piston, and install the dust cover.

13   Install the upper mounting plate and dished washer, and screw on the new piston nut and tighten it securely. Reinstall the trim cap.

INSTALLATION

14   Ensure the upper mounting plate and body contact surfaces are clean and dry, and install a new gasket to the upper mounting plate.

15   Maneuver the shock absorber into position, and install the new upper mounting nuts.

16   Ensure the lower end of the shock absorber is positioned with the mounting bushing spacer washer facing towards the bolt. Screw in the lower mounting bolt, tightening it by hand only at this stage.

17   Tighten the upper mounting nuts to the specified torque setting then reinstall the insulation panel, luggage compartment trim panel, rear light access cover and loudspeaker (as applicable).

18   Reinstall the wheel and lower the car to the ground. With the car resting on its wheels, tighten the shock absorber lower mounting bolt and wheel bolts to the specified torque.

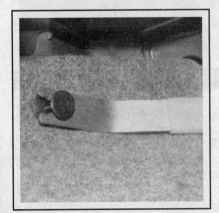

11.2b Lever up the center pin, then pry out the plastic rivets

11.5 Remove the shock absorber lower bolt

11.6 Remove the rear shock absorber upper mounting nuts

12 Rear suspension coil spring - removal and installation

REMOVAL

▶ **Refer to illustrations 12.6 and 12.12**

1   Loosen the rear wheel bolts. Chock the front wheels, then raise the rear of the vehicle and support it securely on jackstands. Remove the relevant wheel.

2   Referring to Chapter 8, loosen and remove the bolts and plates securing the relevant driveaxle to the final drive unit flange. Free the driveaxle and support it by tying it to the car underbody using a piece of wire.

✳✳ CAUTION:

Do not allow the driveaxle to hang under its own weight as the CV joint may be damaged.

3   Detach the fuel tank panel from the rear underside of the vehicle (where installed).

4   On models equipped with suspension ride height sensors, unscrew the nut and detach the sensor link arm from the upper control arm.

5   Detach the rear suspension stabilizer bar (where installed) as described in Section 16.

6   Unscrew the bolt and detach the brake hose bracket from the trailing arm (see illustration).

7   Position a jack underneath the rear of the trailing arm, and support the weight of the arm.

8   Loosen and remove the shock absorber lower mounting bolt.

9   Slowly lower the trailing arm, keeping watch on the brake line/

hose to ensure no excess strain is placed on them, until it is possible to withdraw the coil spring.

10   Recover the spring seats from the car body and control arm. If the car is to be left for some time, raise the trailing back up and reinstall the shock absorber lower mounting bolt.

11   Inspect the spring closely for signs of damage, such as cracking, and check the spring seats for signs of wear. Replace worn components as necessary.

INSTALLATION

12   Install the upper and lower spring seats, making sure they are correctly located on the pegs (see illustration).

13   Apply a little grease to the spring ends and engage the spring with its upper seat. Note that the spring is installed with the smaller diameter opening at the top.

14   Hold the spring in position and carefully raise the trailing arm while aligning the coil spring with its lower seat.

15   Raise the arm fully and reinstall the shock absorber lower mounting bolt, tightening it by hand only at this stage.

16   Reinstall the brake hose bracket to the trailing arm.

17   Reinstall the stabilizer bar (see Section 16).

18   Reinstall the panel to the fuel tank.

19   Referring to Chapter 8, connect the driveaxle to the final drive unit, then reinstall the retaining plates and bolts and tighten them to the specified torque.

20   Reinstall the wheel then lower the car to the ground. Tighten the wheel bolts and shock absorber lower bolt to the specified torque. Tighten the wheel bolts to the specified torque.

12.6 Remove the brake hose bracket bolt

12.12 Ensure that the spring seat is positioned correctly over the peg

13 Rear suspension trailing arm - removal, overhaul and installation

✲✲ WARNING:

Dust created by the brake system is harmful to your health. Never blow it out with compressed air and don't inhale any of it. Do not, under any circumstances, use petroleum-based solvents to clean brake parts. Use brake system cleaner only.

REMOVAL

♦ Refer to illustration 13.11 and 13.15

1   Loosen the wheel bolts. Chock the front wheels, then raise the rear of the vehicle and support it securely on jackstands. Remove the relevant wheel.

2   Remove the relevant driveaxle (see Chapter 8).

3   Unscrew the two bolts securing the brake caliper mounting bracket in position, then slide the caliper assembly off the disc. Using a piece of wire or string, tie the caliper to the rear suspension coil spring, to avoid placing any strain on the hydraulic brake hose.

4   Referring to Chapter 9, disconnect the parking brake cable from the rear wheel.

5   Remove the rear wheel ABS sensor as described in Chapter 9, Section 20.

6   Remove the rear stabilizer bar as described in Section 16.

7   Remove the retaining bolt and release the brake line bracket from the trailing arm.

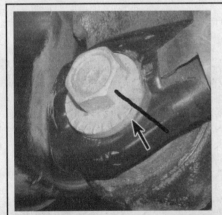

13.11 Make an alignment mark between the eccentric bolt and the lower control arm

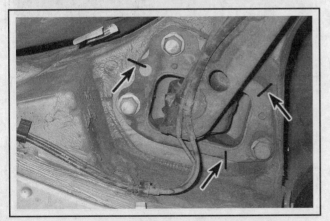

13.15 The trailing arm mounting bracket with alignment marks to the chassis

8   Position a jack underneath the rear of the trailing arm, and support the weight of the arm.

9   Loosen and remove the shock absorber lower mounting bolt.

10 Pry out the plastic expansion rivets, and detach the trim panel adjacent to the fuel tank from the left- or right-hand rear underside of the vehicle.

11 Using paint or a suitable marker pen, mark the relationship between the lower control arm eccentric bolt and the arm itself (see illustration).

➥ **Note: This is necessary to ensure that the rear wheel alignment and camber are correct on installation.**

12 Slowly lower the jack and remove the coil spring.

13 Loosen and remove the nut and washer from the lower control arm pivot bolt. Withdraw the pivot bolt.

14 Loosen and remove the nut and pivot bolt securing the upper control arm to the trailing arm. Note the bolt's direction.

15 Mark the relationship between the trailing arm front mounting bracket and the vehicle chassis (see illustration). Unscrew the three bolts securing the trailing arm mounting bracket to the vehicle body and remove the trailing arm.

➥ **Note: Do not loosen the trailing arm pivot bushing bolt unless replacement of the bushing/mounting bracket is necessary.**

OVERHAUL

♦ Refer to illustration 13.18

16 Loosen and remove the nut and pivot bolt and separate the front mounting bracket and trailing arm.

17 Thoroughly clean the trailing arm and the area around the arm mountings, removing all traces of dirt and underseal if necessary. Check carefully for cracks, distortion or any other signs of wear or damage, paying particular attention to the mounting bushings. If either bushing requires replacement, the arm should be taken to a BMW dealer or suitably-equipped garage. A hydraulic press and suitable spacers are required to press the bushings out of position and install the new ones. Inspect the pivot bolts for signs of wear or damage and replace as necessary.

18 Install the mounting bracket to trailing arm, and install the pivot bolt and nut. Position the bracket using a 5/16-inch (8 mm) rod, and tighten the pivot bolt to the specified torque (see illustration).

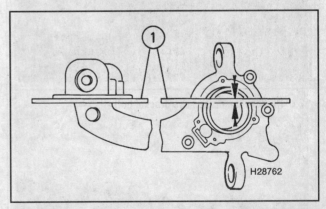

13.18 Place a 5/16-inch (8 mm rod) (1) against the mounting bracket and rest it on the trailing arm to position the mounting bracket

INSTALLATION

19 Position the trailing arm assembly, and reinstall the mounting bracket retaining bolts. Align the marks made prior to removal, then tighten the mounting bracket bolts to the specified torque.

20 Engage the upper control arm with the trailing arm and install the pivot bolt and nut. Note that the bolt should be inserted from the rear. Tighten the bolt by hand only at this stage.

21 Reinstall the coil spring making sure it is correctly aligned with the spring seats, then raise the trailing arm with the jack, and install the lower arm pivot bolt, eccentric washer and nut. Align the washer with the mark made prior to removal, then reinstall the shock absorber lower mounting bolt. Tighten both the pivot bolt and mounting bolt by hand only.

22 Reinstall the fuel tank panel to the underside of the vehicle.

23 Reinstall the brake pipe retaining bracket to the trailing arm, and fully tighten the bolts.

24 Reinstall the rear stabilizer bar as described in Section 16.

25 Referring to Chapter 9, reconnect the parking brake cable to the expander lever and reinstall the ABS wheel sensor. Slide the caliper into position over the disc, making sure the pads pass either side of the disc, and tighten the caliper bracket mounting bolts to the specified torque setting.

26 Reinstall the driveaxle as described in Chapter 8 and lower the car to the ground.

27 With the car on its wheels, rock the car to settle the disturbed components in position, then tighten the shock absorber lower mounting bolt and the upper control arm pivot bolts to the specified torque. Check that the lower arm eccentric washer is still correctly aligned with the mark, then tighten it to the specified torque.

➡Note: On completion, it is advisable to have the camber angle and wheel alignment checked and, if necessary, adjusted.

28 Tighten the wheel bolts to the specified torque.

14 Rear suspension upper control arm - removal, overhaul and installation

➡Note: A new control arm-to-rear subframe pivot bolt and nut will be required on installation.

REMOVAL

◆ Refer to illustrations 14.2 and 14.4

1 Remove the coil spring (see Section 12).

2 Loosen and remove the control arm-to-trailing arm pivot bolt (see illustration). Note the bolts direction.

3 Referring to Chapter 8, support the weight of the unit with a jack, and remove the final drive unit mounting bolts to allow room to withdraw the pivot bolt. Alternatively, remove the driveshaft as described in Chapter 8.

4 Loosen and remove the nut from the control arm-to-rear subframe pivot bolt. Withdraw the bolt, moving the final drive unit slightly to the rear, and remove the control arm from underneath the car (see illustration). Note that on some models it may be necessary to detach the propeller shaft from the final drive unit in order to gain the clearance required to remove the pivot bolt.

➡Note: If the car is to be left for some time, reinstall the final drive unit mounting bolts and tighten securely.

OVERHAUL

5 Thoroughly clean the control arm and the area around the arm mountings, removing all traces of dirt and underseal if necessary. Check for cracks, distortion or any other wear or damage, paying particular attention to the bushing. If the bushing requires replacement, the arm should be taken to a BMW dealer or suitably-equipped garage. A hydraulic press and suitable spacers are required to press the bushing out of position and install a new one.

6 Inspect the pivot bolts for signs of wear or damage, and replace as necessary. The control arm-to-subframe bolt and nut should be replaced as a matter of course.

14.2 Remove the control arm-to-trailing arm bolt

14.4 Remove the control arm-to-subframe bolt

INSTALLATION

7 Maneuver the control arm into position, and install the new arm-to-subframe pivot bolt and nut. Tighten the nut lightly only at this stage.

8 Referring to Chapter 8, Maneuver the final drive unit into position, and tighten its mounting bolts to the specified torque. Where necessary, reconnect the propeller shaft to the final drive unit.

9 Reinstall the pivot bolt and nut securing the control arm to the trailing arm, inserting it from the rear, then tighten it lightly only at this stage.

10 Reinstall the coil spring (see Section 12).

11 On completion, lower the car to the ground and rock the car to settle all disturbed components. With the car resting on its wheels tighten the wheel bolts, shock absorber lower mounting bolt and the control arm pivot bolts to their specified torque settings.

➡**Note: On completion, it is advisable to have the camber angle and wheel alignment checked and, if necessary, adjusted.**

12 Tighten the wheel bolts to the specified torque.

15 Rear suspension lower control arm - removal, overhaul and installation

➡**Note: A new control arm-to-rear subframe pivot bolt and nut will be required on installation.**

REMOVAL

▶ **Refer to illustrations 15.5a and 15.5b**

1 Loosen the rear wheel bolts. Chock the front wheels, then raise the rear of the vehicle and support it securely on jackstands. Remove the rear wheel.

2 Using paint or a suitable marking pen, make alignment marks between the lower control arm pivot bolt eccentric washer and the trailing arm. This is necessary to ensure that the rear wheel alignment and camber are correct on installation.

3 Support the trailing arm with a jack, then remove the nut and washer from the lower control arm pivot bolt. Withdraw the pivot bolt.

4 Referring to Chapter 8, support the weight of the final drive unit with a jack, and remove the unit mounting bolts. Alternatively, remove the driveshaft as described in Chapter 8.

5 Loosen and remove the pivot bolt securing the control arm to the rear subframe. Withdraw the bolt, moving the final drive unit slightly to the rear (where necessary), and remove the control arm from underneath the car. Recover the special nut from the subframe (see illustrations).

➡**Note: On some models it may be necessary to detach the propeller shaft from the final drive unit in order to gain the clearance required to remove the pivot bolt. If the car is to be left for some time, reinstall the final drive unit mounting bolts and tighten securely.**

OVERHAUL

6 Refer to Steps 5 and 6 of Section 14.

INSTALLATION

7 Locate the special nut in the subframe cut-out, and maneuver the control arm into position (with its welded seam facing up). Install the new pivot bolt, tightening it lightly only at this stage.

8 Referring to Chapter 8, Maneuver the final drive unit into position and tighten its mounting bolts to the specified torque. Where necessary, reconnect the propeller shaft to the final drive unit.

9 Install the lower arm-to-trailing arm pivot bolt, eccentric washer and nut. Align the washer with the mark made prior to removal and lightly tighten it.

10 Reinstall the wheel and lower the car to the ground.

11 With the car on its wheels, rock the car to settle the disturbed components in position. Check that the lower arm eccentric washer is still correctly aligned with the mark, then tighten both the control arm pivot bolts to the specified torque wrench setting. Where necessary also tighten the wheel bolts to the specified torque.

➡**Note: On completion, it is advisable to have the camber angle and wheel alignment checked and, if necessary, adjusted.**

15.5a Remove the lower control arm-to-subframe bolt

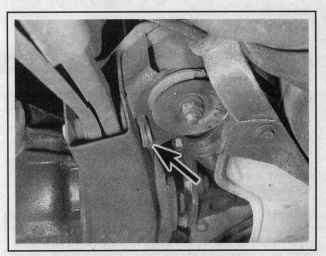

15.5b Recover the special nut from the subframe

16 Rear suspension stabilizer bar - removal and installation

→**Note: New mounting clamp nuts and connecting link nuts will be required on installation.**

REMOVAL

▶ **Refer to illustrations 16.2, 16.3a and 16.3b**

1   Chock the front wheels, then raise the rear of the vehicle and support it securely on jackstands. To improve access, remove the rear wheels.

2   Loosen and remove the nut and bolt securing each connecting link to the upper control arms (see illustration).

3   Make alignment marks between the mounting bushings and stabilizer bar, then loosen the stabilizer bar clamp retaining nuts and bolts (see illustrations).

4   Remove both clamps from the subframe, and maneuver the stabilizer bar and connecting link assembly out from underneath the car. Remove the bushings and connecting links from the bar.

5   Carefully examine the stabilizer bar components for signs of wear, damage or deterioration, paying particular attention to the bushings. Replace any worn components as necessary.

INSTALLATION

6   Install the rubber mounting bushings to the stabilizer bar, aligning them with the marks made prior to removal. Rotate each bushing so that its flat surface is facing forwards.

7   Place the stabilizer bar into position. Locate the connecting links in the upper control arms, and install the new retaining nuts and tighten securely.

8   Reinstall the mounting clamps, ensuring that their ends are correctly located in the hooks on the subframe, and install the bolts and new retaining nuts. Ensure that the bushing markings are still aligned with the marks on the bars, then securely tighten the mounting clamp retaining nuts.

9   Reinstall the wheels then lower the car to the ground and tighten the wheel bolts to the specified torque.

16.2 Remove the nut and bolt securing the stabilizer bar link to the control arm

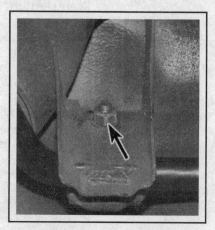

16.3a Loosen the rear stabilizer bar clamp nut

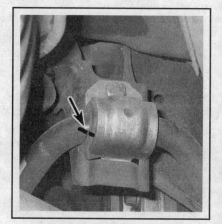

16.3b Mark the relationship of the bushings to the stabilizer bar

17 Steering wheel - removal and installation

❋❋ WARNING 1:

These models are equipped with a Supplemental Restraint System (SRS), more commonly known as airbags. Always disable the airbag system before working in the vicinity of any airbag system component to avoid the possibility of accidental deployment of the airbag(s), which could cause personal injury (see Chapter 12).

❋❋ WARNING 2:

Do not use a memory saving device to preserve the PCM or radio memory when working on or near airbag system components.

❋❋ CAUTION:

Don't allow the steering shaft to turn while the steering wheel is removed.

REMOVAL

▶ **Refer to illustrations 17.3 and 17.4**

1   Disconnect the cable(s) from the battery negative terminal(s) (see Chapter 5, Section 1). Remove the airbag unit from the center of the steering wheel (see Chapter 12).

17.3 Disconnect the electrical connectors and unscrew the steering wheel bolt

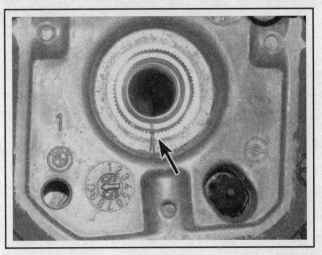

17.4 Make alignment marks between the steering wheel and the column shaft

2   Set the front wheels in the straight-ahead position, and set the steering lock by removing the ignition key.

3   Loosen and remove the steering wheel retaining bolt. Disconnect the electrical connector(s) (see illustration).

4   Mark the steering wheel and steering column shaft in relation to each other, then lift the steering wheel off the shaft splines. If it is tight, tap it up near the center, using the palm of your hand, or twist it from side-to-side, while pulling upwards to release it from the shaft splines (see illustration). The airbag contact unit will automatically be locked in position as the wheel is removed; do not attempt to rotate it while the wheel is removed.

❊❊ CAUTION:

Do not strike the steering wheel or shaft with a hammer or use excessive force to remove it.

5   Inspect the horn contact ring/turn signal canceling cam for signs of wear or damage, and replace as necessary.

INSTALLATION

6   Installation is the reverse of removal, noting the following points.

a) *If the contact unit has been rotated with the wheel removed, re-center it by pressing down on the contact unit and rotating its center fully counterclockwise. From this position, rotate the center back through three complete rotations in a clockwise direction.*

b) *Prior to installation, ensure the turn signal switch arm is in the center (OFF) position. Failure to do so could lead to the steering wheel lug breaking the switch tab.*

c) *Coat the steering wheel horn contact ring with a small amount of petroleum jelly and reinstall the wheel, making sure the contact unit wiring is correctly routed.*

d) *Engage the wheel with the column shaft splines, aligning the marks made on removal, and tighten the steering wheel retaining bolt to the specified torque.*

e) *Reinstall the airbag unit (see Chapter 12).*

18 Steering column - removal, inspection and installation

❊❊ WARNING 1:

These models are equipped with a Supplemental Restraint System (SRS), more commonly known as airbags. Always disable the airbag system before working in the vicinity of any airbag system component to avoid the possibility of accidental deployment of the airbag(s), which could cause personal injury (see Chapter 12).

❊❊ WARNING 2:

Do not use a memory saving device to preserve the PCM or radio memory when working on or near airbag system components.

➡**Note: New steering column shear-bolts, and an intermediate shaft clamp bolt/nut, will be required on installation.**

REMOVAL

▶ **Refer to illustrations 18.6, 18.8a and 18.8b**

1   Park the vehicle with the front wheels point straight ahead. Disconnect the cable(s) from the battery negative terminal(s) (see Chapter 5, Section 1).

2   Remove the steering wheel as described in Section 17.

3   Remove the steering column combination switches (refer to Chapter 12).

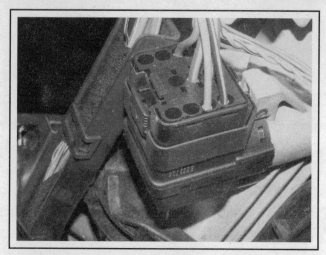

18.6 Disconnect the electrical connector from the ignition switch

18.8a Remove the column retaining bolt (1) and shear-bolt (2) . . .

4   Working in the engine compartment, using paint or a suitable marker pen, make alignment marks between the lower end of the steering column and the intermediate shaft upper joint.

5   Loosen and remove the nut and clamp bolt, and disengage the shaft from the column.

6   Disconnect the electrical connectors from the ignition switch and free the harness from its retaining clips on the column (see illustration).

7   Release the retaining clip and detach the interlock cable (where installed) from the steering column (see illustration 19.6).

8   The steering column is secured in position with two nuts, one bolt and one shear-bolt. The shear-bolt can be extracted using a hammer and suitable chisel to tap the bolt head around until it can be unscrewed by hand. Alternatively, drill a hole in the center of the bolt head and extract it using a bolt/stud extractor (sometimes called an Easy-out). Unscrew the remaining mounting bolt/nuts (see illustrations).

9   Pull the column upwards and away from the firewall, and slide off the rubber mounting, mounting seat, washer and fixing ring off from the column lower end. Remove the collars and rubber mountings from the column mountings.

INSPECTION

10 The steering column incorporates a telescopic safety feature. In the event of a front-end crash, the shaft collapses and prevents the steering wheel injuring the driver. Before installation the steering column, examine the column and mountings for damage and deformation, and replace as necessary.

11 Check the steering shaft for signs of free play in the column bushings. If any damage or wear is found on the steering column bushings, the column should be overhauled. Overhaul of the column is a complex task requiring several special tools, and should be entrusted to a BMW dealer or other qualified repair shop.

INSTALLATION

▶ **Refer to illustrations 18.13 and 18.14**

12 Ensure the mounting rubbers are in position, and install the collars to the rear of the mounting rubbers.

13 Slide the fixing ring, washer, mounting seat and rubber mounting

18.8b . . . followed by the lower mounting nuts

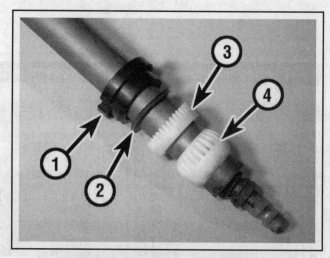

18.13 Slide the fixing ring (1), washer (2), mounting seat (3) and rubber mounting (4) onto the base of the steering column . . .

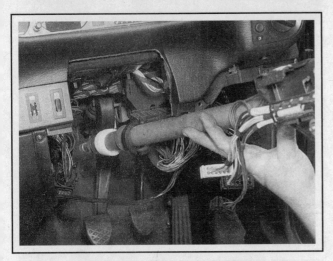

18.14 . . . and reinstall the column to the vehicle

onto the base of the steering column (see illustration).

14 Maneuver the column into position and engage it with the intermediate shaft splines, aligning the marks made prior to removal (see illustration).

15 Locate the lower end of the column in its seat and screw in the mounting bolts and new shear-bolt; tighten them lightly only at this stage.

16 Tighten the column shear-bolt until its head breaks off. Tighten the remaining column mounting fasteners securely

17 Reconnect the wiring connectors to the ignition switch, and secure the wiring to the column, ensuring it is correctly routed.

18 Ensure the intermediate shaft and column marks are correctly aligned, and insert the column into the shaft. Install the new clamp bolt nut and tighten it to the specified torque.

19 Where necessary, reconnect the interlock cable to the switch and secure it in position.

20 Install the combination switches as described in Chapter 12.

21 Reinstall the steering wheel as described in Section 17.

---

19 Ignition switch/steering column lock - removal and installation

LOCK ASSEMBLY

1   Replacement of the lock assembly requires the steering column to be dismantled. This task requires the use of several special tools, and for this reason should be entrusted to a BMW dealer or suitably-equipped specialist.

LOCK CYLINDER

Removal

▶ **Refer to illustration 19.3 through 19.6, 19.7a and 19.7b**

2   Disconnect the battery negative terminal (see Chapter 5, Section 1). Insert the key into the lock and release the steering lock.

3   Loosen the retaining screw and pull it out complete with the plastic rivet, squeeze in the sides of steering column upper shroud as shown, and remove the shroud (see illustration).

4   Push-in the center pins of the two plastic expanding rivets and remove the lower steering column shroud (see illustration).

19.3 Loosen the screw and pull it out complete with the plastic rivet

5   Disconnect the electrical connector then, using two screwdrivers, carefully pry the transponder ring over the end of the ignition switch (see illustration).

6   Depress the retaining clip and detach the interlock cable (where installed) from the ignition switch (see illustration).

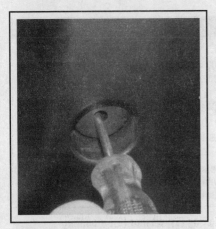

19.4 Press in the center pins of the two expanding rivets

19.5 Carefully pry off the transponder ring

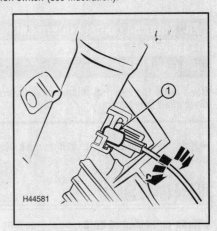

19.6 Depress the retaining clip (1) and detach the interlock cable

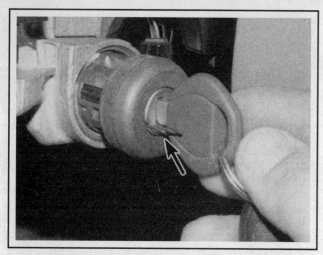

19.7a Insert a 1/8-inch (1.2 mm) (approx) pin into the hole in the cylinder . . .

7 Turn the ignition key to the accessory position (I), then insert a drill bit or other suitable pin into the hole in the cylinder. Depress the lock cylinder detent, and slide the lock cylinder out of position (see illustrations).

Installation

8 Position the lock cylinder as shown in Step 7 and insert the cylinder into the housing until it clicks into position.

IGNITION SWITCH BLOCK

Removal

◆ **Refer to illustration 19.12**

9 Disconnect the cable(s) to the battery negative terminal(s) (see Chapter 5, Section 1).

10 Remove the retaining screw, squeeze in the sides of steering column upper shroud and remove it (see illustration 19.3).

11 Push-in the center pins and pry out the plastic rivets, then remove the lower steering column shroud (see illustration 19.4).

12 Disconnect the electrical connector from the switch, then remove the two set screws and remove the switch block from the lock assembly (see illustration).

19.7b . . . to depress the detent lever (shown with lock removed)

19.12 Disconnect the electrical connector and loosen the two set screws

Installation

13 Installation is the reverse of removal, noting the following points:

a) *Apply varnish to the switch screws prior to installation, to lock them in position.*

b) *Reconnect the battery and check the operation of the switch prior to installation the steering column shrouds.*

20 Steering column intermediate shaft - removal and installation

✳✳ CAUTION:

Don't allow the steering column shaft to turn while the intermediate shaft is removed.

➡ **Note: New intermediate shaft clamp bolts will be required on installation.**

REMOVAL

◆ **Refer to illustration 20.3**

1 Chock the rear wheels, firmly apply the hand-brake, then raise the front of the vehicle and support on jackstands. Set the front wheels in the straight-ahead position. Remove the screws and remove the engine splash shield.

2 Using paint or a suitable marker pen, make alignment marks between the intermediate shaft universal joint and the steering column, the shaft and flexible coupling, and the flexible coupling and the steering gear pinion.

➡ **Note: On some models an alignment mark is already provided on the pinion flange, which aligns with a mark cast into the pinion housing (see illustration 21.3).**

3 Loosen and remove the clamp bolts, then slide the two halves of the shaft together and remove the shaft assembly from the car (see illustration).

4   Inspect the intermediate shaft universal joint for signs of roughness in its bearings and ease of movement. Also examine the shaft rubber coupling for signs of damage or deterioration, and check that the rubber is securely bonded to the flanges. If the universal joint or rubber coupling are suspect, the complete intermediate shaft should be replaced.

INSTALLATION

5   Check that the front wheels are still in the straight-ahead position, and that the steering wheel is correctly positioned.
6   Align the marks made on removal, and engage the intermediate shaft joint with the steering column and the coupling with the steering gear.
7   Insert the new clamp bolts, and tighten them to the specified torque setting. Lower the car to the ground.

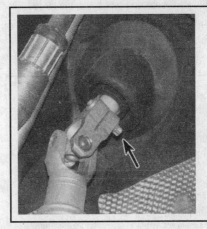

20.3 Steering column intermediate shaft upper clamp bolt

21 Steering gear - removal, overhaul and installation

➡ **Note: New tie-rod balljoint nuts, steering gear mounting nuts, intermediate shaft clamp bolt, and line fitting bolt sealing washers will be required on installation.**

REMOVAL

▶ **Refer to illustrations 21.3, 21.4, 21.5 and 21.6**

1   Loosen the front wheel bolts. Chock the rear wheels, firmly apply the parking brake, then raise the front of the vehicle and support it securely on jackstands. Remove both front wheels, remove the screws and remove the engine splash shield.
2   Loosen and remove the nuts securing the steering gear tie-rod balljoints to the steering knuckles, and release the balljoint tapered shanks using a universal balljoint separator.
3   Using paint or a suitable marker pen, make alignment marks between the intermediate shaft flexible coupling and the steering gear pinion.

➡ **Note: On some models an alignment mark is already provided on the pinion flange, which aligns with a mark cast into the pinion housing (see illustration).**

4   Loosen and remove the flexible coupling pinch-bolt (see illustration).
5   Using brake hose clamps, clamp both the supply and return hoses near the power steering fluid reservoir. This will minimize fluid loss. Mark the unions to ensure they are correctly positioned on reassembly, then loosen and remove the feed and return pipe union bolts and recover the sealing washers. Be prepared for fluid spillage, and position a suitable container beneath the pipes while unscrewing the bolts (see illustration). Plug the pipe ends and steering gear orifices, to prevent fluid leakage and to keep dirt out of the hydraulic system.
6   Loosen and remove the steering gear mounting bolts and nuts, and remove the steering gear from underneath the car (see illustration).

OVERHAUL

7   Examine the steering gear assembly for signs of wear or damage, and check that the gear moves freely throughout the full length of its travel, with no signs of roughness or excessive free play between the steering gear pinion and gear. It is not possible to overhaul the steering gear assembly housing components; if it is faulty, the assembly must be replaced. The only components which

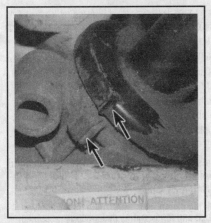

21.3 Align the mark on the pinion flange with the mark on the housing

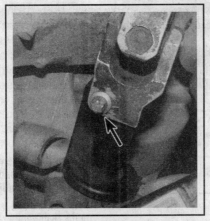

21.4 Remove the flexible coupling pinch-bolt

21.5 Steering gear line fittings

can be replaced individually are the steering gear boots, the tie-rod balljoints and the tie-rods. These procedures are covered later in this Chapter.

INSTALLATION

8   Place the steering gear into position and insert the mounting bolts. Install new nuts on the bolts and tighten them to the specified torque setting.

9   Position a new sealing washer on each side of the pipe hose unions and reinstall the union bolts. Tighten the union bolts to the specified torque.

10   Align the marks made on removal, and connect the intermediate shaft coupling to the steering gear. Insert the new clamp bolt then tighten it to the specified torque.

11   Connect the tie-rod balljoints to the steering knuckles, then install the new nuts and tighten them to the specified torque.

12   Reinstall the wheels, and the engine splash shield, then lower the car to the ground and tighten the wheel bolts to the specified torque.

13   Bleed the power steering system as described in Section 23.

21.6 Remove the steering gear mounting bolts

22   Power steering pump - removal and installation

➡Note: New pressure line fitting bolt sealing washers (if equipped) will be required on installation

REMOVAL

▸ **Refer to illustration 22.6**

1   Chock the rear wheels, then raise the front of the vehicle and support it securely on jackstands (see *Jacking and towing*). Remove the screws and remove the engine splash shield.

2   Loosen the drivebelt pulley fasteners but don't remove them.

3   Release the drivebelt tension and unhook the drivebelt from the pump pulley (see Chapter 1).

4   Remove the drivebelt pulley.

5   Using brake hose clamps, clamp both the supply and return

22.6 Power steering pump details (2004 M56 model shown - others similar)

1	*Drive pulley*	*4*	*Mounting fasteners (one*
2	*Pressure line*		*hidden - attached to*
3	*Feed hose*		*mounting bracket)*

hoses near the power steering fluid reservoir. This will minimize fluid loss during subsequent operations.

6   Mark the pressure line fitting in relation to the pump to ensure it is correctly positioned when reinstalled. Loosen and remove the line fitting bolt and recover the sealing washers (if equipped) (see illustration). Remove the feed hose clamp and then the hose itself. Be prepared for fluid spillage and position a suitable container beneath the line and hose while removing them. Plug the line/hose ends and steering pump orifices to prevent fluid leakage and to keep dirt out of the hydraulic system.

➡Note: Later models use line fittings that do not use bolts to mount to the pump. These types of lines should be removed with a flare nut wrench.

7   Loosen and remove the mounting bolts and then remove the pump.

8   If the power steering pump is faulty, seek the advice of your BMW dealer as to the availability of spare parts. If spares are available, it may be possible to have the pump overhauled by a specialist, or alternatively obtain an exchange unit. If not, the pump must be replaced.

INSTALLATION

9   Where necessary, transfer the rear mounting bracket to the new pump, and securely tighten its mounting bolts.

10   Prior to installation, ensure that the pump is primed by injecting the specified type of fluid in through the feed hose orifice and rotating the pump shaft.

11   Place the pump in position and reinstall the mounting bolts, tightening them to the specified torque.

12   Position a new sealing washer on each side of the line fitting and reinstall the bolt. Tighten the bolt to the specified torque.

13   Remove the hose clamps and reinstall the pump pulley. Ensure the pulley is facing the correct way and securely tighten its retaining bolts.

14   Reinstall the drivebelt and tension it as described in Chapter 1.

15   On completion, lower the car to the ground and bleed the hydraulic system as described in Section 23.

23 Power steering system - bleeding

1   With the engine stopped, fill the fluid reservoir right up to the top with the specified type of fluid.

2   With the engine running, slowly move the steering from lock-to-lock twice to purge out the trapped air, then stop the engine and top-up the level in the fluid reservoir. Repeat this procedure until the fluid level in the reservoir does not drop any further.

3   If, when turning the steering, an abnormal noise is heard from the fluid lines, it indicates that there is still air in the system. Check this by turning the wheels to the straight-ahead position and switching off the engine. If the fluid level in the reservoir rises, then air is present in the system and further bleeding is necessary.

24 Steering gear boot - replacement

▶ **Refer to illustration 24.4**

1   Remove the tie-rod end as described in Section 25. Remove the screws and remove the engine splash shield.

2   Note the correct installed position of the boot on the tie-rod, then release the retaining clip(s) and slide the boot off the steering gear and tie-rod end.

3   Thoroughly clean the tie-rod and the steering gear housing, using fine abrasive paper to polish off any corrosion, burrs or sharp edges, which might damage the new boot's sealing lips on installation. Scrape off all the grease from the old boot, and apply it to the tie-rod inner balljoint. (This assumes that grease has not been lost or contaminated as a result of damage to the old boot. Use fresh grease if in doubt.)

4   Carefully slide the new boot onto the tie-rod end and locate it on the steering gear housing. Position the outer edge of the boot on the tie-rod, as was noted prior to removal (see illustration).

5   Make sure the boot is not twisted, then lift the outer sealing lip of the boot to equalize air pressure within the boot. Secure the boot in position with the new retaining clip(s).

6   Reinstall the tie-rod balljoint as described in Section 25.

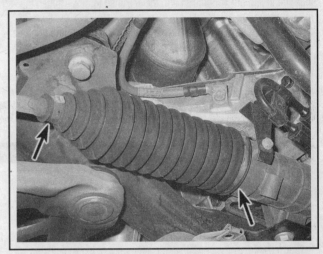

24.4 Position the inner end of the boot on the gear body and the outer end adjacent to the hexagon section of the tie-rod

25 Tie-rod end - removal and installation

➡Note: **A new tie-rod end balljoint retaining nut will be required on installation.**

REMOVAL

▶ **Refer to illustrations 25.2 and 25.4**

1   Apply the parking brake, then raise the front of the vehicle and support it securely on jackstands. Remove the appropriate front wheel.

2   Make a mark on the tie-rod and measure the distance from the mark to the center of the balljoint (see illustration). Note this measurement down, as it will be needed to ensure the wheel alignment remains correctly set when the balljoint is installed.

3   Hold the tie-rod, and unscrew the balljoint locknut.

4   Loosen and remove the nut securing the tie-rod end to the steering knuckle, and release the balljoint tapered shank using a universal balljoint separator (see illustration).

5   Counting the exact number of turns necessary to do so, unscrew the tie-rod end.

25.2 Make a mark on the tie-rod and measure from here to the center of the tie-rod end balljoint

6   Carefully clean the threads on the ballstud. Replace the tie-rod end if the balljoint's movement is sloppy, too stiff, excessively worn or damaged in any way. Also, carefully check the stud taper and threads. If the balljoint boot is damaged, the tie-rod end must be replaced; it is not possible to obtain the boot separately.

INSTALLATION

7   If necessary, transfer the locknut and collar to the new tie-rod end.

8   Screw the tie-rod end onto the tie-rod by the number of turns noted on removal. This should position the balljoint at the relevant distance from the tie-rod mark that was noted prior to removal.

9   Reinstall the balljoint shank to the steering knuckle, then install a new retaining nut and tighten it to the specified torque. Tighten the locknut securely.

10   Reinstall the wheel, then lower the car to the ground and tighten the wheel bolts to the specified torque.

11   Check and, if necessary, adjust the front wheel toe setting as described in Section 28, then tighten the tie-rod end locknut to the specified torque setting.

25.4 Use a balljoint separator to release the tie-rod end

26 Tie-rod - replacement

1   Remove the steering gear boot as described in Section 24.
2   Unscrew the tie-rod from the end of the steering gear.
3   Install the new locking plate to the steering gear, making sure it is locating tabs are correctly seated in the steering gear grooves.
4   Screw in the tie-rod and tighten it to the specified torque.
5   Reinstall the steering boot as described in Section 24.

27 Dynamic Stability Control - general information and component replacement

GENERAL INFORMATION

1   Dynamic Stability Control (DSC) is standard on all models. Strictly speaking, DSC includes ABS and Traction control, but this Section is concerned with Cornering Brake Control (CBC). By monitoring steering wheel movements, suspension ride heights, road speed and lateral acceleration, the system controls the pressure in the brake lines to each of the four brake calipers during braking, reducing the possibility of understeer or oversteer.

COMPONENT REPLACEMENT

Steering angle sensor

2   Replacement of the steering angle sensor involves the complete dismantling of the steering column, which should be entrusted to a BMW dealer or suitably-equipped specialist.

➡Note: After replacing the steering angle sensor, the steering angle offset procedure must be carried out using dedicated BMW diagnostic equipment. Have this procedure carried out by a BMW dealer or suitably-equipped specialist.

Front ride height sensor

3   Remove the nut securing the control rod to the sensor arm (see illustration 12.3 in Chapter 12).

4   Remove the two retaining screws, and withdraw the ride sensor. Disconnect the electrical connector as the sensor is removed.

5   Installation is a reversal of removal. Have the headlight alignment checked on completion.

DSC control unit

6   The DSC control unit is integral with the ABS control unit, replacement of which should be entrusted to a BMW dealer or suitably-equipped specialist (see Chapter 9).

DSC pre-boost pump

➡Note: After replacing the pre-boost pump, the brake high pressure hydraulic system needs to be bled. This necessitates the use of dedicated BMW Service equipment. Have the procedure carried out by a BMW dealer or suitably-equipped specialist.

7   The DSC pre-boost pump is located under the brake master cylinder. Clamp the supply hose from the master cylinder reservoir to the pump, and disconnect the hose from the pump. Be prepared for fluid spillage.

8   Unscrew the line fitting and disconnect the outlet pipe from the pump.

9   Disconnect the electrical connector from the pump and maneuver it from the rubber mounting.

10   Installation is a reversal of removal. Bleed the brake hydraulic system as described in Chapter 9.

Lateral acceleration sensor

▶ **Refer to illustration 27.13**

11 Remove the driver's seat as described in Chapter 11.

12 With the seat removed, lift the floor panel, and move the insulating wedge 10 cm forward to gain access to the sensor.

13 Remove the four screws securing the sensor bracket to the body and, lifting the inner end first, remove the assembly (see illustration). Disconnect the electrical connector as the unit is withdrawn.

➡**Note: The sensor is extremely sensitive to vibration. Handle the unit with care.**

14 If necessary, remove the two screws and separate the sensor from the bracket.

15 Installation is a reversal of removal. Tighten the fasteners to the specified torque where given.

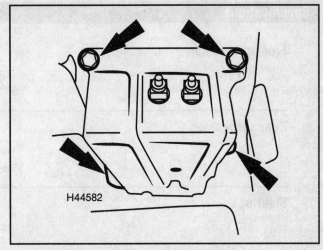

H44582

27.13 Remove the four lateral acceleration sensor bracket bolts

28 Wheel alignment and steering angles - general information

DEFINITIONS

1 A car's steering and suspension geometry is defined in four basic settings - all angles are expressed in degrees; the steering axis is defined as an imaginary line drawn through the axis of the suspension strut, extended where necessary to contact the ground.

2 Camber is the angle between each wheel and a vertical line drawn through its center and tire contact patch, when viewed from the front or rear of the vehicle. Positive camber is when the wheels are tilted outwards from the vertical at the top; negative camber is when they are tilted inwards.

3 The front camber angle is not adjustable, and is given for reference only (see Step 5). The rear camber angle is adjustable and can be adjusted using a camber angle gauge.

4 Caster is the angle between the steering axis and a vertical line drawn through each wheel's center and tire contact patch, when viewed from the side of the vehicle. Positive caster is when the steering axis is

tilted so that it contacts the ground ahead of the vertical; negative caster is when it contacts the ground behind the vertical.

5 Caster is not adjustable, and is given for reference only; while it can be checked using a caster checking gauge, if the figure obtained is significantly different from that specified, the car must be taken for careful checking by a professional, as the fault can only be caused by wear or damage to the body or suspension components.

6 Toe is the difference, viewed from above, between lines drawn through the wheel centers and the car's center-line. Toe-in is when the wheels point inwards, towards each other at the front, while toe-out is when they splay outwards from each other at the front.

7 The front wheel toe setting is adjusted by screwing the right-hand tie-rod in or out of its balljoint, to alter the effective length of the tie-rod assembly.

8 Rear wheel toe setting is also adjustable. The toe setting is adjusted by loosening the trailing arm mounting bracket bolts and repositioning the bracket.

Specifications

Front suspension

Type	Independent, with MacPherson struts incorporating coil springs, telescopic shock absorbers and a stabilizer bar

Rear suspension

Type	Independent, trailing arms located by upper and lower control arms with coil springs, shock absorbers and a stabilizer bar

Steering

Type	Power-assisted rack-and-pinion

Torque specifications	Ft-lbs (unless otherwise indicated)	Nm
Front suspension		
Stabilizer bar connecting link nuts*	48	65
Stabilizer bar mounting clamp nuts*	16	22
Hub nut*	214	290
Lower arm balljoint nut*	65	48
Lower arm rear mounting bracket bolts	44	59
Lower arm-to-subframe	66	90
Reinforcement frame/plate under front subframe*	See Chapter 2A	
Strut mounting-to-body nuts*		
Nuts with 18 mm diameter flange	18	24
Nuts with 21 mm diameter flange	25	34
Strut upper mounting plate/piston rod nut		
M12 thread		
Piston with an external hexagon end (retain with socket)	47	64
Piston with an internal hexagon end (retain with Allen key)	32	44
M14 thread	47	64
Strut-to-steering knuckle bolt*	60	81
Subframe-to-engine crossmember*		
M10		
8.8 strength grade (see head of bolt)	31	42
9.8 strength grade (see head of bolt)	35	47
M12		
8.8 strength grade (see head of bolt)	57	77
10.9 strength grade (see head of bolt)	81	110
12.9 strength grade (see head of bolt)	77	105

Torque specifications	Ft-lbs (unless otherwise indicated)	Nm
Rear suspension		
Control arm-to-subframe pivot bolts*	57	77
Shock absorber lower mounting bolt	74	100
Shock absorber piston rod nut*	120 in-lbs	14
Shock absorber upper mounting nuts		
M8		
8.8 strength grade (see head of bolt)	16	22
10.9 strength grade (see head of bolt)	22	30
Subframe		
M12	57	77
M14	103	140
Trailing arm-to-control arm pivot bolts*	81	110
Trailing arm-to-mounting bracket pivot bolt	81	110
Trailing arm-to-subframe	57	77
Steering		
Lateral acceleration sensor	72 in-lbs	8
Power steering pump mounting bolts	16	22
Power steering line fitting bolts		
M10 union bolt	108 in-lbs	12
M14 union bolt	26	35
M16 union bolt	30	40
M18 union bolt	33	45
Steering column universal joint clamp bolt*	16	22
Steering gear mounting nuts*	31	42
Steering wheel		
Bolt	46	63
Nut	59	80
Tie-rod	74	100
Tie-rod balljoint		
Retaining nut*	48	65
Locknut	120 in-lbs	14
Wheel bolts	See Chapter 1	

*Do not re-use

Notes

Section

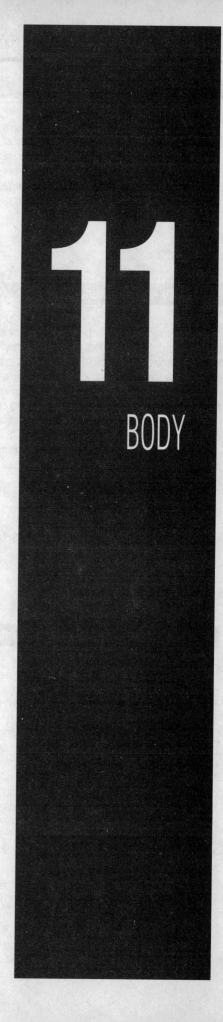

11

BODY

1   General information

The body is made of high strength steel sections. Most components are welded together, but some use is made of structural adhesives.

The hood, door and some other vulnerable panels are made of zinc-coated metal (galvanized steel), and are further protected by being coated with an anti-chip primer before being sprayed.

Extensive use is made of plastic materials, mainly in the interior, but also in exterior components. The front and rear bumpers and front grille are injection-molded from a synthetic material that is very strong and yet light. Plastic components such as wheel arch liners are installed on the underside of the vehicle, to improve the body's resistance to corrosion.

2   Body - maintenance

1   The condition of your vehicle's body is very important, because the resale value depends a great deal on it. It's much more difficult to repair a neglected or damaged body than it is to repair mechanical components. The hidden areas of the body, such as the wheel wells, the frame and the engine compartment, are equally important, although they don't require as frequent attention as the rest of the body.

2   Once a year, or every 12,000 miles, it's a good idea to have the underside of the body steam-cleaned. All traces of dirt and oil will be removed and the area can then be inspected carefully for rust, damaged brake lines, frayed electrical wires, damaged cables and other problems.

3   At the same time, clean the engine and the engine compartment with a steam cleaner or water-soluble degreaser.

4   The wheel wells should be given close attention, since undercoating can peel away and stones and dirt thrown up by the tires can cause the paint to chip and flake, allowing rust to set in. If rust is found, clean down to the bare metal and apply an anti-rust paint.

5   The body should be washed about once a week. Wet the vehicle thoroughly to soften the dirt, then wash it down with a soft sponge and plenty of clean soapy water. If the surplus dirt is not washed off very carefully, it can wear down the paint.

6   Spots of tar or asphalt thrown up from the road should be removed with a cloth soaked in kerosene. Scented lamp oil is available in most hardware stores and the smell is easier to work with than straight kerosene.

7   Once every six months, wax the body and chrome trim. If a chrome cleaner is used to remove rust from any of the vehicle's plated parts, remember that the cleaner also removes part of the chrome, so use it sparingly. On any plated parts where chrome cleaner is used, use a good paste wax over the plating for extra protection.

3   Upholstery and carpets - maintenance

1   Every three months remove the floormats and clean the interior of the vehicle (more frequently if necessary). Use a stiff whisk broom to brush the carpeting and loosen dirt and dust, then vacuum the upholstery and carpets thoroughly, especially along seams and crevices.

2   Dirt and stains can be removed from carpeting with basic household or automotive carpet shampoos available in spray cans. Follow the directions and vacuum again, then use a stiff brush to bring back the "nap" of the carpet.

3   Most interiors have cloth or vinyl upholstery, either of which can be cleaned and maintained with a number of material-specific cleaners or shampoos available in auto supply stores. Follow the directions on the product for usage, and always spot-test any upholstery cleaner on an inconspicuous area (bottom edge of a backseat cushion) to ensure that it doesn't cause a color shift in the material.

4   After cleaning, vinyl upholstery should be treated with a protectant.

➡ **Note: Make sure the protectant container indicates the product can be used on seats - some products may make a seat too slippery.**

✳✳ CAUTION:

Do not use protectant on steering wheels.

5   Leather upholstery requires special care. It should be cleaned regularly with saddlesoap or leather cleaner. Never use alcohol, gasoline, nail polish remover or thinner to clean leather upholstery.

6   After cleaning, regularly treat leather upholstery with a leather conditioner, rubbed in with a soft cotton cloth. Never use car wax on leather upholstery.

7   In areas where the interior of the vehicle is subject to bright sunlight, cover leather seating areas of the seats with a sheet if the vehicle is to be left out for any length of time.

4 Body repair - minor damage

FLEXIBLE PLASTIC BODY PANELS (FRONT AND REAR BUMPER FASCIA)

The following repair procedures are for minor scratches and gouges. Repair of more serious damage should be left to a dealer service department or qualified auto body shop. Below is a list of the equipment and materials necessary to perform the following repair procedures on plastic body panels. Although a specific brand of material may be mentioned, it should be noted that equivalent products from other manufacturers may be used instead.

Wax, grease and silicone removing solvent
Cloth-backed body tape
Sanding discs
Drill motor with three-inch disc holder
Hand sanding block
Rubber squeegees
Sandpaper
Non-porous mixing palette
Wood paddle or putty knife
Curved-tooth body file
Flexible parts repair material

1 Remove the damaged panel, if necessary or desirable. In most cases, repairs can be carried out with the panel installed.

2 Clean the area(s) to be repaired with a wax, grease and silicone removing solvent applied with a water-dampened cloth.

3 If the damage is structural, that is, if it extends through the panel, clean the backside of the panel area to be repaired as well. Wipe dry.

4 Sand the rear surface about 1-1/2 inches beyond the break.

5 Cut two pieces of fiberglass cloth large enough to overlap the break by about 1-1/2 inches. Cut only to the required length.

6 Mix the adhesive from the repair kit according to the instructions included with the kit, and apply a layer of the mixture approximately 1/8-inch thick on the backside of the panel. Overlap the break by at least 1-1/2 inches.

7 Apply one piece of fiberglass cloth to the adhesive and cover the cloth with additional adhesive. Apply a second piece of fiberglass cloth to the adhesive and immediately cover the cloth with additional adhesive in sufficient quantity to fill the weave.

8 Allow the repair to cure for 20 to 30 minutes at 60-degrees to 80-degrees F.

9 If necessary, trim the excess repair material at the edge.

10 Remove all of the paint film over and around the area(s) to be repaired. The repair material should not overlap the painted surface.

11 With a drill motor and a sanding disc (or a rotary file), cut a "V" along the break line approximately 1/2-inch wide. Remove all dust and loose particles from the repair area.

12 Mix and apply the repair material. Apply a light coat first over the damaged area; then continue applying material until it reaches a level slightly higher than the surrounding finish.

13 Cure the mixture for 20 to 30 minutes at 60-degrees to 80-degrees F.

14 Roughly establish the contour of the area being repaired with a body file. If low areas or pits remain, mix and apply additional adhesive.

15 Block sand the damaged area with sandpaper to establish the actual contour of the surrounding surface.

16 If desired, the repaired area can be temporarily protected with several light coats of primer. Because of the special paints and techniques required for flexible body panels, it is recommended that the vehicle be taken to a paint shop for completion of the body repair.

STEEL BODY PANELS

See photo sequence

Repair of minor scratches

17 If the scratch is superficial and does not penetrate to the metal of the body, repair is very simple. Lightly rub the scratched area with a fine rubbing compound to remove loose paint and built up wax. Rinse the area with clean water.

18 Apply touch-up paint to the scratch, using a small brush. Continue to apply thin layers of paint until the surface of the paint in the scratch is level with the surrounding paint. Allow the new paint at least two weeks to harden, then blend it into the surrounding paint by rubbing with a very fine rubbing compound. Finally, apply a coat of wax to the scratch area.

19 If the scratch has penetrated the paint and exposed the metal of the body, causing the metal to rust, a different repair technique is required. Remove all loose rust from the bottom of the scratch with a pocketknife, then apply rust inhibiting paint to prevent the formation of rust in the future. Using a rubber or nylon applicator, coat the scratched area with glaze-type filler. If required, the filler can be mixed with thinner to provide a very thin paste, which is ideal for filling narrow scratches. Before the glaze filler in the scratch hardens, wrap a piece of smooth cotton cloth around the tip of a finger. Dip the cloth in thinner and then quickly wipe it along the surface of the scratch. This will ensure that the surface of the filler is slightly hollow. The scratch can now be painted over as described earlier in this Section.

REPAIR OF DENTS

20 When repairing dents, the first job is to pull the dent out until the affected area is as close as possible to its original shape. There is no point in trying to restore the original shape completely as the metal in the damaged area will have stretched on impact and cannot be restored to its original contours. It is better to bring the level of the dent up to a point that is about 1/8-inch below the level of the surrounding metal. In cases where the dent is very shallow, it is not worth trying to pull it out at all.

21 If the backside of the dent is accessible, it can be hammered out gently from behind using a soft-face hammer. While doing this, hold a block of wood firmly against the opposite side of the metal to absorb the hammer blows and prevent the metal from being stretched.

22 If the dent is in a section of the body which has double layers, or some other factor makes it inaccessible from behind, a different technique is required. Drill several small holes through the metal inside the damaged area, particularly in the deeper sections. Screw long, self-tapping screws into the holes just enough for them to get a good grip in the metal. Now the dent can be pulled out by pulling on the protruding heads of the screws with locking pliers.

23 The next stage of repair is the removal of paint from the damaged area and from an inch or so of the surrounding metal. This is easily done with a wire brush or sanding disk in a drill motor, although it can be done just as effectively by hand with sandpaper. To complete the

These photos illustrate a method of repairing simple dents. They are intended to supplement Body repair - minor damage in this Chapter and should not be used as the sole instructions for body repair on these vehicles.

1   If you can't access the backside of the body panel to hammer out the dent, pull it out with a slide-hammer-type dent puller. In the deepest portion of the dent or along the crease line, drill or punch hole(s) at least one inch apart . . .

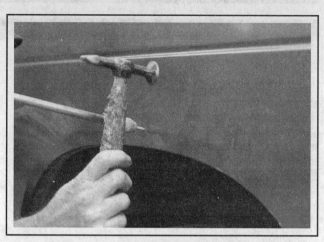

2   . . . then screw the slide-hammer into the hole and operate it. Tap with a hammer near the edge of the dent to help 'pop' the metal back to its original shape. When you're finished, the dent area should be close to its original contour and about 1/8-inch below the surface of the surrounding metal

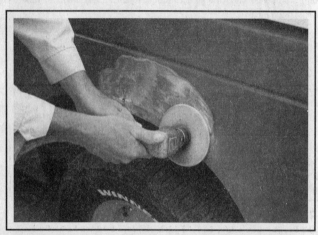

3   Using coarse-grit sandpaper, remove the paint down to the bare metal. Hand sanding works fine, but the disc sander shown here makes the job faster. Use finer (about 320-grit) sandpaper to feather-edge the paint at least one inch around the dent area

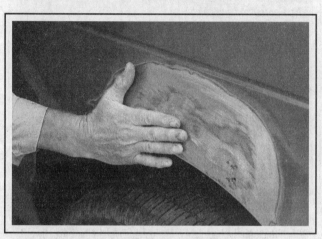

4   When the paint is removed, touch will probably be more helpful than sight for telling if the metal is straight. Hammer down the high spots or raise the low spots as necessary. Clean the repair area with wax/silicone remover

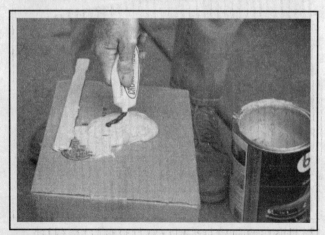

5   Following label instructions, mix up a batch of plastic filler and hardener. The ratio of filler to hardener is critical, and, if you mix it incorrectly, it will either not cure properly or cure too quickly (you won't have time to file and sand it into shape)

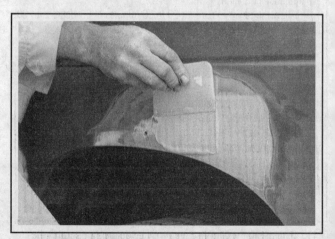

6   Working quickly so the filler doesn't harden, use a plastic applicator to press the body filler firmly into the metal, assuring it bonds completely. Work the filler until it matches the original contour and is slightly above the surrounding metal

7   Let the filler harden until you can just dent it with your fingernail. Use a body file or Surform tool (shown here) to rough-shape the filler

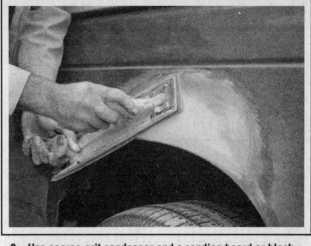

8   Use coarse-grit sandpaper and a sanding board or block to work the filler down until it's smooth and even. Work down to finer grits of sandpaper - always using a board or block - ending up with 360 or 400 grit

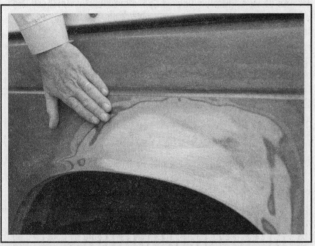

9   You shouldn't be able to feel any ridge at the transition from the filler to the bare metal or from the bare metal to the old paint. As soon as the repair is flat and uniform, remove the dust and mask off the adjacent panels or trim pieces

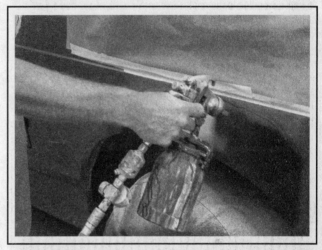

10   Apply several layers of primer to the area. Don't spray the primer on too heavy, so it sags or runs, and make sure each coat is dry before you spray on the next one. A professional-type spray gun is being used here, but aerosol spray primer is available inexpensively from auto parts stores

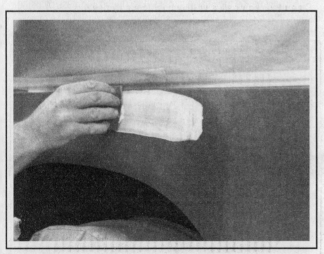

11   The primer will help reveal imperfections or scratches. Fill these with glazing compound. Follow the label instructions and sand it with 360 or 400-grit sandpaper until it's smooth. Repeat the glazing, sanding and respraying until the primer reveals a perfectly smooth surface

12   Finish sand the primer with very fine sandpaper (400 or 600-grit) to remove the primer overspray. Clean the area with water and allow it to dry. Use a tack rag to remove any dust, then apply the finish coat. Don't attempt to rub out or wax the repair area until the paint has dried completely (at least two weeks)

preparation for filling, score the surface of the bare metal with a screwdriver or the tang of a file or drill small holes in the affected area. This will provide a good grip for the filler material. To complete the repair, see the Section on filling and painting.

REPAIR OF RUST HOLES OR GASHES

24 Remove all paint from the affected area and from an inch or so of the surrounding metal using a sanding disk or wire brush mounted in a drill motor. If these are not available, a few sheets of sandpaper will do the job just as effectively.

25 With the paint removed, you will be able to determine the severity of the corrosion and decide whether to replace the whole panel, if possible, or repair the affected area. New body panels are not as expensive as most people think and it is often quicker to install a new panel than to repair large areas of rust.

26 Remove all trim pieces from the affected area except those which will act as a guide to the original shape of the damaged body, such as headlight shells, etc. Using metal snips or a hacksaw blade, remove all loose metal and any other metal that is badly affected by rust. Hammer the edges of the hole in to create a slight depression for the filler material.

27 Wire brush the affected area to remove the powdery rust from the surface of the metal. If the back of the rusted area is accessible, treat it with rust inhibiting paint.

28 Before filling is done, block the hole in some way. This can be done with sheet metal riveted or screwed into place, or by stuffing the hole with wire mesh.

29 Once the hole is blocked off, the affected area can be filled and painted. See the following subsection on filling and painting.

FILLING AND PAINTING

30 Many types of body fillers are available, but generally speaking, body repair kits which contain filler paste and a tube of resin hardener are best for this type of repair work. A wide, flexible plastic or nylon applicator will be necessary for imparting a smooth and contoured finish to the surface of the filler material. Mix up a small amount of filler on a clean piece of wood or cardboard (use the hardener sparingly). Follow the manufacturer's instructions on the package, otherwise the filler will set incorrectly.

31 Using the applicator, apply the filler paste to the prepared area. Draw the applicator across the surface of the filler to achieve the desired contour and to level the filler surface. As soon as a contour that approximates the original one is achieved, stop working the paste. If you continue, the paste will begin to stick to the applicator. Continue to add thin layers of paste at 20-minute intervals until the level of the filler

is just above the surrounding metal.

32 Once the filler has hardened, the excess can be removed with a body file. From then on, progressively finer grades of sandpaper should be used, starting with a 180-grit paper and finishing with 600-grit wet-or-dry paper. Always wrap the sandpaper around a flat rubber or wooden block, otherwise the surface of the filler will not be completely flat. During the sanding of the filler surface, the wet-or-dry paper should be periodically rinsed in water. This will ensure that a very smooth finish is produced in the final stage.

33 At this point, the repair area should be surrounded by a ring of bare metal, which in turn should be encircled by the finely feathered edge of good paint. Rinse the repair area with clean water until all of the dust produced by the sanding operation is gone.

34 Spray the entire area with a light coat of primer. This will reveal any imperfections in the surface of the filler. Repair the imperfections with fresh filler paste or glaze filler and once more smooth the surface with sandpaper. Repeat this spray-and-repair procedure until you are satisfied that the surface of the filler and the feathered edge of the paint are perfect. Rinse the area with clean water and allow it to dry completely.

35 The repair area is now ready for painting. Spray painting must be carried out in a warm, dry, windless and dust free atmosphere. These conditions can be created if you have access to a large indoor work area, but if you are forced to work in the open, you will have to pick the day very carefully. If you are working indoors, dousing the floor in the work area with water will help settle the dust that would otherwise be in the air. If the repair area is confined to one body panel, mask off the surrounding panels. This will help minimize the effects of a slight mismatch in paint color. Trim pieces such as chrome strips, door handles, etc., will also need to be masked off or removed. Use masking tape and several thickness of newspaper for the masking operations.

36 Before spraying, shake the paint can thoroughly, then spray a test area until the spray painting technique is mastered. Cover the repair area with a thick coat of primer. The thickness should be built up using several thin layers of primer rather than one thick one. Using 600-grit wet-or-dry sandpaper, rub down the surface of the primer until it is very smooth. While doing this, the work area should be thoroughly rinsed with water and the wet-or-dry sandpaper periodically rinsed as well. Allow the primer to dry before spraying additional coats.

37 Spray on the top coat, again building up the thickness by using several thin layers of paint. Begin spraying in the center of the repair area and then, using a circular motion, work out until the whole repair area and about two inches of the surrounding original paint is covered. Remove all masking material 10 to 15 minutes after spraying on the final coat of paint. Allow the new paint at least two weeks to harden, then use a very fine rubbing compound to blend the edges of the new paint into the existing paint. Finally, apply a coat of wax.

5 Body repair - major damage

1 Major damage must be repaired by an auto body shop specifically equipped to perform unibody repairs. These shops have the specialized equipment required to do the job properly.

2 If the damage is extensive, the body must be checked for proper alignment or the vehicle's handling characteristics may be adversely affected and other components may wear at an accelerated rate.

3 Due to the fact that some of the major body components (hood, fenders, doors, etc.) are separate and replaceable units, any seriously damaged components should be replaced rather than repaired. Sometimes the components can be found in a wrecking yard that specializes in used vehicle components, often at considerable savings over the cost of new parts.

6 Bumper (front) - removal and installation

▶ **Refer to illustrations 6.2, 6.3, 6.4 and 6.5**

1 Raise the vehicle and support it securely on jackstands.
2 Remove the fog light trim panels. Release the retaining clips and pull the fog light trims forward and away from the bumper (see illustration).
3 Remove the mounting screws and the right and left side trim pieces (see illustration).
4 Remove the retaining screws from the fender splash shield that connect to the bumper assembly (see illustration).

5 Remove the front bumper cover mounting screws (see illustration).
6 Remove the bumper cover forwards and away from the vehicle.
7 Remove the bumper mounting bolts and move the bumper slightly away from vehicle.
8 Note their installed locations, and disconnect the various wiring connectors.
9 Remove the bumper from the vehicle by sliding the bumper off side support brackets.
10 Installation is a reverse of the removal procedure, ensuring that the bumper mounting nuts and screws are securely tightened.

6.2 Push the 'fins' of the trim down, release the clips and pull the fog light trims out

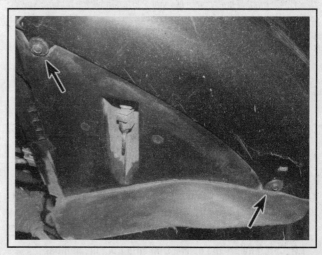

6.3 Remove the two screws at the bumper lower edge

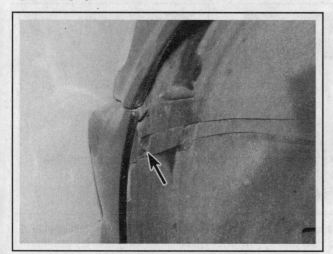

6.4 Remove the screw securing the bumper to the wheel well liner

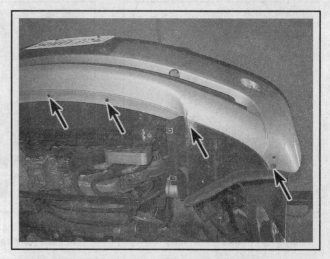

6.5 Location of the bumper cover fasteners on the left side of the vehicle

7 Bumper (rear) - removal and installation

▶ **Refer to illustrations 7.2, 7.5a, 7.5b, 7.6a and 7.6b**

1   To improve access, chock the front wheels, then raise the vehicle and secure it on jackstands.

2   Starting at the left-hand corner, carefully pry the plastic trim strip from the bumper cover (see illustration). On models equipped with parking distance sensors, disconnect the wiring connectors as the panel is withdrawn.

3   Remove the bumper support mounting bolts located under the vehicle behind the bumper assembly near the trunk floor.

4   Remove the rear bumper cover retainers on the lower fenderwells.

 a) *On models built before October 2001, remove the bumper cover*

brackets on the left and right side of the wheelwells. Remove the expansion rivets from the fender splash shield.

 b) *On models built after October 2001, remove the bumper cover from the mounting lugs by rotating the lugs with the detent down.*

5   Remove the fender splash shield fasteners (see illustrations).

6   Pull the front edges of the bumper outwards and slide the bumper slightly to the rear (see illustrations). Disconnect any relevant wiring connectors and remove the bumper.

7   Installation is a reverse of the removal procedure ensuring that the bumper ends are correctly engaged with their slides. Apply locking compound to the bumper mounting bolts and tighten them securely.

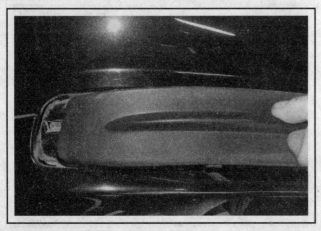

7.2 Carefully pry the plastic trim strip from the bumper

7.5a Pry out the center pin, then remove the expanding rivet

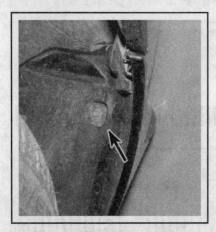

7.5b Remove the screw securing the bumper to the wheel arch liner

7.6a Remove the bumper mounting Torx bolts (one each side) . . .

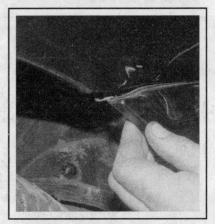

7.6b . . . and pull the front edge of the bumper away from the wheel arch

8 Hood - removal, installation and adjustment

REMOVAL

▶ **Refer to illustration 8.3**

1   Open the hood and have an assistant support it. Using a pencil or felt tip pen, mark the outline of each hood hinge relative to the hood, to use as a guide on installation.

2   Disconnect the hose from the washer jets. On models with heated jets also disconnect the wiring connectors. Tie a length of string to the end of the wiring loom and washer hose, then pull the harness/hose from the hood channel. Free the harness/hose from any retaining clips. As the harness/hose is pulled from the hood channel, untie the string and leave it in place to aid installation.

3   With the aid of an assistant, support the hood in the open posi-

8.3 Pry out the hood strut clip

8.6 Hood hinge ground strap

tion then remove the retaining clips and detach the support struts from the hood (see illustration).

4   Loosen and remove the left and right-hand hinge-to-hood rear bolts and loosen the front bolts. Slide the hood forwards to disengage it from the hinges and remove it from the vehicle. Recover any shims which are fitted between the hinge and hood.

5   Inspect the hood hinges for signs of wear and free play at the pivots, and if necessary replace. Each hinge is secured to the body by two bolts. Mark the position of the hinge on the body then remove the retaining bolts and remove it from the vehicle. On installation, align the new hinge with the marks and securely tighten the retaining bolts.

INSTALLATION AND ADJUSTMENT

▶ **Refer to illustration 8.6**

6   Fit the shims to the hinge and with the aid of an assistant, engage the hood with the hinges. Install the rear bolts and tighten them by hand only. Align the hinges with the marks made on removal, then tighten the retaining bolts securely. Note the ground strap attached to the base of the left-side hinge (see illustration).

7   Close the hood and check for alignment with the adjacent panels. If necessary, loosen the hinge bolts and re-align the hood to suit. Once the hood is correctly aligned, securely tighten the hinge bolts. Once the hood is correctly aligned, check that the hood fastens and releases satisfactorily. Tie the wiring harness/hose to the end of the string and pull them through the hood channel to their original positions. Reconnect the hose and wiring.

9   Hood release cable - removal and installation

REMOVAL

1   The hood release cable is in three sections, the main first cable from the release lever to the connection at the left-hand side (underhood), the second from the connection to the left-side hood lock, and one linking the two hood locks (left side and right side).

Release lever-to-connection cable

▶ **Refer to illustrations 9.6 and 9.9**

2   Open the driver's door and carefully pull up the door sill trim panel.

3   Pull up the rubber weatherstrip from the door aperture adjacent to the footwell kick panel.

4   Unscrew the fasteners and remove the lower panel above the pedals. Disconnect any wiring connectors as the panel is withdrawn.

5   Remove the screw and remove the hood release lever.

6   Remove the screw and remove the footwell kick panel (see illustration).

7   Separate the cable inner end fitting from the release lever.

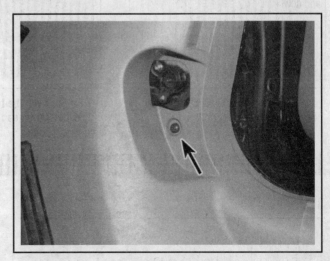

9.6 The kick panel is secured by one screw

8   Push/pull the outer release cable end fitting from the engine compartment firewall, and pull the cable into the engine compartment.

9   Unclip the connection housing from the inner wing. Pry open the connection housing and disconnect the inner and outer cables (see illustration).

Connection-to-hood lock cable

10 Unclip the connection housing from underhood. Pry open the housing and disconnect the inner and outer cables (see illustration 9.9)

11 Remove the driver's side hood lock (see Section 10).

Lock linking cable

12 The linking cable is removed as part of the hood lock removal procedure, as described in Section 10.

INSTALLATION

13 Installation is the reverse of removal ensuring that the cable is correctly routed, and secured to all the relevant retaining clips. Check that the hood locks operate correctly before closing the hood.

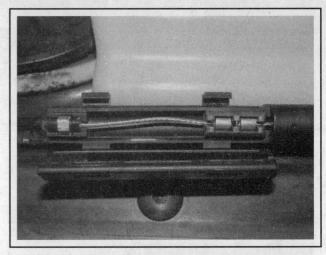

9.9 Disconnect the inner and outer cables from the connection housing

10 Hood latch(es) - removal and installation

REMOVAL

▶ **Refer to illustrations 10.2, 10.3 and 10.4**

1   To gain access to the rear of the latch(es), remove the radiator (see Chapter 3).

2   On models with air conditioning, reach down under the condenser mounts, depress the retaining clips and slide the plastic mount covers down (see illustration). Carefully move the condenser backwards and down.

✳ CAUTION:

Do not disconnect the refrigerant lines.

3   Remove the two screws in the center of the hood crossmember, press down the clips and remove the plastic cover to the rear (see illustration).

4   Loosen and remove the latch retaining screws then free the release outer cable(s) from the latch, then detach the inner cable(s) from the latch (see illustration). Remove the latch from the vehicle.

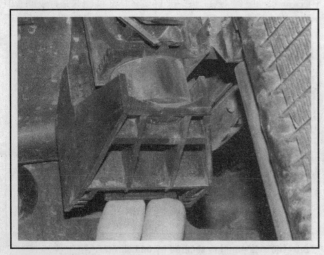

10.2 Depress the retaining clips and slide the plastic mounting covers down

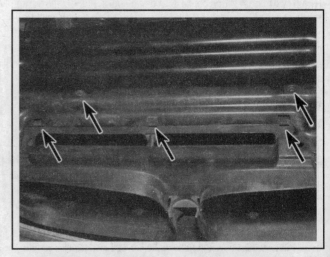

10.3 Remove the screws, release the clips and slide the cover to the rear

INSTALLATION

5   Locate the hood release inner cable(s) in the latch and reconnect the outer cable(s) to the lever. Seat the latch on the crossmember.

6   Align the latch with the marks made prior to removal then install the bolts and tighten them securely.

7   Check that the latches operate smoothly when the release lever is moved, without any sign of undue resistance. Check that the hood fastens and releases satisfactorily.

8   Once the latches are operating correctly, install the condenser (where applicable) and install the radiator (see Chapter 3).

10.4 Hood latch retaining screws

11 Door - removal, installation and adjustment

✳✳ WARNING:

The models covered by this manual are equipped with Supplemental Restraint systems (SRS), more commonly known as airbags. Always disarm the airbag system before working in the vicinity of any airbag system component to avoid the possibility of accidental deployment of the airbag, which could cause personal injury (see Chapter 12). Do not use a memory saving device to preserve the ECM's memory when working on or near airbag system components.

REMOVAL

▶ **Refer to illustrations 11.2, 11.3, 11.4a and 11.4b**

1   Disconnect the cable from the negative terminal of the battery (see Chapter 5, Section 1).

2   Remove the Torx bolt securing the door check link to the pillar (see illustration).

3   Unscrew the hinge nuts from both the upper and lower door hinges (see illustration).

4   Have an assistant support the door, remove the retaining bolt and withdraw the door wiring connector from the pillar. Pull out the locking element and unplug the side airbag connector as the door is withdrawn

11.2 Disconnect the door check strap from the pillar

(see illustrations). If necessary the hinge pins can be unscrewed from the hinges.

INSTALLATION

5   Maneuver the door into position and reconnect the wiring connector. Push the connector into the pillar and secure it in place with the bolt.

11.3 Unscrew the door hinge bolts

11.4a Pull out the locking element and disconnect the door connector

11.4b The hinge pins can be unscrewed from the hinges

6 Engage the hinges with the studs on the door, and tighten the nuts securely. Note that if necessary, the position of the door can be adjusted by inserting or removing shims between the hinge and the door (available from BMW dealers).

7 Align the check link with the pillar, install and tighten the securing bolt.

ADJUSTMENT

8 Close the door and check the door alignment with surrounding body panels. If necessary, slight adjustment of the door position can be made by loosening the hinge retaining nuts and repositioning the hinge/ door as necessary. Once the door is correctly positioned, securely tighten the hinge nuts. If the paint work around the hinges has been damaged, paint the affected area with a suitable touch-in brush to prevent corrosion.

12 Door inner trim panel - removal and installation

✳✳ WARNING:

The models covered by this manual are equipped with Supplemental Restraint systems (SRS), more commonly known as airbags. Always disarm the airbag system before working in the vicinity of any airbag system component to avoid the possibility of accidental deployment of the airbag, which could cause personal injury (see Chapter 12). Do not use a memory saving device to preserve the ECM's memory when working on or near airbag system components.

REMOVAL - FRONT DOOR

1 Disconnect the cable from the negative terminal of the battery (see Chapter 5, Section 1).

Sedan and Sport Wagon

▶ Refer to illustrations 12.2, 12.3a, 12.3b, 12.4a and 12.4b

2 Starting at the rear of the trim, using a trim clip releasing tool or flat-bladed screwdriver, carefully pry the decorative trim from the door panel (see illustration).

3 If you are removing the driver's door trim on models with electrical mirrors, starting at the front edge, carefully pry the mirror switch from the armrest. Disconnect the switch wiring connectors as the

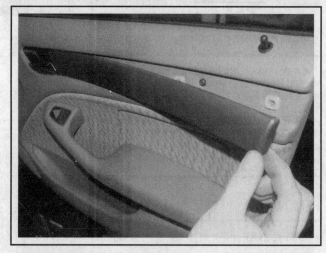

12.2 Starting at the rear, carefully pry the decorative trim from the door trim panel

switch is withdrawn. If removing the passenger's door trim, or non-electric mirror driver's door trim, pry the plastic trim out from the front of the armrest (see illustrations).

4 Pry out the plastic caps from the armrest, then remove the panel retaining screws (see illustrations). Note that the upper front panel retaining screw is longer than the others.

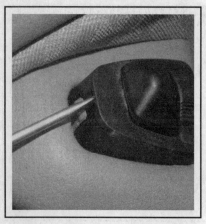

12.3a Carefully pry the mirror switch from the armrest . . .

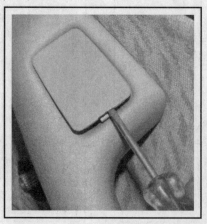

12.3b . . . or remove the plastic trim (as applicable)

12.4a Pry out the plastic caps . . .

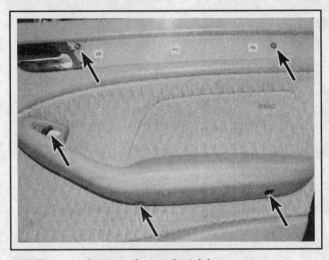

12.4b . . . and remove the panel retaining screws

Coupe

▶ **Refer to illustrations 12.6 and 12.7**

5   If you are removing the driver's door trim on models with electrical mirrors. Starting at the front edge, carefully pry the mirror switch

from the armrest (see illustration 12.3a). Disconnect the switch wiring connectors as the switch is withdrawn.

6   In the interior door handle recess, press-in the rear edge of the plastic cap, and remove the panel Torx screw (see illustration).

7   Carefully lever out the airbag emblem from the panel, and remove the retaining Torx screw behind it (see illustration).

8   Remove the three armrest securing screws.

All models

▶ **Refer to illustrations 12.9a, 12.9b, 12.9c and 12.10**

9   Release the door trim panel clips, carefully levering between the panel and door with a flat-bladed screwdriver. Work around the outside of the panel, and when all the studs are released, ease the panel away from the top of the door, then lift it over the locking knob (see illustrations).

10   Holding the panel away from the door, pull open the inner handle, lever out the cable retaining lock, and remove the cable to the rear (see illustration).

11   Disconnect the speaker wiring connectors as the panel is withdrawn.

12   Where installed, remove the door airbag module (see Chapter 12).

13   If required, carefully pry the sound insulation panel away from the door, using a flat-bladed tool to cut through the sealant.

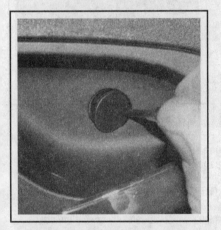

12.6 Press-in the rear edge of the plastic cap in the door handle recess

12.7 Pry out the airbag emblem, and remove the Torx screw

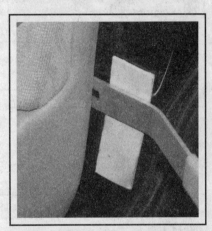

12.9a Carefully lever between the trim panel and the door to release the clips

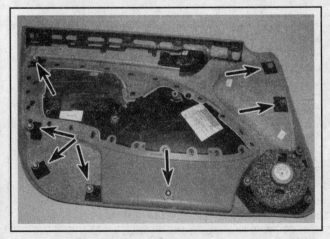

12.9b Door trim panel retaining clips

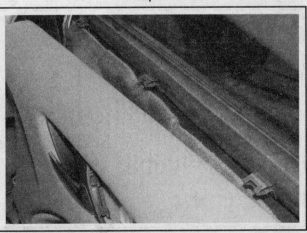

12.9c Pull the top of the trim away before lifting it over the locking knob

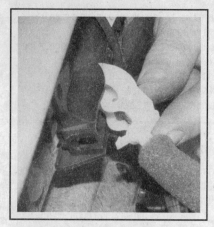

12.10 Lever out the cable lock

12.15 Starting at the rear, pry the trim from the door trim panel

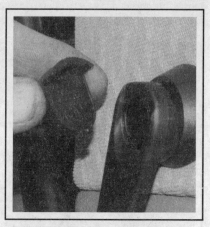

12.16a Pry the plastic cover . . .

12.16b . . . and remove the Torx screw

12.17 On models with rear electric windows, lever the switch from the armrest

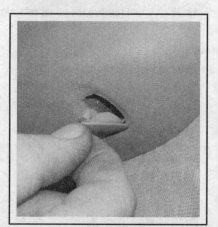

12.18a Pry out the plastic caps . . .

REMOVAL - REAR DOOR

▶ Refer to illustrations 12.15, 12.16a, 12.16b, 12.17, 12.18a and 12.18b

14 Disconnect the cable from the negative battery terminal then open the door (see Chapter 5, Section 1).

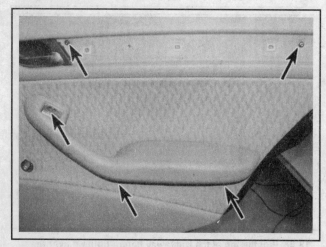

12.18b . . . and remove the five screws

15 Starting at the rear of the trim, using a trim clip releasing tool or flat-bladed screwdriver, carefully pry the decorative trim from the door panel (see illustration).

16 On models with manual windows, carefully pry out the plastic cover from the window handle. Remove the retaining Torx screw and remove the handle complete with circular bezel (see illustrations). Pry the plastic trim from the front of the armrest (see illustration 12.3b).

17 On models with electric windows, using a small flat-bladed screwdriver, carefully lever out the window switch from the armrest. Use a piece of cardboard under the screwdriver to prevent damage to the armrest. Disconnect the switch wiring connector as it is removed (see illustration).

18 Pry out the plastic caps, then remove the five panel retaining screws (see illustrations). Note that the upper front panel retaining screw is longer than the others.

19 Proceed as described in Steps 9 to 13.

INSTALLATION

20 Installation of the trim panel is the reverse of removal. Before installation, check whether any of the trim panel retaining clips were broken on removal, and replace them as necessary. Ensure that where removed, the sound insulation panel is sealed into its original location. If the sound insulation panel is damaged on removal it must be replaced.

13 Door handle and latch components - removal and installation

※※ WARNING:

The models covered by this manual are equipped with Supplemental Restraint systems (SRS), more commonly known as airbags. Always disarm the airbag system before working in the vicinity of any airbag system component to avoid the possibility of accidental deployment of the airbag, which could cause personal injury (see Chapter 12). Do not use a memory saving device to preserve the ECM's memory when working on or near airbag system components.

13.6 Pry the outer cable from the bracket and disengage the inner end from the lever

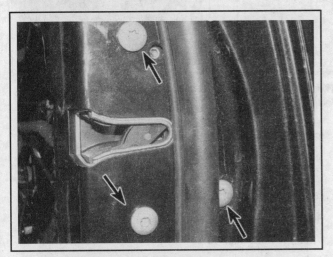

13.7 Remove the door latch retaining screws

13.8a Remove the grommet to expose the handle rear cover bolt - Sedan and Sport Wagon models . . .

REMOVAL

Interior door handle

1   The interior door handle is integral with the door trim, and cannot be replaced separately.

Front door latch assembly

▶ Refer to illustrations 13.7 and 13.8

2   Fully open the window then raise it approximately 140 cm (measured at the rear of the glass). Remove the door inner trim panel as described in Section 12. Carefully peel the plastic sound insulation panel off from the door (carefully cut through the sealant) to gain access to the latch components and continue as described under the relevant sub-heading. If the sound insulation panel is damaged on removal it must be replaced.

3   Loosen the window clamp retaining bolts (see illustrations 14.5a and 14.5b), and tape or wedge the window into the fully closed position. Remove the two nuts securing the window rear support bracket, and maneuver it into the lower part of the door. There is no need to remove the guide rail (see illustration 14.8).

4   If working on the driver's door, remove the lock cylinder as described in Steps 13 to 15.

5   Release the latch assembly wiring retaining clips and disconnect the wiring connector(s).

6   On vehicles from September 2000, pry the outer cable from the retaining bracket, and disconnect the inner end from the lever on the latch (see illustration).

7   Loosen and remove the latch assembly retaining screws then maneuver it behind the rear window support rail, and out from the door complete with the latch button linkage (see illustration).

Front door exterior handle up to September 2000

▶ Refer to illustrations 13.8a, 13.8b and 13.9

8   If working on the driver's door, remove the lock cylinder as described in Steps 13 to 15. If working on the passenger's door, pry out the grommet in the door end panel to expose the outer handle rear cover retaining bolt. On Coupe models, gently fold back the upper door rubber trim to expose the grommet. Remove the bolt with an Allen key and remove the rear cover from the outer handle (see illustrations).

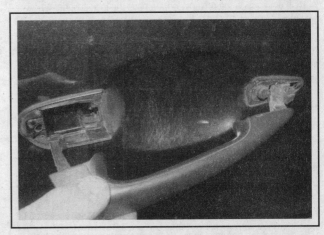

13.8b . . . and Coupe models

13.9 Slide the outer handle to the rear and out of the door

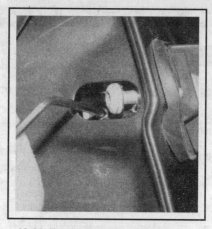

13.11 Turn the actuator screw counterclockwise

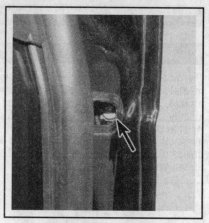

13.13 Pry out the grommet, and remove the lock cylinder retaining bolt

13.14 Remove the bolt and pull the lock cylinder from the door

13.15 Release the retaining clips and remove the lock cylinder cover

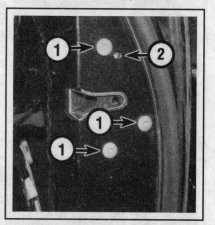

13.17 Rear door latch retaining screws (1) and latch adjusting screw (2)

9   Pull the outer handle outwards and approximately 2 mm to the rear. The latch mechanism is now engaged. Press the outer handle approximately 4 mm inwards, and slide the handle to the rear and out from the door (see illustration).

Front door exterior handle from September 2000

▶ **Refer to illustration 13.11**

10 If working on the driver's door, remove the lock cylinder as described in Steps 13 to 15. If working on the passenger's door, pry out the grommet in the door end panel to expose the outer handle rear cover retaining bolt. On Coupe models, gently fold back the upper door rubber trim to expose the grommet. Remove the bolt with an Allen key and remove the rear cover from the outer handle.

11 The latch must be placed in the 'installation position'. Pull the handle outwards and wedge it in place with a piece of wood or rag. Working through the aperture in the door end panel, turn the actuator screw counterclockwise until it comes to a stop (see illustration). Remove the piece of wood or rag (as applicable).

12 Pull the rear of the handle out, and maneuver it from the door.

Front door lock cylinder

▶ **Refer to illustrations 13.13, 13.14 and 13.15**

13 Pry out the grommet in the door end panel to expose the lock cylinder retaining bolt (see illustration). On Coupe models, gently fold

back the upper door rubber trim to expose the grommet.

14 Remove the retaining bolt with an Allen key, and pull the lock cylinder from the door (see illustration).

15 If required, release the two retaining clips and separate the cylinder from the plastic cover (see illustration).

Rear door latch

▶ **Refer to illustration 13.17**

16 Remove the door inner trim panel and sound insulation material as described in Section 12. Disconnect the door latch wiring connector(s).

17 Loosen and remove the latch assembly retaining screws, then maneuver the latch from the door, complete with the lock button linkage (see illustration).

Rear door exterior handle up to September 2000

▶ **Refer to illustrations 13.18a and 13.18b**

18 Pry out the grommet in the door end panel to expose the outer handle rear cover retaining bolt. Remove the bolt with an Allen key and remove the rear cover from the outer handle (see illustrations).

19 Pull the outer handle outwards and approximately 2 mm to the rear. The latch mechanism is now engaged. Press the outer handle approximately 4 mm inwards, and slide the handle to the rear and out from the door (see illustration 13.9).

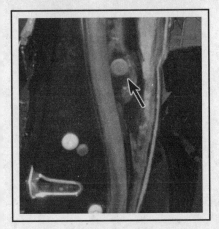

13.18a Pry out the grommet . . .

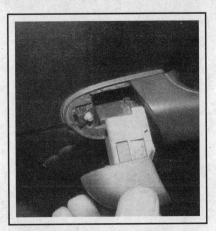

13.18b . . . remove the screw and remove the rear handle cover

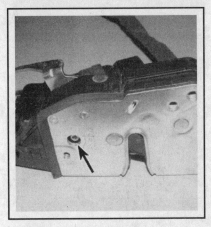

13.26a Loosen the latch adjustment screw - Sedan and Sport Wagon models

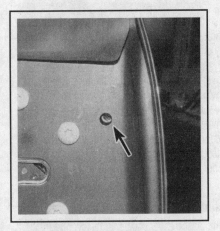

13.26b Latch adjustment screw - Coupe models

13.27 Ensure the latch lever is between the door skin and the support member

13.31 Reconnect the cable to the latch lever

Rear door exterior handle from September 2000

20 Pry out the grommet in the door end panel to expose the outer handle rear cover retaining bolt. Remove the bolt with an Allen key and remove the rear cover from the outer handle.

21 The latch must be placed in the 'installation position'. Pull the handle outwards and wedge it in place with a piece of wood or rag.

22 Working through the aperture in the door end panel, turn the actuator screw counterclockwise until it comes to a stop (see illustration 13.11). Remove the piece of wood or rag (as applicable).

23 Pull the rear of the handle out, and maneuver it from the door.

INSTALLATION

Interior door handle

24 The interior door handle is integral with the door trim panel, and cannot be replaced separately.

Front door latch assembly

▶ **Refer to illustrations 13.26a, 13.26b, 13.27, 13.31 and 13.33**

25 Remove all traces of old locking compound from the latch retaining screws.

26 Prior to installation the latch, loosen the latch adjustment screw.

The screw has a left-hand thread on right-hand door latches, and a right-hand thread on left-hand door latches (see illustrations).

27 Maneuver the latch assembly into position, ensuring that the lock button linkage engages correctly with the hole in the door. Make sure that the latch lever is inserted between the outer door handle support member and the outer door skin (see illustration).

28 Apply fresh locking compound to the latch screws (BMW recommend Loctite 270) then install them and tighten them to the specified torque.

29 Reconnect the wiring connector(s) and secure the wiring in position with the relevant clips.

30 On the driver's door, install the lock cylinder as described in Steps 43 to 45.

31 On all vehicles from September 2000, reconnect the cable to the latch lever, and install the cable outer to the retaining bracket (see illustration).

32 Position the window and rear guide rail, install the nuts and tighten them securely. Lower the window and install it to the clamps as described in Section 14.

33 Do not close the door until the operation of the latch has been set-up and checked as follows:

a) Pry out the small plastic cap adjacent to the latch upper retaining bolt, to access the latch adjusting screw (see illustrations 13.26a and 13.26b).

13.33 Use a screwdriver to 'close' the door latch

13.39 The distance between the mounting and the door plate must not exceed 8 mm

13.47 Loosen the latch adjustment screw

b) *On the left-hand door, tighten the adjusting screw in a clockwise direction. Tighten the driver's door latch adjusting screw counter-clockwise.*

c) *Using a screwdriver 'close' the door latch by pushing in the latch lever (see illustration).*

d) *Using the key, unlock the door.*

e) *Using the outside handle, 'open' the latch.*

f) *If the latch fails to open, loosen the adjusting screw, then tighten it again. Recheck the latch operation.*

g) *Do not close the door until you are completely satisfied that the latch is working correctly. If the door is accidentally closed, it may not be possible to open the door without cutting the door outer skin.*

h) *Install the plastic sealing cap to the door end panel.*

34 Reseal the plastic sound insulation panel to the door. Install the trim panel as described in Section 12.

Front door exterior handle up to September 2000

35 Ensure that the latch lever is positioned correctly (see illustration 13.27). If not, insert a screwdriver through the aperture in the door end panel, and move the lever outwards.

36 Insert the front of the handle into the corresponding hole in the door skin, followed by the rear of the handle. Hold the handle gently again the door and push it forward until it 'clicks' into place.

37 If installation the driver's door handle, install the lock cylinder as described in Steps 43 to 45. If installation the passenger's handle, fit the outer handle rear cover into place, and tighten the retaining bolt securely. Install the grommet to the door end panel.

38 Do not close the door until the operation of the latch has been set-up and checked as described in Step 33. Reseal the plastic sound insulation panel to the door. Install the trim panel as described in Section 12.

Front door exterior handle from September 2000

▶ Refer to illustration 13.39

39 Prior to installation the handle, the door latch must be in the 'installation position'. The distance between the latch actuator mounting and the outer door plate must not exceed 8 mm (see illustration). If the distance is greater, pull the mounting outwards with a finger, until the measurement is correct.

40 Insert the front edge of the handle into the corresponding hole

in the door, and then push the rear of the handle into place. Ensure the seal between the handle and door skin is not distorted. Turn the latch actuator screw fully clockwise to release the handle lock from the installation position.

41 If installing the driver's door handle, install the lock cylinder as described in Steps 43 to 45. If installing the passenger's handle, fit the outer handle rear cover into place, and tighten the retaining bolt securely. Install the grommet to the door end panel.

42 Do not close the door until the operation of the latch has been set-up and checked as described in Step 33. Reseal the plastic sound insulation panel to the door. Install the trim panel as described in Section 12.

Front door lock cylinder

43 If separated, clip the plastic cover back onto the cylinder.

44 Lubricate the outside of the lock cylinder with a suitable grease.

45 Install the lock cylinder into the door latch, and tighten the retaining screw securely. Install the plastic grommet into the door end panel. Before closing the door, check the latch operation as described in Step 33.

Rear door latch

▶ Refer to illustration 13.47

46 Prior to installation, remove all traces of old locking compound from the latch retaining screws.

47 Prior to installing the latch, loosen the latch adjustment screw. The screw has a left-hand thread on right-hand door latches, and a right-hand thread on left-hand door latches (see illustration).

48 Maneuver the latch assembly into position, ensuring that the lock button linkage engages correctly with the hole in the door. Make sure that the latch lever is inserted between the outer door handle support member, and the outer door skin.

49 Apply fresh locking compound to the latch screws (BMW recommend Loctite 270) then install them and tighten them to the specified torque. Reconnect the wiring connector(s) and secure the wiring in position with the relevant clips.

50 On all vehicles from September 2000, reconnect the cable to the latch lever, and install the cable outer to the retaining bracket.

51 Check the operation of the latch assembly as described in Step 33.

52 Reseal the plastic sound insulation panel to the door. Install the trim panel as described in Section 12.

Rear door exterior handle up to September 2000

▸ **Refer to illustration 13.53**

53 Ensure that the latch lever is positioned correctly (see illustration). If not, insert a screwdriver through the aperture at the rear of the handle, and move the lever outwards.

54 Insert the front of the handle into the corresponding hole in the door skin, followed by the rear of the handle. Hold the handle gently again the door and push it forward until it 'clicks' into place.

55 Install the outer handle rear cover into place, and tighten the retaining bolt securely. Install the grommet to the door end panel.

56 Do not close the door until the operation of the latch has been set-up and checked as described in Step 33.

57 Reseal the plastic sound insulation panel to the door. Install the trim panel as described in Section 12.

Rear door exterior handle from September 2000

58 Prior to installation the handle, the door latch must be in the 'installation position'. The distance between the latch actuator mounting and the outer door plate must not exceed 8 mm (see illustration 13.39). If the distance is greater, pull the mounting outwards with a finger, until the measurement is correct.

59 Insert the front edge of the handle into the corresponding hole in the door, and then push the rear of the handle into place. Ensure the seal between the handle and door skin is not distorted.

60 Install the outer handle rear cover into place, and tighten the

13.53 Ensure the latch lever is pulled to the outside of the door

retaining bolt securely. Install the grommet to the door end panel.

61 Do not close the door until the operation of the latch has been set-up and checked as described in Step 33.

62 Reseal the plastic sound insulation panel to the door. Install the trim panel as described in Section 12.

14 Door glass and regulator (Sedan and Sport Wagon) - removal and installation

✳ WARNING:

The models covered by this manual are equipped with Supplemental Restraint systems (SRS), more commonly known as airbags. Always disarm the airbag system before working in the vicinity of any airbag system component to avoid the possibility of accidental deployment of the airbag, which could cause personal injury (see Chapter 12). Do not use a memory saving device to preserve the ECM's memory when working on or near airbag system components.

REMOVAL

Front door window

▸ **Refer to illustrations 14.4, 14.5a, 14.5b and 14.6**

➡Note: BMW states that each time the window is released from the fixing clamps, the plastic 'holders' in the clamps must be replaced.

1 Fully open the window then raise it approximately 140 cm (measured at the rear of the glass).

2 On models with electric windows, disconnect the cable from the negative terminal of the battery (see Chapter 5, Section 1).

3 Remove the inner trim panel and the sound insulation panel (see

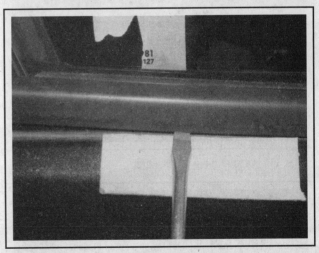

14.4 Place a strip of cardboard between the trim and the screwdriver to prevent damage

Section 12).

4 Starting at the rear using a wide, flat-bladed tool, carefully lever up the window outer sealing strip from the door skin (see illustration). Use a length of cardboard between the door and the tool to prevent damage to the paint.

14.5a Loosen the window rear . . .

14.5b . . . and front clamp bolts

5   Loosen the front and rear window clamp bolts (see illustrations).
6   Lifting the rear first, remove the window from the vehicle (see illustration).

Front door window regulator

▶ Refer to illustrations 14.8, 14.10a, 14.10b, 14.11a and 14.11b

7   Release the door window from the regulator clamps, as described earlier in this Section. Note that there is no need to remove the window from the door, simply use adhesive tape, or rubber wedges, to secure the window in the fully closed position.

8   Remove the bolts securing the rear window guide to the door, and lower the guide to the base of the door (see illustration).
9   On models with electric windows, disconnect the window regulator wiring connectors, and release the harness from any retaining clips.
10 On all models, remove the regulator/motor mouning nuts, release any retaining clips, and lower the assembly to the base of the door.

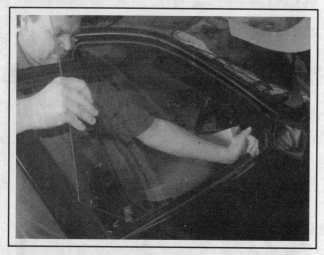

14.6 Lift the rear of the window first

14.8 Remove the rear window guide bolts

14.10a Remove the regulator mounting bolts . . .

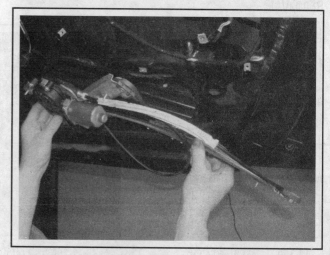

14.10b . . . and maneuver the assembly from the door

14.11a Remove the Torx bolts . . .

14.11b . . . and separate the motor from the regulator

14.13 Carefully remove up the window outer sealing strip

Maneuver the assembly from the door, rear edge first (see illustrations).

11 Where applicable, remove the retaining Torx bolts and separate the motor from the regulator (see illustrations).

Rear door window glass

▶ Refer to illustrations 14.13, 14.14a, 14.14b, 4.14c and 14.16

➡Note: BMW states that each time the window is released from the fixing clamp, the plastic 'holder' in the clamp must be replaced.

12 Remove the door inner trim panel and sound insulation panel (see Section 12).

13 Using a wide, flat-bladed tool, carefully lever up the window outer sealing strip from the door skin (see illustration). Use a length of cardboard between the door and the tool to prevent damage to the paint.

14 Carefully unclip the door inner plastic trim, then peel back the window sealing strip from the front edge of the window opening to gain access to the window trim panel screws. Remove the retaining screws, peel away the door weatherstrip adjacent to the panel, and remove the panel from the door (see illustrations).

15 Fully lower the window, then raise it approximately 115 mm, measured at the front edge. On models with electric windows, disconnect the cable from the negative battery terminal (see Chapter 5, Section 1).

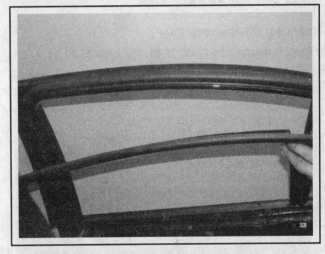

14.14a Unclip the plastic trim . . .

16 Loosen the window clamp screw (see illustration).

17 Maneuver the window out through the top of the door.

Rear door fixed window glass

18 As the rear door fixed window is bonded in place, replacement of the window should be entrusted to a BMW dealer or automotive glass specialist.

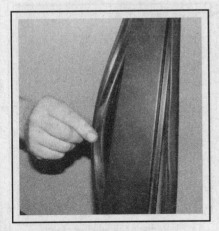

14.14b . . . peel back the sealing strips . . .

14.14c . . . remove the screws and remove the trim

14.16 Loosen the window clamp screw

14.20 Secure the window using tape

14.21 Rear window regulator wiring connector

Rear door window regulator

▶ Refer to illustrations 14.20, 14.21, 14.22 and 14.23

19 Remove the door inner trim panel and sound insulation panel, as described in Section 12.

20 Fully lower the window, then raise it approximately 115 mm, measured at the front edge, so that the window clamp screw is visible. Loosen the window clamp screw and lift the window to the top of the door frame (see illustration 14.16). Secure the window in place using adhesive tape or rubber wedges (see illustration).

21 On models with electric rear windows, disconnect the cable from the negative battery terminal (see Chapter 5, Section 1). Disconnect the regulator motor wiring connector (see illustration), and release the harness from any retaining clips.

22 On all models, remove the regulator/motor securing bolts, release any retaining clips and lift out the lower end of the assembly, and maneuver it from the door (see illustration).

23 Where applicable, remove the two retaining bolts, and remove the motor from the regulator (see illustration).

Rear side fixed window (Sport Wagon)

24 As the rear side fixed window is bonded in place, replacement of the window should be entrusted to a BMW dealer or automotive window specialist.

INSTALLATION

Front door window

▶ Refer to illustration 14.25

25 Installation is the reverse of removal. Smear the window outer sealing strip with a soapy solution (dish soap). Use new window clamp 'holders' (see illustration). Prior to fitting the door sound insulation panel, loosen the window rear guide securing bolts (see illustration 14.8). Reconnect the battery negative lead (where applicable), and fully open the window. Tighten the rear window guide securing bolts. Operate the window and check that it moves easily and squarely in the door frame.

Front door window regulator

26 Installation is the reverse of removal. Install the window glass and adjust as described earlier in this Section.

Rear door window glass

27 Installation is the reverse of removal. Use new window clamp 'holders' (see illustration 14.25). Prior to installing the door sound insulation panel, check that the window operates smoothly and easily.

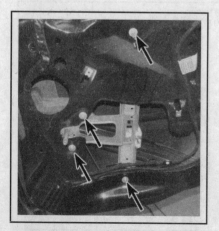

14.22 Remove the regulator mounting bolts

14.23 Rear window motor bolts

14.25 Replace the window clamp plastic holders

Rear door fixed window glass

28 Installation is the reverse of removal making sure the window seal is correctly located in the door.

Rear door window regulator

29 Installation is the reverse of removal. Prior to installation the sound insulation panel, check that the window operates smoothly and easily.

---

15 Door glass, regulator and rear vent window (Coupe) - removal and installation

✳✳ WARNING:

The models covered by this manual are equipped with Supplemental Restraint systems (SRS), more commonly known as airbags. Always disarm the airbag system before working in the vicinity of any airbag system component to avoid the possibility of accidental deployment of the airbag, which could cause personal injury (see Chapter 12). Do not use a memory saving device to preserve the ECM's memory when working on or near airbag system components.

FRONT DOOR GLASS AND REGULATOR

1 Removal of the front door window glass and regulator should be entrusted to a BMW dealer or other qualified repair shop. If the window glass or regulator are disturbed, a complex adjustment procedure must be performed on installation. Failure to adjust the window properly will lead to the glass contacting the body when the door is shut, resulting in breakage of the glass.

REAR VENT WINDOW

Removal

▶ **Refer to illustrations 15.2, 15.3 and 15.5**

2 Using a plastic wedge, carefully lever away the plastic cap over the window link rod (see illustration).

3 Lever the window link rod from the mounting on the window (see illustration).

4 Remove the B-pillar trim as described in Section 27.

5 Lever out the plastic caps, and remove the two hinge retaining bolts in the B-pillar (see illustration).

6 Slide the window to the rear.

Installation

7 Before tightening the hinge bolts, adjust the window position as follows:

   a) *The distance from the rear edge of the front door window to the edge of the rear vent window sealing strip should not exceed 6 mm.*

   b) *The distance from the top edge of the vent window to the rain gutter rail should be 1 mm.*

   c) *The distance from the rear edge of the vent window to the rain gutter rail should be no more than 1.8 mm.*

8 The remainder of installation is a reversal of removal, noting that the plastic cap over the window link rod has an internal lug which must locate over the groove in the window link rod socket.

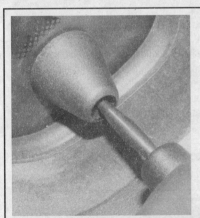

15.2 Lever the cap away from the window along the link rod

15.3 Detach the link rod from the mounting

15.5 Remove the hinge retaining bolts

16 Trunk lid/tailgate and support struts - removal and installation

REMOVAL

Trunk lid

▶ **Refer to illustrations 16.1 and 16.5**

1   Open the trunk, remove the toolbox lid retaining screw and the toolbox hinge screws (see illustration). Remove the toolbox from the trunk trim panel.

2   Pry up the center pins and remove the plastic expanding rivets, then remove the trim panel from the trunk lid.

3   Support the trunk lid in the open position and unclip the support struts (refer to Step 8).

4   Disconnect the wiring connectors from the number plate lights, luggage compartment light switch and central locking servo (as applicable) and tie a piece of string to the end of the wiring. Noting the correct routing of the wiring harness, release the harness rubber grommets from the trunk lid and withdraw the wiring. When the end of the wiring appears, untie the string and leave it in position in the trunk lid; it can then be used on installation to draw the wiring into position.

5   Draw around the outline of each hinge with a suitable marker pen then loosen and remove the hinge retaining bolts and remove the trunk lid from the vehicle (see illustration).

6   Inspect the hinges for signs of wear or damage and replace if necessary; the hinges are secured to the vehicle by bolts.

Tailgate

7   Removal and installation of the tailgate requires special BMW body tools, and the experience to use them. Consequently, we recommend that this task be entrusted to a BMW dealer or suitably-equipped specialist.

Support struts

▶ **Refer to illustration 16.8**

8   Support the trunk lid/tailgate in the open position. Using a small flat-bladed screwdriver raise the spring clip, and pull the support strut

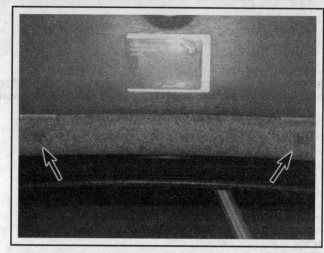

16.1 Remove the toolbox hinge screws

off its upper mounting (see illustration). Repeat the procedure on the lower strut mounting and remove the strut from the vehicle.

INSTALLATION

Trunk lid

9   Installation is the reverse of removal, aligning the hinges with the marks made before removal.

10   On completion, close the Trunk lid and check its alignment with the surrounding panels. If necessary slight adjustment can be made by loosening the retaining bolts and repositioning the trunk lid on its hinges. If the paint work around the hinges has been damaged, paint the affected area with a suitable touch-in brush to prevent corrosion.

Support struts

11   Installation is a reverse of the removal procedure, ensuring that the strut is securely retained by its retaining clips.

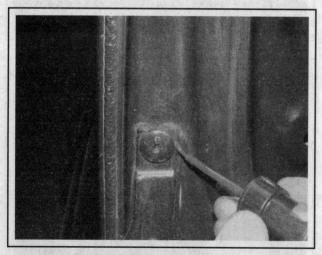

16.5 Make alignment marks around the hinges

16.8 Pry out the strut retaining clip

17 Trunk lid/tailgate latch components - removal and installation

REMOVAL

Sedan/Coupe trunk lid latch

▶ **Refer to illustrations 17.1, 17.3 and 17.5**

1   Open the trunk, remove the toolbox lid retaining screw and the toolbox hinge screws (see illustration). Remove the toolbox from the trunk trim panel.

2   Pry up the center pins and remove the plastic expanding rivets, then remove the trim panel from the trunk lid.

3   Disconnect the wiring connector, remove the two screws and, starting at the edge adjacent to the latch, carefully pull away the cover panel from the latch (see illustration).

4   Disconnect the latch wiring connector.

5   Remove the three screws, and maneuver the latch from the trunk lid. Lever away the actuating rod from the latch as it is withdrawn (see illustration).

Sedan/Coupe trunk lid lock cylinder

▶ **Refer to illustrations 17.10 and 17.11**

6   Remove the trim panel from the trunk lid as described in Steps 1 and 2.

7   Remove the driver's side rear light assembly as described in Chapter 12, Section 7.

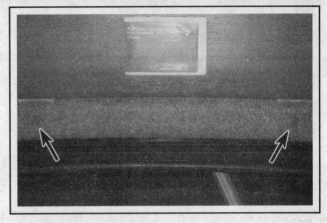

17.1 Toolbox lid hinge screws

8   With the light removed, remove the two retaining screws, and remove the cover from the rear of the lock cylinder.

9   Disconnect the lock cylinder wiring connector.

10 Pull out the locking piece, then carefully pull the actuating rod from the lock cylinder arm (see illustration).

11 Remove the two retaining screws, and rotate the cylinder clockwise until the lock brackets line up with the cut-outs in the panel, then pull the lock from the panel (see illustration).

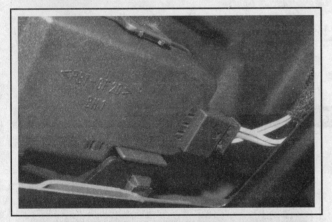

17.3 Disconnect the trunk latch assembly wiring connector

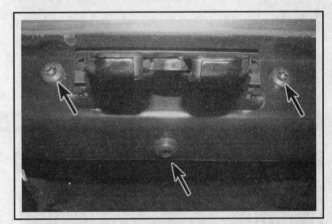

17.5 Trunk lid latch retaining screws

17.10 Pull out the locking piece

17.11 Lock cylinder retaining screws

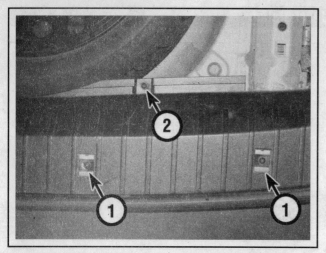

17.13 Pry out the caps and remove the upper screws (1) and lower screws (2)

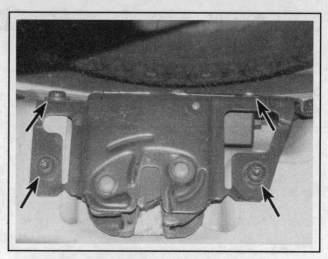

17.14 Remove the tailgate latch retaining screws

Sport Wagon tailgate latch

▶ **Refer to illustrations 17.13 and 17.14**

12 Remove both D-pillar trims as described in Section 27.

13 Pry out the plastic caps, and remove the four retaining screws from the top of the tailgate sill trim panel, then remove the two lower screws. Maneuver the panel from the vehicle (see illustration).

14 Using a marker pen, make alignment marks between the latch and the panel. Remove the four screws and remove the latch (see illustration). Disconnect the wiring connector as the latch is withdrawn.

15 If required, remove the two retaining screws and remove the latch actuator from the latch.

INSTALLATION

16 Installation is a reversal of removal, noting the following points:

a) *Reconnect all wiring connectors, and secure the wiring harnesses using the retaining clips (where applicable).*

b) *Match-up any previously made alignment marks.*

c) *Check the operation of the latches/lock cylinders before installing the trim panels.*

d) *Tighten all fasteners securely.*

18 Central locking components - removal and installation

✳✳ WARNING:

The models covered by this manual are equipped with Supplemental Restraint systems (SRS), more commonly known as airbags. Always disarm the airbag system before working in the vicinity of any airbag system component to avoid the possibility of accidental deployment of the airbag, which could cause personal injury (see Chapter 12). Do not use a memory saving device to preserve the ECM's memory when working on or near airbag system components.

✳✳ CAUTION:

These vehicles are equipped with the Central Body Electronic (ZKE-V) system. Each individual system is linked to a centralized control module that allows efficient and accurate trouble-shooting. This control module governs the windshield wipers and washers, the central locking and anti-theft system, the power windows, the interior lights, the alarm system and the electronic consumer sleep mode. In the event of a malfunction with this system, have the vehicle diagnosed by a dealer service department or other qualified automotive repair facility, as special test equipment is required.

REMOVAL

Electronic control unit (ECU)

1 The central locking system is controlled by the Central Body Electronics (ZKE-V) control unit, known as the General Module (GM V), which is located behind the passenger side glovebox. To access the control unit, remove the glovebox as described in Section 27.

2 Release the retaining clips and lower the ECU out of position.

3 Release the retaining clip then disconnect the wiring connector(s) and remove the ECU from the vehicle.

Door lock actuator

4 The actuator is integral with the door latch assembly. Remove the door latch as described in Section 13.

Trunk lock actuator

5 The trunk lid actuator is integral with the trunk latch assembly. Remove the trunk latch as described in Section 17.

Tailgate lock actuator

6 Remove the tailgate latch as described in Section 17.

7 Remove the two retaining screws and remove the actuator from the latch.

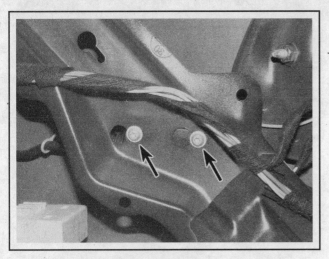

18.10 Fuel filler flap solenoid screws

Fuel filler flap solenoid

8   Rotate the retaining clip 90-degrees and partially remove the right-hand luggage compartment side trim panel.

9   Lift out the first aid box plate and peel back the luggage compartment trim to reveal the solenoid.

10 Disconnect the wiring connector then loosen the retaining screws and maneuver the solenoid out from the luggage compartment (see illustration).

Glovebox lock solenoid

11 Remove the glovebox (see Section 27).

12 Unclip the solenoid rod from the lock and guide, then remove the retaining bolts and remove the solenoid.

INSTALLATION

13 Installation is the reverse of removal. Prior to installation any trim panels removed for access, thoroughly check the operation of the central locking system.

19 Electric window components - removal and installation

✻✻ WARNING:

The models covered by this manual are equipped with Supplemental Restraint systems (SRS), more commonly known as airbags. Always disarm the airbag system before working in the vicinity of any airbag system component to avoid the possibility of accidental deployment of the airbag, which could cause personal injury (see Chapter 12). Do not use a memory saving device to preserve the ECM's memory when working on or near airbag system components.

✻✻ CAUTION:

These vehicles are equipped with the Central Body Electronic (ZKE-V) system. Each individual system is linked to a centralized control module that allows efficient and accurate troubleshooting. This control module governs the windshield wipers and washers, the central locking and anti-theft system, the power windows, the interior lights, the alarm system and the electronic consumer sleep mode. In the event of a malfunction with this system, have the vehicle diagnosed by a dealer service department or other qualified automotive repair facility, as special test equipment is required.

WINDOW SWITCHES

1   Refer to Chapter 12, Section 4.

Sedan/Sport Wagon window motors

2   Remove the window regulator as described in Section 14.

3   Loosen and remove the retaining screws and remove the motor from the regulator.

4   On installation, fit the motor to the regulator and securely tighten its retaining screws.

5   Install the regulator assembly as described in Section 14.

Coupe front window motors

6   Removal and installation of the motors requires the regulator to

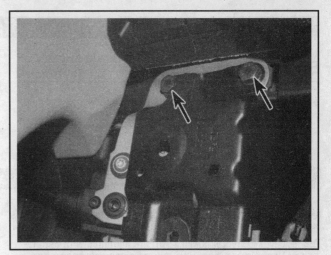

19.10 Remove the motor mounting screws

be removed from the door. This task should be entrusted to a BMW dealer (see Section 15).

Coupe side window motor

▶ **Refer to illustration 19.10**

7   Using a plastic wedge, carefully lever away the plastic cap over the window link rod (see illustration 15.2).

8   Lever the window link rod front the mounting on the window (see illustration 15.3).

9   To remove the plastic trim over the motor, press in the center pin and remove the expanding rivet. Maneuver the trim over the motor link rod.

10 Remove the two mounting bolts, and remove the motor with the bracket (see illustration). Disconnect the wiring connector as the motor is withdrawn.

11 If required, remove the two screws and separate the motor from the bracket.

12 Installation is a reversal of removal, noting that the plastic cap over the link rod has an inner lug which locates in the groove of the window link rod socket.

General Module (GM-V)

▶ Refer to illustration 19.14

13 The electric window system is controlled by the central body electronics (ZKE V) control unit, known as the General Module (GM V), which is located behind the passenger side glovebox. To access the control unit, remove the glovebox as described in Section 27.

14 Release the retaining clips and lower the module out of position (see illustration).

15 Release the retaining clip then disconnect the wiring connector(s) and remove the module from the vehicle.

19.14 Release the clips and remove the module

20 Mirrors and associated components - removal and installation

EXTERIOR MIRROR ASSEMBLY

▶ Refer to illustrations 20.2a, 20.2b and 20.3

1 Remove the door inner trim panel (see Section 12).

2 Carefully pull the plastic trim away from the front inner edge of the door. On Coupe models, carefully pry away the top of the triangular plastic trim over the mirror mounting, then lift it from position (see illustrations).

3 Remove the retaining Torx bolts and remove the mirror from the door. Recover the rubber seal between the door and mirror; if the seal is damaged it must be replaced (see illustration). Disconnect any wiring connectors as the mirror is withdrawn.

4 Installation is the reverse of removal, tightening the mirror bolts to the torque listed in this Chapter's Specifications.

EXTERIOR MIRROR GLASS

▶ Refer to illustration 20.6

➡Note: If the mirror glass is removed when the mirror is cold, the glass retaining clips are likely to break.

5 Tilt the mirror glass fully upwards.

6 Insert a wide plastic or wooden wedge in between the base of the mirror glass and mirror housing and carefully pry the glass from the motor (see illustration). Take great care when removing the glass; do not use excessive force as the glass is easily broken.

7 Remove the glass from the mirror and, where necessary, disconnect the wiring connectors from the mirror heating element.

8 On installation, reconnect the wiring to the glass and clip the glass onto the motor, taking great care not to break it.

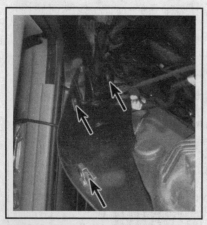

20.2a Note the clips securing the plastic trim at the front of the door edge

20.2b On Coupe models, lift the trim from position

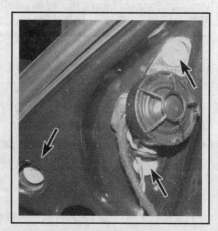

20.3 The mirror is secured by three Torx bolts

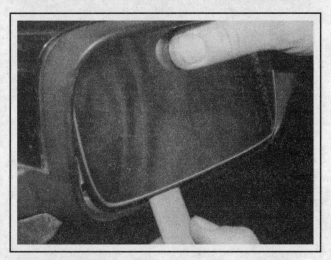

20.6 Carefully pry the mirror glass from the positioning motor

20.11 Remove the three screws and pull the motor, lower edge first, from the housing

EXTERIOR MIRROR SWITCH

9 Refer to Chapter 12.

EXTERIOR MIRROR MOTOR

▶ **Refer to illustration 20.11**

10 Remove the mirror glass as described above.
11 Remove the three retaining screws and pull the motor from position, lower edge first (see illustration). Disconnect the wiring connector as the motor is withdrawn.
12 Installation is the reversal of removal.

EXTERIOR MIRROR HOUSING COVER

▶ **Refer to illustration 20.16**

13 Remove the mirror glass as described above.
14 Release the four retaining clips and remove the mirror housing cover to the front (see illustration).
15 Installation is a reversal of removal.

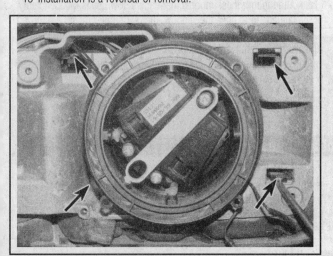

20.14 Release the retaining clips and remove the mirror housing cover

INTERIOR MIRROR

16 There are essentially two different types of mirror arms and mountings. One type has a plastic cover over the plug connection, and the other type has a mirror arm which splits in two to reveal the wiring connector.

Plastic cover type arm

17 Carefully lever out the plastic cover, and disconnect the mirror wiring connector (where applicable).
18 Strike the lower part of the mirror forwards with the ball of your hand to unclip the arm from the mounting.

✳✳ CAUTION:

Do not twist the arm while attempting removal as the clip will be damaged, and do not pull the arm to the rear as the windshield may be damaged.

Split cover mirror arm

▶ **Refer to illustrations 20.19a and 20.19b**

19 Press the two sides of the arm covers towards the mirror and pull the two sides apart. On mirrors equipped with a rain sensor, press up at the base of the covers and pull the two sides apart (see illustrations).

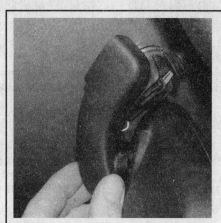

20.19a Pull the two sides of the cover apart

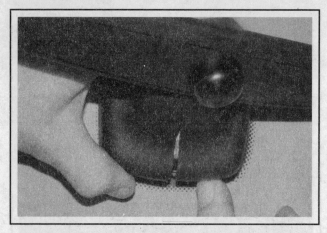

20.19b Press up at the base and pull the two sides apart

20 Push the right-hand side of the mirror upwards and towards the front. Swivel the left-hand arm cover to the left and unclip it from the metal part of the arm.

21 Push the left-hand side of the mirror upwards and towards the front. Swivel the right-hand arm cover to the right and unclip it from the arm.

22 Disconnect the mirror wiring connector.

23 Strike the lower part of the mirror forwards with the ball of your hand to unclip the arm from the mounting.

✳✳ CAUTION:

Do not twist the arm while attempting removal as the clip will be damaged, and do not pull the arm to the rear as the windshield may be damaged.

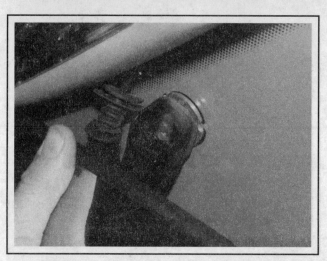

20.24 Position the mirror arm over the mounting at an angle of 45-degrees

All types

▶ **Refer to illustration 20.24**

24 To install the mirrors, position the mirror arm over the mounting at an angle of 45-degrees to the vertical on the driver's side. Push the arm to the vertical and check that it engaged correctly (see illustration). Where applicable, install the covers and reconnect the wiring connector.

21 Windshield and rear window/tailgate glass - general information

1 These areas of glass are secured by the tight fit of the weatherstrip in the body aperture, and are bonded in position with a special adhesive. Replacement of such fixed glass is a difficult, messy and time-consuming task, which is beyond the scope of the home mechanic. It is difficult, unless one has plenty of practice, to obtain a secure, waterproof fit. Furthermore, the task carries a high risk of breakage; this applies especially to the laminated glass windshield. In view of this, owners are strongly advised to have this sort of work carried out by one of the many specialist windshield fitters.

SPORT WAGON REAR WINDOW

2 Although on these models the rear window opens independently of the tailgate, to remove the window, the rear spoiler must be removed. This is a complex task requiring specialist body tools, and experience. Any attempt to remove the spoiler without the necessary equipment is very likely to result in damage. Consequently, we recommend that this work is entrusted to a BMW dealer or suitably-equipped specialist.

22 Sunroof - general information, motor replacement and initialization

GENERAL INFORMATION

▶ **Refer to illustration 22.2**

1 Due to the complexity of the sunroof mechanism, considerable expertise is needed to repair, replace or adjust the sunroof components successfully. Removal of the roof first requires the headlining to be

removed, which is a complex and tedious operation, and not a task to be undertaken lightly. Therefore, any problems with the sunroof (except sunroof motor replacement) should be referred to a BMW dealer or specialist.

2 On models with an electric sunroof, if the sunroof motor fails to operate, first check the relevant fuse. If the fault cannot be traced and rectified, the sunroof can be opened and closed manually using an

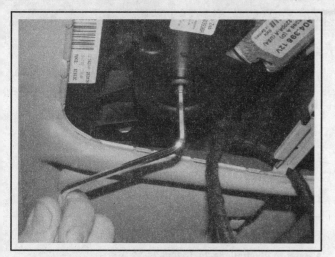

22.2 Insert the tool into the motor spindle

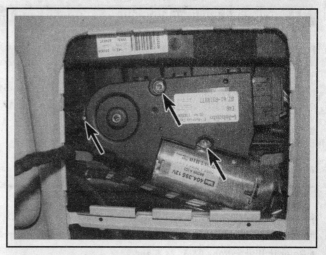

22.5 Sunroof motor screws

Allen key to turn the motor spindle (a suitable key is supplied with the vehicle tool kit). To gain access to the motor, unclip the cover from the headlining. Remove the Allen key from the tool kit and insert it into the motor spindle. Disconnect the motor wiring connector and rotate the key to move the sunroof to the required position (see illustration).

MOTOR REPLACEMENT

▶ **Refer to illustration 22.5**

3   Carefully pry the interior light unit from the headlining between the sun visors. Disconnect the wiring connector(s) as the unit is withdrawn.

4   Carefully pull the front edge of the motor panel down and remove it complete with the switch. Disconnect the wiring connector as the

panel is withdrawn.

5   Remove the three retaining screws, and pull the motor from its location. Disconnect the wiring connector as the motor is removed (see illustration).

6   Installation is a reversal of removal, but carry out the initialization procedure as described next.

INITIALIZATION

7   With the battery reconnected, and the ignition on, press the sunroof operating switch into the 'tilt' position and hold it there.

8   Once the sunroof has reached the 'fully-tilted' position, hold the switch in that position for approximately 20 seconds. Initialization is complete when the sunroof briefly lifts at the rear again.

23 Body exterior fittings - removal and installation

WHEEL ARCH LINERS AND BODY UNDER-PANELS

1   The various plastic covers fitted to the underside of the vehicle are secured in position by a mixture of screws, nuts and retaining clips, and removal will be fairly obvious on inspection. Work methodically around, removing its retaining screws and releasing its retaining clips until the panel is free and can be removed from the underside of the vehicle. Most clips used on the vehicle are simply pried out of position. Other clips can be released by unscrewing and prying out the center pins and then removing the clip.

2   On installation, replace any retaining clips that may have been broken on removal, and ensure that the panel is securely retained by all the relevant clips and screws.

BODY TRIM STRIPS AND BADGES

3   The various body trim strips and badges are held in position with a special adhesive tape. Removal requires the trim/badge to be heated, to soften the adhesive, and then cut away from the surface. Due to the high risk of damage to the vehicle's paint during this operation, it is recommended that this task should be entrusted to a BMW dealer or suitably-equipped specialist.

REAR SPOILER (SPORT WAGON)

4   This is a complex task requiring specialist body tools, and experience. Any attempt to remove the spoiler without the necessary equipment is very likely to result in damage. Consequently, we recommend that this work is entrusted to a BMW dealer or suitably-equipped specialist.

24 Seats and positioning motors - removal and installation

✳✳ WARNING:

The models covered by this manual are equipped with Supplemental Restraint systems (SRS), more commonly known as airbags. Always disarm the airbag system before working in the vicinity of any airbag system component to avoid the possibility of accidental deployment of the airbag, which could cause personal injury (see Chapter 12). Do not use a memory saving device to preserve the ECM's memory when working on or near airbag system components.

FRONT SEAT REMOVAL

▶ **Refer to illustrations 24.3, 24.5 and 24.7**

1   Disconnect the cable from the negative terminal of the battery (see Chapter 5, Section 1).
2   Slide the seat fully forwards and raise the seat cushion fully.
3   On Sedan and Sport Wagon models, remove the bolt and disconnect the seatbelt anchorage bracket from the seat rail (see illustration).
4   Loosen and remove the bolts and washers securing the rear of the seat rails to the floor.
5   Slide the seat fully backwards and remove the trim caps from the seat front mounting nuts/bolts, then loosen and remove the nuts/bolts and washers (see illustration).
6   Slide the seat forward so that the ends of the runners are flush with the rails.
7   Working under the front of the seat, slide out the locking element, and disconnect the seat wiring connector (see illustration).
8   Lift the seat out from the vehicle.

FOLDING REAR SEAT REMOVAL

Sedan and Coupe

▶ **Refer to illustrations 24.10 and 24.12**

9   Pull up on the front of the seat cushion to release the left- and right-hand retaining clips, and remove it forwards and out from the vehicle. Disconnect the seat heating wiring connectors (where applicable) as the seat is withdrawn.
10 If required, pull down the rear seat armrest (where installed) and unbolt it from the seat back (see illustration).

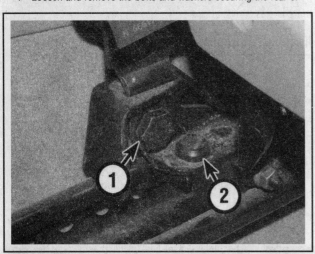

24.3 Front seat belt bolt (1) and seat rail nut cover (2)

24.5 Pry the caps from the seat retaining nuts

24.7 Slide out the locking element and disconnect the seat wiring connector

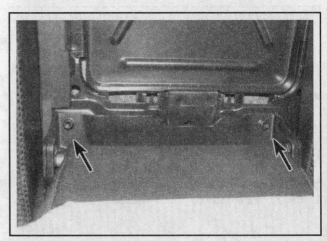

24.10 Remove the Torx bolts and remove the armrest from the seat back

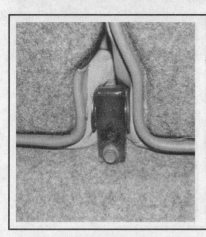

24.12 Remove the rear seat center mounting bolt

11 Loosen and remove the bolts securing the seat belt lower mountings to the body.

12 Fold the seat backs forward, remove the center mounting bolt, and remove the seats (see illustration).

Sport Wagon

▶ Refer to illustrations 24.14, 24.15 and 24.16

13 Release the rear seat backrest, and fold it forward.

14 The trim panel between the seat backrest and the door aperture must be removed. Pull the top of the trim forward to release the retaining clip, and then pull the trim panel upwards to remove it (see illustration). Repeat this procedure on the remaining trim panel on the other side.

15 Remove the screws and remove the rear seat backrest center mounting bracket (see illustration).

16 Remove the two screws securing each side's backrest outer bracket (see illustration).

17 Lift the backrest assembly in the center and disengage the outer pivots from the guides. Maneuver the seats from the vehicle.

FIXED REAR SEAT REMOVAL

▶ Refer to illustration 24.20

18 Pull down the rear seat armrest (where installed) and unclip it from the seat back.

24.16 Rear backrest side mounting bracket

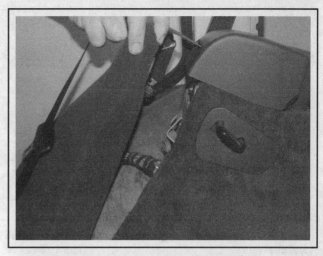

24.14 Pull the top of the trim forward to release it

24.15 Rear backrest center mounting bracket

19 Pull up on the seat base cushion to release the left- and right-hand retaining clips and remove it from the vehicle.

20 Unclip the top of the seat back then slide it upwards to release its lower retaining pins and remove it from the vehicle (see illustration).

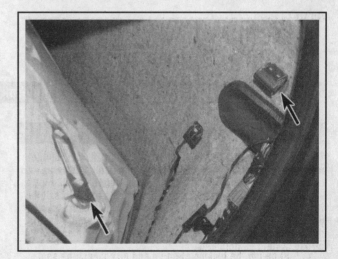

24.20 Note the clips at the top of the fixed seat back

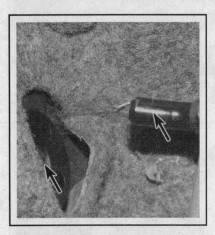

24.22 Rear seat outer locating hole and pivot

24.29a Remove the two Torx screws . . .

24.29b . . . and remove the seat positioning motor

FRONT SEAT INSTALLATION

21 Installation is the reverse of removal, noting the following points.

a) *On manually-adjusted seats, install the seat retaining bolts and tighten them by hand only. Slide the seat fully forwards and then slide it back by two stops of the seat locking mechanism. Rock the seat to ensure that the seat locking mechanism is correctly engaged then tighten the mounting bolts securely.*

b) *On electrically-adjusted seats, ensure that the wiring is connected and correctly routed then tighten the seat mounting bolts securely.*

c) *On Sedan and Sport Wagon models tighten the seat belt mounting bolt to the torque listed in this Chapter's Specifications.*

d) *Reconnect the battery negative lead (see Chapter 5).*

FOLDING REAR SEATS INSTALLATION

Sedan and Coupe

▶ **Refer to illustration 24.22**

22 Installation is the reverse of removal, ensuring that the seat outer pivots engage correctly with the corresponding locating holes in the vehicle body (see illustration). Tighten the seat belt lower mounting bolts to the torque listed in this Chapter's Specifications.

Sport Wagon

23 Installation is the reverse of removal.

24 Twist the upper retaining clip out the metal plate, and slide it into the backrest side section.

25 Locate the lower guides of the side trim panel into the corresponding brackets, and clip the upper edge into place. Install the plastic trim at the top of the side panel.

FIXED REAR SEAT INSTALLATION

26 Installation is the reverse of removal, making sure the seat back lower locating pegs are correctly engaged with the body, and the seat belt buckles and lap belt are fed through the intended openings.

FRONT SEAT POSITIONING MOTORS

Removal

▶ **Refer to illustrations 24.29a and 24.29b**

27 Remove the front seat as described previously in this Section.

28 Disconnect the wiring connector and remove it from the support bracket.

29 Remove the two Torx screws and remove the motor from the drive gearbox (see illustrations).

Installation

30 Installation is a reversal of removal. Tighten the motor mounting screws securely.

25 Front seat belt tensioning mechanism - general information

※※ **WARNING:**

The models covered by this manual are equipped with Supplemental Restraint systems (SRS), more commonly known as airbags. Always disarm the airbag system before working in the vicinity of any airbag system component to avoid the possibility of accidental deployment of the airbag, which could cause personal injury (see Chapter 12). Do not use a memory saving device to preserve the ECM's memory when working on or near airbag system components.

1 Most models are fitted with a front seat belt tensioner system. The system is designed to instantaneously take up any slack in the seat belt in the case of a sudden frontal impact, therefore reducing the possibility of injury to the front seat occupants. Each front seat is fitted with its own system, the tensioner being situated near the seat belt lock.

2 The seat belt tensioner is triggered by a frontal impact above a predetermined force. Lesser impacts, including impacts from behind, will not trigger the system.

3 When the system is triggered, an pyrotechnic device (seatbelt tensioner) retracts and locks the seat belt approximately two additional

inches. This prevents the seat belt moving and keeps the occupant in position in the seat. Once the tensioner has been triggered, the seat belt will be permanently locked and the assembly must be replaced.

4   There is a risk of injury if the system is triggered inadvertently when working on the vehicle. If any work is to be carried out on the seat/seat belt disable the tensioner by disconnecting the battery negative lead (see Chapter 12), and waiting at least two minutes before proceeding.

5   The front seats in convertible models are designed with an integrated seat belt system. This system includes tensioners and seatbelt locks mounted directly to the seat frame along with the seatbelt guide attached to the headrest. This system must be serviced by a dealership or other qualified repair facility.

6   Also note the following warnings before contemplating any work on the front seat.

✳✳ WARNING:

If the tensioner mechanism is dropped, it must be replaced, even it has suffered no apparent damage.

- *Do not allow any solvents to come into contact with the tensioner mechanism.*
- *Do not subject the seat to any form of shock as this could accidentally trigger the seat belt tensioner.*
- *Check for any deformation of the seat belt stalk tensioner, and anchorage brackets. Replace any that are damaged.*

26 Seat belt components - removal and installation

✳✳ WARNING:

Read Section 25 before proceeding.

REMOVAL

Front seat belt - Sedan/Sport Wagon

▶ **Refer to illustrations 26.4 and 26.5**

1   Remove the front seat as described in Section 24.

2   Remove the B-pillar trim panel as described in Section 27.

3   Remove the screws and remove the seat belt guide from the pillar.

4   Remove the screw securing the upper seat belt mount (see illustration).

5   Unscrew the inertia reel retaining bolt and remove the seat belt from the door pillar (see illustration).

6   If necessary, remove the retaining bolts and remove the height adjustment mechanism from the door pillar.

Front seat belt - Coupe

▶ **Refer to illustrations 26.9 and 26.12**

7   Remove the front seat as described in Section 24.

8   Remove the B-pillar trim and the rear side trim panel as described in Section 27.

9   Pry off the plastic cap at the front of the seat belt lower anchorage bar, remove the securing bolt and slide the belt from the bar (see illustration).

10 Remove the screws and remove the seat belt guide from the pillar.

11 Remove the screw securing the upper seat belt mount.

26.4 Front seat belt upper mounting bolt

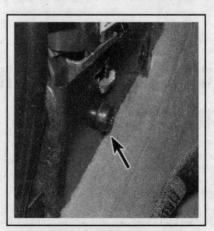

26.5 Front seat belt inertia reel mounting bolt

26.9 Pull off the cap and remove the anchorage bar bolt

26.12 Unscrew the inertia reel retaining bolt

12 Unscrew the inertia reel retaining bolt and remove the seat belt from the door pillar (see illustration).

13 If necessary, remove the retaining bolts and remove the height adjustment mechanism from the door pillar.

Front seat belt stalk

▶ Refer to illustrations 26.15 and 26.16

14 Remove the seat as described in Section 24.

15 Release the tensioner wiring connector from the cable strap, and disconnect it (see illustration).

16 Loosen and remove the stalk assembly retaining nut and remove the assembly from the side of the seat (see illustration).

Fixed rear seat side belts

17 Remove the rear seat as described in Section 24.

18 Loosen and remove the bolts and washers securing the rear seat belts to the vehicle body and remove the center belt and buckle.

19 Unclip the trim cover from the front of the parcel shelf and detach it from the seat belts.

20 Carefully unclip the left and right-hand trim panels from the rear pillars, disconnecting the wiring from the interior lights as the panels are removed.

21 Remove the retaining clips from the front edge of the parcel shelf and slide the shelf forwards and out of position. As the shelf is

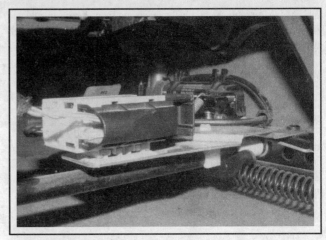

26.15 Disconnect the tensioner wiring connector

removed, disconnect the wiring connectors from the high-level stop-light (where installed).

22 Unscrew the inertia reel retaining nut and remove the seat belt(s).

Folding rear seat side belts

▶ Refer to illustrations 26.24 and 26.25

23 Remove the rear parcel shelf trim as described in Section 27.

24 Loosen and remove the Torx bolt securing the lower end of the belt to the body (see illustration). Feed the belt through the slot in the shelf trim.

25 The inertia reel is secured by one Torx bolt (see illustration). Loosen and remove the bolt and washer. On Coupe models, remove the screw and remove the polystyrene filler piece to expose the bolt.

26 Maneuver the assembly from the mounting bracket and withdraw it from the vehicle.

Rear seat side belt stalk

27 Unclip the rear seat cushion and remove it from the body.

28 Loosen and remove the bolt and washer and remove the stalk from the vehicle.

Rear seat center belt and buckle

29 Unclip the rear seat cushion and remove it from the vehicle.

30 Loosen and remove the bolt securing the center belt/buckle to the body and remove it from the vehicle.

26.16 Remove the stalk retaining nut

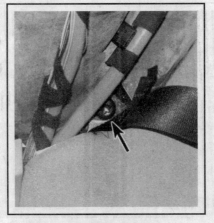

26.24 Rear lower seat belt mounting bolt

26.25 Rear seat belt inertia reel mounting bolt

INSTALLATION

Front seat belt

31 Installation is the reverse of the removal procedure, ensuring that all the seat belt mounting bolts are securely tightened, and all disturbed trim panels are securely retained by all the relevant retaining clips.

Front seat belt stalk

32 Ensure the tensioner mechanism is correctly engaged with the seat and tighten its retaining nut to the specified torque. Install the seat as described in Section 24 and reconnect the battery negative lead.

Fixed rear seat side belts

33 Installation is the reverse of removal, ensuring that all seat belt mountings are tightened to the specified torque and all trim panels are clipped securely in position.

Folding rear seat side belts

34 Installation is the reverse of removal, making sure the inertia reel is clipped securely in position and all seat belt mounting bolts are tightened to the torque.

Rear seat belt stalk

35 Installation is the reverse of removal, tightening the mounting bolt to the specified torque.

Rear seat center belt and buckle

36 Installation is the reverse of removal, tightening the mounting bolts to the specified torque.

27 Interior trim - removal and installation

✳✳ WARNING:

The models covered by this manual are equipped with Supplemental Restraint systems (SRS), more commonly known as airbags. Always disarm the airbag system before working in the vicinity of any airbag system component to avoid the possibility of accidental deployment of the airbag, which could cause personal injury (see Chapter 12). Do not use a memory saving device to preserve the ECM's memory when working on or near airbag system components.

INTERIOR TRIM PANELS

1 The interior trim panels are secured using either screws or various types of trim fasteners, usually studs or clips.

2 Check that there are no other panels overlapping the one to be removed; usually there is a sequence that has to be followed that will become obvious on close inspection.

3 Remove all obvious fasteners, such as screws. If the panel will not come free, it is held by hidden clips or fasteners. These are usually situated around the edge of the panel and can be pried up to release them; note, however that they can break quite easily so new ones should be available. The best way of releasing such clips, without the correct type of tool, is to use a large flat-bladed screwdriver. Note that some panels are secured by plastic expanding rivets, where the center pin must be preyed up before the rivet can be removed. Note in many cases that the adjacent sealing strip must be preyed back to release a panel.

4 When removing a panel, never use excessive force or the panel may be damaged; always check carefully that all fasteners have been removed or released before attempting to withdraw a panel.

5 Installation is the reverse of the removal procedure; secure the fasteners by pressing them firmly into place and ensure that all disturbed components are correctly secured to prevent rattles.

A-pillar trim

◗ **Refer to illustrations 27.7 and 27.8**

6 Due to the head-impact airbag fitted in the area, disconnect the battery as described in Chapter 5, Section 1. Also see The airbag Section in Chapter 12.

7 Using a wooden or plastic flat-bladed lever, carefully pry out the trim insert from the A-pillar trim (see illustration).

8 Remove the three retaining Torx screws, and pull the trim to the rear, starting at the top (see illustration).

9 Installation is the reverse of the removal procedure; secure the fasteners by pressing them firmly into place and ensure that all disturbed components are correctly secured to prevent rattles.

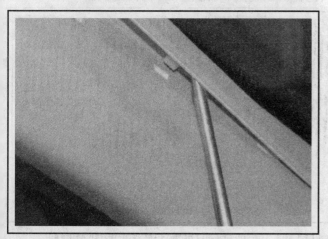

27.7 Carefully pry the insert from the A-pillar trim

27.8 Remove the three screws and remove the pillar trim

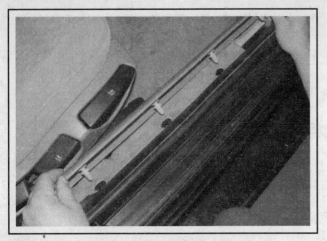

27.10 Pry up the sill trim to release the retaining clips

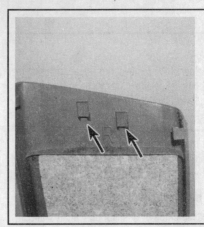

27.11 The B-pillar lower trim has two clips which located behind the upper trim

B-pillar trim - Sedan/Sport Wagon

▶ Refer to illustrations 27.10, 27.11, 27.13 and 27.14

10 Begin by carefully prying up the front door sill trim panel from its retaining clips (see illustration).

11 Starting at the base of the B-pillar trim, pull the trim in towards the center of the cabin, and release it from the two lower retaining clips. Note how the lower part of the trim engages with the upper section of trim (see illustration).

12 Remove the bolt securing the seat belt outer anchorage to the seat rail.

13 The lower edge of the upper trim is secured by two plastic expanding rivets. Pry up the center pins, and lever out the complete rivets (see illustration).

14 Feed the seat belt strap through the upper mounting, and pull the trim down and out. Note how the upper edge of the trim engages with the headlining molding (see illustration).

15 Installation is the reverse of the removal procedure; secure the fasteners by pressing them firmly into place and ensure that all disturbed components are correctly secured to prevent rattles.

B-pillar trim - Coupe

▶ Refer to illustrations 27.19a and 27.19b

16 Carefully pry up the front door sill trim panel from its retaining clips.

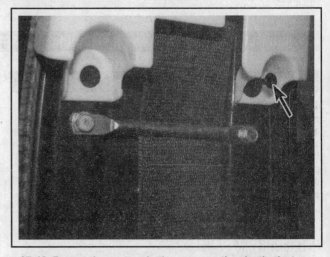

27.13 Pry out the center pin then remove the plastic rivet

17 Pull the rubber weatherstrip from the door aperture adjacent to the trim then, using a clip release tool or flat-bladed screwdriver, carefully release the front edge of the rear side panel trim from its retaining clips.

18 Pry off the plastic cap, and remove the front mounting bolt from the seat belt lower anchorage rail. Slide the belt from the rail.

19 The lower edge of the upper trim is secured by two plastic expanding rivets. Pry up the center pins, lever out the complete rivets, and lower the trim from place (see illustrations).

27.14 The upper edge of the B-pillar trim locates over the two lugs

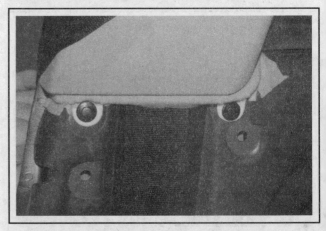

27.19a The lower edge of the B-pillar trim is secured by two expanding rivets . . .

27.19b . . . and the upper edge locates with these clips

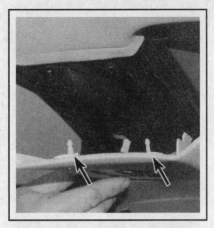

27.21 Pull the C-pillar trim at the top and release the retaining clips

27.23 Pull the top of the trim to release the clip

C-pillar trim - Sedan/Coupe

▶ **Refer to illustration 27.21**

20 Pry out the outer edge of the courtesy light, and remove it from the pillar trim. Disconnect the wiring connector as the unit is withdrawn.

21 Pull the door weatherstrip away from the area adjacent to the pillar trim. Pull the top edge of the pillar trim away, releasing the two retaining clips, and then lift the trim away (see illustration).

22 Installation is the reverse of the removal procedure; secure the fasteners by pressing them firmly into place and ensure that all disturbed components are correctly secured to prevent rattles.

C-pillar trim - Sport Wagon

▶ **Refer to illustration 27.23**

23 Pull the top of the pillar trim towards the center of the cabin to release the top push-on clip (see illustration).

24 With the top released, pull up the lower edge of the trim and remove it.

25 Installation is a reversal of removal.

D-pillar trim - Sport Wagon

▶ **Refer to illustration 27.27**

26 Open the tailgate, press the release button, and fold down the flap

in the luggage compartment side panel.

27 The pillar trim is secured by two screws in the center, and two push-on clips at the top edge. Remove the screws, pull the top of the trim to release the clips, then lift the trim away (see illustration). Disconnect the luggage compartment light as the trim is removed.

28 Installation is a reversal of removal.

Side trim panel - Coupe

▶ **Refer to illustrations 27.31, 27.33 and 27.35**

➡**Note: On models fitted with rear side airbags, due to the proximity of side airbags, disconnect the battery as described in Chapter 5, then wait two minutes before proceeding.**

29 Using a plastic wedge, carefully lever away the plastic cap over the window link rod (see illustration 15.2).

30 Lever the window link rod from the mounting on the window (see illustration 15.3).

31 Push the seat belt to one side, and push down the center pin of the expanding rivet securing the plastic trim at the top of the seat side cushion (see illustration). Maneuver the plastic trim over the hinged window link rod.

32 Remove the rear seat cushion as described in Section 24.

33 Fold the seat backrest forward and, using a screwdriver, release the retaining clip at the top and pull the seat side cushion from its location (see illustration). Note how the fitting at the base of the trim engage with the fitting on the wheel arch.

27.27 Remove the D-pillar trim screws

27.31 Push-in the center pin, and remove the trim

27.33 Release the clip and pull the seat side cushion forward

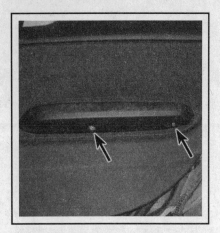

27.35 The armrest is secured by two screws

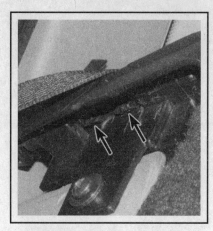

27.40 Release the two clips and remove the trim cover

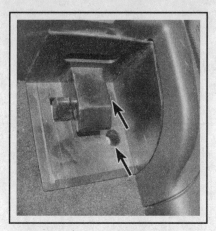

27.42 Remove the two screws and remove the roller cover mounting

34 Carefully pry up the front door sill trim panel from its retaining clips, and pull the rubber weatherstrip from the door aperture adjacent to the trim panel.

35 Where applicable, carefully pry out the airbag emblem from the side panel speaker grill, remove and remove the screw revealed. Remove the two screws securing the armrest (see illustration).

36 The side panel is now secured by 7 push-on clips around its perimeter. Using a trim removal tool or flat-bladed screwdriver, carefully release the clips, and maneuver the panel from the vehicle. Note their fitted locations, and disconnect and wiring connectors as the panel is withdrawn.

37 Installation is the reverse of the removal procedure; secure the fasteners by pressing them firmly into place and ensure that all disturbed components are correctly secured to prevent rattles. Note that the plastic cap on the rear-side hinged window link rod has an internal lug which must locate over the groove in the window link rod socket.

Luggage area trim panel - Sport Wagon

▶ Refer to illustrations 27.40, 27.42, 27.43, 27.44 and 27.45

38 Remove the C- and D-pillar trims as described earlier in this Section.

39 Fold the rear seat forward, unclip the top section of the side trim adjacent to the door aperture, then lift the trim upwards and remove it (see illustration 24.14).

40 Release the two clips at the front edge, and remove the seat belt reel trim cover from the top of the side panel (see illustration).

41 Remove the bolt securing the lower seat belt mounting.

42 Remove the two retaining screws, and remove the luggage compartment roller cover mounting from the side panel (see illustration).

43 Lever out the center pin and pry out the expanding plastic rivet, remove the screws/nut, then remove the cover from the seat belt reel (see illustration).

44 Loosen the retaining screw and remove the trim from the lower edge of the rear side window (see illustration).

45 Lift the trim flap, remove the screws and remove the 'lashing eye' from the side panel (see illustration).

46 Carefully pry the 12V power socket from the side trim, and disconnect the wiring connectors as the socket is withdrawn.

47 Pry out the center pin and lever out the plastic expansion rivet from the lower edge of the trim panel.

48 Lever out the mounting at the top, and remove the trim panel, feeding the power socket wiring through the hole as the panel is removed.

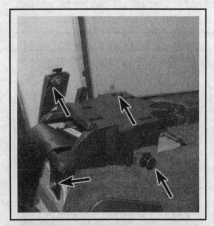

27.43 Pry out the expansion rivet, remove the screws/nuts and remove the cover from the seat belt reel

27.44 Remove the screw and remove the trim

27.45 Lift the flap and remove the lashing-eye screws

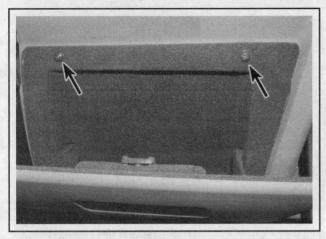

27.49 The driver's glovebox is retained by two screws

27.50 Pull out the pin at the base of the retaining strap/ shock absorber each side

GLOVEBOX

Driver's side
▶ **Refer to illustration 27.49**

49 Open the glovebox, remove the two screws and remove the glovebox (see illustration). Disconnect any wiring connectors as the glovebox is removed.

Passenger side
▶ **Refer to illustrations 27.50 and 27.51**

50 Open the glovebox, and pull out the pin at the base of the retaining strap/shock absorber each side (see illustration).
51 Working in the dash opening, remove the retaining screws, and remove the glovebox complete with hinge and bracket (see illustration). Disconnect all wiring connectors as the glovebox is withdrawn.
52 Installation is the reverse of the removal procedure.

Glovebox lock
▶ **Refer to illustration 27.53**

53 Open the glovebox lid, remove the two retaining screws and remove the lock (see illustration).

CARPETS

54 The passenger compartment floor carpet is in one piece, secured at its edges by screws or clips, usually the same fasteners used to secure the various adjoining trim panels.
55 Carpet removal and installation is reasonably straightforward but very time-consuming because all adjoining trim panels must be removed first, as must components such as the seats, the center console and seat belt lower anchorages.

HEADLINING

56 The headlining is clipped to the roof and can be withdrawn only once all fittings such as the grab handles, sun visors, sunroof (if equipped), windshield, rear quarter windows and related trim panels have been removed, and the door, tailgate and sunroof aperture sealing strips have been pried clear.
57 Note that headlining removal requires considerable skill and experience if it is to be carried out without damage and is therefore best entrusted to an expert.

CUP HOLDERS

58 Squeeze in the sides of the tray and lift it, complete with the cup holders, from the center console.
59 Install the tray first, followed by the cup holders.

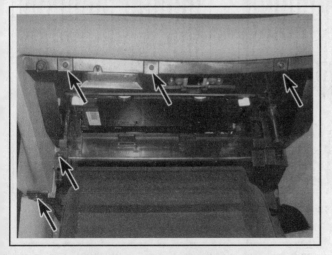

27.51 Remove the screws and remove the glovebox

27.53 The glovebox lock is retained by two screws

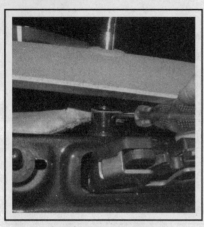

27.62 Lift up the parcel shelf edge and pry out the headrest clips

27.63 Before installation the parcel shelf trim, insert the retaining clips into the headrest holders

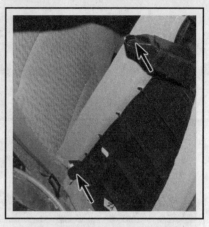

27.65 Rear seat side trim retaining clip and locating lug

REAR HEADRESTS

▶ **Refer to illustrations 27.62 and 27.63**

60 Fold the rear seat forward, or remove the rear seat back as applicable (see Section 24).

61 Pull the center pins down, and pry out the plastic rivets, then remove the plastic trim from the front edge of the parcel shelf.

62 Lift up the front edge of the parcel shelf trim, pull out the retaining clips, and remove the rear headrest (see illustration).

63 Installation is a reversal of removal, but before installation the shelf trim, fit the retaining clips into the rear headrest holders (see illustration).

PARCEL SHELF - SEDAN/COUPE

▶ **Refer to illustration 27.65**

64 Fold the rear seats forward, or remove the rear seat back as

applicable (see Section 24).

65 Pull the top of the rear seat side trim forwards releasing the retaining clips, then lift and remove it (see illustration). Repeat this procedure on the remaining rear seat side trim.

66 Pull the center pins down, and pry out the plastic rivets, then remove the plastic trim from the front edge of the parcel shelf.

67 Remove both C-pillar trims as described earlier in this Section.

68 Lift up the front edge of the parcel shelf trim, pull out the retaining clips, and remove the rear head rests (see illustration 27.62).

69 Carefully pry out the covers over the rear speakers set into the parcel shelf. Remove the bolts, disconnect the wiring connectors and remove the speakers. Lift out the speaker enclosures.

70 Remove the shelf trim to the front. If required, remove the Torx screw securing the lower seat belt anchor, and feed the belt through the parcel shelf trim.

71 Installation is a reversal of removal, but before installing the shelf trim, install the retaining clips into the rear headrest holders (see illustration 27.63).

28 Center console - removal and installation

▶ **Refer to illustrations 28.2, 28.3, 28.4, 28.5, 28.6 and 28.7**

✳✳ WARNING:

The models covered by this manual are equipped with Supplemental Restraint systems (SRS), more commonly known as airbags. Always disarm the airbag system before working in the vicinity of any airbag system component to avoid the possibility of accidental deployment of the airbag, which could cause personal injury (see Chapter 12). Do not use a memory saving device to preserve the ECM's memory when working on or near airbag system components.

1 Disconnect the cable from the negative terminal of the battery (see Chapter 5, Section 1).

2 Roll down the rear storage box/ashtray lid. Press down on the lid edge and lift the box/ashtray from the rear of the center console (see illustration).

28.2 Press down on the edge to remove the ashtray

28.3 Remove the ashtray/storage box surround screws

28.4 Unclip the parking brake lever boot

3   Loosen the retaining screws, pull the screws out complete with the plastic expansion rivets, and remove the ashtray/storage box surround, disconnecting the illumination bulb holder as it is withdrawn (see illustration).

4   On all models unclip the parking brake lever boot from the console (see illustration).

5   Remove the two screws, then pull out the sides and remove the ashtray/storage box surround from the rear of the console (see illustration).

6   Carefully pry out the gear lever boot from the surrounding trim (see illustration). On automatic transmission models, pry the boot up complete with the surrounding trim.

7   Remove the two screws at the rear of the gear lever boot aperture, lift the boot surround trim, and pull the rear section of the console slightly to the rear (see illustration). Note their fitted locations, then disconnect any wiring connectors as the console is withdrawn. Maneuver the center console over the parking brake lever. On models with a center armrest, lift the armrest and pull the rear of the console up and forward.

8   If required, the armrest can now be removed by unscrewing the mounting bolts and disconnecting the parking brake warning switch wiring.

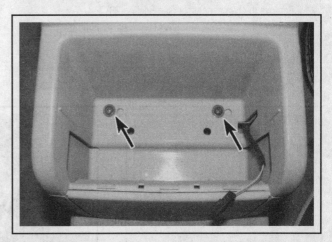

28.5 Remove the ashtray/storage box trim screws

9   Maneuver the center console over the parking brake lever, then over the upright armrest (where installed). The remainder of installation is the reverse of removal, making sure all fasteners are securely tightened.

28.6 Carefully pry up the gear lever boot - on automatic transmission models, remove the trim bezel from around the shift lever

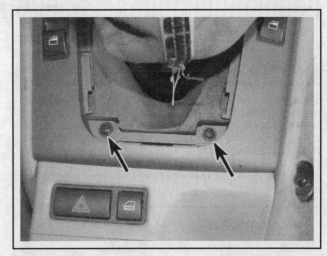

28.7 Remove the two screws at the rear of the gear lever boot aperture

29 Instrument panel assembly - removal and installation

REMOVAL

▶ Refer to illustrations 29.6a, 29.6b, 29.6c, 29.7a, 29.7b, 29.7c, 29.9, 29.10, 29.16, 29.17, 29.19 and 29.20

1   Remove the center console (see Section 28).

2   Remove the gear shift knob from the lever by pulling straight up, grasping the shift knob firmly.

3   Remove the gear lever surround trim. Note their installed locations, and disconnect any wiring connectors as the trim is removed.

4   Remove the steering column combination switch (see Chap-

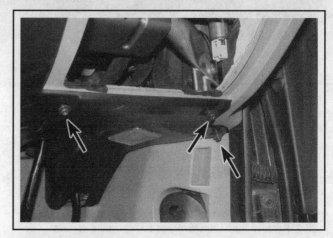

29.6a Remove the three screws . . .

ter 12, Section 4).

5   Remove both gloveboxes (see Section 27).

6   Remove the three screws, one expanding plastic rivet, and one plastic nut, then remove the panel from above the pedals. As the panel

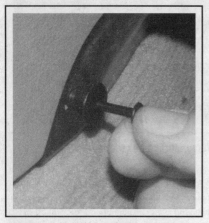

29.6b . . . and the plastic expansion rivet

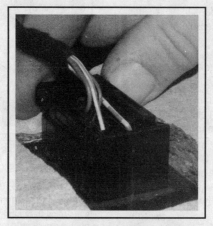

29.6c Slide back the locking element and remove the OBD socket from the panel

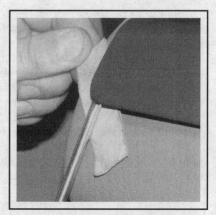

29.7a Use a piece of cardboard to protect the instrument panel when prying up the end of the decorative strip

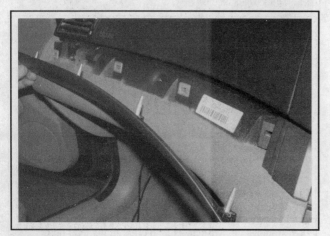

29.7b The decorative strips are retained by 'push-in' clips

29.7c Remove the strip from the center of the instrument panel

29.9 Pry out the lower edge and pull the storage compartment from the instrument panel

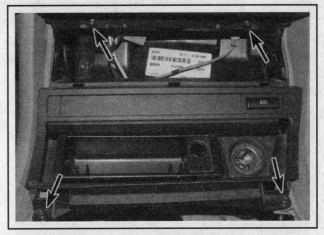

29.10 Remove the four screws and withdraw the storage compartment carrier

is removed, slide back the locking element and remove the OBD socket from the panel. Disconnect the light wiring connector at the same time (see illustrations).

7 Using a wooden or plastic spatula, starting from the outside edges, carefully pry the decorative trim strips from the passenger's and driver's side of the instrument panel, and remove the strip from the center of the instrument panel (see illustrations).

8 Remove the instrument cluster assembly (see Chapter 12).

9 Open the storage compartment lid below the heater controls. Carefully pry out the lower edge of the compartment, starting at the cor-

29.16 Remove the screw in the decorative trim recess

ner, and withdraw it from the instrument panel (see illustration). If you are removing the glasses storage compartment, press the roof of the compartment up slightly, pull it approximately 2 mm to the rear, then press the left and right-hand side of the lid downwards slightly, and pull it from the instrument panel.

10 Remove the four screws and remove the storage compartment carrier from the instrument panel (see illustration). Note their installed positions, and disconnect the wiring connectors as the unit is withdrawn.

11 Remove both A-pillar trims (see Section 27).

12 Remove the light switch from the instrument panel (see Chapter 12, Section 4).

13 Remove the heater control panel (see Chapter 3).

14 Remove the audio unit from the instrument panel (see Chapter 12).

15 Remove the passenger airbag unit (see Chapter 12).

16 On the passenger's side, remove the screw in the decorative trim recess (see illustration).

17 Remove the retaining screw(s) and pull the driver's side air vent from the instrument panel (see illustration).

18 The passenger side end of the instrument panel may be secured by a screw or an expanding plastic rivet. Remove the screw or lever out the rivet.

19 Remove the nut securing the instrument panel to the rear of the gear lever (see illustration).

29.17 Driver's side air vent screw

29.19 Remove the nut at the rear of the gear lever

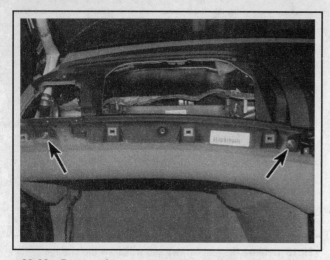

29.20a Remove the two nuts on the passenger side . . .

29.20b . . . and the two nuts on the driver's side

20 Move the front seats as far back as possible, remove the instrument panel mounting nuts, and with the help of an assistant, pull the instrument panel from the firewall (see illustrations). Disconnect the center air vent cable from the side of the heater box where applicable. Note their fitted locations, and disconnect any wiring connectors as the instrument panel is withdrawn.

INSTALLATION

21 Installation is the reverse of the removal procedure, noting the

following points:

a) Maneuver the instrument panel into position and, using the labels stuck on during removal, ensure that the wiring is correctly routed and securely retained by its instrument panel clips.

b) Clip the instrument panel back into position, ensure the center locating lug at the front edge of the instrument panel engages correctly, making sure all the wiring connectors are fed through their respective apertures, then install all the instrument panel fasteners, and tighten them securely.

c) On completion, reconnect the battery and check that all the electrical components and switches function correctly.

30 Convertible top - general information

➡Note: This information is general in nature, as it is intended to apply to all vehicle types, years and models.

ADJUSTMENTS

➡Note: The following are typical adjustments. Some of these adjustments may not be provided for on your vehicle.

Latches

The latches secure the convertible top frame to the upper edge of the windshield frame. If the latches are too loose, the top will rattle and move side to side. If the latches are too tight, they will be difficult or impossible to secure. The hooks on some latches are threaded so they can be screwed in or out to tighten or loosen the latch; pliers are often necessary, so make sure you protect the finish of the hook with a rag. Other latches have set-screws that lock the hooks in place - loosen the set-screws (usually with an Allen wrench), position the hooks as desired, then tighten the set-screws.

Also keep in mind that weatherstrip is attached to the front edge of the top. As this weatherstrip deteriorates over time, it will cause the latches and the front edge of the convertible top to become loose. The proper fix for this problem is to replace the deteriorated weatherstrip, which will also reduce wind noise.

Assist springs

Assist springs are attached between the rear of the top framework and the vehicle body. The springs allow the top to be raised and lowered slowly and evenly, without excessive effort in either direction. If the springs are too loose or too tight, they can cause the top to move very quickly in one direction and very slowly in the other direction. Often, the springs can be loosened or tightened by turning threaded adjusters. The springs are sometimes difficult to locate, especially when they travel into the trunk area or are covered by fabric. Search along the rear portion of the framework and remove any access covers.

Some newer vehicles use gas-filled assist struts in place of springs. These struts are similar in design to the gas-filled support struts used to raise and support the hood on many newer vehicles. While these struts are not adjustable, they do lose their gas charge over time and become less effective. Replace the struts if they are not doing their job.

Center joint

On most vehicles, the center joints of the top framework can be adjusted to align the top weatherstrip with the side windows. This adjustment also slightly affects the forward "reach" of the top. The center-joint adjustment changes the angle between the forward and rear sections of the top framework at each side.

To visualize this adjustment, imagine a standard, flat door hinge lying flat on a table top. If you grasp the hinge on each side at its center pivot and lift slightly, the hinge will flex and appear as an arch, with only its ends touching the table - this also shortens the overall length of the hinge. In this analogy, the hinge plates are the front and rear framework sections and the lifting of the center pivot is the center-joint adjustment.

To make this adjustment, it is usually necessary to position the top at approximately its mid-point between raised and lowered. The adjustment mechanism is located at the joint between the front and rear frame sections on each side. The adjuster usually looks like a notched wheel with a set-screw that secures it in position, although some adjusters are a simple screw-and-locknut setup. Mark the position of the adjuster (in case you have to return to the original setting), then loosen or remove the set-screw or locknut. Rotate the wheel or screw, which will sometimes require an Allen wrench. Usually, you'll make the adjustments in the same small increments, side-to-side, until the correct adjustment is achieved. Raise and lower the top after each small adjustment to check alignment.

If the top alignment is not equal side-to-side (compare the alignment of the top to the upper edges of the side windows on each side), adjust one side more than the other to get the proper adjustment.

Adjusting the center joints also changes the height of the top's front edge, so it is usually necessary to adjust the control link after making a center-joint adjustment.

Control link

This adjustment affects both the forward "reach" of the top and the height of the front edge of the top (how high it sits above the windshield frame before the latches are secured). The control link is located at the rear of the top assembly, usually near the main pivot point. Various methods are used to provide adjustment at the control link, such as slotted mounting screw holes and wheel-type adjusters.

With the top down, locate the adjusters, mark their positions, then remove the set-screws or loosen the mounting bolts. Raise the top, then move the adjusters to provide a slight gap between the front edge of the top and the window frame. Walk all around the vehicle to make sure the adjustment is even from side to side. If it is not even, adjust the low side up until it is even. When adjustment is complete, tighten the set-screws or mounting bolts.

Front frame

Some models have separate framework at the forward end of the top assembly that is adjustable by virtue of slotted mounting bolt holes. If, after all other adjustments are carried out, the alignment pins on the top are too far forward or backward to properly engage the holes in the windshield frame, adjust the frame as follows:

Retract the top part-way, loosen the bolts, slide the framework evenly forward or backward, tighten the bolts, then raise the top and check alignment again. Repeat this process until correct alignment is achieved.

POWER-TOP TROUBLESHOOTING

Power tops are operated by six hydraulic cylinders. The cylinders receive hydraulic pressure from an electric motor/pump assembly that is mounted in the trunk, behind the left-side trim panel. When the switch is pressed to raise the top, the motor drives the pump in a direction that sends hydraulic pressure to the bottom end of each hydraulic cylinder (storage compartment cover, convertible frame, etc.), driving the pistons out of the cylinders, which raises the top. When the switch is pressed to lower the top, the motor turns in the opposite direction, sending hydraulic pressure to the top of each cylinder, driving the pistons down and lowering the top.

As a first step in troubleshooting, listen for the whirring sound of the motor as the switch is pressed. If there is no sound from the motor, refer to *Electrical Troubleshooting* in Chapter 12. If you can hear the motor running but the top does not raise, proceed to Hydraulic/mechanical troubleshooting as follows:

Hydraulic/mechanical troubleshooting

Mechanical and hydraulic problems will cause the top to not open (or close) or to get stuck part-way through the process. If the motor is operating normally, there are generally two possible causes for these problems: 1) A hydraulic system malfunction (low fluid level, air in the system, inadequate pump pressure) or 2) A mechanical binding in the top framework.

Hydraulic system fluid level check

Locate the hydraulic motor/pump behind the left-side trim panel in the trunk. On the side or end of the motor/pump assembly will be a screw-type check plug. Place rags underneath the check plug. Unscrew the plug and verify the fluid level is within 1/4-inch of the bottom of the check-plug hole (the procedure is very much like checking differential fluid level). If necessary, add fluid through the check-plug hole to bring the fluid level to normal. Check your owner's manual, BMW dealer or local auto parts store for specific fluid recommendations. If you find a low fluid level, check for leaks at the pump, hoses and hydraulic cylinders.

Hydraulic system bleeding

Air can get into the hydraulic system through leaks and if the fluid level is too low. Air in the system will generally cause excess noise and, in extreme cases, will cause the top to raise or lower only part-way.

To bleed the hydraulic system, first check the fluid level, then start the engine and raise and lower the top. If the fluid has excessive air, the top might not raise or lower, so you will need an assistant to hold the switch while you raise and lower the top slowly by hand. Raise and lower the top several times to work out all the air. Check the fluid level again, since it will likely drop as the air is expelled.

Checking for binding

If the hydraulic system seems to be operating properly, disconnect the hydraulic cylinders from the top framework and operate the top by hand. The top should go up and down smoothly, without excessive effort. If the top binds during manual operation, make sure all adjustments are correct and spray penetrating lubricant on all framework joints.

If the top is operating smoothly during manual operation but will not raise properly with the hydraulic cylinders connected, suspect a pump/motor assembly that is not providing adequate pressure.

Specifications

Torque specifications	Ft-lbs (unless otherwise indicated)	Nm
Door latch retaining bolts	84 in-lbs	9
Door window glass and regulator fasteners	84 in-lbs	9
Exterior mirror bolts	48 in-lbs	6
Rear vent window hinge bolts/screw (Coupe models)	48 in-lbs	6
Seat belt height adjustment bracket on B-pillar	18	24
Seat belt mounting bolts	23	31
Seat belt tensioner stalk on seat rail	35	48

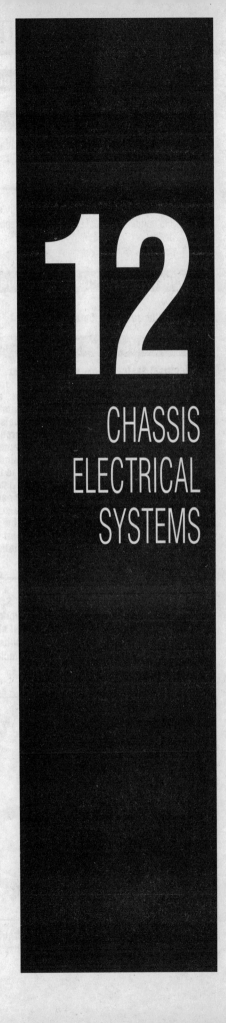

12

CHASSIS ELECTRICAL SYSTEMS

Section

Reference to other Chapters

1 General information and precautions

✳✳ WARNING:

Before carrying out any work on the electrical system, read through the precautions given in "Safety First!" at the beginning of this manual and Chapter 5.

The electrical system is of the 12 volt negative ground type. Power for the lights and all electrical accessories is supplied by a lead-acid type battery which is charged by the alternator.

This Chapter covers repair and service procedures for the various electrical components not associated with the engine. Information on the battery, alternator and starter motor can be found in Chapter 5.

It should be noted that prior to working on any component in the electrical system, the battery negative terminal should first be disconnected to prevent the possibility of electrical short circuits and/or fires (see Chapter 5, Section 1).

2 Electrical troubleshooting - general information

◆ Refer to illustrations 2.5a and 2.5b

✳✳ CAUTION:

The electrical system is extremely complex. Many of the ECMs are connected via a "Databus" system, where they are able to share information from the various sensors, and communicate with each other. For instance, as the automatic transmission approaches a gear ratio shift point, it signals the engine management ECM via the Databus. As the gearchange is made by the transmission ECM, the engine management ECM retards the ignition timing, momentarily reducing engine output, to ensure a smoother transition from one gear ratio to the next. Due to the design of the Databus system, it is not advisable to backprobe the ECMs with a multimeter, in the traditional manner. Instead, the electrical systems are equipped with a sophisticated self-diagnosis system, which can interrogate the various ECMs to reveal stored fault codes, and help pin-point faults. In order to access the self-diagnosis system, specialist test equipment (fault code reader/scanner) is required.

➡Note: Refer to the precautions given in "Safety first!" and in Section 1 of this Chapter before starting work. The following tests relate to testing of the main electrical circuits, and should not be used to test delicate electronic circuits (such as anti-lock braking systems), particularly where an electronic control module (ECM) is used.

A typical electrical circuit consists of an electrical component, any switches, relays, motors, fuses, fusible links or circuit breakers related to that component and the wiring and connectors that link the component to both the battery and the chassis. To help you pinpoint an electrical circuit problem, wiring diagrams are included at the end of this Chapter.

Before tackling any troublesome electrical circuit, first study the appropriate wiring diagrams to get a complete understanding of what makes up that individual circuit. You can often narrow down trouble spots, for instance, by noting whether other components related to the circuit are operating correctly. If several components or circuits fail at one time, chances are that the problem is in a fuse or ground connection, because several circuits are often routed through the same fuse and ground connections.

Electrical problems usually stem from simple causes, such as loose or corroded connections, a blown fuse, a melted fusible link or a failed relay. Visually inspect the condition of all fuses, wires and connections in a problem circuit before troubleshooting the circuit.

If test equipment and instruments are going to be utilized, use the diagrams to plan ahead of time where you will make the necessary connections in order to accurately pinpoint the trouble spot.

For electrical troubleshooting you'll need a circuit tester or voltmeter, a continuity tester, which includes a bulb, battery and set of test leads, and a jumper wire, preferably with a circuit breaker incorporated, which can be used to bypass electrical components (see illustrations).

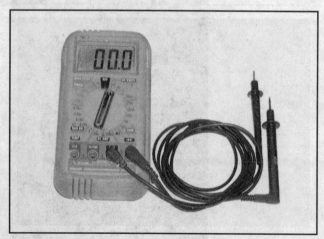

2.5a The most useful tool for electrical troubleshooting is a digital multimeter that can check volts, amps, and test continuity

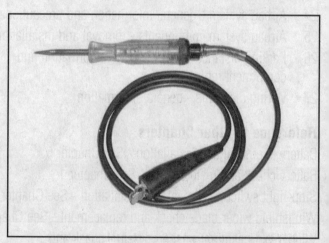

2.5b A simple test light is a very handy tool used for testing voltage

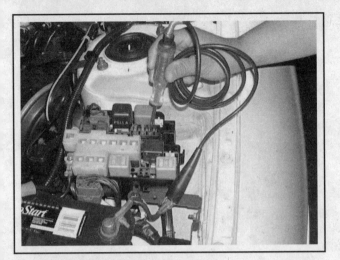

2.6 In use, a basic test light's lead is clipped to a known good ground, then the pointed probe can test connectors, wires or electrical sockets - if the bulb lights, battery voltage is present at the test point

Before attempting to locate a problem with test instruments, use the wiring diagram(s) to decide where to make the connections.

VOLTAGE CHECKS

▶ **Refer to illustration 2.6**

Voltage checks should be performed if a circuit is not functioning properly. Connect one lead of a circuit tester to either the negative battery terminal or a known good ground. Connect the other lead to a connector in the circuit being tested, preferably nearest to the battery or fuse (see illustration). If the bulb of the tester lights, voltage is present, which means that the part of the circuit between the connector and the battery is problem free. Continue checking the rest of the circuit in the same fashion. When you reach a point at which no voltage is present, the problem lies between that point and the last test point with voltage. Most of the time the problem can be traced to a loose connection.

➡**Note: Keep in mind that some circuits receive voltage only when the ignition key is in the ACC or RUN position.**

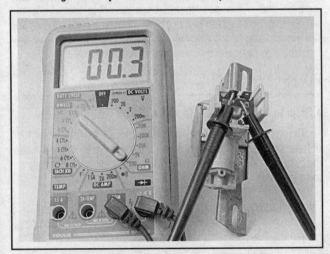

2.9 With a multimeter set to the ohm scale, resistance can be checked across two terminals - when checking for continuity, a low reading indicates continuity, a very high or infinite reading indicates lack of continuity

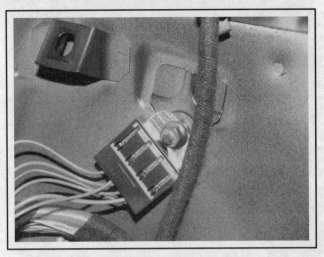

2.8 Luggage compartment ground connection

FINDING A SHORT

One method of finding shorts in a circuit is to remove the fuse and connect a test light or voltmeter to the fuse terminals. There should be no voltage present in the circuit when it is turned off. Move the wiring harness from side-to-side while watching the test light. If the bulb goes on, there is a short to ground somewhere in that area, probably where the insulation has rubbed through. The same test can be performed on each component in the circuit, even a switch.

GROUND CHECK

▶ **Refer to illustration 2.8**

Perform a ground test to check whether a component is properly grounded. Disconnect the battery and connect one lead of a continuity tester or multimeter (set to the ohm scale), to a known good ground. Connect the other lead to the wire or ground connection being tested (see illustration). If the resistance is low (less than 5 ohms), the ground is good. If the bulb on a self-powered test light does not go on, the ground is not good.

CONTINUITY CHECK

▶ **Refer to illustration 2.9**

A continuity check determines whether there are any breaks in a circuit, i.e. whether it's conducting electricity correctly. With the circuit off (no power in the circuit), use a self-powered continuity tester or multimeter to check the circuit. Connect the test leads to both ends of the circuit (or to the power end and a good ground). If the test light comes on, the circuit is conducting current correctly (see illustration). If the resistance is low (less than 5 ohms), there is continuity; if the reading is 10,000 ohms or higher, there is a break somewhere in the circuit. The same procedure can be used to test a switch, by connecting the continuity tester to the switch terminals. With the switch turned on, the test light should come on (or low resistance should be indicated on a meter).

FINDING AN OPEN CIRCUIT

When diagnosing for possible open circuits, it is often difficult to locate them by sight because the connectors hide oxidation or terminal

2.15 To backprobe a connector, insert a small, sharp probe (such as a straight-pin) into the back of the connector alongside the desired wire until it contacts the metal terminal inside; connect your meter leads to the probes - this allows you to test a functioning circuit

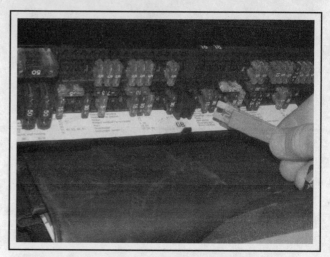

2.18a Use the tweezers provided to extract and install the fuses

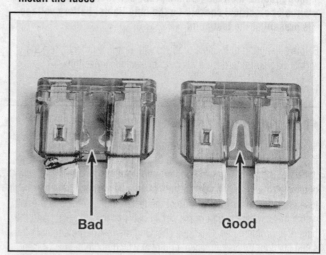

Bad   Good

2.18b When a fuse blows, the element between the terminals melts - the fuse on the left is blown, the one on the right is good

misalignment. Merely wiggling a connector on a sensor or in the wiring harness may correct the open circuit condition. Remember this when an open circuit is indicated when troubleshooting a circuit. Intermittent problems may also be caused by oxidized or loose connections.

Electrical troubleshooting is simple if you keep in mind that all electrical circuits are basically electricity running from the battery, through the wires, switches, relays, fuses and fusible links to each electrical component (light bulb, motor, etc.) and to ground, from which it is passed back to the battery. Any electrical problem is an interruption in the flow of electricity to and from the battery.

CONNECTORS

▶ Refer to illustration 2.15

Most electrical connections on these vehicles are made with multi-wire plastic connectors. The mating halves of many connectors are secured with locking clips molded into the plastic connector shells. The mating halves of large connectors, such as some of those under the instrument panel, are held together by a bolt through the center of the connector.

To separate a connector with locking clips, use a small screwdriver to pry the clips apart carefully, then separate the connector halves. Pull only on the shell, never pull on the wiring harness as you may damage the individual wires and terminals inside the connectors. Look at the connector closely before trying to separate the halves. Often the locking clips are engaged in a way that is not immediately clear. Additionally, many connectors have more than one set of clips.

Each pair of connector terminals has a male half and a female half. When you look at the end view of a connector in a diagram, be sure to understand whether the view shows the harness side or the component side of the connector. Connector halves are mirror images of each other, and a terminal shown on the right side end-view of one half will be on the left side end view of the other half.

It is often necessary to take circuit voltage measurements with a connector connected. Whenever possible, carefully insert a small straight pin (not your meter probe) into the rear of the connector shell to contact the terminal inside, then clip your meter lead to the pin. This kind of connection is called backprobing (see illustration). When insert-

ing a test probe into a male terminal, be careful not to distort the terminal opening. Doing so can lead to a poor connection and corrosion at that terminal later. Using the small straight pin instead of a meter probe results in less chance of deforming the terminal connector.

FUSES

▶ Refer to illustrations 2.18a and 2.18b

The electrical circuits of the vehicle are protected by a combination of fuses and fusible links. The fuses and relay box are located behind the passenger side glove box and in the E-box in the engine compartment (see illustration 3.2a and 3.3a).

Each of the fuses is designed to protect a specific circuit, and the various circuits are identified on the fuse panel itself.

Different sizes of fuses are employed in the fuse blocks. There are regular and fuse pack sizes, with the larger fuse pack located in the E-box in the engine compartment (see illustration 3.3b). The fuse pack consists of fuses that govern a variety of circuits in one assembly (DME control module, EVAP emissions valve, fuel injectors, etc.). Regular fuses require the use of pliers or the small plastic fuse-puller tool (see illustration) found in most fuse boxes. If an electrical component fails,

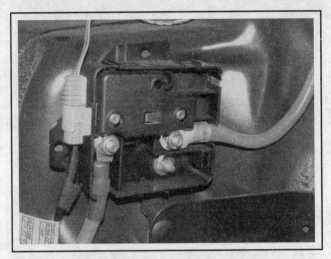

2.21 The main fusible link is located in the luggage compartment

always check the fuse first. The best way to check the fuses is with a test light. Check for power at the exposed terminal tips of each fuse. If power is present at one side of the fuse but not the other, the fuse is blown. A blown fuse can also be identified by visually inspecting it (see illustration).

Be sure to replace blown fuses with the correct type. Fuses of different ratings are physically interchangeable, but only fuses of the proper rating should be used. Replacing a fuse with one of a higher or lower value than specified is not recommended. Each electrical circuit needs a specific amount of protection. The amperage rating of each fuse is molded into the fuse body.

If the replacement fuse immediately fails, don't replace it again until the cause of the problem is isolated and corrected. In most cases, the cause will be a short circuit in the wiring caused by a broken or deteriorated wire.

FUSIBLE LINKS

▶ **Refer to illustration 2.21**

The wiring between the battery and the alternator is protected by a fusible link. A fusible link functions like a fuse, in that it melts when the circuit is overloaded, but resembles a large-gauge wire. To replace a fusible link, first disconnect the negative cable from the battery (see Chapter 5, Section 1). High amperage "fusible links" are located on the top face of the fuse box, while the main fusible link is located adjacent to the battery in the luggage compartment (see illustration). Disconnect the burned-out link and replace it with a new one (available from your dealer or auto parts store). Always determine the cause for the overload that melted the fusible link before installing a new one.

3 Relays - general information and testing

▶ **Refer to illustrations 3.2a, 3.2b, 3.3a and 3.3b**

1   Many electrical accessories in the vehicle utilize relays to transmit current to the component. If the relay is defective, the component won't operate properly. The majority of the fuses and relays are located behind the passenger's side glove box, while some others are located in the "E-box" located in the left-hand corner of the engine compartment.

2   To remove the main fuse box cover, open the glove box, turn the two white quick-release fasteners and pull down the cover. A list of the circuits each fuse protects is given on the label attached to the inside of the main fuse box cover (see illustrations).

➡**Note: When the fuse block is retracted or in the up position, the plastic tabs face each other. When the fuse block is released, the plastic tabs face the rear of the glove box.**

3   The relays and fuse pack in the E-box are accessed once the cover retaining screws have been removed (see illustrations).

4   If a faulty relay is suspected, it can be removed and tested using the procedure below or by a dealer service department or a repair shop. Defective relays must be replaced as a unit.

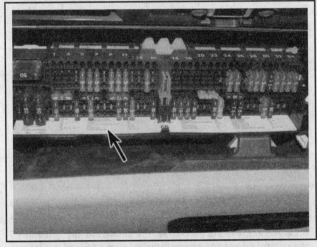

3.2a A list of the fuse allocations is included in the fuse box

3.2b Relays behind the passenger side glove box

3.3a Location of the E-box cover screws

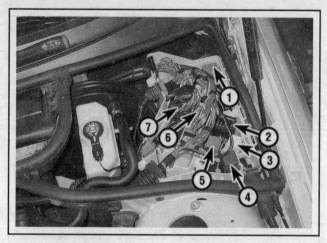

3.3b Lift the cover to access the fuses and relays

1   Windshield washer double relay
2   Engine electronics fuse pack
3   Fuel injector relay (2001 and later models)
4   Back-up light relay (automatic transmission)
5   DME main relay
6   Automatic transmission control module
7   Engine Control Module (ECM)

TESTING

▶ **Refer to illustrations 3.5a and 3.5b**

5   Most of the relays used in these vehicles are of a type often called ISO relays, which refers to the International Standards Organization. The terminals of ISO relays are numbered to indicate their usual circuit connections and functions. There are two basic layouts of terminals on the relays used in the vehicles covered by this manual (see illustrations).

6   Refer to the wiring diagram for the circuit to determine the proper connections for the relay you're testing. If you can't determine the correct connection from the wiring diagrams, however, you may be able to determine the test connections from the information that follows.

7   Two of the terminals are the relay control circuit and connect to the relay coil. The other relay terminals are the power circuit. When the relay is energized, the coil creates a magnetic field that closes the larger contacts of the power circuit to provide power to the circuit loads.

8   Terminals 85 and 86 are normally the control circuit. If the relay contains a diode, terminal 86 must be connected to battery positive (B+) voltage and terminal 85 to ground. If the relay contains a resistor, terminals 85 and 86 can be connected in either direction with respect to

B+ and ground.

9   Terminal 30 is normally connected to the battery voltage (B+) source for the circuit loads. Terminal 87 is connected to the ground side of the circuit, either directly or through a load. If the relay has several alternate terminals for load or ground connections, they usually are numbered 87A, 87B, 87C, and so on.

10 Use an ohmmeter to check continuity through the relay control coil.

a) Connect the meter according to the polarity shown in the illustration for one check; then reverse the ohmmeter leads and check continuity in the other direction.

b) If the relay contains a resistor, resistance will be indicated on the meter, and should be the same value with the ohmmeter in either direction.

c) If the relay contains a diode, resistance should be higher with the ohmmeter in the forward polarity direction than with the meter leads reversed.

d) If the ohmmeter shows infinite resistance in both directions, replace the relay.

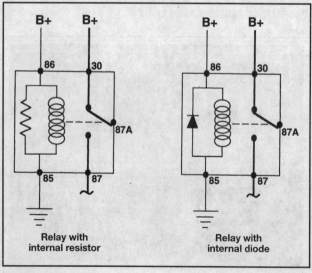

3.5a Typical ISO relay designs, terminal numbering and circuit connections

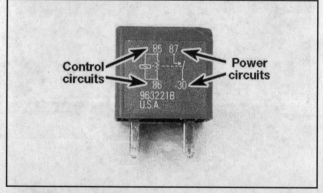

3.5b Most relays are marked on the outside to easily identify the control circuit and power circuits - this one is of the four-terminal type

11 Remove the relay from the vehicle and use the ohmmeter to check for continuity between the relay power circuit terminals. There should be no continuity between terminal 30 and 87 with the relay de-energized.

12 Connect a fused jumper wire to terminal 86 and the positive battery terminal. Connect another jumper wire between terminal 85 and

ground. When the connections are made, the relay should click.

13 With the jumper wires connected, check for continuity between the power circuit terminals. Now there should be continuity between terminals 30 and 87.

14 If the relay fails any of the above tests, replace it.

4 Switches - removal and installation

※※ WARNING:

The models covered by this manual are equipped with Supplemental Restraint systems (SRS), more commonly known as airbags. Always disarm the airbag system before working in the vicinity of any airbag system component to avoid the possibility of accidental deployment of the airbag, which could cause personal injury (see Section 25). Do not use a memory saving device to preserve the PCM's memory when working on or near airbag system components.

1 Disconnect the cable from the negative terminal of the battery (see Chapter 5, Section 1).

STEERING COLUMN SWITCHES

▶ Refer to illustrations 4.3, 4.4, 4.6 and 4.7

2 Place the steering column in the fully lowered and extended posi-

tion. Remove the steering wheel as described in Chapter 10.

3 Loosen the upper column shroud retaining screw and pull out the plastic rivet (see illustration). Gently squeeze together the sides of the trim, lift the steering wheel end of the shroud first, then disengage the front end of the shroud.

4 Place the column in the highest, fully extended position. Using a small screwdriver, push in the center pins of the two expanding rivets securing the lower shroud to the column, gently squeeze together the side of the upper shroud, and remove the lower shroud (see illustration).

5 Disconnect the wiring connectors from the airbag contact unit, wiper and indicator switches.

6 Remove the four retaining screws and lift the switch assembly over the end of the steering column (see illustration).

7 If required, the switches can be removed from the assembly by releasing the two retaining clips (see illustration).

8 Installation is the reverse of the removal procedure, ensuring that

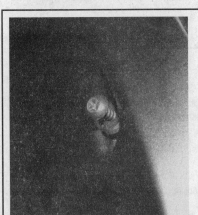

4.3 Loosen the screw and pull it out with the plastic rivet

4.4 Push in the center pins of the expanding rivets

4.6 Remove the four screws and remove the switch assembly

4.7 Depress the retaining clips to remove the switches

4.11a Remove the two screws and remove the light switch

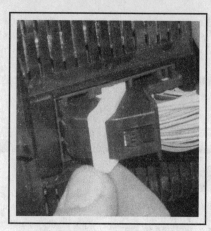

4.11b Lever over the locking catch and disconnect the wiring connector

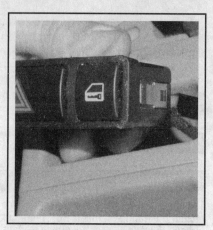

4.16 Press the hazard/central locking switch out from underneath

the wiring is correctly routed. Also, make sure the airbag contact unit is centralized (see Chapter 10, Section 17).

LIGHTING SWITCH

▶ **Refer to illustrations 4.11a and 4.11b**

9   Using a wooden or plastic spatula, carefully pry the decorative strip from the driver's side of the dash, above the light switch. Take care not to damage the dash panels.

10   Open the driver's side glove box, remove the two screws at its upper edge, and maneuver the glove box from the instrument panel. If necessary see Chapter 11, Section 27.

11   Remove the two screws along the top edge of the light switch, lift the switch slightly, pull the top edge of the switch out and remove it from the dash. Lever over the locking catch, and disconnect the wiring connector as the switch is withdrawn (see illustrations). No further disassembly of the switch is possible.

12   Installation is the reverse of removal.

HAZARD WARNING SWITCH AND CENTRAL LOCKING SWITCH

▶ **Refer to illustration 4.16**

13   On manual transmission models, carefully unclip the shift lever

boot from the center console and fold it back over the lever.

14   On models with an automatic transmission, carefully pry up the selector lever boot complete with plastic surrounding trim.

15   Remove the rear ashtray/storage tray, then remove the four screws (two at the front, two at the rear) securing the center console (see Chapter 11 if necessary), lift up the gear/selector lever surround trim.

16   Lift the front edge of the rear center console, and press the switch(es) from place. Disconnect the wiring connectors as the switch(es) are removed (see illustration).

17   Installation is the reverse of removal.

ELECTRIC WINDOW SWITCHES

▶ **Refer to illustrations 4.18 and 4.20**

18   Unclip the gear lever/selector lever boot from the surrounding trim, and pull it up to expose the trim retaining screws (see illustration). Note that on automatic transmission models, the boot should be lifted with the adjacent trim from the center console panel (see Chapter 7B).

19   Remove the two retaining screws and lift up the rear of the trim panel.

20   Press in the locking tabs and remove the switch(es) from the panel (see illustration). Disconnect the wiring connector(s) as the switch is withdrawn.

21   Installation is the reversal of removal.

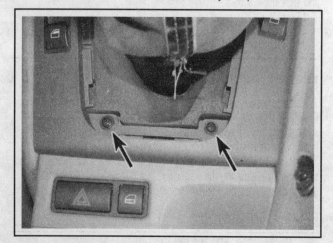

4.18 Remove the trim retaining screws

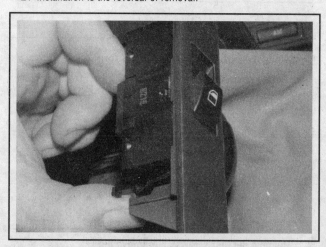

4.20 Press in the locking tabs and remove the switch

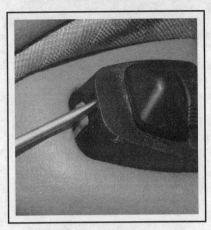

4.22 Carefully pry the mirror switch from the armrest

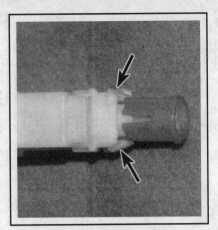

4.28 With the red sleeve fully extended, squeeze together the retaining clips

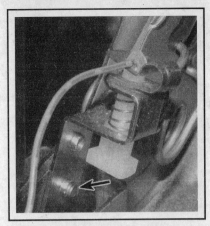

4.44 Remove the screw and remove the parking brake warning switch

EXTERIOR MIRROR SWITCH

▶ **Refer to illustration 4.22**

22 Starting at the front edge, carefully pry the switch out from the armrest (see illustration).
23 Disconnect the wiring connector and remove the switch.
24 Installation is the reverse of removal.

CRUISE CONTROL CLUTCH SWITCH

▶ **Refer to illustration 4.28**

25 Remove the driver's side lower dash panel retaining screws then unclip the panel and remove it from the vehicle. Note their installed positions and disconnect any wiring connectors as the panel is withdrawn.
26 Disconnect the wiring connector from the switch.
27 Depress the clutch pedal, and pull the switch red sleeve out to its fully extended position.
28 Depress the retaining clips and slide the switch out of position (see illustration).
29 Installation is the reverse of removal.

HEATED REAR WINDOW SWITCH

Models with automatic air conditioning

30 On these models the switch is an integral part of the control unit and cannot be replaced. If the switch is faulty seek the advice of a BMW dealer.

Other models

31 On these models the switch is an integral part of the heater control panel printed circuit.
32 Remove the heater control panel as described in Chapter 3.
33 Disconnect the switch wiring connector, release the retaining clips and pull the switch from the panel.
34 Installation is the reverse of removal. Check the operation of the switch before installation the control panel to the dash.

HEATER BLOWER MOTOR SWITCH

Models with automatic air conditioning

35 On these models the switch is an integral part of the control unit and cannot be replaced separately.

Other models

36 Remove the heater control panel as described in Chapter 3.
37 Remove the retaining screws then unclip the switch from the rear of the control panel and remove it.
38 Installation is the reverse of removal. Check the operation of the switch before installing the control panel to the dash.

AIR CONDITIONING SYSTEM SWITCHES

39 Refer to steps 35 to 38.

HEATED SEAT, ELECTRIC REAR SUN BLIND AND TRACTION CONTROL (ASC+T) SWITCHES

40 Remove the storage compartment from the center console.
41 Disconnect the wiring connector then depress the retaining clips and slide the switch out from the panel.
42 Installation is the reverse of removal.

PARKING BRAKE WARNING SWITCH

▶ **Refer to illustration 4.44**

43 Remove the rear section of the center console as described in Chapter 11 to gain access to the parking brake lever.
44 Disconnect the wiring connector from the warning light switch then remove the screw and remove the switch (see illustration).
45 Installation is the reverse of removal. Check the operation of the switch before installing the center console, the warning light should illuminate between the first and second clicks of the ratchet mechanism.

BRAKE LIGHT SWITCH

46 Refer to Chapter 9.

4.49 Pry the switch from the steering wheel

4.50a Remove the switch carrier upper screws . . .

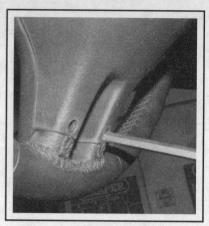

4.50b . . . and lower screws

INTERIOR LIGHT SWITCHES

47 The function of the courtesy light switches is incorporated into the door/trunk lid/tailgate lock assembly. To remove the relevant lock refer to Chapter 11.

STEERING WHEEL SWITCHES

48 Two different types of steering wheels are used on the E46 3-Series range. Either a Multifunction steering wheel, or a Sports steering wheel. To remove the switches, remove the driver's airbag as described in Section 25, then proceed under the relevant heading.

Multifunction steering wheel

▶ **Refer to illustration 4.49**

49 Carefully pry the switch from the steering wheel, and disconnect the switch wiring connectors (see illustration). Note that the horn switch is integral with the airbag unit.

Sports steering wheel

▶ **Refer to illustrations 4.50a and 4.50b**

50 Remove the four retaining screws (two securing the upper section and two securing the lower section), and unclip the switch carrier panel from the steering wheel (see illustrations). Disconnect the wiring connector as the panel with withdrawn.

ELECTRIC SUNROOF SWITCH

▶ **Refer to illustrations 4.51 and 4.52**

51 Depress the clip at the rear of the switch, and pull the switch from the panel (see illustration).
52 Disconnect the switch wiring connector then depress the retaining clips and slide the switch out of position (see illustration).
53 Installation is the reverse of removal.

IGNITION SWITCH/STEERING COLUMN LOCK

54 Refer to Chapter 10.

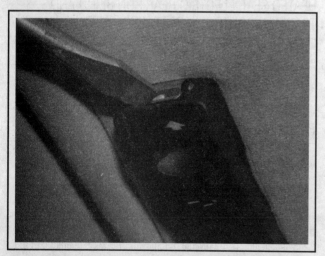

4.51 Press-in the retaining clip and pry the switch from the panel

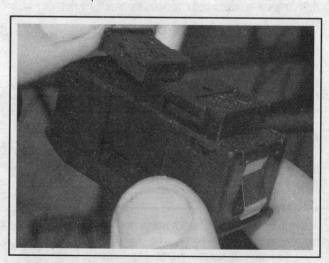

4.52 Disconnect the switch wiring connector

5   Bulbs (exterior lights) - replacement

GENERAL

1   Whenever a bulb is replaced, note the following points.

a) Remember that if the light has just been in use, the bulb may be extremely hot.

b) Always check the bulb contacts and holder, ensuring that there is clean metal-to-metal contact between the bulb and its terminals. Clean off any corrosion or dirt before installing a new bulb.

c) Wherever bayonet-type bulbs are installed, ensure that the contacts bear firmly against the bulb contact.

d) Always ensure that the new bulb is of the correct rating and that it is completely clean before installing it; this applies particularly to headlight/fog light bulbs.

HEADLIGHT

Halogen (conventional) bulbs

▶ **Refer to illustrations 5.2, 5.3 and 5.4**

2   Disconnect the wiring connector from the rear of the bulb holder (see illustration).

3   Squeeze in the retaining clips, turn the bulb holder assembly counterclockwise and remove it from the rear of the headlight (see illustration). To improve access to the left-hand headlight, remove the air filter housing (see Chapter 4).

4   Pull the bulb straight out from the holder (see illustration).

5   When handling the new bulb, use a tissue or clean cloth to avoid touching the glass with the fingers; moisture and oil from the skin can cause blackening and rapid failure of this type of bulb. If the glass is accidentally touched, wipe it clean using rubbing alcohol.

6   Push the new bulb into the holder, ensuring that the bulb's contacts align with the corresponding slots in the bulb holder.

7   Install the bulb holder to the rear of the headlight, rotating it clockwise until the retaining clips lock. Reconnect the wiring connector.

Xenon bulbs

▶ **Refer to illustration 5.10**

8   On models equipped with Xenon bulbs, due to the potential high voltages involved, disconnect the battery negative lead as described in Chapter 5, Section 1. To improve access to the left-hand headlight, remove the air filter housing as described in Chapter 4.

9   Pull the plastic cover from the rear of the headlight.

10 Rotate the bulb igniter unit on the rear of the bulb counterclockwise and disconnect it (see illustration).

11 Twist the bulb retaining ring counterclockwise and remove it, with the bulb, from the headlight.

12 Install the new bulb to the headlight, and secure it in place with the retaining ring.

13 Install the igniter to the rear of the bulb, turning it clockwise to secure it.

14 Install the cover to the rear of the unit. Where necessary, install the air filter housing.

15 Reconnect the battery negative lead as described in Chapter 5, Section 1.

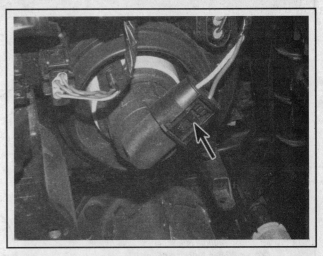

5.2 Disconnect the headlight bulb wiring connector

5.3 Squeeze together the retaining clips, and rotate the bulb holder counterclockwise

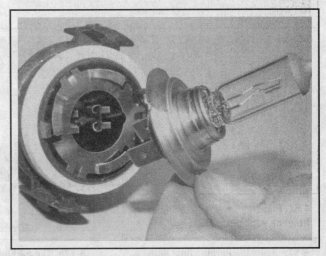

5.4 The headlight bulb is a push-fit in the bulb holder

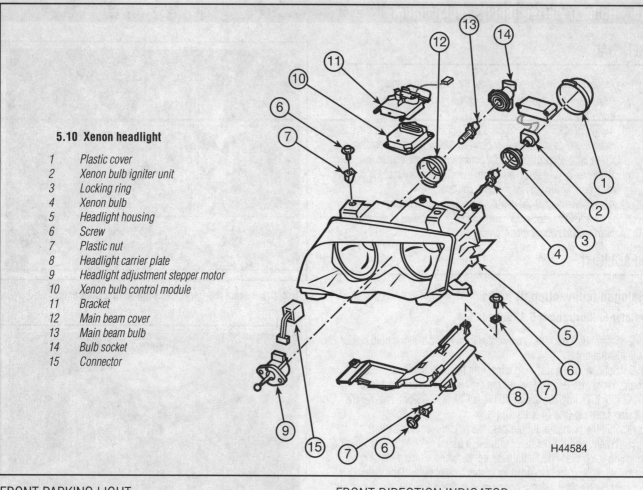

5.10 Xenon headlight

1 Plastic cover
2 Xenon bulb igniter unit
3 Locking ring
4 Xenon bulb
5 Headlight housing
6 Screw
7 Plastic nut
8 Headlight carrier plate
9 Headlight adjustment stepper motor
10 Xenon bulb control module
11 Bracket
12 Main beam cover
13 Main beam bulb
14 Bulb socket
15 Connector

H44584

FRONT PARKING LIGHT

▶ **Refer to illustrations 5.17a and 5.17b**

16 To improve access to the left-hand headlight, remove the air filter housing (see Chapter 4).

17 Rotate the bulb holder counterclockwise and withdraw it from the headlight unit. The bulb is of the capless type and is a push-fit in the holder (see illustrations).

18 Installation is the reverse of removal.

FRONT DIRECTION INDICATOR

▶ **Refer to illustrations 5.19a, 5.19b, 5.19c and 5.21**

19 On all except Coupe models, insert a screwdriver through the hole in the inner fender top, press down and release the light unit retaining clip. Withdraw the direction indicator light from the fender. On Coupe models, the light unit is retained by a single screw (see illustrations).

20 Disconnect the wiring connector, and twist the bulb holder coun-

5.17a Twist the parking light bulb holder counterclockwise and remove it

5.17b The parking light bulb is a push-fit

5.19a Insert a screwdriver through the hole in the fender . . .

5.19b . . . to release the indicator retaining clip (except Coupe)

5.19c On Coupe models, remove the screw

5.21 Push in and twist the bulb counterclockwise

terclockwise to remove it from the light unit.

21 The bulb is a bayonet fitting in the holder. Push the bulb in slightly, then rotate it counterclockwise and pull it from the holder (see illustration).

22 Installation is a reverse of the removal procedure making sure the light unit is securely retained by its retaining clip/screw as applicable.

SIDE MARKER/TURN SIGNAL LIGHT

▶ **Refer to illustrations 5.23 and 5.24**

23 Using finger pressure, push the lens gently forwards. Pull out the rear edge of the lens and withdraw it from the fender (see illustration).

24 Rotate the bulb holder counterclockwise and pull it from the lens. Pull the capless bulb from the holder (see illustration).

25 Installation is a reverse of the removal procedure.

FRONT FOG LIGHT

Sedan and Sport Wagon models

▶ **Refer to illustrations 5.26, 5.28 and 5.30**

26 Using a wooden or plastic tool, carefully pry the fog light from the bumper starting at the inside edge (see illustration). Disconnect the wiring connector as the unit is withdrawn.

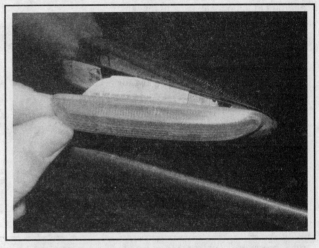

5.23 Push the side marker/turn signal lens forward, and pull the rear edge out

27 Rotate the bulb holder counterclockwise and remove it from the light.

28 The bulb is integral with the bulb holder (see illustration).

29 When handling the new bulb, use a tissue or clean cloth to avoid touching the glass with the fingers; moisture and grease from the skin can cause blackening and rapid failure of this type of bulb. If the glass

5.24 Pull the capless bulb from the side repeater bulb holder

5.26 Carefully pry the fog light from the bumper

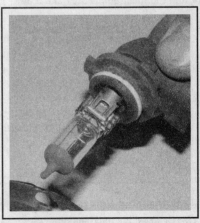

5.28 The fog light bulb is integral with the bulb holder

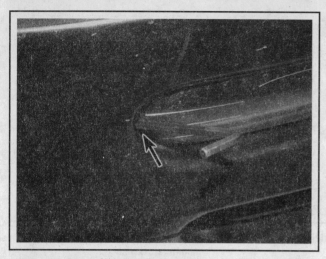

5.30 To adjust the fog light aim, insert an Allen key into the aperture at the outside edge of the lens

5.31 Release the catches and remove the fog light trim

5.34 Rotate the adjusting screw to aim the fog light

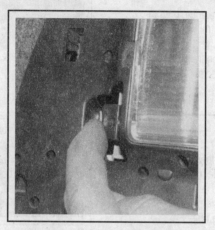

5.35a Release the retaining clip (models up to 09/01) . . .

H44585

5.35b . . . or remove the fastener (models from 10/01)

is accidentally touched, wipe it clean using rubbing alcohol.

30 Installation is the reverse of removal. If necessary, adjust the aim of the light by rotating the adjusting screw adjacent to the lens (see illustration).

Coupe models

▶ **Refer to illustrations 5.31 and 5.34**

31 Lever out the catches, and remove the bumper trim from around the fog lights (see illustration).

32 Remove the screws and remove the fog light. Disconnect the wiring connector as the unit is withdrawn.

33 Rotate the bulb holder counterclockwise, and pull the bulb from the holder.

34 Installation is the reverse of removal. If necessary, adjust the aim of the light by rotating the adjusting screw adjacent to the lens (see illustration).

REAR LIGHT CLUSTER

Body-mounted lights - Sedan/Coupe

▶ **Refer to illustrations 5.35a, 5.35b and 5.36**

35 From inside the vehicle luggage compartment, release the retain-

ing clip (models up to September 2001) or remove the fastener (models from October 2001) and remove the bulb holder from the rear of the light cluster (see illustrations).

36 Press the relevant bulb in slightly, twist it counterclockwise, and remove it from the bulb holder (see illustration).

➡**Note: If replacing the double element stop/tail bulb, the bayonet pins are offset, and the bulb will only fit one way around.**

37 Installation is the reverse of removal.

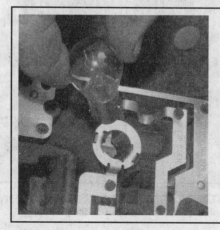

5.36 Press the bulb in, twist it counterclockwise and remove it

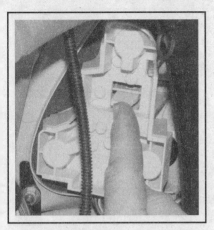

5.39 Release the clip and lift the bulb holder assembly

5.42 Pry out the trunk lid trim retaining clips

5.43 Release the retaining clip and remove the bulb holder

Body-mounted lights - Sport Wagon

▶ **Refer to illustration 5.39**

38 Fold back the flap in the luggage compartment to expose the bulb holder. To improve access to the left-hand light, remove the warning triangle from its location.

39 Release the retaining clip, and lift the bulb holder assembly slightly (see illustration).

5.44 Push in the bulb, and rotate it counterclockwise

40 Press the relevant bulb in slightly, twist it counterclockwise, and remove it from the bulb holder.

41 Installation is the reverse of removal.

Trunk lid-mounted lights - Sedan/Coupe

▶ **Refer to illustration 5.42, 5.43 and 5.44**

42 Pry out the two clips and partially release the trunk lid trim panel behind the light cluster (see illustration).

43 Release the retaining clip, and remove the bulb holder from the trunk lid (see illustration).

44 Press the relevant bulb in slightly, twist it counterclockwise, and remove it from the bulb holder (see illustration).

45 Installation is the reverse of removal.

Tailgate lights - Sport Wagon

▶ **Refer to illustrations 5.47, 5.48 and 5.49**

46 Carefully pry the luggage compartment light unit from the tailgate trim panel. Disconnect the wiring connector as the unit is removed.

47 Pry up the small piece of trim at the top of the panel (see illustration).

48 Remove the two retaining screws at the upper edge, and carefully release the trim panel retaining clips (see illustration). Lift the panel from place.

5.47 Pry up the trim at the top of the tailgate panel

5.48 Remove the two screws

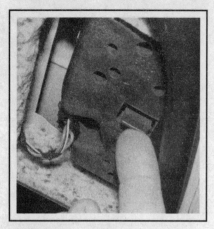

5.49 Release the bulb holder retaining clip

5.53 Slide the retaining clips away from the high-mounted stop-light

5.55 Pry off the license plate light lens

49 Disconnect the rear light cluster wiring connector, release the retaining clip and remove the bulb holder (see illustration).

50 Press the relevant bulb in slightly, twist it counterclockwise, and remove it from the bulb holder.

51 Installation is the reverse of removal.

High-mounted stop-light

▶ **Refer to illustration 5.53**

52 Carefully pull down the front edge, then slide the cover forward and remove it. Two types of cover may be used. The one-piece cover has two patches of Velcro at the front edge, while the split type cover has two push-in clips at the front edge.

53 Slide off the two retaining clips, and remove the light unit (see illustration). Disconnect the wiring connector as the light is withdrawn. The high-mounted stop-light is an LED strip. If a fault develops, consult your local BMW dealer or specialist.

54 Installation is the reverse of removal, ensuring that the lugs at the rear of the cover engage correctly with the corresponding locating holes.

LICENSE PLATE LIGHT

▶ **Refer to illustration 5.55**

55 Using a small screwdriver from the inboard end, carefully pry out the light lens, and remove it from the trunk lid/tailgate (see illustration).

56 The bulb is of the "festoon" type, and can be pried from the contacts.

57 Installation is the reverse of removal, making sure the bulb is securely held in position by the contacts.

---

6   Bulbs (interior lights) - replacement

✳✳ CAUTION:

These vehicles are equipped with the Central Body Electronic (ZKE-V) system. Each individual system is linked to a centralized control module that allows efficient and accurate troubleshooting. This control module governs the windshield wipers and washers, the central locking and anti-theft system, the power windows, the interior lights, the alarm system and the electronic consumer sleep mode. In the event of a malfunction with this system, have the vehicle diagnosed by a dealer service department or other qualified automotive repair facility, as special test equipment is required.

6.2a Carefully pry the courtesy light from the trim panel

GENERAL

1   Refer to Section 5, Step 1.

COURTESY/INTERIOR LIGHTS

▶ **Refer to illustrations 6.2a, 6.2b and 6.2c**

2   Using a small, flat-bladed screwdriver, carefully pry the light unit out of position. When removing the front central interior light or rear central interior light (Sport Wagon models) unit, pry the rear edge of the unit down and pull the light unit free. Rotate the bulb holder pull the capless bulb from the holders (see illustrations).

3   Push the new bulb(s) into the holder(s), and install them in to the light unit. Install the light unit. Note that the front edge of the front central light unit must be installed first, then push the rear edge into place.

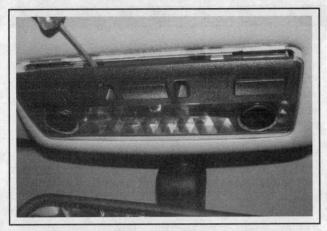

6.2b Pry the main interior light assembly from the headliner

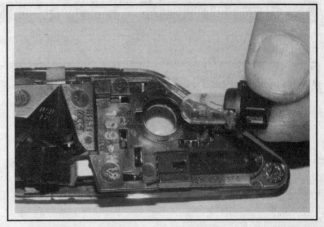

6.2c Rotate the bulb holder counterclockwise and pull out the capless bulb

FOOTWELL LIGHT

▶ **Refer to illustration 6.5**

4   Carefully lever the light lens out from the panel.
5   Pry the festoon bulb from the contacts (see illustration).

❋❋ WARNING:

Only pry on the terminals at the ends of the bulb, not on the glass.

6   Install the new bulb into position and install the lens to the light unit.

LUGGAGE COMPARTMENT LIGHT

7   Refer to steps 4 to 6.

INSTRUMENT ILLUMINATION/WARNING LIGHTS

8   The instrument panel is illuminated by a series of LEDs, which cannot be replaced.

GLOVE BOX ILLUMINATION BULB

9   Open up the glove box. Using a small flat-bladed screwdriver carefully pry the top of the light assembly and withdraw it. Release the bulb from its contacts.
10 Install the new bulb, ensuring it is securely held in position by the contacts, and clip the light unit back into position.

HEATER CONTROL PANEL ILLUMINATION

Models with automatic air conditioning

11 The heater control panel is illuminated by LEDs which are not serviceable. If a fault develops, have the system checked by a BMW dealer or suitably-equipped specialist.

Other models

12 Pull off the heater control panel knobs then remove the retaining screws and unclip the faceplate from the front of the control unit.
13 Using a pair of pointed-nose pliers, rotate the bulb holder coun-
terclockwise and remove it from the vehicle. On some models the panel is illuminated by LEDs which are not serviceable.
14 Installation is the reverse of removal.

SWITCH ILLUMINATION BULBS

15 All of the switches are equipped with illuminating bulbs/LEDs; some are also equipped with a bulb/LED to show when the circuit concerned is operating. On all switches, these bulbs/LEDs are an integral part of the switch assembly and cannot be obtained separately. Bulb/LED replacement will therefore require the replacement of the complete switch assembly.

ASHTRAY ILLUMINATION BULB

16 Pry up the gear/selector lever surround trim. Remove the two screws at the front of the trim aperture securing the ashtray/storage compartment carrier.
17 Pry up the lower edge of the storage compartment and pull the unit from the dash. Remove the two screws at the top of the storage compartment aperture and pull the carrier from the dash.
18 Disconnect the wiring connector, squeeze together the retaining clips and pull the bulb holder from place. The bulb is integral with the holder.
19 Installation is the reverse of removal.

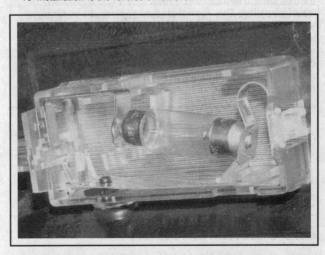

6.5 Carefully pry the festoon bulb from the contacts

7   Exterior light units - removal and installation

HEADLIGHT

▶ **Refer to illustrations 7.3a, 7.3b and 7.5**

1   Remove the relevant direction indicator light (see Step 12).

2   Where applicable, carefully lever out the headlight washer jet from the trim below the headlamp, and pull it out to its stop. With a sharp tug, separate the jet from the washer tube.

3   Unclip the inboard end of the headlight trim, press the trim down slightly to release the center retaining clips, then disengage the outboard end from the front fender (see illustrations). At this point, if required, the headlight lens can be removed by releasing the retaining clips around its circumference.

4   Note their installed positions, and disconnect all wiring connectors from the rear of the headlight.

5   Each headlight is retained by four screws - two hexagon head, and two Torx screws. Loosen and remove the headlight retaining screws (see illustration).

➡**Note: As the screws are removed, do not allow the plastic retaining clips to rotate. If necessary retain the clips with a suitable open-ended wrench.**

7.3a   Unclip the inboard end . . .

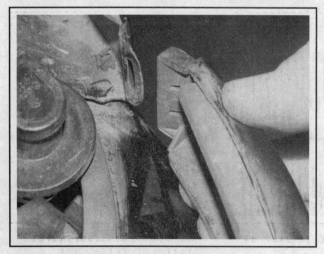

7.3b   . . . and outboard end of the headlight trim

6   Remove the headlight unit from the vehicle.

7   Installation is a direct reverse of the removal procedure. Lightly tighten the retaining screws and check the alignment of the headlight with the bumper and hood. Once the light unit is correctly positioned, securely tighten the retaining screws and check the headlight beam alignment using the information given in Section 8.

XENON HEADLIGHT CONTROL UNIT

8   Remove the relevant headlight as described earlier in this Section.

9   Remove the two retaining screws, slide the control unit to the rear of the headlight and remove it (see illustration 5.10).

10   If required, the control unit can be separated from the mounting bracket by removing the two securing screws.

11   Installation is the reverse of removal.

FRONT DIRECTION INDICATOR LIGHT

12   Insert a screwdriver down through the hole in the inner fender, and release the indicator light retaining clip (see illustrations 5.19a and 5.19b). On Coupe models, the light is secured by a single screw (see illustration 5.19c). Slide the light forward and disconnect the wiring connector from the light unit.

13   Installation is a reverse of the removal procedure, making sure the light retaining clip engages correctly or the screw is securely tightened.

FRONT INDICATOR SIDE MARKER

14   Using finger pressure, push the side repeater lens gently forwards. Pull out the rear edge of the lens and withdraw it from the fender (see illustration 5.23). Disconnect the wiring connector as the unit is withdrawn.

15   Installation is a reverse of the removal procedure.

FRONT FOG LIGHT

Sedan and Sport Wagon models

16   Using a wooden or plastic tool, carefully lever the fog light from

7.5   Remove the headlight retaining screws

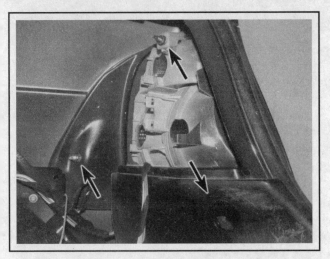

7.23 The rear light is secured by three nuts

the bumper (see illustration 5.26). Disconnect the wiring connector as the unit is withdrawn.

17 Installation is the reverse of removal.

Coupe models

18 Lever out the catches, and remove the bumper trim from around the fog lights (see illustration 5.31).

19 Remove the screws and remove the fog light. Disconnect the wiring connector as the unit is withdrawn.

20 Installation is the reverse of removal.

REAR LIGHT CLUSTER

Body-mounted lights - Sedan/Coupe

▶ **Refer to illustration 7.23**

21 From inside the vehicle luggage compartment, release the retaining clip (models up to September 2001) or remove the faster (models from October 2001) and remove the bulb holder from the rear of the light cluster (see illustrations 5.35a and 5.35b).

22 Release the retaining clips and partially detach the luggage compartment side trim panel around the area of the light cluster (see Chapter 11, Section 27, if necessary).

23 Remove the three retaining nuts and remove the cluster form the fender (see illustration).

24 Installation is the reverse of removal.

Body-mounted lights - Sport Wagon

▶ **Refer to illustration 7.27**

25 Fold back the flap in the luggage compartment to expose the bulb holder. To improve access to the left-hand light, remove the warning triangle from its location.

26 Release the retaining clip, and lift the bulb-holder assembly slightly (see illustration 5.39).

27 Remove the three retaining nuts, and remove the light cluster (see illustration).

28 Installation is the reverse of removal.

Trunk lid-mounted lights - Sedan/Coupe

▶ **Refer to illustration 7.31**

29 Pry out the two clips and partially release the trunk lid trim panel behind the light cluster (see illustration 5.42).

30 Release the retaining clip, and remove the bulb holder from the trunk lid (see illustration 5.43).

31 Remove the securing nut, remove the plastic retainer, and remove the light cluster (see illustration). Note that the edge of the light unit wraps around the edge of the trunk lid.

32 Installation is the reverse of removal.

Tailgate-mounted lights - Sport Wagon

▶ **Refer to illustration 7.37**

33 Carefully pry luggage compartment light unit from the tailgate trim panel. Disconnect the wiring connector as the unit is removed.

34 Pry up the small piece of trim at the top of the panel (see illustration 5.47).

35 Remove the two retaining screws at the upper edge, and carefully release the trim panel retaining clips (see illustration 5.48). Lift the panel from place.

36 Disconnect the rear light cluster wiring connector, release the retaining clip and remove the bulb holder (see illustration 5.49).

37 Loosen the securing nut, press the lock lever in the direction of the light cluster and remove it (see illustration).

38 Installation is the reverse of removal.

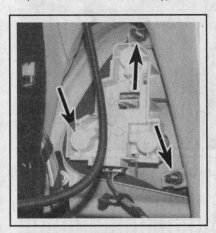

7.27 Remove the three nuts and remove the light unit

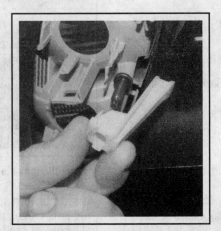

7.31 Remove the nut and remove the plastic retainer

7.37 Remove the nut and press the lever towards the light cluster

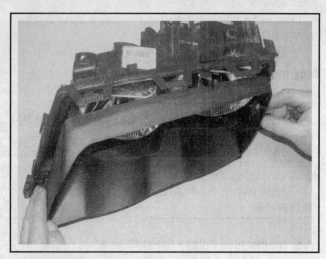

7.43 Pull the "frame" from the headlight

7.46 The headlight range control motor is retained by two screws

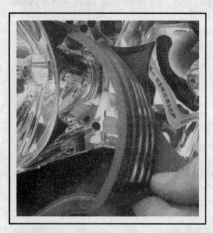

7.47a Remove the black plastic trim . . .

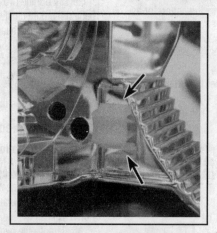

7.47b . . . then squeeze together the retaining clips . . .

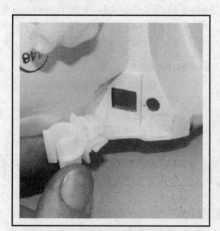

7.47c . . . and remove the control motor socket from the insert

License plate light

39 Using a small screwdriver, carefully pry out the light lens, and remove it from the trunk lid/tailgate (see illustration 5.55). Disconnect the wiring connector as the unit is withdrawn.

40 Installation is the reverse of removal.

HEADLIGHT RANGE CONTROL MOTORS

▶ **Refer to illustrations 7.43, 7.46, 7.47a, 7.47b, 7.47c and 7.48**

41 Remove the headlight lens as described in Steps 1 to 3 earlier in this Section.

42 Remove both bulb holders from the rear of the headlight as described in Section 5.

43 Carefully pull the headlight "frame" towards the front (see illustration).

44 Remove the protective rubber seals around the bulb holders from the rear of the unit.

45 Mark its original position and counting the number of rotations, turn the central adjuster wheel clockwise (maybe 20 to 30 rotations) until the top of the insert is released from the guide slot, then the outer adjuster piece can released from the insert. Carefully disengage the range control motor rod from the socket on the rear of the insert.

7.48 Clip the outer adjuster piece onto the insert

Maneuver the insert from the headlight.

46 Remove the retaining screws, disconnect the wiring connector, and remove the range control motor (see illustration).

47 When installing the headlight insert, release the retaining clips and remove the black plastic trim from the center of the headlight

insert, then squeeze together the retaining lugs, and remove the control motor socket from the insert (see illustrations). Do not install the black plastic trim yet.

48 Locate the socket on the control motor rod, clip the outer adjuster piece onto the insert, and aligning the central adjusting piece with the corresponding slot in the headlamp shell, rotate the central adjusting

wheel back to its original position. Push the insert onto the range control motor socket until its clips into place - guide the socket into place from the front of the insert (see illustration). Install the black plastic trim.

49 When completed, have the headlight beam aim checked, and if necessary adjusted.

8 Headlight beam alignment - general information

♦ Refer to illustration 8.2

1 Accurate adjustment of the headlight beam is only possible using optical beam setting equipment and this work should therefore be carried out by a BMW dealer or qualified repair shop.

2 For reference, the headlights can be adjusted by rotating the adjuster screws on the top of the headlight unit (see illustration). The outer adjuster alters the horizontal position of the beam while the center adjuster alters the vertical aim of the beam.

3 Some models have an electrically-operated headlight beam adjustment system which is controlled through the switch in the dash. On these models ensure that the switch is set to the off position before adjusting the headlight aim.

8.2 Headlight beam adjustment screws

9 Instrument cluster - removal and installation

♦ Refer to illustrations 9.3 and 9.4

1 Disconnect the cable from the negative terminal of the battery (see Chapter 5, Section 1).

2 Move the steering column down as far as it will go, and extend it completely.

3 Loosen and remove the two retaining Torx screws from the top of the instrument cluster, and carefully pull the top of the cluster from the dash (see illustration).

4 Lift up the retaining clips then disconnect the wiring connectors

and remove the instrument cluster from the vehicle (see illustration).

5 Installation is the reverse of removal, making sure the instrument cluster wiring is correctly reconnected and securely held in position by any retaining clips. On completion, reconnect the battery and check the operation of the cluster warning lights to ensure that they are functioning correctly.

➡**Note: If the instrument cluster has been replaced, the new unit must be coded to match the vehicle. This can only be carried out by a BMW dealer or suitably-equipped specialist.**

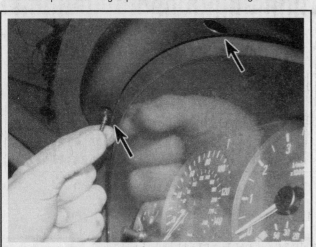

9.3 Remove the two screws from the top of the instrument panel

9.4 Lift the retaining clips and disconnect the wiring connectors

10 Instrument cluster components - removal and installation

Through its connections, via "bus" networks with most of the systems and sensors within the vehicle, the instrument cluster is the control and information center for the BMW 3-Series models. The "K-bus" is connected to the supplementary restraint system, exterior and interior lights, rain sensor, heating/air conditioning, and the central body electrical system. The "CAN-bus" (Controlled Area Network) is connected to the engine management, transmission management, and the ABS/traction control/dynamic stability control systems. The "D-bus" is connected to the diagnostic link connector and EOBD (European On-Board Diagnostics) connector.

The speedometer displays the vehicle's road speed from information supplied by the ABS ECM, generated from the left rear wheel speed sensor.

At the time of writing, no individual components are available for the instrument cluster and therefore the cluster must be treated as a sealed unit. If there is a fault with one of the instruments, remove the cluster as described in Section 9 and take it to your BMW dealer for testing. They have access to a special diagnostic tester which will be able to locate the fault and will then be able to advise you on the best course of action.

11 Rain sensor - removal and installation

▶ Refer to illustrations 11.1 and 11.3

1 The rain sensor is incorporated into the front face of the interior mirror mounting base. Press up on the lower end of the mounting trim, and press the two halves of the mounting trim apart at the base, and release the trim retaining clips (see illustration).

2 With the trim removed, disconnect the sensor wiring connector

3 Pull out the two sensor retaining clips, and pull the sensor to the rear (see illustration).

4 Installation is the reverse of removal.

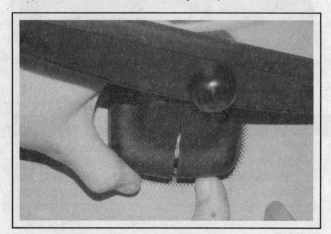

11.1 Press the two halves of the trim apart

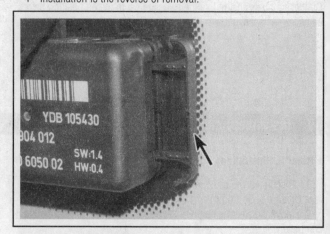

11.3 Pull out the clip on each side and remove the sensor

12 Suspension height sensor - removal and installation

▶ Refer to illustration 12.3

1 Vehicles equipped with Xenon headlights are also equipped with automatic headlight adjustment. Ride sensors at the front and rear suspension provide information on the suspension ride height, while the headlight range control motors alter the headlight beam angle as necessary. The sensors are installed between the suspension subframes, and lower arms. To access the sensors, raise the relevant end of the vehicle, and support securely on jackstands. Where applicable remove the engine splash shield.

2 Remove the nut securing the control rod to the sensor arm, and disconnect the rod.

3 Remove the two mounting nuts and remove the sensor. Disconnect the wiring connector as the sensor is withdrawn (see illustration).

4 Installation is the reverse of the removal procedure, ensuring all the wiring connectors are securely reconnected.

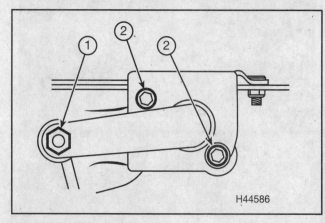

12.3 Suspension height sensor

1   Control rod nut   2   Height sensor nuts

13 Tire pressure control system (RDC) - information and component replacement

INFORMATION

1 A tire pressure monitoring system (RDC) is available as an option on most of the 3-Series range. The system consists of a transmitter in each wheel, attached to the base of the inflation valve, a receiver behind the wheel arch liner adjacent to each wheel, and a control module behind the passenger side glove box. A warning light in the instrument cluster, alerts the driver should the tire pressure deviate from the set pressure. Note that due to the weight of the wheel-mounted transmitter unit, it is essential that any new tires are balanced correctly before use.

COMPONENT REPLACEMENT

2 Disconnect the cable from the negative terminal of the battery (see Chapter 5, Section 1).

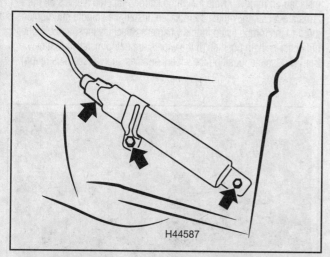

H44587

13.8 Disconnect the wiring connector, remove the two screws, and remove the receiver

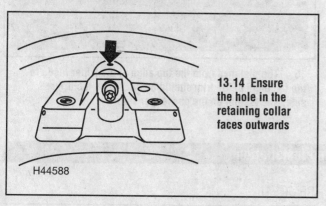

13.14 Ensure the hole in the retaining collar faces outwards

H44588

Control module

3 Remove the passenger side glove box as described in Chapter 11, Section 27.

4 Carefully unclip the plastic panel behind the glove box.

5 Unlock the wiring connector catch, and disconnect it. Depress the retaining clip and slide the control unit from the carrier.

6 Installation is the reverse of removal. Reprogram the system's reference pressure settings as described in the Owner's Handbook.

Receiver

▶ **Refer to illustration 13.8**

7 Loosen the wheel lug nuts, raise the vehicle and support it securely on jackstands, then remove the wheel. Release the retaining clips/screws and remove the wheel arch liner.

8 Disconnect the receiver wiring connector, remove the two retaining screws, and withdraw the unit (see illustration). Note that the right-hand side front and the rear receivers are mounted on the inside of the front section of the wheel arch liner.

9 Installation is the reverse of removal.

Transmitter

▶ **Refer to illustration 13.14**

10 A transmitter is located on the base of each inflation valve. Have the relevant tire removed by a suitably-equipped specialist.

11 Remove the Torx screw and slide the transmitter from the base of the valve. Note the following precautions:

a) *Do not clean the transmitter with compressed air.*
b) *Do not clean the wheel rim (tire removed) with high-pressure cleaning equipment.*
c) *Do not use solvent to clean the transmitter.*
d) *If tire sealing fluid has been used, the transmitter and valve must be replaced.*
e) *It is not possible to use the valve with the transmitter removed.*

12 Insert a rod into the hole in the valve body retaining collar, unscrew the body and remove the valve.

13 Install the new valve body (with collar) into the transmitter, only finger-tighten the Torx screw at this stage.

14 Insert the assembly into the hole in the wheel, ensuring that the hole in the valve body retaining collar faces outwards. Tighten the valve body nut, using a rod in the hole in the collar to counterhold the nut (see illustration).

15 Tighten the transmitter Torx screw to the torque listed in this Chapter's Specifications.

16 Have the tire installed.

14 Horn(s) - removal and installation

1   The horns are located behind the left- and right-hand ends of the front bumper.

2   To gain access to the horn(s) from below, apply the parking brake then jack up the front of the vehicle and support it on jackstands. Remove the retaining screws and remove the lower front section of the wheel arch liner. Unclip and remove the brake disc cooling duct.

3   Remove the retaining nut/bolt and remove the horn, disconnecting its wiring connectors as they become accessible.

4   Installation is the reverse of removal.

15 Wiper arm - removal and installation

REMOVAL

▶ **Refer to illustration 15.3**

1   Operate the wiper motor then switch it off so that the wiper arm returns to the "at rest" position.

2   Stick a piece of masking tape along the edge of the wiper blade to use as an alignment aid on installation.

3   Pry off the wiper arm spindle nut cover then remove the spindle nut. Lift the blade off the glass and pull the wiper arm off its spindle. If necessary the arm can be levered off the spindle using a suitable flat-bladed screwdriver or suitable puller (see illustration).

➡**Note: If both windshield wiper arms are to be removed at the same time, mark them for identification; the arms are not interchangeable.**

15.3 Remove the wiper spindle nut and pull or pry off the wiper arm

INSTALLATION

▶ **Refer to illustration 15.4**

4   Ensure that the wiper arm and splines are clean and dry then install the arm to the spindle, aligning the wiper blade with the tape installed on removal. Note that if the knurled-tapered sleeves on the arms are loose, they must be replaced. Install the spindle nut, tightening it to the torque listed in this Chapter's Specifications, and clip the nut cover back in position. If the wipers are being installed to a new front windshield, position the wipers arms as shown (see illustration).

15.4 The distance from the top edge of the wiper blade to the top edge of the trim should be 44 mm on the driver's side, and 24 mm on the passenger side

16 Windshield wiper motor and linkage - removal and installation

⁜⁜ **CAUTION:**

These vehicles are equipped with the Central Body Electronic (ZKE-V) system. Each individual system is linked to a centralized control module that allows efficient and accurate troubleshooting. This control module governs the windshield wipers and washers, the central locking and anti-theft system, the power windows, the interior lights, the alarm system and the electronic consumer sleep mode. In the event of a malfunction with this system, have the vehicle diagnosed by a dealer service department or other qualified automotive repair facility, as special test equipment is required.

REMOVAL

Front windshield wiper motor

▶ **Refer to illustrations 16.3a, 16.3b, 16.9 and 16.10**

1   Remove the wiper arms as described in the previous Section.

2   Open the hood.

3   Remove the heater air inlet housing as follows (see illustrations):

16.3a Lift the rubber strip and remove the two fasteners

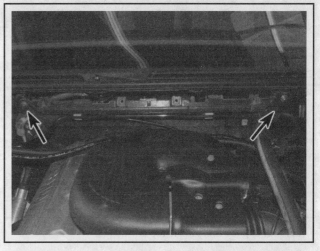

16.3b Remove the two screws and remove the inlet ducting

16.7 Remove the screw securing the wiper linkage

16.9 Maneuver the linkage from the firewall

a) Rotate the three fasteners 90-degrees counterclockwise and remove the in-cabin air filter cover from the rear of the engine compartment (see Chapter 1). Pull the filter forward and remove it.

b) Remove the four retaining clips and thread the cable out of the ducting.

c) Unscrew the four screws and pull the filter housing forwards and remove it.

d) Pull up the rubber strip, rotate the two fasteners counterclockwise, and move the dividing panel in the left-hand corner of the engine compartment forward a little.

e) Remove the two screws and remove the inlet ducting upwards and out of the engine compartment.

4   Carefully pull the scuttle panel trim up, releasing it from the retaining clips.

5   Release the two retaining clips, remove the screw and remove the front cover from the heater (see Chapter 3 if necessary).

6   Disconnect the wiper motor wiring connector.

7   Remove the screw securing the linkage assembly to the underside of the scuttle panel (see illustration).

8   Unscrew the large nuts from the wiper spindles and remove the washers.

9   Maneuver the motor and linkage assembly out of position (see illustration). Recover the rubber grommets from the spindles, inspect them for signs of damage or deterioration, and replace if necessary.

10   If necessary, mark the relative positions of the motor shaft and crank then pry the wiper linkage from the motor balljoint. Unscrew the retaining nut and free the crank from the motor spindle. Unscrew the motor retaining bolts and separate the motor and linkage (see illustration).

16.10 Remove the three bolts and remove the wiper motor

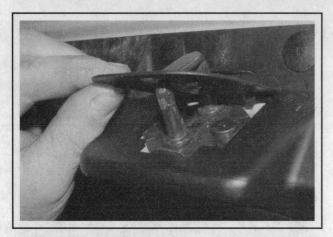

16.14 Unclip the trim around the latch striker

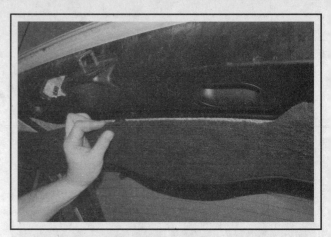

16.15a Remove the trim insert from the inner panel

Rear windshield wiper motor

▶ **Refer to illustrations 16.14, 16.15a, 16.15b, 16.16, 16.18a and 16.18b**

11 Open the tailgate, and carefully pry the luggage compartment light unit from the tailgate trim panel. Disconnect the wiring connector as the unit is removed.

12 Pry up the small piece of trim at the top of the panel (see illustration 5.47).

13 Remove the two retaining screws at the upper edge, and carefully

release the trim panel retaining clips (see illustration 5.48). Lift the panel from place.

14 Unclip the trim around the tailgate latch striker (see illustration).

15 Remove the panel insert from the inner trim panel. Note how the insert engages with the trim panel (see illustrations).

16 Remove the seven screws, release the four retaining clips, and remove the tailgate inner trim panel (see illustration).

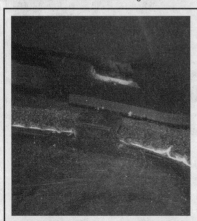

16.15b The trim insert lugs must engage correctly with the holes in the inner panel

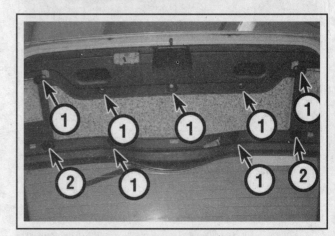

16.16 Release the screws (1) and clips (2)

16.18a Rear wiper motor screws

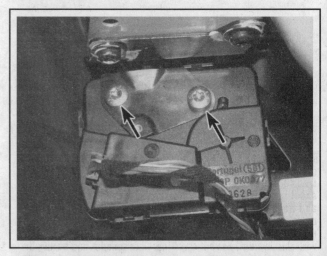

16.18b Remove the screws and remove the window latch from the wiper motor

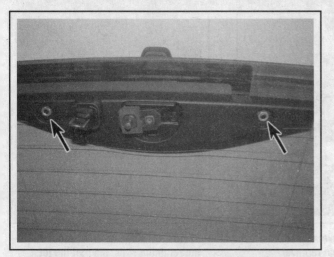

16.20 Pry out the plastic caps and remove the two nuts

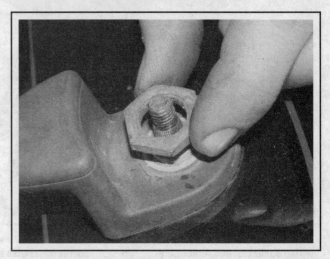

16.21 Loosen and remove the wiper spindle nut

16.22 Remove the nut and remove the housing complete with spindle

17 Disconnect the wiper motor wiring connectors.

18 Make alignment marks where the motor and bracket touch the tailgate, to aid installation. Remove the four screws, and remove the wiper motor. If required, the window latch can be separated from the wiper motor by removing the two retaining screws (see illustrations).

Rear wiper arm spindle and housing

▶ Refer to illustrations 16.20, 16.21 and 16.22

19 Remove the rear wiper arm as described in the previous Section.

20 Open the tailgate, pry out the two plastic caps, and remove the two nuts securing the plastic cover over the spindle (see illustration). Remove the cover.

21 On the outside of the windshield, loosen and remove the wiper arm spindle nut. Recover any washers (see illustration).

22 On the inside of the windshield, remove the retaining nut and maneuver the housing and spindle from position (see illustration). No further disassembly is recommended.

INSTALLATION

23 Installation is the reverse of removal. On completion install the wiper arms as described in Section 15.

17 Windshield/headlight washer system components - removal and installation

❋❋ CAUTION:

These vehicles are equipped with the Central Body Electronic (ZKE-V) system. Each individual system is linked to a centralized control module that allows efficient and accurate troubleshooting. This control module governs the windshield wipers and washers, the central locking and anti-theft system, the power windows, the interior lights, the alarm system and the electronic consumer sleep mode. In the event of a malfunction with this system, have the vehicle diagnosed by a dealer service department or other qualified automotive repair facility, as special test equipment is required.

FRONT WASHER SYSTEM RESERVOIR

1 The windshield washer reservoir is situated in the engine compartment. On models equipped with headlight washers, the reservoir also supplies the headlight washer jets via an additional pump.

2 Empty the contents of the reservoir or be prepared for fluid spillage.

3 Release the heat shield retaining clip, and disconnect the wiring connector(s) from the washer pump(s). Carefully rotate the pump(s) clockwise and pull them up from the reservoir and position them clear.

17.8 Disconnect the washer pump wiring connector and remove the heat shield

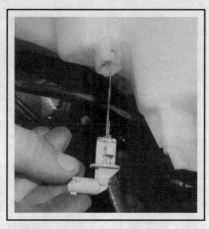

17.11 Rotate the level switch counterclockwise and remove it from the reservoir

17.13a On some models, squeeze the retaining clips and pull the jet down from the hood . . .

Inspect the pump sealing grommet(s) for signs of damage or deterioration and replace if necessary.

4 Disconnect the wiring connector from the reservoir level switch.

5 Loosen and remove the reservoir fastener and lift the reservoir upwards and out of position. Wash off any spilt fluid with cold water.

6 Installation is the reverse of removal. Ensure the locating lugs on the base of the reservoir engage correctly with the corresponding slots in the inner fender. Refill the reservoir and check for leakage.

WINDSHIELD AND HEADLIGHT WASHER PUMPS

▶ **Refer to illustration 17.8**

7 Empty the contents of the reservoir or be prepared for fluid spillage.

8 Release the heat shield retaining clip, and disconnect the wiring connector(s) from the washer pump(s). Carefully rotate the pump(s) clockwise and pull them up from the reservoir. Inspect the pump sealing grommet(s) for signs of damage or deterioration and replace if necessary (see illustration).

9 Installation is the reverse of removal, using a new sealing grommet if the original one shows signs of damage or deterioration. Refill the reservoir and check the pump grommet for leaks.

FRONT WASHER RESERVOIR LEVEL SWITCH

▶ **Refer to illustration 17.11**

10 Remove the reservoir as described earlier in this Section.

11 Rotate the level switch counterclockwise and remove it from the reservoir (see illustration).

12 Installation is the reverse of removal, using a new sealing grommet if the original one shows signs of damage or deterioration. Refill the reservoir and check for leaks.

WINDSHIELD WASHER JETS

▶ **Refer to illustrations 17.13a and 17.13b**

13 On early models, squeeze together the retaining clips and carefully ease the jet out from the hood, taking great care not to damage the paint. On later models disconnect the washer hose(s) and wiring connectors then, working under the hood, push the rear edge of the washer

assembly forward and up, press in the clip at the front edge and remove the washer from the hood (see illustrations).

14 Disconnect the washer hose(s) from the base of the jet. Where necessary, also disconnect the wiring connector from the jet.

15 On installing early models, securely connect the jet to the hose and clip it into position in the hood; where necessary also reconnect the wiring connector. On later models, push the jet into place and reconnect the hose(s) and wiring connectors. Check the operation of the jet. If necessary adjust the nozzles using a pin, aiming one nozzle to a point slightly above the center of the swept area and the other to slightly below the center point to ensure complete coverage.

HEADLIGHT WASHER JETS

▶ **Refer to illustrations 17.17 and 17.19**

16 Using a wooden or plastic lever, carefully pry out the washer jet cover from below the headlight, and pull it out to its stop.

17 With a sharp tug, separate the jet assembly from the washer tube (see illustration). Be prepared for fluid spillage.

18 Where applicable disconnect the jet heater wiring connector.

19 If required, the trim can be separated from the jet by releasing the retaining clips on each side of the jet (see illustration).

17.13b . . . while on others, push up the rear edge of the jet, and depress the clip at the front, then pull the jet up from the hood

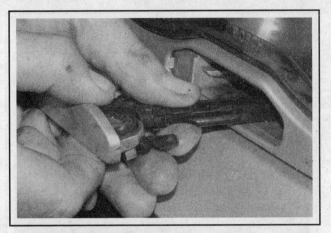

17.17 With a sharp tug, separate the washer jet from the tube

17.19 Release the retaining clips and separate the jet from the trim

17.22a Some control module wiring connectors have locking levers . . .

17.22b . . . while others have sliding locking elements

17.23 Release the retaining clip and slide the General Control Module from position

20 On installation, pull out the washer tube and push the jet into place. Where applicable, reconnect the wiring connector. Adjustment of the jets requires use of BMW tool 00 9 100.

WASH/WIPE CONTROL MODULE

▶ Refer to illustrations 17.22a, 17.22b and 17.23

21 The wash/wipe system is controlled by the central body electronics (ZKE V) control module, known as the General Module (GM V), which is located behind the passenger side glove box. To access the control unit, remove the glove box as described in Chapter 11, Section 27.

22 Disconnect the module wiring connectors. Some connectors have locking levers, and some have sliding locking elements (see illustrations).

23 Release the retaining clip then remove the ECM from the vehicle (see illustration).

24 Installation is the reverse of removal.

REAR WINDOW WASHER RESERVOIR

▶ Refer to illustration 17.29

25 Remove the right-hand side luggage compartment trim panel as described in Chapter 11, Section 27.

26 Empty the contents of the reservoir or be prepared for fluid spillage.

27 Disconnect the pump wiring connector.

28 Carefully detach the reservoir filler tube and pump delivery tube.

29 Remove the top mounting nut, and loosen the lower mounting nuts (see illustration). Remove the reservoir.

30 Installation is the reverse of removal.

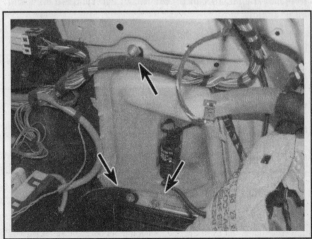

17.29 Rear washer reservoir nuts - Sport Wagon models

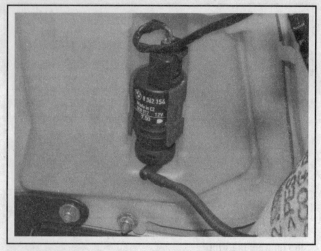

17.34 Rear washer pump - Sport Wagon models

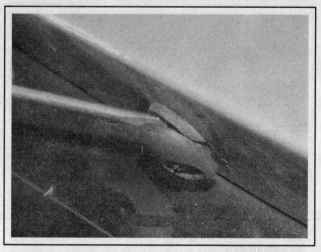

17.36 The rear washer jet is a push-fit into the tailgate

REAR WINDOW WASHER PUMP

▶ **Refer to illustration 17.34**

31 Remove the right-hand side luggage compartment trim panel as described in Chapter 11, Section 27.

32 Empty the contents of the reservoir or be prepared for fluid spillage.

33 Disconnect the pump wiring connector.

34 Disconnect the pump delivery tube, and carefully pull the pump up and out of the reservoir (see illustration).

35 Installation is the reverse of removal.

REAR WINDOW WASHER JET

▶ **Refer to illustration 17.36**

36 The washer jet is a push-fit into the end of the washer tube fitting. Using a plastic or wooden lever, carefully pry the washer jet from the rubber fitting at the top of the window (see illustration).

37 Installation is the reverse of removal. Aim the jet to an area 4-inches (100 mm) from the top, and 12-inches (300 mm) from the edge of the window.

18 Radio unit - removal and installation

→**Note: The following removal and installation procedure is for the range of standard equipment radio/cassette/CD units. Removal and installation procedures of non-standard units will differ slightly.**

1 Disconnect the cable from the negative terminal of the battery (see Chapter 5, Section 1).

REMOVAL

Dash-mounted unit

▶ **Refer to illustrations 18.3 and 18.4**

2 Using a wooden or plastic lever, carefully pry away the decorative trim above the passenger side glove box, followed by the trim above the radio unit.

3 Remove the two screws and pull the unit from the dash (see illustration).

4 Note their installed positions, and disconnect the wiring connectors from the rear of the unit (slide out the locking element on the main connector) (see illustration).

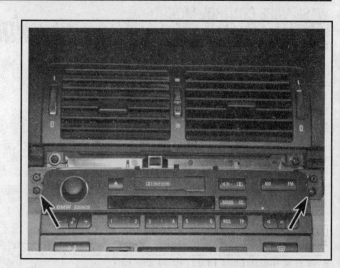

18.3 Remove the two screws that secure the radio unit

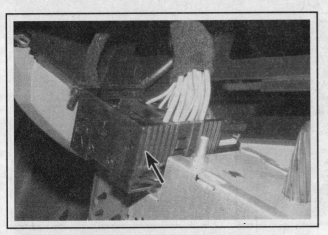

18.4 Slide out the locking element and disconnect the wiring connector

18.6 The CD autochanger is retained by these four screws

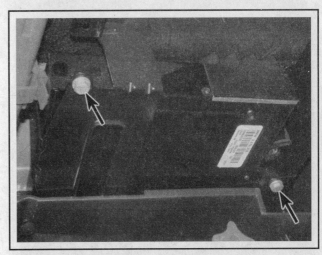

18.9 The amplifier is retained by two bolts - Sport Wagon model

CD autochanger

▶ **Refer to illustrations 18.6**

5 Remove the left-hand side luggage compartment trim panel as described in Chapter 11, Section 27.

6 Loosen the four mounting screws, and lift the unit from position (see illustration). Disconnect the wiring connectors as the unit is withdrawn.

Amplifier

▶ **Refer to illustration 18.9**

7 The amplifier (on models so equipped) is located behind the left-hand side luggage compartment trim panel. Press the button, and remove the first aid kit trim panel.

8 Remove the storage/tool kit tray.

9 Disconnect the amplifier wiring connectors, remove the retaining bolts and remove the unit (see illustration).

INSTALLATION

10 Installation is the reverse of removal.

19 Speakers - removal and installation

DOOR PANEL SPEAKER(S)

▶ **Refer to illustrations 19.2 and 19.3**

1 Remove the door inner trim panel as described in Chapter 11.

2 Unscrew the three screws and remove the speaker from the door trim (see illustration).

3 Where present, unscrew the large retaining collar and remove the small speaker from the trim panel (see illustration).

4 Installation is the reverse of removal.

DOOR UPPER SPEAKER

▶ **Refer to illustrations 19.5a, 19.5b and 19.7**

5 Carefully unclip the plastic panel from the front inner edge of the door (see illustrations).

19.2 The door speaker is retained by three screws

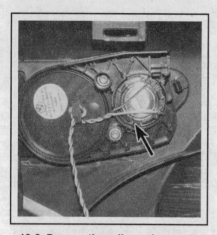

19.3 Remove the collar and remove the speaker

19.5a Note the clips retaining the plastic trim at the front edge of the door . . .

19.5b . . . and the clip at its lower edge

6   Remove the door inner trim panel as described in Chapter 11.

7   Disconnect the speaker wiring connector, remove the two screws and remove the speaker (see illustration).

8   Installation is the reverse of removal.

19.7 Remove the door upper speaker bolts

LUGGAGE AREA SPEAKER

▶ Refer to illustration 19.10

9   Remove the relevant luggage compartment side trim panel as described in Chapter 11, Section 27.

10 Remove the retaining screws and remove the speaker, disconnect its wiring connectors as they become accessible (see illustration).

11 Installation is the reverse of removal making sure the speaker is correctly located.

REAR SPEAKER

▶ Refer to illustration 19.12

12 Carefully pry the speaker grille out from the rear parcel shelf (see illustration).

13 Remove the retaining screws and lift off the speaker. Disconnect the wiring connector as the speaker is withdrawn.

14 Installation is the reverse of removal.

19.10 Rear speaker - Sport Wagon models

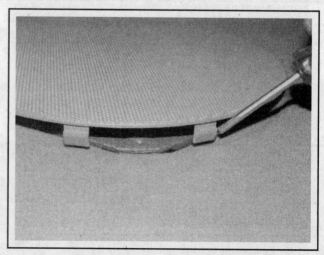

19.12 Carefully pry up the parcel shelf speaker grille

20 Radio antenna - general information

▶ **Refer to illustration 20.1**

The radio antenna is built into the rear window. In order to improve reception, an amplifier is used to boost the signal to the radio/cassette unit. The amplifier unit is located behind the left hand rear C-pillar trim panel.

To gain access to the antenna amplifier unit, carefully remove the C-pillar trim panel as described in Chapter 11, Section 27, disconnecting the wiring from the interior light as the panel is removed. Disconnect the antenna lead and wiring, then remove the retaining screws and remove the amplifier (see illustration). Installation is the reverse of removal.

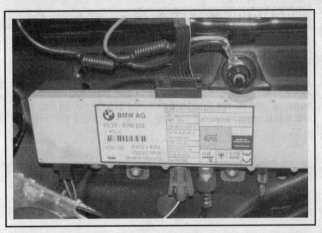

20.1 Antenna signal amplifier is located behind the left-hand C-pillar trim panel

21 Cruise control system - information and component replacement

INFORMATION

1 The cruise control function is incorporated into the engine management ECM. The only replaceable external components are the clutch pedal switch, and the throttle actuator.

COMPONENT REPLACEMENT

Clutch pedal switch

2 The trim panel above the pedals is secured by one plastic expanding rivet, two screws, and a retaining clip. Pry out the center pin and lever out the plastic expanding rivet, remove the two screws, rotate the retaining clip 90 degrees counterclockwise and remove the panel. Note their installed positions, and disconnect the wiring connectors as the panel is withdrawn.

3 Disconnect the switch wiring connector.

4 Depress the clutch pedal, and pull out the switch plunger to its full extent. Squeeze together the retaining clips and pull the switch from the bracket.

5 Installation is the reverse of removal, but slowly allow the pedal to return to its "at rest" position.

Throttle actuator (M54 and M56 engines)

▶ **Refer to illustrations 21.6a and 21.6b**

6 The actuator is located on the left-hand side inner fender. Ensure the ignition is switched off, remove the nut and bolt, then remove the actuator from the inner fender. Squeeze together the sides of the grommet and separate the throttle cable from the throttle lever (see illustrations).

21.6a Remove the nut and bolt that retain the cruise control actuator

21.6b Squeeze together the sides of the grommet, and remove the cruise control cable from the throttle lever

22 Anti-theft alarm system - general information

✳✳ CAUTION:

These vehicles are equipped with the Central Body Electronic (ZKE-V) system. Each individual system is linked to a centralized control module that allows efficient and accurate troubleshooting. This control module governs the windshield wipers and washers, the central locking and anti-theft system, the power windows, the interior lights, the alarm system and the electronic consumer sleep mode. In the event of a malfunction with this system, have the vehicle diagnosed by a dealer service department or other qualified automotive repair facility, as special test equipment is required.

These models are equipped with a sophisticated anti-theft alarm and immobilizer system. Should a fault develop, the system's self-diagnosis facility should be interrogated using dedicated test equipment. Consult your BMW dealer or other qualified automotive repair facility.

23 Heated front seat components - removal and installation

HEATER MATS

On models equipped with heated front seats, a heater pad is present in the both the seat back and seat cushion. Replacement of either heater mat involves peeling back the upholstery, removing the old mat, sticking the new mat in position and then installing the upholstery. Note that upholstery removal and installation requires considerable skill and experience if it is to be carried out successfully and is therefore best entrusted to your BMW dealer or specialist. In practice, it will be very difficult for the home mechanic to carry out the job without ruining the upholstery.

HEATED SEAT SWITCHES

Refer to Section 4.

24 Airbag system - general information and precautions

The models covered by this manual are equipped with a total of six airbags and two extra as an option on Sport Wagons and Sedans. There is a driver's airbag mounted in the center of the steering wheel, a passenger's airbag located behind the dash, two head protection airbags located in each A-pillar (headliners), two side impact airbags located in each front door trim panel and, on some Sport Wagons and Sedans models, behind each rear door trim. The airbag system consists of the airbag unit(s) (complete with gas generators), impact sensors, the control unit and a warning light in the instrument panel.

The airbag system is triggered in the event of a heavy frontal or side impact above a predetermined force; depending on the point of impact. The airbag(s) is inflated within milliseconds and forms a safety cushion between the cabin occupants and the cabin interior, and therefore greatly reduces the risk of injury. The airbag then deflates almost immediately.

Every time the ignition is switched on, the airbag control unit performs a self-test. The self-test takes approximately 2 to 6 seconds and during this time the airbag warning light on the dash is illuminated. After the self-test has been completed the warning light should go out. If the warning light fails to come on, remains illuminated after the initial period, or comes on at any time when the vehicle is being driven, there is a fault in the airbag system. The vehicle should be taken to a BMW dealer for examination at the earliest possible opportunity.

- *Note that the airbag(s) must not be subjected to temperatures in excess of 194°F (90°C). When the airbag is removed, ensure that it is stored the correct way up to prevent possible inflation (padded surface uppermost).*
- *Do not allow any solvents or cleaning agents to contact the airbag assemblies. They must be cleaned using only a damp cloth.*
- *The airbags and control unit are both sensitive to impact. If either is dropped or damaged they should be replaced.*
- *Disconnect the airbag control unit wiring connector prior to using arc-welding equipment on the vehicle.*

25 Airbag system components - removal and installation

GENERAL INFORMATION

1   All models are equipped with a Supplemental Restraint System (SRS), more commonly known as an airbag. This system is designed to protect the driver, and the front seat passenger, from serious injury in the event of a head-on or frontal collision. It consists of airbag sensors mounted on the seat crossmember for models equipped with side impact airbags and a sensing/diagnostic module mounted in the center of the vehicle, near the floor console. The airbag assemblies are mounted on the steering wheel and the right side top surface of the passenger's side dash. Side-impact airbags are located in the sides of the seat backs, and head protection airbags located in the headliner A pillars. The airbag control module is mounted in the center console near the parking brake handle.

2   Two different types of driver's airbags may be installed. Models from September 1999 are equipped with "Smart" airbags with two stages of inflation. Where a low speed impact is detected and airbags provide "soft" deployment, and "hard" deployment in high speed impacts. Thus ensuring that the airbag deployment is no greater than necessary to provide protection.

25.8 Rotate the steering wheel to access the two Torx screws

25.9 Release the retaining clip and disconnect the airbag wiring connector

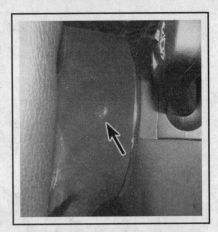

25.11a Insert a screwdriver through the hole in the side of the steering wheel . . .

DISARMING THE SYSTEM AND OTHER PRECAUTIONS

✴✴ WARNING:

Failure to follow these precautions could result in accidental deployment of the airbag and personal injury.

3   Whenever working in the vicinity of the steering wheel, steering column or any of the other SRS system components, the system must be disarmed. To disarm the system:

a) *Point the wheels straight ahead and turn the key to the Lock position.*

b) *Disconnect the cable from the negative battery terminal(s) (see Chapter 5, Section 1).*

c) *Wait at least two minutes for the back-up power supply to be depleted.*

4   Whenever handling an airbag module, always keep the airbag opening (the trim side) pointed away from your body. Never place the airbag module on a bench or other surface with the airbag opening facing the surface. Always place the airbag module in a safe location with the airbag opening facing up.

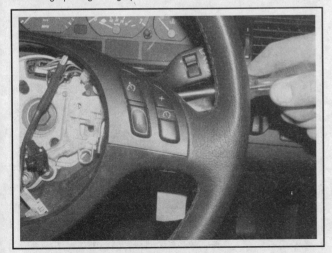

25.11b . . . so that the screwdriver goes behind the metal plate . . .

5   Never measure the resistance of any SRS component. An ohmmeter has a built-in battery supply that could accidentally deploy the airbag.

6   Never use electrical welding equipment on a vehicle equipped with an airbag without first disconnecting the yellow airbag connector, located under the steering column near the combination switch connector (driver's airbag) and behind the glove box (passenger's airbag).

7   Never dispose of a live airbag module. Return it to a dealer service department or other qualified repair shop for safe deployment and disposal.

DRIVER'S AIRBAG REMOVAL AND INSTALLATION

Models equipped with a conventional steering wheel

▶ **Refer to illustrations 25.8 and 25.9**

8   Loosen and remove the two airbag retaining Torx screws from the rear of the steering wheel, rotating the wheel as necessary to gain access to the screws (see illustration).

9   Return the steering wheel to the straight-ahead position then carefully lift the airbag assembly away from the steering wheel. Release the locking clip and disconnect the airbag wiring connector from the steering wheel (see illustration). Note that the airbag must not be knocked or dropped and should be stored the correct way up with its padded surface uppermost.

10 On installation reconnect the wiring connector and seat the airbag unit in the steering wheel, making sure the wire does not become trapped. Install the retaining screws and tighten them to the specified torque setting and reconnect the battery.

Models equipped with a sport steering wheel

▶ **Refer to illustrations 25.11a, 25.11b, 25.11c and 25.12**

11 With the steering wheel in the straight-ahead position, insert a screwdriver through the hole in the rear-side of the steering wheel at 90-degrees to the steering column to release the spring clip, and pull that side of the airbag away from the wheel (see illustrations). Repeat this process on the other side of the wheel.

12 To disconnect the airbag wiring connectors, using a small flat-bladed screwdriver, lift the connector locking flap and pull the connector from position (see illustration). Note that the airbag must not be knocked or dropped and should be stored the correct way up with its

25.11c ... and pushes against the retaining clip (airbag removed for clarity)

padded surface uppermost.

13 On installation, reconnect the wiring connectors, and ensure that connectors are locked in place. Note that the connectors are color-coded to ensure correct installment. The connector plugs into the socket of the same color. Position the airbag on the wheel and push the unit home until it locks in place. Reconnect the battery negative terminal.

PASSENGER AIRBAG

▶ **Refer to illustrations 25.16, 25.17a and 25.17b**

14 Using a wooden or plastic level, carefully pry off the decorative strip above the passenger's glove box.

15 Remove the two screws and pull out the air vent on the passenger's side.

16 Carefully pull the lower edge of the airbag cover from the dash. Remove the two screws and remove the cover (see illustration). Note that after airbag deployment, a new cover must be installed.

17 Remove the retaining nuts and remove the airbag. Press the locking tab and disconnect the wiring connector as the unit is withdrawn (see illustrations).

25.12 Lift the locking flap and disconnect the airbag wiring connector

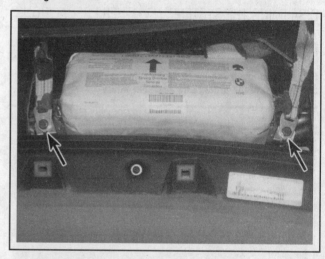

25.16 Remove the screws and remove the cover

18 Installation is the reverse of removal. Tighten the airbag retaining screws to the torque listed in this Chapter's Specifications, and reconnect the battery negative terminal.

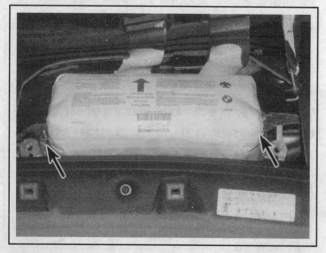

25.17a Remove the airbag nuts

25.17b Press the retaining clip and disconnect the airbag wiring connector

DOOR AIRBAGS

▶ **Refer to illustrations 25.20a and 25.20b**

19 Remove the door inner trim panel (see Chapter 11).

20 Remove the three screws and lift the airbag from position. Pull the wiring connector from the airbag as it is removed (see illustrations). Where applicable, release the wiring from any retaining clips.

21 Installation is the reverse of removal. Tighten the airbag retaining screws to the torque listed in this Chapter's Specifications, and reconnect the battery negative terminal.

HEAD AIRBAGS

22 On each side of the passenger cabin, a Head Protection Airbag (HPS) is present. The airbag runs from the lower part of the windshield pillar to above the rear door, is approximately 5-feet (1.5 meters) in length, and 5-inches (130 mm) in diameter when inflated. To remove the airbag, the entire dash and headlining must be removed. This task is outside the scope of the DIYer, and therefore we recommend that the task be entrusted to a BMW dealer or specialist.

AIRBAG CONTROL UNIT

▶ **Refer to illustration 25.25a and 25.25b**

23 Remove the rear section of the center console as described in Chapter 11.

24 Cut the carpet in front of the parking brake lever to expose the control unit.

25 Remove the retaining nuts and lift the module. Note the ground strap under one of the mounting nuts. Disconnect the wiring connector as the unit is withdrawn (see illustrations).

26 Installation is the reverse of removal. Note that the control unit must be installed with the arrow pointing towards the front of the vehicle, and that the ground strap is installed under one of the module mounting nuts.

IMPACT SENSOR

▶ **Refer to illustration 25.29**

27 There are two impact sensors, one on each side of the passenger cabin. Remove the seats (see Chapter 11).

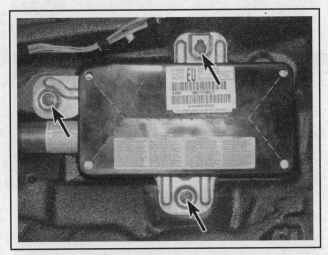

25.20a Door airbag retaining nuts

25.20b Unplug the yellow connector from the side airbag

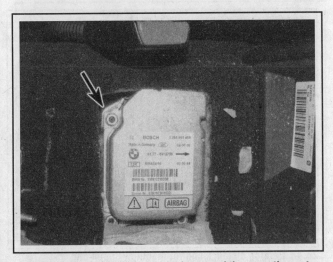

25.25a Note the ground strap under one of the mounting nuts

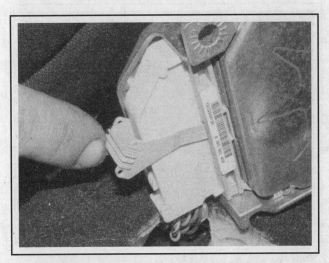

25.25b Unlock the catch and disconnect the control unit wiring connector

28 Unclip the door sill trim panel, and fold the carpet away from the side. To improve access if required, remove the floor level heater duct.

29 Remove the two retaining screws, and remove the sensor (see illustration). Disconnect the wiring connector as the sensor is withdrawn.

30 Installation is the reverse of removal, noting that the arrow on the sensor must point towards the door sill.

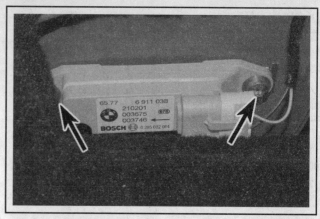

25.29 Remove the two screws and remove the impact sensor

26 Parking distance control (PDC) - information and component replacement

GENERAL INFORMATION

1 In order to aid parking, a models in the 3-Series range can be equipped with a system that informs the driver of the distance between the rear of the vehicle, and any vehicle/obstacle behind while reversing. The system consists of several ultrasonic sensors mounted in the rear bumper which measure the distance between themselves and the nearest object. The distance is indicated by an audible signal in the passenger cabin. The closer the object, the more frequent the signals, until at less than one foot (30 cm), the signal becomes continuous.

PDC ELECTRONIC CONTROL MODULE

Removal

▶ **Refer to illustration 26.3**

2 On Sedan and Coupe models, remove the right-hand luggage compartment trim panel as described in Chapter 11, Section 27.

3 On Sport Wagon models, lift out the panel from the luggage compartment floor. Remove the wing nut and lift out the spare wheel cover. Remove the two retaining nuts and lift the rear edge of the panel between the spare wheel and the rear seats sill (see illustration).

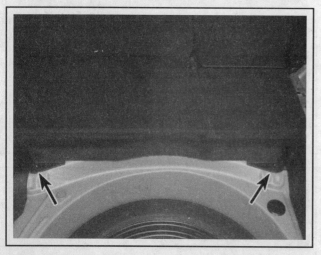

26.3 Remove the two screws and lift the panel between the spare wheel and rear seats

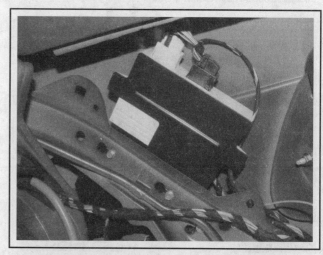

26.4a Parking distance control module - Sedan and Coupe models

4   On all models, note their installed positions, and disconnect the unit's wiring connectors. Remove the mounting screws and remove the control unit (see illustrations).

Installation

5   Installation is the reverse of removal.

ULTRASONIC SENSORS

Removal

6   Remove the rear bumper as described in Chapter 11.

7   Disconnect the sensor wiring connectors, release the retaining clips and remove the sensors from the bumper.

Installation

8   Installation is the reverse of removal.

**26.4b Parking distance control module -
Sport Wagon models**

27 Wiring diagrams - general information

1   The wiring diagrams which follow only offer limited coverage of the electrical systems on these models.

2   At the time of writing, no more wiring diagrams were available from BMW, so the inclusion of more information has not been possible.

3   Bear in mind that, while wiring diagrams offer a useful quick-reference guide to the vehicle electrical systems, it is still possible to trace faults, and to check for supplies and grounds, using a simple multimeter. Refer to the general fault finding methods described in Section 2 of this Chapter (ignoring the references to wiring diagrams if one is not provided for the system concerned).

Specifications

Component location

Air conditioning blower relay	Behind passenger's glove box
Air conditioning clutch relay	Behind passenger's glove box
Airbag control module	Under carpet beneath center console
Airbag crash sensor	Front seat crossmember under carpet
Alarm control module	Above main fuse box behind glove box
Automatic transmission control module	E-box in engine compartment
Engine management ECM	E-box in engine compartment
Engine management main relay	E-box in engine compartment
Fog light relay	Behind passenger's glove box
Fuel injector relay	E-box in engine compartment
Fuel pump relay	Behind passenger's glove box
General Module (GM V)	Behind passenger's glove box
Headlight dimmer relay	Light switch on light control center
Heated rear window relay	Right-hand side of luggage compartment
Horn relay	Behind passenger's glove box
Ignition relay	E-box in engine compartment
Instrument cluster control unit	Instrument cluster
Parking distance control module	Right-hand side of trunk near battery
Reversing light relay (automatic transmission)	E-box in engine compartment
Seat control module	Base of seat cushion
Secondary air injection pump relay	Behind passenger's glove box
Tire pressure control module	Behind passenger's glove box
Windshield washer relay	E-box in engine compartment

Note that not all models are equipped with all of the components listed.

Torque specifications	Ft-lbs (unless otherwise indicated)	Nm
Airbag system items:		
Door airbag retaining screws	72 in-lbs	9
Driver's airbag retaining screws	71 in-lbs	8
Impact sensor mounting bolts	84 in-lbs	10
Passenger's airbag cover straps screws	72 in-lbs	9
Passenger's airbag retaining nuts	16	22
Head Protection Airbag (HPS) bolts	96 in-lbs	11
Tire pressure transmitter Torx screw	30 in-lbs	4
Wiper arm-to-wiper spindle nut	22	30

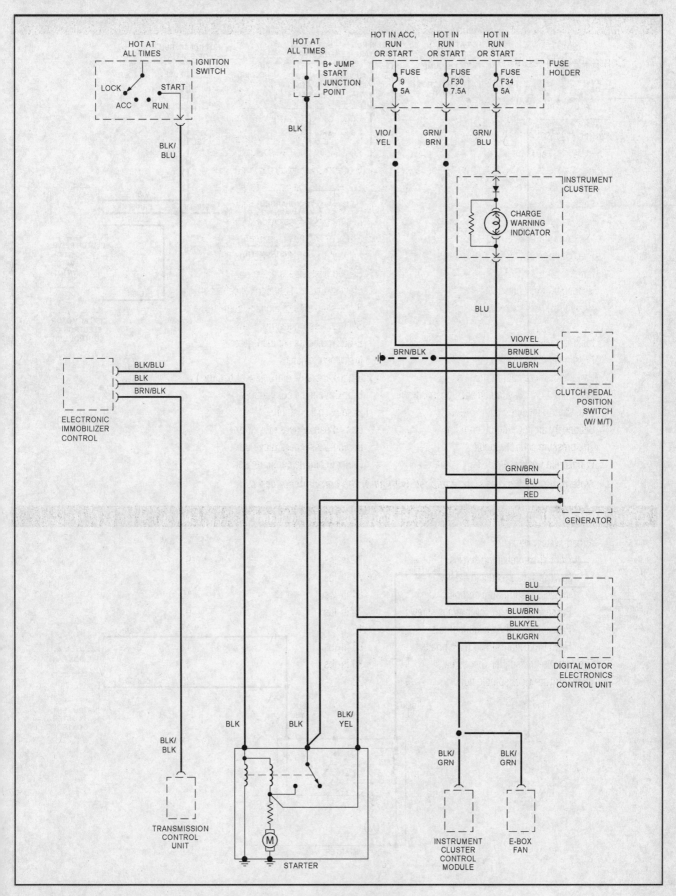

Starting and charging systems - 1999 and 2000 323i, 323ci, 328i and 328ci models

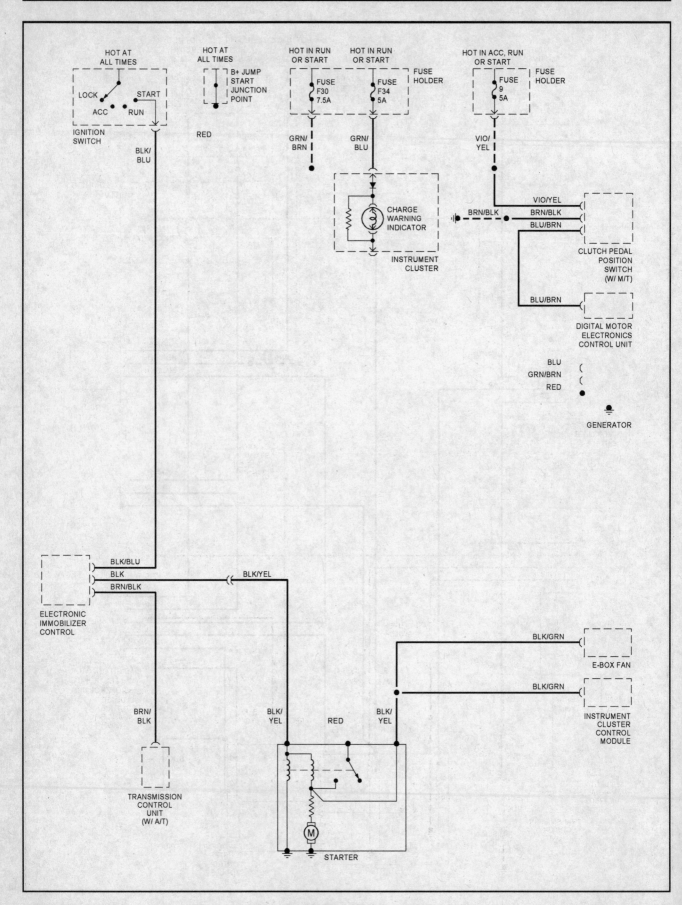

Starting and charging systems - 2001 and later 325i, 325ci, 330i and 330ci models

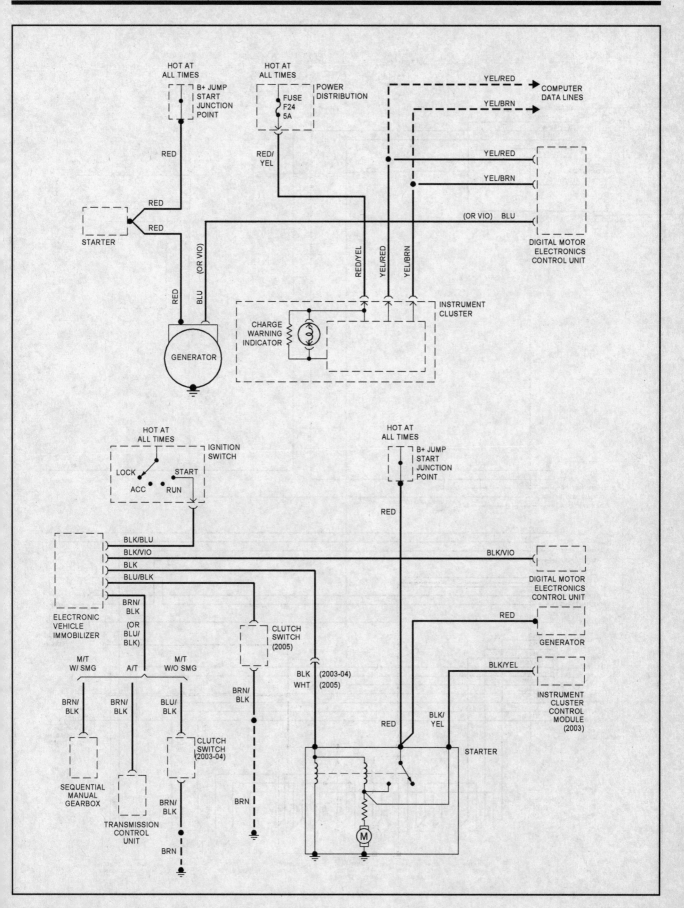

Starting and charging systems - 2003 and later Z4 models

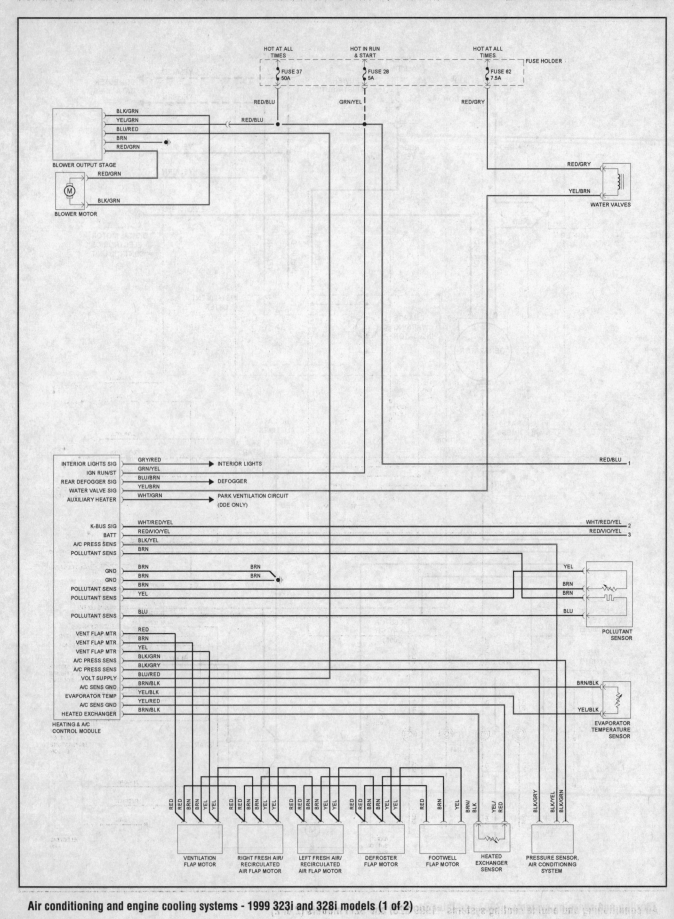

Air conditioning and engine cooling systems - 1999 323i and 328i models (1 of 2)

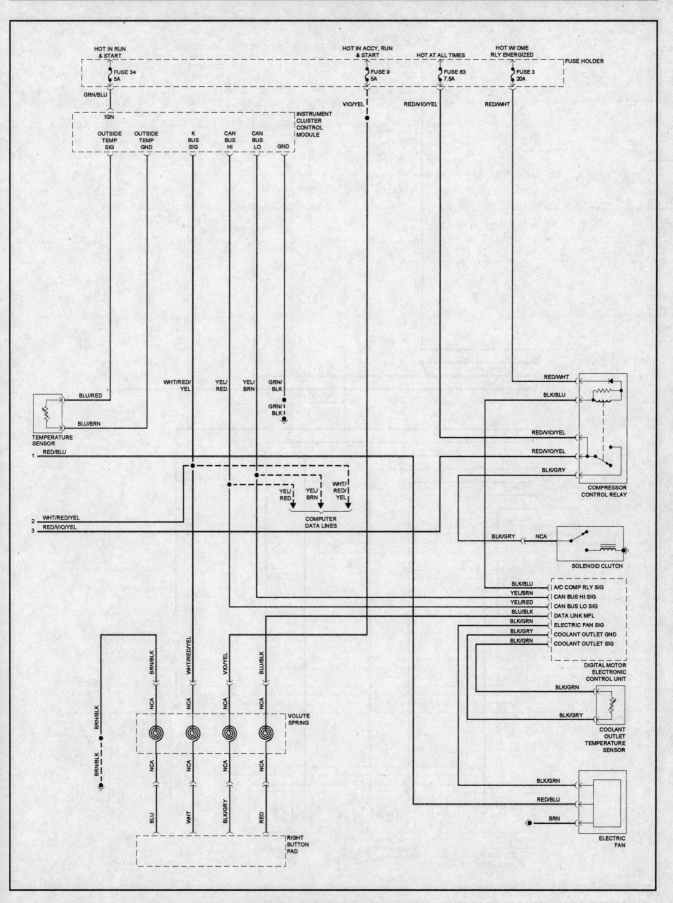

Air conditioning and engine cooling systems - 1999 323i and 328i models (2 of 2)

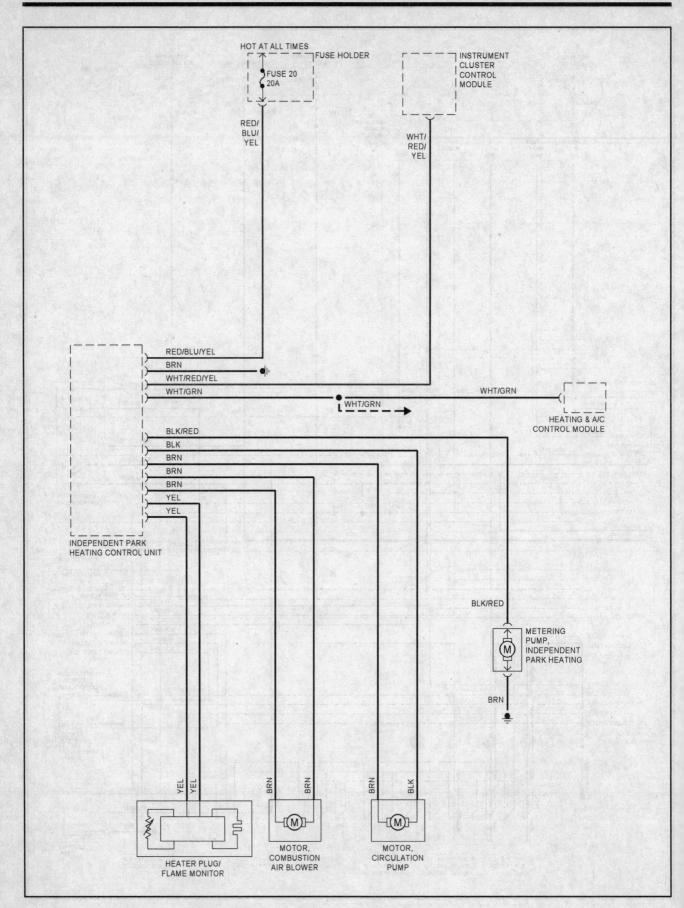

Park ventilation/heater circuit - 1999 323i and 328i models

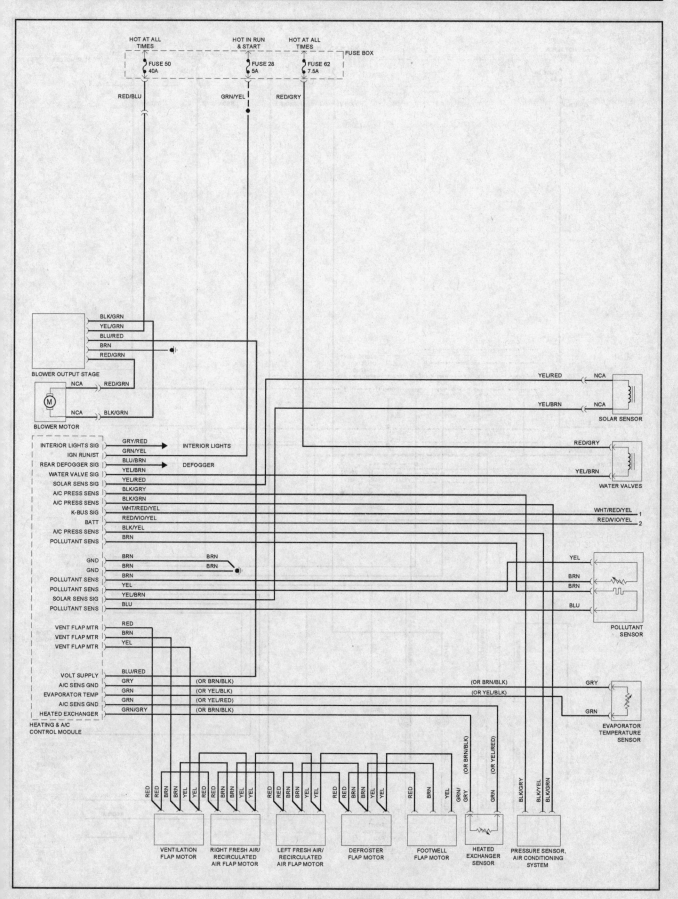

Air conditioning and engine cooling systems with automatic A/C - 2000 and later 3-Series (1 of 2)

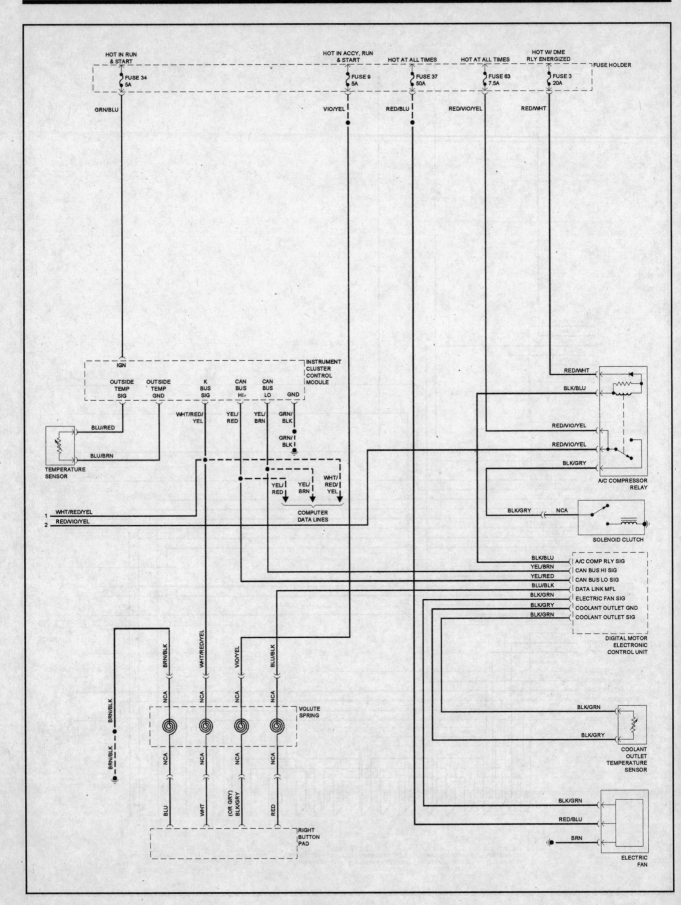

Air conditioning and engine cooling systems with automatic A/C - 2000 and later 3-Series (2 of 2)

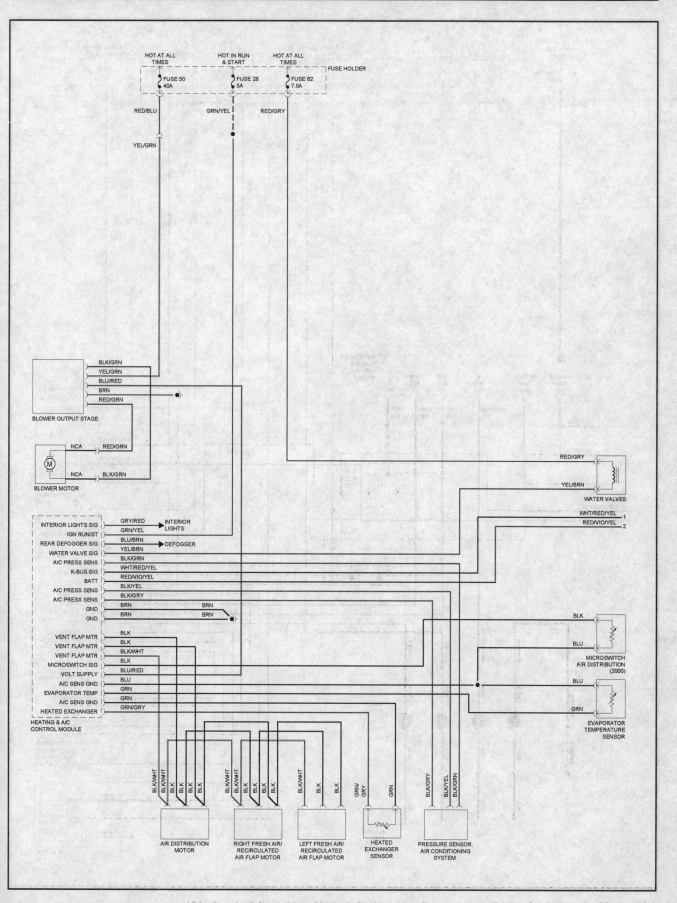

Air conditioning and engine cooling systems with manual A/C - 2000 and later 3-Series (1 of 2)

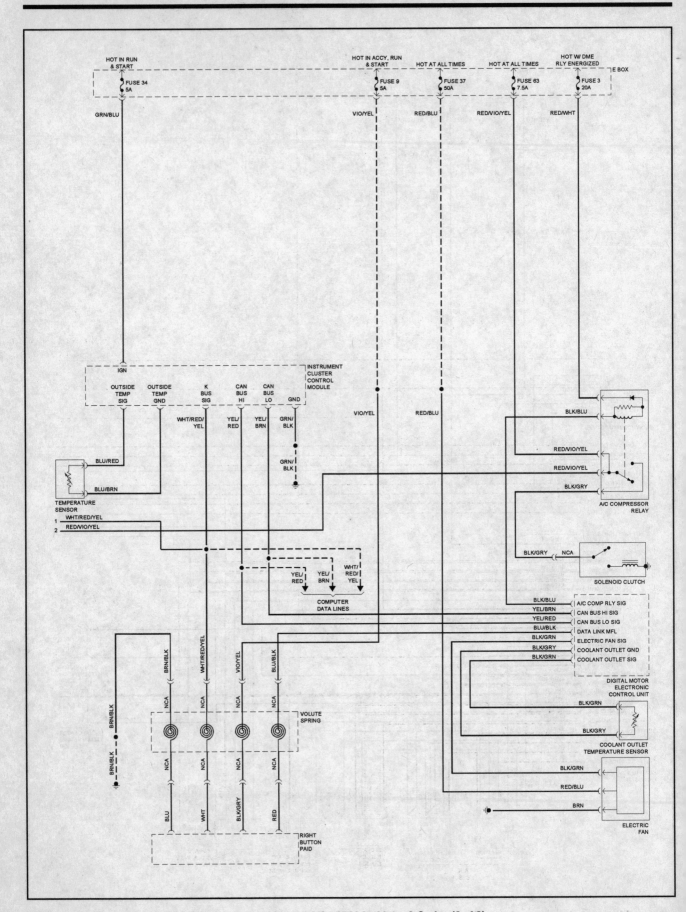

Air conditioning and engine cooling systems with manual A/C - 2000 and later 3-Series (2 of 2)

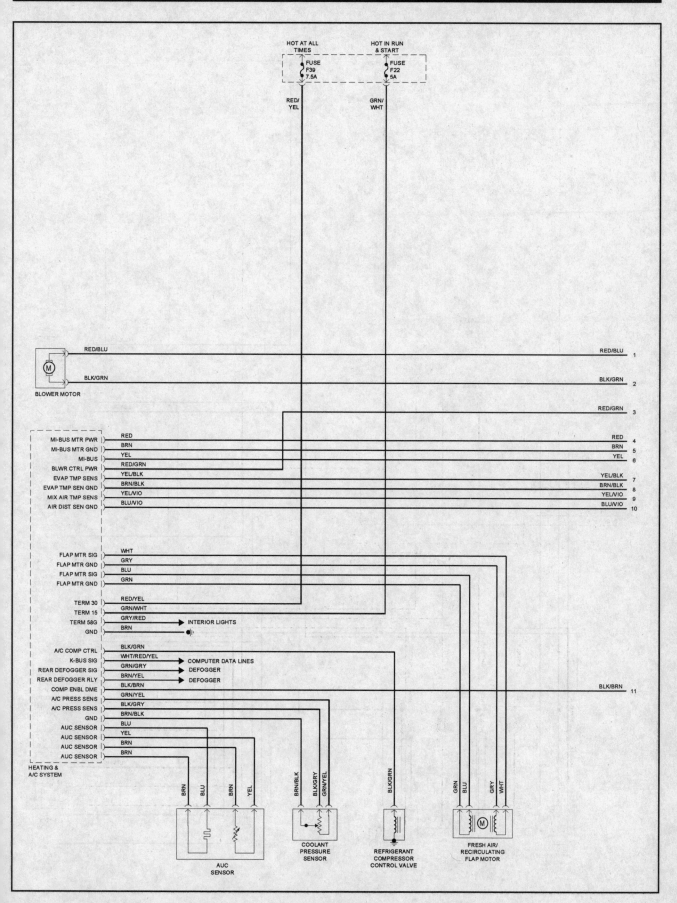

Air conditioning and engine cooling systems with automatic A/C - 2003 and later Z4 models (1 of 2)

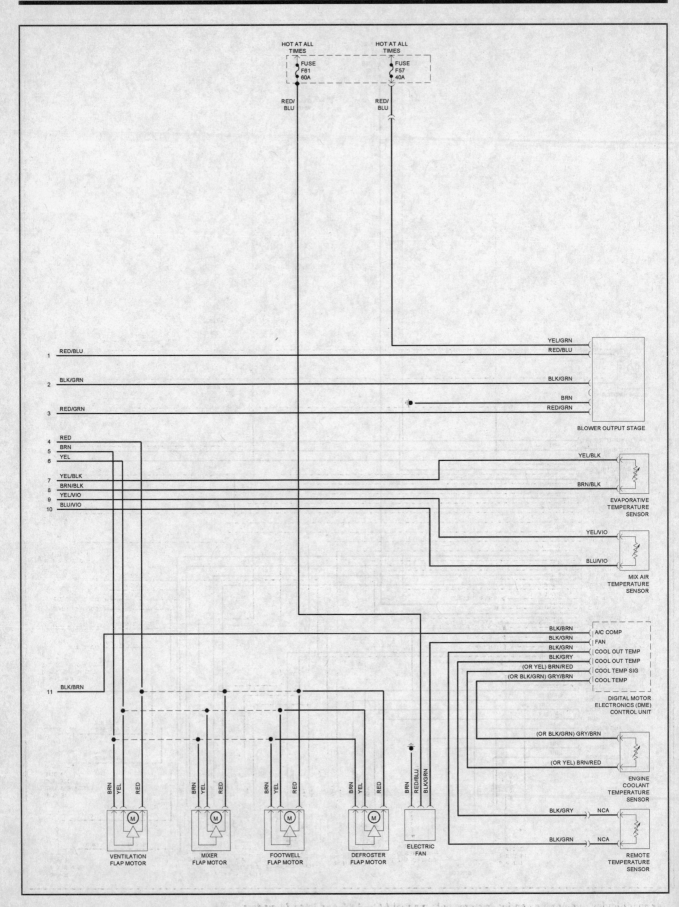

Air conditioning and engine cooling systems with automatic A/C - 2003 and later Z4 models (2 of 2)

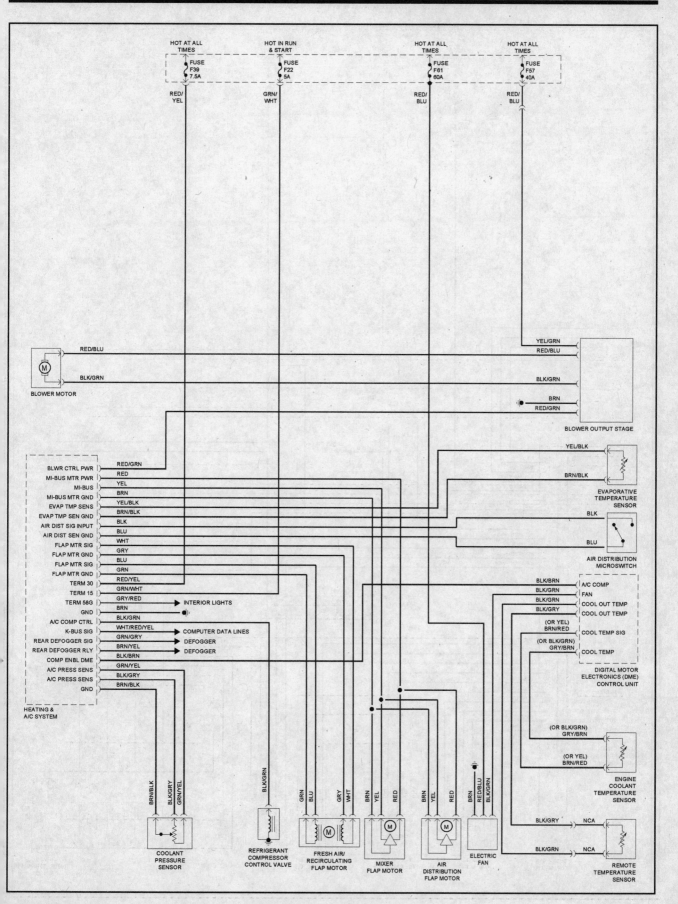

Air conditioning and engine cooling systems with manual A/C - 2003 and later Z4 models

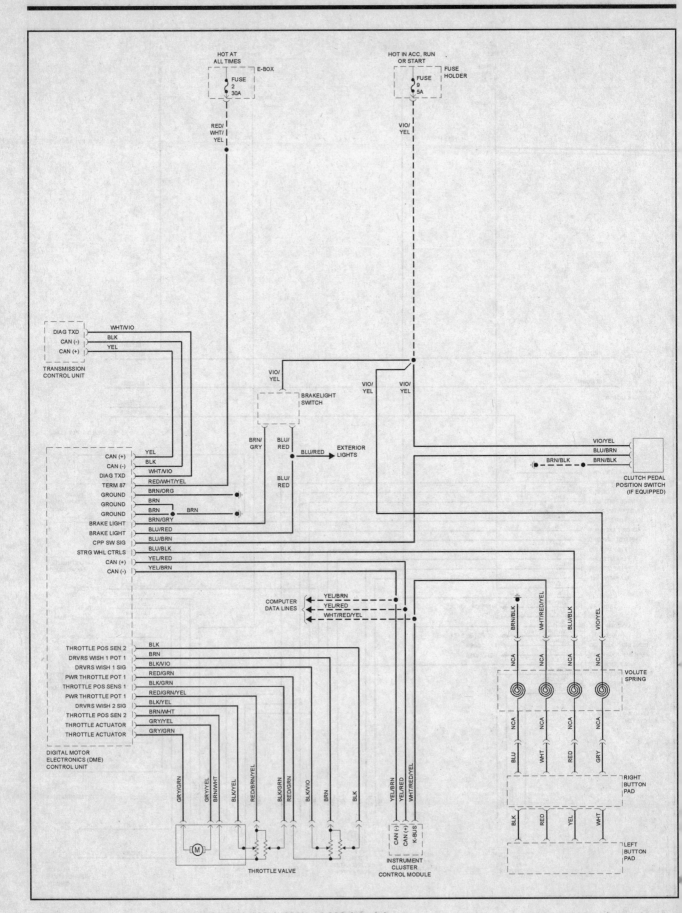

Cruise control system - 1999 and 2000 323i, 323ci, 328i and 328ci models

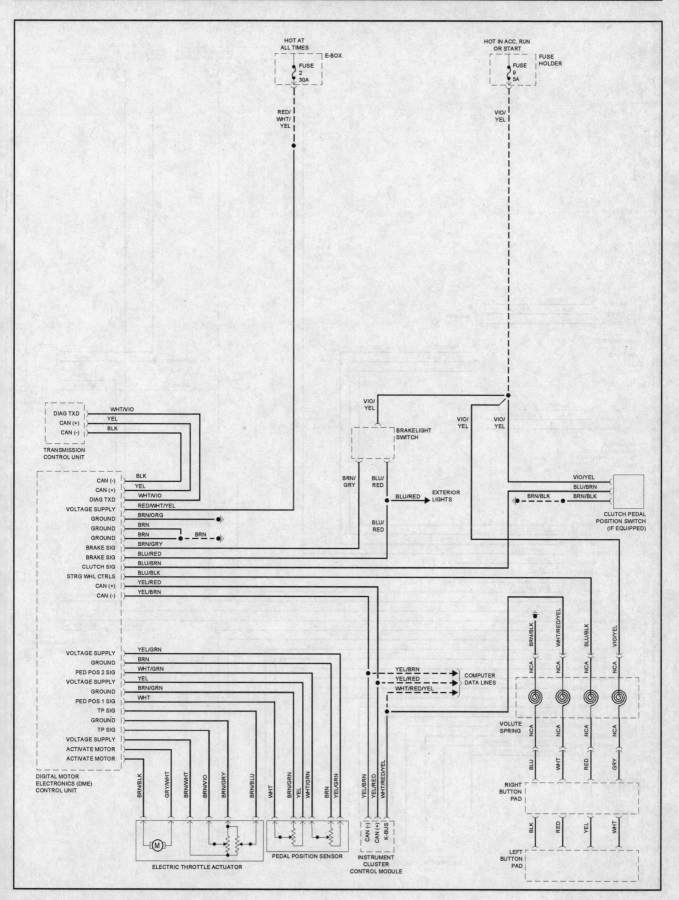

Cruise control system - 2001 and later 3-Series

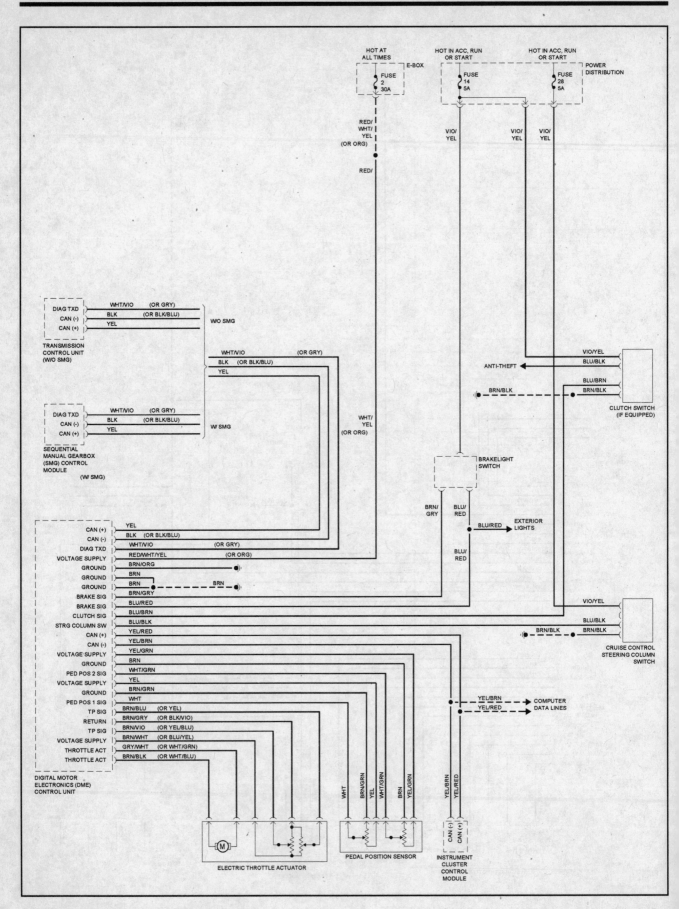

Cruise control system - 2003 and later Z4 models

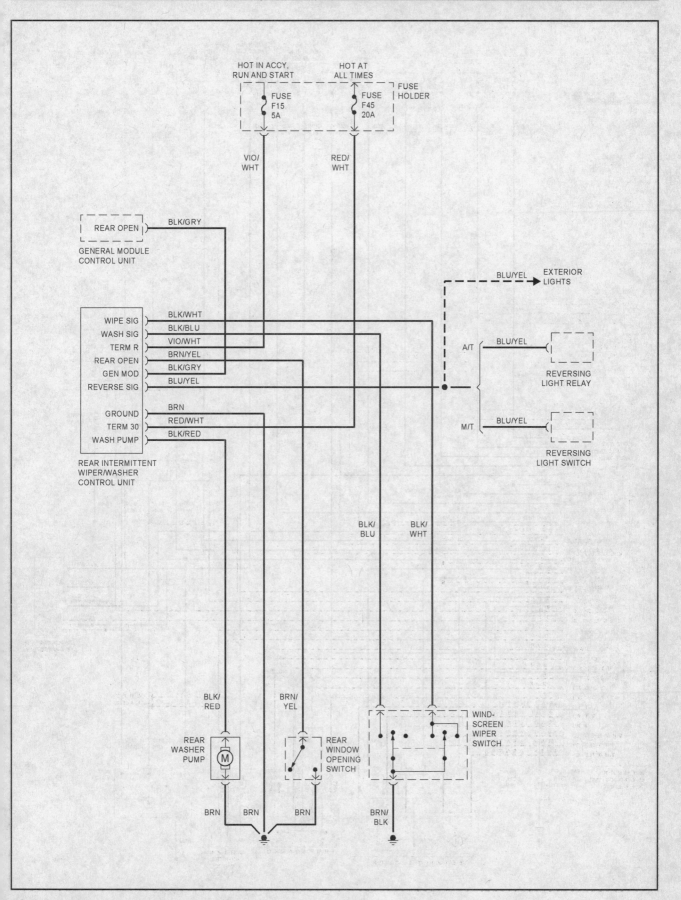

Windshield wiper and washer systems - 1999 and later 3-Series wagons

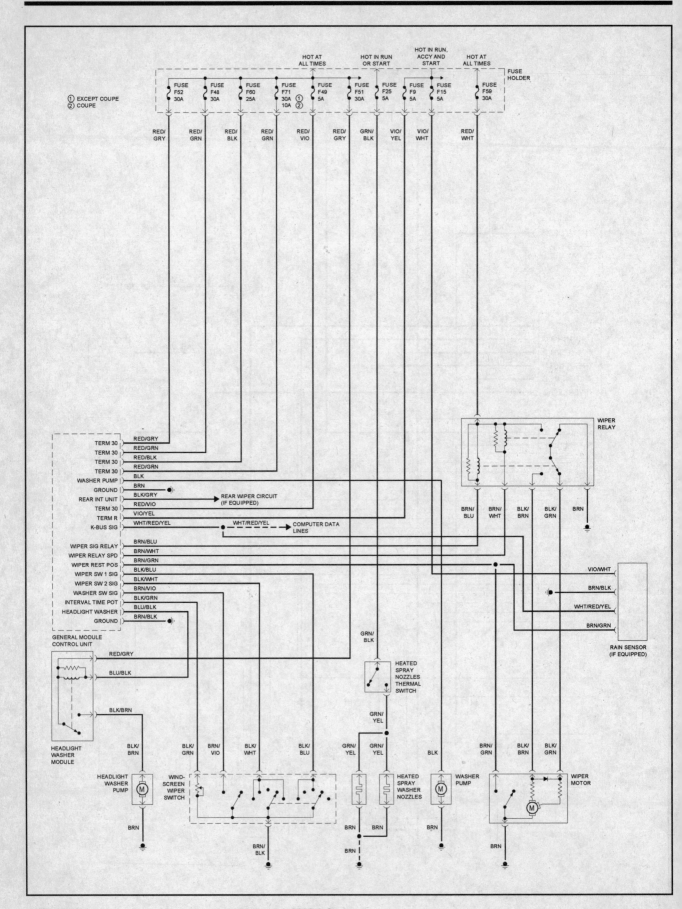

Windshield wiper and washer systems - 1999 through 2002 3-Series

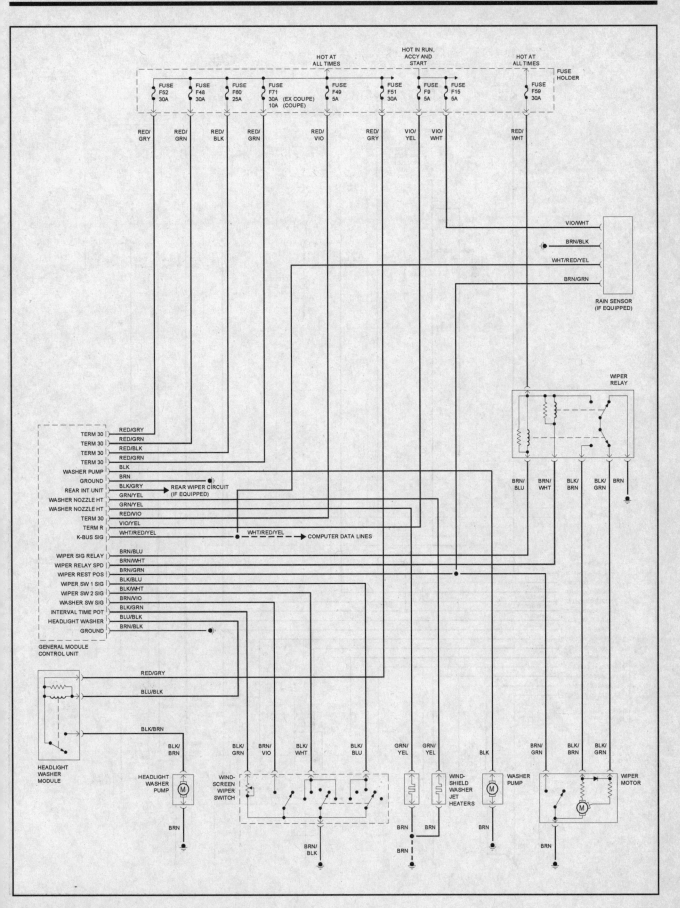

Windshield wiper and washer systems - 2003 and later 3-Series

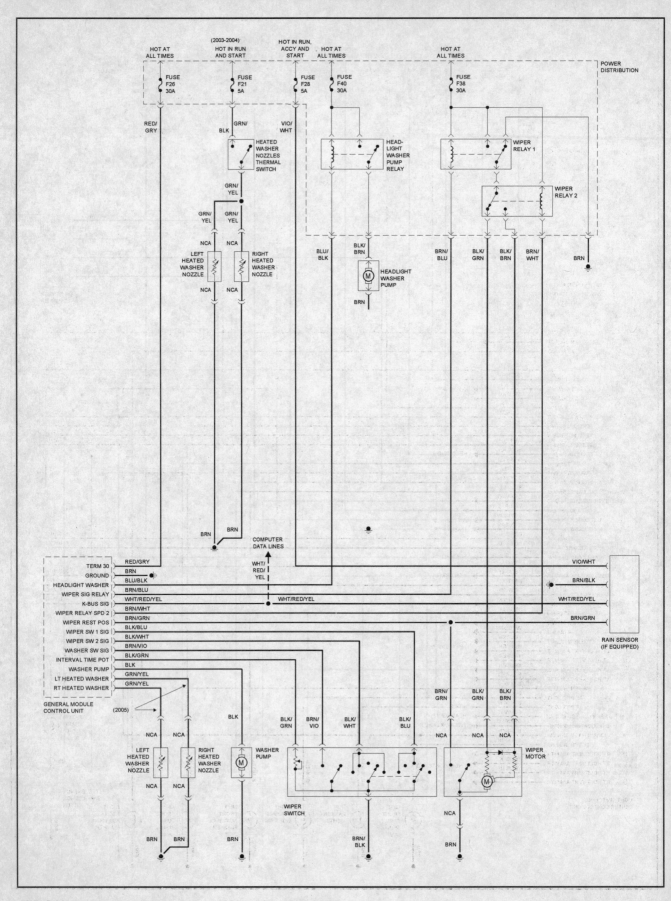

Windshield wiper and washer systems - 2003 and later Z4 models

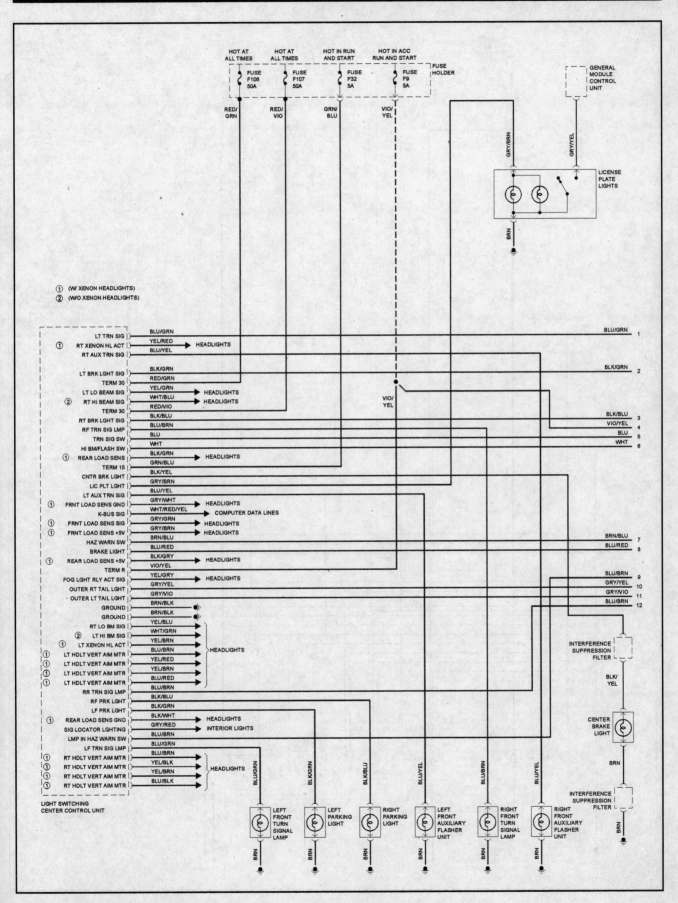

Exterior lighting system - all 1999 through 2001 3-Series, 2002 and later coupes (1 of 2)

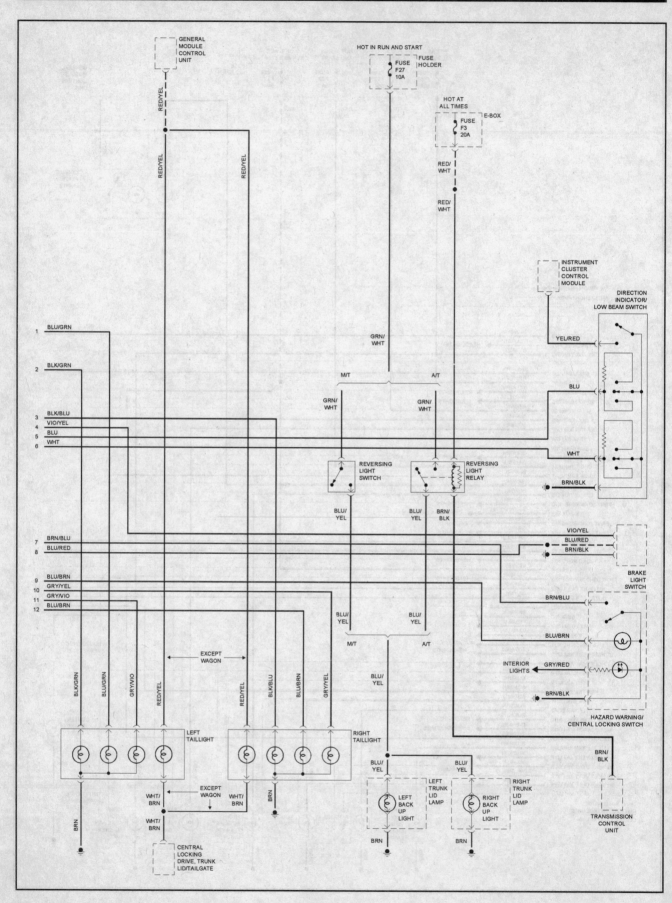

Exterior lighting system - all 1999 through 2001 3-Series, 2002 and later coupes (2 of 2)

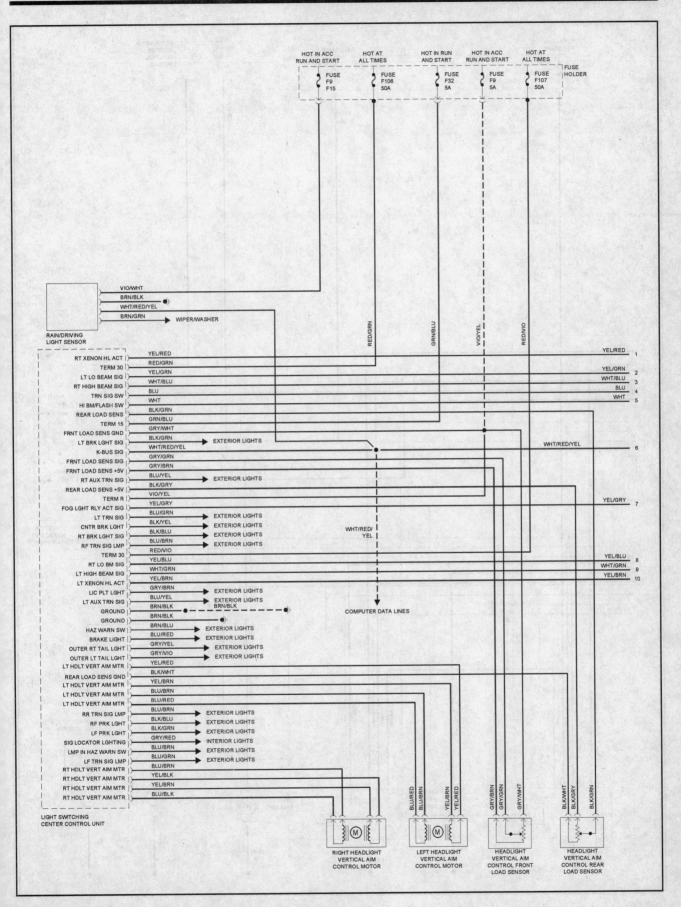

Headlight system with Xenon lights - 1999 through 2001 3-Series (1 of 2)

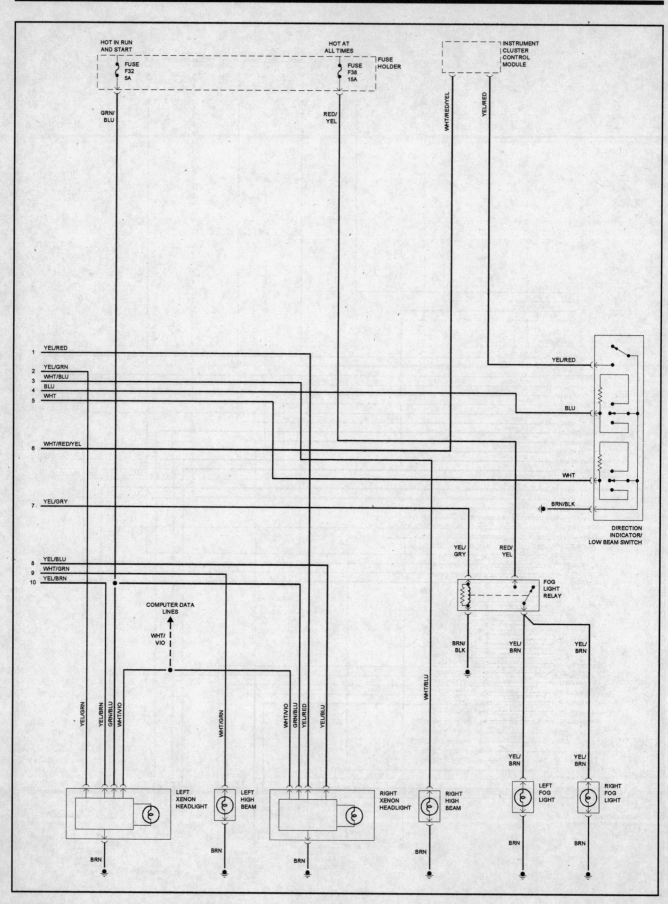

Headlight system with Xenon lights - 1999 through 2001 3-Series (2 of 2)

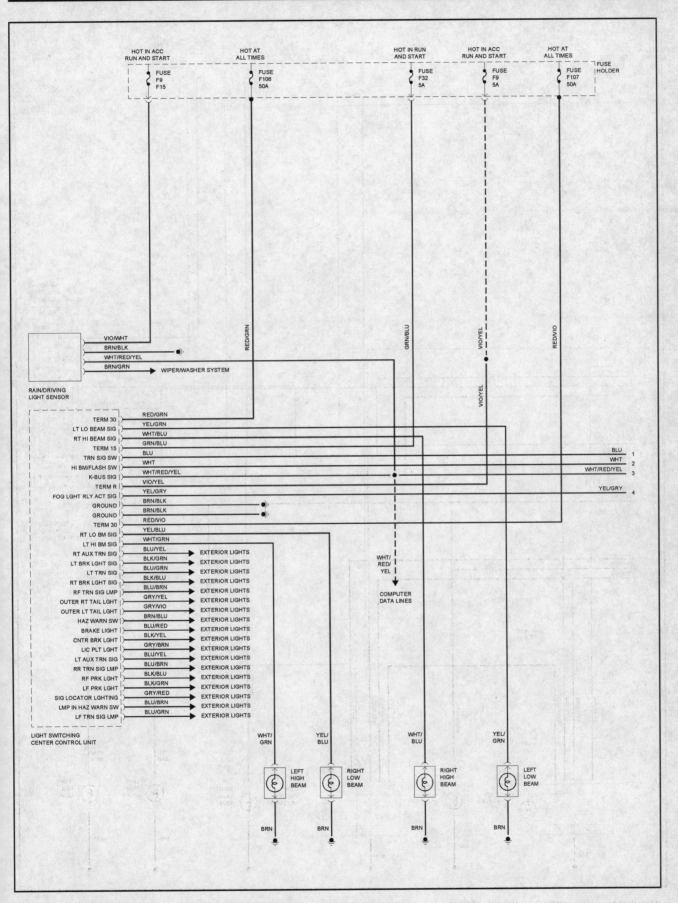

Headlight system without Xenon lights - 1999 through 2001 3-Series (1 of 2)

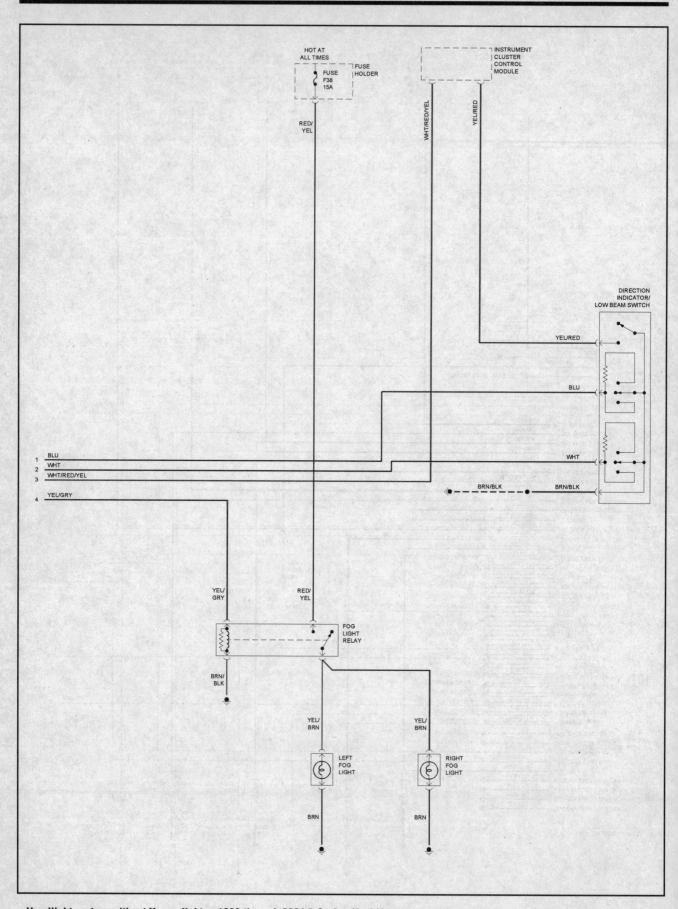

Headlight system without Xenon lights - 1999 through 2001 3-Series (2 of 2)

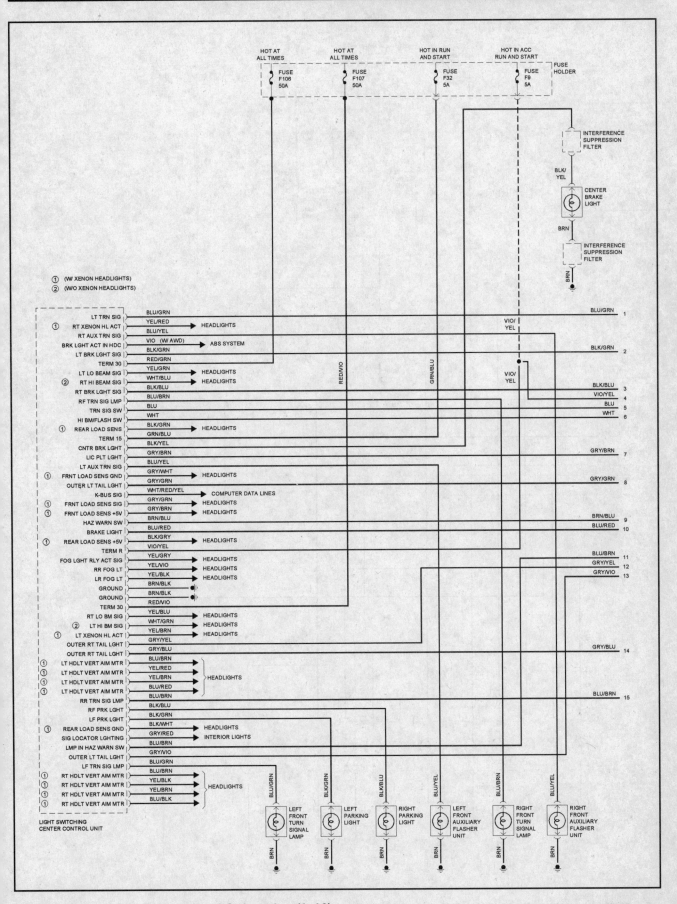

Exterior lighting system - 2002 and later 3-Series sedans (1 of 2)

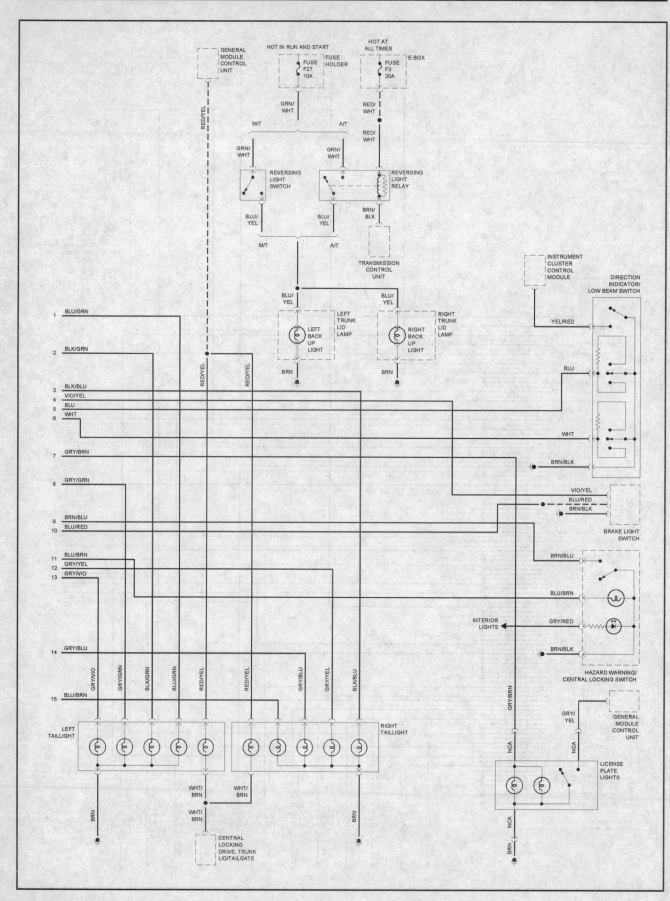

Exterior lighting system - 2002 and later 3-Series sedans (2 of 2)

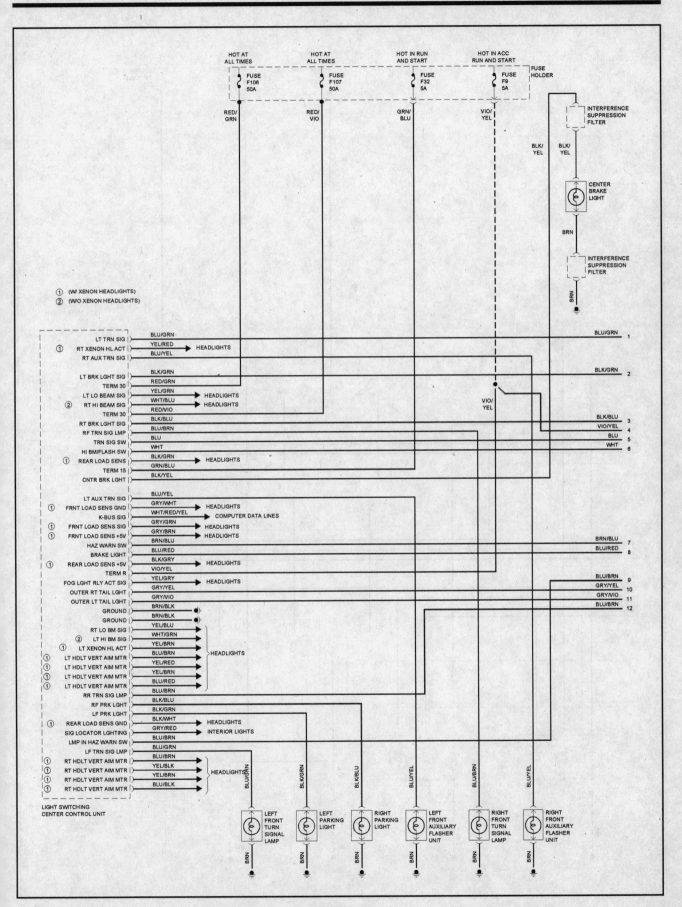

Exterior lighting system - 2002 and later 3-Series wagons (1 of 2)

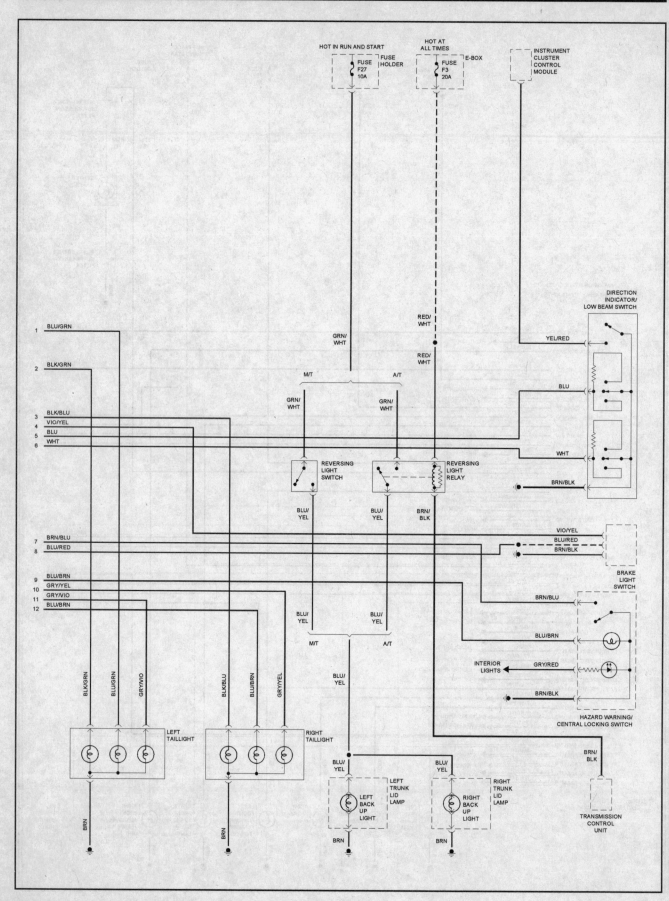

Exterior lighting system - 2002 and later 3-Series wagons (2 of 2)

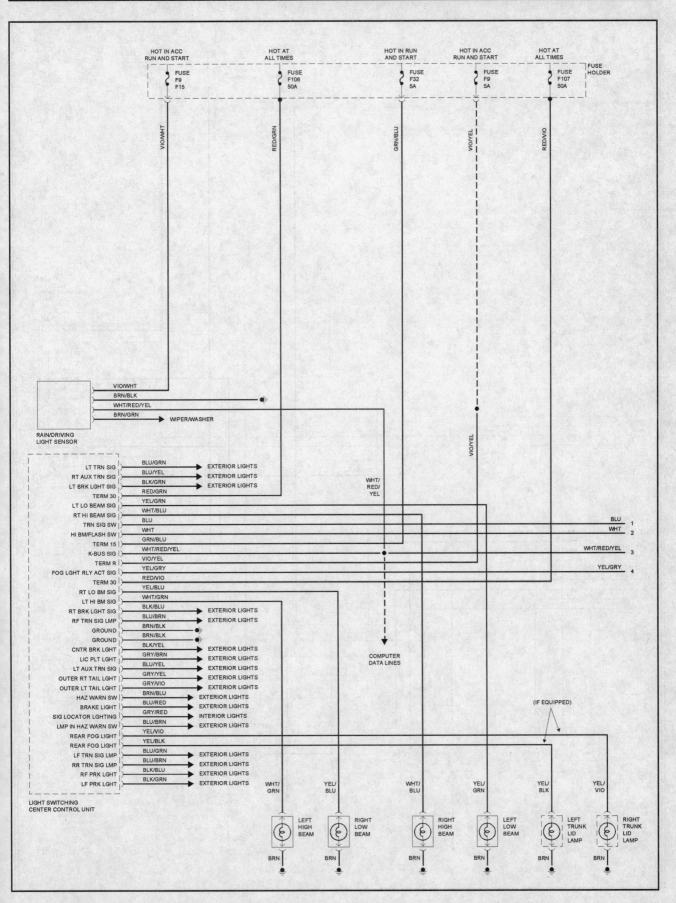

Headlight system without Xenon lights - 2002 and later 3-Series (1 of 2)

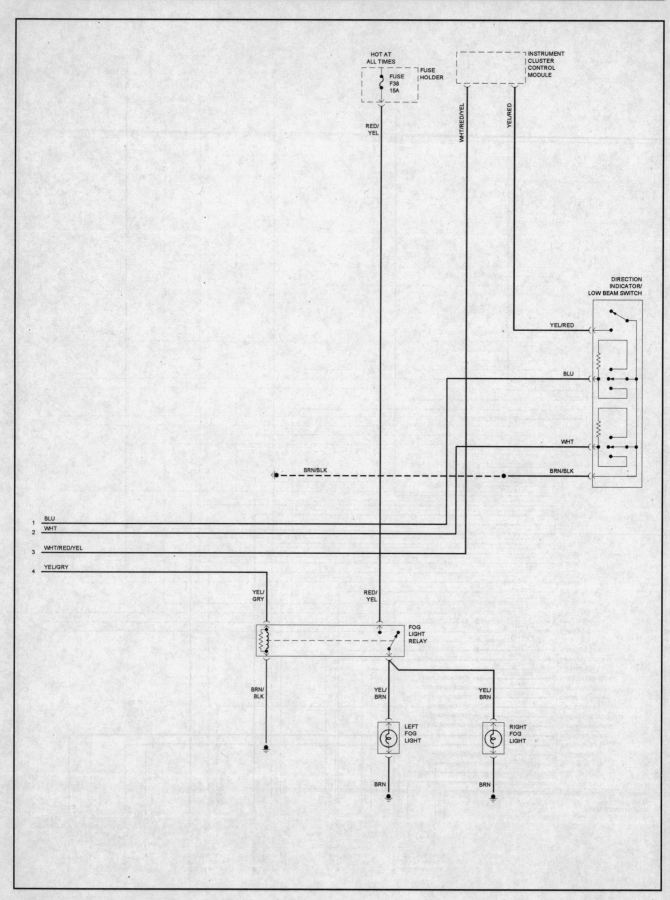

Headlight system without Xenon lights - 2002 and later 3-Series (2 of 2)

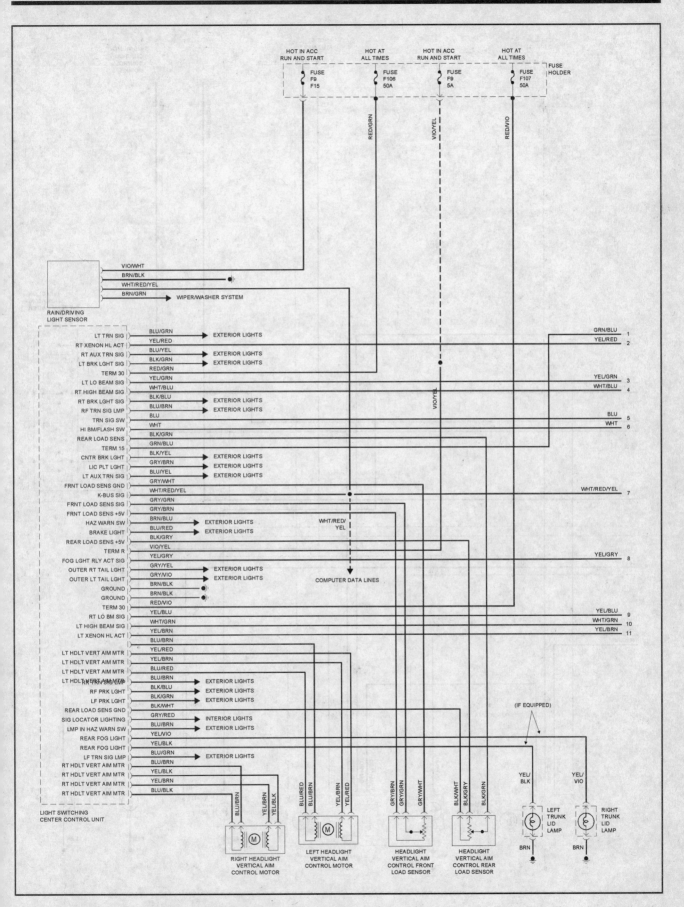

Headlight system with Xenon lights - 2002 and later 3-Series (1 of 2)

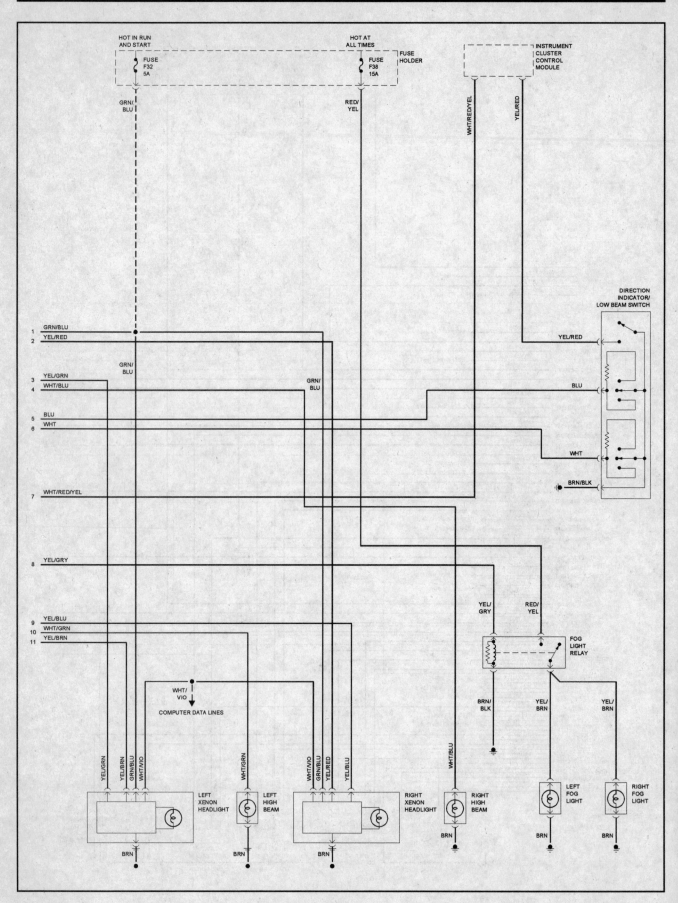

Headlight system with Xenon lights - 2002 and later 3-Series (2 of 2)

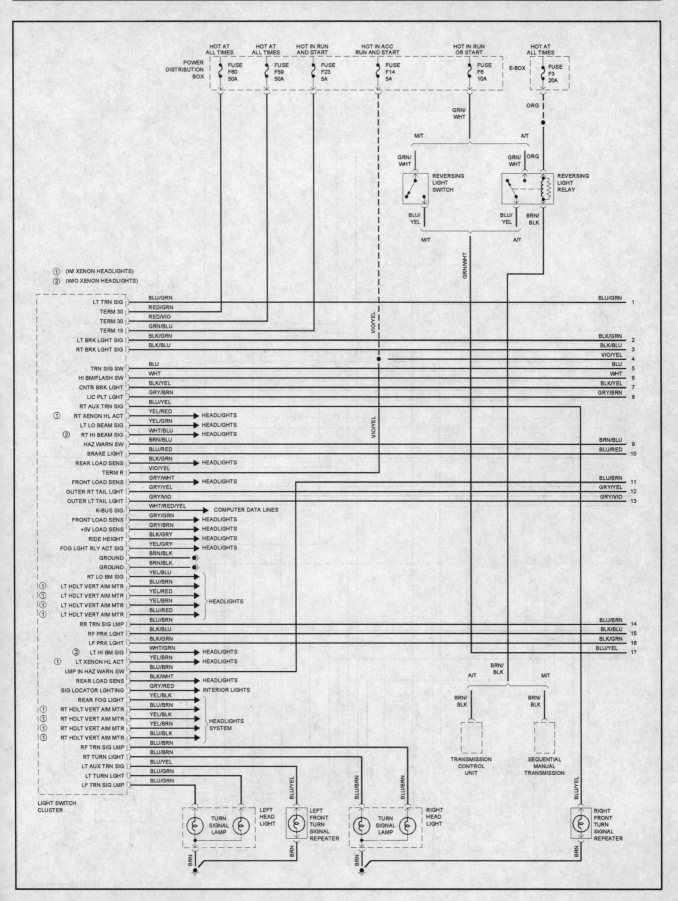

Exterior lighting system - 2003 and later Z4 models (1 of 2)

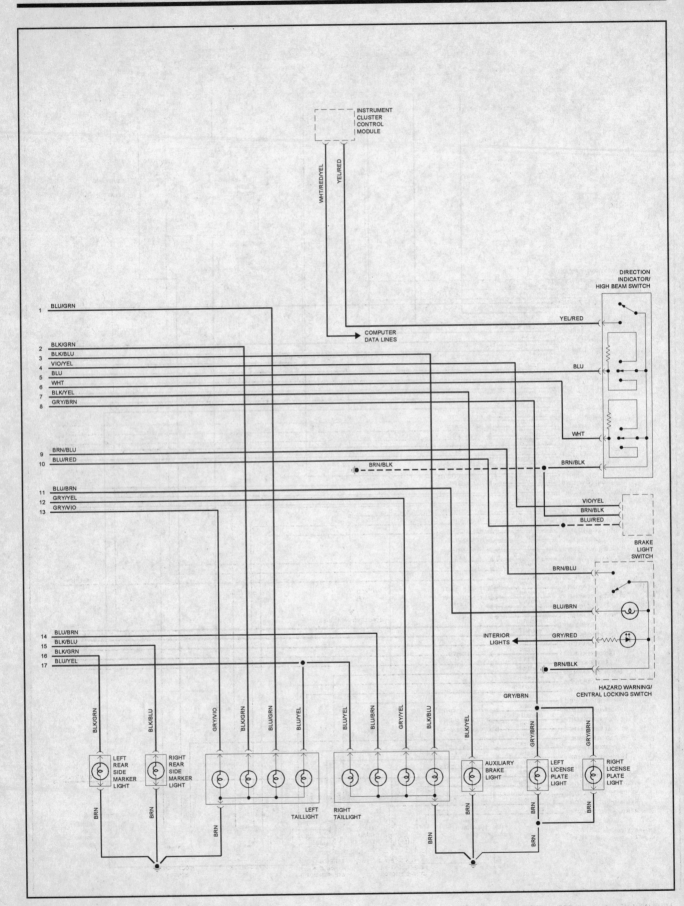

Exterior lighting system - 2003 and later Z4 models (2 of 2)

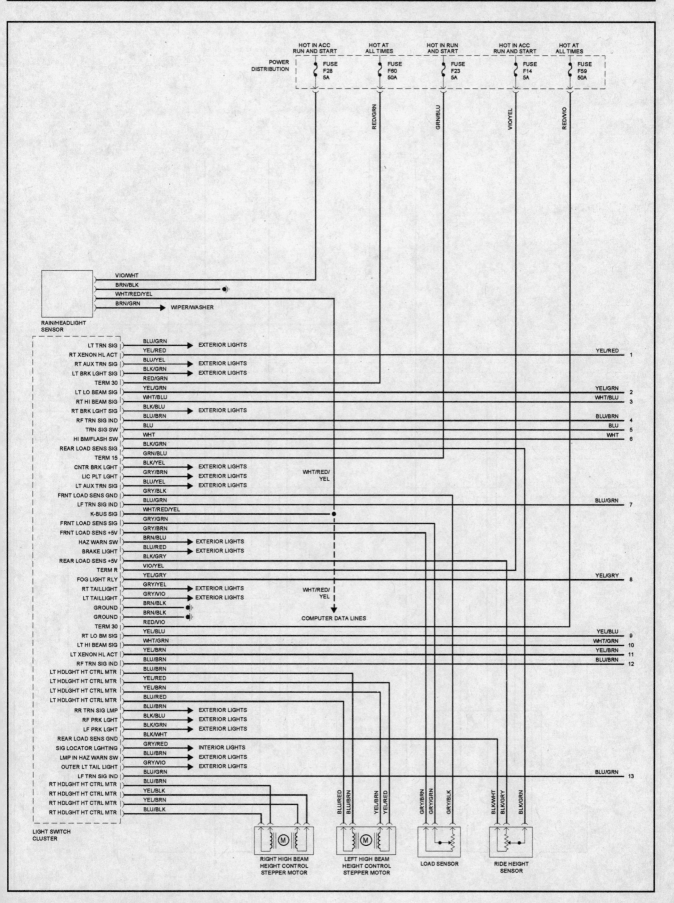

Headlight system - 2003 and later Z4 models (1 of 2)

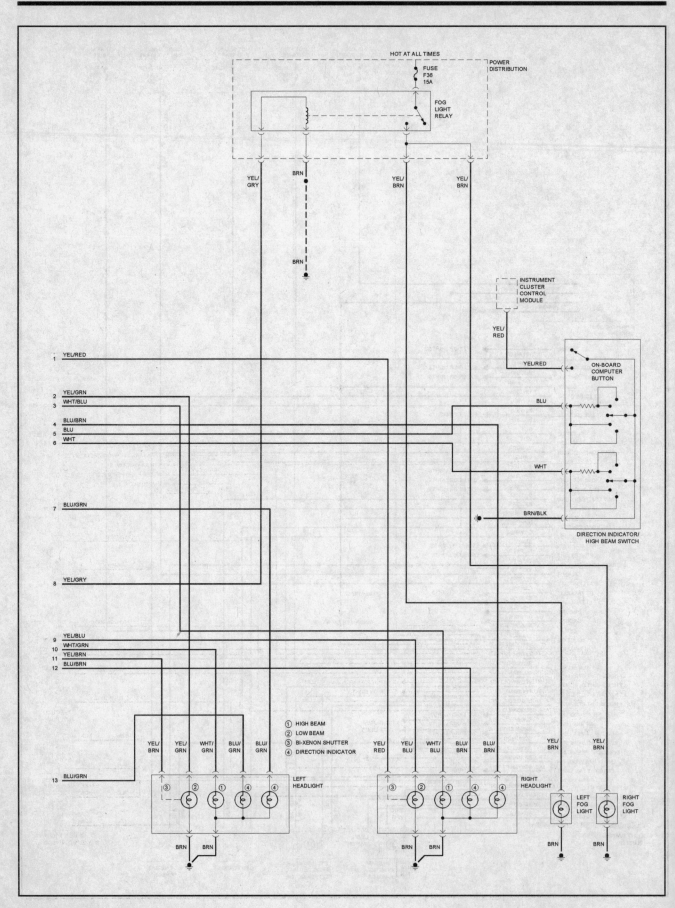

Headlight system - 2003 and later Z4 models (2 of 2)

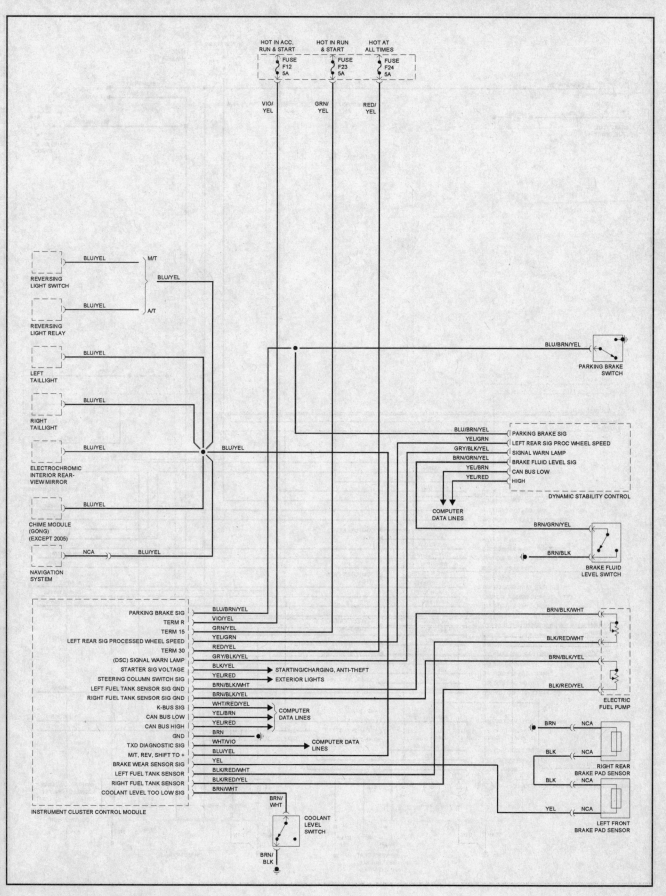

Warning light systems - 2003 and later Z4 models

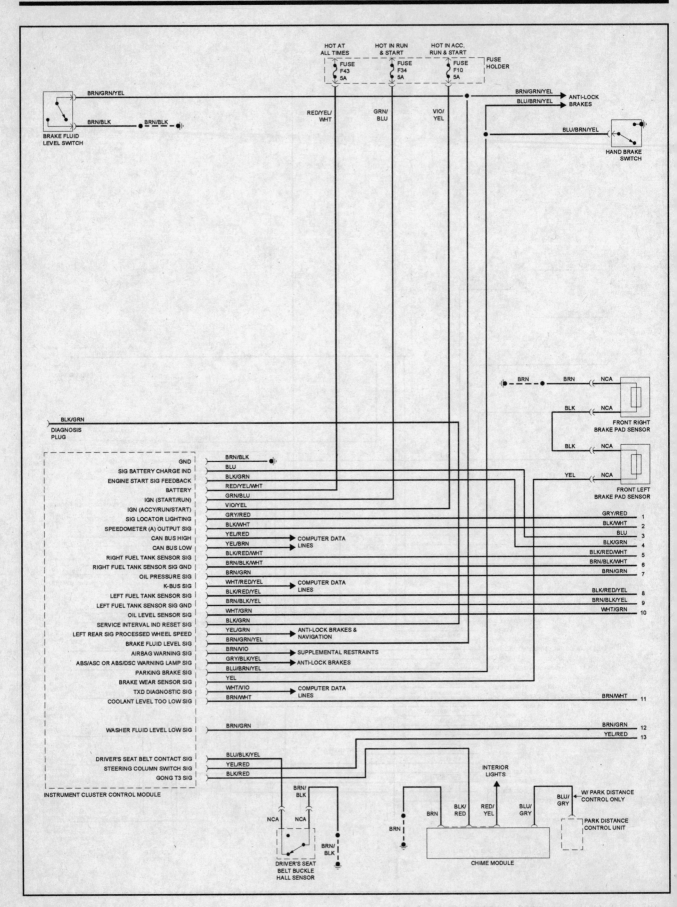

Warning light systems - 1999 and 2000 3-Series (1 of 2)

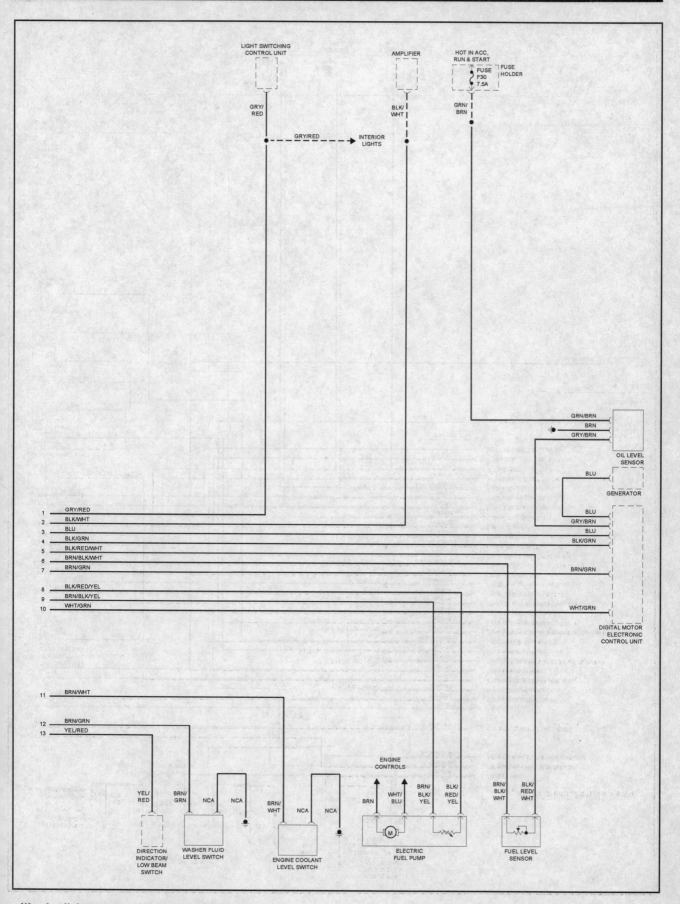

Warning light systems - 1999 and 2000 3-Series (2 of 2)

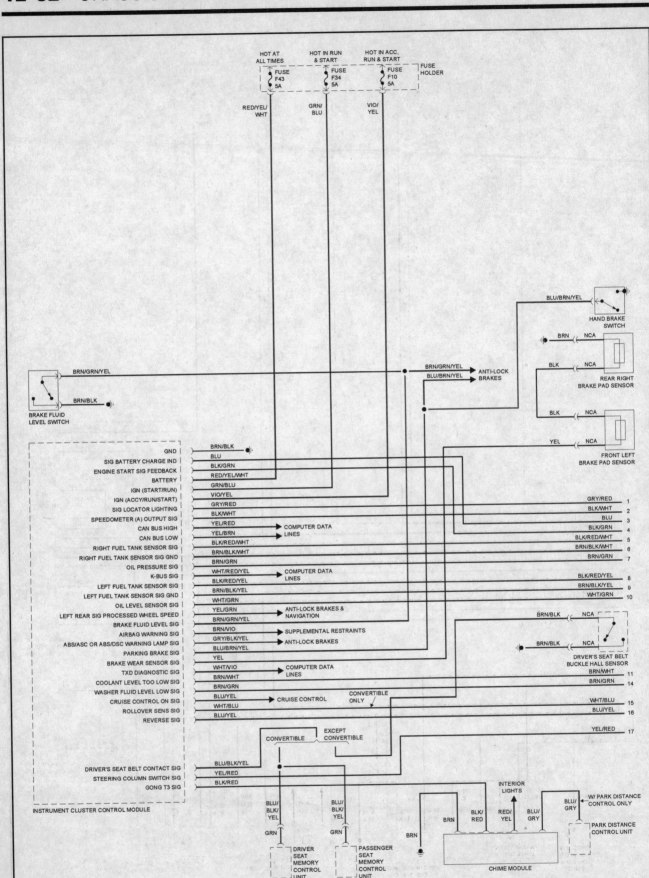

Warning light systems - 2001 and later 3-Series (1 of 2)

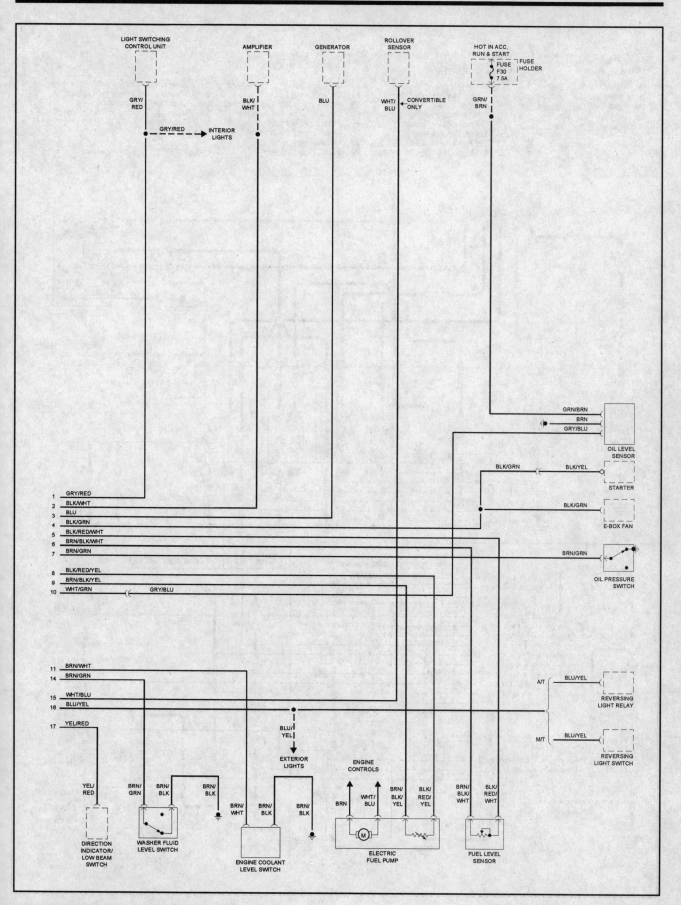

Warning light systems - 1999 and later 3-Series (2 of 2)

Wire colors

Bl	Blue	**Vi**	Violet
Br	Brown	**Ws**	White
Ge	Yellow	**Or**	Orange
Gr	Grey	**Rt**	Red
Gn	Green	**Sw**	Black

Key to items

1	Battery
2	Ignition switch
77	General control unit
78	Interior/map reading light
79	Central locking switch
80	LH rear interior light
81	RH rear interior light
82	LH luggage compartment light
83	RH luggage compartment light
84	Glovebox light switch
85	Passenger's footwell illumination
86	Driver's footwell illumination
87	Front cigar lighter illumination
88	Rear ashtray illumination
89	LH storage tray light
90	RH storage tray light
91	Driver's vanity mirror light
92	Driver's vanity mirror light switch
93	Passenger's vanity mirror light
94	Passenger's vanity mirror light switch
95	Cigar lighter
96	Charging socket

H32738

Storage tray and vanity mirror illumination

Cigar lighter & charging socket

Typical interior lighting system

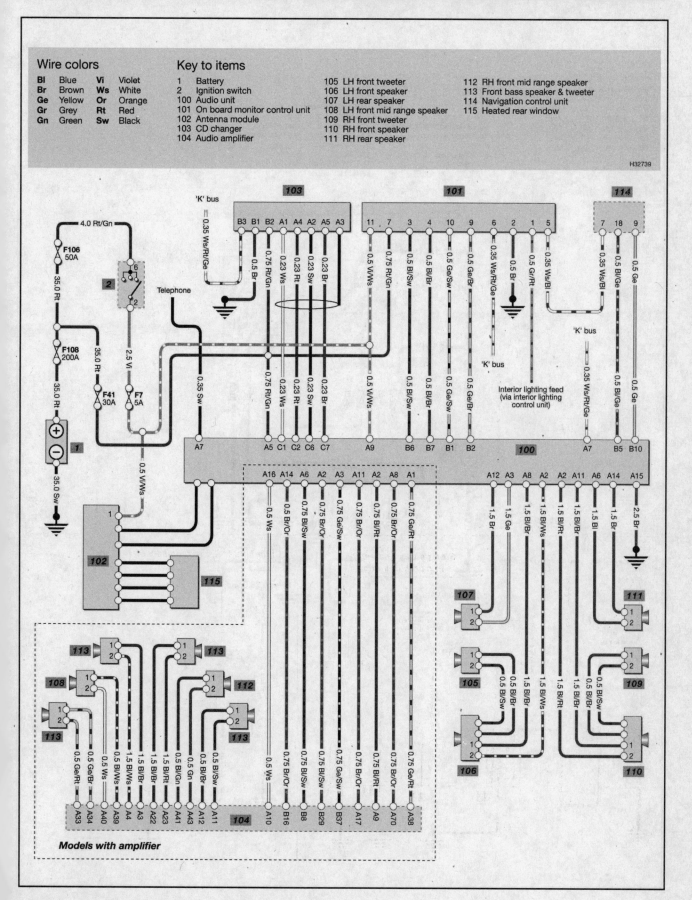

Typical audio system and rear window defroster

Wire colors

Bl	Blue	**Vi**	Violet
Br	Brown	**Ws**	White
Ge	Yellow	**Or**	Orange
Gr	Grey	**Rt**	Red
Gn	Green	**Sw**	Black

Key to items

1	Battery	123	Thermal switch
2	Ignition switch	124	Headlight washer relay
77	General control unit	125	Headlight washer pump
118	Horn relay	126	Heater blower control module
119	Horn	127	Heater blower motor
120	Steering wheel clock spring	128	Wash/wipe switch
121	Horn switch	129	Front wiper relay
		130	Front wiper motor

H32740

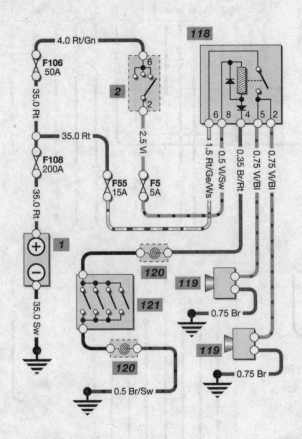

Typical horn system

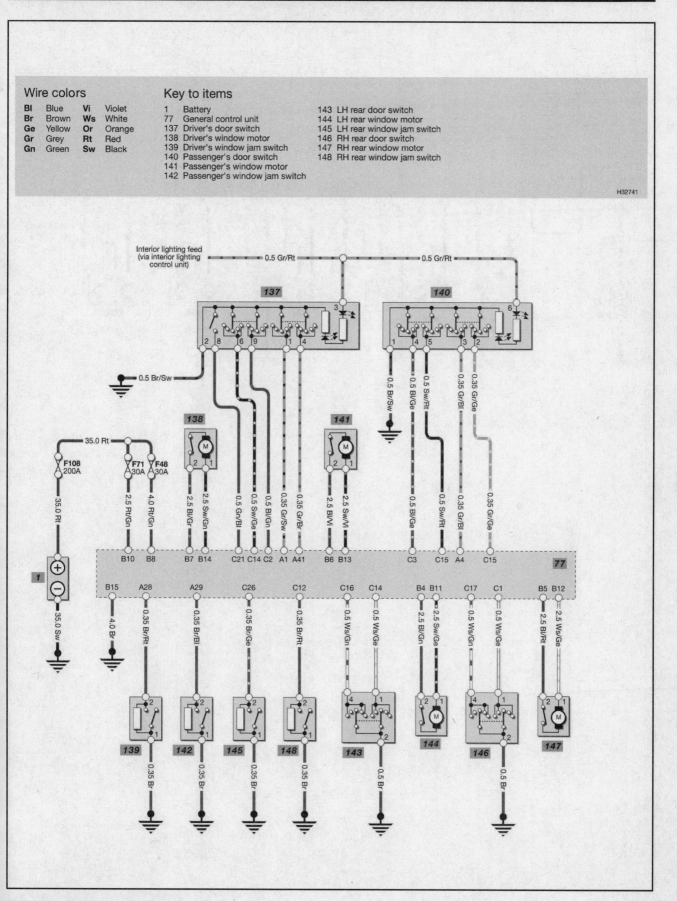

Wire colors

Bl	Blue	**Vi**	Violet
Br	Brown	**Ws**	White
Ge	Yellow	**Or**	Orange
Gr	Grey	**Rt**	Red
Gn	Green	**Sw**	Black

Key to items

1 Battery
77 General control unit
137 Driver's door switch
138 Driver's window motor
139 Driver's window jam switch
140 Passenger's door switch
141 Passenger's window motor
142 Passenger's window jam switch
143 LH rear door switch
144 LH rear window motor
145 LH rear window jam switch
146 RH rear door switch
147 RH rear window motor
148 RH rear window jam switch

H32741

Typical power window system

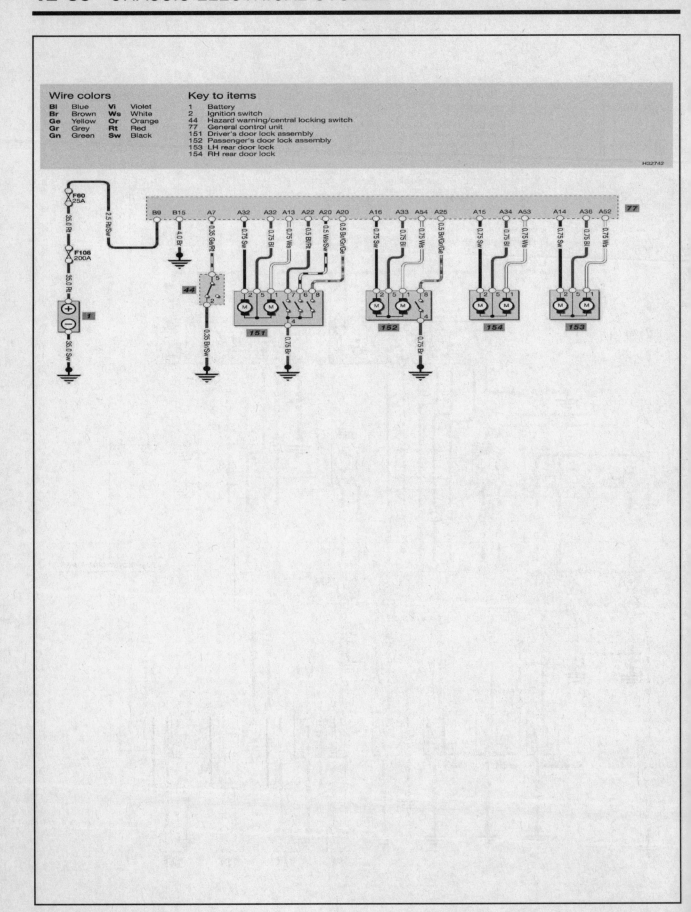

Wire colors

Bl	Blue	**Vi**	Violet
Br	Brown	**Ws**	White
Ge	Yellow	**Or**	Orange
Gr	Grey	**Rt**	Red
Gn	Green	**Sw**	Black

Key to items

1   Battery
2   Ignition switch
44 Hazard warning/central locking switch
77 General control unit
151 Driver's door lock assembly
152 Passenger's door lock assembly
153 LH rear door lock
154 RH rear door lock

H32742

Typical central locking system

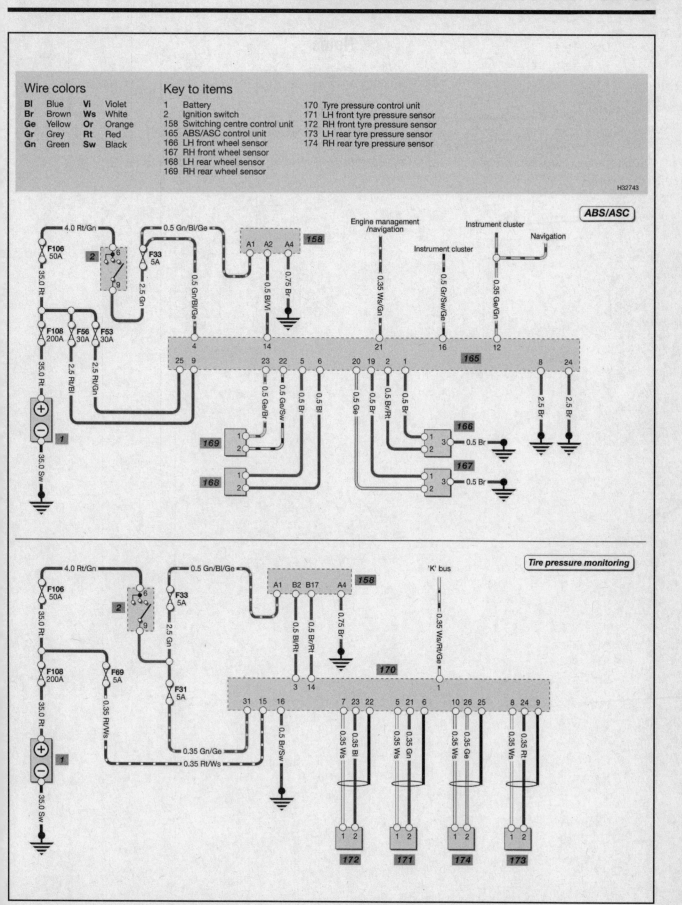

Wire colors

Bl	Blue	**Vi**	Violet
Br	Brown	**Ws**	White
Ge	Yellow	**Or**	Orange
Gr	Grey	**Rt**	Red
Gn	Green	**Sw**	Black

Key to items

1 Battery
2 Ignition switch
158 Switching centre control unit
165 ABS/ASC control unit
166 LH front wheel sensor
167 RH front wheel sensor
168 LH rear wheel sensor
169 RH rear wheel sensor

170 Tyre pressure control unit
171 LH front tyre pressure sensor
172 RH front tyre pressure sensor
173 LH rear tyre pressure sensor
174 RH rear tyre pressure sensor

H32743

ABS/ASC

Tire pressure monitoring

Typical ABS and tire pressure monitoring systems

Notes

GLOSSARY

AIR/FUEL RATIO: The ratio of air-to-gasoline by weight in the fuel mixture drawn into the engine.

AIR INJECTION: One method of reducing harmful exhaust emissions by injecting air into each of the exhaust ports of an engine. The fresh air entering the hot exhaust manifold causes any remaining fuel to be burned before it can exit the tailpipe.

ALTERNATOR: A device used for converting mechanical energy into electrical energy.

AMMETER: An instrument, calibrated in amperes, used to measure the flow of an electrical current in a circuit. Ammeters are always connected in series with the circuit being tested.

AMPERE: The rate of flow of electrical current present when one volt of electrical pressure is applied against one ohm of electrical resistance.

ANALOG COMPUTER: Any microprocessor that uses similar (analogous) electrical signals to make its calculations.

ARMATURE: A laminated, soft iron core wrapped by a wire that converts electrical energy to mechanical energy as in a motor or relay. When rotated in a magnetic field, it changes mechanical energy into electrical energy as in a generator.

ATMOSPHERIC PRESSURE: The pressure on the Earth's surface caused by the weight of the air in the atmosphere. At sea level, this pressure is 14.7 psi at 32°F (101 kPa at 0°C).

ATOMIZATION: The breaking down of a liquid into a fine mist that can be suspended in air.

AXIAL PLAY: Movement parallel to a shaft or bearing bore.

BACKFIRE: The sudden combustion of gases in the intake or exhaust system that results in a loud explosion.

BACKLASH: The clearance or play between two parts, such as meshed gears.

BACKPRESSURE: Restrictions in the exhaust system that slow the exit of exhaust gases from the combustion chamber.

BAKELITE: A heat resistant, plastic insulator material commonly used in printed circuit boards and transistorized components.

BALL BEARING: A bearing made up of hardened inner and outer races between which hardened steel balls roll.

BALLAST RESISTOR: A resistor in the primary ignition circuit that lowers voltage after the engine is started to reduce wear on ignition components.

BEARING: A friction reducing, supportive device usually located between a stationary part and a moving part.

BIMETAL TEMPERATURE SENSOR: Any sensor or switch made of two dissimilar types of metal that bend when heated or cooled due to the different expansion rates of the alloys. These types of sensors usually function as an on/off switch.

BLOWBY: Combustion gases, composed of water vapor and unburned fuel, that leak past the piston rings into the crankcase during normal engine operation. These gases are removed by the PCV system to prevent the buildup of harmful acids in the crankcase.

BRAKE PAD: A brake shoe and lining assembly used with disc brakes.

BRAKE SHOE: The backing for the brake lining. The term is, however, usually applied to the assembly of the brake backing and lining.

BUSHING: A liner, usually removable, for a bearing; an anti-friction liner used in place of a bearing.

CALIPER: A hydraulically activated device in a disc brake system, which is mounted straddling the brake rotor (disc). The caliper contains at least one piston and two brake pads. Hydraulic pressure on the piston(s) forces the pads against the rotor.

CAMSHAFT: A shaft in the engine on which are the lobes (cams) which operate the valves. The camshaft is driven by the crankshaft, via a belt, chain or gears, at one half the crankshaft speed.

CAPACITOR: A device which stores an electrical charge.

CARBON MONOXIDE (CO): A colorless, odorless gas given off as a normal byproduct of combustion. It is poisonous and extremely dangerous in confined areas, building up slowly to toxic levels without warning if adequate ventilation is not available.

CARBURETOR: A device, usually mounted on the intake manifold of an engine, which mixes the air and fuel in the proper proportion to allow even combustion.

CATALYTIC CONVERTER: A device installed in the exhaust system, like a muffler, that converts harmful byproducts of combustion into carbon dioxide and water vapor by means of a heat-producing chemical reaction.

CENTRIFUGAL ADVANCE: A mechanical method of advancing the spark timing by using flyweights in the distributor that react to centrifugal force generated by the distributor shaft rotation.

CHECK VALVE: Any one-way valve installed to permit the flow of air, fuel or vacuum in one direction only.

CHOKE: A device, usually a moveable valve, placed in the intake path of a carburetor to restrict the flow of air.

CIRCUIT: Any unbroken path through which an electrical current can flow. Also used to describe fuel flow in some instances.

CIRCUIT BREAKER: A switch which protects an electrical circuit from overload by opening the circuit when the current flow exceeds a predetermined level. Some circuit breakers must be reset manually, while most reset automatically.

COIL (IGNITION): A transformer in the ignition circuit which steps up the voltage provided to the spark plugs.

COMBINATION MANIFOLD: An assembly which includes both the intake and exhaust manifolds in one casting.

COMBINATION VALVE: A device used in some fuel systems that routes fuel vapors to a charcoal storage canister instead of venting them into the atmosphere. The valve relieves fuel tank pressure and allows fresh air into the tank as the fuel level drops to prevent a vapor lock situation.

COMPRESSION RATIO: The comparison of the total volume of the cylinder and combustion chamber with the piston at BDC and the piston at TDC.

CONDENSER: 1. An electrical device which acts to store an electrical charge, preventing voltage surges. 2. A radiator-like device in the air conditioning system in which refrigerant gas condenses into a liquid, giving off heat.

CONDUCTOR: Any material through which an electrical current can be transmitted easily.

CONTINUITY: Continuous or complete circuit. Can be checked with an ohmmeter.

COUNTERSHAFT: An intermediate shaft which is rotated by a mainshaft and transmits, in turn, that rotation to a working part.

CRANKCASE: The lower part of an engine in which the crankshaft and related parts operate.

CRANKSHAFT: The main driving shaft of an engine which receives reciprocating motion from the pistons and converts it to rotary motion.

CYLINDER: In an engine, the round hole in the engine block in which the piston(s) ride.

CYLINDER BLOCK: The main structural member of an engine in which is found the cylinders, crankshaft and other principal parts.

CYLINDER HEAD: The detachable portion of the engine, usually fastened to the top of the cylinder block and containing all or most of the combustion chambers. On overhead valve engines, it contains the valves and their operating parts. On overhead cam engines, it contains the camshaft as well.

DEAD CENTER: The extreme top or bottom of the piston stroke.

DETONATION: An unwanted explosion of the air/fuel mixture in the combustion chamber caused by excess heat and compression, advanced timing, or an overly lean mixture. Also referred to as "ping".

DIAPHRAGM: A thin, flexible wall separating two cavities, such as in a vacuum advance unit.

DIESELING: A condition in which hot spots in the combustion chamber cause the engine to run on after the key is turned off.

DIFFERENTIAL: A geared assembly which allows the transmission of motion between drive axles, giving one axle the ability to turn faster than the other.

DIODE: An electrical device that will allow current to flow in one direction only.

DISC BRAKE: A hydraulic braking assembly consisting of a brake disc, or rotor, mounted on an axle, and a caliper assembly containing, usually two brake pads which are activated by hydraulic pressure. The pads are forced against the sides of the disc, creating friction which slows the vehicle.

DISTRIBUTOR: A mechanically driven device on an engine which is responsible for electrically firing the spark plug at a predetermined point of the piston stroke.

DOWEL PIN: A pin, inserted in mating holes in two different parts allowing those parts to maintain a fixed relationship.

DRUM BRAKE: A braking system which consists of two brake shoes and one or two wheel cylinders, mounted on a fixed backing plate, and a brake drum, mounted on an axle, which revolves around the assembly.

DWELL: The rate, measured in degrees of shaft rotation, at which an electrical circuit cycles on and off.

ELECTRONIC CONTROL UNIT (ECU): Ignition module, module, amplifier or igniter. See Module for definition.

ELECTRONIC IGNITION: A system in which the timing and firing of the spark plugs is controlled by an electronic control unit, usually called a module. These systems have no points or condenser.

END-PLAY: The measured amount of axial movement in a shaft.

ENGINE: A device that converts heat into mechanical energy.

EXHAUST MANIFOLD: A set of cast passages or pipes which conduct exhaust gases from the engine.

FEELER GAUGE: A blade, usually metal, of precisely predetermined thickness, used to measure the clearance between two parts.

FIRING ORDER: The order in which combustion occurs in the cylinders of an engine. Also the order in which spark is distributed to the plugs by the distributor.

FLOODING: The presence of too much fuel in the intake manifold and combustion chamber which prevents the air/fuel mixture from firing, thereby causing a no-start situation.

FLYWHEEL: A disc shaped part bolted to the rear end of the crankshaft. Around the outer perimeter is affixed the ring gear. The starter drive engages the ring gear, turning the flywheel, which rotates the crankshaft, imparting the initial starting motion to the engine.

FOOT POUND (ft. lbs. or sometimes, ft.lb.): The amount of energy or work needed to raise an item weighing one pound, a distance of one foot.

FUSE: A protective device in a circuit which prevents circuit overload by breaking the circuit when a specific amperage is present. The device is constructed around a strip or wire of a lower amperage rating than the circuit it is designed to protect. When an amperage higher than that stamped on the fuse is present in the circuit, the strip or wire melts, opening the circuit.

GEAR RATIO: The ratio between the number of teeth on meshing gears.

GENERATOR: A device which converts mechanical energy into electrical energy.

HEAT RANGE: The measure of a spark plug's ability to dissipate heat from its firing end. The higher the heat range, the hotter the plug fires.

HUB: The center part of a wheel or gear.

HYDROCARBON (HC): Any chemical compound made up of hydrogen and carbon. A major pollutant formed by the engine as a byproduct of combustion.

HYDROMETER: An instrument used to measure the specific gravity of a solution.

INCH POUND (inch lbs.; sometimes in.lb. or in. lbs.): One twelfth of a foot pound.

INDUCTION: A means of transferring electrical energy in the form of a magnetic field. Principle used in the ignition coil to increase voltage.

INJECTOR: A device which receives metered fuel under relatively low pressure and is activated to inject the fuel into the engine under relatively high pressure at a predetermined time.

INPUT SHAFT: The shaft to which torque is applied, usually carrying the driving gear or gears.

INTAKE MANIFOLD: A casting of passages or pipes used to conduct air or a fuel/air mixture to the cylinders.

JOURNAL: The bearing surface within which a shaft operates.

KEY: A small block usually fitted in a notch between a shaft and a hub to prevent slippage of the two parts.

MANIFOLD: A casting of passages or set of pipes which connect the cylinders to an inlet or outlet source.

MANIFOLD VACUUM: Low pressure in an engine intake manifold formed just below the throttle plates. Manifold vacuum is highest at idle and drops under acceleration.

MASTER CYLINDER: The primary fluid pressurizing device in a hydraulic system. In automotive use, it is found in brake and hydraulic clutch systems and is pedal activated, either directly or, in a power brake system, through the power booster.

MODULE: Electronic control unit, amplifier or igniter of solid state or integrated design which controls the current flow in the ignition primary circuit based on input from the pick-up coil. When the module opens the primary circuit, high secondary voltage is induced in the coil.

NEEDLE BEARING: A bearing which consists of a number (usually a large number) of long, thin rollers.

OHM: (Ω) The unit used to measure the resistance of conductor-to-electrical flow. One ohm is the amount of resistance that limits current flow to one ampere in a circuit with one volt of pressure.

OHMMETER: An instrument used for measuring the resistance, in ohms, in an electrical circuit.

OUTPUT SHAFT: The shaft which transmits torque from a device, such as a transmission.

OVERDRIVE: A gear assembly which produces more shaft revolutions than that transmitted to it.

OVERHEAD CAMSHAFT (OHC): An engine configuration in which the camshaft is mounted on top of the cylinder head and operates the valve either directly or by means of rocker arms.

OVERHEAD VALVE (OHV): An engine configuration in which all of the valves are located in the cylinder head and the camshaft is located in the cylinder block. The camshaft operates the valves via lifters and pushrods.

OXIDES OF NITROGEN (NOx): Chemical compounds of nitrogen produced as a byproduct of combustion. They combine with hydrocarbons to produce smog.

OXYGEN SENSOR: Use with the feedback system to sense the presence of oxygen in the exhaust gas and signal the computer which can reference the voltage signal to an air/fuel ratio.

PINION: The smaller of two meshing gears.

PISTON RING: An open-ended ring with fits into a groove on the outer diameter of the piston. Its chief function is to form a seal between the piston and cylinder wall. Most automotive pistons have three rings: two for compression sealing; one for oil sealing.

PRELOAD: A predetermined load placed on a bearing during assembly or by adjustment.

PRIMARY CIRCUIT: the low voltage side of the ignition system which consists of the ignition switch, ballast resistor or resistance wire, bypass, coil, electronic control unit and pick-up coil as well as the connecting wires and harnesses.

PRESS FIT: The mating of two parts under pressure, due to the inner diameter of one being smaller than the outer diameter of the other, or vice versa; an interference fit.

RACE: The surface on the inner or outer ring of a bearing on which the balls, needles or rollers move.

REGULATOR: A device which maintains the amperage and/or voltage levels of a circuit at predetermined values.

RELAY: A switch which automatically opens and/or closes a circuit.

RESISTANCE: The opposition to the flow of current through a circuit or electrical device, and is measured in ohms. Resistance is equal to the voltage divided by the amperage.

RESISTOR: A device, usually made of wire, which offers a preset amount of resistance in an electrical circuit.

RING GEAR: The name given to a ring-shaped gear attached to a differential case, or affixed to a flywheel or as part of a planetary gear set.

ROLLER BEARING: A bearing made up of hardened inner and outer races between which hardened steel rollers move.

ROTOR: 1. The disc-shaped part of a disc brake assembly, upon which the brake pads bear; also called, brake disc. 2. The device mounted atop the distributor shaft, which passes current to the distributor cap tower contacts.

SECONDARY CIRCUIT: The high voltage side of the ignition system, usually above 20,000 volts. The secondary includes the ignition coil, coil wire, distributor cap and rotor, spark plug wires and spark plugs.

SENDING UNIT: A mechanical, electrical, hydraulic or electro-magnetic device which transmits information to a gauge.

SENSOR: Any device designed to measure engine operating conditions or ambient pressures and temperatures. Usually electronic in nature and designed to send a voltage signal to an on-board computer, some sensors may operate as a simple on/off switch or they may provide a variable voltage signal (like a potentiometer) as conditions or measured parameters change.

SHIM: Spacers of precise, predetermined thickness used between parts to establish a proper working relationship.

SLAVE CYLINDER: In automotive use, a device in the hydraulic clutch system which is activated by hydraulic force, disengaging the clutch.

SOLENOID: A coil used to produce a magnetic field, the effect of which is to produce work.

SPARK PLUG: A device screwed into the combustion chamber of a spark ignition engine. The basic construction is a conductive core inside of a ceramic insulator, mounted in an outer conductive base. An electrical charge from the spark plug wire travels along the conductive core and jumps a preset air gap to a grounding point or points at the end of the conductive base. The resultant spark ignites the fuel/air mixture in the combustion chamber.

SPLINES: Ridges machined or cast onto the outer diameter of a shaft or inner diameter of a bore to enable parts to mate without rotation.

TACHOMETER: A device used to measure the rotary speed of an engine, shaft, gear, etc., usually in rotations per minute.

THERMOSTAT: A valve, located in the cooling system of an engine, which is closed when cold and opens gradually in response to engine heating, controlling the temperature of the coolant and rate of coolant flow.

TOP DEAD CENTER (TDC): The point at which the piston reaches the top of its travel on the compression stroke.

TORQUE: The twisting force applied to an object.

TORQUE CONVERTER: A turbine used to transmit power from a driving member to a driven member via hydraulic action, providing changes in drive ratio and torque. In automotive use, it links the driveplate at the rear of the engine to the automatic transmission.

TRANSDUCER: A device used to change a force into an electrical signal.

TRANSISTOR: A semi-conductor component which can be actuated by a small voltage to perform an electrical switching function.

TUNE-UP: A regular maintenance function, usually associated with the replacement and adjustment of parts and components in the electrical and fuel systems of a vehicle for the purpose of attaining optimum performance.

TURBOCHARGER: An exhaust driven pump which compresses intake air and forces it into the combustion chambers at higher than atmospheric pressures. The increased air pressure allows more fuel to be burned and results in increased horsepower being produced.

VACUUM ADVANCE: A device which advances the ignition timing in response to increased engine vacuum.

VACUUM GAUGE: An instrument used to measure the presence of vacuum in a chamber.

VALVE: A device which control the pressure, direction of flow or rate of flow of a liquid or gas.

VALVE CLEARANCE: The measured gap between the end of the valve stem and the rocker arm, cam lobe or follower that activates the valve.

VISCOSITY: The rating of a liquid's internal resistance to flow.

VOLTMETER: An instrument used for measuring electrical force in units called volts. Voltmeters are always connected parallel with the circuit being tested.

WHEEL CYLINDER: Found in the automotive drum brake assembly, it is a device, actuated by hydraulic pressure, which, through internal pistons, pushes the brake shoes outward against the drums.

A